A COMMENTARY O?

O?

Michael Inwood, an eminent scholar of German philosophy, presents a full and detailed new commentary on a classic work of the nineteenth century. *Philosophy of Mind* is the third part of Hegel's Encyclopaedia of the Philosophical Sciences, in which he summarizes his philosophical system. It is one of the main pillars of his thought. Inwood gives the clear and careful guidance needed for an understanding of this challenging work. In his editorial introduction he offers a philosophically sophisticated evaluation of Hegel's ideas which includes a survey of the whole of his thought and detailed analysis of the terminology he used. This volume is issued simultaneously with a companion volume containing Inwood's translation of the *Philosophy of Mind*.

Michael Inwood is Fellow and Tutor in Philosophy at Trinity College, Oxford.

A Commentary on Hegel's Philosophy of Mind

M. J. INWOOD

CLARENDON PRESS · OXFORD

OXFORD
UNIVERSITY PRESS

Great Clarendon Street, Oxford OX2 6DP

Oxford University Press is a department of the University of Oxford.
It furthers the University's objective of excellence in research, scholarship,
and education by publishing worldwide in

Oxford New York

Auckland Cape Town Dar es Salaam Hong Kong Karachi
Kuala Lumpur Madrid Melbourne Mexico City Nairobi
New Delhi Shanghai Taipei Toronto

With offices in

Argentina Austria Brazil Chile Czech Republic France Greece
Guatemala Hungary Italy Japan Poland Portugal Singapore
South Korea Switzerland Thailand Turkey Ukraine Vietnam

Oxford is a registered trade mark of Oxford University Press
in the UK and in certain other countries

Published in the United States
by Oxford University Press Inc., New York

© Michael Inwood 2007

British Library Cataloguing in Publication Data
Data available

Library of Congress Cataloging in Publication Data
Data available

Typeset by Laserwords Private Limited, Chennai, India
Printed in Great Britain
on acid-free paper by the
MPG Books Group, Bodmin and King's Lynn

ISBN 978-0-19-957566-4 (pbk.)

1 3 5 7 9 10 8 6 4 2

Abbreviations

DGS   *Dictionary of German Synonyms*, by R. B. Farrell (3rd edn.: Cambridge: Cambridge University Press, 1977)

Enc.   Hegel's *Encyclopaedia of the Philosophical Sciences in Outline*. The three parts are usually published separately. The first part ('Enc. I')is translated by William Wallace as *The Logic of Hegel* (2nd edn.: Oxford: Oxford University Press, 1892) and by T. F. Geraets, W. A. Suchting and H. S. Harris as *The Encyclopaedia Logic* (Indianapolis: Hackett, 1991). The second part ('Enc. II') is translated by A. V. Miller as *Hegel's Philosophy of Nature: Being Part Two of the Encyclopaedia of the Philosophical Sciences* (1830; Oxford: Oxford University Press, 1970) and by M. Petry as *Philosophy of Nature* (London: Allen & Unwin, 1970). The third part ('Enc. III') is translated by W. Wallace and A. V. Miller as *Hegel's Philosophy of Mind* (Oxford: Oxford University Press, 1971) and in part by M. Petry as *The Berlin Phenomenology* (Dordrecht: Reidel, 1981). These works translate the third (1830) edition of Enc., but also translate the *Zusätze*. In my quotations from Enc. I, I have usually followed Wallace's translation

HP   *Lectures on the History of Philosophy*, 3 vols., trans. E. S. Haldane and F. H. Simson (London: K. Paul, Trench, Trubner, 1892–6; repr. London: University of Nebraska Press, 1995)

ILA   *Introductory Lectures on Aesthetics*, trans. B. Bosanquet, ed. M. Inwood (Harmondsworth: Penguin, 1993). This is Hegel's introduction to his lectures. The complete text is translated by T. M. Knox as *Hegel's Aesthetics: Lectures on Fine Art* (Oxford: Oxford University Press, 1975)

LPR   *Lectures on the Philosophy of Religion*, 3 vols., trans. E. Speirs and J. Sanderson (London: K. Paul, Trench, Trubner, 1895)

PH   *The Philosophy of History*, trans. J. Sibree (New York: Dover, 1956). This is the only complete translation of Hegel's lectures on 'world history'

PR   *Philosophy of Right*, trans. T. M. Knox (Oxford: Oxford University Press, 1957). Also translated by H. Nisbet as *Elements of the Philosophy of Right*, ed. A. Wood (Cambridge: Cambridge University Press, 1991). Hegel's major work on ethics and politics. As in the case of the *Encyclopaedia*, Hegel's posthumous editor added *Zusätze* or 'additions' from lectures

PS   *Phenomenology of Spirit*, trans. A. V. Miller (Oxford: Oxford University Press, 1977)

SL   *Science of Logic*, trans. A. V. Miller (London: Allen & Unwin, 1969)

Editor's Introduction

This book is concerned with *Geist*. *Geist* is both 'mind' and 'spirit'. It is the 'mind' of an individual. It is the 'spirit' of a people. It is art, religion, and philosophy. It is the Holy Spirit. *Geist* is the dominant concept in Hegel's philosophy. It propels his thought onward and upward. *Geist* itself, in Hegel's view, propels humanity onward and upward. If there is any 'secret of Hegel', that secret is *Geist*.[1] But what is *Geist*? Can it bear all the meanings Hegel assigns to it? Can it perform the multitude of tasks that Hegel requires of it? Such are the questions that this Introduction attempts to answer.

HEGEL

Georg Wilhelm Friedrich Hegel was born in Stuttgart in 1770. After leaving the local high school, he enrolled in the philosophy faculty of Tübingen university in 1788, but later transferred to the theological faculty with the aim of becoming a Lutheran pastor. On graduating in 1793, he followed the common practice of serving as a private tutor to the children of a wealthy family, first in Berne and later in Frankfurt. During this period he wrote some essays on Christianity, which in general regret, and attempt to explain, its degeneration into a 'positive' religion, a religion of prescribed dogmas, rules, and rituals, in contrast to the 'folk-religion' of ancient Greece that it supplanted. The most important of these essays, 'The Spirit of Christianity and its Fate', argued that Jesus originally preached a religion of love, but that it had to become a religion of law, a positive religion, in order to convert mankind. Despite the occurrence of the word 'spirit' (*Geist*) in its title, as yet spirit plays only a subordinate role in Hegel's thought. He invests more hope in 'love' as a means of overcoming the alienating oppositions—between simple faith and ecclesiastical authority, between reason and the heart—that he so deplored. As yet, Hegel doubts the capacity of conceptual thought to do justice to the insights of Christianity.[2]

Early in 1801 Hegel moved to Jena to lecture at the university where his younger, but more precocious friend Friedrich Schelling already held a professorship. It was here that *Geist*, along with conceptual thought, secured a more prominent place in Hegel's thought. The upshot of his Jena period was his first major work, the *Phenomenology of Spirit*, that he published in 1807. In this work

---

[1] *The Secret of Hegel* (London: Longman, 1865), by James Hutchison Stirling, was the first book about Hegel in the English language.

[2] These essays were not published until 1907. Most of them are translated by T. M. Knox in *Hegel's Early Theological Writings* (Chicago: University of Chicago Press, 1948).

Geist has many of the meanings that it is given in the *Encyclopaedia*. (But not all
the meanings, since the *Phenomenology* does not contain anything corresponding to the section on 'anthropology' in the *Encyclopaedia* or to the section on
'psychology'.) In a brief advertisement for his book Hegel said that it

conceives the various forms of the spirit as stations on its way into itself, the way by
which it becomes pure knowledge or absolute spirit. Thus the main sections of the
science... consider: consciousness, self-consciousness, observing reason and active reason, spirit itself as ethical spirit, cultured and moral spirit, and finally spirit as religious
spirit in its different forms. The wealth of appearances of spirit, which at first sight seems
chaotic, is presented in its necessity: imperfect appearances dissolve and pass into higher
ones that are their proximate truth. They reach the ultimate truth initially in religion, and
then in science, the result of the whole.[3]

By the time the book was published, Hegel had left Jena, because the university
was closed after Napoleon's victory at the battle of Jena in 1806. For about a
year he edited a Napoleonic newspaper in Bamberg in Bavaria. Then, in 1808,
he was appointed headmaster of a gymnasium in Nuremberg. There he gave
lectures on various philosophical themes, including phenomenology of spirit
and 'philosophical encyclopaedia'.[4] He married Marie von Tucher in 1811 and,
between 1812 and 1816, published the *Science of Logic*. This work won him a
professorship at Heidelberg, where in 1817 he published his *Encyclopaedia of
the Philosophical Sciences in Outline* as a textbook to accompany his lectures.
It consisted of three parts: logic (a shorter and modified version of the *Science
of Logic*), philosophy of nature, and philosophy of *Geist*. It was divided into
consecutively numbered paragraphs, often brief and obscure, but to be expanded
and explained in his lectures. To some paragraphs he added 'Remarks', which
illustrate the theme of the paragraph in a less formal, less cryptic way and were
intended to appeal to a wider readership.

In 1818 he took up a professorship in Berlin, which he held until his death in
1831. In 1821 he published the *Philosophy of Right*, covering roughly the same
ground, in greater detail, as the section 'Objective Mind' in the *Encyclopaedia*. In
1827 he published the *Encyclopaedia* in a second edition that was nearly twice as
long as the first, mainly as a result of increasing and expanding the Remarks. He
published a slightly longer third edition in 1830. The work reached its present
form in the 1840s, when it was edited for the collected edition of Hegel's works
published by his pupils and friends. The three parts were produced separately, the
Logic in 1840 by Leopold von Henning, the Philosophy of Nature in 1842 by

[3] 'Science', in Hegel, often means 'philosophy'. Here it refers, in its first occurrence, to what is
presented in the *Phenomenology* itself, and, in its second occurrence, to the philosophy proper (logic,
philosophy of nature, and philosophy of mind) to which the *Phenomenology* was originally intended
as an introduction.
[4] Hegel's notes for these lectures were published by Karl Rosenkranz in 1844. They are translated
by A. V. Miller in *Philosophical Propaedeutic* (Oxford: Blackwell, 1986).

Karl Ludwig Michelet, and the Philosophy of Mind in 1845 by Ludwig Bou-
mann. It was these editors who added the *Zusätze*, 'Additions', from Hegel's
lectures on these subjects. Some of his lectures were also published separately:
on aesthetics, on the history of philosophy, on philosophy of history, and on
philosophy of religion. These too shed light on the corresponding sections of the
Encyclopaedia, especially on the Philosophy of Mind.[5]

THE *ENCYCLOPAEDIA*

The 1830 edition of Hegel's *Encyclopaedia* has the following overall structure.
It begins with the Prefaces to all three editions. The most interesting of these is
the second, which discusses the relationship between religion and philosophy and
the question whether philosophy is pantheistic.[6] There follows a long introduction, discussing the general nature of philosophy and of logic in particular. Then
Hegel supplies a critique of his predecessors—primarily Leibniz and his followers, Kant and F. H. Jacobi[7]—which, he suggests, may be a better introduction
to his system than the *Phenomenology of Spirit* was (Enc. I, §25). After a brisk
account of the three aspects of the logical method—'intellect', 'dialectic' or 'negative reason', and 'speculation' or 'positive reason'[8]—the Logic proper begins at
§84.

Like the *Encyclopaedia* as a whole, the Logic is divided into three parts. The
first is the 'Doctrine of Being'. It begins with 'pure being', the simplest of all
concepts, without which we cannot begin to conceive the world. But *pure* being,
being with no specifications, is equivalent to 'nothing' and passes over into nothing. 'Nothing', however, is equivalent to being, so it passes back into being. This

---

[5] Hegel's posthumous editors published only his lectures on subjects that were not dealt with at
length in his published works. More recently his lectures on other subjects, such as logic, nature,
and right have been published. Attempts have also been made to distinguish the courses that
Hegel gave in different years—his original editors stitched together materials from different years.
Especially relevant to *Encyclopaedia* III are his Jena lectures on *Geist*, translated by L. Rauch as *Hegel
and the Human Spirit: A Translation of the Jena Lectures on the Philosophy of Spirit (1805–6) with
Commentary* ((Detroit: Wayne State University Press, 1983).

[6] In Wallace's translation of the first part of the *Encyclopaedia*, *The Logic of Hegel* (2nd edn.,
Oxford: Oxford University Press, 1892), the Prefaces are summarized, but not translated. They are
now translated in a more recent version, *The Encyclopaedia Logic* (Indianapolis: Hackett, 1991),
trans. T. Geraets, H. Harris and W. Suchting.

[7] Friedrich Heinrich Jacobi (1743–1819) argued that immediate feeling and faith are the basis
of all our beliefs, including in particular religious beliefs.

[8] 'Reason' translates *Vernunft*, which contrasts with the more rigid and static *Verstand*.
Translators of Kant and Hegel usually render *Verstand* as 'understanding'. I depart from
tradition, preferring 'intellect' for three reasons: (1) 'Intellect' generates an adjective, 'intellectual'
(*verständig*)—and also others from the same stem such as 'intelligent' and 'intelligible'—that is not
easily confused with the noun. (2) 'Intellect' conveys the ideas of separation and clarity, which Hegel
associates with *Verstand*, better than 'understanding' does. An intellect may be 'sharp', 'penetrating',
or 'piercing', whereas 'understanding' suggests agreement and sympathy. (3) The medieval ancestor
of Hegel's (and Kant's) distinction between *Verstand* and *Vernunft* was the distinction between
intellectus and *ratio*.

oscillation between the two amounts to 'becoming'. But becoming subsides and congeals into *Dasein*, 'determinate being', a fusion of being and nothing.[9] An entity has a definite nature or quality (its 'being') that excludes a range of other natures or qualities (its non-being or 'nothing'). From the categories of quality we proceed to those of quantity (magnitude, number, etc.), and finally to 'measure', where quality and quantity intertwine. (A human being, for example, necessarily changes its shape as it increases in size.)

The second division of Logic is the 'Doctrine of Essence'. It considers concepts that capture, more obviously than those in the first division, the relationships between entities, and the inner nature underlying their outer appearance. Thus these concepts come in correlated pairs, such as essence–appearance, identity–difference, thing–properties, substance–accidents, and cause–effect.

The third and final division of the Logic is the 'Doctrine of the Concept'.[10] Like the preceding divisions, this contains three sections. The first deals with the 'subjective concept'. It considers the subject matter of traditional logic, the varieties of concepts, judgements, and inferences or syllogisms. (Despite his use of the word 'subjective' Hegel tends to regard concepts, judgements, and syllogisms as objective in a way that traditional logic does not. A concept is, for him, not simply a mental or a linguistic entity, but is embedded in things and determines their structure and their growth. Judgements and syllogisms are similarly implanted in the nature of things and not simply our ways of representing the nature of things.) The second section deals with the 'object'. There are three main types of object. The lowest type is mechanical. An example of this is the solar system, though higher types of entity, such as the mind, are often regarded as mechanical—in Hegel's view, inappropriately. Next comes the chemical object—for example, the compounding of an acid and an alkali to form a salt. Finally, there is 'teleology', in which an agent exploits the mechanical and chemical properties of an object to impose its purpose on it. With this unification of a purpose (i.e. the agent's concept) and an object, we reach the third section: the 'Idea', the unity of the concept and the object.[11] The first case of this is life or the living organism, which cannot, in Hegel's view, be explained mechanically or chemically, but

[9] Heidegger has since adopted the word '*Dasein*' to refer specifically to human being(s) and sometimes stresses its literal meaning: 'being [*sein*] there [*da*]'. Hegel's use of the word is different. He applies it to anything that has a definite character. In Enc. III, it usually contrasts with the 'concept' of something, and I have generally translated it as 'reality' or 'embodiment'.

[10] Hegel's word for 'concept', *Begriff*, is often translated (by, for example, Wallace and A. V. Miller) as 'Notion', in part because Kant used '*notio*' as its Latin equivalent. I prefer to translate it as 'concept', a word that has a more secure position in English philosophical discourse.

[11] The initial capital in 'Idea' is intended to distinguish Hegel's word *Idee* from the word *Vorstellung*, which I usually translate as 'representation', but, when this becomes unbearable, as 'idea'. A *Vorstellung* is roughly an idea in the ordinary sense of the word 'idea', whereas an *Idee* is more like a Platonic idea. In Hegel's usage an *Idee* is the unity of a *Begriff* and its *Objekt*, though he often uses other words, such as *Realität* ('reality') or *Dasein* ('reality, embodiment') in place of *Objekt*.

only in terms of the concept that it embodies. A more advanced case is 'cognition' and the 'will', which, in their different ways, unify a concept or concepts with objects. The final case, and the climax of the Logic as a whole, is the 'absolute Idea'. This represents Hegel's own Logic, which, as thought about thought, is a perfect match between the object, the thought that is thought about, and the concept, the thought that thinks about it. The Logic thus in a way returns to its beginning, to pure being.

There is another way in which the Logic returns to its beginning. The absolute Idea represents not only the Logic itself, but also the way in which logical categories or thoughts inform and structure the world. The convergence, within logic, between the concept and the object prefigures and explains the convergence between logic (or the 'logical Idea') and the world outside logic. Thus at the end of the Logic we turn to Philosophy of Nature and this begins with an account of space, which embodies (though only approximately) the first category of logic, pure being. In this part of the *Encyclopaedia* Hegel ranges through the science of his day, considering such topics as time, motion, the solar system, crystals, electricity, plants, and animals. He concludes with the death of an animal and this provides him with a (somewhat fanciful) transition to *Geist*, the theme of the third part of the *Encyclopaedia*.

Mind, like nature, embodies the logical Idea and is structured by it. In particular, the Philosophy of Mind follows the path prescribed in the third division of the Logic. It begins with the *concept* of mind: the mind is essentially something that strives to know itself. This essential characteristic of mind generates (Hegel assures us) its whole development: its emergence from its 'soulful' state in the womb and in infancy, its drive to comprehend the world, its capacity for perception, thought, and will, its conquest of the natural world and its formation of families, societies, and states. Eventually, it rises above the secular world to find itself as 'mind as such', mind freed from the confines of nature. It does this in religion, especially the Christian religion, which displays in a pictorial form the tripartite structure of reality that Hegel's philosophy presents in a prosaic form. So finally mind turns to philosophy. Now mind not only becomes fully aware of the concept of *mind*. It also gains knowledge of the concept as such, of the logical Idea that underlies both nature and mind. For philosophy begins with logic, and this takes us right back to the beginning of the *Encyclopaedia*. The *Encyclopaedia* circles back on itself, and in doing this (Hegel believes) it reflects the circular structure of reality.

SUBJECTIVE MIND

The *Encyclopaedia* presents, then, an ordered system that returns to its own beginning, a circular system. The driving force behind this movement is the mind itself. For mind (Hegel believes) is implicit even in nature and accounts for its hierarchical structure. In nature, however, mind is only implicit. Nature is not conscious. The mind in it is no more than the thoughts or categories embedded in it. Mind emerges explicitly only in human beings. And this is the theme of the third part of the *Encyclopaedia*.

But what is the mind? Hegel's word is *Geist*, which does not exactly correspond to the English word 'mind', which has in fact no single equivalent in the English language. The most common translations are 'mind' and 'spirit', one or other of which is usually appropriate for Hegel's use of the term. But within this broad range *Geist* takes on a bewildering variety of apparently distinct senses. In its most general sense, 'mind' contrasts with 'nature' and with such terms as 'matter'. Nature and matter are the concern of the Philosophy of Nature. This deals with space, time, plants, animals, and so on. (Animals do not, in Hegel's view, have minds nor are they in his sense 'conscious'. But this does not imply that they do not, for example, feel pain.) Philosophy of Mind, by contrast, deals with what is specifically human, including for example the state, art, and religion—topics that do not usually fall within the range of what we call 'philosophy of mind'. 'Mind' also contrasts with 'logic'. It does so in at least two respects. First, logic is 'abstract'. It deals with concepts of great generality, the concept of 'substance' for example, which apply equally readily to both nature and mind. Secondly, although logic governs our thought and is something that we think about, Hegel's Logic is not, officially at least, concerned with our *thinking* about, or in terms of, logic. It is concerned only with logical concepts and forms themselves, and these do not fall within the scope of the human or therefore of the philosophy of mind.

There is, secondly, a more restricted sense of *Geist* in which it contrasts with *Seele*, 'soul'. Philosophers before Hegel often regarded the 'soul' as a spiritual substance distinct from, though temporarily lodged in, the human body. In Hegel's preferred sense, '*Seele*' is closer in meaning to Aristotle's word '*psuche*', which is what makes something *alive*. Aristotle concluded that plants and animals, as well as men, have souls simply because they are alive, though he did not believe that their souls were immortal. Hegel discusses plants and animals in his Philosophy of Nature, but he hardly raises the question whether they have souls or not. In fact, Hegel is less inclined than Aristotle is to regard human beings as 'rational animals', that is, as similar to animals, only with reason added to them. For him men differ from animals all the way down. Nevertheless for Hegel 'soul' refers primarily to those aspects of human beings in which, though they differ from animals and a fortiori from plants, they are still closely connected to nature. Thus 'Anthropology', literally the 'study of man', but for Hegel the study of the soul, deals with such themes as the foetus, racial differences, the course of a human life, sleep and waking, and sexuality. *Geist*, by contrast, refers to the more intellectual or rational features of humanity. One important difference between *Seele* and *Geist* is this. *Geist*, the mind, differentiates itself more or less sharply both from other minds and from the external world of which it is conscious. A properly working mind knows that the objects of which it is conscious—trees, houses, rivers—are distinct from itself. It knows that they exist even when it is not conscious of them. It knows that they have aspects which it does not currently, and perhaps never will, perceive. It distinguishes between the hot fire and the pain it receives from it, locating the heat in the external world and the pain in itself. It also knows that other people are similar to, yet distinct from, itself. They perceive roughly the same objects as it itself does, but perceive them from a different perspective. Other people, I come to realize, do not know everything I know. That is why I can lie to them. They know things that I do not know. That is why they can lie to me.

The soul, by contrast, does not draw a boundary between itself and other things or between itself and other people. This is especially true of the foetus, and to a lesser extent of the infant. It is the job of the mind, not the soul, to mark these boundaries. It begins to do this in the section that Hegel calls the 'Phenomenology of Mind'.[12] 'Phenomenology' is literally the 'study of appearance(s)'. Characteristically, Hegel probably has in play several different senses of the word 'appearance'. Among other things, it means the 'emergence' of mind. The mind appears on the scene. It emerges from the self-enclosed, self-absorbed soul-state of infancy to make contact with a world distinct from itself and with people other than itself. It both differentiates itself from its 'other' and enters into relationship with it. When the mind has fully emerged, it retreats (Hegel implies) back into itself. In the section called 'Psychology, the Mind' Hegel gives an account of the powers and development of the mind that makes only occasional reference to the external world on which these powers are exercised. The relationship of 'psychology' to 'phenomenology' differs radically from the relationship of 'anthropology' to either. The soul constitutes, and anthropology describes, a stage or level of the human being distinct from and prior to the fully developed mind. A human being, a foetus for example, might be a soul without yet being a mind. Conversely, in a fully developed mind, the soul plays only a subsidiary and subdued role. But 'phenomenology' and 'psychology'

---

[12] The relationship between this section of the *Encyclopaedia* and Hegel's 1807 book of the same title is a vexed problem. The book was originally intended as an introduction to the 'system of science', which was to consist of logic, philosophy of nature, and philosophy of mind. But Hegel did not complete this plan. In a 'Remark' to the *Encyclopaedia* added to the 1827 edition (§25) he says that the book expanded beyond his original design and came to incorporate much of the material intended for inclusion in the philosophies of nature and mind. This explains why he abandoned the idea of making his book the introduction to his system. But why did he then include a truncated version of the book in his encyclopaedia? The answer is this. The book, roughly speaking, describes the ascent of mind from innocence to philosophy. This is clearly an appropriate introduction to philosophy: an account of how philosophy emerges is one way of leading Hegel's pupils to philosophy from their relative innocence. But it is also an appropriate, perhaps indispensable, part of the story of mind. Mind does, after all, ascend from innocence to philosophy. So when the *Phenomenology* drops out as an introduction to philosophy, it naturally finds a place in the Philosophy of Mind. It might even occupy both positions, serving both as an introduction to philosophy as a whole and as a strand in the philosophy of mind. But since Hegel's *Encyclopaedia* is circular, it implicitly occupies both positions anyway. Nevertheless, Hegel still remained attached to the book. He began to revise it for a second edition shortly before his death.

do not describe different stages or levels of the mind. They simply describe the mind from different points of view. No one could have the powers that Hegel includes under the heading of psychology without also being conscious of objects and other people, without being self-conscious. Conversely, no one could be conscious and self-conscious without having those powers.

OBJECTIVE MIND

Nevertheless, Hegel regards 'psychology' as a distinct stage of mind, a stage in which the mind withdraws into itself, in order to examine itself without regard to the external world. This withdrawal of the mind is the culmination of what Hegel calls the 'subjective mind', which is (roughly speaking) the individual mind. The soul, consciousness (the subject matter of 'Phenomenology') and the 'free' mind (the subject matter of 'Psychology') all fall under the general heading 'Subjective Mind'. It is within the sphere of 'subjective mind' that the soul is distinguished from the mind proper. Now we come to *objective* mind. In a typically Hegelian transition the withdrawal of the mind into itself is succeeded by the mind's return to the external world. The mind has already ventured into the external world, in the form of 'consciousness'. But now it is the external world with a difference. The world of which the mind was 'conscious' was initially a strange and alien world, a world of natural entities and of uncivilized, hostile people. Even when the mind came to understand this world it remained the natural rather than the social world. Its relations with other people were relations of dominance and subjection. Such understanding, dominance and subjection are essential steps on the way to objective mind. But they are not the same as objective mind. When mind is objective it has completed its task of taming and permeating the world. The world is no longer a world of merely natural entities and antagonistic people. Such natural entities as figure in it are the raw materials from which we produce goods for consumption and exchange. They are transformed in the houses we dwell in, the parks in which we stroll, and the buildings in which we conduct our public affairs. The people we primarily encounter are not our enemies, but the members of family: our parents, spouse, and children. They are, again, in 'civil society', our employers or employees, our business partners or rivals, our fellow guild-members, and so on. And finally we encounter or are at any rate affected by the various officials who manage the affairs of state. All this is the work of objective mind.

Objective mind is closely related to the *Volksgeist*, the 'mind of a people' or 'national mind'. The social and political order that Hegel describes under the heading 'Objective Mind' does not embrace the whole of humanity. Human beings are divided into 'peoples', the Germans, the French, the Italians, the English, and so on, each of them united by their shared customs, sentiments, language, and history. Some of these peoples are organized into societies of roughly the type that Hegel describes. (What Hegel actually describes is probably no existing society, but an idealized version of the Prussian constitution.[13]) A people's society—its family arrangements, its laws, and so on—is informed and permeated by the 'mind' or 'spirit' of that people, by its general way of looking at things and doing things. It is, in Hegel's view, neither desirable nor possible for the whole of humanity to unite in a single society governed by a single world-state. If humanity were to retain their present diversity of cultures, religions, languages, etc., the bonds between them would be too loose for them to form a single cohesive society. If humanity were to adopt a single language, culture, and perhaps religion, then the bonds between them would also be loosened, since there would be no significant conflicts to weld them together. In either case, Hegel might argue, this all-embracing world-state would share the fate of the Roman Empire, disintegrating into a collection of self-engrossed individuals. The unity of the state, he believes, depends on its being one among several such states, whose occasional bouts of warfare wrest their citizens from absorption in their private affairs out into the public realm. There are, then, a diversity of 'national minds' and Hegel sees no prospect of their homogenisation into a single mind with the same degree of coherence and unity as a national mind.

There is, however, a single mind at work in all this. Hegel calls it the *Welt-geist*, the 'world-mind'. It embraces not so much the variety of national minds in existence at any given time, but the national minds that have emerged over the course of history. A national mind does not, in Hegel's view, last for ever. It arises, flourishes, and declines, summoned for judgement before the court of the world. At any given period of world-history, one national mind is dominant, representing the cutting edge of the advance of humanity. First it was China, then India, then Persia, Egypt, Greece, Rome, and finally the 'Germanic peoples', the Christian civilization of Western Europe. One might object that these supposedly successive civilizations are for the most part too disparate, too disconnected, to constitute the work of a single mind or spirit in the way in which a single civilization could be regarded, with some plausibility, as the work of a single national mind. This objection may be intensified into the doubt whether there has been, until quite recently, such a thing as 'world-history'. Until some way into the nineteenth century, events in, say, China had little if any effect on events in, say, England. Events in China could not become known in England until several months after their occurrence, if they ever became known at all. So, we might say, there was Chinese history, Indian history, English history, perhaps even European history, but hardly any world-history. And without world-history it makes little sense to speak of a 'world-mind'. A mind must have more coherence than we can plausibly attribute to most of humanity's history. But Hegel has

---

[13] Allan W. Wood argues, in his *Hegel's Ethical Thought* (Cambridge: Cambridge University Press, 1990), 13, that the state that Hegel describes in his *Philosophy of Right* 'bears a striking resemblance' not to the actual Prussian state, but to the plan for a new constitution drafted by Wilhelm von Humboldt and K. A. von Hardenberg in 1819, but never put into practice.

given an answer to this. It is the dominant culture of each epoch that is the main focus of the world-mind's spotlight. Other civilizations, even if they have been dominant in the past, recede into the background. It does not matter if Western Europe, in the period of its dominance, knows little of what is happening in China. Nothing of great significance is happening in China, and China has descended into what we might call the subconscious of world-mind. What matters, therefore, is not primarily the coherence of cultures contemporary with each other, but the coherence of the historical sequence of dominant cultures: China, India, Persia, Egypt, Greece, Rome, Western Europe.

ABSOLUTE MIND

Hegel associates this world-mind with 'divine providence'. Sure enough God makes his final appearance shortly afterwards in 'Absolute Mind'. Absolute mind comprises art, religion, and philosophy, though religion, Hegel says, is the dominant term of the triad. (In Hegel's view, art, especially pre-Christian art, has a more or less close connection with religion.) Why is this mind 'absolute'? It is the final term of a triad: subjective mind—objective mind—absolute mind. So we might expect, from our acquaintance with Hegel's other triads, that absolute mind will be a combination of subjective and objective minds or, what may amount to the same thing, a restoration of subjective mind on a higher level. One obvious difference between subjective and objective mind is this. Subjective mind is the same for everyone. Every normal human being, whether in China, India, Persia, Egypt, Greece, Rome, or modern Europe has more or less the characteristics outlined under the heading 'Subjective Mind'. What Hegel describes may in fact be a peculiarly European mind, and a nineteenth-century mind at that. But that is surely not his intention. His intention is to describe the individual mind as such. With objective mind it is otherwise. More or less every individual mind, at least in the period of recorded history, belongs to a community that is an objectification of mind. But individuals do not all belong to the same community nor do they all occupy the same role in their community. Human beings are divided up into groups—'peoples'—with distinctive cultures. They are divided up into historical epochs. Within their society individuals are divided up into nobles and commoners, traders and farmers, and so on. Worst of all, in some societies, in fact in practically all pre-Christian societies and in some Christian ones too, people are divided up into slave and free. Now the aim of mind, Hegel insists, is to know itself, to know mind as such. This is what Hegel claims to have done in his *Philosophy of Mind*. But how can we know mind as such if mind is divided in this way? Surely all that we can know is some particular type of mind, the Roman mind, the mind of the free man, the mind of the worker, the mind of the nobleman, and so on. We have already seen that Hegel despairs of uniting everyone in a single society. Nor would this help much unless everyone had the same role. Even then, if mind was to know itself, everyone would have to reflect on themselves, reflect, that is, on mind as such.

At this point absolute mind resolves our dilemma. Here the mind attempts to rise above its historical and social setting to consider mind as such. At first it is not very successful in this. It cannot easily extricate mind from its entanglement in nature, let alone its social context. The Greeks achieved a rounded, realistic portrayal of human beings, but they presented their surface appearance, not their inner depths. The man they presented was Greek man, Greek mind, not mind as such. But Christianity is different. Christianity reveals the inner depth of man. It also reveals the breadth of mind. It appeals to all men, Greek and Jew, male and female, slave and free. It presents, or at least begins to present, mind as such, mind purified of nature and of local peculiarities. Philosophy, the highest term of the triad, completes this process. A philosopher inevitably belongs to a nation. Philosophers are Chinese, Indian, Greek, Roman, German, or French. But the philosophy they produce does not appeal essentially only to members of their own nation. Greek religion is specifically Greek. It makes little sense for a Jew or a Persian, embedded in Jewish or Persian culture, to worship the gods of Greece. But Greek philosophy, Platonism for example, is not specifically Greek. It is presented as true for everyone. Anyone, whether Jew or Greek, male or female, slave or free, can become a Platonist. If someone converts from Platonism to, say, Cartesianism, they do not need to change their nationality from Greek to French. A philosophy may of course consider the differences and affinities between Greek minds, Chinese minds, and German minds. It may also argue, as Hegel does, that its capacity to do this adequately and its capacity to consider mind as such, stem from the objective mind of Western Europe and its Christian religion. But in doing so, philosophy is not identifying itself with, or appealing to, any particular type of mind, not even Western European mind. It presents its findings as true for anyone and everyone, true for mind as such.

There is therefore a peculiar affinity between Christianity and philosophy. Both are concerned with mind as such and are presented to mind as such, to everyone. But there is a difference. Christianity tells a story about God, who is himself a mind distinct from any human mind. He then generates a son, who is again a mind. And when, after his death and resurrection, the son has returned to God, another mind descends on humanity, the holy 'spirit'. Philosophy is grateful for this story, but does not take it literally. It interprets God the father as the 'logical Idea', which underlies 'nature'—the philosophical counterpart of God the son[14]—and then the development of the human mind (the Holy Spirit, as it were), whose highest phase is philosophy, which comprehends the logical Idea, nature, and mind itself.

---

[14] For Hegel, Christ or the 'son' represents both nature and man. See Enc. III, §381.

HEGEL'S MYTH?

Hegel, we might protest, has reworked the Christian story into another story, which though less pictorial is no less fanciful. It is a story of mind's endeavour to disentangle itself from the natural world and from the local peculiarities of the social world in order to know itself in its purity, to achieve, as Hegel puts it, its 'freedom' and 'truth'. Why should we accept this story? Does it have any objective status? Or is it just Hegel's way of arranging the multifarious facts about humanity into a satisfying narrative? Even as a narrative, it has conspicuous defects. In the first place, it does not follow a single time-sequence. It begins with the soul, and this (apart from its anomalous resurgence in deranged adults) precedes in time the 'appearance' of mind, described in the 'Phenomenology'. Then the powers of the mind are considered in 'Psychology', but these do not, very obviously, temporally follow the 'appearance' of mind. Objective mind comes next. Within objective mind there is a temporal sequence driven by the world-spirit, one culture giving way to the next. But objective mind as such does not follow subjective mind in time. There was no time that Hegel knew of when human beings with the powers considered by 'Psychology' did not form social groups. (Objective mind may temporally follow the state of nature described in the early part of the 'Phenomenology', but Hegel does not regard that as serious history.). Next comes absolute mind: art, religion, and philosophy. Art does not emerge later than objective mind, let alone the specific institutions that Hegel describes under the heading 'Objective Mind'. Art has been around as long as anything Hegel could recognize as humanity. The same is true of religion. But Hegel avoids this difficulty by speaking here primarily of 'revealed religion', that is Christianity, and by merging earlier religions into his account of art. Finally we come to philosophy. This emerged later than art and religion. Its beginnings in Europe are generally located in Greece in the sixth century BC. But it pre-dates revealed religion by at least 500 years. Even the first indisputably great philosopher, Plato, was born 427 years before the supposed birth of Christ. Perhaps Plato did not get to the bottom of mind as such. But Hegel had a high esteem for the philosophy of mind of his pupil, Aristotle.

Hegel's Philosophy of Mind does not follow a single temporal sequence. Suppose we accept, nevertheless, that Hegel presents a single narrative of a journey from the natural soul to mind's full self-knowledge. Is there a single subject of this narrative? What is that subject? It is *Geist*, Hegel says. But '*Geist*', as Hegel uses it, seems to be applied too liberally to denote a single subject. Subjective mind, objective mind, national mind, world-mind, absolute mind, the holy spirit: what links these together to form a single developing mind? Perhaps they bear a family-resemblance to each other, But that is surely not enough for them to constitute a single subject. In any case, it easy to doubt whether there is such a thing as objective mind, national mind, or world-mind, let alone the holy spirit. This doubt operates at two levels. First, one might question the ontological status of societies, nations, world-history, even of philosophy. Do they amount to anything more than arrangements of individuals—citizens, historical agents, philosophers, and their audience? Secondly, one might resist the suggestion that such entities, whatever their ontological status, are 'minds' in a sense sufficiently close to that of an individual 'mind' to constitute a prolongation of the individual mind. Yet this is what Hegel requires. It is mind, a single mind, that makes the journey from nature to self-knowledge. It begins as soul, and here it is more or less continuous throughout humanity, in fact (Hegel suggests) throughout nature as a whole. There are no clear boundaries between one soul and another soul, or between the soul and its natural environment. With the 'appearance' of mind (in contrast to 'soul') boundaries are established, between one mind and another mind, and between a mind and the world. Mind 'as such', considered in 'Psychology', withdraws into itself as a distinct, individual mind. Then, as objective mind, it re-establishes its connections with other individual minds and with the surrounding world. But now the individual mind retains its individuality. It is not lost in other minds and in the world. Its relations with other minds are intelligibly structured, and the world it inhabits is permeated and ordered by mind. But this objective mind is localized in space and time. It is not mind as such, not even the objectification of mind as such. The closest that we come to mind as such in this sphere is the temporal sequence of dominant national minds presented by the world-mind. However, the peoples whose minds are thus objectified are not content to remain within the confines of their secular social and political life. They try to make sense of the cosmos and of their own place in it. They express their attempt and its outcome in their religion and their art, which in its early stages is closely intertwined with religion. They worship gods who represent their conception of mind as such. But their religion is not entirely separate from their secular life. It informs and sustains their political and social institutions. Religion is a sort of bridge between localized objective mind and mind as such. Pre-Christian religions, as we have seen, tend to project their localized objective mind onto the divine plane. But Christianity purports to avoid this. It presents mind as such for all human beings. Philosophy does this too, only purged of the pictorial elements of Christianity. Mind has returned to the unity from which it began, but now on a higher level. Mind now knows itself inside and out. It can compose a philosophy of mind, something of which it is not capable at any lower stage of itself. Mind has thus become 'true' mind. It has become its own object.

IN DEFENCE OF HEGEL

In the hope of avoiding these criticisms of Hegel's procedure, we might consider the stages of mind not as temporally successive stages but as aspects of an individual person. The person begins life as a soul. Here he is not clearly differentiated from other persons and their souls or from the external world. A person's soul-life persists into adult life. But then, except in cases of derangement, the soul is subordinate to the person's objective consciousness. The emergence of objective consciousness is described in the 'Phenomenology of Mind'. Here a person becomes aware of himself as one person among other persons distinct from, though similar to, himself, inhabiting an orderly world to which they are cognitively and practically related. Such objective consciousness depends on the mental powers considered in 'Psychology'. Hegel presents this section as a sort of withdrawal of mind into itself. But there is, at this stage, really no such withdrawal. The person we are considering does not yet describe his own mental powers and activities. He can only do this properly when he becomes a philosopher.

So far we have focused more or less on the single individual, albeit an individual whose self-consciousness requires an awareness of other individuals. Now we turn to 'Objective Mind' and consider the person as a property owner, as a family member, a participant in civil society, and a citizen of a state. All this does not leave the individual unchanged. The social and political structure permeates the individual mind. Even non-Hegelians acknowledge this:

> The whole process of choosing has itself an influence on one's identifications, therefore on the self, and therefore on the goals one seeks to maximize. On the whole, the process of making market choices tends to narrow one's identifications to the individual or, at the most, to the family. The process of voting, on the other hand, with all that it presupposes in the way of discussion and techniques of reciprocity, tends to broaden one's identifications beyond the individual and the family.[15]

We need not insist, then, that a social order is itself a 'mind' larger than the minds of the individuals composing it. We need only refer to the enlargement of the individual mind stemming from its relationships to other individual minds. We can, if need be, individualize the 'world-mind' in a similar way. An individual in a society, say a German individual in nineteenth-century Prussia, not only absorbs the culture of his own society. He also contains within him, more or less implicitly, the cultures or mentalities of the societies that preceded it. The German mentality has developed out of the Greek mentality, in such a way that although it is more complex than the Greek mentality it is intelligibly related to it and retains the Greek mentality as a subordinate part or element of itself. And similarly with other historic cultures. Scratch a modern German and you will find a Roman, a Greek, and even an Egyptian buried within him. This is why he can understand them. At this stage the individual is of course only dimly aware of the history that lies behind him and which, in a way, lies buried within him. It takes a historian to unearth and clarify the details. But he is likely to be aware that his

---

[15] Robert A. Dahl and Charles E. Lindblom, *Politics, Economics and Welfare* (New York: Transaction Books, 1953), 422, quoted from Brian Barry, *Political Argument* (London: Routledge, 1965), 299.

social order has not been around from eternity and also that it will not endure everlastingly.

RELIGION

Germans of the early nineteenth century were religious. Humans throughout history have for the most part been religious. They believed in a supernatural, supersocial realm inhabited by one or more gods and they engaged in rituals directed towards these gods. Such beliefs and conduct seem to come as naturally to human beings as does their association with their own kind. Human beings are religious almost as inevitably as they are gregarious. (Not everyone is religious, of course. But nor is everyone gregarious.[16]) Why this should be so is far from clear. No religious beliefs are obviously true, and religious conduct does not provide any obvious benefits comparable to those we derive from cooperation with others. The crucial factor, Hegel believes, is man himself. Man is a finite creature. He lives at a particular time in a particular place. He has a particular position in a society, a society that is, moreover, only one of the very many societies that there are and have been. For the most part man views the world from the particular position he occupies in it, from what we might call the 'worm's-eye view'. But man is also 'infinite'. He can, in thought and imagination, survey the world from a perspective independent of his particular location in the world, adopting the bird's-eye view or, as we might call it, the 'God's-eye view'. That humans are able to adopt such a perspective is one of their main differences from other animals. Non-human animals, we might plausibly suppose, are aware only of their immediate surroundings in the more or less immediate present. They do not reflect on the past or the future. They do not consider how things look from the viewpoint of their prey or their predator. Humans are different. They range in imagination over remote times and places. They enter sympathetically into the viewpoints of others, of other people, other tribes, even other species, and even the gods. Naturally their attempts to do this are only sporadic and generally imperfect. When they ascribe such a viewpoint to a god or gods, the gods they concoct are too similar to themselves to be properly godlike. Their gods are too Egyptian, too Greek, or even too human. (The mythical transformations of gods into animals are, in part, an attempt to overcome such limitations.) But at least they tried. They were attempting, Hegel would say, to rise to the standpoint of 'mind as such', mind unhampered by local peculiarities and limitations. And this attempt, he would add, is not simply an agreeable addition to their everyday worm's-eye view of things. Their worm's-eye view could not be what it is if it were not for their ability to adopt the God's-eye view. Even in their everyday, unreflective life, men do not see things and conduct themselves in the way that other animals do. And this

---

[16] Nevertheless: 'As a gregarious animal, man is excited both by the absence and by the presence of his kind' (William James, The Principles of Psychology (New York: Dover, 1950), ii. 430.)

xxiv   *Introduction*

is because of their ability to rise above their everyday, unreflective life. We can, for example, critically assess our everyday desires and also our everyday beliefs. What I, as a worm, desire may not be worthy, and what I believe may not be true, when surveyed from a higher standpoint. In doing this, we need not, of course, ascend, or even purport to ascend, all the way up to the God's-eye view—as, say, Descartes claimed to do. We can go some way up the ladder, without going right to the top. But Hegel would say that our ability and readiness to advance up the ladder at all presupposes that we have some conception, however vague or fanciful, of what can be seen from the top of the ladder.

But why, it might be asked, should we ascribe the bird's-eye view to gods? And even if we do, why should we worship them? Some scientists and philosophers seem eminently capable of adopting the 'infinite' viewpoint, without assigning it to any god except perhaps metaphorically. The infinite viewpoint seems a distinct matter from God. One can adopt the viewpoint without the god, though one cannot, conversely, adopt the god without something of the viewpoint. Hegel's response is this. Religious believers often regard a god as a mind, and a mind quite distinct from any human mind. The Christian God, for example, is regarded as an infinite mind, very different and quite distinct from the finite human mind. But this is a mistake, albeit an entirely intelligible mistake. Gods may be minds, but they are not distinct from the human mind. This is because the human mind is not exclusively finite. It is *both* finite *and* infinite. So in a way man is not exclusively *man*. He is *both* man *and* God. This becomes more or less explicit in Christianity. Christ is both man and God. And Christ represents, in Hegel's view, man in general. In pre-Christian religions man's divinity is only implicit, obscured, for example, by the representation of gods in animal forms. In fact, for most of human history man's essential divinity is only implicit. Divinity is not, for Hegel, an all or nothing matter. Man *ascends* to God over the course of history. And this means not simply that man becomes aware of God or of his own divinity, but that he gradually becomes God.

This might be taken as atheism in disguise. If God or gods are simply an aspect of man, then God and gods do not really exist. They are on a par with other human fictions such as Sherlock Holmes, flying saucers, and pink rats. But Hegel would deny this. Sherlock Holmes, flying saucers, and pink rats are not essential creations of the human mind. It may be essential to us that we create fictions, but not these particular fictions. Our ability to adopt the 'infinite' viewpoint is, by contrast, essential to us. We would not be recognizably human if we lacked it altogether. It is then natural enough to ascribe this viewpoint to a superhuman mind or minds, conceived in accordance with the level of our culture. To deny flatly the existence of gods or God is to underrate the reach and depth of the human mind. The human mind is expansive and effervescent. It does not remain lodged within our skulls. It ranges out to coalesce with the minds of other human beings, and it ascends to the infinity of mind as such. So Hegel does not deny the existence of these gods. He regards belief in them as a 'representation', a pictorial version of the truths attained by the pure thinking of the philosopher, especially the Hegelian philosopher, who is perhaps more godlike than the rest of humanity.

CHRISTIANITY

What is so special about Christianity? One of its merits is that Christianity establishes what Hegel regards as a proper relationship between the finite and the infinite, between the secular world and the world beyond. There are two main ways in which we can go wrong about this. First, we may view them as separated by an unbridgeable gulf. Then we might respond to this in various ways. We might focus exclusively on the secular world, more or less ignoring the world beyond as unknowable and/or irrelevant. We might focus primarily on the world beyond, regarding this secular world as valueless or evil, to be redeemed, if at all, only if it is thoroughly subordinated to the world beyond. (In the 1807 *Phenomenology of Spirit* Hegel had called this attitude the 'unhappy consciousness'.) Or we might oscillate between these two worlds, without discerning or establishing any significant relation between them. The second way in which we may go wrong about the relation between the finite and the infinite is by failing to distinguish them sufficiently from each other, by making their relationship too close. Then we shall not regard the secular world as a properly independent world. We shall see the hand of gods or God everywhere, and neglect the scientific exploration of the natural world and the secular development of the world of mind. In contrast to each of these errors, Christianity—especially, in Hegel's view, Lutheran Christianity—distinguishes the two realms, but establishes an intelligible rational relationship between them. It inspires us to explore the world of nature for its own sake, guided by our religious beliefs but not overwhelmed by them. It encourages us to establish secular, constitutional regimes, keeping the church (and religious spirituality) in its proper place and giving adherents of other religions, or of none, a share in public life.

That non-Christians as well as Christians are granted a share in public life and, more generally, that Christianity does not ultimately tolerate the exclusion of any human being from the community is a crucial step on the way to the discovery of mind as such.[17] But what is a human being? Non-Christians or 'humanists' tend to take human beings for granted, as a sheer biological fact. Whatever fundamental equality is ascribed to them is to be established by empirical inquiry. Even when such equality is denied it is generally assumed at least that no human being

[17] In Hegel's Germany women did not have civic or citizen rights, though they had human rights and were not seen as slaves. However, the exclusion of women from the affairs of state and, more or less, from civil society is not an essential feature of Christianity. Genesis 2: 27 seems to imply that women are as godlike as men: 'So God created man in his own image, in the image of God created he him; male and female created he them'. (I owe this reference to the Revd Canon Trevor Williams.)

should be enslaved by another human being or, presumably, by any other sort of being. 'Slavery is not natural', we say. 'There are no natural slaves', not, at any rate, *human* natural slaves. Hegel disagrees. Slavery, he thinks, is natural. What could be more natural than enslaving one's defeated foe—except perhaps killing and eating him? No matter whether the slave is a natural slave in Aristotle's sense, deficient in rationality.[18] Whether or not there are natural slaves, there are at any rate natural enslavers. It comes naturally to us to enslave our opponents. But the naturalness of slavery, Hegel insists, is not a point in its favour. It is precisely its naturalness that is wrong with it. In opposing slavery Christianity appeals not to nature, but to supernature. It postulates a God-man, a sort of Platonic paradigm of humanity as such, who marks out the boundaries of humankind by recognizing them and preaching to them. What this means is that mind is extricated from its natural integument, so that mind alone can decide what belongs to it. Of course neither Christ nor mind can dispense altogether with the natural and the biological. How does Christ decide to preach to men but to ride on a donkey, to cast the demons into swine and not the swine fever into men? Only by empirical observation of the differences between men, donkeys and swine. But on this basis Christ extends and sharpens the boundaries of humanity, overriding the superficial variations, gradations, and borderline cases that empirical inquiry might find. Man is then elevated to God's right hand, while the donkey is left with nothing but a cross on its back.

PHILOSOPHY

Hegel was a profoundly religious philosopher. Philosophy, he believes, has the same 'content' as religion, though it presents it in a different 'form'. This does not mean, however, that Hegel is ensnared in religious dogmas or subservient to ecclesiastical authority. For according to Hegel's interpretation of Christianity, Christianity sets man free: free to engage in worldly intellectual and scientific inquiry, free to set up secular states, free to produce non-religious, even irreligious art, free to be enlightened. It is a mistake to think that Christianity enslaves us to God and his arbitrary requirements. Previous religions may have done that, but Christianity, properly interpreted, does not. It sets us free. Freedom is not our natural condition. Our natural condition is oppression—oppression by nature, by our rulers, by our community, even by the gods. Freedom has to be striven for, and religion is, in Hegel's view, the central arena in which the battle is fought. The outcome of the battle is the liberation granted us by Lutheran Christianity.

This liberation extends to philosophy too. Besides being a religious philosopher, Hegel is also a profoundly secular philosopher. His study of nature follows,

---

[18] Hegel avoids a head-on confrontation with Aristotle's definition of a natural slave by assuming (incorrectly) that a slave was always the offspring of slaves and that, conversely, the offspring of slaves was always a slave. He therefore inferred that it was parentage, rather than defective capacity for rational deliberation, that made someone a natural slave. See Enc. III, §433.

by and large, the science of his day. The state that he describes, and endorses, in his *Encyclopaedia* and in the *Philosophy of Right*, is a thoroughly secular state. He is alive to the historic importance of technology, though (unlike Karl Marx) he regards it as an instrument of humanity's spiritual advance rather than as the force that drives it on.[19] His interpretation of Christianity (a conventional Christian might well say) all but obliterates the distinction between God and man; it makes man too much a God and God too much a man; and ultimately the object of Hegel's worship is not God, but man.

It is the liberation bestowed by Christianity that enables Hegel to be both religious and secular. For the beneficiaries of this liberation need not leave the orbit of Christianity. The Christian God, in Hegel's view, embraces what is other than himself. For example, what seems to us secular art (such as Shakespeare's plays) is for Hegel a sort of religious art: in presenting the deeds and thoughts of men it reveals an aspect of God. What seems to us a thoroughly secular state (such as that described by Hegel) is a state nurtured and sustained by Christianity. Even the atheist or agnostic discloses an aspect of God whose expression is generally stifled or prohibited by other religions.[20] Hegel did not profess atheism or agnosticism. But he did excuse his frequent failure to engage in public worship by saying: *Das Denken ist auch Gottesdienst*, 'Thinking too is service to God'.

[19] 'Another invention also tended to deprive the nobility of the ascendancy which they owed to their accoutrements—that of *gunpowder*. Humanity needed it and it made its appearance forthwith' (PH, p. 402). 'These novel ideas met with a principal organ of diffusion in the newly discovered *art of printing*, which, like the use of gunpowder, corresponds with modern character, and supplied the desideratum of the age in which it was invented, by tending to enable men to stand in an ideal connection with each other' (PH, p. 410).

[20] 'What strikes the mind so forcibly and so painfully is His [God's] absence . . . from His own world. It is a silence that speaks' (J. H. Newman, *An Essay in Aid of a Grammar of Assent* (2nd edn. London: Longman, 1892), 396–7).

Commentary

The Philosophy of Mind begins at §377, since it is the third part of the *Encyclopae-dia of the Philosophical Sciences in Outline*: the first part is Logic (§§1–244) and the second the Philosophy of Nature (§§245–376). Hegel published three editions of the *Encyclopaedia*, in 1817, 1827, and 1830. In 1840 the 1830 edition was reprinted together with *Zusätze* or 'Additions' put together from notes taken by students at his lectures. What is translated here is the 1830 edition together with the *Zusätze*.

1. This echoes the opening sentence of Aristotle's *de anima* (402^a1 ff.), which also stresses the importance and difficulty of the subject. However, Aristotle and Hegel have different things in view. For Aristotle the difficulty lies in the rela-tionship between form and matter, between the mental and the physical. For Hegel the difficulty lies primarily in the the mind's reflexivity, in the fact that the mind studies itself. (On this, see Alfredo Ferrarin, *Hegel and Aristotle* (Cam-bridge: Cambridge University Press, 2001), 258).

    Hegel's word for 'mind', *Geist*, is often translated more appropriately as 'spir-it' (as in 'the Holy Spirit', 'the spirit of the age', etc.), but its range of meaning is wider than that of either 'mind' or 'spirit'. Knowledge of mind is more 'con-crete', and less abstract, than logic or than philosophy of nature, since it presup-poses and in some way involves both logic and philosophy of nature. ('Concrete' originally meant 'grown together': cf. §396, n. 3.) In particular, *Geist* essentially 'knows itself' in a way that merely natural entities do not.

2. *Gnôthi sauton*, 'know thyself', was inscribed at the entrance to the sixth-century temple of Apollo at Delphi, next to *mêden agan*, 'nothing too much'. Herac-litus ('It belongs to all men to know themselves and have good sense') and Plato (*Charmides*, 164e7) associate the dictum with *sôphrosunê*, which meant, in the Homeric epics, 'good sense' in contrast to folly, but later acquired the mean-ing of 'temperance', a 'decent sense of one's place within the social setting and one's limitations as a human being' (C. H. Kahn, *The Art and Thought of Herac-litus* (Cambridge: Cambridge University Press, 1979), 13, cf. 116–17). *Gnôthi sauton* was not originally intended to recommend anything like Hegel's philo-sophy of mind.

3. Hegel distinguishes three types of self-knowledge: (1) One's knowledge of one's own individual characteristics. (2) 'Understanding of human nature' (*Menschen-kenntnis*)—the sort of knowledge displayed by novelists and in practical dealings with others. (*Kenntnis* usually means 'knowledge', but I have translated it as 'understanding' here to differentiate it from *Erkenntnis*, the more systematic 'knowledge' that Hegel speaks of elsewhere in this Paragraph.) (3) 'Knowledge' (*Erkenntnis*) of 'man's genuine reality, etc.'. (1) and (2) are knowledge of what

is 'particular', that is, of features peculiar to one person or to some people, while (3) is knowledge of the 'universal', of 'man as such'. To pursue (1) or (2) to the neglect of (3) is like, say, acquiring a knowledge of the stylistic peculiarities of a particular German writer, or of various types of writer, without a grasp of the structure and grammar of the German language as such, when it is this underlying structure that makes possible the various peculiarities. Hegel says both that (2) presupposes an *implicit* knowledge of the 'universal', and that it neglects *explicit*, conceptual knowledge of it, in favour of insignificant details. Knowledge of type (3), i.e. Hegelian philosophy of mind, is not simply knowledge of man's reality. It is also knowledge of 'genuine reality in and for itself—of the 'essence as mind': mind or spirit is the 'essence' of reality as a whole, not simply of the human species. (On the difference between *Kenntnis* and *Erkenntnis*, see §448, n. 2.)

4. The 'logical Idea' is the fundamental logical structure of reality and is presented in Hegel's Logic (Enc. I). 'Idea' is *Idee*, a word that is, in Hegel's usage, distinct in meaning from *Vorstellung*, 'representation, idea'. Roughly, a *Vorstellung* is an idea in one's mind, while an *Idee* is more like an objective Platonic idea. (I have followed the custom of capitalizing the first letter of 'Idea' as *Idee* in order to differentiate it from 'idea' as *Vorstellung*.) In Hegel's official usage an *Idee* is a 'concept' (*Begriff*) together with its corresponding 'reality'. An analogy that he often uses is this: a concept is like the plan or code embedded in a seed, while the full-grown tree actualizes the plan in the seed. Hegel often calls the logical Idea 'the concept', since in relation to nature and mind it is somewhat like an undeveloped seed. But it is usually called an 'Idea', because within itself it undergoes a development comparable to the growth of a tree from a seed. Starting from the simple concept of 'being', it unfolds into an elaborate logical system. However, this development is not, like the growth of a tree, a temporal process. The development is logical or, as Hegel says, 'eternal'. Despite this internal development, the logical Idea is still 'comparatively abstract', because it has yet to 'actualize' itself in the world, namely in nature and mind. The way in which this actualization occurs is mysterious, but it is, in Hegel's view, prefigured and explained by the internal development of the logical Idea. (In Enc. III, §§565–9, Hegel compares the logical Idea's self-actualization to God's creation of the world: the creation is prefigured and explained by God's internal complexity.) Enc. II has already dealt with its actualization in nature. About mind, Hegel makes two claims. First, the mind, 'finite' mind (roughly, the individual mind and also society, §§387–552) as well as 'absolute' mind (art, religion, and philosophy, §§553–77), is an actualization of the logical Idea. Secondly, mind is a 'copy' of the logical Idea. That is, the mind develops from simple beginnings in the same way as the logical Idea develops internally, except that the development of mind is, in part at least, a temporal process. What the mind develops from is the 'concept of mind'. The concept of mind is not the logical Idea as a whole, since the mind is a 'copy' of the logical Idea and should therefore develop from its concept in a similar way to that in which the logical Idea develops from *its* concept. It is rather the initial plan or outline of

mind (described in §§381–4), from which the mind develops in a sequence of necessary stages that parallel the stages of the logical Idea. It is the seed from which the mind grows.

5. The 'concept' of mind, which mind is destined to 'cognize' (*erkennen*), is now a wider notion than simply the initial plan from which the mind develops, because mind is destined to know not only its initial plan, but also the stages of its development from this plan. But Hegel could reply that the mind's whole development is implicit in and determined by its initial plan (as the growth of a tree is implicit in and determined by the plan in the seed), and so, in knowing the plan, the mind knows its whole development. The 'self-knowledge' (*Selbsterkenntnis*) to which the mind is summoned has several meanings:

   (1) The mind is aware or conscious of itself and its states, etc.: if I am angry, I am aware that I am angry, and so on. It is not implausible to say that in this sense 'all activity' of the mind is an 'apprehension of itself'. But it would be an exaggeration to say that it is 'only' this, and the Delphic oracle could hardly summon us to this type of self-knowledge, since we inevitably have it in any case.

   (2) When the mind, whether of the individual or of human beings generally, reaches a certain stage of its development, it reflects on the stage it has reached and gains knowledge of it. Adolescents reflect on their adolescence, a historian reflects on the spirit of the age, and so on. In Hegel's view, such reflection plays an important part in the mind's progression to a higher stage and thus in the development of mind both in the individual and over the course of history. Since not everyone is so reflective, it is something the oracle might reasonably recommend. But again it is an exaggeration to say that 'all' the mind's activity consists 'only' in self-knowledge of this type.

   (3) The mind engages in scientific or philosophical investigation of itself in contrast to other things. This is what Hegel does in Enc. III. But this is not all that the mind does. It investigates many things beside itself.

   (4) In dealing with other, non-mental, things ('everything in heaven and on earth') the mind does, or should, know or 'recognize' (*erkennen*) itself in them: they are not 'out-and-out Other'. In science the mind discovers in the world the structures of its own thought and in its practical activity it makes things conform to its own needs and purposes. In this sense it is plausible to say that 'all' the mind's activity is 'only' an 'apprehension of itself', since in dealing with any object, not only scientifically but also practically, the mind recognizes itself in it.

Thus Hegel moves from a conception of 'self-knowledge' according to which the mind knows itself in contrast to other things—self-knowledge in sense (1), (2), and/or (3)—to a conception of it according to which the mind knows or recognizes itself in everything else. This recognition of mind in what is other than mind is one of the things that Hegel means by the 'actualization' of the concept of mind: cf. §377, n. 4. What accounts for this move? Why cannot mind know itself without knowing other things, or at least without recognizing itself in them? Hegel believes that the mind can only put itself in order to the extent that it finds order in the world. To gain self-knowledge in sense (1), to become aware, that is, of one's mental states and of one's ownership of them, and to gain self-knowledge in sense (2), that is, to reflect on the mind's current stage of development, the mind must view the world as conforming to a certain type of order, an order that corresponds to the mind's own internal order. Hegel derived some of this from Immanuel Kant, who argued (in his *Critique of Pure Reason*) that the orderly conceptualization of phenomena, enabling us to have 'objective experience' of them, is a necessary condition of our self-consciousness, roughly in sense (1) above. However, Kant tended to regard such conceptualization as a fait accompli, whereas Hegel regards it as a task which we complete gradually throughout our lives and throughout history.

6. 'Oriental' refers primarily to Hinduism, but Hegel may also have in mind Buddhism, Zoroastrianism, etc. see §§389Z, and 393Z. Hegel's point is not so much that the oriental worshipper does not forget himself in his worship, but that the object of worship is not wholly unanthropomorphic and alien to the worshipper. The Greek gods were anthropomorphic, but are regarded as distinct from mortal men. They are thus not 'infinite', but other than and hence bounded ('finite') by men, who, in worshipping what is other than themselves, are not related to the gods 'freely'. One can be related freely only to what is seen as somehow identical to oneself. Christianity resolves this defect: God becomes man and the Holy 'Spirit' (*Geist*) descends into the community of believers. Thus the divine is now infinite: it embraces the believers and is not bounded by them; they freely worship what is in a way themselves.

7. In his *Histories* (1.2.8, 9.2.4, etc.) Polybius described his enterprise as *pragmatikê historia*, 'pragmatic history', probably in the sense of political and military history. F. W. Walbank, *Polybius I: A Historical Commentary on Polybius* (Oxford: Oxford University Press, 1970), 42, says that it means 'little more than "history", and bears no overtones of "didactic" or "politically useful"'. Hegel uses the term to mean the treatment of history with a view to its lessons for the present, i.e. the historian's contemporaries (PH, pp.5 ff.). Pragmatic history, he believes, tends to belittle great men, explaining their deeds in terms of petty motives (PH, pp.29 ff.): petty, everyday motives are more constant from epoch to epoch than the grand designs of heroes, and heroes are thus made more relevant to the present if they are cut down to size (PH, p.6). Here he offers two arguments against such a reduction: 'great things can only be accomplished through great characters', and it reduces history from the work of providence to 'pointless activity and contingent occurrences'. Prima facie it is not clear why providence could not lead agents, each of whom was intrinsically insignificant, to perform together great and significant deeds. A poet, after all, can produce a great poem from letters that are severally quite insignificant. Hegel does not, however, regard providence as external to agents and their actions in the way that a poet is external to the poem. Thus heroes are required to guide humbler actors in

great historic upheavals, and heroes must be in part aware of and motivated by the rationality of their goals, and not simply by, say, boredom or greed. On the question of the extent to which the historical agent is aware of the role assigned to him by providence, see Shlomo Avineri, 'Consciousness and History: *List der Vernunft* in Hegel and Marx', in Warren E. Steinkraus (ed.), *New Studies in Hegel's Philosophy* (New York: Rinhart & Winston, 1971), 108–18.

In this Paragraph 'individual' sometimes translates the adjective *einzeln* and the noun *(der) Einzelne*, sometimes (das) *Individuum*. '*Der Einzelne* is the general term for "the individual". *Das Individuum* is used in more strictly philosophical contexts, and not like English "individual" in the sense of "person"' (DGS, p. 297 n. 1). Hegel often uses the words indifferently, but *Einzelne* is less elevated than *Individuum* and can suggest triviality. Hence the 'world-historical individual' is always a *weltgeschichtliche Individuum*. Hegel's stock examples of such individuals are Alexander, Caesar, and Napoleon.

NOTES TO §378

1. *Pneuma* is Greek for 'wind, air, breath (of life), life, soul, (a) spirit'. Pneumatology is thus the 'study of spirit'. The word was also current in Britain: 'The branch [of knowledge] which treats of the nature and operations of minds has by some been called Pneumatology' (Thomas Reid, *Essays on the Intellectual Powers of Man*, Preface). Pneumatology or *rationelle Psychologie* ('so-called', because it is not, in Hegel's view, rational) was an a-priori discipline attempting to prove that the human soul is a substance, simple, numerically identical over time, immortal, etc. Kant criticized what he called the 'paralogisms' of rational psychology in *Critique of Pure Reason*. Hegel criticizes it in a similar vein: rational psychology employs inappropriate categories (such as force and activity), and, in part owing to these intrinsic defects, does not explore the 'concrete' mind. The 'metaphysic of the intellect' is *Verstandesmetaphysik*, the metaphysics of the hard and fast, unilinear *Verstand*, 'intellect, understanding', in contrast to the fluid, lateral *Vernunft*, 'reason'. Hegel attacks not metaphysics as such, but the pre-Kantian metaphysics of Leibniz and such followers as Christian Wolff, Moses Mendelssohn, and Alexander Baumgarten. The reference to the 'Introduction' is to Enc. I, §34.

2. Empirical psychology studies what rational psychology neglects, namely the 'concrete' powers of the mind such as perception. Sometimes the two types of psychology were practised by the same people: Christian Wolff wrote on empirical as well as rational psychology. However, empirical and rational psychology are not brought together, in such a way that the powers of the mind are derived from the underlying nature of the mind. Nevertheless, empirical psychology presents its findings in the inadequate garb of the *Verstandesmetaphysik*. Hegel's own approach is 'speculative': see §378, n. 5. It will remedy the deficiencies of empirical and rational psychology by deriving the empirical manifestation of the mind from its nature or 'concept', and it

will apply to the mind adequate categories, categories that reveal the connection between the concept of mind and its concrete reality.

3. Aristotle's *de anima*, 'On the Soul', consists of three 'books'. Aristotle also wrote shorter works on such topics as perception, memory, dreams, etc. Aristotle's *psuchê*, 'soul', differs in two important respects from Hegel's *Geist*. First, a *psuchê* is what makes something alive. So plants and animals as well as men have a *psuchê*, though the human soul is distinguished by its possession of *nous*, 'intellect'. In a wide sense, *Geist* includes our lower psychological aspects, the *Seele*, 'soul' (§§388 ff.), but in its more usual narrower sense it is more intellectual and is restricted to humans. It is thus closer to *nous* than to *psuchê*. Secondly, Hegel's *Geist* includes objective mind and absolute mind. But these do not appear in Aristotle's psychological writings, and have no special connection with the *psuchê* apart from presupposing ensouled human beings. Aristotle considers objective mind (though not under this title) in his works on ethics and politics. In so far as he deals with absolute mind at all, he does so in various works: poetry in his *Poetics*; God, though not religion, in the *Metaphysics*; and the history of philosophy throughout his works, but especially in the *Metaphysics*.

4. *Begriff*, 'concept', also suggests unity, since the cognate verb *begreifen*, 'to comprehend, etc.', also means 'to encompass, include'. Hegel's point is twofold. His philosophy of mind will introduce the concept: §377, n. 5. It will thereby unify the concerns of rational and of empirical inquiry in a way that resolves the defects of each taken in isolation. Aristotle drew no distinction between philosophy and empirical science. His *de anima* combines both types of inquiry.

5. *Spekulativ* comes from the Latin *speculari*, 'to spy, observe, etc.'. In German, as in English, it often refers to risky financial dealings and also to bold conjectures. In medieval philosophers *speculativus* often means 'theoretical' in contrast to 'practical'. Hegel applies it to his preferred philosophical method. It retains a suggestion of boldness, but no hint of the conjectural. It contrasts with the merely empirical, with the cut-and-dried thinking of *Verstand*, and with merely sceptical, 'negative' dialectic that advances to no positive conclusion. See Enc. I §82. (The Latin word *speculum*, derived from *speculari*, means a 'mirror', and some commentators associate Hegel's notion of *Spekulation* with mirroring. Hegel himself does not link 'speculation' with mirrors, however. If he links mirrors with anything, it is with *Reflexion*, which is, in Hegel's usage, a less elevated idea than *Spekulation*.)

6. The empirical 'approach' which Hegel here rejects is not the empirical psychology discussed in §378 and below (see §378, n. 8), but the 'understanding of human nature' discussed in §377, n. 3. This deals only with the surface appearances of the mind, while rational psychology deals only with the mind's 'essence' or 'in itself' (*Ansich*), what it is 'in itself' (*an sich*), apart from its appearances and its relations to other entities. Enc. I, §§112–14 presents general objections to attempts to separate an essence from its appearance(s). An essence, such as electricity, essentially appears or manifests itself in such phenomena as light and heat. Conversely, electrically generated light, heat, motion, etc. depend on an underlying essence, electricity. Similarly, a psychology dealing only with the

essence of mind and a psychology dealing only with its appearance are both deficient.

7. This is why Hegel excludes the 'understanding of human nature' of §377. Speculative philosophy cannot simply take things over from *Vorstellung*, 'representation', here empirical observation. It must in some way or other derive them from the concept of mind. The same objection is raised below against the empirical psychology of §378.

8. Rational psychology regards the mind as a static 'thing' rather than 'pure activity'. The mind is conceived in terms of the categories of *Verstand*, as simple to the exclusion of all complexity, as immaterial to the exclusion of all materiality, etc. In general, if the mind is F, then rational psychology takes this to exclude entirely the 'negation' or opposite of F-ness. This explains rational psychology's neglect of the 'appearances' of the mind. If the mind is a self-contained 'essence' it has no essential connexion with its appearances. If it is simple and immaterial to the complete exclusion of their opposites, it can be related to the body only 'externally'. To remedy this we need the fluid, self-negating categories of reason. The mind is simple, but it also 'distinguishes itself from itself' in a variety of ways: it is conscious of itself, it counterposes to itself an object that it apprehends, it ramifies into a diversity of functions and activities, it is intimately, and not just externally, related to its body. It is an essence, but an essence that requires appearance for its completion. The internal defects of rational psychology account for its seclusion from the 'empirical'.

9. The empirical psychology of §378 is distinct from, and lies between, the 'understanding of human nature' rejected in §377 and rational psychology. Whereas the 'understanding of human nature' considered only the peculiarities of certain types of men (e.g. that men often resent their benefactors), empirical psychology considers 'faculties' that are common to all human beings, such as thought, perception, and memory. It simply assumes, on the basis of empirical observation, that there are minds and that minds have just these faculties and no others, without attempting to demonstrate the necessity of this from the concept of mind.

10. The inability to derive logically the mind's faculties and the consequent dependence on *Vorstellung* goes with a 'despiritualization' (*Entgeistigung*) of the 'mind' (*Geist*), treating it as a bundle of 'forces' that interact, but are essentially independent of each other. No one mental force can be logically derived from the others, or from the concept of mind itself.

11. The modes of treatment already described are 'understanding of human nature', which considers the 'individual', and rational psychology, which considers the 'universal'. Empirical psychology deals with neither of these, but with 'particular forms' (*Besonderungen*), that is the mind's faculties. Hegel distinguishes the objects of the three rejected types of psychology as respectively individual, universal, and particular. 'Particularity' combines the idea of a particular judgement ('Some men are wise'), in contrast to the singular ('Socrates is wise') and the universal ('All men are wise') judgement, and the idea of a determinate or specific property (dog, green) in contrast to a determinable or generic property

(animal, coloured). But Hegel uses the triad in cases, such as this one, where neither of these ideas is especially appropriate. A faculty, such as perception, is a *particular* (type of) way in which the mind works. On this triad see Enc. I, §§163–4.

12. The 'harmonious interconnexion' (*harmonische Zusammenhang*) is something that the empirical psychologist expects each mind to achieve for itself, not something that the psychologist hopes to achieve in his own theory. In this respect it is analogous to the 'perfection' that followers of Leibniz, in particular Wolff, urged us to strive for. If the mind were simply a bundle of independent forces, it could never achieve such integration. In Hegel's view, by contrast, the mind has an 'original unity', the 'concept of mind' itself, and this particularizes itself in a 'necessary and rational' way, not into a bundle of forces, but into a rationally articulated structure. The 'concept' (*Begriff*) is here conceived not as a concept that we form, but as rather like the plan embedded in a simple seed that ramifies into a full-grown tree: cf. §377, n. 4.

NOTES TO §379

1. 'Self-feeling' (*Selbstgefühl*) is dealt with in §§407–8. Here it is the mind's feeling of its own unity, a unity that persists throughout the variety of its states and activities.

2. The opposition between freedom and determinism concerns the 'mind' (*Geist*), whereas the second opposition is between the body and the 'soul' (*Seele*). If Hegel is here distinguishing between the mind and the soul, the distinction is that while the 'mind' is our rational and intellectual principle, the 'soul' is our animating principle, making the body a living body. That is, *Geist* is close to *nous* in Aristotle's sense, while *Seele* is close to *psuchê* in Aristotle's sense, but not in the sense of rational psychology: cf. §378, n. 3. On the first opposition, Hegel implies that if the mind is a collection of independent forces, it can hardly be any more free than a similar collection of physical forces, each determining and determined by the others. (See also F. H. Bradley, 'The Vulgar Concept of Responsibility', in *Ethical Studies* (2nd edn., Oxford: Oxford University Press, 1927)). But he also means that the mind is *both* free *and* determined, and that the unilinear 'intellect' cannot accommodate this apparent incongruity. §382 considers freedom of the mind in more detail. On the second opposition, Hegel suggests that the soul is *both* free *and* intimately connected with the body—another incongruity that the 'intellect' cannot handle. See §389 on the soul and its 'community' with the body. To deal with both of these problems we must resort to 'comprehension' (*begreifen*).

3. A Viennese physician, Franz Anton Mesmer (1734–1815), attempted to cure nervous illnesses by hypnosis, induced by e.g. the patient's grasping a suitably 'magnetized' iron bar. Animal magnetism was, in his view, a physical force permeating the whole universe. Illness resulted from an imbalance between the animal magnetism in the patient's body and that in the external world, and

was to be cured by directing animal magnetism into the patient from outside. 'Animal magnetism' is thus equivalent to 'mesmerism'. §406Z. considers animal magnetism in detail. It is the 'phenomena' of magnetism, rather than Mesmer's cranky theory, that, in Hegel's view, suggest the 'unity' of the soul and baffle the 'rigid distinctions' of the intellect—such phenomena as 'clairvoyance', enabling the patient to foretell such world events as Napoleon's defeat at Waterloo, though not the winning numbers in a lottery (§406Z.). The mesmerized patient, Hegel explains, withdraws into the inner depths of his psyche, which are more sensitive to such matters than our normal waking consciousness. The 'substantial unity' of the soul is primarily the soul's internal unity, the fact that it is not divided into separate faculties nor divisible in the way that the body is. But Hegel may also be referring to the fact that under hypnosis one person's soul merges with another's: cf. §406, n. 7. The 'ideality' (*Idealität*) of the soul is its ability to surmount or negate distinctions within itself, whether between its supposedly distinct faculties or between the rigid categories applied to it: cf. §403, n. 2.

4. 'Finite' (*endlich*) means 'bounded'. The forces or faculties of empirical psychology are distinct from, and thus bounded by, each other. A category of the intellect, such as simplicity, is bounded by its opposite, complexity. The self-contained essence of the mind and the mind's appearances, as they are conceived by rational psychology, bound each other. The mind itself transcends these boundaries, and so does speculative philosophy. In doing so, they are 'infinite': cf. §386, n. 1.

5. Christian Wolff (1679–1754) is for Hegel the paradigmatic practitioner of 'reflective thinking', which sharply separates concepts from each other. (On *Reflexion*, see §§384, n. 2; 389, nn. 9, 12.) Johann Gottlieb Fichte (1762–1814), though not in Hegel's sense a 'reflective' thinker, did, in his *Science of Knowledge* (*Wissenschaftslehre*) of 1794 (§§1–2), speak of the I (or the proposition 'I am I') and the non-I (or the proposition 'A is not = A') as 'facts of empirical consciousness' (*Tatsachen des empirischen Bewusstsein*). To regard something as a 'fact' is to imply that it is not capable of further derivation or explanation. Hegel makes the same point more explicitly at §415 and Z. He treats Fichte rather unfairly, since Fichte expresses reservations about the concept of a 'fact of consciousness' in 'A Comparison between Prof. Schmid's System and the *Wissenschaftslehre*' of 1795 (see *Fichte: Early Philosophical Writings*, ed. D. Breazeale (Ithaca: Cornell University Press, 1988), 316–35).

6. The mind is an Idea, because it is a concept which develops into a reality corresponding to it: cf. §377, n. 4. The mind's development consists in differentiating itself in a 'necessary' way and then overcoming these differences to unify itself once more by attaining knowledge of its own concept in 'absolute mind', especially philosophy. The development of the mind from its concept is like the growth of a plant from a seed. This suggests that the development of the mind is a process in time, initially the development of an embryo into a complete human being, but in later sections the development of man over history. But

for much of the work Hegel follows the logical order of the mind's unfolding, with no indication that this is also the temporal order of its growth, that, say, recollection (§452) emerges first and is then followed in time by imagination (§455).

In this passage Hegel seems to identify the concept of mind with the 'logical' or 'eternal Idea', expounded in Enc. I. At first sight this is odd, since the logical Idea is seemingly a neutral logical system, with no more to do specifically with mind than with nature. Hegel has, however, several reasons for identifying them. First, the logical Idea has to bifurcate into nature and mind, so that the mind emerges from the logical Idea in much the same way as it emerges from the concept of mind, whatever that might be. Secondly, the development of the mind throughout Enc. III follows, in Hegel's view, the same pattern as the development of the logical Idea: the logical Idea is, as it were, the plan of the mind's development. Thirdly, the logical Idea, an implicit system of thoughts, forms the core of the mind; it is not just the plan of the mind's development, but also 'propels' its development. Hence the concept embedded in the embryonic mind is the logical Idea. On the relationship between the logical Idea and the mind as the 'self-knowing, actual Idea', see also §381, n. 3.

What makes the implicit logical Idea develop, whether temporally or non-temporally, into a fully fledged mind is its intrinsic contradictoriness, the 'contradiction' between the 'difference' implicit in the logical Idea (like the roots, branches, leaves, etc. implicit in the seed) and the simple, homogeneous form in which it occurs. This 'impels' it to develop actually into the 'whole' that it is potentially. Speculative philosophy follows the mind's development like a spectator, and, unlike empirical psychology, shows how every phase is derived necessarily from the logical Idea. Like the mind itself, it starts from the logical Idea, and traces the development of mind from it owing to contradictions immanent in the logical Idea and in any phase of its development short of the mind's complete actuality. Thus philosophy, if properly done, mirrors the development of the mind itself: we 'merely look on. . . at the object's own development', but in a quite different way from that in which an empirical psychologist might observe the development of the mind from infancy to adulthood.

Non-speculative philosophy has to appeal to empirical observation or 'subjective ideas and notions' in order to develop a coherent account of the mind. This depends especially on the seclusion from each other of the 'individual', 'particular', and 'universal': cf. §§378, n. 11; 389, n. 2. Non-speculative philosophy acknowledges no a-priori path from the universal (e.g. animal) to the particular species of it (e.g. dog, cat) and from there to the individual (e.g. Fido and Tibbles, with all their individual features). In a similar way it acknowledges no a-priori route from the universal concept of mind as such to the particular powers of the mind, such as perception, nor from there to the individual mind and its individual features. Hegel, by contrast, believes that the particular powers, or rather stages, of the mind develop with a discernible 'necessity' from the concept of mind. It is less clear, however, what part he assigns to individuality: see §389, n. 2.

7. The development of a seed is complete when the plant produces another seed of the same type. The seed is the 'sensuously present concept', and in general a concept completes its development in generating an 'actuality' that perfectly corresponds to it. The concept of mind does this not by producing offspring with minds of their own, but by gaining 'complete consciousness of its concept', that is, by gaining, as absolute mind, philosophical comprehension of its own nature and development.

Hegel exaggerates in saying that the final stage of mind is 'one and the same' as the concept that produces it. The seed or germ produced by an organism, though numerically distinct from the seed or germ from which the organism developed, is (more or less) qualitatively identical to it. But a mind that knows its own concept is not qualitatively identical to that concept before it is known. Moreover, the philosophical mind that emerges at the end of Enc. III knows a lot more than simply its own concept; it knows about nature and also about the development of mind. This perhaps does not impair Hegel's main point, which is that the development of mind comes to a close when it knows all about itself. But Hegel seems to have a more ambitious point in view, namely that the final stage of mind is just the logical Idea from which the mind originally developed and that the system outlined by Enc. thus forms a circle, beginning and concluding with the logical Idea. For more on this, see §577, nn. 1 and 2.

8. For Hegel truth is not the truth of a judgement such as 'This rose is red', when the rose referred to is in fact red. Such a judgement is 'correct' (*richtig*) rather than 'true' (*wahr*): see Enc. I, §172. Truth is the 'agreement of the concept with its actuality': a true tree is a fully grown tree, a true friend is a friend who fully satisfies the concept of a friend. This passage gives three accounts of what this amounts to in the case of mind: true mind, in contrast to merely 'immediate', namely undeveloped, mind (1) makes its concept an 'object' (*gegenständlich*) to itself, (2) transforms what is 'immediate' into something 'posited' (*Gesetzten*, from *setzen*, 'to set, put, posit') by itself, (3) makes its 'actuality' appropriate to its concept. These accounts are not equivalent: a true friend need not know the concept of a friend, and a true tree does not know the concept of a tree. However, because self-knowledge is of the mind's essence, to be appropriately actualized the mind must become its own object. It is not very clear what account (2) means. It may mean that the mind's inner, 'immediate', nature has to be developed, 'posited', externally, as the inner nature of the seed is posited as a tree. Or it may mean that the mind has to recognize itself in things other than itself: Cf. §377, n. 5 on self-knowledge.

9. The 'natural side' (*Naturseite*) of the mind is its knowledge, usually perceptual, of objects and events located at specific times and places, in contrast to science and philosophy. The intellect can explain, more or less, everyday knowledge of this sort in terms of causality, etc. But it cannot explain the 'magnetized' patient's knowledge of events remote in space and time. Although the magnetized patient sinks below the level of 'ordinary consciousness', since it cannot distinguish itself from surrounding nature, it is akin to philosophy in that its knowledge is not restricted by its position in space and time.

NOTES TO §380

1. Nature, like mind, involves an ascending series of 'stages' which develop its concept. A lower stage, such as 'matter and movement' is involved in higher stages, such as organic life. But the lower stage also occurs in isolation. The solar system involves matter and motion, but not, in any way relevant to our theories about it, higher stages such as life. The 'determinations of the senses' are the colours perceived by sight, the hardness perceived by touch, etc., and are thus involved in a relatively advanced stage of nature, the five senses characteristic of animals: see Enc. II, §358. But they also appear independently of the senses in lower stages: as the 'properties of bodies' and as 'elements', presumably the four Greek elements (earth, air, fire, water), which, in defiance of Lavoisier (1743–94), Hegel was reluctant to abandon: see Enc. II, §281. By contrast, the lower stages of mind are not found separately, but only as ingredients in higher stages.

   It is not clear that this is true. Even if most stages of mind occur together, animals (and perhaps infants) have sense-perception, or at least sensation, while lacking higher stages of mind. However, Hegel argues that human sensation differs significantly from that of animals, in that e.g. our inability to sense stimuli above or below a certain level of intensity suggests that we have an 'internal determinacy' that animals lack, that we are less fully determined by our surroundings and our awareness more selective: see §401, n. 15.

2. A lower stage of mind shows signs of a higher stage, 'even empirically', that is, not just to the philosopher, who knows a priori that the lower stage must eventually give rise to the higher stage, but in empirically observable combinations of the lower with the higher stage. For example, feeling or 'sensation' (*Empfindung*: cf. §§390, n. 5; 402, n. 1) is a low grade of mind, involving primarily outer sensations of e.g. heat and cold, and inner sensations of e.g. anger (§401 and Z.). But its 'content or determinacy' is often of a higher grade: we have as 'sense' of justice, a religious or moral 'sense', and religious 'feeling', etc. Some philosophers, such as F. H. Jacobi and Friedrich Schleiermacher, are misled by this into supposing that morality and religion are essentially a type of feeling or sensation (cf. Enc. I, §§61 ff.). This is a mistake, but all the same, lower grades of mind cannot be considered without reference to 'content' of higher grades for which the lower serve as 'forms' or vehicles. Thus in discussing 'natural waking' (§398 and Z.) we refer to consciousness, a higher grade dealt with fully at §§413 ff., and 'derangement' (§408 and Z.) involves reference to 'intellect' (§§422–3, 467 and Z.).

   Hegel here assimilates different types of case. (i) It is entirely possible to discuss sensations of heat, anger, etc. without referring to religious and moral feeling. In religious or moral feeling, low grade feeling is a 'form' for a high grade 'content'. It is no doubt important to note that sensation or feeling does accommodate high grade content, but it might well be discussed when religion and morality come up for consideration rather than in the context of a discussion of sensations of heat, etc. (ii) Waking is not a 'form' with consciousness as its content, but the event or process of becoming conscious after sleep. Waking and sleep are related to consciousness, not simply 'in their empirical existence', but conceptually: one cannot wake up, or be asleep, unless one is capable of being conscious. (But *Bewusstsein*, like 'consciousness', is ambiguous: the consciousness discussed later at §§413 ff. is consciousness *of* objects, but the consciousness to which one awakes may simply be consciousness in contrast to unconsciousness, where 'consciousness' can include e.g. feeling pain, with no or little awareness of one's surroundings.) (iii) 'Derangement' or insanity is related to 'intellect' as sleep (not waking) is related to consciousness. Insanity is a privation or perversion of intellect, not a form in which it appears. Their relationship is again conceptual, not empirical: only those capable of intellect can become insane.

NOTES TO §381

1. On the concept of mind, cf. §379, n. 6. 'For us' (*für uns*) mind presupposes nature and thus nature is in some way prior to mind. But since mind is the 'truth' of nature, mind is nature's *absolut Erstes*, literally its 'absolutely first', and thus 'absolutely' prior to nature: cf. §381, n. 23. 'For us' contrasts with 'absolutely'. It is not clear whether it means 'for us human beings in general' or 'for us philosophers'. In either case, the point is that looking on from the outside, we cannot yet see how mind transfigures nature. As philosophers, we have to show how mind emerges from nature: cf. §381, n. 3.

2. Mind is the truth of nature: mind achieves an agreement of the concept with its actuality, such as nature strives towards but never attains: cf. §379, n. 8 on truth. The Idea is the concept together with its actuality, but here its constituents are described as the 'subject' and the 'object', each of which is the 'concept'. In nature the 'concept' (*Begriff*) has its object(ivity) outside itself. But in mind this 'externalization' is nullified or 'sublated' (*aufgehoben*) and the concept becomes identical with itself. This identity is 'absolute negativity', since it is reached by way of a negation of nature's externality and a return from nature.

   Hegel conflates two ideas: (i) the actualization of a concept, and (ii) the object of, or apprehended by, a subject. The mind, unlike any natural entity, is a subject with itself as its own object: cf. §377, n. 5 on self-knowledge. Hegel assimilates this to a concept whose actualization is internal to itself, a concept which is its own actualization. This is one of the reasons why Hegel assumes that the actualization of the concept of mind consists in the mind's gaining complete knowledge of itself. And since nothing other than mind can gain knowledge of itself, nothing other than mind can fully actualize itself.

3. The concept of mind, the 'self-knowing, actual idea', must be derived from the 'universal concept', the logical Idea, by way of nature. One might think that mind precedes nature, since a 'cognition' (*Erkennen*) is contained in the logical Idea (cf. Enc. I, §§223 ff.) and cognition has to do with mind. But this was

not actual cognition, only our concept of cognition. So we cannot introduce the concept of mind by appeal directly to the Logic. We have to derive its necessity from logic and philosophy of nature. (This corresponds to the first of the three 'syllogisms' described at the end of Enc. III: cf. §575.) Conversely, philosophy of mind must 'authenticate' (*bewähren*) the concept of mind by developing and actualizing it. It authenticates it by showing that what is derived from the concept of mind presents us with an adequate and complete account of the mind, that the mind is in fact the 'self-knowing idea'.

4. The Idea appears in logic, in nature, and as mind. The Idea as mind must have a differentia or 'determinacy' (*Bestimmtheit*) to distinguish it from the logical Idea and the Idea in nature. This is 'ideality' (cf. §379, n. 3), its 'sublation' (*Aufheben*) of its own 'otherness'. The logical Idea is still 'within-self', and so has not yet become other than itself. In nature the Idea becomes external to itself and thus other than itself. In mind the Idea overcomes this otherness or self-externality. The Idea thus undertakes a return journey: the logical Idea has not yet set out; the Idea in nature has reached its destination; the Idea as mind has returned to its starting-point from its destination, enriched by the journey there and back. The otherness of the Idea is not simply cancelled. It is 'sublated'. The verb *aufheben* means 'to lift; to cancel; to keep'. Hegel generally uses it in all three senses at once, so that what is sublated is elevated, cancelled, and preserved—rather like someone who is 'kicked upstairs'. It is often translated as 'sublate', because *sublatum* is the perfect participle of the Latin verb *tollo*, which means both 'to lift, raise up' and 'to remove, destroy annul'.

5. In nature the Idea is external to itself, because it is external to the mind and to the mind's essential 'inwardness', and thus cannot have the unity characteristic of the mind. Hegel's reference to the 'Greeks' is unspecific, but he presumably means that Greek philosophers, especially Plato and Aristotle, distinguished nature from mind and regarded natural phenomena as extended in space and time. More generally, Hegel believed that the Greeks achieved a midway position between the unity of mind and nature, as conceived by their predecessors, and the withdrawal into 'subjectivity' characteristic of modernity.

6. The relation between natural entities is sufficiently close for any one of them to be comprehensible only by reference to others, but sufficiently 'external' for them to remain 'independent existences'. Thus we cannot understand the motions of planets without the sun, but the sun and the planets are distinct entities and each could exist, in some form or other, without the other. The relation is 'external', because it does not affect the essence or interior of the related entities. The relation is also 'internal', because it is kept inside each entity and not fully expressed overtly. Hence natural entities are governed by necessity, not free: a planet's movement, is not self-determined, but determined by something other than itself, the sun. The 'contradiction' between the relation (attraction by the sun) and the independence (centrifugal force) is 'displayed' by the planet's motion round the sun. On the view that what is 'only' external is also 'only' internal, see Enc. I, §140 and Z. On necessity and freedom, see Enc. I, §158 and Z. For the idea that motion is the result of contradiction, see

Enc. I, §119Z.(2). On planetary motion, see Enc. II, §270. On relation between light and the elements, see Enc. II, §§281–2.

7. Unlike a rock, a plant develops from a seed into an articulated whole. But 'each part is the whole plant'. Not only is each leaf or flower similar to every other leaf or flower on the plant. A part of a plant can be detached (without detriment to the rest of the plant) and will grow into a distinct whole plant, if it is planted. Hegel is indebted to Goethe's *Versuch die Metamorphose der Pflanzen zu erklären* (*Attempt to Explain the Metamorphosis of Plants*) (1790), which argued that every part of a plant, and the plant as a whole, is a modified leaf: cf. Enc. II, §345 and Z.

8. No significant part of an animal can be removed without detriment to the whole or survive in isolation: each part both causes and is caused by, is both end and means for, every other part. Thus the parts, unlike those of a plant, are genuinely 'other' than each other. But what happens to any part, its 'determinacy', is also 'ideal' (cf. §379, n. 3): what happens to one part of a plant hardly affects the plant as a whole, but what happens to one part of an animal affects the whole animal. The animal is a unified 'universal' subject, not identical with any one part or with the aggregate of all the parts, but permeating each part of the whole. It is thus a subject in a different sense: it is 'subjectivity' and has 'sensation'. The presence of the whole in each part is secured by the messages sent to it from the parts. Hence animals are more self-determined, less exposed to external influences than plants are: the animal as a whole can actively respond to messages received from its parts.

9. The animal's development is driven by a series of 'contradictions' and their resolution. The first is this. In virtue of its 'determinate' sensation (e.g. hunger or pain) the animal involves a 'difference', a difference and thus a contradiction between its universal nature (which is susceptible to various types of sensation, but not identical to any one of them) and its specific hunger or pain. This difference is at first only 'ideal', a difference within the animal and not between two distinct entities. That is, the animal feels the pain or hunger but does not recognize the source of the pain or the remedy for the hunger. If the contradiction is to be resolved, however, the difference cannot remain ideal; it must be 'posited' as a difference, felt by the animal as a difference. This can only happen if the animal enters into opposition to nature, making explicit the difference between itself and nature, i.e. the source of the pain or the remedy for its hunger.

10. The explicit difference between the animal and the external object contradicts the 'unity of the concept', which the animal is. It resolves this by consuming and thus annihilating the object. On the 'unity of the concept', see §378, n. 8.

11. The first contradiction now returns and can only be resolved in the same way. The animal is engaged in a labour of Sisyphus, a task that it can never complete. It resolves this 'contradiction' by encountering something like itself, of the same species or 'genus' (*Gattung*). In the 'sexual relation' animals have a feeling or 'sensation' (*Empfindung*) of their unity and are not mutually 'external'.

12. The soul of the animal, e.g. a dog, is 'one with', wholly absorbed in, its determinate sensation. It 'senses' the genus, since it desires another dog, not (usually) a

cat or a rabbit. But it is not aware of the genus, since its desire is focused on this individual dog, not caninity or dog as such. Again, what results from the union is an individual dog or, more likely, dogs, not dog as such. These new dogs go through the same processes as their parents, a 'perpetual cycle'.

13. The death of an animal is only the 'annihilating negation' of it, not its 'preserving sublation'. On *Aufhebung*, 'sublation', from the verb *aufheben*, 'to destroy', 'to preserve', and 'to elevate', see §381, n. 4. In Hegel's usage it generally combines all three senses, as the addition of *erhaltende*, 'preserving', here indicates. He perhaps implies that the death of a human is a 'preserving sublation' of individuality, that death gives significance to the individual's life. But his main concern is with 'the universality that is in and for itself'. The preceding discussion would lead us to expect this to refer to mankind aware of itself *as* mankind, in the way that dogs are not aware of themselves as dogs. But the 'individuality that is universal in and for itself, i.e. 'the subjectivity that has itself for object', can only refer to an individual self-conscious human, an I aware of itself as I. Hegel moves from the universality of a species or genus to the universality of the 'I'. The individual I is 'universal', because it is intrinsically indeterminate and can accommodate any of a wide range of contents: cf. §381, n. 15; 412, n. 3. A dog is neither aware of itself as I nor does it have universal thoughts about its own or other species. Hegel believes there is a connexion between these two disabilities, but he does not make clear what it is.

14. Since a dog is unaware of the dog as such, it does not distinguish dogs from things that are not dogs. It is we who draw this distinction by our 'external reflection' on dogs. The mind, by contrast, distinguishes itself from nature by its 'overcoming' (*Überwindung*) and 'sublation' (*Aufhebung*) of 'externality'. Overcoming and sublation are related but not identical. In *overcoming* externality the mind becomes aware of itself as mind, becomes its own 'object', thus achieving the self-duplication of the concept that nature cannot provide. It does this by *sublating* externality, that is, by reducing to 'inwardness', 'idealizing', or 'assimilating', everything external to itself. The mind can achieve rational self-awareness only in so far as it is aware of external reality. Cf. §377 on self-knowledge. On ideality, see §§379, n. 3; 381, nn. 4, 8.

15. In lower phases of mind, the mind cannot refer to itself as 'I' (cf. §§402 Z., 413 Z.), but then it is strictly 'soul' (*Seele*) rather than 'mind' (*Geist*). Everyone is an 'I', and to speak of oneself as 'I' implies no more about oneself than that one is a mind. Thus the I can 'abstract from everything, even from its life'. I can ignore the distinguishing features of myself and my experience; I can imagine that they are all different, yet I am still myself. I can 'abstract' from my life not, primarily at least, because I would still be myself if I were dead, but because I can choose to risk or surrender my life (cf. §432). The I or ego is not just simple, like light in contrast to a composite body. (See Enc. II, §275Z. for the affinity of the ego to light.) It involves two types of differentiation:

(1) The I is aware of itself as an I. The I is here 'infinite': it is not bounded by an other, but circles back on itself. This corresponds to 'overcoming' in §381, n. 14.

(2) The I is aware of 'manifold material confronting it'. It 'poisons', i.e. degrades, this material by depriving it of its independence, but it also transfigures, i.e. elevates, it by spiritualizing it. This corresponds to 'sublation in §381, n. 14.

The I proves or 'authenticates' its differentiated 'being-together-with-itself' (of stage (1)) by sublating the 'manifold material' (at stage (2)) and by remaining simple and self-aware throughout the 'multiplicity' that it 'pervades'.

16. Mind is as yet still 'finite'. (See §386 and Z. on finitude.) Objective as well as subjective mind is finite. But here Hegel is thinking especially of subjective mind. This is made to sound unsatisfactory by speaking of its 'representational activity' and by the suggestion that mind simply transposes things from outside into its inner 'space', where they remain as diverse and unorganized as they were in external space. The mind is confronted by a multiplicity other than itself, which it then proceeds to internalize in an 'external' manner, that is, leaving the multiplicity more or less unchanged, but also with the suggestion that the finite mind does all the work itself, without the cooperation of the external world: cf. §381, n. 20. At the stage of absolute mind, by contrast, the multiplicity of the world is conceived as intrinsically unified and self-unifying. To discern this unity requires work on the part of the mind, but once it has done this work, it sees the world as a structured whole rather than a disorganized mess. We might ask why the mind needs religion and philosophy to see the world as an organized whole. Subjective mind itself contains resources for unifying the multiplicity of the world, especially language (§459) and thought (§§465 ff.), stages of subjective mind that go beyond mere representation. Elsewhere, Hegel himself shows an awareness of the mind's capacity to bring order into the world below the level of absolute mind: cf. §402, n. 8.

17. Hegel moves directly to absolute mind, bypassing the stage of objective mind. For 'religious consciousness' things are held together by God, no longer simply juxtaposed in inner or outer space. In this way things lose their 'absolute independence' and thus become ideal, that is, intrinsically interconnected and interdependent. This 'idealization' is brought about by religious consciousness, rather than by God—though Hegel tends not to distinguish sharply between God and religious consciousness, between the human mind and the divine mind. Philosophy completes this idealization in terms of the logical or 'eternal' Idea, the categories presented in Hegel's logic: cf. §379, n. 6. Philosophy shows in 'determinate' detail how the eternal Idea manifests itself in things, whereas religion (Hegel implies) invokes God's power in a general way and does not explain in detail how it works. The eternal Idea is not equivalent to the 'actual' Idea. The eternal Idea does not begin or develop in time, nor (in Hegel's view) does its operation in nature have a temporal beginning or development. By contrast, the

Idea becomes actual only when the mind discerns or 'cognizes' the eternal Idea in things, that is, in nature and ultimately in mind itself.

18. Finite mind involves a return journey from immediate unity with nature (*Position*) to nature as its Other (*Negation*) and back to itself in unity with its Other, whose otherness is now overcome ('negation of negation'): cf. §381, n. 4. Finite mind is thus an 'actual Idea'. How does it differ from philosophy? Earlier (cf. §381, nn. 16, 17) Hegel's answer was that the other is overcome only 'externally'. Now the answer is that finite mind is 'one-sided': the Idea apprehends itself in the form *either* of subjectivity (concept) *or* of objectivity (actuality), but not both together. It may be that Hegel has in view the distinction between theoretical mind (§§445 ff.) and practical mind (§§469 ff.). The former absorbs external objects into the mind, while the latter projects the mind or the will into the external world: cf. §443, n. 3. Hegel's point would then be that absolute mind gives equal weight to these two 'moments' or aspects: it combines theory and practice, proceeding both from world to mind and from mind to world. However, the reference to absolute mind and Hegel's discussion of 'world-history' below (see §381, n. 21) suggests that he has in view the distinction between subjective mind and objective mind. This is not the same as the distinction between theoretical mind and practical mind, since although objective mind is in a broad sense 'practical' rather than theoretical, practical mind falls within the realm of subjective mind in so far as the object it works on is alien to the mind and not yet formed and structured by our theoretical and practical activity. Then Hegel's point would be that absolute mind somehow combines the one-sided accomplishments of subjective and objective mind.

19. Christianity illustrates, for those who need it, the philosophical account of mind. Hegel controversially suggests that God develops, needing to create nature and to send his son to be properly and fully God. He fuses together two triads traditionally regarded as distinct: Father–Son–Holy Spirit and God–Nature–Man. Holy Spirit and man are combined in the idea of the 'Christian community'. Nature and Son are harder to combine. Nature is, on the face of it, quite different from God, while the Son is 'his other I'. But Hegel views nature too as God's 'other I', especially in virtue of the presence of the 'eternal Idea' in nature. The Son symbolizes this affinity of nature to God. The Holy Spirit then symbolizes man's intellectual and practical conquest of nature, and this is conceived as God's own reconciliation with nature and his return to himself in it.

If this third stage, the Holy Spirit, is omitted, then God may be conceived in either of two unsatisfactory ways: in the form of 'mere concept, of abstract being-within-self' *or* of an 'individual actuality in disagreement with the universality of its concept'. It is not clear how these conceptions differ from each other. Assuming that the second stage (Nature, Son) is in place, then the situation seems to be the same in both conceptions: God and Nature are out of accord with each other. Hegel may allude to the distinction between 'acosmism' (the doctrine that only God really exists) and 'atheism' (the doctrine that only nature really exists): §573, n. 7. If so, then the first unsatisfactory conception of God would be acosmism, while the second would be atheism. More likely, Hegel has in view the contrast between 'subjectivity' and 'objectivity' discussed in the previous paragraph: cf. §381, n. 18. Then the two unsatisfactory conceptions of God would correspond to the two 'one-sided' ways in which the mind can overcome its Other. Christianity represents an appropriate combination of theoretical understanding of the world and practical transformation of it, and/or of subjective mind and objective mind.

20. This suggests that the two 'one-sided' ways in which finite mind idealizes nature are not theoretical and practical mind, but subjective and objective mind. The will is practical, while thinking is theoretical, but in so far as they both belong to subjective mind, thinking and the will have the same defect, that all the work is done by the mind, whether as will or thought, while nature is merely passive. Nature's indifference to our alteration of it does not mean that it is due solely to our way of viewing them that e. g. the planets revolve, or seem to revolve, around the sun, but that, although the planets really do go round the sun, they do nothing special to enable us to view them in this way. Similarly, a field that we cultivate, though it is intrinsically cultivable, does not help us to cultivate it; it passively endures our work on it.

21. Heroes such as Alexander and Caesar did not actively work on their passive people and their time in the way that we work on nature. The people actively prepared itself for the deeds of the hero; the hero is a product of his people as much as it is his instrument. The mind or spirit that 'produces world-history' is a stage of objective mind, in fact its highest stage (§§548 ff.). This raises a problem. Earlier, Hegel has assigned the 'perfect unity' of subjectivity and objectivity not to objective mind, but to absolute mind: see §381, n. 18. Objective mind was plausibly assumed to be as one-sided as subjective mind. How then can the reconciliation of objectivity and subjectivity take place within objective mind? One answer might be that the reconciliation takes place only at the final stage of objective mind, when it is on the brink of becoming absolute mind, that earlier phases of objective mind are as one-sided as subjective mind. This reply fails, however. It is not only historic heroes who work on an object that cooperates with them. Social actors regularly deal with objects that meet them halfway. A farmer who ploughs a field finds the field passive and uncooperative. But a farmer who claims a field as his property may well find that others recognize his claim. A politician who calls an election relies on the cooperation of the citizens. Hegel attempts *both* to reserve the 'perfect unity' for absolute mind *and* to locate its beginnings in the highest stage of objective mind. The attempt is unsuccessful.

22. Philosophy of nature resembles world-history more than does our prephilosophical idealizing of nature. Nature cooperates with philosophy in the way that a people cooperates with its hero. The philosopher is, however, an onlooker, who has only to observe how nature itself overcomes its externality. Hegel makes at least four claims: (1) The logical Idea or the concept is not simply the categories we apply to nature, but is embedded in nature itself. (2) Nature develops

(though not over time) from lower to higher stages, and as it advances it sheds its 'asunderness' (*Aussereinander*) or 'externality' (*Äusserlichkeit*), 'liberates the concept', and becomes increasingly 'free'. It culminates in the animal's 'sensation' (*Empfindung*), which takes us to the brink of mind. (3) Mind proper thus emerges from nature, in a way not wholly unlike the emergence of a hero from the people. (4) This (non-temporal) development is driven by mind, not the philosopher's mind, but the mind in itself or 'implicit mind' (*an sich seiende Geist*) at work in nature, which is equivalent to the 'eternal Idea immanent in Nature'. All this remains true during our prephilosophical idealization of nature, but it is not apparent to the non-philosopher, who does not discern the Idea in nature or survey nature in all its ascending phases. The analogy with world-history is tenuous. Alexander and Caesar were leaders, not onlookers. Without them their battles would not have been won nor their empires founded, whereas the development of nature does not require the philosopher of nature.

23. Hegel's doctrine involves at least three claims: (1) Mind proper, mind that is 'in and for itself', is the 'truth' or fulfilment of its presuppositions, of the logical Idea (the mind that is only 'within itself'), and of nature (the mind that is only 'outside itself'), in something like the way in which the tree is the fulfilment of the seed: cf. §379, n. 7. (2) However, mind proper is not simply a smooth continuation of nature. Mind becomes independent of nature and reacts against it, by cultivating it, for example, and by studying it. (3) Despite appearances, it is really mind proper that posits the logical Idea and nature in the first place. Its 'presuppositions' (*Voraussetzungen*) are its 'positings [-*setzungen*] in advance [*voraus*]'. The tree, as it were, produces the seed from which it emerges.

   Claims (1) and (2) are intelligible enough, or at least respectably Aristotelian. Claim (3) is problematic. How can the fully developed human mind 'posit' the conditions of its own emergence, if to 'posit' means to 'establish' rather than simply to 'overcome' or 'sublate'? Even if mind is implicitly at work in nature, steering it towards the emergence of the human mind, it does not follow that the fully developed human mind produces nature and its implicit mind. Hegel is perhaps conflating two distinct doctrines. First, there is his theological doctrine that God is a sort of implicit and undeveloped mind, which establishes the conditions (nature) that will eventually enable it to become a fully fledged, actualized mind in the shape of human beings. Secondly, there is the doctrine that human beings, when they reach the level of absolute mind, gain complete philosophical insight into the conditions of their own emergence, namely the logical Idea and nature. On the first of these interpretations claim (3) entails claim (1) and at least suggests claim (2). But claim (3), so interpreted, is not entailed by claims (1) and (2). On the second interpretation of claim (3), claim (3) is not very different from claim (2): it says that mind proper fully understands the conditions of its own emergence, not that it literally 'posits' them or sets them up.

24. The transition from nature to mind is a return to itself of externalized mind, but mind is radically different from nature. Hegel expresses this difference by saying

that the mind emerges from, or in, the death of the animal: Enc. I, §222, and also Enc. II, §376. This emergence is not 'fleshly', as if a mind emerged from a dead animal like a butterfly from a chrysalis. It is, like all the transitions in Enc., a 'development of the concept'. Nature culminates in two 'one-sided' aspects that it cannot fuse together: the individual animal and the universal genus that emerges in the death of its members. Mind, by contrast, combines universality and individuality. Human beings do what dogs cannot do; they become aware of their own genus or species as such: cf. §381, n. 13. An animal species requires the death of individuals if it is to become explicit or 'for itself': cf. Enc. I, §221. But the human species becomes explicit in the minds of individuals and so does not require their deaths for this purpose. Why, then, do human individuals die? Hegel shows little interest in the Christian doctrine of individual immortality, but he has a two-part reply to this objection. First, human individuals do not die in the same way as animals do. They are remembered as individuals and their achievements are preserved and developed. Secondly, the death of individuals is required by the development of mind over history: cf. my 'Hegel on Death', *International Journal of Moral and Social Studies*, 1 (1986), 109–22.

25. An animal is entirely engrossed by each current individual 'sensation' or feeling (*Empfindung*). It therefore lacks 'self-knowledge', etc. Cf. §381, n. 12, and J. S. Mill, *The Philosophy of Sir William Hamilton* (6th edn.: London: Longmans, 1889), 248: 'If. . . we speak of the Mind as a series of feelings, we are obliged to complete the statement by calling it a series of feelings which is aware of itself as past and future; and we are reduced to the alternative of believing that the Mind, or Ego, is something different from any series of feelings, or possibilities of them, or of accepting the paradox, that something which *ex hypothesi* is but a series of feelings, can be aware of itself as a series'. The importance of the 'universality of thought', in contrast to the 'individuality of sensation', for our self-awareness, explains why Hegel regards mind as the 'individuality which is in and for itself universal'.

NOTES TO §382

1. Because an animal is aware of nothing except its current sensation, it is entirely determined by it. It cannot ignore or resist the sensation, since it has no basis for doing so, no inner citadel to which it can withdraw away from the sensation. An animal has no persisting identity underlying its sensations; it is nothing but a sequence of sensations. Consequently, it is entirely at the mercy of the external things that produce its sensations. Humans, by contrast, can, and at some level invariably do, 'negate' external things. Negativity, the negation of the external things of nature, is a necessary condition of proper self-identity: it is only if entanglements with other things are severed that something can be genuinely identical with itself. Negativity is also a sufficient condition of self-identity: it is not just that there is nothing for the mind to be, once its external relationships are severed, except self-identical, but that negativity presupposes a withdrawal

into oneself. We might then expect Hegel to say that the mind inevitably *does* abstract from 'everything external', but he says that it *can* do so: I can ignore external circumstances; imagine them to be otherwise; doubt whether things are as they appear to me to be; risk my life; steadfastly endure pain. If my tormenter extracts my fingernails, the pain is the 'negation' of my 'individual immediacy', the sensory surface of my existence. ('Infinite pain' means 'any amount of pain'.) But owing to my own intrinsic negativity, I can retreat from this immediacy into my inner citadel, my 'abstract universality'.

2. The 'unity of concept and objectivity' in which mind's freedom consists is also Hegel's account of truth: cf. §§379, n. 7; 381, n. 2. If the mind were dependent on other things, this would impair the unity, since the mind would have features resulting from other things, not just its concept. At John 8: 32, Christ says: 'And ye shall know the truth, and the truth shall make you free'.

3. If freedom is not being dependent on an other, there are three ways in which the mind might be free: (i) It is simply isolated from and independent of other things, through no special effort on its part. The mind's negativity towards nature means that it is never free in this sense. (ii) The mind negates nature and anything other that presents itself. This is 'fleeing from the Other' and reposing in its 'abstract universality', being aware of itself simply as a bare I or ego. The mind cannot attain 'actuality' in this way. Hegel does not strictly exclude the possibility of its remaining in this condition. In the Addition to PR, §5, he suggests that the Hindu devotee and the Jacobin, who smashes every determinate institution, are instances of this. But they are only imperfect instances of it, and by and large Hegel believes that the mind must adopt a different strategy. (iii) The mind 'posits' something other than the I, e.g. the idea of 'house', thus producing a difference in itself. In overcoming this other, the mind lives up to its concept, the 'ideality of the external'. Hegel leaves it unclear what this overcoming involves, whether it consists simply in not being wholly absorbed by the other in the way that an animal is by its sensation (cf. §381, n. 25) or in some complex conceptual mastery of the other. Cf. §382, n. 7.

4. This 'rupture' (*Entzweiung*) between the I and its other makes 'pain' (*Schmerz*) possible. It follows that animals do not have pain, or pain of the type in question (on animal pain see Enc. II, §359Z.). Is the pain in question ordinary physical pain, or is it mental pain of a special sort arising from our rupture? A pure I, wholly oblivious to anything else, could have no pain. Only a human can have a pain that is felt to be distinct from himself. An animal, by contrast, is engrossed in the pain and draws no distinction between itself and the pain. Rupture is thus a necessary condition of pain. It does not follow, as Hegel implies, that it is also a sufficient condition of pain, that pain does not come to the mind 'from outside', but only that an internal condition is required if an external stimulus is to result in pain. Later in the *Zusatz* Hegel speaks of 'pain aroused by evil, as well as by the disagreeable', suggesting that the pain in question is mental pain or grief, something less readily attributable to animals than physical pain.

5. The 'infinite mind', the negative of which is 'evil' (*das Böse*), is not God, but the mind in its pure universality, 'infinite' in that it is not 'bounded' by its other.

An animal may steal food, but it has no choice in the matter, being wholly engrossed in its sensation or desire. A man who steals from a desire for wealth is not engrossed by desire or by his project. He chooses to act on this desire, to pursue this project, when he might have chosen otherwise. He opts for extreme 'individuality', since he puts his own desires above those of everyone else, and therefore suffers extreme rupture, since his individuality now is as far as it could be from his universality and his 'ethical nature'. Nevertheless, the thief remains universal and ethical by nature: otherwise he would be no better, and no worse, than an animal.

6. A piece of metal cannot have both the specific gravity of gold and a different specific gravity; this would be a plain contradiction. It cannot have (or acquire) a different specific gravity from that of gold and yet be (or remain) gold; this would contradict the essential nature of gold. Gold, like other natural stuffs and entities, cannot sustain such 'contradictions'. A mind sustains what are (Hegel believes) comparable contradictions. I am not a house, nor am I the idea or 'representation' of a house. But I can have the idea of a house, something 'contradictory to my I', while still remaining an I. (Not all such 'contradictions' are painful but, Hegel believes, every pain is, or presupposes, a contradiction.) This is perhaps not peculiar to minds. A mirror can mirror things quite different from itself: trees, houses, etc. But Hegel adds (somewhat sweepingly) that the mind is aware of having posited every such 'determination' and of its ability to 'sublate', i.e. get rid of it. This differentiates a mind from a mirror.

   Pace Hegel, 'ordinary logic' does not in fact deny that we can assert or even believe a contradictory proposition, only that such a proposition can be true. Nor does it deny that the mind can sustain 'contradictions' of the sort Hegel has in view. It does not deal with the question that concerns Hegel, namely, what distinguishes specifically human consciousness from the 'consciousness' of animals?

7. The distinction between mind 'in its immediacy' and mind in 'actual freedom' is different from the distinction between mind 'fleeing from the Other' and mind that posits and overcomes its other in §382, n. 3. Mind in its immediacy posits the idea of 'house' and overcomes it by being able to endure and sublate it. But it has to do more than this to gain 'actual freedom', overcoming all the forms of its 'reality' (*Dasein*) that fall short of its concept. Since mind, even in its immediacy, is not determined by external things, mind's ascent to actual freedom is effected by the mind itself.

NOTES TO §383

1. The mind's 'abstract universality' is not only mind's possibility (cf. §382, n. 1), but also its *Dasein*, its 'reality'(cf. §382, n. 3). '*Dasein*' is here close to '*Wirklichkeit*', 'actuality'. The mind's universality cannot remain merely potential; it has to be actualized, since it has a being of its own, is *für sich*, 'for itself'. (Other types of universal, triangularity say, need not be actualized—there need be no actual triangles—since this universal is not 'for itself'.) If it is actualized, it must be

particularized, actualized in a particular sort of way. (This applies to other types
of universal too. An actual triangle must be a particular sort of triangle.) If it is
actualized and particularized, it must particularize itself, since it is independent
of other things. (By contrast, the particular way in which triangularity is actualized depends on factors extraneous to the universal itself.) 'For itself' combines
the ideas of independence, actuality, and self-awareness.

2. The 'determinacy' of something is its intrinsic nature or content. In many
cases this determinacy may either be manifested or remain hidden. A scar, for
example, may be revealed or concealed. But mind has no such determinacy.
Its determinacy is manifestation (*Manifestation*) or revelation (*Offenbaren*).
Manifestation combines the idea of being manifest to oneself (i.e. self-awareness)
and the idea of manifesting oneself by 'positing' or producing something
definite. Hence 'manifestation' is close to 'actualization'. A scar may remain
hidden, even from its bearer, and may in this sense be merely potential. But
a mind cannot remain hidden. Its 'possibility' or potentiality is *ipso facto* its
actuality. This actuality is 'infinite', because it is self-generated, independent of
anything else, and also because it is reflexive: the mind manifests not something
other than mind, but the mind itself.

The idea that the mind is intrinsically indeterminate extends from Aristotle
(*nous*, 'intellect') down to Sartre (the *pour-soi*, 'for itself').

3. On 'ideality', see §381, n. 4. It is unclear whether the otherness of the Idea is
the otherness of the logical Idea or the otherness of the Idea in nature. 'Earlier'
(§381Z.) it was the otherness of the Idea in nature. Here it seems to be the
otherness of the logical Idea. But it must be the otherness of the Idea in nature
that is to be 'sublated'. The logical Idea is not yet other than itself. It is enclosed
within itself and is thus not revealed to itself. It can only be revealed to itself
by first externalizing itself in nature and thus becoming other than itself. This is
the mind that is 'in itself'. Then the mind sublates this otherness and this is the
mind's 'ideality'. But in doing this the mind becomes 'for itself' (i.e. self-aware,
as well as independent and actualized), and so it is 'revealed to itself'. This is self-
knowledge in sense (4) distinguished in §377, n. 5. In our conceptual mastery of
nature, we become aware of our own mental structures and capacities.

4. Hegel here distinguishes two questions which he has so far conflated: (1) Why
must the I 'posit' anything other than itself, i.e. reveal itself? In other words,
why can I not just be *me*, a pure ego, without bothering about anything else?
(2) Why is the mind self-aware, i.e. revealed *to* itself? So far his answer to (1) has
been: Mind has to posit its other in order to 'sublate' it. And, implicitly: Mind
is wholly empty unless it posits its other, it has to give itself some content. His
answer to (2) has been: The pure I must be self-aware, since there is nothing to
it except self-awareness. If it is *für sich*, in the sense of 'independent', it must be
für sich, in the sense of 'self-aware'. And: It has to posit its other within itself (not
outside, like an egg it has laid), and it can only do this by remaining aware of it.
Now Hegel distinguishes the two questions. The mind reveals or manifests itself
in two different ways: I can just focus on myself as an I. Then the I is manifest
to itself. But the I also posits its other and puts its mark on it (e.g. converts the

many trees it has seen into the idea of 'tree') and thereby attains 'concrete being-for-self', 'determinate revelation to itself'. Since its other bears the stamp of the mind, in positing its other the mind manifests itself, and in being aware of its other it is aware of itself, i.e. manifests itself to itself.

This seems to conflict with Hegel's earlier claim that the logical Idea is really embedded in nature and is not simply imposed on it by us: see §381, n. 22. But his view is this. The logical Idea is embedded both in nature and in our minds. However, in our initial encounter with nature we do not recognize the logical Idea in it. We thus need to impose our categories on nature. But in doing this, we make contact with the categories implicitly present in nature. Nature comes out to meet us, as it were. In this respect, understanding nature is comparable to doing a jigsaw puzzle. We start with a rough idea of what the picture should be and try to impose this on the pieces. At first, our imposition is somewhat forcible, but eventually the picture emerges from the pieces more spontaneously and we realize that it was implicit in the pieces all along.

5. Hegel advances at least four propositions: (1) A 'content' of the mind is essentially revealed. (2) Such a content has no intrinsic character apart from its occurrence in the 'form' of revelation. (3) Whatever the mind reveals is, or belongs to, the mind itself. (4) The content revealed is just the revelation itself. Proposition (1) is plausible. It is at least plausible that a pain must be revealed to one who has it and so must the idea of a tree. Proposition (2) is doubtful. Surely there must be a residual content, something besides the sheer revelation, to distinguish a revealed pain from a revealed itch or the idea of a tree from the idea of a dog. But perhaps this is to misinterpret Hegel. Perhaps he meant that whatever it is that distinguishes a pain from an itch or the idea of a tree from the idea of a dog must itself be revealed, that no feature of any content can remain unrevealed. This would be a comparatively benign version of proposition (2). However, this benign interpretation seems to be excluded by proposition (4). If all that is revealed is revelation, then nothing else is revealed, not pains, itches, trees, dogs, nor the ideas of them. Perhaps Hegel did not mean proposition (4) quite literally, but only as an extravagant expression of proposition (1), along with its converse, proposition (3): Whatever is revealed by mind is a 'content' of mind, not something distinct from mind. The arguments advanced in the rest of this *Zusatz* do not support the literal version of (4), but only (1), (2), and (3).

6. Revelation is a 'form' and what is revealed is a 'content'. The Logic, Hegel believes, has established that every content has some form (Enc. I, §133). In one sense, a content may have any one of several forms. A book, for example, may be published in writing, in print, or electronically, though it must have some such form if it is to exist at all. In another sense, a content can only have one form or, at least, only one appropriate form. The content of Virgil's *Aeneid*, for example, can only appear in the form of an epic poem in hexameters; any other form is wrong and would make the work 'formless'. Another idea that Hegel perhaps has in view is that, say, a particular colour or a particular sound has its 'content' in virtue of its formal relationships to other colours or other sounds: cf. Enc. I, §§91–2.

Conversely, Hegel implies, every form has some content. Initially this seems less plausible than his view that every content has a form. To take examples from modern logic, any proposition or 'content' has a logical form, whether it be simply 'p' or some more complex form such as 'If p, then q' or 'Everything that is F is also G'. A propositional form, such as 'If p, then q', may be given a content, such as 'If Hegel is German, then Kant is a philosopher'. The form perhaps 'makes the content into the content': the proposition could not have that content unless it had that form, or at least some form or other. However, the propositional form 'If p, then q' does not as such have a content: I cannot by uttering this expression make any definite assertion. But to this Hegel will reply as follows: The form itself is, or at least can become, a content. I can think about it and make assertions about it just as I do about anything else. In fact, the form must have a content to differentiate it from other logical forms, such as 'Not-p and not-q'.

Even if we grant Hegel all this, however, why does it follow that a mental content must be revealed? A content may require a form if it is to exist at all and to differ from other contents. But revelation is surely only one type of form, and not one that need accompany every content: books may remain unpublished and secrets may be kept fast. However, Hegel here regards revelation not simply as one form among others, but as the common structure of all form. Content is a 'being-within-itself', the intrinsic nature of a thing, while form is the thing's relations to other things, its external revelation, for example, the relations of red to blue, green, yellow, and so on, or of 'If p, then q' to 'Not-p and not-q'.

It is not very easy to move from this general notion of revelation to the more specific notion pertaining to the mind. Perhaps a pain and an itch need formal relations to each other to account for their distinctive content. But why must either be revealed in any further sense, either to oneself or to others? Some help is given by Hegel's account of the 'inner' and the 'outer': see Enc. I, §140. If something is only inner, that is, unexpressed, then it is only 'in itself', potential and undeveloped. Rather than pains and itches, Hegel has in view such things as an idea. An idea comes to me before I express it. But it is not fully formed in my mind before I express it. Until I express it, in words or paint or in manipulation of objects in my environment, the idea is inchoate and undeveloped. When I express it, the idea may be revealed to others. But it is also revealed to myself: I only see what my idea really amounts to when I see it embodied before me. Only when my idea is expressed can it come into contact with other ideas and define itself in relation to them. The mind's drive to reveal itself is therefore a drive to actualize itself: cf. §383, n. 8. However, Hegel will not let matters rest at such generalities: we have to 'get to know' (*erkennen*) mind, etc., i.e. show in detail how the mind works.

7. If Christ is just the 'instrument' (*Organ*) of the revelation, then 'what is revealed' (*das Geoffenbarte*, i.e. God) is different from 'what reveals it' (*das Offenbarende*, i.e. Christ). Similarly if I say 'I have a good idea', my words are quite distinct from my good idea; I can easily have a good idea without saying so, or say so without having one. If, by contrast, I express my idea in a painting, my painting

reveals not just my idea but also its tendency (albeit not unfailing) to reveal itself in paint. Similarly, in begetting a Son, God reveals his (unfailing) tendency to beget a Son. Although God is somehow different from the Son he nevertheless maintains his 'unity' with it. Analogously, the mind, though it is somehow different from the painting it has produced, recognizes itself, its idea, in the painting and thus 'reveals only itself' in its other. However, in neither case is it plausible to maintain proposition (4), in §383, n. 5: 'The content revealed is just the revelation itself'. That God is revealed by a Son, rather than a daughter, a volcano, or whatever, implies a content independent of the sheer form of revelation. So does the mind's revelation of itself in this particular painting rather than some other painting or a brick wall. What Hegel perhaps means is that God and the mind are wholly revealed, nothing is kept back.

8. An acorn is a 'possible' or potential oak-tree. The 'possibility' of the oak-tree is the 'concept' of an oak-tree embodied in the acorn. As the plant grows, it gradually actualizes this concept and becomes an actual oak-tree. An oak-tree, however, is presumably not the 'unity of possibility and actuality', not at least in the way that a mind is. But how does Hegel think they differ? One difficulty in the way of answering this question is the difficulty of saying what a merely potential, merely 'inward' mind would be. There are at least three possibilities:

   (1) *A pure I or ego with no other states or activities.* This would differ from an acorn in that, while an acorn may remain undeveloped, there cannot be a mind that is only a pure ego. A mind has to actualize itself in this sense if it is to be a mind at all. An ego that does have states and activities differs from an oak-tree, however, in that whereas the oak-tree has left its possibility behind and retains nothing of the acorn, a developed mind still has the ego underlying it, its possibility is preserved in its actuality.

   (2) *A mind with states and activities that it expresses or reveals neither to itself nor to others.* Again, Hegel does not believe that there could be such a mind. Acorns need not grow, but minds have to actualize themselves in this sense. Nevertheless, a developed mind retains its inner side in a way that a developed oak-tree does not.

   (3) *The mind of an embryo or an infant.* This resembles the acorn, in that it need not develop further. If it does develop, however, it differs from the acorn, in that it is retained, below the surface, in the rational adult mind: see §408 on insanity.

There are, therefore, several ways in which the mind might be said to be the 'unity of possibility and actuality'. Probably, Hegel has them all in view. See also §384, n. 7.

NOTES TO §384

1. This is the first of three forms of 'revelation', in which three different things happen to nature. The revelation of the 'abstract', i.e. logical, Idea is an immediate transition to nature, not mediated by mind (cf. Enc. I, §244). This is nature's 'becoming' or coming to be (*Werden*). See also §384, n. 5.

2. In the second revelation, mind 'posits' (*Setzen*) nature as its, namely the mind's, world: cf. §384, n. 6. But since this positing is *Reflexion* it also 'presupposes' (*Voraussetzen*: lit. 'posits in advance') this world as mind-independent nature. *Reflexion* combines the ideas of reflecting back something (primarily light) and of reflecting on something. Mind reflects on nature, nature and mind are each reflected back into themselves, as independent spheres. *Reflexion* on things is an inferior mode of thought, closer to *Verstand* than to reason: cf. Enc. I, §112.

3. This is presumably the third revelation discussed in §384, n. 7. 'In the concept' (*im Begriffe*) may mean something like 'implicitly', but it also indicates the conceptual rather than reflective character of the third revelation. It is a 'creation' (*Erschaffen*) of 'nature' (*derselben*, which might alternatively refer to 'the world'), not as an independent nature, but 'as its being' (*als seines Seins*), i.e. as an extension of itself. The mind perfects its freedom in the third revelation, because it finds that its other, nature, is itself mind. This revelation is undertaken by 'absolute mind', ambiguously God and human art, religion and philosophy. For Hegel, man and his efforts to understand the world, himself, God, etc., are not distinct from God, but the culminating phase of God, God's self-consciousness. At their highest phase—absolute mind—God and man coincide.

4. This remark added in the second, 1827, edition relates to the third revelation, discussed in §384, nn. 3 and 7. That God is mind or spirit was, in Christianity, presented to our imagination or 'representation' (*Vorstellung*); philosophy grasps it in the 'concept' or conceptually. Absolute mind (§§553 ff.) recognizes with increasing clarity that ultimate reality—God, the 'absolute' or the 'essence'—is mind. (The three revelations are associated with the Holy Trinity, but do not exactly match it: the Son, the second member of the Trinity, corresponds to the emergence of nature, i.e. the first revelation: cf. §381, n. 19.)

5. This is the revelation of the logical Idea in nature: cf. §384, n. 1. It too is a revelation of mind, since the logical Idea is mind 'in itself'. Because nature as such is in contradiction with the 'Idea', nature has to develop into a mind that is no longer just in itself, but awake and self-conscious. This development is not itself a revelation. It sets the stage for the second revelation.

6. Mind emerges from nature, but nature still remains as something other than mind. This leaves a rift between mind's 'consciousness' of nature and its 'self-consciousness', corresponding to the rift between nature and mind. Mind does its best, at the level of natural science and non-philosophical understanding, to close this rift. But the rift still persists, because mind fails to see (1) that a mind, with which it is in 'unity', is active in nature, and (2) that nature is the creation of 'infinite mind'. These two claims, that mind is active in nature and that nature is the creation of mind, are not identical. Claim (1) does not entail claim (2): mind might be active in nature, without creating nature. Claim (2) does not entail claim (1): mind might create something that does not itself contain mind. Claim (2) is an explicitly religious doctrine. Claim (1) is the philosophical version of it, and means roughly that the logical structure of nature is the same as the logical structure of our thought.

7. The third revelation of 'absolute mind': cf. §384, nn. 3 and 4. In the first revelation mind remains 'in itself', *an sich*. In the second it becomes *für sich*, 'for itself', but fails to see its unity with mind in itself within nature. The third revelation unites mind's being-in-itself and its being-for-itself. It is now in and for itself. Being in itself is equated with its 'concept' or possibility, being for itself with its actuality. This unity of possibility and actuality differs from that discussed in §383, n. 8. §383 primarily refers to the mind's drive to reveal itself or become 'for itself', a drive involved in mind's 'in itself' or concept. This is the second revelation of §384. §383 conceded, however, that 'finite' mind does not attain the 'absolute unity' of possibility and actuality. This was reserved for 'absolute' mind. That is the third revelation, under discussion here: the mind's recognition of its unity with mind in itself, or nature. The oak-tree provides no counterpart to this. However high it grows, it never recognizes its unity with the acorn.

8. 'Mind absolutely revealed to itself, etc.' is contrasted with mind in itself (the first revelation) and mind for itself (the second revelation). Such lower types of mind might be man's mind at early stages or God's mind, according to non-Christian accounts of God. God and man, so conceived, are distinct from each other. But they coincide at the level of absolute mind: cf. §384, n. 3.

9. Three 'conceptions of the eternal' display the pattern: unity—difference—unity in difference. (Hinduism is omitted, since it does not fit this pattern: cf. §377, n. 6.) (i) In oriental monotheism (and later atavisms such as the Enlightenment) God is self-enclosed and abstract, God the Father shorn of his tendency to generate Son and Holy Spirit. God is 'in himself', quite distinct from nature and from man. (ii) In Greek religion God begins to be 'revealed'. The rift between God and nature is closed, since nature is 'raised to the level of mind', i.e. used to portray gods in a lifelike human form. But since Greek religion operated only with 'sensory intuition' or 'representation', the 'totality of mind' takes the form of polytheism, with independent gods related only by a 'power' that eludes their control and is thus not subdued by mind. (iii) Christianity combines the merits of oriental and Greek religion, while avoiding their defects. It reveals God as a differentiated unity, at first in the form of 'representation', but later in the 'form of the concept'.

   This sequence of religions corresponds roughly to philosophy's progress 'from the imperfect forms of mind's revelation' to its highest form. The self-enclosed oriental God faintly resembles mind implicit in nature—but also the mind as considered by rational psychology: cf. §378 and nn. 5 and 7. Greek religion resembles the mind as it unfolds in the bulk of Enc. III—and also mind as treated by empirical faculty psychology: cf. §§378, 379. Christianity resembles, and virtually coincides with, 'absolute mind'. But it also symbolizes Hegel's own philosophy of mind, combining the merits and excluding the defects of the rational and faculty psychologies. In Hegel's view, Christianity permeates his whole philosophy as well as constituting its final phase.

NOTES TO §385

1. As the *Zusatz* says, mind is 'always Idea'. But the first stage is associated with
   the concept, the second with reality, and the third with their combination, the
   Idea proper. The third is said to be 'in and for itself'; hence the first is implied
   to be 'in itself' and the second 'for itself'.The freedom of subjective mind is as
   yet exempt from the social and ethical constraints that in objective mind merge
   freedom and necessity: cf. §§385, n. 6, and 469; 482. In stage II, 'world' refers
   not (as in §384) to the natural world, but to the human world that we create.
   The *Zusatz* suggests that the development is chronological. It is not straightforwardly so. At every stage of human history, subjective, objective, and, even if in a
   rudimentary form, absolute mind go hand in hand. Long before a child displays
   all the capacities considered under the heading of 'subjective mind', it has been
   initiated into the social and cultural life of its community. Hegel tends to assume
   that the development of his own thought runs parallel to the development of the
   object of his thought.
2. The undeveloped indeterminacy of the mind in its earliest stage is associated
   with the concept (the indeterminate seed in contrast to the plant), with the
   'being' (*Sein*) common to everything that is—the opening phase of Hegel's
   logic (cf. Enc. I, §§84–6), and with universality in contrast to particularity. The
   seeds of different types of plant (and plants themselves at the beginning of their
   growth) do not differ, at least to a cursory inspection, nearly as much as full-
   grown plants. Their concepts differ, but what we perceive of them, their 'reality',
   does not. A seed is thus 'universal', presenting the common features of a group
   of plants, but no 'particular' plant. Particularity involves a 'One and an Other' in
   that one particular thing, such as a daffodil, contrasts with another, such as a lily.
   However, more relevant here are the particular aspects of a single organism. In
   a seed, the particulars (leaves, stem, root, etc.) that will emerge in contrast with
   each other in the plant, are not yet differentiated. Analogously particular aspects
   of the mind—memory, recollection, reason, etc.—are not yet discernible in the
   embryo or, in their full development, in children.
3. On children, cf. §396 and Z. Hegel is here describing the early stages of subjective mind rather than subjective mind as a whole.
4. The concept of mind has two 'realities' corresponding to it: A. its first quasi-
   natural reality, which is 'immediate' in the sense that it is not 'mediated' by a
   preceding development; B. the 'totality of the developed moments [i.e. aspects]
   of the concept', the adult mind, in which the concept is still the unifying 'soul'
   of these 'moments'. The mind's advance from A to B is driven by the 'contradiction' between the concept itself and and the 'immediacy' of reality A. The words
   'what seems to be immediately present in the mind is not anything genuinely
   immediate, but is in itself something posited, mediated' might refer to reality B,
   the adult mind, which appears immediate, but results from a transition from, a
   'sublation' of, reality A. But they might also mean that reality A is posited, not
   (as it appears) immediate. Reality A is posited or mediated by the concept of

mind, which has initially to appear in this simple guise, as a prince may have to assume the guise of a beggar before he ascends the throne. But mind must advance to reality B, driven on by the contradiction between its concept and reality A, and so too the prince must shed the beggarly garb that contradicts his regal destiny. Then reality A can be stripped of its immediacy, 'posited', in another way. When we advance from, say, mere natural hunger to rational self-control, then hunger can be posited (or 'preposited') in the form (or as the basis) of a rational decision to eat. Perhaps too the king will employ the humility he learnt as a beggar in his regal decisions.

5. Here the mind parts company with the prince. The prince knows all along that he is a prince. But in reality A, mind does not know that it is mind, has not grasped its concept, and does not know what it is. Since mind is 'essentially only what it knows itself to be', at stage A it is only mind 'in itself' or potentially. It becomes 'for itself', actual, but also self-aware, by 'particularizing' itself. It advances to reality B, which is not universal and indeterminate, like reality A, but differentiated and determinate. Then it regards reality A (which is not simply its past state, but persists as the natural foundation of the mind) not as itself, but as its presupposition, as its 'other'. At first it treats A (e.g. its hunger) as simply other than itself, but then it 'sublates' it as other, by transforming it into, say, a rational decision to eat and thus incorporating the hunger into itself. But cf. §385, n. 6.

6. Mind is 'subjective', when it is related to itself as an other, that is, when it is not wholly absorbed in reality A, but has not yet sublated it. In 'grasping itself as itself', not as an other, mind sublates reality A, making it 'ideal' and thus 'proving itself' to be its 'ideality': cf. §379, n. 3; §381, nn. 4 and 8. When it achieves this, and becomes 'for itself', it is 'objective' mind. The claim that subjective mind is 'unfree' or free only 'in itself' need not contradict the claim in the Paragraph that at stage I mind is 'free'. The Paragraph uses 'free' in the different sense of 'together with itself' (*bei sich*), i.e. cut off from the other. (It is also possible that it says only that freedom is *in the concept* of subjective mind.) Objective mind is free in the different sense that it has sublated or taken over the other, and therefore knows that it is free. 'Objective' thus combines two ideas: that the mind objectifies or realizes itself in the world and that the mind thereby becomes objective, or an object, to itself. The two ideas are connected. The other (nature) is sublated, by the transformation of natural objects into property and in general by the construction of a human world. In this world mind finds and knows itself, not simply alien nature, and sees its own freedom objectified. 'Other' refers to two apparently distinct things: (i) natural aspects of the mind, e.g. raw urges such as hunger; (ii) external nature. Both are sublated, (i) by the development of the rational self, (ii) by the construction of a human world. Hegel is attempting to explain the connection between these twin sublations.

7. The *Person*, constituted by ownership, is the initial phase of objective mind: cf. §§488 ff. and PR, §§34 ff. Mind is not here exclusively objective. It is also subjective: 'we see a subjective entity' and also 'an external reality of

this freedom'. Hegel conceives the freedom(s) one has in a society as the 'reality' of the concept of freedom, of one's intrinsic freedom or 'free will': cf. §469 and Z. On the state, cf. §§535 ff. and on the 'ethical world' in general, §§513 ff.

8. Absolute mind does not (as the Paragraph suggests) simply unify subjective and objective mind: objective mind is also subjective in any case (cf. §385, n. 7). Absolute mind releases the world, which as an ethical world is 'posited' by mind, so that it is now conceived as 'having an immediate being', i.e. as existing independently, *as well as* ('at the same time') posited by mind. Perhaps cf. §554: '*Religion*, as this supreme sphere [i.e. absolute mind] can in general be designated, is to be regarded as issuing from the subject and situated in the subject, but is equally to be regarded as objectively issuing from the absolute spirit, which as spirit is in its community.' The ethical world is obviously a product of human beings, and is regarded by us as a product of human beings. God—the theme, in Hegel's view, of art and philosophy, as well as religion—is not so obviously a human product. At least, God is not regarded by worshippers as a human product. To say, as Voltaire did, that man made God in his own image, naturally implies that God does not really exist, whereas to say that man creates the state does not imply that the state does not exist.

NOTES TO §386

1. Mind as subjective and as objective is 'finite', i.e. displays a concept–reality mismatch, as do flatly finite entities such as the sun and the solar system: cf. §386, n. 7. But unlike these entities, mind as such is 'infinite Idea', able and destined to have its concept and reality in accord. Hence the mind's finitude, its inadequate reality, is a barrier or limitation set up by the mind itself, enabling it eventually to recognize its own 'freedom', which is not sharply distinct from its 'infinity', since it too consists in the adequacy of mind's reality to its concept. In saying how mind erects the barrier Hegel exploits *Schein* and *scheinen*, which mean both 'glow, shine; to shine' and 'semblance, illusion, show; to seem'. He may be thinking of light, which also needs an obstacle—a material surface or medium—to manifest its nature, though it does not itself posit the obstacle: cf. §§381, n. 15; 384, n. 2; Enc. II, §§275 ff.

2. Mind's activity of erecting and clearing hurdles involves three main stages:(i) finding a world before it as 'presupposed', i.e. subjective mind; (ii) 'generating' a world, i.e. objective mind; (iii) liberation from and in this world, i.e. absolute mind. These are stages of mind's liberation; it has to linger in, and pass through, each stage. Stage (iii) is the complete fulfilment, the 'absolute truth' of its liberation, and this stage involves the identification of all three stages, the realization that they are 'one and the same', i.e. are all necessary parts of a single process. The 'semblance', i.e. subjective, objective, and perhaps the early phases of absolute mind, 'purifies itself' and ends up as the 'infinite form' of this truth, i.e. as philosophical 'knowledge' (*Wissen*) of the truth. By this stage it is no longer 'semblance'.

3. On 'reason' (*Vernunft*) and understanding or 'intellect' (*Verstand*), cf. §378, nn. 1 and 2. Hegel's opponents make two claims: that (1) the human mind is unable to know the 'infinite', and (2) the human mind is not, as Hegel believes, both finite and infinite, but exclusively finite. Claim (1) was endorsed by Kant and his followers, with added support from the religious objection that it is impious to attempt to know too much about God. Claim (2) is maintained by the intellect, insisting that anything must be either finite or infinite, and that nothing can be both finite and infinite. (Hegel and his opponents agree that the mind is not *exclusively* infinite.) This too has moral and religious support: to ascribe infinity to the human mind is to liken ourselves to God. Hegel and his opponents agree that the two claims entail each other: if the human mind can know the infinite, then it is itself infinite, and if the mind is infinite, then it can know the infinite.

   Hegel's objections to these claims are that they regard the finite as 'fixed and absolute' and they make our knowledge superficial by confining it to the finite, to what has its ground in something else, namely the infinite, not in itself. (Hegel has no strong aversion to likening man to God.) His opponents might reply as follows. First, there may still be something infinite (e.g. God, the universe as a whole), even if it is not the human mind and even if we do not know much about it, and this is enough to prevent the finite from being 'absolute'. Secondly, knowledge of the finite, however superficial it may be, is the best we can hope for. But see also §386, n. 4.

4. On finitude, see Enc. I, §§92–4. Logic considers 'thought-forms of finitude', such as 'whole and parts' (Enc. I, §135) and causality (Enc. I, §153). Such categories are themselves finite, in that they are bounded or limited by other categories, into which they tend to mutate owing to their internal incoherence. They also apply to the 'concrete forms' of finitude, the finite entities and stages studied by the philosophies of nature and mind. The finite, i.e. the forms themselves and the entities they apply to, are shown not to be 'true', i.e. their reality does not correspond to their concept (cf. §379, n. 7). Hence finite entities dissolve into other entities, and finite thought-forms pass over into other, usually equally finite, thought-forms. This is the 'dialectic' considered in Enc. I, §81, a dialectic immanent in things and forms that makes them pass away through and in an 'other'. But some things are exempt from this dialectic. The 'concept' itself embraces all the 'thought-forms of finitude' and so, although it develops in accordance with their 'transitions', it does not change into something else in the way that they do. Nor can the concept itself be characterized in terms of any of the finite thought-forms that it embraces. Similarly the mind cannot be adequately described in terms of causality or as a whole consisting of parts. The mind develops and expands as its finite stages succumb to dialectic, but it does not itself succumb to this dialectic or change into anything other than mind. Thus mind and the concept endure to demolish things and forms that are intrinsically friable. (The German *eitel* means 'vain' both in the sense of 'conceited' and in the sense of 'futile'.) To insist that the mind is merely finite denies the mind this power of demolishing the finite and thus retains the finite intact.

In clinging to the finite, what purports to be modesty is really a sort of vanity. On 'evil', overvaluing the finite, cf. §§382, n. 5, 396Z., 472.

5. On the inseparability of gold from its specific gravity, cf. §382, n. 6. Elsewhere animal species are said to be classified according to their teeth and claws, since these are what the animals themselves use to distinguish themselves from other animals: Enc. I,§230Z. and Enc. II, §370Z. But the two cases differ. No piece of stuff with a specific gravity other than that characteristic of gold is gold. But a toothless and clawless animal may well be a freak or damaged tiger. Hegel's point is just that such a tiger would not survive for long.

6. The mind is not simply indeterminate. It enters into various determinate states. Such states are 'finite', distinct from, and excluding, other states. Sensation is distinct from thought: if I am doing arithmetic I cannot at the same time be wholly absorbed in contemplating a sunset. But no given state constitutes the mind in the way that a certain specific gravity constitutes gold or teeth and claws constitute an animal. The finite states into which the mind enters are 'sublated' or reduced to a moment, an element, of the mind and its 'genuine infinity', the infinity that does not exclude but embraces the finite. On infinity, cf. §386, n. 8. On ideality, cf. §379, n. 3.

7. This definition of the finite is more or less the converse of the earlier definition of truth as 'agreement of the concept with its actuality': cf. §379, n. 7. 'Finite' is thus equivalent to 'untrue'. The definition is applied somewhat liberally. The sun is finite, because its reality expands beyond its concept to include the solar system, without which the sun 'cannot be thought'. The solar system itself is finite for the different reason that, while its concept, like any concept, is essentially 'ideal', its reality disperses into seemingly independent bodies. The reality of the mind, by contrast, is ideality; the mind does not tolerate independent elements in itself but sublates them. It is thus in absolute unity with the concept. Or at least it fulfils one condition of such unity. Hegel has not yet shown that the mind can be thought without other entities and is not finite in the way that the sun is finite. But his answer to this is that any other entity which the thought of the mind involves is itself taken up into the mind, by being thought, and thus reduced to a 'moment' of mind.

8. Hegel implies an apparently different definition of finitude: to have a 'limitation' (*Schranke*). If the limited entity is not aware of its limit, it is simply finite and not infinite. If the limited entity is aware of its limit, it is primarily infinite, though secondarily and temporarily finite. (The third possibility, a wholly unlimited entity, would be a case of 'bad infinity' and entirely indeterminate, as, for example, a mind that has no definite thoughts.) Hegel intertwines three lines of thought:

   (1) The connection between this definition and the previous one should be this: A finite entity, such as the sun, is divided by a limit from other things, from, say, the rest of the solar system. What is beyond the limit helps to determine the nature of the sun. Hence the sun is not fully determined by, but exceeds, its own concept. A mind too is divided by a

limit from other things than itself: rocks, trees, desks, etc. But it becomes aware of the other by 'receiving' it into its 'consciousness', and thereby transcends the limit. The mind's infinity then consists in its ability to become aware of things other than itself.

(2) Unlike the sun, the mind does not have a determinate intrinsic nature, contrasting with the natures of other things. It is thus intrinsically 'infinite' (*unendlich*), lacking an 'end' or limit. Therefore, when it becomes conscious of an other, such as the sun, it does not thereby overcome finitude, but rather makes itself finite, limits itself; it gives itself a determinate nature contrasting with other possible natures, such as (being conscious of) rocks, trees, etc. It overcomes this limit and displays its infinity, not by its continuing consciousness of the sun, by knowing this other, but by knowing its own limit, by knowing, that is, that it is conscious of the sun. Knowing one's own limit is a sufficient condition of transcending it. If one knows that one is conscious of the sun, then one does not have to be conscious of the sun, but can become conscious of other things instead. Conversely, if one's thought were permanently fixed on some single object, one could not be aware that one was thinking of that object.

(3) There can be no known limits to our knowledge of the sort postulated, for example, by Kant. As soon as one knows of a limit, it ceases to be an impassable barrier. For to know of a limit is to know what is beyond the limit, i.e. to cross the limit. See Enc. I, §60.

(1) and (2) are easily reconciled. That the mind can become aware of a variety of things suggests that it is in some sense indeterminate, like the eye that does not see itself. (3) is not easily salvaged. That a limit is known does not in all cases imply that we can cross the limit. Knowing that I cannot, say, run a mile in two minutes does not increase my speed. Why should it be any better with knowledge than with running? Knowing that I cannot know the exact contents of every book ever written does not remove this limit. In these cases I know that there is a limit, but I do not know precisely where the limit lies, that I can run a mile in exactly five and a half minutes, but no less, or read exactly six million books, but no more. But that is enough for my powers to be finite.

9. It is unclear whether or not Hegel means to differentiate God from the human mind in respect of finitude. He has said that mind 'as mind *is* not finite, it *has* finitude within itself': cf. §386, n. 6. This makes us like God, who 'posits finitude within himself', but does not 'become a finite entity'. But Hegel has also said that we 'make ourselves into a finite entity': cf. §386, n. 8. This makes us different from God. Moreover, even if both God and man avoid becoming a finite entity, they do so for different reasons. God avoids finitude because the 'reality' he adopts is 'perfectly conformable to him'. But if I contemplate, say, the sun, the reality I give myself is not perfectly conformable to me. The sun is only one of the many things I can think about and is far below me in the ontological hierarchy. What prevents me from becoming a finite entity is my awareness of all this, my knowledge of my 'limit'.

Even at the level of traditional theology, it is not clear whether the finitude God posits is 'perfectly conformable to him'. If God thinks, then he thinks about everything at once, not, as we do, about different things successively. He creates the whole world, though it is not obvious that the world is 'perfectly conformable to him': if it were, it would be a second God. Christ is more or less finite, though a finitude that it is entirely appropriate for God to posit. But what Hegel has in view is probably this. At the level of subjective and objective mind, we are different from God. The realities we posit are not 'perfectly conformable' to us. What saves us from the sun's type of finitude is our awareness of our limit and our consequent tendency to overcome our limit. Eventually we ascend to absolute mind and then we converge with God. Like God, we become aware of the whole of reality in art, religion, and above all philosophy. According to traditional theology, this still leaves a gulf between ourselves and God; God is never entirely revealed to us; we see only the tip of the iceberg, not its hidden depths. Hegel disagrees: eventually God is entirely revealed to us and in receiving this revelation we become God.

10. The fact that the mind overcomes every limit that it sets itself does not entail that it will ever achieve complete liberation from limitation. Each of the lines of thought considered in §386, n. 8 suggests an infinite progression: (1) The mind becomes aware of one object after another to infinity. (2) In the case of any object of which it is aware, it knows of its own awareness of it, and hence transcends this limit, only to become aware of another object and another limit, and so on to infinity. (3) It surmounts one hurdle on its path to complete knowledge, only to encounter another hurdle, and so to infinity. The 'intellect' denies that we can escape from such infinite progressions: we make progress, but we will never reach the final goal. (Enc. I, §94 attributes this view to Kant and Fichte.) However, the mind 'wrests itself' out of such progressions. In philosophy and, in a less satisfactory way, in art and religion, mind achieves a state which is not one of finitude, where its reality fully matches its concept.

NOTES TO §387

1. These sentences present three problems: (i) Is the mind cognitive throughout its career or only at a certain stage? (ii) What is the force of 'cognitive' (*erkennend*)? Often, though not invariably, Hegel contrasts *Erkennen*, as scientific knowledge or 'cognition', with *Wissen*, as simple knowledge or awareness. Does it implicitly contrast with *wissend* here (as in §445Z.)? Or is Hegel just insisting that the mind knows itself and is not only known by an external observer? (iii) What is the relevance of these sentences to the rest of §387? Do they relate to the mind's own development, or to our philosophical cognition of this development?

Hegel's dominant thought is this: Since the mind develops 'in its ideality', it does so in virtue of knowledge, because knowing things, both itself and other entities, makes them 'ideal'. 'Cognition' as a feature of the logical Idea is primarily scientific knowledge. The mind does not have scientific knowledge throughout its career, but 'determines itself to' it by way of various more rudimentary forms of knowledge, attaining cognition proper in the third stage of subjective mind (§445). Cf. §381, n. 3 on 'cognition' (*das Erkennen*) as a 'determinacy' of the logical Idea, and §445, nn. 1 and 6 on *Erkennen* or *Erkenntnis* in philosophy of mind.

2. Subjective mind starts off as 'soul' (*Seele*), which is self-enclosed and dimly aware of its own states rather than its surroundings. It then bifurcates to become 'identical [i.e. even-handed?] reflection' into the mind itself and other things, with which it is in 'relationship' and of which it is conscious. Finally it withdraws away from objects back into itself, as a 'subject' that is 'for itself', i.e. independent and self-reflective. This triad exemplifies the pattern: simple unity—opposition—restored unity (cf. §387, n. 14). 'Reason' (*Vernunft*) emerges at the end of the section on Phenomenology of Mind in §§438–9. In that context, reason combines subjectivity and objectivity, and thus forms the transition to the Psychology section, in which the mind is conscious not of external objects but of itself.

3. A 'determinacy' (*Bestimmtheit*) is a specific feature or differentia which, when added to a concept, makes that concept more specific. For example, if we start with the concept 'animal' and then add to it the determinacy 'herbivorous', we make an 'advance of development' of the concept 'animal' towards the concept 'horse', though we shall have to add other determinacies to the concept 'animal' before we reach our goal. But Hegel is thinking primarily not of such concepts as 'animal' or 'horse', but of the logical Idea, of which cognition is one 'determinacy' among others: cf. §387, n. 1. Something similar happens to the mind. As the mind develops it acquires more and more 'determinacies', such as 'sensation' in §399. Each such determinacy is a step towards the mind's long-term goal of becoming for itself what it is in itself, i.e. to gain complete self-knowledge. Moreover, each stage within this long-term process, such as the stage of 'soul', is itself a process of the same type. At the beginning of the stage the mind has a certain character 'in itself' or implicitly. We (i.e. we philosophers) can see that it has this character, but the mind itself cannot. But by the end of that stage the mind itself, in the form that it has at that stage, sees what it is, and has implicitly been all along. This self-knowledge is limited, however, and does not constitute the final goal of the mind. It drives the mind on to the next stage of its development.

4. Ordinary psychology treats what the 'soul' (here equivalent to 'mind') does simply as 'expressions' of faculties that it has all along. Such psychology can therefore describe the soul only 'in a narrative fashion', i.e. unsystematically. It considers the faculties in no methodical order nor are there any systematic pathways between different faculties. For Hegel, by contrast, the soul is not a 'ready-made subject'. It develops. First it has a certain character or determinacy, then it expresses it. This expression is not just for the benefit of us psychologists, not simply our way of telling that the soul has a certain character. It also presents the soul's own character to the soul itself. It does not present it to the soul very explicitly, but only 'in its concept', in germ. The soul does not yet know as much about itself as we psychologists do. But it knows enough to be promoted to a higher level. This provides Hegel with a systematic way of studying the soul. We

start with determinacy no. 1, the expression of this leads to determinacy no. 2, the expression of no. 2 leads to no. 3, and so on. The main problem is that Hegel does not make clear whether this development is a development undergone by the soul over time or whether it is simply a logical development enabling Hegel to describe what is, in effect, a 'ready-made subject': cf. §440, n. 3. Sometimes the development of Hegel's account of the mind seems to coincide, more or less, with the development over time either of the individual mind or of the human mind in general, but sometimes it does not. He gives no clear account of the relationship between the two types of development.

5. Cf. §§395Z. and 396Z., where Hegel stresses that education should initiate individuals into the the general culture of the time, i.e. the 'universal mind'. Philosophy is concerned not with individuals, but with the mind as such. It asks not 'How does the universal mind come to exist in individuals?' but 'How does the universal mind arise in the first place?' 'What is its structure and mode of development?' and 'How is it related to the individual minds that participate in it?' This gives a partial answer to the problem raised in §387, n. 4: Hegel is not much concerned with the development over time of a human individual, not at least after the time at which education proper begins.

6. Mind is at first 'subjective' for two reasons: (i) its concept or concept is 'undeveloped', i.e. the mind here is comparable to an acorn or a sapling; (ii) it has not made its concept 'an object for itself' (*sich. . . gegenständlich*). These are connected: the mind becomes aware of its concept not by direct inspection of it, but in view of its development (rather as *we* learn the species of the seed from the full-grown plant), and, at least in later stages, it develops by becoming aware of its current state. The mind is never exclusively subjective; even at the start it is 'Idea', concept plus reality, hence both subjective and objective. But this 'immediate reality' is inadequate and must be overcome if the mind is to grasp its own concept or subjectivity. Why does this imply that we could 'just as well say that mind is. . . objective and has to become subjective'? The case of the acorn helps to explain. An acorn has two aspects. First, it contains implicitly the concept of a full-grown oak. This is its 'subjectivity'. Second, it is a small brown lump, not in the least like an oak-tree. This is its 'reality' or 'objectivity'. Because the concept is so inadequately expressed by its current reality, i.e. the small brown lump, we can say that the acorn (qua concept-container) is subjective and has to become objective, i.e. develop a reality adequate to the concept it contains. Because the acorn so inadequately expresses the concept, we can say that the acorn (*qua* small brown lump) is objective and has to become subjective, i.e. develop into a reality adequate to the concept. Unlike an acorn or oak-tree, a mind is also 'subjective' in another sense: it has an inner life, a dim awareness, even if not 'consciousness' in Hegel's sense. This is quite different from the *concept* the mind contains. The inner life of, say, an infant falls far short of its concept, of the full-grown mind of a rational adult. The mind's inner life may not be very adequately expressed in its outer life, its bodily form and behaviour, in which case the mind might also be described as only subjective (owing to its ill-expressed inner life) or as only objective (owing to its inadequately expressive

outer life). Hegel may also have this sense of subjectivity in view, but it is not the dominant sense in this context.

7. The series of 'formations' are indicated empirically, but they express a series of 'determinate concepts'. The series is necessary in that it has a fixed order, and no term in it can be absent, rather like the series $1, 2, 3, \ldots n, n+1, \ldots$ The determinate concepts are segments of the logical Idea and are thus less specific than the formations that express them. The details of a formation that go beyond its corresponding concept are known to us empirically, but the determinate concept is a priori. Hegel is not trying to deduce the mind in all its details from the logical Idea. He gives similar accounts of the collaboration of experience and a priori thought in Enc. I, §12 and in Enc. II, §246.

8. On universality, particularity, and individuality, cf. §§378, n. 11; 379, n. 6; 385, n. 2. The concept develops, in Hegel's Logic, from 'abstract universality' to individuality, by way of particularity: cf. Enc. I, §163. At the simplest level, a generic concept, e.g. 'animal', is universal; specific concepts, e.g. 'dog', 'horse', are particular; and 'Fido', 'Neddy', etc. are individual concepts. But Hegel's account involves further complexities that help to explain, if not justify, the use made of the triad here. In particular, mind that is 'for itself' is not individual in the sense that it is the mind of Tom, Dick, or Harry. It is individual in the sense that, unlike the soul, it is intrinsically determinate and, unlike consciousness, not dependent on external objects. It stands on its own two feet.

9. 'Ideality' often refers to the mind's ability to surmount or negate distinctions, as in §379, n. 3. 'Ideality' in this sense does not contrast with 'reality', except in so far as reality presents the distinctions that are to be surmounted. Conversely, 'reality' often refers to the specific stage of development that the mind has currently reached. 'Reality' in this sense contrasts with the 'concept', but not with 'ideality' in the above-mentioned sense. Here, however, 'ideality' and 'reality' are contrasted and are roughly equivalent to 'inner life' and 'outer life' or to 'mind' and 'body'. It may be, however, that Hegel is running together two different questions:

(1) Why can we not begin with the concept of mind, that is, with a general account of the mind that does not specify any particular stage of it—or, perhaps, with an account of the fully developed rational mind? Why must we start with the soul? (Aristotle raises a similar question in *de anima*, II. 3, 414^{b}20–7.)

(2) Why must we consider the physical side of the soul, its body, as well as its inner, mental side?

The two questions are connected at least to the following extent. Once we have decided that we have to consider not just the concept of mind, but the first stage of its actualization, we have to consider its physical embodiment. For the mind has just emerged from nature and from nature it inherits a body that is not yet 'mediated' or 'posited' by mind. It has not been shaped or trained by mind, still less has it been downgraded by 'abstract thinking', in the way that, say, philosophers attach relatively little importance to their bodies. The body is still 'abstract', i.e. ill-formed and undifferentiated, as is the 'ideality' or inner life that it has in its grip.

10. *Anthropos* is Greek for 'man' (covering both sexes), and *Anthropologie* is the study (*logos*) of man. 'Man' (*Mensch*), or '*anthropos*', contrasts with 'mind', in that it also includes the body and psychical features directly related to the body. 'Anthropology' in Hegel (and Kant) is not restricted to 'ethnology'.

11. Anthropology involves a movement from immediate unity (the 'natural' soul, §§391–402) through opposition (the feeling soul, §§403–10) to restored unity (the actual soul, §§411–12). Quality is the first division of the Logic (Enc. I, §§86–98), and thus the mind is initially 'qualitatively determined', marked by qualities impressed on it by its natural surroundings: cf. §392. On racial differences cf. §393 and Z. On somnambulism cf. §§398Z. and 406 and Z. On insanity cf. §408 and Z. On the body as a 'sign' of the soul, cf. §411. Here the distinction between ideality and reality comes close to the distinction between soul and body. The reality is 'posited ideally' in so far as the soul is expressed by bodily deportment, gestures, etc.

12. While the natural soul was aware of nature only by way of the qualities nature impressed on it, the mind now extrudes the natural aspect of itself out into the external world and pares itself down to the bare 'I' or ego (*das Ich*, from the first-person pronoun, *ich*), which is conscious of its 'Other'. The natural mind is now an object for the mind itself, not just for us (philosophers), but the I does not yet recognize it as the natural mind. The I thus has 'being-for-self' (*Fürsichsein*), in that it is now detached from nature and has some self-awareness. But it is not 'for itself' (*für sich*), fully independent and aware only of itself, since it depends on an other. On freedom, cf. §385, n. 6.

13. *Phänomenologie*, from the Greek *logos* ('doctrine, study, etc') and *phainomena*, 'things that seem, appear, are manifest', is the 'doctrine of appearances'. Other philosophers (such as Husserl) use the term with reference to things that appear *to* the mind. But for Hegel it is primarily the mind itself that appears, not its objects. 'Appearance' (*Erscheinung*) and 'appear' (*erscheinen*) are different from 'semblance' (*Schein*) and 'seem' (*scheinen*): cf. §386, n. 1, and Enc. I, §131. That the mind 'only appears' does not mean that it only seems to be mind. Nor does it mean that the mind is manifest. It means that the mind is only 'emerging' or 'coming into view' and is not yet fully 'actual.'

14. The I is reflected back, rebounds off, the other into itself. The subjective and the objective are no longer, as in anthropology, mind and body, but the I and its other, i.e. its objects. The mind's aim, as in anthropology, is to equalize and harmonize the two sides. This is achieved especially by a rational culture that informs *both* the mind, filling up the empty I, *and* the external world, rendering it subjective as well as objective. The mediated universality of self-consciousness thus attained (cf. §§436–7) is quite different from the 'abstract universality' of the natural soul. Consciousness here follows the pattern of immediate unity (the I)—opposition (the I and its other)—restored unity (self-consciousness). Cf. §§424 ff. on self-consciousness.

15. Here 'an object' translates *gegenständlich*. German has two words for 'object', *das Objekt* and *der Gegenstand*, and two words for 'objective', *objektiv* and *gegenständlich*. When 'object(ive)' is contrasted with 'subject(ive)' (*Subjekt, subjektiv*), Hegel always uses *Objekt* or *objektiv*. What is objective in this sense, need not be known to the subject or be *its* object. When he means that an object is known to, or is the object of, the mind, he uses *Gegenstand* and *gegenständlich*.

16. Subjective mind as a whole, like each of its three forms, follows the pattern: immediate unity (soul)—opposition (consciousness)—restored unity (actual mind), which is also the movement: universality—particularity—individuality: cf. §387, n. 8. On truth, see §379, n. 7.

17. 'Reason' (*Vernunft*) is essential to mind as weight is essential to a body and freedom essential to the will. A mind is always rational, though it is only 'mind as such', the mind studied by psychology, that recognizes this. Earlier Hegel defined truth as 'agreement of the concept with its actuality': cf. §379, n. 7. 'Idea' is the concept together with its corresponding reality: cf. §377, n. 4. So 'truth' and 'Idea' roughly coincide. 'Reason' is sometimes equated with 'Idea': cf. Enc. I, §214. And when Hegel said, in the Preface to PR and again in Enc. I, §6, 'What is rational [*vernünftig*] is actual, and what is actual is rational', he could easily have used 'true' instead of 'actual' or instead of 'rational'. However, 'reason' is not, in Hegel's usage, always equivalent to 'truth' and 'Idea'. Reason, both as a mode of thinking and as an objective process, has a 'negative', sceptical or destructive, role as well as a positive role: cf. Enc. I, §§81–2. Only in its positive role can reason be assimilated to truth or the Idea. In its negative role it sublates untrue thoughts or things that fall short of the Idea. In its positive role it reaches the truth or the Idea itself. This happens in §§438–9. What Hegel there has in view is that the mind combines subjectivity and objectivity by imposing its own rationality on what is initially other than itself.

18. Mind as such exemplifies the pattern: immediate unity—opposition—restored unity. It begins by embracing both subjectivity and objectivity, but then bifurcates into a subjective side, 'intelligence' (*Intelligenz*), i.e. theoretical mind, and an objective side, will or practical mind. Intelligence imposes rationality on the scattered material given to it, i.e. simply presented to it, and transforms it into a 'concrete universal', i.e. not a thin, 'abstract' universal, whether it be a universal derived from the logical Idea (such as 'being') or a universal applicable to the untransformed empirical given (such as 'green'), but a complex universal, such as 'animal', 'horse', etc. (Cf. §393, n. 8, for a different but related conception of the abstract universal.) What the intelligence then knows is not an 'abstraction' (i.e. the untransformed given or perhaps the abstract universal) but the 'objective concept', i.e. the conceptualized world that it has helped to produce.

This account of intelligence casts doubt on the claim that it is 'subjective'. Theoretical and practical mind are regarded as respectively subjective and objective, because they are seen as proceeding in opposite directions: theoretical mind receives content from the external world, while practical mind discharges its own content into the world and thereby changes it. But Hegel rejects this sharp dichotomy. In his view, theoretical mind proceeds in the same directions as practical mind. It too projects its own content onto the world and thereby trans-forms it. Only then does it receive the content into itself. Intelligence thus seems objective as well as subjective.

19. Since intelligence 'imposes rationality' on the 'content' presented to it, it may be said (with some exaggeration) to derive the content from itself. When intel-ligence becomes aware of this, it decides to focus on itself, in particular on its 'urges, inclinations', material which is, like the preconceptual external materi-al, 'individual' and disorderly, but which mind immediately recognizes as 'its own', before any conceptual processing. Its treatment of this material is analog-ous to its treatment of the external material. It reflects 'itself into itself' out of these urges, etc., i.e. it distinguishes itself from them and does not automatic-ally endorse them. It brings order into them by relating them to a universal, especially the idea of happiness (§§479–80.). Finally it wills the 'universal in and for itself', etc., a rational social order that coincides with its own freedom (§§481–2.), an order whose 'determinations' are not natural but conceptual. Then mind has returned to a unity with itself comparable to the unity of the natural soul and of actual mind before its bifurcation into intelligence and will, but a unity on a higher level. This is objective mind.

NOTES TO §388

1. Hegel probably means not that mind came into being in time—he has at best only a hazy conception of the temporal origins of mind—but that it has emerged in the logical order of things. On mind as the 'truth of nature', cf. §381, nn. 1 and 2. The 'Idea in general' is the logical Idea as a whole, in which a result is always prior to, and the 'truth of', what it results from—roughly in the way that the oak-tree is the 'truth' or fulfilment of, and thus prior to, the acorn. Applied to the mind, this means that mind is the truth of and prior to what went before (namely nature). The 'concept', on the other hand, is here the third section of the logical Idea, in which the transition from one stage to the next is a 'development' or unfolding, illustrated in Enc. I, §161 by the development of a seed into a plant. However, this third section of the logical Idea also contains, as one of its subdivisions, the 'judgement'. The German for 'judgement' is *Urteil*, and Hegel takes this to mean an 'original division' from *ur-* ('original') and *teilen* ('divide'). (That this etymology is incorrect does not significantly impair Hegel's argument.) Hence the development characteristic of the concept can be seen as a sort of self-division of a primitive unity, in the way that a unitary seed divides into the various parts of a plant. Analogously nature can be regarded as dividing in two, one of the divisions being nature itself and the other division becoming mind. Furthermore, Hegel distinguishes several types of judgement. The highest type of judgement, in his view, is the 'judgement of the concept' (Enc. I, §178). In this type of judgement, a thing is assessed or evaluated by comparison to its concept. For example a painting is judged to be good or bad, according to whether or not it accords with the concept of a painting. This suggests that what

leads nature to generate mind is an evaluation of itself, the judgement that it is 'untrue'. That this judgement is 'free' means at least that nature judges *itself*, and so sublates itself.

Why is nature 'untrue'? It is not obvious that it falls short of the concept of *nature*; it does what we would expect nature to do. But nature, in Hegel's view, embodies the logical Idea, which he often calls the concept, and this concept is not adequately expressed in nature: it is outside itself, 'self-externalized', in various bodily individuals. Something is needed to draw it back together again, something that, owing to its 'concretion' or concreteness, embodies the whole of the concept in a simple form.

In Hegel's account, the mind's emergence from nature already involves mental functions such as self-evaluation. This suggests a fairly literal interpretation of his claim that mind 'presupposes' itself, namely that mind is at work in nature all along: cf. §§381, n. 23; 384, n. 2. The mind pulls itself up by its own bootstraps.

NOTES TO §389

1. 'For itself' (*für sich*) here means 'by itself, independently'. The soul is not just one solitary immaterial entity among many material entities. It is, as the *Zusatz* explains, the 'universal immateriality' of nature in two senses. First, nature itself, as it develops, becomes increasingly 'immaterial': cf. §389, n. 3. The soul is the culmination of this development. Second, the soul 'overarches' and transfigures the whole of nature: cf. §389, n. 16.
2. Aristotle draws a distinction between passive and active 'intellect' (*nous*) in *de anima*, III. 5. Passive intellect is 'potentially all things': it can acquire the concept of anything and think about anything. But it needs the active intellect to supply concepts to it and perhaps to prod it into thinking about something in particular. However, the passive intellect is not much like the soul in Hegel's sense. It does not supply the 'stuff' from which the active intellect forms concepts. ('Stuff' here translates Hegel's *Stoff*. 'Material' would be more elegant, but too easily confused with 'material' in the sense in which it contrasts with 'immaterial', whereas '*Stoff*' is used here for matter in the more Aristotelian sense in which 'matter' or 'material' contrasts with the 'form' it takes.) This stuff is supplied, in Aristotle's view, by the five senses and then converted into concepts by the active intellect. Moreover, the passive intellect does actually think, albeit under the tutelage of the active intellect. By contrast, Hegel's soul is the lowest level of the human mind and it does not think about anything. Rather, it somehow absorbs material from its surroundings without selection or discrimination. It does not differentiate itself from the external world. This distinction is drawn only with mind's 'particularizing', when the mind becomes 'conscious' of objects which it distinguishes from itself: cf. §§413 ff. These objects are composed of the stuff that the mind absorbed as soul and which it now projects out into the external world. (This does not mean that the objects are just *subjective*: they really are in the external world, only the soul did not realize this.) Nor does the soul distinguish itself from other souls. This happens only with

mind's 'individualizing', when the mind becomes 'self-conscious' (§424 ff.) and especially when it becomes 'actual mind' (§§440 ff.).

3. Hegel attacks the view that matter is, or is regarded as, 'something true' (*ein Wahres*) by arguing that types of matter form a series, whose members become progressively 'thinner', shedding, one after another, the features characteristic of matter: cf. Enc. II, §337Z. (That the soul is not a 'thing' is argued in the *Zusatz*: see §389, n. 10.) Heat and light (and perhaps space and time) lack weight or gravity and the power of resistance—'in a sense': a lighted or hot room is no harder to enter than a dark or cool room, but it may be too bright or hot to enter. But heat and light remain perceptible and 'self-external': they spread throughout an area. 'Vital matter' (*Lebensmaterie*), the matter supposedly responsible for the life of plants and animals, implicitly lacks 'self-externality' too. What Hegel perhaps has in mind is the fact that if, say, someone's hand is cut off, the hand immediately ceases to be alive, whereas it does not immediately lose its temperature: cf. Enc. I, §216Z. This suggests that 'vital matter', or whatever it is that animates the whole body, is not spread out through the body in the way that heat is. However, animal life is still closely attached to the body that constitutes its 'existence or objectivity'. This is also true of the soul, the lowest phase of human life. So Hegel now speaks of the mind instead of the soul. Here self-externality has disappeared altogether, since the mind (or the 'concept') is not related to an extended body in the way that the life of an animal is. It is related to itself. Thus mind is not material at all. It shows that matter has no truth, since it is the terminus of progressive dematerializations of matter, i.e. the 'truth of matter': cf. §389, n. 14.

Hegel's argument uses outdated science. Antoine Lavoisier (1743–94) regarded light and heat as elements and therefore material; heat was an 'imponderable fluid' called 'caloric'. Heat and light are now regarded as nonmaterial, in the sense that they are not stuffs. The idea of 'vital matter' or 'vital force' was endorsed by Jöns Jakob Berzelius (1779–1848), but is now generally rejected. However, the force of Hegel's argument does not essentially depend on these obsolete doctrines. A more serious objection is this. The mind can transcend the body in the sense that it can think about things that are remote from it in space and time or not even in space and time at all. The mind can also think about itself. Hegel tends to run together two relations that are, on the face of it, distinct: the relation of the mind to the body and the relation of the mind to the object of which it is conscious (cf. §389, n. 15). The mind's relation to itself as an object does not replace its relation to the body. The mind cannot think without a body. This body, moreover, is not 'imponderable'. It has a weight, along with many other properties characteristic of matter.

4. Two answers are considered to the question: How do soul and body combine?

(1) Soul and body are two distinct substances. Then, Hegel objects, they cannot combine, except—like two pieces of matter—by fitting into each other's 'pores' or interstices (cf. Enc. I, §130), and then they make no real contact. Epicurus (*c*.341–270 BC) located the gods not in the pores

of bodies, but in the interstices between worlds; they therefore take no interest and play no part in human affairs, though they do appear to us in dreams.

(2) Descartes (1596–1650), Malebranche (1638–1715), Spinoza (1632–77), and Leibniz (1646–1716) located the body–soul relation in God. If body and soul were still regarded as independent substances, 'God' would just be a name for the mystery involved in (1). But their dependence on God implies that the finite soul and finite matter are not really independent substances. This enables God to relate them in a comprehensible way, as their 'identity'. However, Spinoza's God is (Hegel implies) insufficiently 'creative': see §389, n. 6. Leibniz's God, the 'monad of monads', is creative, but only by a 'judgement'. It does not advance to the syllogism or 'conclusion'.

As is often the case with Hegel's criticisms of other philosophers, it is hard to see to which of Leibniz's doctrines he is objecting. Elsewhere Hegel interprets *urteilen*, *Urteil*, 'judge(ment)', as 'original' (*ur*) 'division' or 'partition' (*teilen*) of a unitary concept: cf. §388, n. 1, and Enc. I, §166. The two parts, the subject and the predicate, are then joined together, even identified, by the copula, 'is'. The German for 'syllogism' or 'inference', *Schluss*, primarily means 'close, end, conclusion'. Hence Hegel regards it as joining together again what the judgement has divided. It joins them more adequately than the copula does: cf. Enc. I, §§181 ff. For whereas a judgement involves only two terms, a syllogism involves three: two extremes and a middle term that joins them together. In traditional logic, these terms are contained in judgements or propositions, of which there are usually three: two premises and a conclusion. But for Hegel what matters is just the three terms. Hence he is apt to describe any three terms, one of which joins the other two, as constituting a syllogism: see Enc. I, §198 on the individual, civil society, and the state. In the 'absolute syllogism', the three terms are the logical Idea, nature, and mind: cf. §§574–7. However, Hegel seems to have in mind a more specific objection to Leibniz than that he failed to arrive at the full-scale Hegelian philosophy. The *Zusatz* (cf. §389, n. 11) suggests that it is this. For Leibniz the soul and the body are not radically different. The body consists of monads that have only subliminal perceptions, while the soul or mind is the dominant monad, which has 'apperception', self-conscious awareness. The dominant monad has no causal relation to the body-monads. Mind and body are related only by a 'pre-established harmony', established, that is, by God: the perceptions of the mind and those of each body-monad harmonize with each other in a sort of psycho-physical parallelism. Hegel's objection seems to be that Leibniz has made the mind too similar to the body and too closely related to it. This results from Leibniz's exclusive reliance on 'judgement'. Once the mind and body are divided by a judgement, they have to remain similar and closely related, joined, as it were, by a copula. If the mind were to transcend the body, in the way that Hegel requires, the unity of mind and body would be lost. If, however, we bring in the syllogism, then the mind can transcend the body and become very dissimilar to it, and yet still be united, or reunited, to the body by a syllogism. Hegel's own attempt to fulfil this programme, in §§574–7, is deeply obscure and of doubtful success. But he gives in §573 a discerning account of different types of unity, especially the type that allows considerable free play to the united terms. This type of unity is relevant not only to the mind, but also to the modern state: cf. §539.

5. Hegel did say, in the Paragraph, that the soul is 'substance', but not that it is a 'unity of thinking and being'. The soul in Hegel's sense does not actually think. What he means is that the soul combines a natural, bodily element ('being') with a low-grade mind that absorbs 'stuff' from its surroundings. It thus constitutes an underlying fund ('substance') from which the mind draws resources for its 'particularization' and 'individualization'. On Persian religion, cf. §377, n. 6, and PH, pp.173 ff.

6. In his *Ethics*, Spinoza argued that there is only a single substance. It has an infinity of attributes, only two of which are known to us: extension (Hegel's 'being') and thought. Thus mind is 'implicitly [an sich] in that unity' of thinking and being, though it may 'withdraw into itself', disengaging itself in a Cartesian way from extended things. Spinoza (Hegel argues) does not show how the mind achieves this or how, in general, substance differentiates itself into a 'manifold' of various things and people. This manifold is simply tacked on to substance in an 'external manner'. What in fact happens, according to Hegel, is that substance develops the difference between thinking and being into an actual difference and then unifies it again. Showing how this occurs occupies the whole of Enc. III, but especially §§572–7. If it did not happen, mind would remain an unconscious soul and not get to 'absolute being-for-self'. Hegel is trying to explain how human beings get beyond the dim awareness of their surroundings that he supposes animals to have to a fully human understanding of the world and of themselves. Spinoza, he believes, did not explain this, primarily because he did not see that to understand something—nature, the world, even ourselves—we must first take our distance from it and then return to it.

7. Anaxagoras (*c*.500–428 BC) held that the cosmos was originated and is governed by a supreme intellect or *nous*. His view differs from that of Spinoza, who never suggests that the attribute of thought originates or governs the world and is averse to explanations of things in terms of purposes. The criticism that Anaxagoras's *nous* does not develop is less apt than the corresponding criticism of Spinoza. *Nous* does not create matter or 'seeds' but merely organizes them into an ordered cosmos. Hegel may be influenced by Socrates, who, in Plato's *Phaedo*, 97b10 ff., regrets that Anaxagoras did not fulfil his promise to supply purposive explanations of things, but relied instead on mechanical explanations, and invoked *nous* only to initiate motion.

8. 'Pantheism' is not an apt term for Anaxagoras, both because he does not identify *nous* with matter and because he nowhere, in the surviving fragments, calls *nous* 'god'. That pantheism does not systematize its content stems from its logical defects, especially that it operates only with individuality and universality, with no mediating particularity to explain their connexion. This defect is shared

by Spinoza, but he is not in the least 'bacchanalian'. This aspect of pantheism emerges only when pantheism takes the more pictorial form of 'representation'. Hegel is perhaps thinking of Hinduism, which he discusses at length in §573.

9. *Reflexion* deals in hard and fast opposites such as the I and the body: cf. §§384, n. 2; 389, n. 12. For the sake of his argument, Hegel tends to equate the soul and the I, which belongs to a later stage of the mind's development. But the word 'soul' (*Seele*) fluctuates between Hegel's own sense (in which it is quite distinct from the 'I') and the sense in which it was used by the rational psychology described in §378.

10. If we regard the soul as immaterial and the body as material, both 'equally substantial', we cannot explain how they are united. The 'former metaphysics' of pre-Kantian thinkers such as Christian Wolff avoided the difficulty by making the soul a 'thing', with many of the features of a physical thing: a spatial location, a beginning and end in time, and a persistent nature capable of bearing properties (cf. §378). It is unclear why this should be supposed to resolve the difficulty, given Hegel's doubts about the possibility of combining two pieces of matter. But two bits of matter can at least fit into each other's pores, whereas a soul that had no location in space or time could hardly fit into a body at all.

11. A monad is a mind, and Leibniz really held that only minds exist, albeit minds of varying degrees of sophistication. Hegel offers two criticisms: (i) Since a soul-monad is as stable and persistent as a material thing, it is just as hard to see how it can be united to body-monads as it is to see how a soul can be united to a body or one body to another body. (ii) The difference between a soul and a material thing is made a difference of degree rather than kind, a soul-monad having perceptions that are clearer and more distinct than those of other monads. Cf. §389, n. 4.

12. On 'speculative' logic, see §378, n. 5. It contrasts with 'reflective' thinking and with the understanding or 'intellect' (*Verstand*): cf. §378, n. 1. *Reflexion* is often similar to *Verstand*. But *Verstand* is regularly contrasted with *Vernunft*, 'reason', and, unlike *Reflexion*, has no special connection with light. On the mind's ideality and its bearing on opposites, cf. §§379, n. 3; 381, nn. 4 nd 8.

13. The 'old' (*alte*) metaphysics may be the pre-Kantian metaphysics of Wolff, etc., but Hegel usually calls this the 'former' (*vormalige*) metaphysics: cf. §389, n. 10. More probably, he means 'ancient' metaphysics, and is thinking of passages such as Plato's *Phaedo*, 78b4 ff., where Socrates argues that the soul is non-composite and thus indissoluble. He may also have in view Plato's theory of ideas or forms, according to which each form is 'one', in contrast to the 'many' things that 'participate' in it.

14. This repeats the progressive dematerialization of matter described in §389: cf. n. 3. But earlier weight or 'gravity' (*Schwere*) was a feature 'characteristic of matter', while now it is the first step in overcoming it: the attraction of one body to another is a sort of 'refutation' of their separate individuality. Mind plays two roles in this: mind that is 'in itself and at work within nature' gradually overcomes materiality, and mind as soul completes the process. Given this dual use of 'mind', Hegel's conclusion is ambiguous. If the mind at work in nature

overcomes materiality, then matter has no independence in face of this mind. But it does not follow that matter has no independence in face of the human soul or even the developed human mind. Gravity, heat, light, etc. are not at our beck and call. Conversely, it is not clear why we could not have such control over matter as we do have even if there is no mind implicitly at work in nature.

15. The 'indeterminate universal soul' is not the mind at work in nature, but the human soul discussed in the Paragraph. The opposition between mind and its other is an essential feature of mind, especially as consciousness *of* something other than itself. Hegel again tends to run together two apparently different relations: the relation between the soul or mind and the body, and the relation between the mind and the object of which it is conscious. (See also §389, n. 3.) One reason for this may be that Hegel here uses, for 'body', the word *Körper*. This word 'excludes any implication of human feelings, sentiments and life in its non-physical aspects. It is *Leib* which conveys this suggestion and is conceived as the vessel of the soul' (DGS, p. 45). Unlike *Leib*, *Körper* can apply to a piece of matter as well as to a human body. This means that the distinction between the relation of the soul to a body of which it is conscious and its relation to *its* body is less clear than it might be. However, the two relations are also connected. *My* body (*Leib*) is also *a* body (*Körper*). If I am to ask about the 'communion' of my soul and my body, then I must distinguish my soul or myself from my body. That is, my body must become an object of which I am conscious. So I must in general be conscious of objects 'other' than myself. For Hegel, the philosophical question about the soul's relation to the body is rooted in a fundamental and necessary capacity of the human mind, the ability to distinguish itself from other objects.

16. The material is 'particular' and the immaterial 'universal'. Thus the immaterial 'overarches' the material in something like the way in which the universal 'colour' overarches and embraces particular colours such as red and green. This might suggest the Aristotelian view that the soul is the form of the body, fitting together with the body with no special need for divine help. But Hegel neglects Aristotle here, preferring Descartes *et al.* and their resort to God. Mind and matter are originally united in God, wholly dependent on him, so that they are not independent substances. But since God is himself 'mind' or spirit, mind is predominant: God as mind is the universal that overarches 'particular' mind and 'particular' matter. The claim that mind 'idealizes' its other, etc. refers to our conceptual and other ways of processing the material world. God, it might be thought, is not needed for this. But Hegel (unlike Descartes *et al.*) does not sharply distinguish between God and man. Unlike them too, Hegel is trying to answer *two* questions: (i) Are mind and matter in an 'original unity' and if so, how? This is the question of Descartes et al. Hegel is less interested in it, but his answer is that they are united in nature and in the natural soul, as well as in the logical Idea. (ii) Once mind and matter have emerged from their original unity, in consciousness and other stages of the developed mind, how are they to be reunited again? To this Hegel does not reply by referring again to their original unity, but instead to the mind's idealizing activity.

Thus for Hegel the mind–matter relationship follows the pattern: original unity—opposition—restored unity: cf. §387, n. 14. (Hegel might say that Descartes gave a similar answer: the mind is wrested from its 'original unity' with body by scepticism, but recovers belief in external bodies by appealing to God's veracity.)

According to Malebranche's 'occasionalism', no event causes any other event. It is God who causes all events. Thus there is no causal interaction between mind and body. Rather, whenever God causes a mental event, he causes a corresponding physical event. 'We see everything in God', because our seeing is caused by God, not by the objects seen. On Plato, Hegel is perhaps alluding to *Timaeus*, 35a–b, which he paraphrases at Enc. I, §92Z.

17. Hegel offers three criticisms of materialism:

   (1) If thought is a result of matter, the relation of matter to thought is, or resembles, a relation of cause to effect, or of means to end. But a cause is sublated in its effect: e.g. the rain that causes the wetness of the street also constitutes the wetness (cf. Enc. I, §153). The means to an end is sublated in the end once it is realized: e.g. the paint and canvas are contained in the finished painting (Enc. I, §§204 ff.). Thus if thought is a result of matter, matter is sublated in thought. (There is thus no special reason for calling such a doctrine 'materialism' rather than, say, 'mentalism'.)

   (2) Mind has its own peculiar way of sublating other things, including the conditions of its own emergence: it coverts them into something 'posited by itself': cf. §379, n. 7.

   (3) 'Mind as such' develops of its own accord out of its 'being-in-itself', i.e. out of its earlier forms, soul and consciousness: cf. §387, esp. n. 18.

Points (1) and (2) concern the development from its earliest beginnings. Point (3) concerns the subsequent development of mind. Hegel disagrees with traditional materialism in two essential respects. First, although mind emerges from matter, the matter from which it emerges is already pervaded by mind. Second, mind does not develop in accordance with the laws even of this mind-pervaded matter; it breaks free of it and develops autonomously.

NOTES TO §390

1. On the three stages of soul, cf. §387, n. 11. That the natural soul 'only *is*' implies that it involves no opposition and thus does not sense or feel anything. At stage (b) the soul is related to the soul of stage (a), its immediate 'being' (*Sein*). This has 'determinacies' which produce feelings. Hence the soul is 'abstractly for itself', i.e. it has a hazy self-awareness. (On 'for itself', cf. §383, n. 1.) At stage (c) the soul takes over its body and makes it its own. Since it is expressed by the body, it is now 'actual', not merely potential.

2. The natural soul, stage (*a*), itself undergoes a development which Hegel divides into three phases, following the pattern of unity—opposition—restored unity. Phase I of stage (*a*) falls into two: (i) A wholly universal, undifferentiated,

unidividualized soul, with its 'explication in nature and in mind': see §391 n. 2 for the meaning of this expression. It corresponds to pure being in the Logic (Enc. I, §86). (ii) Soul with 'universal, qualitative determinations'. They correspond to the reality or 'determinate being' (*Dasein*) to which 'being' (*Sein*) passes over in Logic (cf. Enc. I, §§89 ff.). Racial and national differences belong here, since they are deep, subconscious differences between *types* of soul, and not between, or within, individual souls. See §§392–5.

3. Hegel is trying to combine two different accounts of the transition from phase I to phase II of stage (a). The first sentence implies that it follows the pattern: unity (phase I: the 'universal natural soul')—opposition (transition: 'divergent universal particularizations')—restored unity (phase II: the particularizations taken back into the soul, which is then individual). This is what the correspondence to the Logic or 'concept' would suggest. But the second sentence implies that the 'universal natural soul' directly 'splinters' into individual souls, without the help of any mediating 'particularizations'. This second account is more plausible. It is hard to see how racial or national differences mediate the division of the universal soul into individual souls.

   On the stars, see Enc. II, §269Z: 'This eruption of light is as little worthy of wonderment as an eruption on the skin or a swarm of flies'.

4. Three phenomena belong to phase II: (i) The 'particularizations' no longer characterize different types of soul, but different stages, or 'alterations', in the life of a single, persisting subject: cf. §396. (ii) Individuals are of different sexes. Here difference becomes 'actual particularization', because the sexes are opposite to each other in a way that different races and different ages are not: cf. §397. Individuals are explicitly distinguished from, yet related to, each other. (iii) The soul is opposed to its 'natural qualities', i.e. phase I, and relegates it to the sleeping state.

5. Phase III reunites the opposition that opened up in phase II. In phase II, the soul's other was a 'state' (*Zustand*), sleep, in opposition to the waking state. Now the other is made 'ideal', i.e. the object of the soul's 'sensation' (*Empfindung*): cf. §§399 ff. *Empfindung* is often closer to 'feeling' than to 'sensation'. But it needs to be translated as 'sensation' to distinguish it from *Gefühl* in stage (b), the 'feeling soul', the theme of the 'second part of Anthropology' (§§403 ff.). *Gefühl, fühlen*, 'feeling; to feel' are close to *Empfindung, empfinden*, but not synonymous. Hegel tries to distinguish them in §402. The 'boding soul' translates *ahnende(n) Seele*, which appears as the 'feeling soul in its immediacy' at the end of §402Z. and in §405 and Z. The verb *ahnen* is 'to foresee, suspect, etc.'. Here it is intended to suggest a vague awareness of one's surroundings, not necessarily of future events.

NOTES TO §391

1. If we call the universal soul a 'world soul', we treat it as a subject. It is not a subject, but the 'universal substance' which essentially requires completion in individual subjects. (It is not unlike 'prime matter' in medieval philosophy, wholly

indeterminate matter that cannot exist in isolation but only as constituting some specific kind of matter.) When it becomes an individual, it is not aware of anything other than itself: it just *is*. The 'natural determinacies' that it has in it play a double role: (i) They have a 'free existence' as natural features which can be objects of our consciousness (§§413 ff.). (ii) In the soul they are 'ideal', i.e. qualities in the soul itself. The soul cannot perceive them as 'external', but it is affected by them as qualities impressed on it.

2. The soul, as the microcosm, has compressed in it as qualities the phenomena that range freely in nature, the macrocosm. But the microcosm, the 'little world', stands opposed not just to one 'big world', nature, but also to the 'world of ethical freedom'. As natural phenomena are compressed in the soul, so urges, etc. are compressed in the 'individual man'. These are developed, in the 'political state', into an ethical world that is as expansive and differentiated as nature. The soul or the individual man is like a funnel, into one end of which is squeezed the natural world, while the ethical world emerges from the other end. On 'urges', see §473. They are not, in the adult, unconscious, but Hegel presumably means that an urge is not something one is conscious of as an object distinct from oneself. It is 'simply something he is' (*ein Sein*).

NOTES TO §392

1. Here Hegel considers man's general susceptibility to his natural environment. Correspondingly, §393 considers racial differences, and §395 the temperament, etc. of individuals. Climatic variations, etc. affect the soul, but in the mind for the most part produce only 'dark', or perhaps 'vague', moods. On moods, cf. §401Z.
2. 'Cosmic' pertains to the universe as a whole, 'sidereal' to the stars, and 'telluric' (*tellurischen*, from the Latin *tellus*, 'earth') to the earth. 'Cosmic' perhaps refers more specifically to the solar system, in contrast to the earth and the stars.
3. 'World-history' is not the history of the planet Earth, but human history and, since it depends on the survival of written records, the history of relatively sophisticated humans who are fairly immune to planetary influences.
4. On insanity or 'derangement', cf. §408 and Z.
5. The soul shares in the life of the universe, but the mind does not. The mind fights back and liberates itself from nature by subjecting it to concepts. But in primitive people and psychologically disturbed people, the natural soul, the persisting substratum of our personality that usually manifests itself only in unimportant 'moods', rises to the surface in the form of intense moods, prophecy, etc. On prophecy, see §406.
6. Leibniz held that the mind and the world mirror each other. The doctrine was also expounded by philosophers of nature such as Lorenz Oken (1779–1851) and by F. W. J. Schelling (1775–1854) in e.g. *On the World-Soul: A Hypothesis of the Higher Physics on the Explanation of the Universal Organism* (1798). J. G. Herder was attracted by the idea, and so were Goethe, Friedrich Schlegel, and Novalis.

7. Hegel rejects astrology because he rejects physical determinism. Entities are ranged in a hierarchy, the levels of which embody increasingly complex categories and are governed by increasingly complex laws. A higher level is determined by a lower only within a certain range, never fully. At the bottom are the planets, whose motion is 'free', determined solely by (the concept of) space and time, and nothing else. (Cf. Enc. II, §§269 ff., where Hegel expresses his support for Kepler and hostility to Newton.) Above the planets is the 'physical individual'. This does not change in the same way as the planets. The time taken by e.g. a crystal to form depends not on the nature of time as such but on the nature of the crystalline substance. The angles at which the faces of a crystal meet depend not on space as such, but its chemical composition: cf. Enc. II, §§310Z. and 315Z. Higher still is the animal: on the course of fevers, see Enc. II, §372 and Z. Finally the mind is virtually exempt from the influence of abstract space and time, though not from more concrete forms of them. Hegel connects two apparently distinct questions: (i) Does the mind work on the same principles as planetary movements? (ii) Is the mind influenced by planetary movements? If the mind did work on the same principles as the planets, then even if it were not significantly influenced by them, it would nevertheless keep in step with them, and also there would be nothing, apart from distance, to insulate it against their influence. Conversely, if the mind were significantly influenced by planetary movements, then it would work on the same principles, being determined, at least indirectly, by space and time as such. It is not clear that our dependence on a certain distance from the sun amounts to dependence on a merely spatial factor, for what matters is not distance as such, but warmth and energy. Nevertheless it is a case of our dependence on a lower level in the hierarchy.

8. Apis was an Egyptian god in the form of a bull, and Hegel associates astrology with Egypt: 'All astrological and sympathetic superstition may be traced to Egypt' (PH, p. 211). (This claim is false. Astrology probably originated Babylon in the third and second centuries BC, not in Egypt.) The zodiac is a belt of the heavens outside which the sun, moon, and major planets do not pass. It is divided into twelve equal areas, each named after a constellation that once occupied it but no longer does. These names or 'signs' are usually taken from animals. ('Zodiac' comes from the Greek *zôon*, 'animal', and means 'circle of animals'.) One such constellation is Taurus or the bull and this is one sign of the zodiac. Another such sign is the adjacent Aries or the ram. The apparent course of the sun in relation to the zodiac changes (owing to a wobble in the earth's rotation on its axis), and this is called the 'precession of the equinoxes', since it results in a change in the positions of the equinoxes, the times at which the sun crosses the equator and day and night are of equal length. The equinoxes move back along the zodiac, traversing one constellation in 2,160 years and the whole zodiac in 25,920 years. Nowadays the vernal or spring equinox is in Pisces or the fish. From about 4000 BC to 2000 BC it was in Taurus; and about 2000 BC it moved into Aries, remaining there until well into the Christian era. Thus the view that Hegel rejects is that the movement of the spring equinox from

Taurus to Aries foretells the replacement of Egyptian bull-worship by Christian lamb-worship. See also David Ulansey, *The Origins of the Mithraic Mysteries* (2nd edn. Oxford: Oxford University Press, 1991).

9. 'Lunatic', from the Latin *luna*, 'moon', originally denoted a person subject to bouts of insanity supposedly influenced by phases of the moon. The German *Wahnsinnigen* involves no reference to the moon.

10. The Spartan Pausanias, acting as regent for his child-cousin Pleistarchus, led a force of Spartans, Athenians, and their allies against a Persian force led by Mardonius. They met at Plataea in August 479 BC. When the Persians attacked, the Greeks hesitated, since the sacrificial animals were unfavourable. Pausanias eventually turned towards the temple of Hera, prayed to her, and after this favourable omens were obtained. Such superstition was not confined to Spartans. The Athenian general Nicias postponed his departure from Sicily—with disastrous results—owing to a lunar eclipse on 27 August 413 BC.

11. Hegel's point is not that the moderns can invariably discover by rational argument what to do and when to do it, but that even in cases of uncertainty we make our own decisions and do not leave it to entrails, etc. Often there are 'grounds' or reasons for doing something and reasons for not doing it, but the 'subjective will' curtails them and decides to act. The ancients were not prepared to do this. Even when they did seem to have overwhelming reasons for doing something, they still paid heed to omens, often (like Pausanias) repeating the sacrifices to get the right result, but abandoning the project if they could not do so.

12. Hegel here gives a different account of sacrifices, etc. The morale of ancient soldiers was crucial and it depended on external conditions whose effects are more easily discernible in animals. But they still made too much of entrails owing to their superstition.

13. In 401 BC Xenophon, an Athenian, led ten thousand Greek mercenaries to help Cyrus's rebellion against his elder brother, Artaxerxes, the Persian emperor. He told the story of the expedition and the retreat in his *Anabasis* or 'Up-going', i.e. an expedition up from the coast.

NOTES TO §393

1. Gottfried Reinhold Treviranus published his *Biologie, oder Philosophie der lebenden Natur für Naturforscher und Ärzte* (Biology, or Philosophy of Living Nature for Natural Scientists and Physicians) in Göttingen between 1802 and 1822. Hegel often cites him in Enc. II, e.g. §344Z.

2. It is significant that Hegel describes the question of human origins as a *historische*, not a *geschichtliche*, question. *Geschichte* and *geschichtlich* are his favoured words for 'history' and 'historical', while he often uses *Historie* and *historisch* as terms of mild contempt for what is unsystematic and merely empirical. The question of human origins could not be a question for *Geschichte*, since this depends on written records.

3. For Hegel's view that human equality is not 'natural', cf. §539.

4. On the 'geographical basis of history', cf. PH, pp. 79 ff.

5. The most that Hegel has done to show that the differences between the continents of the Old World are 'necessary' is to suggest that they form a triad of the universal—particular—individual type. Africa is an undifferentiated unity, Asia an unmediated contrast between highlands and river valleys, and Europe a differentiated unity of interpenetrating mountains and valleys.

6. Classifications of human races were attempted by Carolus Linnaeus (1707–78) and by Georges Louis Leclerc, comte de Buffon (1707–88), but Hegel acquired his information about skulls from Johann Friedrich Blumenbach (1752–1840), an anatomist and anthropologist, who became known as the father of physical anthropology. In his *De Generis Humani Varietate Nativa* (1775) (On the Natural Variety of the Human Race) he distinguished five races: Caucasian, Mongolian, Ethiopian, Malayan, and American. (The name 'Caucasian' was applied to the 'white' race, which Blumenbach believed to come from the Caucasus region.) He collected sixty skulls of various races, and these were published in his *Collectionis Diversorum Gentium Illustratae Decades* (1790–1828) (Parts of his Collection of Crania of Various Races). Hegel's official criterion for distinguishing the races, the angle of intersection of the horizontal and vertical lines drawn within the skull, is a refinement of the 'cephalometric lines' introduced by Adriaan van der Spiegel (1578–1625). A later refinement was the 'cranial index' devised by Anders Adolf Retzius (1796–1860) in 1846, the ratio of skull width to skull length.

7. For a longer, but equally derogatory, account of Africans, see PH, pp. 91 ff. However, Hegel does not suggest that the psychological characteristics that he attributes to Africans are hereditary, as their physical characteristics are. They are connected, in a way that he does not adequately explain, with the geography of Africa.

8. On Asia and oriental religions, see §377, n. 6 and PH, pp. 111 ff. For Hegel, a religion or a conception of God is essentially related to a conception of the person, and with the value and rights assigned to the person. On the 'concrete universal' in contrast to the 'abstract universal', cf. §387, n. 18. An abstract universal is thin and empty. Hence the temptation to identify it with an individual (in Buddhism) or with nature as a whole (in Hinduism). (Hegel seems to confuse the creator god, Brahma, with a 'Brahmin', or more properly 'Brahman', a member of the caste from which priests were drawn, but who was not regarded as a god.) What is needed for a universal to be concrete is a particularization that mediates its relationship to the empirical world. But for this to occur, the universal must particularize or develop itself, and this requires that the mind become genuinely independent of nature and that it make 'its concept into its object'. This also applies, in Hegel's view, to an individual mind. An infant, with its undeveloped mind, absorbed in its immediate surroundings, is barely in control of its body and makes little sense of, and has little mastery over, the external world. As its mind becomes more independent of its immediate surroundings, and acquires more awareness of itself, it makes sense of and masters its environment. That the mind properly connects with what is other than mind only when

it is fully independent of it exemplifies Hegel's principle that opposites turn into each other at their extreme points: cf. Enc. I, §81Z.(1).

9. On Mohammedanism, cf. PH, pp. 355 ff. Mohammedans have no inclination to identify God with the empirical world or with some entity in it. But their failure to particularize their abstractly universal God goes with a failure to develop a differentiated political system and a tendency to oscillate between religious self-denial and the relentless pursuit of worldly aims. It is worth noting that Hegel does not attempt to distinguish 'West Asiatics' from Europeans by physiological criteria. For him, as for his contemporaries, Mohammedanism and Judaism were primarily religious categories. In particular, the classification of Jews as a physiologically distinct race is a later development, entirely alien to the founders of physical anthropology.

10. God or 'thought' or the 'universal' is 'self-determining' and can thus unite with the 'particular', a process expressed in the 'representation' of the Trinity. Non-Christian religions do not display the immanent development characteristic of thought. Something similar happens on the secular plane. The mind frees itself from the world, then returns to imbue it with thought. It masters the world by acting on 'universal principles' and develops a differentiated state. (For a different view of the relationship between Christianity and science, see 'Religion and Science', in Anthony Quinton, *From Wodehouse to Wittgenstein* (Manchester: Carcanet, 1998), 3–22, arguing that modern science was made possible by the Christian idea of a rational God 'behind the perceptible surface of the world' but governing it 'in accordance with a unitary system of intelligible laws' (p. 12).)

NOTES TO §394

1. The 'racial variations' of §393 are 'determined by the concept' in that Africans are abstractly and uniformly universal; Asiatics (including Mohammedans) are particularized into an abstractly universal deity and unredeemed particularity; and Europeans restore the unity of universality and particularity into something that Hegel might have called 'individuality'. The natives of America are an embarrassing afterthought, but logic is saved by their imminent extinction. (Despite his predilection for triads, Hegel often accommodates four elements by treating one as trivial or five by grouping three together: cf. §401Z. on the five senses.) Further differentiations of the natural mind, not into 'races' (*Rassen*) but 'peoples' (*Völker*), are not determined by the concept, though Hegel finds triads wherever possible. He allocates these differences to two sciences: (i) the 'natural history of man' (a science to which Hegel did not contribute) describes and explains national and local characteristics; (ii) the 'philosophy of history' portrays the spiritual climax of a people's underlying natural character, its culture and historic deeds. 'Philosophical anthropology', Hegel's current enterprise, is distinct from these sciences and supplies only as much of (i) as is required for an understanding of (ii).

2. On the Hindu caste system, see PH, pp. 144 ff.

3. PH does consider differences between China, India, etc., but not between different black African peoples. Hegel's words for 'Germanic peoples', 'germanic' are *Germanen, germanisch(en),* derived from the Latin *germania, germanus,* are quite different from the normal word for 'german', *deutsch.* They embrace, besides Germans proper (the *Deutschen*), peoples speaking Germanic languages (such as the English and Scandinavians) and also Romance-speaking peoples such as the French, Spanish, and Italians. All are germanic, because the Roman Empire was overrun by German tribes in the fifth century AD. See PH, pp. 341 ff., esp. 347–55.

4. The Greek 'nation' was divided into many small city-states, of which the most important were Sparta, Thebes, and Athens. Hegel here follows the practice, common both in antiquity and today, of using 'Lacedemonians' as equivalent to 'Spartans'. He briefly describes Spartan institutions, including communal meals and restrictions on the disposal of property, at PH, pp. 262 ff., where he distinguishes the 'Spartans', the inhabitants of the city, from the 'Lacedemonians', the 'perioeci' or 'dwellers round about', who lived in the region under Spartan control, Laconia, and were dependent on Sparta in external affairs but retained considerable local autonomy. (The perioeci are distinct from the helots, serfs working the land of the Spartans.) 'Ethical substance' implicitly contrasts with 'subject', and implies that the Spartans were not developed as individuals, but immersed in their institutions. On Sparta and its institutions, see J. B. Bury and R. Meiggs, *A History of Greece* (4th edn., London: Macmillan, 1975), ch. 3.

5. Thebes became the dominant state in Greece after the Thebans under Epaminondas defeated the Spartans at Leuctra in. 371 BC. But Theban hegemony did not survive the death of Epaminondas in the battle of Mantinea in. 362. In PH, p. 267, Hegel takes Theban dependence on Epaminondas as one more sign of their 'subjectivity'. He regards lyric poetry, whose greatest practitioner was the fifth-century Theban Pindar, as the 'expression of subjectivity'. Around 377 BC Thebes created the 'Sacred Band', a force of 300 hoplites or heavy-armed infantry fighting in close formation, to form the spearhead of the Theban army. Each had his closest friend beside him, so that the band consisted of 150 pairs of comrades, ready to fight and die together. It is the efficacy of these 'amatory bonds' that Hegel regards as evidence of Theban subjectivity.

6. Athens is a mean between two extremes: Sparta to the south, with its 'objectivity of ethical life' and the state, and Thebes to the north, with its subjectivity and individualism. It is also a mean between the eastern, 'Ionian', Greeks of the coast of Asia Minor and its islands, and the western Greeks of Italy. The Ionian philosophers were materialists, finding the 'absolute' in some natural substance, such as water (Thales), air (Anaximenes), or fire (Heraclitus), of which they supposed everything ultimately to consist. The western philosophers found their 'principle' in an abstract thought, such as being or the one (Parmenides) or number (Pythagoras). Plato attempted to combine the 'natural element' and 'abstract thought' as 'moments' in his own philosophy. Hegel sees the Platonic 'Idea' as effecting this synthesis, since the Idea is, in Hegel's vocabulary, the 'concept'

together with its 'reality': cf. §377, n. 4. Many of the Greeks in Italy originally came from the East as refugees from Lydian and, later, Persian pressure. Pythagoras left Samos, ruled by the tyrant Polycrates, and settled in Croton, in southern Italy. Xenophanes left Colophon, on the coast of Asia Minor, for Elea, on the west coast of Italy. Not all western Greek philosophers fit Hegel's stereotype: Empedocles of Akragas (Agrigento), in Sicily, was a materialist, believing things to consist of four elements: earth, air, fire, and water.

7. Hegel here uses two approximate synonyms, *Individualität* and *Einzelheit*: cf. §377, n. 7. Usually I have translated these two words and their cognates as 'individual(ity)', but here, where a distinction needs to be drawn, I have translated *Individualität* as 'individuality' and *Einzelheit* as 'idiosyncracy'. Idiosyncracy is uninhibited by 'universal purposes', whereas *Individualität* might be governed by general norms, even if it is not in this case.

8. 'With African inhumanity' is *mit afrikanischer Unmenschlichkeit*. This is probably to be associated with his account of black Africans in PH, pp. 93 ff., though it may allude to the earlier Islamic conquest of Spain.

9. '*Esprit*' is the closest French equivalent of the German '*Geist*'. But *esprit* suggests wit, while *Geist* suggests profundity, though it acquired the connotation of wit under the influence of *esprit*. Hence Hegel is here supporting his claim about French 'wit'. In bringing together what the 'intellect' (*Verstand*) separates, *esprit* resembles reason and 'the rational' (*das Vernünftige*), but it does not amount to 'conceptual cognition'. This is not entirely fair to Charles de Montesquieu, whose *De l'Esprit des Lois* (1748) (On the Spirit of the Laws) exerted a considerable influence on Hegel: cf. PR, §§3, 261, 273.

10. Here Hegel supports his claim that the French display 'firmness of intellect' as well as wit. In the Revolution, the French intellect took 'one-sided' principles to extremes—one-sidedness being a characteristic of intellect. But this resulted in the sublation of 'one-sidednesses' in the Napoleonic state. This sublation itself was the work not of the French intellect, but of the 'dialectic of world-historical reason'. Hegel's idea is that if the intellect pursues its work thoroughly and consistently enough, then it turns into reason automatically, breaking down one-sidedness by developing it to its limits.

11. 'Intellectual intuition' (*intellektuelle(n) Anschauung*) is an expression coined by Kant for a type of 'intuition', or grasp of individual entities, which is not sensory and dependent on sense-perception, but purely intellectual: cf. §§415, n. 2; 449, n. 4. Kant supposed that God (if he exists) has intellectual intuition, but we humans have only sensory intuition, and our intellect is general and conceptual, grasping individuals only with the aid of sense-perception. Hegel is less inclined than Kant to deny that we possess intellectual intuition and is thus only half-joking when he ascribes it to the English. It is intellectual, because it grasps 'the rational', and intuition, because it focuses on individuals rather than universality.

12. The Germans like to define the 'principles' (*Grundsätze*) on which they act, and also to find 'grounds' or reasons (*Gründe*) for what they do. The first procedure means that often 'the better kills the good', i.e. the search for perfection leads

them to act in a worse way than they otherwise would have done. The second means that, since reasons (though not conclusive reasons) can be found for anything, in practice such principles and reasons do not genuinely determine what they do, but rely on external input. For example, some invoke a principle such as the 'sanctity' of human life in order to oppose the death penalty for murder. Others invoke the same principle in order to support the death penalty, arguing that the principle requires us to deter or punish the unlawful killing of a human being very severely. In reality the principle is a reason for either view, but a conclusive reason for neither. Thus it can be used to support whichever alternative one favours on other grounds. Hegel implies that the 'immanent development' of the 'universal thought of right' will solve some of these dilemmas, but he does not believe that every decision that we have to make (e.g. on precise rates of taxation) can be determined in this way: cf. §529, n. 4.

13. 'Formalism' here refers not to abstract principles or reasons, but to formal rights that confer no real benefit on the right-holder. Hegel may be thinking of the Holy Roman Empire, which until Napoleon abolished it in 1806, formed a loose framework of German unity: the emperor was elected by the seven electoral princes of Germany, though for centuries the emperor had been supplied by Austria.

NOTES TO §395

1. The natural mind 'opposes itself to itself' as 'individual soul' in that one individual soul differs by nature from another in temperament, etc. This opposition is quite different from the opposition between consciousness and its object, which is no longer a matter of nature: cf. §§413 ff.

2. 'Bad' infinity is distinguished from 'good' or 'true' infinity. The bad infinite goes on for ever and it is also, in some cases, sharply distinct from the finite; the true infinite forms a circle and embraces the finite: cf. Enc. I, §§94–5. The claim that individual indiosyncracy is a matter of bad infinity implies, for Hegel, that it is of secondary importance. He is arguing against educational views inspired especially by Rousseau's *Émile* (1762), which emphasized the natural development of a child's abilities: cf. PR, §153Z. (On educational theories and practices current in Germany at this time, see 'F. A. Wolf', in Mark Pattison, *Essays*, (Oxford: Clarendon Press, 1889), 337–414.) Hegel makes two distinct claims:

    (1) The aim of education is not to cultivate the child's idiosyncrasies, but to induct it into the general or 'universal' culture.
    (2) In educating children one should not begin from their idiosyncrasies, adapting the teaching to them, but teach them in a uniform way.

One might well agree with (1), while rejecting (2), arguing that the best way of leading children to a uniform end-point is to adapt one's teaching to their different starting-points. To this Hegel objects that there is 'no time'. In claiming, with regard to (1), that education tends to eliminate eccentricity, he does not mean that everyone is to be educated to exactly the same level or that no one should learn special skills. But the ability to lecture on philosophy of mind or to make violins are aspects of the general culture, shared by a class, albeit a small class, not simply individual peculiarities.

3. 'Predisposition' translates *Naturell*, a seventeenth-century borrowing from the French *naturel*, a nominalized adjective meaning 'natural predisposition, natural character, disposition, temperament'.

4. Hegel argues that talent or genius is not a sufficient condition of success in e.g. painting or philosophy. He also seems to doubt whether talent or genius is a necessary condition for success, at least in philosophy. Someone who lacks any special gift (e.g. Hegel?) can achieve results by strenuous and systematic reasoning, while a genius (e.g. Schelling?) who does not submit to the 'discipline of logical thinking' will not get far. Hegel resists the idea that logical thinking might require talent or genius. He believes that thought is a function of the mind at its highest level and involves the natural mind only minimally; in philosophical thinking the mind soars above the natural constraints of talent, genius, and their absence, into a realm of freedom. Pure thought is autonomous and self-developing. Thus once one has started to think, thought as it were takes one over and there is no reason why one should not think to the highest level, as long as one puts in the effort to think properly and not be distracted by other things. The capacity for thought, reason, is present in every human being. Hence every human being is, after a suitable education, able to think to the highest level, more slowly perhaps than a gifted person, but just as surely.

5. Hegel spoke above of 'reason which by its own activity has come to a knowledge of its concept' as 'absolutely free thinking and willing'. He dealt with 'thinking' under the heading of 'philosophy'. Now he comes to 'willing'. He gives two reasons for denying a 'genius for virtue': that virtue is required of everyone and that virtue is not innate but acquired by one's own efforts. It might be objected that the virtue required of all is a fairly humble affair, but that genius may be required for the performance of supererogatory acts, such as those performed by saints and heroes. Hegel might reply that the respect we accord to saints and heroes implies that they achieved this status by their own efforts, not by a natural gift. Here too, he is influenced by his belief that the rational will, in contrast to everyday likes and dislikes, belongs to the higher reaches of the mind that have broken loose from natural constraints and must therefore be free.

6. This account of temperament sounds like Heidegger's account of *Befindlichkeit*, 'how one finds oneself', and of mood: 'The mood overwhelms. It comes neither from "without" nor from "within", but arises as a mode of being-in-the-world from being-in-the-world itself' (*Being and Time*, p. 136). In the final paragraph of this *Zusatz*, Hegel speaks of 'temperamental moods' or perhaps attunements of temperament (*Temperamentsstimmungen*). But Hegel downgrades temperament, mood, and everything that Heidegger associates with *Geworfenheit*, 'thrownness', relegating them to the 'natural mind' that culture overcomes: cf. §§392, nn. 1 and 5; 401Z.

7. The word *Temperament* comes from the Latin *temperare*, 'to combine, blend, keep in due proportion', and *temperamentum*, 'a mixing in due proportion, a due measure'. It was then used especially for the proportion in which the four human bodily fluids or 'humours' are mixed. This in turn corresponds to the mixture of four elements: hot, cold, dry, wet. For example, a choleric temperament depends on a preponderance of heat and dryness: the blood is overwhelmed by bile, overheated, and burnt. This medieval theory goes back to the Greek physician Hippocrates. Kant dealt with the temperaments in *Anthropologie in pragmatischer Hinsicht* (1798) (Anthropology from a Pragmatic Point of View), Part Two, B 256–63.

8. *Charakter*, like 'character', oscillates between something that every adult human being has, even if it is a weak, vacillating character, and something that only strong, distinctive, consistent people have, while some people are lacking in character. Hegel concentrates on the latter. Unlike temperament, which can be overcome by culture, character is indispensable: strength of character enables us to pursue the ends that our culture requires of us or presents to us as possibilities. Character requires, first, energy and consistency. This need not exclude the 'trimmer', who (like Halifax) supports what is for the moment the weaker party, so as to avoid either side gaining the preponderance. But it excludes vacillation that has no respectable 'universal' aim, resulting only from overriding concern for one's own safety or inability to make up one's mind. Secondly, character requires that one's guiding aims have a 'universal content' and be 'inwardly justified', if it is to have 'complete truth'. This excludes the pursuit of a trivial enterprise (such as the man who devotes himself single-mindedly to throwing lentils through the eye of a needle, referred to in ILA, p. 49). The enterprise also needs some respectable justification. This does not exclude the devotee of a controversial cause, such as the consistent revolutionary, the consistent restorationist, or the consistent trimmer. The cause need only have some general justification, not a conclusive and overriding justification. 'Complete truth' means the harmony of the will's form and content, not the manifest correctness of the content to the exclusion of all other contents. The 'form' of the lentil thrower's will, his energy, is at odds with the triviality of its 'content'. Hence he displays self-will or 'obstinacy' (*Eigensinn*), not character. See also ILA, pp. 74–5. and 160 ff. on the weak characters favoured by Romantic art.

9. Hegel considers *Idiosynkrasien* for the sake of completeness, but they are not as important to him as the other three categories and are not mentioned in the next paragraph.

10. The triad predisposition—temperament—character is rationally necessary, since predisposition is opposed to temperament, and character overcomes the opposition by combining features of both. A predisposition is, first, immediately 'fixed', with the form of 'something that merely is' (*eines bloss Seienden*), i.e. just there, not produced or altered by us, and, secondly, its 'inner differentiation is related' to an external difference. That is, talent is always talent *for* something, a talent for painting differs from a talent for music by reference to the difference between painting and music; genius is not for something specific, but it

manifests itself in one's actions and products. Temperaments, by contrast, are not fixed, but flow into each other, and differentiated by reflection within, not externally. In each of these dimensions character resembles both predisposition and temperament. First, it is fixed (like predisposition), but also changeable (like temperament). That is, its fixity depends not on nature but on the will. If character were no more than an 'even blending of the various temperaments', it would be natural and not need development by the will. Secondly, it refers outwards (like predisposition), but the soul is reflected into itself (as in temperament). That is, one's character essentially affects how one behaves, but also involves an inner power, strength of will, that a talent *as such* need not involve. Predisposition too needs to be developed by the will to manifest itself, but it exists whether or not it is developed, whereas character exists only if it is developed. One may have an undeveloped talent for painting, but not an undeveloped strong character. The products of talent or genius manifest not simply the talent or genius, but the strength of character to develop and exercise it.

NOTES TO §396

1. The 'differences' are the ages of life (§396), sexual differences (§397), and sleeping and waking (§398). The differences are primarily natural and thus the concern of anthropology. But to describe fully e.g. waking, we need to know what it is like for a cultured adult to be awake, not simply an infant.
2. Hegel distinguishes four ages of life: (1) Childhood: mind is 'wrapped up in itself'. (2) Youth: a gulf or 'opposition' opens up between the world and the individual; the world does not measure up to the youth's ideals and the youth is not yet equipped for his part in the world. (3) Manhood: the opposition is reconciled by the individual's recognizing the necessity and rationality of the world and finding a respectable position in it for which he is well equipped. This is a sophisticated contentment with the world, in contrast to the immediate contentment of childhood. ('World' here refers not to raw nature but to the world already formed by human beings.) (4) Old Age: the reconciliation between world and individual goes beyond the 'genuine relationship' of middle age to a 'unity' that brings with it the inertia of 'habit' (a concept first considered in §§409–10.) and freedom from the concerns of the present. (Such sophisticated super-contentment with the world is something Hegel did not live to experience.) On the pattern: immediate unity—opposition—restored unity, see §387, n. 14.
3. The 'natural soul' is to begin with 'completely universal'. It particularized and then individualized itself in the stages described in §§391 ff. However, the soul as an individual retains an 'inner universality', its 'substance'. Between individuality and universality there is 'opposition' and 'contradiction'. The 'life-process' of the individual soul is driven by this contradiction and eventually overcomes it. As individuality and universality are brought together, the original simple unity of the (child's) soul with itself becomes a unity (in adulthood) mediated by

opposition (in youth), and universality becomes concrete rather than 'abstract'. The elderly become even more 'universal' than the adult, since they lose interest in individual details of the present and focus almost exclusively on the 'universal': cf. §396, n. 19.

This passage presents two difficulties. First, the universality to which the individual needs to be reconciled is not the universality of the natural soul, but the universality of the objective, primarily cultural, world. The former is 'abstract', the latter 'concrete'. 'Concrete' (*konkret*) comes from the Latin *concretus*, 'grown together', the perfect participle of *concrescere*, ' to grow together'. The universality to which the adult attains is the universality 'grown together' out of youthful opposition, not the abstract universality that presupposes no prior opposition. Secondly, the soul that is 'completely universal' is not the child, but the natural soul that is prior (logically, though not temporally prior) to individuality. The child is individual but not in opposition to the universal. Opposition arises in youth. If the life-process stems from the contradiction between individuality and universality, and in childhood there is no such contradiction, it is not clear what propels the advance from childhood to youth. See §396, n. 8.

4. The life-process of an animal is also propelled by a contradiction between the individual and universality, i.e. the 'genus' or species. (Hegel uses *Gattung*, the usual word for 'genus', rather than *Art*, 'species', owing to its connection with *Begattung*, 'copulation'.) The individual cannot actualize the genus or represent it perfectly. Hence the individual dies, killed as it were by the power of the genus, attempting to actualize itself. This realization of the genus is 'abstract'; the genus destroys the individual, which is also 'abstract' owing to its incompatibility with the genus; individual and genus cannot grow together. Cf. §381.

5. Humans realize the genus in two ways. It is genuinely realized when we think about it, think universal thoughts: cf. §381, n. 25. But we also realize it at the anthropological level, not as adequately as in thought, but better than an animal does. Unlike its realization in thought, this is a gradual realization in time. Hegel conceives of thought as non-temporal for several reasons. The thought one thinks, if not the thinking of it, is non-temporal. It does not take time to think a thought, though Hegel believes that to think a 'concrete' thought properly one must also think the thoughts that grow together to form it. In philosophical thinking one does not think about specific times and dates.

6. 'Impression' translates *Einbildung*, which has come to mean 'imagination', but is literally 'forming, moulding [*Bildung*] into [*ein*]', especially, but not exclusively, into the soul. The animal dies because it cannot otherwise realize its genus, the human dies because it does realize its genus. In each case the individual dies when it has done as much as it can to realize its genus.

7. The genus and 'the rational' both have 'inner universality'. That is, they are self-developing universals that constitute the entities to which they belong and determine the course of their development. A dog's caninity, unlike its brown colour, significantly determines the pace and stages of its growth. Cf. §§383, n. 8; 387, n. 6; and Enc. I, §§163–4. Reason or the rational similarly develops autonomously, and significantly determines pace and order of the development

of an individual mind. Since an animal has no significant mental development and since the genus applies to animals as well as men, the genus concerns primarily the 'physical alterations' of an individual. The rational concerns, by contrast, 'mental phenomena'. But the stages of our physical and mental growth tend to 'correspond', because genus and rationality are both inner universals. The correspondence between a person's physical age and mental development is closer than that between the physical and mental characteristics of a race, since an individual's soul affects its body, i.e. soul (or the rational) and body (or genus) do not develop independently of each other. But the physique and mentality of a race are 'fixed' independently of each other and are less likely to coincide in any given individual. Child prodigies are a not very significant exception to the general correspondence of bodily and mental age.

8. Hegel reruns the four ages of man outlined above. The 'genus', on the 'different relationship' to which the different ages depend, has changed its role and is now primarily man's rationality and general culture, not his physical structure: cf. §396, n. 7. The ages present the 'differences of the concept' only roughly, since there are four ages, but usually only three differences of the concept: immediate unity (universality)—opposition (particularity)—individuality (unity restored). The first is presented by childhood. Opposition appears in youth between the individual and the 'universal' or 'world'. The youth assigns opposed values to the opposites. He regards himself as true, good, substantial, and the world as 'contingent, accidental'. That is, he believes the world needs to be perfected in conformity with his ideals. This, Hegel believes, is a mistake. The world is not a blank canvas waiting for the youth to fill it in as he pleases, or an imperfect sketch in need of completion. It is already 'complete', an 'ethical world-order' imbued with the 'Idea' that the youth mistakenly transfers to himself. Hence in trying to reform the world the youth is banging his head against a brick wall. Nevertheless the opposition and the perverse valuation are essential for the emergence of the independent adult. One has to aim beyond one's target in order to hit it. The opposition persists into manhood, which is thus also a phase of particularity. But the valuation is reversed. The world is now substantial, the individual an accident. Now the process of reconciliation can begin, since it is far easier to bring oneself into conformity with the world than to bring the world into conformity with oneself. As above (cf. §396, n. 2) the transitions from youth to manhood and from manhood to old age are better motivated than the passage from childhood to youth. But the passage becomes clearer in Hegel's more detailed account of childhood: see §395Z. and §396, n. 13 on the child's desire to grow up.

9. Cf. Enc. II §344Z: 'The plant is the immediate organic individuality, in which the genus has the preponderance and the reflection is not individual; the individual does not return into itself as such, but is an Other, and so has no *self-feeling*'. More generally, plants are dealt with in Enc. II, §§343–9 and animals in Enc. II, §§350–76.

10. Hegel's idea is not that the external world is mind-dependent in the sense of traditional idealism, but that it is ready for colonization by mind, vulnerable

to our practical and cognitive interventions. But in PS, p. 65, he attributes this attitude to animals, since they 'do not just stand idly in front of sensuous things as if these possessed intrinsic being, but, despairing of their reality, and completely assured of their nothingness, they fall to without ceremony and eat them up'.

11. Hegel's considers 'sensation' in §§399 ff., and 'intuition' in §§446 ff.—esp. §§448–9. on the transition from sensation to intuition. Intuition is similar to 'perception', which is dealt with in §§420–1, and the transition from sensation to intuition is similar to the transition from 'sensory consciousness' to perception in §418–19. But the two pairs of terms and their respective transitions belong to different phases of Hegel's thought and are not explicitly brought together.

To say that the child 'casts the external out of itself' does not mean that it *creates* the external, but that it becomes aware of the external world by referring its inner sensations to things outside it: cf. §389, n. 2. Its awareness of an external world, distinct from itself and its sensations, is essential for its awareness of itself as an I. But see William James, *The Principles of Psychology* (New York: Dover, 1950), ii. 31–43, for a rejection of what he calls the 'eccentric projection' of sensations.

12. Hegel returns to the upright posture distinctive of human beings, in §§410–11, where he discusses habit. It is important primarily because it comes to us less naturally than crawling or walking on all fours, so that it requires a special effort of will that only humans can muster. Specifically human walking presupposes the upright stance. It sublates the 'asunderness' of space in that I can walk from one place to another, thus overcoming their separateness, and also decide where I want to place myself. Animals also walk, but they do not, in Hegel's view, acquire a language. Language enables one both to view things as instances of a universal type and to regard oneself as 'I'. 'I' itself is universal in that it expresses the bare individual, what is common to all human beings, in contrast to its particular states and activities. Thus if one regards oneself as 'I', one can detach oneself from one's particular states and activities and also from the external things that produce the states and provoke the activities. On the I or ego, see also §§413 ff.

13. Hegel has two arguments against the view that learning should be sweetened by play: (1) What makes the child educable is its desire to become like the adults in its surroundings. If the adults present themselves as playful, i.e. childlike, this desire is not exploited to the full. (2) Children thus educated will as adults treat everything 'disdainfully'. Against the view that children should be encouraged to raise quibbles about what they are taught, there are also two objections: that this diminishes the ideal towards which the child is striving, and that it makes them 'impudent'. Hegel believes that to become a proper adult one needs instruction in 'the substance' (*die Sache*), the culture of the age. This is a serious, not a playful matter. Only when one has imbibed it are one's thoughts and objections worth considering. See also §395, n. 2.

14. Hegel believes in discipline for two reasons: (1) If children are allowed to follow their own inclinations they go wrong and do not learn what is right. (2) Uninhibited indulgence in one's own inclinations is intrinsically bad; one has to learn to overcome them. Hegel assumes, not unreasonably, that one's own inclinations tend to be selfish. Innocence consists in ignorance of good and evil. An ignorant infant (or animal) is innocent whatever it does. When it acquires knowledge of good and evil, then 'self-will' (*Eigenwille*) is the source of evil. Enc. I, §24Z. illustrates this with the biblical story of the fall. On the benefits of discipline, see also Hegel's account of mastery and bondage in §435 and Z., and at greater length in PS, pp. 104–11.

15. On language and the alphabet, see §459. The child rises above 'the sensory' in a variety of ways. In contrast to an ideographic script (such as Chinese), an alphabet consists of intrinsically meaningless signs standing for sounds that are themselves signs. In contrast to a syllabic script (such as Japanese) it analyses spoken sounds as far as possible. Spoken language itself is both sensory and unsensory, in that while the sounds of which it consists are sensory, they are intrinsically meaningless and bear no non-conventional relationship to what they express or denote. Language consists of universals: phonemes and letters are universals, types that may be instantiated by indefinitely many tokens. Language also *expresses* universal concepts or thoughts, not simply individual entities and states of affairs.

However, a youngster gets only as far as 'representation(al thinking)', that is, such universal but nevertheless 'representational' thoughts as 'animal' and 'The horse is an animal', but not such pure thoughts as 'being' or such claims about the 'world in its inner connectedness' as 'Spirit came into being as the truth of nature' (§388). But they appreciate the 'supersensory world' in this representational form and should be introduced to religion, and to 'right' (namely law and formal morality), early on. This is best done at school, where the child is not valued simply as the individual it is, but is assessed according to general rules and criteria. It is subjected to universal regulations, which forbid things (such as walking on the lawn), which though harmless if done by one individual, are harmful if done by many. This prepares it for the transition from the family (cf. §§518 ff.) (which usually forbids only activities that are in themselves harmful) to the rules and regulations of 'civil society' (cf. §§523 ff.).

Hegel seems to operate with two distinct conceptions of the non-sensory. First, there is abstract thought about the sensory world and abstract rules for our conduct in it. Second, there is the 'supersensory world' of Christianity, a world located beyond the sensory world. That Hegel connects the two conceptions closely is indicated by his claim that religion, as well as 'right', is best taught in school, where we are governed by abstract regulations. At the level of representation, the supersensory world of Christianity seems to rise above the sensory in a quite different way from abstract thinking and abstract practices. At the level of philosophical thought, however, the two conceptions converge. To be a Christian is to think about this world and about oneself in a certain way, and also to act in a certain way. On Christianity, see §§564 ff., and on Christianity's greater 'exaltation above the sensory' and 'absorption in its own inwardness' in contrast to Greek religion, see §§557 ff.

16. The 'life of the genus' here combines the ideas of universality and of sexual desire: cf. §396, n. 4. That the youth's ideal is detached from any individual person enables the youth to view the ideal as unrealized. (If an ideal is embodied in a particular person, the ideal is at least actualized in that person.) But it is still unclear why the youth must regard the ideal as unrealized, when (in Hegel's view) it is already realized. Four answers are implicit in the text: (1) One of the youth's aims, sexual love, is at this stage likely to be unrealized. This dissatisfaction is transferred to the youth's assessment of the world as a whole. (2) The youth wants 'his own personality' to be 'recognized by the world'. This aim is not yet realized, and never will be in the egocentric form that youth requires. (3) The youth is out of tune with world, not yet equipped to play a part in it. He blames the world for this, not himself. (4) The youth needs an unrealized ideal to motivate his ascent to manhood. He becomes a man in attempting to equip himself to realize the ideal. But why could he not become a man by simply continuing to model himself on his father? Perhaps because the youth's ascent requires more energy than is now discernible in his father, who is by now a complacent middle-aged bourgeois.

17. On 'civil society', in contrast to the family, the state, and, presumably, the university, cf. §§396, n. 15; 523 ff. The 'hypochondria' induced by the descent from generalities to 'details' and by the inability to realize one's ideals seems to be depression or malaise rather than a tendency to imagine that one is ill. Hegel makes at least three claims about the 'world': (1) It is 'independent' (*selbständige*) and 'complete' (*fertige*). It cannot easily be altered in accordance with the 'subjectivity'—the hopes and wishes—of the individual. To try to change it as one might e.g. (re)build or (re)furnish one's house is both impracticable (since the world is independent) and superfluous (since it is already complete). Hence (2) it is necessary to adapt to the world and its ways. But it is also *desirable* to do so. The world embodies a rationality far exceeding the bright ideas of any single individual. This rationality is 'divine' rather than human. This is connected with Hegel's first point. That such rationality is divine implies that it is embodied in an independent and complete world. God does not need any particular Tom, Dick, or Harry to realize his plan, though he does of course need human beings in general. Thus (3) individuals need to act, and their activity serves three purposes: (i) It gets the individual what he wants, as long as his aims are realistic and his behaviour adapted to the ways of the world. (ii) Along with the activity of many other individuals it preserves the world. (iii) In addition it helps to change or develop the world. The world develops like a living organism; individuals and their conduct develop along with it. Such change is discernible only over large areas and long (fifty-year) periods. Hegel calls this change 'progress', and in retrospect the individual derives satisfaction from his contribution to it and to the rationality embodied in it. Such progress fulfils what is 'true' in our youthful ideals; the rest is dross

to be discarded. Different individuals have different callings, but common to them all is right, ethics, and religion: they perform their civic and familial duties and the duties attached to their particular calling, and, as well as performing specifically religious duties, they preserve and promote the work of God as it manifests itself in the world. To be a fully fledged adult an individual must complete his education and earn his own living. For an individual to live in idleness and dependence is comparable to a people's being ruled by paternalistic temporal and spiritual authorities rather than attending to its own interests by free trade and the Protestant religion.

This paragraph expands on Hegel's claim that 'What is rational is actual, and what is actual is rational' (PR, Preface, Enc. I., §6). The claim does not entail that *every* fifty-year period exhibits, in retrospect, progress or improvement in the human condition. This rationality allows for, and even requires, periods of apparent decline and collapse. When St. Augustine died in 430, the invading Vandals were besieging Hippo. Who sees progress since 380? The Vandals no doubt. Perhaps St. Augustine, if he considers his own uncommonly large contribution to Christianity and to thought in general, and if he reflects on the vicissitudes ordained by divine providence and the possibility that the Vandals will eventually adopt the culture they are attempting to destroy. But the ordinary citizen of Hippo might reasonably see nothing but the destruction of fifty years' work.

18. That in the course of one's career one discerns the universal in one's tasks and thus becomes perfectly familiar with them is more plausible of some jobs than of others: playing chess, teaching philosophy, and possibly political activity are not easily mastered or exhausted in a single lifetime, especially if the progress mentioned in §396, n. 17 implies that the tasks themselves change.

19. The elimination of the opposition between subject and object is for Hegel something to be striven for. But when it becomes complete and no further object arises to offer resistance to the subject, the subject lapses into inactivity. Life requires opposition and conflict. Death is an 'abstract negation', since (unlike a 'concrete' negation) it terminates what it negates, and does not develop it into something new.

NOTES TO §397

1. The distinction between 'subjectivity' and 'activity' corresponds to the distinction between the two sexes. Women are more closely associated with subjectivity and abstain from public life; men are associated with activity and public life: §398, n. 7. But the distinction also corresponds to two aspects of any human being, whether man or woman. A man needs a private, emotional life as well as public engagement. A woman also needs to make her mark on the public world, if only by proxy. Hence men and women cannot dispense with each other. Each needs the other to satisfy both aspects of their nature. The family is treated at §§518 ff., where §§518 and 519 correspond approximately to 'subjectivity', while §520 on property corresponds to 'activity'.

NOTES TO §398

1. 'Judgement' (*Urteil*) is here used in two senses. First, the individual judges, in the ordinary sense of 'judge', that it is awake and distinguishes this waking state from the state of sleep from which the soul has just emerged. This judgement is immediate, i.e. not based on an inference. Secondly, 'judgement' has the Hegelian sense of an 'original partition' or division. (For Hegel's account of 'judgement', cf. §§388, n. 1; 389, n. 4; 467.) The soul divides into the soul as it merely *is*, its 'mere being', and the soul as it is *for itself*: cf. §383, nn. 1 and 4. In the undivided state the soul merely *is*, and is then asleep. When it divides it 'confronts' its 'self-absorbed natural life', which is *both* its undivided sleeping state *and* a stratum of its divided state that persists when it is awake. Although sleep is associated with the 'natural life' of the soul, waking as well as sleeping is a natural state, and, at this stage of his exposition, Hegel tries to exclude higher, spiritual aspects of waking life.

2. Sometimes the water is warm, sometimes it is cold. This distinction is only 'for us', because (1) the water is unaware of its states, (2) which state it is in depends not on the intrinsic nature of water, but on external conditions, and (3) the distinction between warmth and cold is drawn by, and for the purposes of, the observer or user of the water. Similarly, whether I am ugly or handsome, even if I am aware of my condition and even if it depends on my own nature, is a matter to be decided by others, and it is they who draw the distinction between ugliness and beauty. The distinction between sleep and waking is not just 'for us'. The soul is aware that it is awake, aware that it has been asleep, and, perhaps, that it will later go to sleep again. The distinction between the two states is drawn by the soul's own bifurcation into its 'mere being', and being for itself. That the states alternate also depends on the soul's own bifurcation, which does not imply, of course, that the passage from one state to the other is voluntary. This bifurcation of the soul into being-for-itself and its 'being' or 'undifferentiated universality', and its relating or 'relation' (*Beziehung*) of the latter to the former, are essential to the soul's being-for-itself.

3. Waking involves 'dispersion' (*Zerstreuung*) in various 'determinacies' and 'individual details'. Sleep is withdrawal back into the undifferentiated 'substance' underlying the details of waking life. The details are, as it were, bubbles on the surface of their substance, which thus has power over them. On substance, cf. Enc. I, §§150–1.

4. *Ideologie* here has its original sense of the 'doctrine of ideas' that Destutt de Tracy gave to the French *idéologie* when he coined it (from the Greek *idea* and *logos*, 'word, study, etc.') in 1796. The ideas in question were 'ideas' in the sense of Locke and Condillac, what Hegel would call 'representations', and the aim of the science was to investigate empirically the origins and relations of ideas. On this basis practical rules were to be established for education, ethics, and politics.

5. Dreams consist of 'representations' and waking life involves representations. Representations are, in dreams at least, connected by laws of 'association of

ideas': cf. §455. As long as we regard waking life, as well as dreams, as consisting *only* of representations, there is no essential difference between waking and dreaming. Any test suggested for distinguishing waking reality from a dream (such as coherence or pinching oneself) can be met with the 'trivial observation' that the apparent success of the test is itself just a representation that might occur in a dream. According to Hegel, waking differs from dreaming in two respects: (1) The waking mind is not simply a canvas on which various representations appear, or an observer of such representations, but 'consciousness' and 'intellect', a 'concrete I' or ego. (On consciousness and the I or ego, cf. §§413 ff.; on 'intellect', cf. §§422-3, 467.) (2) Owing to the intellect, 'intuition' forms a 'concrete totality' of systematically cohering and mutually supporting entities, rather than a collection of ideas linked by association. Our consciousness of this coherence, however hazy, is implicit in our 'self-feeling'. (On self-feeling, cf. §§407-8.)

6. Hegel alters Kant's treatment of the categories and expands their number, but he agrees with Kant that objectivity is conferred on our experience or on our representations by their ordering by categories, general thoughts, such as causality, which give representations a coherence beyond anything that can be supplied by association of ideas. That we are not explicitly conscious of the categorial structuring of our experience does not entail that it is not 'actually present in the mind'. Similarly the feeling mind need not be explicitly aware of the proofs of God's existence even though they express its ascent to God. (See Enc. I, §§50–1.) The proofs do not simply explicate the concept of God or establish his existence; they explicitly map the route by which we ascend to God from finite things and concerns. The expression 'ascent . . . to God' (*Erhebung . . . zu Gott*) primarily means our ascent to *awareness* of God, though it also suggests that we *become* God. God, in Hegel's view, is not sharply distinct from our awareness of him: see my 'Introduction' to ILA. Thus whereas Kant sharply distinguished between the finite objects of our experience, whose objectivity is secured by the categories involved in them, and an infinite God, whose objectivity cannot be captured by categorial cognition, Hegel presents religion as a continuation of our conceptual apprehension of the world.

   Whatever the merits of Hegel's theology, he is right to insist that our experience (and our language) involves features of which we are not explicitly conscious. More controversial is his suggestion that it is the lack of certain of these features, notably of category-generated coherence, that explains the 'subjectivity' of dreams. A fictitious story is 'subjective', rather than 'objective', but it need not lack category-generated coherence. Thus, a dream might be as coherent as such a story, yet still lack objectivity.

7. The alternation of sleep and waking is the third and most satisfactory of the ways in which a human individual, at the level of natural mind, is related to the 'genus' or 'substantial universality' from which it emerges. To become a proper mind, the individual has to establish its mastery over the genus, to domesticate the 'natural mind' and thus liberate itself from it. The first relation between individual and genus was the 'ages of life', in which the soul is a single 'subject' persisting through 'transient . . . differences'. In the second relation of individual

and genus, the sexual relationship, there is a 'fixed difference' and an 'opposition'. Male and female are opposites, not simply different. Ages of life, by contrast, cannot be opposites, because there are more than two ages of life, and a single thing cannot have more than one opposite. Thus infancy cannot be the opposite of adolescence, since adulthood has an equally strong claim to this status, and the two claims cancel each other. Male and female are, moreover, permanent, not transient, conditions: people do not routinely change their sex in the way that they change their age. The permanence of the opposition comes at a cost, however. One and the same individual cannot be both male and female. There must be two individuals, one of each sex. Thus the terms of the individual's relation to its 'genus' are distinct individuals of opposite sexes. In sleeping and waking, there is opposition, since there are two, and only two, alternating 'states', but the opposition is not so 'fixed' that it cannot occur in a single individual. Hence the alternation of sleep and waking is a genuine relation of the individual to its substance. It is the 'unity' of the first two relations, combining the opposition of sexuality with the 'simplicity' of the subject of the ages of life.

Hegel conflates two different accounts of the 'dialectical progress' from sexuality to the alternation of sleep and waking:

(1) Before their sexual union, each individual, the male and the female, has only 'being in itself'. But each individual, when it finds itself in the other, ascends to 'being for itself'. That is, each of them, the male and the female, undergoes a transition analogous to waking from sleep.

(2) The female remains 'in immediate unity with its substance', while the male enters into opposition to it. That is, the female is in a condition analogous to sleep, while the male's condition is analogous to waking.

Account (1) is, for Hegel's purposes, defective, since the change from being-in-itself to being-for-itself occurs within a single individual, even though it is stimulated by the encounter with another individual. Account (2) fits his schema better, but is rather implausible. For example, even the most compliant wife is usually aware of her husband's worldly activity, whereas a sleeper is not aware of the waking state. Here, as often, Hegel's ambition to link together disparate phenomena in a chain of necessity leads him to the brink of absurdity.

8. Having said that the alternation of sleep and waking is the most satisfactory of the three relations between the individual and its genus, Hegel now complains of its inadequacy. Waking is simply a 'state' of the soul, alternating with another state, sleep. Thus the waking mind has no more control over the sleeping state than Dr Jekyll has over Mr Hyde. The waking mind cannot decide when it will emerge from sleep and is, to that extent, not even in control of itself. The 'free mind' can voluntarily wake up: I can set an alarm, drag myself out of half-sleep, or perhaps will myself, successfully, to wake after a certain interval. But these abilities presuppose will and intelligence, which are not available to the soul at the level of anthropology. On waking the soul simply 'finds'

(*findet*) itself and, in opposition to itself, the world. Waking essentially involves 'sensation' (*Empfindung*), but not the will and intelligence needed to integrate the world into one's own thought and activities. (Moreover, even when one is fully endowed with mental equipment, it generally takes some time, after waking, to orient oneself in the world.) So the mind, in waking as well as sleep, is still encumbered with a natural aspect and is not yet as it is 'in its truth', namely 'pure activity'.

9. Hegel's '*Unterscheidung der Seele von sich selbst und von der Welt*' could mean, as Miller translated it, the 'distinguishing of the soul... from [*von*] itself and from the world' or the soul's 'distinguishing of [*von*] itself and of the world', i.e. 'between itself and the world'. The latter seems preferable here: the preceeding two sentences speak only of a distinction between the soul and the world, not between the soul and itself. Nevertheless, waking depends on the soul's 'distinguishing-itself-from-itself' (*das Sich-von-sich-selbst-Unterscheiden*) in contrast to its 'undifferentiatedness' in sleep. This enables it to distinguish itself from the world and, aided by daylight, between different things in the world.

10. Marie François Xavier Bichat (1771–1802) was a French physician whose discoveries arose from the post-mortems he conducted. He presents the distinction between organic and animal life in *Recherches physiologiques sur la vie et la mort* (Paris, 1800; 4th ed. 1822), 7–8. (The work was reprinted in 1973 by Éditions Gérard, Verviers, Belgium.) The 'irritability' of nerves and muscles was discovered earlier by a Swiss physiologist, Albrecht von Haller (1708–77). A slight stimulus to a muscle produces a sharp contraction. Nerves are even more irritable, responding to a lesser stimulus. A stimulus to a nerve produces a sharp contraction in the muscle to which it is connected, suggesting that muscular movement depends on nervous, rather than directly muscular, stimulation.

11. Bichat discusses this difference in the 'second article' of his *Recherches*.

12. In sleep the soul does not distinguish itself from itself or from the external world. This 'definition' (*Bestimmung*) is not derived from or answerable to 'experience'; it is intrinsically 'necessary'. But it is 'confirmed' by the fact that sleep is induced by an object that is either monotonously simple or incoherent. The waking mind and the world that keeps it awake are symmetrically related. Each is an 'internally differentiated totality', in 'opposition' to and 'unity' with the other. Hegel gives no answer to the objection that we may be bored yet remain awake, unless we suppose, implausibly, that wakeful boredom only occurs at the level of 'representational thinking' and that our intellect is always aroused, when we are awake. His answer to the objection that we may find a dream interesting is inadequate. Even if we grant that dreams, for example erotic dreams, stimulate only one's representational thinking, the same may well be true of a waking erotic experience that is not at all boring and has no tendency to send one to sleep.

13. What distinguishes waking is not the clarity of 'intuition' in its 'immediacy', regardless of its mediations, its interconnections with other intuitions, but the overall coherence of the intuited object as a 'rational totality'. Cf. §398, n. 5, and on 'intuition', §§449–50.

14. Hegel does mean that we think all the time, even in dreamless sleep. (If he had meant this he would have referred to Descartes or to Leibniz.) He means rather that any human mental activity, whether in sleep or in waking, involves thought. In seeing a mountain, for example, thought or categories enable me to see it as a unitary object, as a mountain, and to assign the perception to myself, to be aware that I can see the mountain. The doctrine stems from Kant, but it is also present in Plato's *Theaetetus*, 184–6, where Socrates argues that perception of a unitary object by a unitary self involves such concepts as being, identity, and difference. In dreams, Hegel argues, our mental activity, e.g. dreaming about a mountain, also involves thought, albeit to a lesser degree: cf. §398, nn. 5 and 6.

15. The waking soul does two things. (1) It frees itself from the external world and develops into an independent 'totality'. (2) It frees objects from its own 'subjectivity' and regards them as totalities belonging to an all-embracing totality, as an 'interconnection of necessity'. The two achievements are connected. As long as the soul is absorbed in nature it is confined to individual items with no coherent order. We have, as it were, to step back from the world, detaching ourselves from it, in order to survey it as an ordered whole. Hegel associates this independence from the world with being an I, being able to think and speak of oneself as 'I'. He here assigns the two accomplishments to 'intellect' (*Verstand*) rather than 'reason' (*Vernunft*), since intellect is primarily responsible for orderly arrangement, reason being more free-wheeling. The 'objectivity' of a representation depends on its 'agreement' or coherence with the 'totality', both of the world and of the mind. The word *Totalität*, derived from the Latin adjective *totus*, 'whole', suggests for Hegel a systematically ordered whole.

16. Cf. §§380 n. 1 and 401, n. 15 on the greater susceptibility of animals to sensory stimuli.

NOTES TO §399

1. On the distinction between 'being-for-self' (*Fürsichsein*) and mere 'being' (*Sein*), see §398, n. 2. The sleeping soul is mere being and is a 'substance' with certain accidents or 'determinacies', which are 'particular' rather than universal. These determinacies are also in the waking soul, but there they are 'for itself', not simply 'implicitly' or in itself (*an sich*). But the waking soul just 'finds' them in itself; it does not produce them itself or decide what they are to be. In the waking soul, though not in the sleeping soul, the determinacies are an 'ideal moment'; they do not constitute its nature, but are distinct from the self-identity of its 'being-for-self'. The redness of a rose, e.g., is not (immediately at least) ideal, but real; it partly constitutes the nature of the rose. When, in looking at the rose, I have a sensation of redness, this is ideal, in no way constitutive of my nature; even if I must have some sensations, I need not have this one. On 'ideality', see also Enc. I, §95.

   'Sensation' translates *Empfindung*, a word that hovers between 'feeling' and 'sensation'. It comes from the verb *empfinden*, 'to sense, feel'. Hegel exploits its link with *finden*, 'to find': a sensation is simply 'found' by the soul, not produced by it. §402 explains the difference between *Empfindung* and *Gefühl*, 'feeling'.

2. Sleep and waking alternate in what is (or would be, were it not for death) an infinite progression. This is one case of what Hegel calls 'bad' or 'false' infinity, the other being the sharp separation of the infinite (God) from the finite (the world). The solution to such unsatisfactory infinity is 'good' or 'true' infinity, in which the infinite is not cut off from the finite and which does not go on for ever. Cf. Enc. I, §§94-5 (where, however, the solution to bad infinity is, albeit temporarily, being-for-self) and §104. Here the solution is facilitated by the fact that sleep and waking, as Hegel initially described them, are both 'one-sided'. Sleep is undifferentiated and waking is 'abstract' and 'empty' being-for-self. The waking soul is self-aware, but has no definite nature to be aware of. It distinguishes itself from the external world, but has no means of acquiring definite information about the world. It is these deficiencies that motivate the endless alternation, though it can no more relieve them than one can relieve financial problems by endlessly borrowing more money to pay off old debts. To get its filling or 'fulfilment', the waking soul appropriates the 'determinations' or 'determinacies' that occur unconsciously in the sleeping soul. They are now 'immersed in the soul's universality' and occur in an 'ideal' form, as 'semblance', *Schein*—a term whose difference from *Erscheinung*, 'appearance', is explained in Enc. I, §131. (By contrast, sleep does not incorporate any features of waking. Hegel regards dreams not as an essential feature of sleep, but as a problem in the way of distinguishing it from waking.) The waking soul has now become in a way infinite. It incorporates its 'other' in itself. It forms a sort of circle: it goes out from itself to its other, is at home or 'together with itself' (*bei sich*) in its other, and then returns to itself and 'posits' itself in contrast to the sleep-derived determinations. It now has true 'individuality' (*Individualität*), a combination of universality and particularity: cf. §§379, n. 6; 394, n. 7. It does not of course cease to sleep, but it now sleeps because it is tired, not in order to repair some intrinsic deficiency in itself.

The 'dialectical progress' from waking to sensibility is not a temporal process in history or in the life of the individual. It is, first, a progression in Hegel's thought. If we suppose the soul to be subject to two alternating states, blank substantiality and sheer being-for-self, then we must suppose that it is driven to such endless alternation by the deficiency in each of the states, more particularly in the waking state. These deficiencies cannot be successfully resolved by the endless alternation fuelled by them. So to resolve the difficulty, we need to allow to the waking soul something of the substantiality of sleep—a result which coincides with what we otherwise know as sensibility. Secondly, nature itself is driven by this dialectic, which thus explains why we have sensations as well as sleep and waking. If we alternately wake and sleep, then we must have sensations; nature is driven by its internal logic to supply sensations once it has introduced sleep and waking. If one is awake, one must be awake *to* something or (as Hegel might have said had he not reserved the term 'consciousness' for a higher stage of mind) conscious *of* something.

3. The 'immediate determinacy' in the soul, e.g. a sensation of red, is particular and definite, one of an indefinite range of possible sensations. The soul itself is 'universal', capable of accommodating any sensation in the range and irretrievably attached to no particular one of them. It maintains its universality even in the face of a particular sensation. Water too is intrinsically universal, colourless, that is, yet capable of assuming any particular colour. But when it is given a particular colour, e.g. red, it does not maintain its universal nature, and hence does not have a sensation of red.

4. A *Schluss*, an inference or 'syllogism', is literally a 'closure' or 'conclusion', 'putting 2 and 2 together': cf. §389, n. 4. In the syllogism 'All men are mortal; all Greeks are men; all Greeks are mortal', we join the term 'Greeks' together with the term 'mortal', by way of the middle term 'men'. Hegel tends to regard two terms joined or 'mediated' as forming a syllogism, even when the terms do not occur in propositions, just as he spoke of the bifurcation into sleep and waking as a 'judgement', even though no propositional judgement is involved: cf. §§389, n. 4; 398, n. 1. Here there seem to be two 'syllogisms' in play: (1) The soul is united with the external world by way of its sensations. The soul's 'other' is no longer merely sensations, but external things 'distinct from ourselves'. By getting in touch with them we assure ourselves that we are awake. (2) The soul is united with itself by way of the other. The other may be a sensation or external things. In either case the process is the same as that mentioned earlier, where the 'other' from which the soul 'reflects' itself is sensation.

NOTES TO §400

1. In sensation the mind is 'unconscious' not in the sense that it is unaware of its sensation, but that sensation does not involve consciousness of an object distinct from oneself. Hence it belongs to the mind's ownness or 'peculiarity' (*Eigenheit*), its private possessions rather than public property. In sensation mind is also without understanding or 'unintellectual', since sensation involves no intellectual discrimination or argument: it is just what I sense or feel, and that is that. What I sense or feel thus tends to be thin and indeterminate, as well as ungrounded. It is 'qualitative': I sense e.g. redness, not the whole rose to which it belongs. It is 'finite' or piecemeal: I sense the redness alone, not together with other qualities with which it is connected. Cf. Enc. I, §90.

2. *Empfindung* now takes on the flavour of 'feeling', as well as 'sensation', but where 'sensation' seemed inappropriate, I preferred to translate it as 'sentiment' to maintain the distinction between *Empfindung* and *Gefühl*, 'feeling'. (Cf. §§380, n. 2; 381, n. 25; 390, n. 5; 399, n. 1.) *Empfindung* is a 'form' which can have various types of 'content'. I can sense redness, or again blueness. Redness and blueness are the content, sensing is the form. The form of *Empfindung* is the immediate or direct, 'unconscious', i.e. non-objectifying, intellectually undeveloped apprehension of a quality. Some types of content are intrinsically appropriate to the form of *Empfindung*. Colours, e.g., are simple, directly apprehended qualities that naturally fit into this form. We

do not normally ask for reasons why something is thought to be of a certain colour; we just see that it is e.g. red. However other contents, such as moral principles and religious doctrines, contents that are not usually regarded as simple and directly apprehended, can also assume the form of *Empfindung*. I feel that God is merciful, I see that theft is wrong, I intuit that knowledge is good. Hegel does not deny that mental states or acts corresponding to such claims occur, but believes that their natural home is the form of thought, rather than *Empfindung*. He considers three reasons for denying this: (1) The empiricist dictum 'Everything is in Empfindung': everything is based on or rooted in sensation-feeling. Hegel agrees, without conceding that everything can appropriately *remain* in the form of *Empfindung*. (2) Principles, religion, etc. must be in the 'heart', as well as the 'head', to ensure that they are 'my very own' (*mein Eigenstes*). What I am merely conscious or aware of intellectually (e.g. the existence of God) can be kept at a distance from myself, leaving me unmoved; I may cease to believe it without loss to myself. By contrast, what I sense or feel becomes an inseparable accompaniment of my whole self. Hegel replies that 'will, conscience, etc.' have a superior sort of 'being-my-own' (*Mein-eigen-Seins*). He reveals what this is at the end of the Remark: *thinking* is our 'very own' (*das Eigenste*), our distinctive characteristic. The appropriate form for what is our very own is thus the form of thought. Hegel's opponent might reply that thought may be *our* very own—human in contrast to bestial—and may make will and conscience our very own, but it is not *my* very own, in contrast to the common property of humanity. However, Hegel sets little store by what is *my* very own, the private possession of an individual. (3) Religion, etc. can be justified by appeal to the heart. No, replies Hegel. Feelings and the heart may be bad or wrong, as Matthew 15: 19 implies.

3. Hegel operates with four contrasting pairs of terms; the first of each pair characterizes spiritual or 'mental' content, the second the form of *Empfindung* and the content appropriate to it: (i) mediated—immediate; (ii) universal—'individual(ized)' (*Vereinzelt(es)*); (iii) necessary—contingent; (iv) objective—subjective. (i) *Empfindung*, primarily sensation, but also feeling or 'sentiment', is immediate or direct. I just have a sensation of red, without regard to argument or to other qualities in my environment. Hence what is sensed, the redness, is not connected with, 'mediated' by, other qualities or other instances of the same quality. So (ii) what I sense is individual, not universal. (When 'individuality' contrasts with 'universality', Hegel tends to use *einzeln* and its relatives; when individuality involves universality, he tends to use *individual* and its relatives: cf. 377, n. 7.) I sense this red and that red, not redness as such or colour as such. (iii) What is merely individual is 'contingent'. Contingency involves two ideas, the possibility of being otherwise and dependence on something else: 'we consider the contingent to be what may or may not be, what may be in one way or in another, whose being or not-being, and whose being on this wise or otherwise, depends not upon itself but on something else' (Enc. I, §145 Addition). What is sensed in isolation, e.g. a red patch, might easily have been otherwise, e.g. green. There is no

argument or causal context to establish the necessity of its redness. Does not its being contingent *upon* something else secure the necessity of the redness? If Hegel intends to introduce this second component of contingency here, he may mean that whatever necessity there is to the redness of the patch cannot be discerned by isolated sensation, but only by ascending (by thought rather than sensation) to a larger whole in which individual items appear as necessary elements in a system. Or he may mean that what the sensation is contingent upon is not sufficient to determine the necessity of what is sensed. Someone's feeling that abortion is wrong, e.g., may be *both* contingent upon something else (upbringing, personal experiences, etc.) *and* capable of being otherwise (a feeling e.g. that abortion is not wrong), if the upbringing, personal experiences, etc. had been otherwise. The causal history of the feeling, and such necessity as it confers on the feeling, is not relevant to the status of what is felt. Since what is felt, the wrongness of abortion, is merely *felt*, it could as well be otherwise, and would have been felt to be otherwise if different circumstances had obtained. (iv) For similar reasons, *Empfindung* is subjective, in a sense which excludes its objectivity. The sensation is confined to an 'individual subject', not 'common to all'. Hence what is sensed or felt has no objective status conferred on it. One type of subjectivity, 'free, etc.' subjectivity, 'following its own law', is compatible with objectivity. This is the autonomous subjectivity of the mathematician or the philosopher; their thoughts are the thoughts of the individual thinker, but they are also objective thoughts, 'common to all', or at least to all who consider the matter in an appropriate way. 'Natural' subjectivity, by contrast, is confined to and determined by particular times, places, and circumstances. I cannot expect others to share my precise sensations, pangs of hunger, or moral feelings.

Whatever content assumes the form of *Empfindung* takes on these characters of immediacy, individuality, contingency, and subjectivity. What is properly the concern of rational thought, e.g. the morality of abortion, is withdrawn from it in so far as it is merely felt.

4. The soul that does no more than feel or sense does not distinguish itself or its feeling from what is sensed or felt. To do this requires 'consciousness' of an object as distinct from myself, and this in turn requires thought, the 'abstract thought of its I': cf. §402 Addition. This is connected with the subjectivity of feeling even when the subject can distinguish itself from its object: mental states or acts belonging to a stratum of the mind which lacks the resources for drawing the subject–object distinction are themselves 'subjective'. The distinction between subject and object is considered in §§413 ff. Anthropology, and specifically §401, considers not this distinction, but the distinction to be found in the content of *Empfindung*, namely between sensations that originate in the body and those that originate in the soul.

NOTES TO §401

1. Hegel associates sensing with finding, since *empfinden*, 'to sense, feel', comes from *finden*, 'to find' (with the prefix *ent-*): cf. §402. Sensation has two aspects:

(i) a psychological aspect, in which it is 'natural and immediate', 'ideally' or ideal (*ideell* may be either an adjective or an adverb) in the soul, i.e. belongs to 'being-for-self'; (ii) a physical aspect, in which it acquires the 'bodiliness' or embodiment necessary for it to be sensed or felt. 'Being-for-self' (*Fürsichsein*) is the beginning of the 'I of consciousness' since, though it is not yet conscious of external objects or able to distinguish itself from its sensations as 'I' or 'me', it is a unitary centre aware of all its feelings and sensations.

2. The embodiment of sensations proceeds in two directions, from body to soul and from soul to body. (i) A sensation, especially a perceptual sensation, is a 'determination' of a part of the body, which is then internalized in the soul's 'being-for-self'. 'Recollected' translates *erinnert*, the perfect participle of *erinnern*, 'to remind [someone of something]' and in the reflexive form, *sich erinnern*, 'to remember, recollect, etc.' But for Hegel *erinnern* has the flavour of 'internalize, make inner'. Hence he means primarily that the bodily modification is internalized. (ii) A sensation, or what we would more naturally call a 'feeling' or 'sentiment', begins in the 'mind' and is then embodied, and thus 'found' (*gefundene*) and 'felt' (*empfundene*), placed in the 'subject', the 'soul'. 'Mind' here seems to be relatively independent of the body, while 'soul' is intertwined with it.

   The senses form a system, different types of sensation originating in different sense-organs. This is also true of the bodily organs that accommodate feelings stemming from the mind; they too form a system, and different types of feeling are embodied in different parts of the body, depending on their 'content'.

3. So far in §401 'bodiliness' has translated *Leiblichkeit*, from *Leib*, the word most commonly used for the human 'body', owing to its affinity to *Leben*, 'life': cf. §401, n. 18. But 'corporeal functions' translates *Körperlichkeit*, more literally 'corporeality', from *Körper*, 'body' in the sense in which it applies also to non-human bodies. *Körper* 'refers to matter and is applied as an anatomical term to the body of living beings, also to anything considered as an entity (e.g. the planets). . . . It excludes any implication of human feelings, sentiments and life in its non-physical aspect. It is *Leib* which conveys this suggestion and is conceived as the vessel of the soul' (DGS, p. 45). *Körperlichkeit* is the right word here, since Hegel considers the senses in terms not primarily of their bodily organs, but of the aspects of external bodies that they apprehend. The corporeality of external bodies is specified or particularized, not by Hegel but intrinsically, into aspects ranged along the ideal–real spectrum. 'Determinate' light, i.e. light as differentiated into various colours and shapes, and sound are more 'ideal': their involvement with the bodily material that reflects or emits them is minimal. That there are two such aspects, rather than one, has no special explanation. If they were aspects of the mind, of 'subjective ideality', there would have to be some explanation of their twoness and their difference, some logical relation between them. But as it is they are simply different, simply 'diversity' (*Verschiedenheit*). Smell and taste are closely linked and apprehend aspects of bodies nearer to the reality end of the spectrum; they absorb material particles. Touch apprehends the least ideal aspects of bodies, those most intimately associated with

their bodily reality. The aspects apprehended by the senses are more fully discussed in the §§ of Enc. II to which Hegel refers. There they are discussed in the
order of their development in 'natural corporeality', i.e. as they occur in physical bodies and without reference to senses, which are not dealt with until §358.
Their order in Enc. II does not correspond to their place on the ideal–real spectrum. Hence in §401 they are arranged 'more simply', 'around the centre of
sentient individuality'.

4. 'Psychical physiology', dealing with the 'relation' of sensations and their
   embodiment, would consider at least four themes:

   (i) Some sensations are pleasant, some unpleasant. An 'immediate sensa-
       tion', e.g. a sound, is pleasant or unpleasant depending on whether or
       not it is appropriate to our sensory 'interior', which has a 'determination'
       or constitution of its own, independently of the particular sensations that
       it receives. This 'sensory interior' also explains why humans and animals
       are sensitive to different stimuli: cf. §401, n. 15. The appropriateness or
       inappropriateness of the sensation is itself something felt, giving rise to an
       Empfindung of pleasure or pain. The relevance of this to the relationship
       between the psychical and the physiological is this. Sensations are primar-
       ily physiological, stemming from changes in our sense-organs. They are
       related, as appropriate or inappropriate, to our sensory interior. But our
       sensory interior stems from the soul or mind. Hence the pleasure or pain
       derived from sensations belongs to psychical physiology, but tenuously,
       not centrally, involving only 'something of a relation of this type'.

   (ii) Sensations are associated with certain moods and are used to symbolize
        them, e.g. black is gloomy and symbolizes grief: cf. §401, n. 16. Again
        this belongs to the margins of psychical physiology, since what is primar-
        ily physiological, sensations, is correlated with what is primarily mental,
        moods and emotions.
        Both (i) and (ii) are examples of *Sympathie*, rather than of embodiment.
        Sympathie is used in its original Greek sense, 'suffering/being affected
        with', the idea being that certain feelings or sensations go together with
        certain others, giving rise to either a feeling of pleasure (or pain) or to a
        symbolic affinity.

   (iii) 'Emotions' (*Affekte*) are felt in certain regions of the body. On the irrit-
         able and sensible systems, see §§398, n. 10; §401, n. 23.

   (iv) Passions, emotions, etc. express themselves in bodily ways 'from out of
        the soul'. 'Physiognomy' is the art of 'judging' or interpreting ('-gnomy',
        from the Greek *gnōmē*) someone's character or 'nature' (*phusis*) from
        their physical, especially facial, characteristics. Johann Kaspar Lavater
        (1741–1801) popularized the idea in his *Physiognomische Fragmente zur
        Beförderung der Menschenkenntnis und Menschenliebe* (Physiognomical
        Fragments for the Promotion of the Knowledge of Human Nature and
        the Love of Mankind: Leipzig, 1775–8). He was a friend of Goethe,

vividly described in Goethe's autobiography, *Wahrheit und Dichtung* (Truth and Poetry). Hegel attacks Lavater's doctrine of physiognomy in PS, pp. 185–95. *Pathognomie* is the art of judging or interpreting a person's passions or emotions from their bodily expressions.

5. Internal 'sensations' (*Empfindungen*), i.e. feelings, are considered in §§447-8.
6. Two related points show the 'universal nature' of the sentient individual: (i) A single sense can perceive a wide range of qualities. e.g. sight can sense red, blue, etc. (ii) The sense, or the individual, is not 'tied' to a single quality, e.g. blue, since it can also perceive red, etc., and thus does not take on blue, or any other colour, as its 'quality'—unlike coloured water: cf. §399, n. 3. It is universal in the sense of 'indeterminate', it remains aloof, at home or 'together with itself' (*bei sich*), in any determinate perception, and this enables it to perceive any quality in the range. Hegel is influenced by Aristotle's *de anima*, II: cf. §378, n. 3.
7. The sensory, e.g. perceived colours, is 'self-external': the colours are spread over a field, such that any given colour occupies a two-dimensional area, not simply a point or a line, and different colours occupy different areas: cf. Enc. I, §20. Hegel connects this sort of 'externality' with externality of a different sort. The content of sensation divides into different types of sensation, e.g. colours and temperatures, which are (unlike the contents of a single type) 'mutually indifferent', in that something can be, say, red and hot all over (or alternatively red and cold all over), but not red and green all over. Internal sensations are also mutually external. Anger and grief are felt in different parts of the body. But one emotion, e.g. anger, tends to dampen, if not exclude, another, e.g. grief.
8. The three groups of senses correspond only roughly to the three 'moments' of the concept: 'physical ideality' corresponds to universality, 'real difference [*Differenz*]' to particularity, i.e. the division of universality into different particulars or species, 'earthly totality' to individuality, the full-bodied, earthy physical entity. Cf. §379, n. 6.
9. Each group of senses 'must' form a totality, a whole, since the 'moment' of the 'concept' which it represents is itself a single moment, not a collection of concepts. A 'concrete' (namely 'grown together') totality is a coherent whole, each of whose parts implies, and is incomplete without, the others. An animal organism e.g. is a concrete totality; from a single part, or a bone, we can infer a good deal, though not of course everything, about the rest of the organism. However, the first group, sight and hearing, do not form a concrete totality. Sight and hearing have something in common; each perceives its object from a distance. But the acuteness of sight and hearing vary quite independently of each other. Thus sight and hearing form only a 'sundered' totality. This is because they are the sense, or senses, of what is *abstractly* universal and ideal, i.e. abstracted, or cut off, both from each other and from the body that reflects or emits them. Light and sound are 'ideal' in quite different ways: sound results from the 'negation of the material', i.e. from a movement of the object heard and of the intervening medium, whereas light involves no prior negation of what is other than itself, no disturbance of the object seen or of the medium.

The second group corresponds to the division of the concept into particulars, and so it is easier to explain why it contains two members—smell and taste—than in the case of the first group. Nevertheless, smell and taste are more closely related than sight and hearing. Both respond to the 'decomposition and dissolution' of a concrete body. Smell functions at a distance from the body and senses the 'abstract' process of decomposition, etc; taste requires contact and thus senses the 'concrete' process.

Touch or 'feeling' (*das Gefühl*) is a single sense, since it senses the 'concrete totality', i.e. the full-bodied object. However, in view of the variety of independent features discerned by touch (temperature, texture, etc.), it is unclear why we should regard it as a single sense.

10. Hegel's account of light and colour is influenced by Goethe. Newton had argued that colour is a property of light and that all the colours are formed out of white light. He based this on his discovery that sunlight can be bent through a prism so as to give a spectrum of colours. Goethe rejected this view, insisting that white light is not a mixture of colours. He adopted a view close to Aristotle's, that colour arises in the passage from light to darkness, being a mixture of white and black, or, as Hegel puts it, light's 'obscuration by the dark'. See Goethe's *Farbenlehre* (1810), translated by C. L. Eastlake as *Theory of Colours* (London: John Murray, 1840; Cambridge, Mass., MIT Press, 1970). See also Enc. II, §§275–8, 317–20. The connection of light with space corresponds to the connection between sound and time: cf. §401, n. 11. Light occupies space that is otherwise empty. Hegel seems to reject the view that 'empty' space is filled with 'ether': cf. Enc. II, §276.

11. The connection of sound with time depends on the fact that sound requires movement, and movement takes time. (In Enc. II, §276, Hegel seems to acknowledge that light takes time to travel, but this is less obvious than the fact that sound takes time to travel.) More generally, Hegel opposes the view that time is a neutral medium. It depends on features of bodies or other entities such as mind. See my 'Kant and Hegel on Space and Time', in S. Priest (ed.), *Hegel's Critique of Kant* (Oxford: Oxford University Press, 1987). That sound passes through other substances, besides air, and does not require a medium of a specific constitution is important for the 'ideality' of sound, as Hegel explains in Enc. II, §300.

12. On smell and taste, cf. Enc. II, §§321, 322, and 358.

13. 'Heaviness' (*Schwere*) is not simply a body's tendency to attract and be attracted by other bodies, especially the earth, but a force that makes it a cohesive, solid, independent body, offering 'resistance' to other bodies, especially to the sentient subject. It is this solid resistance that is the primary object of touch; even in feeling the warmth of a body, we feel its solidity, since a body's temperature corresponds to its 'specific gravity' and 'cohesion'. The objects of touch are dispersed throughout Enc. II: §§262 gravity; 290–4 specific gravity; 295–9 cohesion; 303–7 warmth; 310–15 shape, with a brief mention of touch in §358.

14. The triad quality—quantity—measure is treated in Enc. I, §§86 ff., esp. 103 on intensive magnitude and 107–9 on measure. 'Measure' (*das Mass*) is a union

of quality and quantity or a restoration of quality, on a higher level, after its passage into quantity. A village e.g. may have a varying number of inhabitants. But if their number is sufficiently reduced, it ceases to be a village and becomes an isolated dwelling, while if their number is increased sufficiently it becomes a town or a city. 'Measure' involves the idea of due measure or proportion. The intensity of a sensation, e.g. the loudness of a sound, may vary within limits, but if it decreases too far it becomes inaudible, and if it increases too far it becomes deafening. (Although loudness is an 'intensive' magnitude, it 'also exists extensively' as a certain number of decibels.) It is unclear why the 'quantitative side of sensation' is of no philosophical interest. It may be because it is the quasi-qualitative measure that is interesting, not quantitative variations that do not proceed *beyond* 'measure', or because quantitative variations that go beyond the threshold of sensibility lack interest.

15. Cf. §§380, n. 1; 398, n. 15. Hegel's example suggests that some animals can sense stimuli that humans (without special training) cannot, but not that animal sensibility is wholly unselective and 'measureless' or even that it is less selective than our own. But our sensory 'measure' differs from those of other species. Cf. §401, n. 18 on the connection between measure and 'inner sensation'.

16. Hegel gives three cases of the 'relation' of outer sensation to our 'mental interior': (i) A sensation is pleasant or unpleasant according as it satisfies or dissatisfies our independently determined 'nature': cf. §401, n. 4.This is treated in §472, within the section of 'psychology' entitled 'practical mind' (§§469–82). (ii) Sensations arouse our impulses or 'urges'. These are treated in §§473 ff. (iii) Sensations often arouse a 'mood': cf. §401, n. 4. Moods produced by the general environment, e.g. climate, were discussed in §§392 (cf. nn. 1 and 5) and 395 (cf. n. 5). A mood aroused by a sensation is more determinate or definite, but still 'unconscious' in two respects. First, I need not be aware of the relationship between the sensation and the mood; certainly I need not, by 'conscious intelligence', infer from the sensation that e.g. things are going badly and acquire the mood as a result. The sensation simply has an 'inner meaning' for me, and that arouses the corresponding mood. Second, there is here no 'external object', distinct from myself, of which I am conscious; I am aware simply of a sensation, and that does not amount to 'consciousness' *of* something. In virtue of its inner meaning, the sensation is 'symbolic'. But it is not a symbol in the strict sense, namely a distinct external object (e.g. a black armband) in which I am conscious of an inner 'determinacy' or which I refer to an inner determinacy (such as grief). On symbols proper, see §457.

17. §458 distinguishes between a 'sign' and a 'symbol'. Here their relationship is this. Black symbolizes grief in virtue of its general tendency to arouse grief or at least sadness. Hence black is conventionally supposed to stand for grief. So one chooses black clothing as a *sign* of one's 'present' (*vorhandenen*) mood. One's grief exists before one puts on black clothing; it is not likely to have been aroused by the sight of black, but by the death of a loved one. Nevertheless black is suitable for the 'expression' of grief. Of course, one need not oneself feel any

actual grief. What makes black dress appropriate for a funeral is that it is the conventional expression of the grief one is supposed to feel.

18. The 'measure' of human sensibility (cf. §401, nn. 14 and 15) suggested that I am not simply a blank tablet, but have a determinate inner nature. That external sensations arouse moods confirms this. Our 'interior' has a 'content', to feel which, we need (i) an 'external occasion' (e.g. a colour sensation to arouse a mood—or possibly Hegel means an external stimulus to produce a sensation), and (ii) an 'embodiment' (*Verleiblichung*) of the content. Embodiment and symbolization proceed in opposite directions: symbolization goes from outer to inner, embodiment from inner to outer. Moods, etc. must embody themselves, since they belong to the natural soul, thus are 'simply in being' (*seiende*), and so must acquire an immediate 'reality' (*Dasein*) in which the soul becomes 'for itself'. Hegel here conflates two questions: (a) Why must moods be felt? Because otherwise they would not be states of the natural soul, not states in which the soul is for itself. (b) Why is embodiment needed for a mood to be felt? Because, Hegel implies, a subject cannot directly sense or feel itself. A mood, if it is to be felt, must be 'identical' with the subject, but also 'distinct' from it, not *flatly* identical with it. It achieves this through embodiment. But why only through embodiment? Why not by simply distinguishing my *mood* from *myself*, or by painting a gloomy picture? The natural soul cannot yet dissociate itself from its inner states, it is not an 'I': cf. §381, n. 15. Nor can it yet paint pictures. Hence its feelings must be externalized in its 'corporeal body' (*Körper*). Here, as in §389 (on the 'communion' of soul and *Körper*), the body is thought of in contrast to the soul and thus in its material aspect. Nevertheless, the body is not 'for itself', i.e. independent, but permeated by soul, for which it is 'an ideality' (*ein Ideelles*), i.e. an inseparable part of the whole living organism: cf. §387, n. 11.

19. Anger is primarily displeasure over some injury or offence to *myself*. Revenge is a desire to retaliate for some offence to *myself*. Envy is displeasure at someone's doing better than *myself*. Shame is displeasure at *my* own shortcomings, especially in view of the actual or possible disapproval of others. 'Remorse' or regret (*Reue*) is displeasure at something that *I* have done. Each of these emotions involves an essential reference to my- or oneself. Hegel gives no examples of the second type of feeling, but he mainly has in mind such feelings as respect for (or 'sense of') justice, religious awe, love of beauty, etc., rather than occurrent feelings on specific occasions and directed upon specific objects. But feelings of the first type can often be modified, so that they too refer to a 'universal in and for itself'. Anger may concern an offence against e.g. morality or religion, not something I just happen to dislike. Nor need the offence be to myself or my associates, but e.g. the desecration of an altar or a massacre of innocents. Revenge too may be a desire to retaliate for an offence contravening rules of justice, morality, or religion, though it must be an offence to myself or my connexions. Envy is irremediably egocentric: the displeasing advantage is always an advantage over myself, and even if the advantage relates to a 'universal'—I envy, e.g., another's moral superiority to myself—this confers no respectability on the displeasure. Shame always concerns the faults of myself or my connexions; what

I am ashamed about is usually something *conventionally regarded* as bad, though it may be (either *in addition* or *instead*) regarded as bad intrinsically or 'in and for itself'. If what I am ashamed about is regarded as intrinsically bad, by e.g. moral standards, shame comes close to remorse. Remorse is for something done by *myself* that offends against morality, religion, etc. Regret, by contrast, may be for something done by myself that offends no universal standard, though (unlike remorse) it may also be for something for which I am not responsible, such as the decline of religion or inclement weather.

Both types of feeling are such that I 'find' them in myself, i.e. I do not decide to have them, they come and go of their own accord. They come close to each other in two ways. (i) The second type becomes like the first if its moral, etc. content acquires the form of 'individualization' (*Vereinzelung*), if e.g. the moral norm to which I appeal (perhaps to justify my request for a salary increase or my indignation at not receiving it) commends itself to me only because it favours my individual interests. Conversely, feelings of this type differ more starkly from feelings of the first type to the extent that they involve less of the 'subject's particularity'. (ii) The first type becomes like the second if subject-oriented feelings acquire universal content, if e.g. my anger at the treatment I have received is genuinely based on moral disapproval of this treatment. In general, the bodily expression of a feeling becomes less important to the extent that the feeling concerns a universal matter rather than oneself. My reddening face and quivering lip adequately express my anger at an insult. But to convey my moral indignation over injustice to others I need to resort to words.

20. The 'content' of outer sensations is treated in Enc. II (cf. §401, n. 3). The content of inner sensations is considered briefly in the third part of the 'doctrine of subjective mind', namely 'psychology', in §447, but the 'universal' content of feelings of the second type—right, morality, etc. —appears in the accounts of 'objective' and 'absolute' mind. 'Embodiment' occurring 'involuntarily', e.g. the reddening face and quivering lip, is distinct from 'gestures' (*Gebärde*), e.g. the shaking of a fist, which are dependent on my will. On gestures, cf. §411. Involuntary embodiment may become a 'sign' of e.g. anger, but its involuntariness differentiates it from the wearing of black as a sign of grief: cf. §401, n. 17.
21. For Bichat's distinction, in his *Recherches physiologiques sur la vie et la mort*, between *la vie animale* and *la vie organique*, cf. §398, n. 9. The 'precious viscera' or vital organs (*edlen Eingeweide*) are also considered by Bichat, especially in his sixth article, where he relates them to the 'passions'.
22. Bichat, in his sixth article, cites linguistic evidence for the internal embodiment of the passions and draws attention to their destructive possibilities.
23. The connexion between a feeling and its organ is not merely contingent; it depends on the relation between 'physiological significance' of the organ and the 'content' of the feeling. There may be exceptions to the general 'rule' (*Regel*). But these stem from the 'impotence of nature' (*Ohnmacht der Natur*) and do not affect the rule. Hegel invokes the 'impotence of nature' at Enc. II, §250 to account for the inability of philosophy to account for the 'infinite wealth and

variety of forms' in nature. In German, as in English, usage a *rule* admits of exceptions—'as a rule', 'the exception proves the rule'—whereas a *law* does not.

The quality of each type of feeling fits the 'physiological significance' of the organ in which it primarily resides. Hegel assumes that a feeling is felt or sensed in the organ in which it is primarily embodied. (i) Grief, as the soul turning inward, resides in the abdomen, the 'reproductive system'. *Reproduktion* is not breeding or propagation, but the self-maintenance of the organism. Along with sensibility and irritability, it is one of the three main functions of life: Enc. II, §354; cf. Enc. III, §398, n. 10. (ii) Anger is outward-turning and thus resides in the heart, the centre of 'irritability'. But repressed anger involves the reproductive system once more, which vents its own 'anger' or 'irritability' on food, by means of bile and pancreatic secretions, and is thus an appropriate seat for anger, as well as grief: cf. Enc. II, §§384-5 on digestion, and Enc. III, §395, n. 7 on bile. (iii) Like outward-turning anger, shame is associated with the circulatory or 'blood' system, and thus the heart. Hegel puns on 'appearance' (*Erscheinung*). What one is ashamed of is not necessarily one's physical appearance or how one appears to others, but one's appearance in the sense of what one has done and made of oneself, the manifestation of one's essence: cf. Enc. I, §131 on appearance. Blushing changes one's appearance, but not that aspect of it of which one is ashamed, nor is it the only feeling to do so. (iv) Terror is inward-turning, and thus, in consistency, should perhaps (like grief) reside in the abdomen. But, instead, it too involves the blood, which in this case withdraws inwards. That we blush from shame and blanch from fear, rather than the other way about, is, despite occasional 'irregularities', a 'law' (*Gesetz*), though Hegel should perhaps have said a 'rule'. (v) Thinking, a definite person's thinking, occurring at a definite time, is felt in the head. On the connection between sensibility and the brain, see Enc. II, §354.

24. 'Show' (*Zeigen*) refers to embodiment as a 'sign' (*Zeichen*) of a feeling: cf. §401, n. 20. *Äusserlichwerden* ('externalization') is close to *Entäusserung*, 'elimination', but also one of Hegel's words for 'alienation' or 'estrangement'. Here the idea is that by expressing or 'externalizing' a feeling one sometimes gets rid of it. This does not invariably involve vocal externalization. Punching one's adversary or breaking his furniture relieves anger better than shouting at him. Conversely, giving voice to a feeling does not invariably get rid of it. Love often outlasts the lover's sighs. On voice, see §401, nn. 27 and 28.

25. The physiological 'phenomena' (*Erscheinungen*) whose connection with emotions or 'motions of the soul' is hard to explain are vocal expressions, such as laughter, that relieve the feeling. What (supposedly) arouses laughter is the transformation of an intrinsically worthless or 'null' purpose into its opposite. It is not funny if a hungry man chokes on his food, since his end is not intrinsically worthless. It is not funny if a fallen man gets up again, since this is not something 'self-annihilating'. Nor is it funny (to me at least, though it may be to others) if I myself fall over. (Hegel seems to disallow the possibility of laughing at oneself.) It is funny if a proud man, whose end is, say, to cut

a fine figure, suddenly falls over (without, presumably, breaking his leg or skull). This is a sort of 'dialectic', a 'contradiction', within pomposity, becoming 'immediately obvious' in prostration. (Dialectic is, for Hegel, not primarily an activity that we philosophers engage in, but the intrinsic dynamic of concepts, things, and events: cf. Enc. I, §81.) What succumbs to this dialectic is the finite, a 'limited content', pomposity, say, in contrast to prostration and to other more significant ends. The spectator is not confined to any such restricted content. He observes the pomposity, but does not associate himself with it. If the spectator shares and respects the demeanour of the victim, he will not find his fall funny. (If he were to find it funny, this would be like laughing at himself.) Hence the spectator's 'subjectivity' is absolute 'ideality', 'infinite power'. It stands aloof above the fray, identifying with none of the contestants in the game of life and transcending them all: cf. §§379, n. 3; 381, nn. 4, 8, 14 on ideality. (Hegel's account is close to Hobbes's view of laughter as a self-glorifying gesture of triumph over one's inferiors.) Laughter has two aspects, a lighting-up of the face embodying the pure self's enjoyment of itself, and an 'expulsion of the breath' embodying the soul's repulsion of the 'ridiculous' from itself. Hegel gives no reason why self-enjoyment alone would result in laughter rather than a gentle smile. Hence the repulsion of the ridiculous is required to account for proper laughter. But why does the soul need to repel the ridiculous? Suppressed amusement can be painful and needs relief. But Hegel's account of the pure self's self-enjoyment seems to leave no room for such obtrusive mirth. His idea (influenced perhaps by Aristotle's doctrine of katharsis) is that laughing gets rid of obtrusive mirth and of its finite object, thereby maintaining the purity of the self's enjoyment.

Hegel's aversion to loud or involuntary laughter was shared by Lord Chesterfield ('there is nothing so illiberal, and so ill-bred, as audible laughter'). It coheres with his account of amusement: why should the self's pure self-enjoyment produce laughter? Pericles was traditionally regarded as austere. See further Jan Bremmer, 'Jokes, Jokers and Jokebooks in Ancient Greek Culture', in Jan Bremmer and Herman Roodenburg (eds.), *A Cultural History of Humour* (Cambridge: Polity, 1997), 11–28.

26. 'Critical outburst' is *kritische Ausschlag*. *Ausschlag*, from *ausschlagen*, 'to knock out, etc.', means a 'rash, eruption of the skin', the 'swing' of an indicator, or the 'decisive factor' that tips the scales. *Kritisch*, like 'critical', means 'skilled in or given to rigorous assessment', 'censorious', 'serious, dangerous', 'decisive, deciding'. Hegel may have in mind the sense of 'separating, dividing', the root-meaning of its Greek parent-verb, *krinein*, also 'to discern, judge, etc.' Thus tears are a selective or discriminating eruption, and this explains why they are not only the 'expression' (*Äusserung*) of pain, but also its 'elimination' (*Entäusserung*).

27. 'Voice' (*Stimme*) does not, like laughter, 'form' (*formiert*) an external object (presumably one's own face), nor, like crying, discharge a material stuff such as water, but produces an 'incorporeal bodiliness' (*unkörperliche Leiblichkeit*), which leaves the subject's interior internal, while nevertheless externalizing it.

Voice is especially suitable for 'eliminating' (*Entäusserung*) feelings, because sound is fleeting. Here 'ideality' (*Idealität*) contrasts with 'reality' (*Realität*), as inner feelings to their outward expression, though owing to its incorporeality this reality is also 'ideal' (*ideelle*). In the accounts of laughter and weeping *Idealität* contrasted not with *Realität*, but with the 'finite': cf. §401, n. 25.

28. *Sprache* is both 'speech' and 'language'. Hegel's main discussion of it in Enc. is at §459. Animals have 'voice' (*Stimme*) but not speech. Speech is usually voluntary; the sounds produced by mere voice are involuntary, 'immediately' or directly produced by the feeling. Speech is 'articulate' (*artikulierte*), divided into significant elements such as syllables and words; voiced sounds admit 'modifications' (a cry of pain differs from a cry of pleasure, and different types of pain elicit different types of cry), but are not 'articulate'. Unlike mere voice, speech expresses feelings 'in their entire determinacy'. Hence speech more effectively objectifies and externalizes feelings, raising them into 'representation' and making them extraneous or 'alien' (*fremd*) to the subject. Goethe's *Sorrows of Werther* is the best known *Gedicht* (which can apply to a novella as well as a 'poem') in which he overcame the pain of unsatisfied love by transforming it into literature.

It is not true, however, that speech can invariably convey a feeling in its entire determinacy, nor can it always convey it more accurately than non-verbal sounds. Intense pain or the pleasure of love-making cannot be described at the time by the person experiencing them, only in retrospect. Even then I cannot express the exact intensity and quality of my pain in words. But words can convey some things that a cry cannot: that a wasp has stung my right hand, for example, or that I am upset about the death of my father. It is also untrue that expressing one's feeling in words always eliminates the feeling. If this were so, no lover could declare his love without thereby forfeiting it. Whether expressing a feeling in words diminishes it, enhances it or leaves it as before depends on such factors as these: Can one expect to satisfy the feeling, e.g. fulfil one's love, take revenge, revive a sick loved one? If one can, it is hard to see why verbal expression of the feeling should diminish rather than enhance it and prepare for its fulfilment. Funeral hymns may reduce the feelings they address; war cries and patriotic songs do not. What is the nature of the verbal expression? A simple profession of love or hatred may only fuel one's passion. But if one writes a novel about it, one's attention is redirected to one's new literary enterprise and the raw passion falls into neglect.

NOTES TO §402

1. This paragraph supplies a transition from *Empfindung* ('feeling, sensation') to *Gefühl* ('feeling'), words which, in ordinary usage, are close in meaning. But Hegel differentiates them. For him, *Empfindung* is 'individual' (*einzelne*) and 'transient', not a feeling of the soul as a whole. *Gefühl*, by contrast, is directed on the soul as a whole, on the self. Sensations are fleeting accidents in the substance of the soul: cf. Enc. I, §§150–1 on substance and accidents. Sensations are *gesetzt in ihrem mit derselben identischen Fürsichsein*. Grammatically this can

be taken in three ways: (i) They are 'posited' (*gesetzt*) in its (the soul's) 'being-for-self' (*Fürsichsein*), which is identical with the soul's 'substantiality'. (ii) They are posited in its [substantiality's] being-for-self, which is identical with the soul. (iii) They are set in their [the sensations'] being-for-self, which is identical with it [the soul or, less probably, its substantiality]'. Wallace's (i) is plausible. Version (ii) is less plausible—why should being-for-self be ascribed not to the soul, but to its *substantiality*? —but otherwise differs little from (i). Version (iii) differs more significantly from (i); that Hegel's next sentence implies that *Fürsichsein* belongs to 'sensation' (*Empfinden*) tells in its favour. This 'being-for-self' is not just a 'formal' (*formelles*, i.e. 'superficial') feature of sensation, since in itself (*an sich*, 'implicitly') the soul is 'reflected totality of sensation' (or just possibly 'of being-for-self': *reflektierte Totalität desselben*). That is, the soul is not just a collection of independently felt sensations, but a coherent totality of sensations with a single centre of awareness. 'Reflected' means not that the totality is 'reflected upon', but that the diverse sensations are, like light-rays, 'reflected back' to the centre: cf. Enc. I, §112 on 'essence' and reflexion. Hence 'within itself' (*in sich*) the soul 'feels', or is sensation of, the whole substance which it is implicitly or 'in itself' (*an sich*). It is thus 'feeling' (*fühlende*) soul, not merely sensing soul. It feels itself as a whole, not only fleeting sensations. On *Fürsichsein*, combining the ideas of independence, self-awareness and actuality, cf. §§387, n. 12; 398, nn. 2, 7. On *an sich*, combining the ideas of independence, latency, and potentiality, cf. §§378, n. 5; 389, n. 17; 398, n. 7.

2. *Gefühl*, 'feeling' and *fühlen*, 'to feel' are not clearly distinct from *Empfindung*, *empfinden*. But German speaks of *Gefühl des Rechts*, 'sense of right or justice', and *Selbstgefühl*, 'feeling of self, self-esteem', not *Empfindung des Rechts* or *Selbstempfindung*. *Empfindung* is related to *Empfindsamkeit*, 'sensitivity, sentimentality'. Hence *Empfindung* suggests passivity, 'finding', *Finden*, from which it derives: cf. §401, n. 1. It stresses the immediacy of what we feel, the fact that we just 'find' it there and do not infer or derive it from anything else. By contrast, *Gefühl* stresses 'selfishness'. In ordinary German, *selbstisch*, like 'selfish', implies a deficiency of concern for others, motivation by self-interest, by one's own pleasure and profit. This connotation is, in Hegel's usage, suppressed, if not wholly excluded. *Selbstischkeit* refers to orientation towards oneself that contrasts not with orientation towards others, but with lacking a conception of oneself—and also of others.

Farrell gives a different account of the distinction: '*Fühlen* refers simply to the strength or weakness of the feeling, *empfinden* to one's capacity to react to or to be aware of stimuli, therefore to one's sensitiveness and powers of subtle discrimination, particularly *(a)* with regard to pain; *(b)* aesthetic experience. At times "to be sensitive to" is a more suitable English equivalent than "to feel"'(DGS, p. 123). But this is not wholly at odds with Hegel's account. The strength or weakness of a feeling depends on the *self* rather than on the stimuli to which it is sensitive.

3. In Enc. I, quality (§§86–98) involves three stages: being (§§86–8), 'determinate being' or *Dasein* (§§89–95), and being-for-self (§§96–8), which is closely connected to ideality (§§95–6). The soul determined 'wholly qualitatively'

corresponds to the stage of *Dasein*, where no distinction is drawn between an entity and its current quality. Cf. §§387, nn. 11, 12; 390, nn. 1, 2, and 4. Now the soul has distinguished itself from its quality or 'determinacy': it posits it as 'ideal' (*ideell*), not flatly identical with the soul itself, but only an aspect of it, and becomes 'for itself', i.e. the 'sentient [*empfindenden*] individual [*individuellen*] soul'. The soul is opposed to its 'substantiality', i.e. the level at which it is just qualitatively determined, and to 'itself' as qualitatively determined. In its sensations, i.e. its qualities, it gains not just single sensations but the 'feeling' (*Gefühl*) of itself, 'consciousness' of its totality, albeit a subjective consciousness: cf. §402, n. 5. The soul is no longer merely 'sentient', since *Empfindung* is tied to 'the individual' (*das Einzelne*), i.e. we sense this and that, not the whole. The soul is now divided or ruptured, involved in a 'contradiction' between, on the one hand, 'unfreedom', its lingering substantiality and naturalness, and, on the other, 'freedom', its burgeoning objective consciousness. This conflict is itself a sort of 'disease'. Much insanity is in fact a reversion to this primitive psychical level. Hence insanity should be considered in this context and will, in turn, shed light on this transitional state: see §408.

4. Here Hegel considers the extreme states between which the 'feeling' soul is intermediate: 'sensation' and 'consciousness'. Sensation, dealing only with the 'individual', etc., draws no distinction between the objective and the subjective. Hence the 'sentient soul' takes what is sensed to be its 'own concrete actuality', not anything distinct from itself. Consciousness, by contrast, confronts an ordered objective world, extending far beyond the fragments that we fleetingly sense. Thus consciousness achieves considerable 'independence' of the 'material of sensation', being aware, for example, of remote times and places. It does so by raising it to the 'form of universality', excluding the contingent and retaining the essential, transforming what is sensed into something 'represented'. What is 'represented' here hovers between an individual entity, such as Porky, and a general idea of e.g. a pig. I sense a shimmering pink patch and guess that it is a pig, though I do not see the whole pig, only enough to identify it as a pig. I omit the 'contingent', the particular shape and shade I see owing to my angle of vision, etc. I do not omit its pinkness, though pigs are not essentially, only usually, pink. I fill in the parts of the pig that I do not perceive, in their main outlines, but not all their detail, from my knowledge of the essential nature of a pig. Here I may go wrong, believing it to have four legs, when it has in fact only three. Perhaps there is no pig there; it is a pink rag or a trick of the light. I may take what I sense for a centaur, one of those 'representations' to which 'no actuality' corresponds. This transformation of sensation into representation is 'subjective', so open to error. However, the world I project by this subjective process is objective, a world 'outside' me about the contents of which I can be mistaken. But the 'interconnection of things' will usually enable me to correct my mistakes.

5. The feeling soul differs from sensation in that it feels or 'glimpses' itself as a whole, not just individual states or 'accidents' of itself. It differs from representational consciousness in that what it feels is not an objective world, which requires thought-mediated universality, but a conglomerate of subjectivity and objectivity

with the soul at its centre. This is the raw material that representational consciousness will turn into an objective world.

6. *We*, 'reflecting' (*reflektierende*) consciousness, distinguished in §401 external and
internal sensations, but the feeling and sentient souls cannot draw that distinction, since they are unaware of anything outside themselves. Unbeknown to itself,
the soul has 'ideality', is 'ideal', in the sense that it is internal and subjective, not
external and objective or real. In another sense of 'ideality' (cf. §§379, n. 3; 381,
n. 15; 386, n. 7), it is the 'ideality' or 'negativity' of its sensations. Each sensation 'seems' to be 'for itself', independent, and 'indifferent' to the others, but
the soul negates this independence, interconnects them, and submerges them in
itself. The soul and sensations are analogous to the objective world and objects
within it. The world is 'a concrete' (*ein Konkretes*, from the Latin *concrescere*,
'grow together') divided into distinct, but interrelated objects (pigs, trees, etc.).
Each of these objects is 'for itself', i.e. in its own right, a 'concrete', 'a complex'
(*ein Konvolut*, a bundle, something rolled together) of 'determinations' (pinkness,
snout, trotters, etc.). Similarly the soul is a 'totality' of 'distinct determinacies',
i.e. sensations. (Hegel rightly refrains from adding that each sensation is, like a
worldly object, itself a complex of determinations. The soul–world analogy does
not extend that far.) Since these determinacies all unite in the soul, the soul does
not split up into parts each corresponding to a sensation, but remains a unified
whole. It is 'infinite', i.e. self-contained, not limited or bounded by anything else.
It is 'being-for-self', independent and unified, not just a bundle of sensations.
The 'interior' of the soul is 'timeless', unchanging, while the sensations 'crowd
each other out'. Past sensations, now supplanted by others, remain in the soul,
'sublated' (*aufgehobene*: cf. §381, n. 13) and merely 'possible' or potential. A
sensation becomes 'actual' if it becomes 'for' the soul or the soul is 'for itself'
in the sensation, i.e. if the soul becomes aware of (itself in) the sensation. Past
sensations are thus preserved. This 'preservation' differs from 'recollection'. Preservation concerns only sensations conceived as states or accidents of the soul,
while recollection internalizes an external, intuited (i.e. perceived) object. This
caveat concerns 'recollection [*Erinnerung*] proper' or in the strict sense, which
Hegel takes to be the 'making internal', *Er-innerung*, of the recollected object:
cf. §401, n. 2. (This is etymologically incorrect. The idea is rather that of 'making oneself internal' to, getting inside, the recollected object.) On *Erinnerung*,
see §§452–4.

7. The soul, at this stage unbeknown to itself, is in the world or universe, in it at
a definite standpoint, and thus related to it in a definite way. These relations are
distinct from the residual content of past sensation, and need not figure in our
present sensation or 'representation', yet they constitute the content of the soul
and are not just an environment external to it. The world or its content has an
'infinite periphery', i.e. it is boundless, or possibly of indeterminate extent, but
with the individual soul at its centre. The soul that encapsulates this world is a
'soul of a world', an 'individually determined world-soul'. The 'world-soul', *Welt-
seele*, also appears in §§389 and 392. But in those passages the soul is not, as here,
an individual soul correlated to a unique perspective on the world. Hegel seems

to combine two ideas: (i) Leibniz's doctrine that a mind or monad mirrors the universe from a certain point of view: cf. §392, n. 6. (ii) A post-Enlightenment doctrine, associated with J. G. Herder and the Romantics, that people are not purely rational cosmopolitans, but essentially attached to a particular place and time, their homeland or *Heimat*, detachment from which can induce 'home-sickness' (*Heimweh*). People differ in their ability to endure transplantation or even homelessness, but even the 'strongest natures' need for their 'self-feeling' (*Selbstgefühl*) a portion of the world (or an 'individual world') that they can call their own. Without it the soul would lack 'actuality', a 'determinately distinct individuality [*Einzelheit*]'. (Here *einzel(heit)* and *individuell/-ität* seem to be used interchangeably: cf. §§394, n. 7; 400, n. 3.) A *Heimat*, a country, town, or village, differs from a Leibnizian perspective on the world in that it is usually occupied by more than one person. How then can it *individualize* a soul? A *Heimat* radiates outwards from a chair in which one usually sits, a family in which one has a unique position, a cottage in which they live. Rational egohood alone is not sufficient for individuality. As rational I's or egos people do not differ from each other: 'The rational is the high road where everyone travels, where no one is conspicuous' (PR, §15Z.) Attachment to one's *Heimat* lies at a deeper level than rationality or objective consciousness.

8. 'Natural differences' are here the differences between one individual and another depending on the difference of their 'individual world'. In the feeling soul there is as yet no other difference. Its world is within itself. Gradually, however, it divides itself, separates its world from itself, and counterposes it to its 'subjective' self. It does this, so that it or the 'mind' can be 'for' itself what it already is 'in itself'. In this process the mind as well as the world undergo a parallel change. The 'manifold . . . content of its individual world' becomes 'a simple entity', 'an abstract universal'. Correspondingly, the soul too becomes 'universal', 'the I that is for itself, etc.'. The I is freed from its worldly 'material', and can thus allow this material to subsist independently of itself. Now we can fill out our account of the soul's 'aim'. It aims not just to be for itself, consciously, what it is in itself, but to be adequate to its 'concept', viz. 'self-related, simple subjectivity'. Only such subjectivity can be conscious of objectivity.

Why does the soul, in becoming a conscious and self-conscious I, come into conformity with its concept? One idea is that the concept is rather like the programme of development embodied in, say, an acorn. The acorn is 'in itself or by its concept' an oak-tree. But since it is not yet actually (*für sich* in one of its senses: cf. §383, n. 1) an oak-tree, it does not yet correspond to its concept. Is a soul like an acorn? Is there any reason to suppose that its destiny is to become an I—apart from the empirical fact that human souls, unlike animal souls, tend to become I's? Hegel's idea is this. A mere feeling soul is burdened with its 'individual world'. Its world is extraneous to its concept. For one thing, while all (human) souls should share the same concept, each soul's individual world is different. Thus in shedding its individual world a soul becomes simply what it is, with no contingent, extraneous material. It thereby becomes 'universal', not different from other souls. It also becomes 'for itself' in another sense, self-aware or self-conscious. A soul that is wholly embedded in its individual world cannot be conscious of itself as distinct from this world.

Why is the world 'projected out of myself' (*aus mir herausgesetzten*) 'simple' and an 'abstract universal'? Soul–world symmetry requires this. Fundamental to Hegel's thought is the idea that world and self go in tandem, that there is a systematic correlation between the nature of the subject and the nature of its world. He owes this in part to Kant, and it differentiates him from, say, Descartes. The soul becomes simple and universal, so therefore must the world that is for the soul and somehow mirrors the soul. The world is simple in at least two ways. It is one and the same world for every soul or I, and it is unified by concepts and categories into a single orderly structure: or 'interconnection of things': cf. §402, n. 4. The world is universal: it is the same for all, not perspectivally differentiated. It is 'abstract', perhaps because its 'content' is no longer 'concrete', as it is in the soul, but expanded or unfolded, or perhaps because it is, like the I, 'for itself' or self-aware.

9. The three stages of elevation from the feeling soul to consciousness are: the 'feeling soul in its immediacy' (§§405–6), 'self-feeling [*Selbstgefühl*]' (§§407–8), and 'habit' (§§409–10).

The stages follow the pattern: immediate unity–division–restored unity: cf. §387, n. 14. Immediate unity is associated with universality; division with 'particularity' (*Besonderheit*), here qualified as 'individual' (*einzelnen*), perhaps because it occurs within an individual soul; and restored unity with 'individuality' (*Naturindividualität*): cf. §387, n. 16. At the third stage the soul habituates its body and thus acquires control of it. It casts or 'projects' from itself the 'content' that does not belong to its body to form the 'objective world'. For the anticipation of higher phases of mind in the description of lower ones, cf. §§380, nn. 1, 2; 398, nn. 1, 5.

NOTES TO §403

1. Ideality or subjectivity contrasts with substantiality: cf. §398, n. 7. What belongs to substantiality alone is merely in itself or 'implicit', not something that the soul is aware of. Since the 'feeling individual' (*fühlende Individuum*) is ideality, it has to realize its potentiality, to raise its substantiality to subjectivity and thus take control of itself. 'Formal' (*formelle*) is used loosely. Here it amounts to 'implicit' or 'in itself' (*an sich*). In §402, by contrast, 'formal' seems to contrast with '*an sich*' and to mean something like 'superficial': cf. §402, n. 1.

2. On ideality, cf. §379, n. 3. *Idealität* contrasts with *Realität*, and *ideell* with *reell*. (*Ideell* is, for Hegel, distinct from *ideal*, 'ideal' in the sense of 'perfect', but *Idealität* serves as the noun for both adjectives. By contrast, he uses *reell* and *real* interchangeably.) Something is *ideell* or *Idealität* if it 'negates' the 'real', that is, retains it 'virtually' (*virtualiter*, here equivalent to *an sich*), but suppresses it, so that it does not 'exist'. (Elsewhere, but not here, Hegel uses *aufheben*, 'sublate', for this preserving suppression: cf. §381, n. 13.) Hegel uses 'exist(ence)' (*existieren*, *Existenz*) in the sense of 'to come forth, to have/having come forth', relying on

the literal meaning of its Latin ancestor, *ex(s)istere*, 'to step forth, etc': cf. Enc. I,
§123. The sensations, representations, etc. 'stored up' (*aufbewahrt*, cf. §402, n. 6)
in the featureless 'cavern' or mine of the I are the 'real' that is suppressed and preserved. At this stage the soul is not yet an I nor a consciousness, but a unity which
underlies the consciousness that later emerges from it.

The passage raises a problem. When Hegel said that the soul has to raise its
substantiality to subjectivity, did he mean that it has to suppress and preserve its
sensations, etc. or that it has to become explicitly aware of sensations, etc. that are
so far suppressed and preserved? The former seems more plausible, since ideality
is the 'negation' of the real, not awareness of it, and the soul is supposed to take
possession of *itself*, not of its sensations, etc. It is its suppression of sensations,
rather than its recalling them to awareness, that unifies the soul.

3. Hegel here rejects the view, essentially the Cartesian view, that the soul is an
intrinsically non-bodily thing conjoined with a material body quite different in
nature from itself. Consciousness and the intellect regard the body as material,
extended, and divisible, and as 'outside the soul'. 'Consciousness' sees the body
in this way, because it views the body from the outside, just as it views other objects from the outside. 'Intellect' agrees, since it draws a sharp distinction
between body and soul, just as it draws sharp distinctions between other entities
and concepts. But the feeling soul views the body differently. It contains a 'bodiliness', which involves no plurality of separate parts. This unitary bodiliness is
compatible with the material body, just as the unitary ego is compatible with the
multiplicity of its 'representations'. As the feeling soul suppresses and preserves
its sensations, etc., so it suppresses and preserves the various parts of the material body. To have sensations the soul needs the material body, through which it
is 'immediately determined'. But the material body does not count for the soul
as 'anything real', or as a 'barrier' confining its activity. Similarly, the material
body does not count as real for 'the concept'. The soul is 'the existent concept',
i.e. the concept stepping forth or actualized. The soul is like a unitary code or plan
determining the growth and structure of its bodily realization. It is thus the 'existence of the speculative' (*die Existenz des Spekulativen*). Unlike the intellect, with
its cut-and-dried distinctions, speculation discerns the unity of things in their
opposition: cf. §378, n. 5 and Enc. I, §82. Analogously, the soul does this in
reality, not simply in thought. It joins together with what is apparently opposed
to itself, namely the material body. Since this body is not a barrier for the soul, the
soul is in the body as an 'omnipresent unity'. Every part of the body is animated
by the soul, but the soul itself does not consist of parts, each occupying a part of
the body. The amputation of a left arm does not entail the amputation of a part of
the soul; the severed arm simply loses its vitality. For 'representation' (*Vorstellung*)
the 'body' (*Leib*) is a single 'representation' (*Vorstellung*) and has attained to one
'determinate concept'. We do not see or conceive the body, even when we view it
from the outside, as a conglomerate but as a single entity. Similarly, 'bodiliness'
(*Leiblichkeit*) is reduced in the feeling soul (which does not have representations
or concepts) to 'ideality', i.e. to a unity in which the 'natural multiplicity' of bodiliness is overcome. (It is because the feeling soul *idealizes* bodiliness in this way

that we are able to *represent* the material body as a unity.) 'In itself' the soul is the whole of nature. The individual soul is a 'monad', which, as Leibniz says, mirrors the world from a certain point of view. (On monads, cf. §§388, n. 11; 402, n. 7.) The soul receives sensations from what it will later come to regard as the external world by way of its body. The body receives sensations, however faint and suppressed, from the whole of nature, however remote. But it receives them always in a certain position and from a certain point of view. Hence the world it contains is its own 'particular' world. At this stage the soul does not yet distinguish its own body from the rest of nature. Hence Hegel speaks of the *Leib*, 'body', only once in this paragraph—when the body is an object of 'representation', a faculty that the feeling soul does not yet possess. Elsewhere he prefers *Leiblichkeit*, 'bodiliness', and *das Leibliche*, 'the bodily', because the unity of the body, implied by *Leib*, is under consideration, not presupposed.

Enc. I, §34Z. makes Hegel's point in a simpler way: 'In philosophy at present we hear little of the soul: the favourite term now is mind [*Geist*]. The two are distinct, soul being as it were the middle term between body and mind, or the bond between the two. The mind, as soul, is immersed in bodiliness, and the soul is the animating principle of the body.' The view that Hegel is criticizing operates with only two terms, 'body' and 'mind', or 'body' and 'soul', where the soul is more or less equated with the mind, and conceived as an incorporeal intellectual principle. Hegel insists that we need three terms: 'body', the 'soul' that animates the body, making it a single living body, and the more intellectual 'mind'. The soul–mind distinction then comes close to, though it does not exactly coincide with, Aristotle's distinction between *psuche* ('soul') and *nous* ('intellect'): cf. §378, n. 3. When it has been idealized and unified by the soul, the body is not starkly opposed to the mind, but is fit to accommodate it.

NOTES TO §404

1. The 'difference' between the soul and what is other than itself is a distinction drawn by the soul itself 'within itself': §398, n. 2. Hence it is 'exclusive': it expels or extrudes material from itself to become its object. This exclusivity is connected with the soul's individuality: it sustains its individuality by expelling what makes it one with the world rather than 'individual' (*individuell*). The differentiation is a 'judgement', *Urteil*, which Hegel interprets as an 'original' [*ur-*] division [*teil*]': cf. §389, n. 4. At first the distinction was between the subject (the soul) and its object, though not yet an 'external object'. Now that the distinction is a 'judgment' it is also a distinction between the subject (the soul) and its predicate (the soul's 'substance': cf. §§394, n. 4; 397; 398 nn. 2, 3). In its 'natural life' (*Naturleben(s)*), which is associated with sleep (cf. §398, nn. 1, 7), the soul is not *individuell*, since there is no object opposed to it. It becomes individual when it becomes 'sensation-packed': cf. §402, n. 3. The soul's substance is now the 'content' of this individual sentient soul, not just that of its 'natural life'. This content is excluded from the soul as its object and its 'predicate'. The soul (or, less plausibly, the substance: *sie*) is not only individual; it is also 'particular':

cf. §§378, n. 10; 402, n. 7. Hence the content is the 'particular world' that the subject implicitly carries with it: cf. §403, n. 3. This 'particular' world is the same as the 'individual' world discussed in §402, nn. 7 and 8.

2. *Form* and *formell* are used unclearly, if not ambiguously. That 'this stage of mind' is 'altogether formal' might mean: (i) it is just a form with no content of which it is conscious; (ii) it has no *specific* content of its own: it has *some* content, but there are no restrictions on the content that it can take; or (iii) it does not occur in isolation as a state of a soul, but only as an element in more complex mental conditions. To be 'formal' is not the same as becoming a 'form'. When the feeling soul 'becomes a form' (*als Form ist*), it occurs as a distinct mental condition, not just an element in a more complex condition. It is a 'state' (*Zustand*) of its own, not an aspect of some other state. Hegel does not mean, however, that the feeling soul occurs *unadulterated* in, say, the infant or embryo (cf. §405), or in adults who have relapsed into a totally infantile condition. He means that a person who has advanced to a 'more genuine form [*Form*] of mind', in particular that of intellectual consciousness, may retain the *content* appropriate to the higher form, but present this content in the 'more subordinate and abstract' *form* of mind, i.e. the feeling soul. Then there is a 'discrepancy' between the content and the form which amounts to a disease. 'Consciousness and intellect' are, unlike feeling soul, a healthy form of mind, not simply 'formal'. Although they are superimposed on feeling soul and do not dispense with it altogether, they usually keep it in its proper, subordinate place.

NOTES TO §405

1. On monads and monadicity, see §389, n. 11. A monad (from the Greek *monas*, a 'unit') is (according to Leibniz) a mind, a unitary mind, and every mind 'perceives'. But only some minds 'apperceive', are self-consciously aware of things. Mere 'perception' is below the threshold of awareness. Hegel avoids the term 'apperception' (except when speaking of Leibniz, Kant, etc.) in favour of *Selbstbewusstsein*, 'self-consciousness'. The 'feeling individuality' is not 'reflected into itself' and is thus 'immediate' rather than mediated by such reflection. Hegel does not explain why it necessarily has a 'selfish' (*selbstische*, with the flavour of egocentricity: cf. §402, n. 2) individuality at all. But given that it has one, this must be located in a different subject, even 'another individual', primarily its mother. 'Predicate' usually contrasts with 'substance' as well as with 'subject'. But the embryo is a substance, a passive object of influence, not an active 'subject'. It is a predicate, and again not a subject, since it depends wholly on its mother, the real subject. A *Genius* is a protective spirit. The word derives from the Latin *gignere*, 'to generate, procreate'. Hence in Roman mythology a genius presides over one's procreation and birth and then accompanies one throughout one's whole life as a tutelary deity. It is quite distinct from the 'genius' or special mental endowment (*Genie*) discussed in §395Z.

2. That the genius is the 'totality of reality, etc.' as 'activity', not just 'possibility', suggests that the feeling soul is the seat of reality, etc. as *potentiality*, which is

then activated by the genius. Hegel is here thinking not only of mother and embryo, but also of the feeling soul and genius as components of a single adult: cf. §405, n. 5.

3. On 'judgement' as original (*ur-*) division, see §§388, n. 1; 389, n. 4. Monocotyledons are a family of flowering plant with a single 'cotyledon', seed leaf in their embryo.

4. On 'magnetic' phenomena, see §379, n. 3

5. The feeling soul has, as an embryo, its controlling genius in its mother. But it is 'destined' (*bestimmt*) to develop so that it provides its own 'rational, etc.' controlling genius in 'one and the same individuality'. By now, however, the 'life of feeling' (*Gefühlsleben*, no longer the 'feeling soul', since it has its own internal controller) has become so 'determinate', containing its whole 'character', that the roles are reversed. The 'being of feeling' (*Gefühlsseins*) is the genius, which has the 'final determination', the last word, in the 'show' of 'mediations, etc.' The overall course of our life is determined by our *Gefühlsleben*. Reason provides a justification for what we do and works out the details. But the justifications are rarely conclusive and feeling has the casting vote.

   This is connected with 'heart' or 'breast'. 'Breast' translates *Gemüt*, which denotes the 'seat of certain types of feelings, particularly those which embrace the world and its objects with warmth and affection. . . . English lacks an equivalent term and resorts to approximations such as "soul", "heart", "disposition"' (DGS, pp. 217–18). (I have usually translated it as 'heart', but this was not possible here, where Hegel explicitly mentions the 'heart'.) Everyone has a *Gemüt*, but not everyone indulges it to the same extent. Thus people are 'heartless', deficient in *Gemüt*, when they pursue their ends with cool, or cold, rationality. They are 'good-hearted' (*gemütlich*), if they put their heart and soul into what they do. This 'good nature' (*Gemütlichkeit*) is not itself the genius, but indulgence of it, since even the 'heartless' have a genius. The Latin phrase *indulgere genio* occurs in the comic dramatist Plautus, in the sense of 'to indulge one's spirit of enjoyment, to enjoy oneself, let one's hair down'.

6. The end of the *Zusatz* to §402 refers to the soul's 'dreaming away' and 'intimation' (*Ahnen*) of its 'concrete natural life', the first of three stages of feeling soul: cf. §402, n. 9. *Ahnen*, 'to presage, suspect, etc.', suggests dim awareness rather than explicit consciousness. It need not imply foretelling or foreboding, but Hegel also has this in mind: cf. §390, n. 5.

7. 'Absolute' magic would be magic that is wholly immediate or direct, with no mediation or intervention whatsoever. This would be the magic 'of the mind as such', of the mind without the involvement of anything else. The magical influence of one mind on another is not for the most part 'absolute'. It involves mediation as well as immediacy: thought, language, etc. The influence of adults on children is 'predominantly' but not wholly immediate. In Shakespeare's *King Lear*, the Earl of Kent refuses to accept the banishment Lear has imposed on him and continues to accompany him in disguise. 'Does thou know me fellow?' asks Lear. Kent replies: 'No sir, but you have that in your countenance, which I would fain call master' (Act I, Scene 4). The queen of France referred to was

Catherine de' Medici, the wife of Henri II. (I owe this information to Dr Peter
Carey of Trinity College, Oxford.)

 8. Hegel now turns to the mind's magical influence on 'objects'. His attitude to
    what is commonly called 'magic', the mind's more or less 'immediate' influ-
    ence on natural objects, is clearly sceptical. The mind's ability to move its own
    body fits the general definition of magic, the unmediated influence of a mind
    on something else, as well as does what is commonly called 'magic', or even
    better, since it involves no words, chants, or spells. So does man's influence
    on animals, since it works by a mere 'gaze'. But even these types of magic
    are not said to be entirely devoid of mediation. In general, Hegel is reluct-
    ant to admit that anything is wholly and exclusively immediate: cf. Enc. I,
    §§66–74.

 9. The view that early man had scientific knowledge is attributed in PH, pp. 57–8,
    to Friedrich von Schlegel, who said: 'Nature ... like a clear mirror of God's
    creation, had originally lain revealed and transparent to the unclouded eye
    of man' (*The Philosophy of History in a Course of Lectures* (1828), trans. J.
    B. Robertson (London: Bohn 1846), 91). The myth of the fall is discussed
    at PH, p. 57 and in Enc. I, §24 Addition(3). God forbids Adam to eat the
    fruit of the tree of knowledge of good and evil (Genesis 2: 9, 17). He eats
    the fruit and is then expelled from Eden. Knowledge, Hegel infers, is not our
    primeval condition but the result of our fall, which he interprets as a circuitous
    ascent. Hegel knew nothing of Babylonian astronomy, which was at its height
    when Greek astronomy was just beginning. The Babylonians made careful
    observations, but did not (like the Greeks) produce theories. The best known
    Babylonian astronomer is Kiddinu (in Strabo's *Geography*) or Kidenas (in Pliny's
    Natural History). He was born *c.*340 BC and worked out the precession of the
    equinoxes: cf. §392, n. 8. The 'mysteries' were associated with Greek cults
    devoted to the gods of the underworld, primarily those established at Eleusis
    from about the seventh century BC and later incorporated in Athenian state
    religion. They are discussed in a similar way in PH, pp. 247–8.

10. This Addition, like §405, deals only with 'the formal [formelle] subjectivity of
    life'. The second, oppositional, and hence pathological, form of magic is the
    subject of §406.

11. 'Impressions' (*Affektionen*) are more or less equivalent to 'sensations' (*Empfind-
    ungen*): cf. §402, n. 1. As 'individualized' (*vereinzelten*) they are contrasted with
    the 'feeling' (*Gefühle*) of the soul's 'whole individual nature'. But Hegel does not
    consistently distinguish *fühlen* from *empfinden* in this respect, since he says that
    the soul's 'individual totality' is 'sensed' (*Empfundenwerden*).

12. The undivided 'soul–unity' (*Seeleneinheit*) of two individuals, one of them an
    'actual self', the other having a '*formal* [ie.potential] being-for-self', is a mystery
    to the 'intellect', but not to genuine philosophy.

13. 'Fate' translates *Schicksal*, 'destiny' *Verhängnis*, which today means 'doom' or
    'unhappy fate', but is here used in a neutral sense more or less equivalent to that
    of *Schicksal*. General principles and objective circumstances never fully determ-
    ine what a given individual does or how he fares. Reason or 'grounds' are given

for one's actions, but one's genius determines what one sees as good reasons: cf. §405, n. 5.

1. This is an account of the second phase of feeling soul, promised in §405Z: cf. §405, n. 10. 'Magnetic somnambulism' is sleepwalking induced by mesmerism: cf. §379, n. 3. When the subject wakes up he has no memory of the events that occurred in the trance. A follower of Mesmer, the Marquis de Puységur, is said to have given the first account of such post-hypnotic amnesia: cf. §406, n. 24.

2. Hegel raises two problems: (1) Is the 'determination' or definition of magnetic somnambulism given in the Paragraph correct? Does it fit the reported 'experiences'? This problem is not fully resolved, but is at least considered in the rest of the Remark and in the Addition, in which he attempts to bring the phenomena 'under their universal points of view', i.e. to describe their general features. (2) Does magnetic somnambulism really occur? Hegel says no more about this problem, but assumes that the number and authority of the reports establish its occurrence beyond reasonable doubt. Sceptics are in thrall to the 'intellect' and its rigid 'categories': cf. §378, nn. 1, 4, 7.

3. On the 'individually determined world', cf. §402, n. 7. On this sense of 'genius', cf. §405, n. 5.

4. The non-somnambulist is aware, in a rational, self-conscious way, of the world in which the somnambulist is wholly and unreflectively absorbed. This world is seen as intelligibly ordered, and distinct from, though connected to, oneself and one's 'subjective ideas [*Vorstellungen*] and plans': cf. §398, esp. n. 5, on the world of waking consciousness. Hegel refers to Marcus Porcius Cato Uticensis (95–45 BC), a Stoic hostile to Julius Caesar. He killed himself at Utica after the battle of Thapsus. In PH, p. 311, he is quoted as saying: 'To hell with his [Caesar's] virtues; they have ruined my country!'

5. On the state of mind here described cf. §379, n. 3. A person in this state is at some level aware of the world inhabited by the normal person, but bereft of its normal intelligible structure. The somnambulist, because he has been an adult consciousness, does not simply revert to the condition of the embryo. He retains 'the formality' (*das Formelle*) of being-for-self. But he draws no distinction between himself and the world, between the subjective and the objective. Hence he is a self-enclosed 'monad', aware only of its own 'actuality': cf. §402, n. 7. He discerns none of the usual rational interconnexions of things. Hence what we know only by inference and conjecture, the somnambulist knows directly. 'Clairvoyance' (*Hellsehen*) is the ability to acquire information that is not at the time known to anyone else and is not accessible to the senses as we know them. We ordinarily learn of, say, a distant earthquake from the howling of dogs or later reports. But a clairvoyant might know of it directly. How can he do that if we cannot perceive the tremors and if his world is the same as ours, except that it is compressed into uniform subjectivity? It is presumably because he, like

animals, senses stimuli that are below the threshold of our conscious awareness: cf. §§380, n. 2; §401Z.

6. Hegel's citations from *Timaeus* 71d ff. are not accurate quotations, even when they appear in quotation marks, but summaries. 'Sobriety' translates *den Besonnenen*, which in turn translates Plato's *sôphroni*: cf. §377, n. 2.

7. The 'somnambulist' is not here a sleepwalker in particular, but anyone in a hypnotic, or quasi-hypnotic, state. (Hegel often uses *Somnambulismus* in a general way, while *Schlafwandeln* applies specifically to 'sleepwalking'.) 'Genius' is used in two senses. In its first occurrence it denotes the conscious, self-aware person, the 'magnetizer' or hypnotist, comparable to the pregnant woman (in contrast to the embryo) in §405. But the two 'genii' with which the somnambulist is in 'relationship' are the deep feeling-lives of the somnambulist and the magnetizer. On this ambiguity, see §405, n. 5. Hegel takes the 'substantial identity' established between the two souls as evidence for the immateriality of the soul. The argument is this: the souls merge into one; their respective bodies remain distinct; so the soul is distinct from its body. It is not clear, however, why the relationship between somnambulist and magnetizer need differ significantly from the relationship between a computer and its operator. Hegel also conflates two arguments against the reliability and/or extraordinariness of the somnambulist's pronouncements: (1) It is unclear whether the pronouncements stem from the somnambulist or the magnetizer. (2) The pronouncements vary according to the culture of the somnambulist. This would cast doubt on the authority and extraordinariness of the pronouncements even if no magnetizer were involved. One way of approaching problem (1) might be to see what happens if the somnambulist and the magnetizer are of different cultures.

8. In 'feeling substantiality' barriers come down and oppositions are abolished. There is no 'contrast' between oneself and the external world. The usual contrast between different senses also disappears. The senses are normally allocated to distinct sense-organs; we see with our eyes, not with our ears or our fingers, etc. But the sense-organs are now in abeyance, and their role is assumed by the 'common feeling' (*Gemeingefühl*), which uses various unusual parts of the body for this purpose. The 'common feeling' is a descendant of the 'common sense organ of all the sense-organs' postulated by Aristotle (*On Youth and Old Age, On Life and Death*, 467^{b}27–8, 469^{a}12; *On Sleep and Waking*, 455^{a}15 ff. Cf *de anima*, III. 1, 425^{a}13 ff.), which unites and coordinates the perceptions of the special senses. Aristotle locates it in the heart. It is especially associated with the sense of touch or feeling, since this sense is presupposed by the other senses (*On Sleep and Waking*, 455^{a}23; *de anima*, III. 13, 435^{a}12 ff.). Hence Hegel can appropriately refer to it as the common 'feeling', though the *Zusatz* calls it the 'common sense': cf. §406, n. 13.

9. 'Comprehend' is *begreifen*, the parent verb of *Begriff*, 'concept, notion': §378, n. 4. *Begreifen* means tracing the connexions between one phenomenon and another, but only for 'intellectual reflexion' (*die verständige Reflexion*), not necessarily for speculative reason. On the 'intellect', see §378, n. 1. On *Reflexion*, see §§384, n. 2; 389, nn. 9, 12. This account of comprehension bears on

somnambulism in two respects. (1) The somnambulist cannot 'comprehend' anything, since for him no phenomenon, e.g. rain, is related to another, e.g. clouds, by a series of 'mediations'. (2) We non-somnambulists cannot comprehend the somnambulist, since he is not related to anything else by mediations. The external world and everything in it is available to him *immediately* and *directly*.

It might be objected that it is only from his own point of view that the somnambulist is related immediately to everything to which he is related. For the somnambulist the magnetizer is a part of himself, not something related to him. But *we* can see that the magnetizer is distinct from the somnambulist, causally affecting him by his words and gestures. Why can *we* not 'comprehend' the somnambulist from outside, in terms of his ('intellectual') relationship to the magnetizer? Because, Hegel implicitly replies, the 'laws and relationships of the intellect', 'relationships of finitude', i.e. external relations between things that are distinct from each other and therefore bounded or finite, cannot do what we require of them. Entities distinct from and outside the somnambulist cannot explain how he is immediately aware of all of them. To comprehend the somnambulist we must abandon the assumption that such things—personalities, the objective world—really are quite distinct from and independent of him. This type of comprehending will then be quite different from the comprehending of 'intellectual reflexion'. Cf. §406, n. 18.

10. On magic, see §405, nn. 7, 8, and on the distinction between 'formal' subjectivity and what is now called 'real' subjectivity, see §405, n. 10. In formal subjectivity, only the 'soulful' side (*das Seelenhafte*) is involved, while the 'mind' is that of another individual (the mother) if it is in play at all. In real subjectivity, both the soul and the mind are initially in play, but the soul supplants the mind. The healthy mind projects material from itself into the external world and then 'sublates' (i.e. abolishes *and* preserves) its externality, thus establishing a 'relationship' between itself and an objective world distinct from itself. When the soul takes control, the distinction between mind and world is obliterated, and so too is the relationship between them. Everything goes into one melting-pot. On physical disease, see Enc. II, §§371–4.

11. The separation of the soul and the mind is a general or 'universal' condition which appears in various forms, such as 'catalepsy' (or 'catatonic schizophrenia', in which the patient remains immobile for long periods), St Vitus's dance (a disorder involving convulsive movements) and experiences associated with the approach of death, e.g. 'out of body experiences'. On animal magnetism, see §379, n. 3. The Cévennes are a range of mountains in southern France. The 'war of the Cévennes' was an armed uprising in the early eighteenth century in the Bas-Languedoc and Cevennes regions in response to Louis XIV's persecution of Protestants following his revocation in 1685 of the Edict of Nantes, which had guaranteed Protestants' religious and civil liberties.

12. Carlo Amoretti (1741–1816), an Italian scholar, is mentioned by Hegel only here.

13. In this paragraph the 'common sense' is *Gemeinsinn*, not, as in the Remark, *Gemeingefühl:* cf. §406, n. 8. Hegel uses the expression in its original meaning

of a central reserve into which the five senses pool their contributions so that the unification of their results can give rise to coherent perception. The expression stems from Aristotle's *de anima*, the idea goes back to Plato's *Theaetetus*, 184–6.

14. Christoph Friedrich Nicolai (1733–1811) was a writer, a champion of the Enlightenment and an opponent of Romanticism.

15. The reference is to §389, and perhaps also to §403, which discussed the relationship of the feeling soul to the body. Here Hegel makes the more ambitious claim that the soul pervades not only its body but everything. If it pervaded only its body, it might still exist only in a definite individual, and this would not be sufficient to account for its awareness of remote events, etc. Moreover, there is, in some sense, only one soul, and this too is required to account for such 'somnambulistic' phenomena as the rapport between the magnetizer and his patient. However, Hegel's model for the all-pervading universal soul seems to be the relation of an individual soul to its body. My left arm is distinct from my right foot, but pervaded by a single soul they belong to a single, unitary body. My body is 'other' than my soul, but the soul 'overarches' (see §389, n. 16) the body, animating it, controlling its movements, and feeling simultaneous pains, say, in my left arm and my right foot. In a not wholly dissimilar way the somnambulist 'feels' the ocurrence of far-off events. I too would feel them, if only I did not establish the distinction between the subjective and the objective, myself and the world. On the soul as 'the entirely universal', see §406, nn. 16 and 18.

16. The soul as such is 'entirely universal' (*das ganz Allgemeine*). It therefore involves the two other 'moments' or phases of the 'concept', 'particularity' and 'individuality'. First, then, it involves 'determinations' or 'particularizations' such as love of friends. Love of friends is not universal in the way that the soul as such is, since it it only one determination or particularization of the soul, distinct from others, such as love of parents. But such determinations are still 'universal', indefinite in their content and capable of exemplification by several individuals. The final step is to assign love of friends to a definite individual. Then it is 'this' person's love of 'these' friends, etc. (Hegel rashly assumes that the individualization of love entails the individualization of its object. Love of parents is normally love of one's own definite parents; love of women may be love of no definite women, but of women in general.)

These 'individualized' determinations 'constitute my actuality' and are not 'left to my discretion'. Even the fact that I am sitting here is 'exempt from the wilfulness of my representation [*Vorstellens*]'. Can I not choose my friends or where to sit? Or imagine sitting somewhere else or having different friends? Hegel seems to have three points in mind: (1) As he argues in §406 (ββ), 'threads' connecting me to the external world make me what I am. This applies, however, only to certain special relatives, friends, etc., and to broad features of my world—such as the fact that it is the Roman republic, not to such matters as the precise place at which I am sitting. (2) These determinations are linked together in a 'chain' in such a way that if any one were different, all the others would be different. Thus if I were not now sitting here, then I would not have the friends that I do, etc. Hence I cannot coherently suppose or imagine that I am not sitting here, without supposing or imagining a radical change in my individual world, the world that makes me what I am. (3) We are here concerned with 'feeling'. I can suppose or imagine that I am somewhere else, I can choose my friends and where to sit. But these capacities presuppose a higher level of mind than that of feeling, the detachment of myself as an I or ego from my surroundings and my relationships. I cannot do these things merely as a feeling soul. Even when I become a self-conscious ego, establishing an 'opposition of the subjective and objective'and 'sublating' it as I get to know more about the world, the level of feeling still persists. Some changes in my world induce malaise in me—the disintegration of my favourite chair perhaps, though not usually a change in its position.

17. Edward Young (1683–1765), *The complaint, or Night-thoughts on life, death, & immortality* (1742).

18. Space and time are 'forms of asunderness' (*Formen des Aussereinander*) in that they separate one thing from another. London and Oxford are in a different places and, since they are not adjacent, they are separated by a spatial interval. I can see things happening at some distance from myself, but if I am in Oxford I cannot know about small-scale events so far away as London, unless I 'sublate the distance' by a mediation, e.g. a newspaper or, almost simultaneously, by television. The 'clairvoyant [*schauende*] soul' does not need to do this. It can be immediately aware of a remote event. This is possible because space, the medium that separates a normal person from remote events, pertains to 'external nature', not to the soul. Hegel leaves unclear the sense in which his claim, that space does not pertain to the soul, is to be understood. When I feel, or otherwise apprehend, something at a distance, it is, in a manner of speaking, no longer at a distance but in me. Again, I am immediately aware of the position of my left foot and of a pain in it. As far as my soul extends, its awareness is 'immediate'. This may help to explain what such clairvoyance is like. But how does it explain the extension of its immediate awareness beyond the confines of my body to remote places? My soul may have no specific location in my body, but it is located where my body is. How can it, if I am in Oxford, 'feel' events in London? Hegel's implied answer is that 'the soul' is universal in a more substantial sense than that in which, say, redness is universal. There is, first, universal redness. Then there are specific or 'particular' shades of red. Finally there are individual red things. Universal redness does not exist apart from individual red things. But universal soul does exist apart from individual souls. Souls are made individual, in the case of humans at least, by 'free intellectual consciousness'. Two individualized souls, one in Oxford, the other in London, are separated by the spatial interval. But if one of them 'sinks to the form of the merely feeling soul', the barriers are down and it enters the network of the 'all-pervading' universal soul. It can now feel events both in Oxford and in London, and perhaps read the mind of the other soul, even if the other soul is still restricted by intellectual consciousness.

This theory is so bizarre that one hesitates to attribute it to Hegel. Nevertheless, this, or something like it, is what he seems to propose. Moreover, if we accept the authenticity of the phenomena in question, this theory is a reasonable, if not inevitable, way of explaining them. In §380 Hegel implies a different explanation: that people who sink from 'intellectual consciousness' to the feeling soul are sensitive to stimuli which we usually overlook: cf. §380, n. 1; 406, n. 6. This account would not require a substantial universal soul, only an acute, if normally latent, sensitivity of individual souls. It is, however, easy enough to doubt the authenticity of the phenomena. In particular, Hegel tends to stress the successes of supposed clairvoyants and to ignore their failures, and neglects the question whether their success-rate is statistically significant.

19. Apart from recovery of buried past knowledge, Hegel discusses three types of knowledge that transcend time. (1) Perceptual acquaintance with a future event comparable in vivacity to our preception of present events. This would make life impossibly boring. It also cannot occur. A future event is 'merely in itself', while only what 'exists' can be properly perceived. (2) 'Cognition' of the 'eternal' or of 'truths of reason'. These presumably include not only philosophical and mathematical truths, but also general truths about e.g. astronomy that enable us to predict future events. Such cognition occurs, but not in the 'magnetic state'. (3) The clairvoyant's 'conditioned' (i.e. limited to personal affairs) and hazy awareness of future events. This too, Hegel believes, occurs, especially in less than fully civilized, but not primitive, cultures such as prevailed in the Scottish Highlands. (For a sympathetic, not to say credulous, account of 'second sight', see Dr Samuel Johnson's *Journey to the Western Islands of Scotland*.)

One difficulty with (3) is this. The clairvoyant is elevated above time. This is why he can see future events. But how then can we or he tell that the vision refers to a future event rather than a past event or a spatially remote present event? One answer might be that the vision has no temporal index, that from its intrinsic character we cannot tell whether it refers to a future event or not. But we can search our memories and records to see whether such an event has occurred in the past, and wait to see whether it happens in the future. (John William Dunne in *An Experiment With Time* (1927) and *The Serial Universe* (1934) describes his attempts to assess the predictive power of his dreams in such ways as this.) Hegel believes, however, that the clairvoyant's visions have a flavour of futurity, an intrinsic quality that points to, but does not explicitly indicate, its future occurrence. This is possible, since in the 'concentrated state' of the clairvoyant the 'determinations of space and time are also contained', albeit 'under a veil'. But these confer on the experience only a certain temporal 'quality', not a 'quantum'. That is, no definite date or period of time is attached to the vision. The distance in the future to which it refers must be inferred from the 'intensity' of the vision, in the way in which we can infer from the intensity of a fever how long it will last. The clairvoyant is able to make such an inference and to state the time of the event in terms intelligible to 'waking consciousness', because he is 'a representer' (*ein Vorstellendes*) as well as an intuitive feeler. The fallibility of clairvoyants depends on their interpretation of the vision rather than on the vision itself.

20. On Mesmer and his procedures, see §379, n. 3. The name 'animal magnetism' derives from Mesmer's use of a single magnet. In 'inorganic magnetism' two

distinct 'existences', i.e. magnets, are immediately attracted to each other. In 'animal magnetism' two distinct 'animals' (including human beings) are immediately attracted to each other. Since the patient and the hypnotist are immediately attracted, or at least related, to each other, the state is still called 'animal magnetism', despite the disuse of an actual magnet. *Solarismus* relates the phenomenon to the sun, *Tellurismus* relates it to the earth, especially since the earth is magnetized. On the sun, see §392, n. 7. On the earth, see §392, n. 2.

21. This account of illness is expounded more fully in the first paragraph of this *Zusatz*: cf. §406, n. 10. Physical illness shows the 'finitude' of the organism, i.e. its vulnerability to external forces and its ultimate mortality. Mental disease, even if the 'rupture' between mind and soul occurs spontaneously, similarly exposes the subject to an 'alien power', not only the events and objects to which the somnambulist is sensitive, but also and primarily the hypnotist, who can manipulate the subject as he will, since the subject's 'intellectual consciousness' and therefore his 'freedom' to resist are in abeyance. This rupture between mind and soul is latent in everyone. Hence the states that arise spontaneously can also be artificially induced by an 'alien power'. Sometimes this is a power of the same type as that to which a spontaneous somnambulist can be subjected, such as a hypnotist. But sometimes it is a power of a different sort, such as 'henbane', a poisonous and narcotic plant. The subject then becomes, though often only temporarily, an 'epopt [Epopt(en)]'. The Greek word *epoptês*, originally a 'seer' or 'overseer', was used for an advanced initiate in the Eleusinian mysteries (cf. §405, n. 9); for Hegel it is a 'visionary'. 'Baquet' is, in French, a 'tub' or 'bucket'.

   Hegel's general account of mental illness perhaps explains the hypnotism of humans, but it does not explain the hypnotism of animals. If an animal has only a soul and no mind, how could its hypnotized state differ from its normal state?

22. PH, pp. 171–2 and LPR i. 296 discuss the Mongolian Shamans. At Delphi in Phocis, at the foot of Mt Parnassus, was an oracle of Apollo, mentioned in PH, p. 236. The priests who interpreted the utterances of the priestess were not themselves in a trance. A sober awareness (or 'intuition') of the realities of Greek life guided their interpretations.

23. Luigi Galvani (1737–98), an Italian anatomist, observed that the legs of a dead frog twitch when they come into contact with two different metals, e.g. iron and brass. He supposed that the electricity came from the frog muscles, but Count Alessandro Volta (1745–1827) showed that it came from the metals alone, that two metals in contact set up an electric current ('galvanism'). Hegel compares the contact of patient and magnetizer to the 'immediate' contact of two metals. Galvanism is discussed in Enc. II, §330.

24. Armand Marie Jacques Puységur (1751–1825) was a follower of Mesmer: cf. §406, n. 1. Karl Alexander Ferdinand Kluge (1782–1844) published *Versuch einer Darstellung des animalischen Magnetismus als Heilmittel* (An Attempt to Expound Animal Magnetism as a Cure) in 1811. Pierre Gabriel van Ghert (1782–1852) was a Dutch politician and a friend of Hegel. Karl Eberhard von Schelling (1783–1854) was a senior medical officer of health and the brother of Friedrich Wilhelm Joseph von Schelling.

25. On sleep, cf. §398. On the *Repoduktionssystem*, §401, n. 23; it is primarily concerned with the self-maintenance of the organism rather than with breeding, but
it seems here to include sexuality. Jan Baptista van Helmont (1577–1644), a
Flemish physician and alchemist heavily influenced by Paracelsus (1493–1541),
coined the word 'gas' from the Greek *chaos*, and is sometimes called the 'father of
biochemistry' for his experiments on the growth of plants.

26. On the 'individual world', cf. §402, n. 7. A fully fledged magnetic experience
has the following stages: (1) Intellectual consciousness; (2) Sleep; (3) Clairvoyance; (4) Interpretation of the clairvoyant's visions by the clairvoyant and/or the
magnetizer; (5) The re-emergence of the clairvoyant to intellectual consciousness, when he does not, without special measures, remember anything about
stages (2), (3), and (4).

'Most magnetic persons will be in this clairvoyant state [stage (3)] without
recalling it'. 'Without recalling it' translates *ohne sich desselben erinnern*. Miller
translated this phrase as 'without remembering it afterwards', so that it refers
to stage (5). This is what *sich erinnern* would normally mean and it is a
possible rendering here. But (i) *sich erinnern* could mean 'become aware of'
something, which need not be in the past; (ii) the following sentence, 'The
presence . . . sleeping', concerns the question how we know, *at the time of stage
(3)*, that the patient is in a clairvoyant state; and (iii) the question of subsequent
recollection is dealt with at the end of the paragraph.

'[Y]et these individuals can be aware of what they are as objective
consciousness' (*so können diese Individuen doch von dem wissen, was sie als
objektives Bewusstsein sind*). Miller translated this as: 'yet these individuals can
only have knowledge of what they, *qua* objective consciousness, know'. This
would imply that genuine clairvoyance does not occur. Hegel's point is that
clairvoyants at stage (3) know about themselves at stage (1), often speaking of
themselves at stage (1) as 'another person'.

The 'battle of Belle-Alliance' is the battle of Waterloo. Belle-Alliance was a
nearby farm, where Wellington and Blücher, the Prussian leader, met after their
victory over Napoleon.

27. The magnetized state is itself a disease. But Hegel believes that it can directly
effect a cure of other diseases, physical and mental. Such cures are distinct from
those in which the subject clairvoyantly diagnoses his own illness and proposes
a remedy for it. In the cases that Hegel discusses here clairvoyance plays no
essential part. A disease is, according to Hegel, a separation between one part
of the organism and the rest. This is true also of the magnetized state, which
is itself a separation of the feeling soul from intellectual consciousness. How
then can the separation involved in one disease cure the separation involved in
another? The feeling soul, though only one aspect of the mind, is associated
with unity, with 'simple universality', while intellectual consciousness involves
dispersal in the 'external world'. Thus the temporary suppression of intellectual consciousness tends to restore the unity of the mind or the body, breaking
down barriers within them. Once this has been achieved, the subject can 'involve
itself once more in separation and opposition', i.e. engage in worldly affairs with

intellectual consciousness. It is not clear from this account why the magnetized state is a more effective cure than ordinary sleep.

NOTES TO §407

1. 'Judgement' is *Urteil*, which, as in e.g. §389, n. 4, is here primarily a *Teilung* ('division'). Since the 'feeling totality' is an individual, it divides itself into 'particular' feelings, on the one hand, and, on the other, a 'subject' that posits them as 'its' feelings. The feelings are 'ideal', i.e. sublated or submerged in the subject. Thus the subject closes the rift opened up by the 'judgement'. It returns out of the particular feelings to join together with itself as 'subjective unit' and becomes 'self-feeling'. It is self-feeling 'only in the particular feeling', i.e. self-feeling is itself a particular feeling; the subject has not yet attained a conception of itself as distinct from any feeling that it may have. *Selbstgefühl*, 'self-feeling', can also mean 'self-esteem'. This sense is also in play here, since madness often consists in a misconception about oneself, especially in overestimating one's own importance.

NOTES TO §408

1. Self-feeling is 'immediate', that is, it has not, like higher aspects of the mind, broken loose from the body. A particular feeling, unlike, say, a thought, involves a particular part of the body. Even when a person has advanced to 'intellectual consciousness', he still retains self-feeling and the particular feelings that go with it. Hence an intellectual consciousness may become obsessed by a feeling which it cannot 'refine to ideality', integrate into its overall view of things ('put in its proper perspective'), and thus overcome. Owing to their physical embodiment feelings can resist rational control. In this case there is a 'contradiction' between the subject's 'individual world-system' and its recalcitrant feeling. This is *Verrücktheit*, 'insanity', but since it comes from *verrücken*, 'to move, disarrange', also 'derangement'. There are no pieces missing from the subject's mind; the pieces are simply in disarray.
2. A subject that has only self-feeling, but no intellectual consciousness, cannot be insane, since derangement involves a 'contradiction' between intellectual consciousness and self-feeling. Hence intellectual consciousness, a later stage of mind, must be introduced into this account of derangement. There are not two selves here, one the self of self-feeling, the other the self of intellectual consciousness. Intellectual consciousness, though not itself 'natural', is also the 'natural self' (*natürliches Selbst*) of self-feeling. Because of this a contradiction can arise between these two aspects of the self. Older metaphysicians (especially such followers of Leibniz as Christian Wolff, Alexander Baumgarten, etc: cf. §378, n. 1) equated the mind with the soul and conceived it as a 'thing' (*Ding*). They were wrong about this. The mind is 'free', not a lump of stuff that might have a thought or a feeling stuck in it like a nail in a shoe. 'For itself' or on its own the mind is not capable of derangement. Only if it is 'natural and in being [*Seiendes*]' can the mind become insane, with a 'finitude' fixed in

it. Derangement involves the soul and its bodily accompaniment as well as the mind; it is a 'psychical', not a purely mental, disease. It occurs only because intellectual consciousness is also the natural self of self-feeling.

3. The difference between the healthy and the insane subject is like the difference between waking and dreaming. But derangement is not simply dreaming. A normal dream does not usually come into conflict or contradiction with intellectual consciousness, since intellectual consciousness is in abeyance. Derangement is dreaming and waking together. A dream is incorporated into what is otherwise a normal waking life. Error is embedded in the objective world. But we all make mistakes. Where does 'madness' (*Wahnsinn*) begin? An unjustified surge of e.g. hatred at odds with one's usually calm demeanour may seem like madness, but really it is not. Madness requires a 'feeling that has come into *being* in a bodily form' (leiblich, *seiend* gewordenen Gefühls) stubbornly resistant to incorporation in the 'mediations' of consciousness, such as hatred that persists despite one's realization that its object has done nothing to deserve it. In this case the mind is in a state of 'being' (*seiend*), with an indigestible 'being' (*Sein*) that it cannot dissolve, though it retains the general principles and the rational resources for overcoming it. Phillipe Pinel (1745–1826), a French physician, viewed insanity as 'mental alienation', a mind alienated from its proper function, and advocated treating the insane as persons to be cured rather than objects of amusement or fear.

Hegel holds that derangement stems initially from a feeling, passion, or emotion. This view is challenged by Anthony Quinton in 'Madness', in his *From Wodehouse to Wittgenstein* (London: Carcanet, 1998), 213–38, who argues that emotions (or at least emotions characteristic of madness) embody beliefs and that madness consists in the 'systematic unreasonableness of a person's practical beliefs'. (Beliefs, not emotions, are 'primary', since an emotion can only be said to be unreasonable or inappropriate if it embodies an unreasonable belief (ibid. 219–20). But it is not clear why this, even if it is true, implies the *causal* primacy of beliefs. Might we not say that an emotion is unreasonable if it *generates* an unreasonable belief?) Hegel has a deep-seated reason for rejecting this account, his conviction, namely, that the mind is intrinsically immune to 'systematic unreasonableness' and that its apparent unreasonableness depends on intrusions from lower levels of the psyche. He can agree that emotions are accompanied by beliefs, that e.g. the 'manic's wild elation embodies a belief in his own supreme qualities of intelligence, etc.' (Quinton, 'Madness', 221). But he would argue that the belief is powered by the elation rather than the other way round. Analogously, love is love of someone and love embodies certain beliefs. If a youth falls in love with a girl, his love embodies the belief, say, that she is the most beautiful girl in the world, or that he cannot live without her. But it seems unlikely that the youth's love is driven by, and to be explained by, such a belief. In all probability the youth would have fallen in love with another girl, had he met her instead. He was in the mood for love, harbouring feelings ready to be aroused by any object falling within a certain range of acceptability. Again, the beliefs that accompany the youth's love are (in all probability) absurd.

That an otherwise sane youth should adopt them would be quite inexplicable in the absence of an appropriate feeling. Here the belief is generated by the emotion, not the emotion by the belief. It is not obvious that it need be otherwise in the case of those systematically unreasonable practical beliefs that constitute madness.

Hegel also holds (along with Plato, Aristotle, Kant, etc., but in opposition to, say, Pascal or Rousseau) that passions or the 'heart' are intrinsically evil and self-seeking. It is not obvious that this is so. Insanity can be altruistic, expressing itself in, say, excessive generosity. Generosity may be inconvenient if unrestrained by reason, but it is not inherently evil or 'self-seeking'. Socrates, in Plato's *Phaedrus*, detects an affinity between madness and love. In the eyes of a dispassionate observer, love involves a passion for an object wholly disproportionate to its merits, manifestly false beliefs about the loved object, and strangely impractical behaviour. But love is surely a benign emotion, inconvenient if wholly unrestrained by reason, but not intrinsically malignant and possibly beneficial. Hence we are more tolerant of blind love than of blind hatred.

4. On the stages of the soul's development, see §402, n. 9. Crime is considered in Hegel's *Philosophy of Right* (1821), §§90–103, and in Enc. III, §§496–502. The cases of crime and derangement differ. Derangement is a 'contradiction' between the intellectual consciousness and self-feeling. These are constituents of every human mind. Hence every human individual has the seeds of derangement in him, even though the seeds do not usually burgeon. Derangement is for Hegel an individual, not a social, matter. By contrast, the necessity of crime is a social matter. Hegel does not argue that every individual contains the seeds of criminality, only that given that there are laws, some people are bound to break them. Despite Hegel's explanation, it remains unclear in what sense derangement is a 'stage in the development of the soul'. A person cannot be insane if he is not already an intellectual consciousness, that is, if he has not yet completed his development, since there is then nothing for self-feeling to contradict. Thus self-feeling may be a stage in the soul's development. But to infer from this that derangement is a stage in our development is comparable to saying that because the feeling soul in its immediacy is a stage in our development, so is animal magnetism. A given stage, Sn, is distinct from a reversion to it at a later stage, $S(n+m)$. Sn is still, in normal minds, latently present in $S(n+m)$. In abnormal minds it acquires an undue prominence, giving the diseased state $S(n!+m)$. Sn is a stage in our development, and so is $S(n+m)$. But $S(n!+m)$ is not; it is a perversion of $S(n+m)$. Here too crime differs from derangement. Crime is not a reversion to an earlier stage of development.

5. The difference between somnambulism and derangement is discussed in the first paragraph of the *Zusatz* to §405. The 'concept' of derangement applies to derangement in general. It contrasts with the particular species of derangement considered below. Hegel argues for the 'necessity' of his procedure as follows. The soul is a 'contradiction'. It is *both* a single individual *and* 'immediately identical with the universal natural soul, with its substance'. However, at the stage of the 'feeling soul in its immediacy', this contradiction is only 'in itself',

or latent. Moreover, a 'contradiction' is an 'opposition' (*Entgegensetzung*), and opposition stands in contrast to identity. Yet here the contradiction or opposition exists in a form that contradicts it, in the 'contradictory form of identity', the identity of the individual with the universal. To be a proper contradiction it must become explicit, appear in a form that does not contradict it—as an opposition or as a contradiction.

Why must a contradiction become explicit? The point that the 'form of identity' contradicts its content, namely, the contradiction, is not sufficient. If contradictions can subsist at all, why not a contradiction between a contradiction and the form in which it appears? Possibly Hegel believes that to sharpen a contradiction into an opposition is to go some way towards resolving it. If the selfsame person supports both the Government and the Opposition, we have what Hegel would regard as a contradictory (though not necessarily impossible) state of affairs. If we split him in two, leaving one wholehearted Government-supporter and one wholehearted Opposition-supporter, we have an opposition, and perhaps a 'contradiction', but not, at least in its upshot, an unusual state of affairs. Or, less fancifully, transforming a latent contradiction into an explicit contradiction, though not itself a resolution of the contradiction, is a step towards a resolution. I cannot begin to resolve a contradiction in my thought or my writing until I make it explicit, get it out in the open. Analogously, the more explicit contradictoriness of self-feeling and/or insanity is a step on the road to harmonious consciousness. That an explicit contradiction is closer to resolution, i.e. to ceasing to be a contradiction, exemplifies a general principle of Hegel's thought, that one opposite veers over into the other at its extreme point. e.g. if you travel as far northwards as possible, you start travelling southwards. (But traveling to the East never veers over into traveling westwards!)

In Hegel's Logic identity is not immediately followed by opposition; an intervening stage is 'difference' (*Unterschied*), so that the order is (roughly): identity–difference–polarity/opposition (Enc. I, §§115–20). We might then expect here an intervening stage in which the individual soul is different from the universal soul, but not in opposition to it, giving the order: feeling soul in its immediacy/somnambulism—intermediate stage—self-feeling/derangement. But Hegel does not supply such an intervening stage. Instead, he describes somnambulism in different ways. Sometimes it involves a difference (but not an opposition) between the individual soul and the universal: 'the relationship to it of something different' in the first paragraph of §405Z; 'relationship . . . of mere difference' at the beginning of the second paragraph of §408Z. Sometimes the somnambulist soul is 'immediately identical' with its 'substance', as later in the second paragraph of §408Z. This ambiguity is clarified in the first paragraph of §406Z. and later in this paragraph of §408Z. The 'feeling soul in its immediacy' as an early stage in our development (e.g. the soul of the foetus) is immediately identical with its world. In the adult reversion to this state, the soul is divided. On one side it is, like the foetal soul, immediately identical with its 'individual world', its 'substance'. On the other side it has a 'mediated' relationship to the objectively ordered world. These two sides are just 'different', not opposed. The individual is sometimes in a magnetic state, sometimes in a normal state; when he is in a magnetic state he is controlled by someone in a normal state. The two states never come into collision. They can therefore be 'mixed' (§405Z., first paragraph; *vermischt*, §408Z, first paragraph). Here Hegel tends to conflate the feeling soul in its immediacy as a stage in our development with later reversions to it in intellectual consciousness, *Sn* with *S(n!+m)*, in the terminology introduced in §408, n. 4.

In derangement the 'subjectivity of the soul' separates itself from and comes into opposition to that with which it is, in somnambulism, 'immediately identical'. What it opposes is described in two ways, first as 'its substance', and secondly as 'the objective'. The first description suggests what is called above 'the universal natural soul, . . . its substance'; the second suggests the objective world accessible to 'objective consciousness'. The first suggests that Hegel is dealing with self-feeling as a stage in our development, the second suggests the adult reversion to self-feeling in derangement. An opposition occurs in both states. In simple self-feeling the soul attempts to extricate itself as an individual from its individual world and from its feelings and sensations. In derangement there is a parallel movement of extrication and opposition: the individual extricates itself from the objective world. But the movements are more than simply parallel. The movement of derangement is driven by a re-emergence of the self-feeling characteristic of the earlier stage. Self-feeling is a healthy development, an essential stage in our advance to full self-consciousness. Derangement is an obtrusive perversion of it.

Hegel's account is conducted in terms of derangement, involving an impaired objective consciousness, not of simple self-feeling. The soul enters into opposition to the objective world, a world in which it is, say, a pauper. In this opposition its 'subjectivity' is 'purely formal, empty, abstract'. It is not a pauper, but nor is it anything else. It has no role, no place in the world. So it adopts a role, a place: it supposes it is in reality a prince. Then it is a 'unity of the subjective and objective', it is a simple, subjective self, with subjective opinions, but also, objectively, a prince, with a palace and retainers, from which it has perhaps been temporarily ousted by a usurper. 'Actually objective consciousness' is not so defective. An actual prince is aware (subjectively) that he is (objectively) a prince. He is thus 'for' himself, 'an object [*gegenständlich*]', to himself, just as the pauper is. This is 'a subjective identity of the subjective and objective'. But unlike the deranged pauper, the real prince has 'disconnected' (*abgeschieden*) this subjective identity from himself, 'placed it over against' himself as an 'actually objective' identity. Sanity involves not just the unity of the two sides that it shares with insanity, but also a 'separation'. The insane cannot effect this separation, since they are still encumbered by 'immediacy', 'naturalness' and 'bodiliness'. But the sane consciousness overcomes them, makes them 'ideal', 'makes them its own' (*sich zu eigen machen*), and transforms them into 'an objective unity of the subjective and objective'. In this way it frees itself from 'its Other', namely *corporeality*, etc., and releases its 'Other', namely *objective reality*, from identity with itself. The feeling soul and the insane distinguish themselves from and relate themselves to a quasi-objective world. But this world in which they live is a world of their own, a *subjective* objective world. It must be so, since the feeling soul is still anchored to its bodily feelings. Only by overcoming them can the subject reach out to what is genuinely objective, extruding its private world and its subjective view of it out of itself into genuine objectivity. It is thus extricated from its 'other', that is, from both its corporeality and the objective world. Self-feeling, by contrast, is still immersed in its corporeal feelings and thus has no access to an objectivity that is more than a projection of its feelings, while the insane combine a consciousness of the objective world with its 'negative', their private, feeling-dependent world.

Hegel tends to conflate the 'substance' of the feeling soul, its naturalness and corporeality, with the objective world disclosed to consciousness. He refers to each as the soul's 'other'. It seems to be corporeality, etc. that are transformed into 'an objective unity of the subjective and objective'. (But here the object of the verb 'transform', *umbilden*, is uncertain. It may be, as Miller supposed, the soul 'itself'. This depends on whether *sich* in the clause *sich zu eigen machen* is a dative, with 'them' understood —'make them its own' —, or an accusative —'appropriate itself' —which can then be taken as the direct object of *umbilden* in the following clause.) Hegel's general idea is that one can only know about something if one is not immersed in it, but sets it at a distance. A natural objection is that the soul's corporeality is not the same as the objective world, but at most a part of it. But the conflation is mitigated by the following considerations: (1) Hegel tends to believe that the *substance* of the soul is not a clearly demarcated individual distinct from the rest of the world, but extends throughout the world: cf. §406, n. 18. (2) Since the objective world is an interconnected whole, and the soul's corporeality is at least a part of that whole, objective knowledge of one's own corporeality involves at least a rough objective knowledge of the world. (3) The illusions of the insane usually concern themselves, their surroundings, and people close to them, that is, that portion of the objective world that is closely connected to their soul's corporeality, etc.

6. 'Being-together-with-itself', like 'together with itself' in the preceding paragraph, is *Beisichsein*, 'being (at home) with [*bei*] oneself'. The term implies that the consciousness of the insane is, though fractured, nevertheless somehow unified.

7. Psychical or 'soulful consciousness' and 'intellectual consciousness' are each the 'negative' of the other. Hence the deranged are 'together with' themselves in their 'negative', namely soulful consciousness or self-feeling. There are, however, other types of 'negative'. For example, pains and hardships are a 'negative'. Is it therefore insane to endure hardships voluntarily? (If one endures them involuntarily, one is perhaps not 'together with oneself' in them.) Clearly not, if the hardships are endured for a worthwhile end which can be achieved with them and not without them. In contrast, pilgrims to the Holy Sepulchre and 'Indians crawling on their stomachs' either have no worthwhile end or their end can be attained as easily without the hardships. Hegel is inclined to regard these as cases of derangement or at least 'folly'. But this involves at least two difficulties:

(1) The sense of 'negative' in which hardship is 'negative' is different from the sense in which the delusions of the insane are 'negative'. Delusions are the negative of intellectual consciousness, but hardships, as such, are not; they may be an integral part of a rational plan. Conversely, insane delusions need not be painful; the pauper enjoys the thought of being a prince. What may qualify Christian and Hindu devotees for insanity is not the pains they endure, but the delusions motivating their endurance, delusions presumably at odds with their intellectual consciousness. That what they endure is painful is not strictly relevant to the question of their sanity, except in so far as it is evidence for their delusions. (2) The Christian and Hindu beliefs that sustain their endurance are not isolated beliefs of solitary individuals, but parts of a large-scale, and not wholly irrational, widespread ideology. The pauper's belief that he is a prince can perhaps be explained by the untimely intrusion of self-feeling into his intellectual consciousness. But a shared ideology depends also on education, etc. This is not simply a matter of the number of individuals who have the beliefs. In principle, very many individuals might succumb to the delusion that they are a prince; their numbers would not mitigate their insanity. Their belief would not be a shared belief, propagated by education, but a belief adopted more or less independently by each individual and to be explained by his individual defects. Individual insanity might be widespread. But genuinely shared insanity is more problematic. This is not to deny that an ideology may provide an arena for the display of individual insanity. Not all Christians undertake an arduous pilgrimage, perhaps only those who are insane; the sane are less consistent in the pursuit of their (presumably less intense) beliefs. Hegel might also insist that a shared ideology can be insane, arguing perhaps that it arouses the latent self-feeling of its adherents.

The force of the final sentence is this: In rationally endured pains, the intellectual consciousness 'finds itself again' (*sich wiederfindet*), i.e. achieves overall satisfaction by gaining an end that is worth the pain. This is not insanity. In irrationally endured pains only the 'sentient' (*empfindende*) consciousness finds itself again, i.e. gets the satisfaction of doing what it wants, or thinks it ought, to do. This can qualify as insanity. Hegel's point is again impaired by the slide in the sense of 'negative'.

8. This seems to distinguish the negativity of pain from the negativity constituting derangement. The former is not reciprocal: pain is the negative of mind, but mind is not the negative of pain. Psychical and intellectual consciousness are each the negative of the other. Their cohabitation in an individual is distinct from 'error' and 'folly'. Hegel perhaps implies that excessive religious devotion is error and folly rather than insanity. Cf. §408, n. 10.

9. Hegel has spoken above of 'somnambulistic consciousness' and 'soulful [*seelenhafte*] consciousness' above. But 'consciousness' unqualified is a higher state, involving opposition of thinking and 'externality', an outer world. In the 'natural soul' these are in immediate unity; no distinction between subjectivity and objectivity is drawn. In 'reflective' (*reflektierenden*) consciousness the 'two worlds' *seem*, and at some level *are*, distinct and independent. This is 'finite

thinking'. To it the 'two worlds' seem distinct and thus 'finite', each bounded by the other. Initially it is concerned with finite individuals, individuals not intelligibly related to their environment. 'In truth', however, the two worlds are 'identical'. Consciousness goes on to display their identity by converting the mass of isolated contingencies, 'what is found and sensed [*das Gefundene und Empfundene*]', into general 'representations' and thus into a coherent interrelated whole, in which things that at first seemed contingent become 'necessary' and 'objective'. (Taken by itself, it seems a mere contingency that I am not a prince. But in the context of my ancestry, the law of succession, etc. it is necessary.) This order is produced by the activity of my reason and intellect. Hence the two worlds are once more identical. Their identity is not 'immediate' identity as it was for the natural soul, but 'mediated' by our intellectual activity. This exemplifies the pattern: immediate unity–division–restored unity: cf. §387, n. 14.

What Spinoza actually wrote was: 'The order and connexion of ideas is the same as the order and connexion of things' (*Ordo et connexio idearum idem est, ac ordo et connexio rerum*, *Ethics* II, proposition vii). Spinoza meant that the order and connexion of ideas and things is the same constantly, whereas for Hegel the identity is the result of human cognitive activity.

10. This would seem to acquit religious devotion (cf. §408, nn. 7, 8) of insanity. It is not trying to become a prince that is insane, but tenaciously believing against all the evidence that one is a prince. Hence trying to fortify one's soul by a pilgrimage would not be insane, but believing against all the evidence (whatever this might be) that one's soul has been fortified by it. This distinction does not seem plausible, however. Trying to catch the moon's reflection with a fishing rod seems hardly more sane than believing one has caught it. After all, the mere attempt implies a belief that the reflection is the sort of thing that can be caught in this way, a belief that itself defies the evidence. However, it is harder to present evidence against the belief that souls are fortified by pilgrimages, especially to someone whose whole view of the world is coloured by this system of beliefs.

11. If I am not a king, then in the context of the 'totality of my actuality' it is both certain and necessary that I am not a king, evidenced and determined by my actuality. But taken by itself, it is possible that I am a king, since some men are kings. This bare logical possibility is the only 'ground' of my belief, though Hegel does not deny that such factors as my regal feeling of superiority over others help to cause it.

12. On the 'abstract' I, see §§412–17. The abstract I or ego bears a resemblance to the consciousness that is confronted by a mass of contingencies that it has not yet subjected to rational ordering: cf. §408, n. 9. Consequently it has not yet assigned itself a stable place in concrete actuality. Many a rational adult is an abstract I to the extent that he can *imagine* being a king and imagine being, or at least entertain the proposition that he is, a dog. But a *merely* abstract I can not only imagine these possibilities but also believe them. This is because, as an

abstract I, it has no determinate belief about itself (e.g. that it is a commoner, or that it is a rational biped) to exclude these possibilities. (Hegel seems to hold that we cannot believe, or even imagine, what is logically impossible.) In the early stages of consciousness the I (an essential ingredient of consciousness) is merely abstract. It advances by degrees to concrete egohood or 'concrete, sober self-consciousness': cf. §§424–5. (This bears a resemblance to the consciousness that has ordered the world by its intellectual activity.) But even after it has reached this stage, it can revert to merely abstract egohood and lose it bearings in the objective world. It can become stubbornly attached to such a subjective idea as that it is a king.

What is the connexion between this account of insanity, as a reversion to the abstract I, and the earlier account of it as a reversion to self-feeling? The abstract I is needed in order to explain how a person can *believe* e.g. that he is a king, rather than simply having feelings of superiority that do not affect his conscious beliefs. It explains the effects of self-feeling at the level of consciousness. Self-feeling is needed in order to explain the descent from the concrete to the abstract ego, and why the abstract I opts for one belief rather than another. It is possible that I am a king and equally possible that I am a commoner. As a merely abstract I, I can believe either. My obstinate belief that I am a king stems from my particular self-feeling. But cf. §408, n. 14.

13. There are two unresolved contradictions: First, the 'individualized representation' or isolated idea contradicts the 'abstract universality of the immediate I'. It is not clear why this is so. The abstract I can after all accommodate any idea. Perhaps the point is that I can find no intelligible connexion between my abstract self and the concrete king I believe myself to be. Why should I be a king rather than a commoner or a dog? (But see also §408, n. 14.) Secondly, the isolated idea, together with the abstract I, contradicts the 'internally harmonious total actuality'. Here Hegel introduces three propositions and one 'sensation':

    (1) 'What I think is true'. In one sense this is true and defended by 'conceptual reason'. The world achieves its objectivity and coherence by our thinking. This is the third stage discussed in §408, n. 9. At the highest level, what conceptual reason thinks, is true in 'form' and 'content', a perfect unity of 'what is thought' and 'what is': cf. §§465–8, 574–7. Interpretation of this claim is bedevilled by two ambiguities: Does 'true' mean 'fitting the facts', i.e. 'correct', or does it have Hegel's special sense of (roughly) 'coherent and self-contained' (cf. §379, n. 7)? Is what is 'thought' by reason the object of its thinking (e.g. God) or the content of its thinking (e.g. that God is good)? At this elevated level 'truth' bears Hegel's special sense, and the distinction between the object ('content'?) and the content ('form'?) of the thinking is transcended. On 'conceptual', from *begreifen*, 'comprehend', cf. §406, n. 9.

    (2) 'What I think is true' in the 'deranged' sense given it in insanity. This implies that if I think I am a king, then I am a king. The 'concrete content

of actuality' is 'excluded' from this merely 'formal' unity-in-difference. If 'actuality' were taken into account it would be obvious that I am not a king.

(3) 'The subjective and objective are absolutely divorced'. This is asserted by the 'unintelligence [*Unverstand*] of the intellect [*Verstand*].' This is the separation of the 'two worlds', the second stage discussed in §408, n. 9.

(4) A healthy mind's feeling or 'sensation' (*Empfindung*) contains, but does not assert, the 'actual unity of the subjective and objective'. That is, it draws no distinction between them and, usually at least, they coincide: I feel hot and I am hot. This is the first, pre-conscious, stage discussed in §408, n. 9.

14. The subjective–objective unity characteristic of derangement is 'immediate', i.e. the unity asserted in proposition (2) in §408, n. 13. It is not the unity resulting from 'infinite mediation', i.e. the unity asserted in proposition (1) in §408, n. 13. (The force of 'infinite', *unendliche*, may be that owing to mediation the objective and subjective are not 'finite', bounded by each other, *or* that everything is included in the mediation, *or* that the mediation is very complex.) The deranged I is the peak or 'tip' of self-feeling, and is in a way thin and 'acute'. But owing to its relation to self-feeling it is 'natural, immediate, a being'. 'A being' translates *Seiendes*, a nominalization of the present participle of *sein*, 'to be'. Hegel's point is that the I just *is*, involving no negation or mediation with what it is not, with what is other than itself: cf. Enc. I, §§84–6. Hence the I is abstract, cut off from its other and therefore thin and empty and therefore exposed to the intrusion of an unruly feeling, such as a feeling of superiority. This feeling too is a 'being', impervious to mediation and therefore hard to dislodge. Instead of being 'posited ideally', put in its proper place, it is held fast as an objective fact, the belief that I am a king. Hence there is a duality of 'being', of the feeling, on the one hand, and objective consciousness, on the other. They contradict each other, but the disparity between them, because it just *is*, has no tendency to dispel the feeling, any more than, say, my objective consciousness can remove a headache or a physical entity such as a boil. The mind alone, Hegel believes, cannot accommodate unmediated lumps of indigestible being, since it is fluid and free. An unsurmountable 'barrier' between two parts of the mind must therefore stem from a bodily intrusion. On 'being', cf. §410, n. 1.

15. Hegel's second question is answered in §§409–12, i.e. the last four Paragraphs of Anthropology.

16. Hegel asks two questions: (1) Why must the soul, in particular self-feeling, be discussed before objective consciousness? (2) Why must derangement, which presupposes objective consciousness, since it consists in the intrusion of the soul into consciousness, be discussed before objective consciousness? The answer to (1) is that the soul or 'natural self' is relatively 'abstract', while consciousness is relatively 'concrete', involving, among other things, the latent natural self 'in potentiality'. Presumably the natural self also precedes consciousness in time,

at least as a stage in the life of an individual. Neither of these considerations answers question (2). Derangement is no less 'concrete' than objective consciousness, nor does it precede consciousness in time.

PR, and the summary of it in Enc. III, §§469–552, follows the order: concept of will; abstract or 'formal' right (property, personhood, etc.); 'morality' (*Moralität*, i.e. the morality of individual conscience); 'ethical life' (*Sittlichkeit*, i.e. social morality), which develops into: family; civil society; state. This parallel helps to answer question (1). Each stage is more abstract and less concrete than its successors. Morality, e.g., is less concrete than ethical life, just as the natural self is less concrete than objective consciousness. There are, however, differences. Morality does not precede ethical life in time, but the natural self does precede objective consciousness. Again, while there can be no consciousness without a latent natural self, there can, in Hegel's view, be an ethical life without morality. Hegel supposed ancient Greece to be an ethical society without morality, without an individual conscience. Does the parallel help to answer question (2)? If so, an earlier stage in PR must be not only more abstract than later stages, but also a diseased version of a later stage. e.g. morality is perhaps not simply an abstraction as compared to ethical life, but an abstraction that can reassert itself, unduly and deleteriously, within ethical life. This is what happens, in Hegel's view. Morality is the most obvious case of a stage that recurs as a disease in a later stage. But other stages might also recur in this way. Although e.g. abstract right is an essential element in a healthy political state, it may, in some states (e.g. imperial Rome), gain undue prominence, and so too might the family or civil society.

However, even if the parallel is sound, and early stages of right and of mind are *both* healthy abstractions *and* diseases parasitic on later stages, this is no conclusive reason for considering the disease at the same time as its healthy counterpart and *before* the later stage, the host on which it is parasitic. Hegel could as well have discussed derangement under the heading of consciousness, and morality as a malignant excrescence under the heading of ethical life. The deranged idea and malignant morality may be an '*abstraction* held on to in opposition' to objective consciousness and ethical life respectively. But derangement and morality-infected ethical life themselves are no less concrete than healthy consciousness and ethical life. Hegel's real reason for treating derangement earlier is that it gives him an insight into self-feeling and the soul in general that he could not otherwise have had. He cannot, after all, remember what it was like to be just self-feeling. So he looks for clues in adult regressions to it.

17. The differentiation of derangement into types is to be 'necessary' and 'rational', based on its inner nature, not on its external 'expressions', nor on the 'particular content of the formal' subjective-objective unity, distinguishing indefinitely many varieties of derangement according to whether the patient thinks he is, say, a king, a dog, or a building. Classification into types begins with a fundamental feature common to all types of derangement. The deranged mind is invariably enclosed within itself, sunk into itself. This sounds similar to somnambulism

and the mind's 'being-within-self'. But it is quite different. The somnambulist is deaf to all voices except the hypnotist's, but this is because he is in immediate contact with 'actuality', from which the deranged mind, by contrast, is decisively separated.

18. 'Submergence within itself' is *both* the 'universal' feature common to all types of derangement *and* a 'particular' type of derangement. The idea that the genus is one of its own species, which occurs frequently in Hegel, perhaps owes something to Aristotle, who argued that plants are *both* a type of living creature (in contrast to animals and humans) *and* possess only those generic life functions (nutrition and growth) that are common to all living creatures (*de anima*, II. 3, 414^{b}27 ff.). Cf. §408, nn. 21, 22, 23.

19. The indeterminate submergence- or being-within-itself that constitutes the first form of derangement becomes the second form, when it attaches itself to a 'particular' idea and regards it as objective. Cf. §408, nn. 24, 25.

20. The third main form of derangement is just the second form together with awareness of it and the endeavour to escape it. Cf. §408, n. 26.

21. If cretinism is diagnosed in infancy, it can be avoided by treatment with thyroid extract. Once it has developed it is not curable. It is not related to insanity or to catatonic schizophrenia, which afflicted the anonymous 'Englishman'. On Pinel, see §408, n. 3.

22. Distraction or 'absent-mindedness' is *Zerstreutheit*, from *zerstreuen*, 'to scatter, disperse'. Its relationship to insanity seems remote, as long as, say, Newton does not persist in claiming that the finger is a tobacco-stopper. Hegel connects it with insanity by ascribing some versions of it to absorption in 'abstract self-feeling' and to obsession with one's 'subjectivity' at the expense of the objective surroundings.

23. 'Rambling' is *Faselei*, primarily '(talking) drivel', but here applied to what is now termed 'attention-deficit disorder' and to some types of schizophrenia. (The term 'schizophrenia', meaning 'split mind', was coined in. 1911 by a Swiss psychiatrist, Eugen Bleuler, reflecting his not entirely unhegelian view that the symptoms stem from a split, a dissociation or lack of coordination, between feeling or emotion, on the one hand, and thought and cognition, on the other.)

24. Throughout this paragraph, Hegel speaks of *Narrheit* and *Narren*, literally 'folly', 'fools', but he clearly means 'madness' and 'madmen' and uses them synonymously with *Verrücktheit* and *Verrückten*. Hegel is searching for words to designate different types of insanity, words which in the language of his day were not clearly differentiated. Perhaps he is also implying that this form of insanity is superior to at least some varieties of the first form. Unlike the idiot and the rambler, this madman can 'hold on to' something definite and has a largely 'coherent consciousness'. In effect, Hegel treats the varieties of derangement as a progression towards sane consciousness.

25. Again, Hegel speaks of *Narrheit* and *Narren*, meaning 'madness' and 'madmen'. 'Weariness with life' is 'indeterminate' in that it involves no particular idea. Even the 'fixed idea [*Vorstellung*] of the loathsomeness of life', which Hegel introduces in order to assimilate it to other types of madness, lacks a definite object.

26. 'Mania' is *Wahnsinn*, 'lunacy' is *Tollheit*. But the words are not used with great precision or discrimination. This type of insanity is marked by an awareness of the 'contradiction' that afflicts the subject. Earlier the contradiction was said to be between a subjective idea and objective consciousness: cf. §408, n. 20. Now it is said to be between the subjective idea and 'objectivity'. When the madman becomes aware of this contradiction, his response is not to seek help in removing his subjective idea, but (at least when he does not wallow in 'tranquil pain') to make his idea an 'actuality' or to destroy 'what is actual'. Hence Hegel is not simply describing the type of madness fostered by the French Revolution, which also afflicted those attached to the old order and now living 'in the past', but also the madness of French revolutionaries themselves, who feel an acute contradiction between the present state of things and their subjective ideas about how things ought to be. The 'rage of reason against unreason' is the rage, not of reason in Hegel's preferred sense, but of the reason of the Enlightenment, against the irrationality of the old order. The rage of unreason against reason may be the rage of restorationists against revolutionaries, but more probably Hegel is suggesting that the reason of the revolutionaries is really unreason. The revolutionary suffers from another contradiction. He flouts 'ethical laws' but retains 'moral [*moralische*] and ethical [*sittliche*] feelings'. This 'unmediated opposition' corresponds to the contradiction between a subjective idea and objective consciousness or reality. Ethical laws stem from the 'rational will that wills the universal' or the 'genuinely universal will', not the private will of any given individual, rather as objective consciousness reveals a world that is necessary and 'universal', not the idiosyncratic ideas of any individual: cf. §§396, n. 3; 400, n. 3; 401, n. 19; 402, n. 4. Hence the two 'contradictions' afflicting the revolutionary, and perhaps other maniacs, tend to converge. Their mind is torn between attachment to objective reality and values, on the one hand, and devotion to its private ideas and desires, on the other.

27. In this section Hegel distinguishes between *Verrücktheit* or *Narrheit*, 'insanity' proper, and *Wahnsinn*, 'mania'—the second and third main forms of derangement. But he does not distinguish between the types of cure for them. Both can respond to a 'talking cure'. Bernard de Montfaucon (1655–1741), whose problem was stupidity rather than insanity, was a pioneer in Greek paleography and archaeology, as well as a patristic scholar. Pinel's 'publication' on the subject is: *Traité médico-philosophique sur l'aliénation mentale ou la manie* (Paris, 1801). It was soon translated into German: *Philosophisch-medizinische Abhandlung über Geistesverirrungen oder Manie* (Vienna, 1801).

NOTES TO §409

1. In self-feeling (§407) the self is not distinguished from its particular feelings. But 'implicitly', or in itself, the self is not just a particular feeling or a collection of particular feelings, but a 'simple relation of ideality to itself'. (On ideality, cf. §379, n. 3. See also §398, n. 7 on a self-relation mediated by opposition, and §401, n. 9 on light as simple self-relation.) The self-relation is 'simple', because

the self does not relate to itself by way of mastering or negating its feelings; it simply withdraws from its feelings and communes with itself. When it does this it is universality 'for itself'. This universality is the 'truth' of the feelings; it is the realization of their nature: cf. §379, n. 7. The feelings and their satisfaction have become familiar and habitual, as we learn from §410. That is why the self can withdraw from them. But the universality is not their 'content-packed' (*gehaltvolle*) truth, since the 'content' of the feelings is left as it was. Now the soul consists of two components, the self as abstract being-for-self and the feelings as the soul's particular being or immediacy. Feelings are essentially bodily. So in distinguishing itself from its feelings, the self is distinguishing itself from its body. In §389 the soul was simply the 'substance' of the body, but now it is more: it is the 'ideal, subjective substantiality' of the body. In fact in §389 Hegel also described the soul as 'ideality', but there the soul is conceived as uniformly animating the body, without distinguishing *itself* from it or, as it is beginning to do here, contracting into a single centre of consciousness.

2. The I or ego is 'the universal that is for the universal': cf. §387, n. 12. The soul has not yet reached this stage. It still involves the body, in a way in which the I does not, but the body is 'reduced to its pure ideality', a form in which it can belong to the soul without disturbing the soul's 'universality'. Hegel here gives an account of space and time similar to Kant's, but restricts it to empty space and time, as abstract 'asunderness' (*Aussereinander*). Each is pure 'intuition' (*Anschauen*). Analogously, the pure 'being' (*Sein*) of the soul is 'entirely pure intuition'. This differentiates it from the I and from consciousness. Space and time are, for Kant, quite distinct from the 'I' or the 'I think', which neither he nor Hegel regard as an 'intuition'. But after the 'sublation' of its bodiliness, the soul is well on the way to consciousness and thus to egohood. Consciousness and the I are correlative: an I must be conscious and only an I can be conscious. A 'subject', by contrast, may, but need not, be conscious: cf. §381, n. 8.

NOTES TO §410

1. 'Habit' is *Gewohnheit*. It reduces feelings (of e.g. the normal temperature of the room) or things one is conscious of (e.g. one's right arm) to a determination 'that just *is*' (*seienden*). Here the force of *seienden*, the present participle of *sein*, 'to be', is that the feature unobtrusively *is*, and does not intrude into one's sensation or consciousness. (cf. §408, n. 14 for a different use of *seiend*.) Hence it leaves the soul free for other things. See also William James, *The Principles of Psychology* (New York: Dover, 1950), ch. iv.

2. Constant 'repetition' of the same feeling or sensation makes it habitual and incorporates it into the 'being' of the soul. 'Self-incorporation' is *Sicheinbilden*, which would normally mean 'imagining', but Hegel often stresses its derivation from *bilden*, 'to form, mould, etc.' and gives it the sense of 'building or moulding itself [*sich*] into [*ein*]'. In Enc. I, §175, Hegel discusses the 'judgement of reflexion', the third form of which is a universal judgment such as 'All men

are mortal'. 'Universality of reflexion' (*Reflexions-Allgemeinheit*) is thus the sort of universality that applies to all the members of a given class. For example, humanity applies to all men. This universality owes its name in part to the fact that the diverse entities to which the universal applies are collected together by our 'reflection' on them and do not spontaneously form themselves into a group. Hegel does however distinguish between a universal such as 'man', which constitutes the individuals to which it belongs such that they would not exist without it, and a universal such as 'having ear-lobes', which although it may be possessed by all men, does not constitute them: they would still be distinct individuals, even men, if they lacked ear-lobes. Universality of reflexion is distinct from merely 'abstract universality', which need not be applied to 'the natural-particular material' (*das Natürlich-Besondere*). The being of the soul is, in itself, 'abstract universality', the intrinsically indeterminate recipient of a variety of sensations. A type of sensation (e.g. the sensation of room temperature or of one's arm) is repeated many times; this is the 'natural-particular material' and, before it becomes habitual, an 'external plurality of sensation' (*Äusserlich-Vieles des Empfindens*), i.e. each sensation is distinct from the others, even though qualitatively similar to them. But repetition brings out or 'posits' the unity of these sensations, and in this form they are incorporated into the 'being' of the soul: this is 'universality of reflexion'. Cf. §410, n. 10.

3. 'Memory' (*Gedächtnis*), like habit, is 'mechanical' or automatic. I just remember e.g. a word without thinking about it. But memory is more intellectual and objective than habit: one remembers words, but is in the habit of cleaning one's teeth. (On memory see §§461 ff.) 'Mechanism' (*Mechanismus*) implies being mechanical; in Enc. I mechanism (§§195 ff.) is distinguished from 'chemism' (§§200 ff.) and 'teleology' (§§204 ff.).

   Ageing, sleeping and waking are 'immediately natural', not made natural by habituation. On 'self-feeling' see §§402, n. 7; 409, n. 1. 'Intelligence' and will are involved in habitual actions such as cleaning one's teeth and cleaning them in a certain way. One acquires certain habits of thinking and willing that 'belong to self-feeling' or are 'embodied' in so far as they are idiosyncratic, not determined by the objective nature of things. 'Habit is a second nature' was said by Montaigne (1533–92) in his *Essays*, III, ch. 10.

4. What I do out of habit I do unfreely in the sense that it just comes naturally: I do not deliberately decide to do it and do not consciously control my performance. I do it freely in so far as what I do (e.g. walking, teeth-cleaning) or experience (e.g. room temperature) has become a part of myself, my 'being' (*Sein*), so that I am not determined by something (a sensation, a requirement, a practice, etc.) different from myself, but act of my own accord. (Hegel here uses *Differenz*, which means both 'difference' and 'non-indifference', an ambiguity which I have attempted to convey with my 'no longer different from it, is indifferent to it'.) Consequently habitual action or experience does not engage my interest or attention: 'habit diminishes the conscious attention with which our acts are performed' (James, *Principles of Psychology*, 114). The unfreedom in

habit is 'formal': it concerns the form of what I do, but not its 'content'. What I do is done automatically, since it pertains to the being of my soul; but what I do out of habit (e.g. obey the law, clean my teeth) need not differ in content from what I would, or should, do even if I had not formed such a habit. Hence unfreedom only becomes serious, when the content of the habit is 'bad' or at odds with 'another purpose' of mine.

5. Hegel's classification is not very systematic and it is not always clear how what he says about the forms of habit squares with his general account of habit in the Paragraph. The 'immediate sensation' is the sensation as I feel it before I have become accustomed to it. When I harden myself against it, it is 'reduced to an externality and immediacy', that is, it no longer affects me conspicuously, it does not intrude into the 'abstract being-for-self' of the soul's 'universal being'. It does not follow that the sensation is not 'incorporated' into the being of the soul (see §410, n. 2). It is because the soul somehow incorporates the sensation that it has become relatively indifferent to it.

6. The first form of habit concerned our habituation to unpleasant sensations. This second form concerns our habituation to desires for pleasant things and to their satisfaction. Frequent satisfaction of a type of desire reduces the intensity of the desire and also of the pleasure of satisfying it. If we renounce the satisfaction, the desire remains intense and it is not, in any case, rational to forgo e.g. sexual satisfaction entirely, as long as we keep the desire a 'finite determinacy', and so not the dominant or exclusive principle of one's life. As Hegel says, an ascetic cannot become habituated to the *satisfaction* of desire, since he does not experience the satisfaction. But he may often experience the *pain* of *unsatisfied* desire, and it is not clear why he cannot become habituated to this pain and, according to the *first* form of habit, achieve 'liberation' from it. Moderate consumption of tobacco may be rational, but it is not, as Hegel's argument would imply, the only way to achieve liberation from the desire to smoke. Perhaps he would distinguish between natural desires, where one has the desire for x or to φ independently of getting x or φ-ing, and artificial desires, where the desire arises from getting x or φ-ing. But the distinction is not sharp: sexual desire is often intensified, and may even be acquired, by sexual activity, and conversely a desire to smoke might be extinguished by actually smoking. On 'monkish renunciation', see further §552.

7. In the first and second forms of habit, the abstract being of the soul was retained in the face of bodily pain and desire for pleasure. Habituation of the body was not essentially involved. In fact, the unresponsiveness of one's body to one's wishes might be one of the pains to which one becomes habituated. In this third form the soul does not just remain insulated from bodily intrusions; it takes over the body. The process has three stages: (1) The soul has 'being-for-self within itself', its 'initial naturalness and immediacy', its 'initial immediate identity', in which it is entirely contented with its self-enclosed condition. (2) It loses this immediate identity, when it forms a 'subjective purpose' or 'internal determination' that is frustrated by the body. One wants, e.g., to grasp something over there, but one's arms and legs will not cooperate. This is the 'more determinate breach' (more determinate, that is, than the breach that occurred in the first and

second forms of habit) with its naturalness and immediacy. (3) The soul subjugates the body and incorporates its purpose in it. It learns to move its arms at will, to grasp things, to walk, to whistle a tune, etc. This restores the 'identity' that it lost at stage (2). Specific purposes are 'incorporated' in specific parts of the bodily organism. I walk with my legs and feet, grasp with my hands, whistle with my lips, etc. Before I learn to do such things, the 'material', i.e. my corporeal body and its parts, has 'implicit' or potential 'ideality'. Afterwards the ideality is 'posited' or actualized. On 'ideality', see §§379, n. 3; 381, nn. 4, 8; 385, n. 6; 403, nn. 1, 2. The soul then 'exists as substance' in the body. 'Exists' (*existiere*) is used in accordance with its Latin prototype, *exsistere*, 'to step forth' (cf. §403, n. 2): the soul does not simply reside in the body, but expresses itself in its bearing and movements. Hegel continues to speak of the embodiment of 'sensations' or feelings (*Empfindungen*) here, when they do not seem to play a prominent role. His reasons for doing so are: (i) Sensations figure prominently in the first and second forms of habit. (ii) At this early stage of the mind, Hegel is reluctant to hand the soul over entirely to the will and its purposes. (iii) Sensations do play a role in habitual activities. Sensations are involved in walking, grasping, etc. Before these activities become habitual, the sensations are quite conspicuous. When habit sets in, they become less noticeable, but they do not disappear entirely: walking or grasping with numb legs or hands is quite different from ordinary walking or grasping. (iv) In some habitual activities, sensations play another role. Whistling and singing involve the production of sounds that give rise to auditory sensations both in the whistler and in his audience. (These are not the only sensations felt by the whistler. The sensation of air passing through his lips is not a part of his performance and belongs under heading (iii).) Such cases perhaps led Hegel to give sensations undue prominence in this form of habit.

8. On our upright posture, see also §§396, 411. On sight and other senses see §401 and Z. If I am not accustomed to thinking or I am thinking about unfamiliar topics, my thought is impeded, not 'pervaded' (I do not know my way around in it), not really my own property or 'possession' (*Eigentum*), since it feels strange and alien to me. When I overcome this by increasing habituation, I 'exist for myself as thinking', I am entirely familiar with my own thoughts and thinking. This is the 'immediacy of thinking togetherness-with-oneself': immediate, because I do not have laboriously to work things out or find my way around, and together with oneself, because I am entirely at home in my own thinking. The claim that habit makes thinking the property of my 'individual self' seems at odds with what Hegel says elsewhere, e.g. Enc. I, §§20 and 24Z.(1): that thoughts are not really my own individual thoughts, for the reason (among others) that I cannot denote, in terms of pure thought at least, myself as an individual I. But the two claims are not incompatible. A system of thoughts, e.g. arithmetic, is not mine or anyone's in particular, —and not only because I cannot express my own determinate individuality in arithmetical terms. But I as an individual need to habituate myself to it and make it my own 'possession'. The fact that it is now my property does not exclude others from simultaneously making it *their* property. Once I have made it my property, my own determinate

individuality recedes; my individuality is more prominent in my defective thinking than when I have perfected it.

  On 'recollection', see §§452 ff., and on 'memory', §§461 ff.

9. Habit is 'lifeless': if I do something out of habit, my heart is not really in it. It is
  'contingent': almost anything can become a habit. It is 'particular' (*Partikuläres*):
  what is habitual need not be what is essential to everyone, e.g. morality, religion, but the customs of a particular region or tribe, the peculiar habits of an
  individual, perhaps 'particularist'. Cf. §396 and Z., and nn. 2 and 19, on death
  as (the result of) habituation to life—an example of a bad, or at least strange,
  habit, though (in Hegel's view) a habit most of us eventually acquire. 'Existence',
  with the flavour of 'stepping forth' (cf. §410, n. 7), contrasts with 'implicitly',
  'predisposition' (*Anlage*: cf. §395, n. 2, where, however, 'predisposition' translates *Naturell*), etc. Habit makes the subject a 'concrete immediacy'. My ability
  e.g. to speak English is immediate—I do not usually have to search for words
  and constructions (as I do when I speak e.g. French), they come to me, as it
  were, naturally—and concrete: I know a lot of English, not just the odd word.
  It is not only a predisposition needing development, such as an infant has. Habit
  makes me a 'soulful ideality'. On 'ideality', cf. §§379, n. 3; 410, n. 10. But the
  stress here is on 'soulful' or psychical (*seelische*: 'pertaining to the soul') rather
  than 'ideality': the habitual is part of my (second) nature, not something I need
  to work out by explicit deliberation.

10. On 'mania' (*Wahnsinn*) see §408, n. 26. On 'absolute ideality', cf. §401Z. and
  n. 25. In mania the subject is trying to overcome a 'contradiction' between its
  'objective consciousness' and a 'fixed representation' or idea (e.g. the groundless
  belief that everyone is persecuting me). 'In itself' the soul is absolute ideality,
  which does not allow any such stubborn fixations, so the 'concept' of the soul
  requires it to overcome the idea and the contradiction, though it may of course
  fail in the attempt. On 'genius' (*Genius*), cf. §§405 and nn.; 406, n. 7. The
  genius is an individual outside the soul, initially the mother of the embryo,
  then the hypnotist or 'magnetizer'. The genius is rational and self-aware, and so
  supplies the dominated soul's 'being-for-self'. Hegel presents habit as a state of
  sanity, 'being-for-self' and 'being-together-with-one's-own-self', emerging from
  the overcoming of the contradiction or 'disruption' involved in madness or
  'derangement'. Thus he compares our condition before the formation of habit
  to madness, and more specifically 'mania'. Before habituation a 'representation',
  sensation, or whatever engrosses one's attention, because it is excessively painful,
  pleasant, desirable, or interesting. The soul loses itself in it, is 'evicted by it from
  the centre of its concrete actuality', in something like the way in which a maniac
  is engrossed by his fixed idea. (Cf. §§381, n. 25; 382, nn. 4, 5; and also Heidegger's account of an animal's *Benommenheit*, 'captivation', by stimuli in contrast
  to our own freedom in relation to them, discussed in my 'Does the Nothing
  Noth?', in A. O'Hear (ed.), *German Philosophy since Kant* (Cambridge: Cambridge University Press, 1999), 271–90.) Habit universalizes and internalizes
  the external stimulus, so that one is no longer captivated by it and, in any case,
  one is now dealing with oneself rather (or at least more) than a series of external

stimuli and is therefore free, since freedom is, for Hegel, self-determination (cf. §382, n. 3). The universality of reflection in which habit consists is still 'abstract universality', in contrast to the 'concrete universal' (*dem . . . konkret Allgemeinen*: literally, 'the concretely universal'). 'Concrete' is literally 'grown together' (§377, n. 1, 396, n. 3). So the concrete universal grows together into internal complexity without direct reliance on external input, and is thus 'self-determining'. (Hegel is thinking mainly of the procedure of his own Logic.) Habit involves both freedom and unfreedom. Freedom, in so far as it is 'posited' by the soul, and an 'ideality of beings' (*Idealität des Seienden*), i.e. 'beings', or what is, are taken up into the soul. Unfreedom, in so far as it is 'immediate', i.e. not simply 'posited', 'nature', and has the form of 'being'. 'Being' (*Sein*) is here contrasted with 'ideality', as *simply* being, inexplicable and intellectually indigestible: cf. §408, n. 3. ('Why did you do that?' 'No reason at all. It's just a habit of mine.')

Thomas Reid says of habit: 'I conceive it to be part of our constitution, that what we have been accustomed to do, we acquire, not only a facility, but a proneness to do on like occasions; so that it requires a particular will and effort to forebear it; but to do it, requires very often no will at all' (*Essays on the Active Powers of the Human Mind*, Essay III, i, ch. 3. Cf. Essay III, ii, ch. I: 'Some habits produce only a facility of doing a thing, without any inclination to do it. . . . Other habits produce a proneness to do an action, without thought or intention. . . . There are other habits which produce a desire of a certain object, and an uneasy sensation, until it is obtained.'). Roughly speaking, the facility increases our freedom, while the proneness diminishes it.

11. Here there are (as in §410, n. 7) three stages: (1) When the soul is 'immediately identical' with its body, it has no 'objective consciousness' of 'a world it finds before it'. It is aware only of its own bodily states and of the external stimuli that immediately impinge on its body. (2) It enters into opposition to the body, finding it alien and inadequate. It extrudes its 'bodiliness' and releases it to 'immediacy': the body is seen as just *there*, unmediated by the soul. (3) It reclaims the body by habituating it to sensations, movements, etc., exerting the 'power of its ideality' on it. Eliminating the conspicuous obtrusiveness of the body enables the soul to acquire objective consciousness of the world as a whole.

An 'Idea' (*Idee*) is, for Hegel, the unity of a 'concept' (*Begriff*) and its 'reality' (here *Dasein*, but elsewhere *Realität*) (cf. §394, n. 6), though he sometimes uses *Idee* informally as equivalent to *Begriff*. Here the soul is the concept, the body its reality. Hence the body 'belongs to my Idea'. The most famous expression, in Western philosophy, of hostility towards the body occurs in Plato's *Phaedo*, but Hegel probably has Catholicism in mind: cf. §410, n. 6. Hegel conflates two questions: (i) Would it be better if we did not have bodies with physical needs? (ii) Given that we do have bodies should we take care of them? One might consistently answer 'Yes' to both questions. Hegel answers (i) with 'No', (ii) with 'Yes'. This is consistent with his disbelief in a disembodied afterlife: see my 'Hegel on Death', *International Journal of Moral and Social Studies*, I (1986), pp.109–122.

'Negative' activity on the body is 'finite', since it sets the soul apart from the body, sets up a boundary or limit between them, which a proper attitude towards the body obliterates and is thus infinite or unbounded: cf. §§395, n. 2; 399, n. 3; 412, n. 1.

In reading the passage it needs to be borne in mind that 'spirit' and 'mind' both translate *Geist*, and that 'spiritual' is the related adjective *geistig*.

12. 'Nevertheless [*Dennoch*], etc.' is surprising, since Hegel has mentioned the habituation of the body, i.e. the soul's mediated unity with it, in the preceding paragraph. But the need to care for the body depends on the soul's immediate unity with the body, not its mediated unity with it. Even an unhabituated body needs to be looked after. So this new paragraph moves to a theme different from its immediate predecessor. In the immediate unity, the body is pervaded by the soul only in an 'indeterminately universal way', i.e. the body is alive and moves, but with insufficient precision for the soul's purposes. In the preceding paragraph 'my concept' required a body. Now the 'concept of the soul' requires the habituation of this body. The two cases differ. I or my soul could not exist at all without a body; I do not first exist as a soul and then acquire a body. But I do first exist with an untrained body, and one might conceivably live one's whole life (no doubt with the help of others) with a more or less untrained body. The 'concept' explains both why something is the case at any given time (e.g. the soul's having a body) and why something, though it is not always and invariably the case, tends over time to become the case (the soul's having a trained body). To use an analogy much favoured by Hegel, the concept embodied in the seed explains both why seeds invariably have some material component and why seeds tend to develop into full-grown plants (cf. §379, n. 5). The body is to become 'an accident brought into accord with its substance, freedom'. The body is not to be an independent substance nor an accident at odds with its substance, but a subordinate part of a coherent whole: cf. Enc. I, §§150-1 on substance and accidents. That this whole is called 'freedom' imples that Hegel is thinking of the 'facility' involved in habit rather than the 'proneness': cf. §410, n. 10. After all, whereas one is likely to do with facility what one is prone to do out of habit, one need have no overwhelming proneness to do what one does with facility. The artistic 'talent' that Hegel has in mind (cf. §395) may express itself only occasionally and reluctantly, albeit with facility.

13. On the 'magical relationship', cf. §405, n. 7. Here and in the previous paragraph, habituation makes the body one's own 'possession' or 'property'. Hegel adopts Locke's view of the acquisition of a property right: mixing one's labour with a natural object. He then applies this to one's own body. In this case the property right is exclusive (unlike the case discussed in §410, n. 8): only one person can own each body. Moreover, I can only enter into possession of my own body, i.e. the body with which I am initially immediately identical: I cannot gain ownership of someone else's body by mixing my labour with it.

14. 'Recollection' (*Erinnerung*) has, for Hegel, the sense of 'internalization' as well as 'recollection': cf. §402, n. 6. When I write (by hand) the letter 's', the 's' I produce will differ to some degree from every other 's' I produce. This does

not matter to me, in fact I do not usually notice it; I am only concerned to produce an adequate token of the universal type 's'. If I teach someone else to write the letter 's' (and not to imitate my handwriting), I want him to produce acceptable tokens of the type 's', not to produce marks that are exactly similar to some individual 's' of mine, or even very similar to my s's in general. His s's may resemble my z's more than they do my s's, but that does not matter as long as his script is legible. Only if differences between individual tokens are ignored can I hand on a 'rule' (*Regel*) to others. I cannot prescribe as a rule that others should write s's exactly similar to some individual s of mine; even I cannot follow that rule. I might tell others to write their s's in a similar way to mine, if I am teaching them to forge my handwriting. But more usually I give them greater latitude, allowing a tolerable range of variation between their s's and mine. Consciousness or the soul is absent from the inessential detail of handwriting, and this makes it seem mechanical. Ordinary handwriting differs in this respect from painting, where the fine detail matters. An artist's various paintings of the same theme, e.g. Cezanne's paintings of Mount St Victoire, are not expressions of a habit.

NOTES TO §411

1. The soul is now 'actual' (*wirkliche*), not just potential, since it has an adequate external expression in its trained body. That it is an individual subject 'for itself' also suggests that it is actual rather than potential, but 'for itself' also conveys the ideas that it is aware of itself and that it is independent, a subject in its own right or by itself: cf. §383, n. 1. Characteristically, Hegel moves freely between the human subject (often contrasted with an *object*) and the subject of a predicate in a judgement or proposition; the predicate, here the body, is subordinate to and dependent on the 'subject'. In Enc. I the account of 'inner' and 'outer' (§§138–41) is immediately followed by 'actuality' (§142). 'Pathognomic' expression is expression of occurrent emotions and feelings; 'physiognomic' expression is expression of dispositions, such as mental abilities, character, etc. See §411, n. 2.
2. On 'sign', cf. §§401, n. 17; 411, n. 4. On speech, cf. §401, n. 28. What the body primarily cannot express is our thoughts, the mind 'in its universality for itself'. But it is also a 'contingency' in its 'physiognomic and pathognomic determinacy': features of the body, especially the face, are not an infallible indication of emotions and dispositions, which can be feigned, especially by actors and confidence tricksters. The most famous attempt to make a science of physiognomy was *Physiognomische Fragmente* (1775–8; translated as *Essays on Physiognomy*, 1793) by Johann Kaspar Lavater (1741–1801). Hegel criticizes physiognomy in PS, pp.185–95. The main proponent of 'cranioscopy' or phrenology, the art of reading character from bumps on the skull, was Franz Josef Gall (1758–1828). It depends on three dubious assumptions: (1) mental functions are located in specific regions of the brain; (2) the bigger the brain region, the more developed the mental function; and (3) the shape of the skull corresponds to the shape of the brain. Hegel also attacked this theory, especially assumption (1), in PS,

pp.195–210. The *signatura rerum* ('signature of things') refers to the external quality of things that indicates their inner nature, e.g. the brainlike appearance of the walnut that indicates its benefits for the brain. Hegel mentions it in his LPR i. 280–1 and argues that animals and uncivilized peoples are more sensitive to the beneficial and harmful properties of plants than civilized human beings are. *De signatura rerum* was also the title of a book written by Jakob Böhme (1575–1624) in 1622 and published in 1635, referring to the clues provided by the external qualities of things to their inner nature. But Hegel is probably not alluding to Böhme here, both because Böhme was a mystic more interested in the symbolism of natural entities than in their medicinal properties, and because Hegel has a deep respect for Böhme. In both versions, the *signatura rerum* is related to St Augustine's view, influential in the Middle Ages and persisting into German Romanticism, that nature is, in addition to the Bible, a second form of divine revelation, a sort of book written in a script that we need to decipher. Cf. Sir Thomas Browne, *Religio Medici*, i. 12: '*Beware of philosophy* is a precept not to be received in too large a sense; for in this Mass of Nature there is a set of things that carry in their Front, though not in Capital Letters, yet in Stenography and short Characters, something of Divinity, which to wiser Reasons serve as Luminaries in the Abyss of Knowledge, and to judicious beliefs as Scales and Roundles to mount the Pinacles and highest pieces of Divinity'.

3. Aristotle described the hand as the 'tool of tools' (*organon . . . organōn*) in *de Anima*, III. 8, 432ᵃ1-2.

4. These 'looks and gestures' are not signs, but have a 'symbolic nature', since their relationship to their 'meaning' is not (in Hegel's view) purely conventional, but depends on an intrinsic resemblance between the gesture and the meaning. In the Paragraph and the Remark, the body is said to be a 'sign' of the mind, rather than a symbol. If Hegel is thinking here of his later distinction between sign and symbol (cf. §457), he may mean that the human body as a whole has no special resemblance to the mind, even though such a body is peculiar to humans and is specially suited for the production of gestures that *do* have a resemblance to their mental counterparts.

5. On the animal's absorption in its current 'sensation', cf. §381, nn. 12 and 25. It is not clear why expressing a sensation or feeling should immerse one in it rather than liberate one from it, as Hegel suggests elsewhere: e.g. ILA, pp. 52 ff. Nor is it clear whether the superiority, in this respect, of speech consists in the fact that one does not usually express one's feelings in language as readily and fully as one does in gestures or in the fact that linguistic expression of a feeling keeps it in its proper place and does not let it take over one's entire 'reality' (*Dasein*).

6. On Lavater see §§401, n. 4; 411, n. 2. 'Beware of him whom God hath marked' (*Hüte dich vor dem, den Gott gezeichnet hat*) refers to Genesis, 4: 15, where God puts a mark on Cain, and Ezekiel, 9: 4–6, where he puts a mark on the foreheads of those who 'sigh and cry for all the abominations' perpetrated in Jerusalem. In both cases the mark is intended to protect its bearer from being killed. (This mark is distinct from the 'mark of the beast' of Revelation 16: 2, etc., though this is similarly designed to elicit favourable treatment from the beast, but not of course

from God.) Hence the dictum is 'misused', when it is taken to advocate mistrust of marked people. It is also misused, because no such mark is an infallible sign of the character of its bearer.

NOTES TO §412

1. This Paragraph summarizes the process described in §411, but adds that the culmination of the process is a change from soul to 'consciousness' (*Bewusstsein*). Consciousness involves two additional features: (1) awareness of oneself as 'I'; (2) awareness of an 'object' (*Objekt*), a world, external to oneself. However, the transition from the soul's separation from and 'incorporation' (*Einbilden*) into its body to the I's consciousness of a world is unclear. Could not someone (or something) master their body without becoming an I or conscious of a world? Could not someone even be conscious of a world without being an I, or, conversely, be an I without being conscious of a world? In the Paragraph Hegel's argument seems to depend on ambiguities. When the 'ideality of [the soul's] determinacies' is said to be 'for itself' (*die für sich seiende Idealität ihrer Bestimmtheiten*), this might mean that it is actual rather than potential (as the two preceding occurrences of 'in itself', which presumably mean 'potentially', suggest) or it might mean that the ideality is aware of itself, which at once brings in something like egohood. When this ideality is said to be 'recollected' (*erinnert*: cf. §401, n. 2) in its externality and 'infinite relation to itself' (cf. §410, n. 11 on 'finite'), this might simply mean that in its habituated body it is together with and related to itself, rather than that it is internalized into egohood. Hegel's train of thought seems to be that what is left in the soul, once its determinate states have been extruded into the body, can only be 'free universality', which amounts to egohood. This 'awakening to the I' is 'higher' than the soul's 'awakening' from sleep of §398. On the 'judgement' (*Urteil*) as original division (*Ur-teil*), and the corresponding conflation of the human 'subject' with the subject of a judgement, see §§389, n. 4; 407, n. 1; 411, n. 1. An argument that Hegel might have used, but apparently does not, is that habituation of one's own body implies a distinction between one's body and other external material over which one does not have a similar control.

2. Here Hegel presents an argument for the transition to egohood that is not apparent in the Paragraph. (1) Even habituation leaves a distinction between soul and body. (The reference to the 'logical Idea' may be to a specific phase of the logical Idea, e.g. Enc. I, §§213–15 on the Idea or §§216–21 on life, or more generally to the fact that the logical Idea is not flatly identical with what develops out of it: cf. §§574–7) (2) 'Therefore' (*daher*) the body resists, to some extent, control by the soul. (3) The soul responds to this by a withdrawal into itself, a 'reflection-into-self', which makes it 'essence' (*Wesen*), the I, rather than 'being'. (Roughly speaking, 'being' is the outer surface of something, 'essence' is its inner nature. On the complex relationship between being, essence, and reflection—which Hegel associates with the reflection of light—see Enc. I, §§112–14.) Proposition (1) seems true. The step from (1) to

(2) looks plausible. Exploiting Hegel's analogy in §411 —the habituated body as the 'soul's work of art' —we can ask: Why is the artist distinct from his work? There are at least two possible answers. (i) The artist has produced and will produce other works apart from this one, or at least other *things*. This is not relevant to the soul and its body, since the soul has only one body and it does not have or produce anything else on a par with the body; its actions, utterances, etc. are all states of the body. (ii) As soon as a work is embodied it has features out of the artist's control: a large painting is difficult to lift, the song cannot be heard ten miles away, etc. Additionally, the work is open to interpretation, misinterpretation, neglect, etc. by others. (The latter is also true of the body, though Hegel does not mention it here.) Proposition (2) is also true. The step from (2) to (3) is questionable. Why must the soul withdraw into itself? The artist (to continue the analogy) need not differentiate himself from his works, feeling that they are not a complete expression of himself. He may be content with his dispersal among products not fully in his own control. If the soul does withdraw into itself and thereby become the 'essence' of the body or the living creature, why must this amount to the I? Proposition (3) seems true (more or less), but it does not follow from (1) and/or (2). Animals too, after all, have a similar mixture of control and lack of control over their bodies, but they do not become I's. At the very least Hegel needs an extra premiss concerning the peculiar response of an implicit *mind* to its imperfectly habituated body.

3. On 'selfishness', cf. §402, n. 2. The I is universal, because it is intrinsically featureless ('simple') and exactly similar in everyone who is an I: cf. §396, n. 12. Someone is an I if, and only if, they think of themselves as (an) I. So the universal is related to the universal. In 'external nature' the universal emerges *as* a universal with the death of an individual, especially an animal, instantiating it. The universal does not become *for itself*: a dog is not aware of its caninity, only of individuals. But in humans it emerges as a universal by being for itself, without the death of the individual: cf. §381, and nn. 24, 25. The relationship between the I's universality and the universality of caninity or animality, in virtue of which they are both called 'universality', is this: just as caninity disregards or abstracts from the particular and individual features that differentiate one dog from another, so the I disregards features differentiating one person from another. Caninity and animality are not featureless or 'simple' in the way that the I is: an animal e.g. is a living being capable of sensation and movement. Perhaps a closer parallel to the I is the universal '(being an) entity', which disregards any feature differentiating anything from anything else. Many things are entities without thinking of themselves as entities, though none think of themselves as entities without being entities. Hence, despite its intrinsic featurelessness, the 'entity' differs from the I. 'Natural awakening' is awakening from sleep: cf. §§398; 412, n. 1.

4. The human soul transcends 'sensation' in two ways: (i) in habit it universalizes individual sensations, etc., makes them 'into a being' (*zu einem Sein*: a verbal noun); (ii) by becoming an I, it distances itself from its sensations, even habitual sensations: it is no longer wholly absorbed in each sensation, but has 'posited' it 'ideally' (*ideell*: cf. §403, n. 2). As an I, the soul is an 'empty space' with no

determinate content of its own, but it fills this with a universal content, presumably the 'world external to it' (cf. §412, n. 1), which is universal both because it is objective and thus shared by all I's, and because it, and our consciousness of it, involve universal thoughts: cf. §377, n. 5. The soul is thus an 'individually [*individuell*] determined' universal, since it has its own perspective on the world and its own body. In the case of the sentient soul 'the self' (*das Selbst*: here more or less equivalent to the I) was the 'genius' acting on it 'only from outside' and 'only from within'. On the duality of the genius, see §§405, n. 5; 406, n. 7. Here Hegel's idea is that if the controlling genius (the embryo's mother, the mesmerizer) is only outside the soul, it is also inside the soul, but deep inside it, so that it does not manifest itself in the outer behaviour of the organism. But now the self enters into the soul's body and posits 'being' in itself. So the self is now unitary. On 'being' (*das Sein*), see §§408, n. 3; 410, nn. 4 and 10; 412, n. 4. In §§408 and 410, n. 10, *Sein* indicated sheer givenness, intellectual or psychical indigestibility. In §412 *Sein* indicates stability of habit (in contrast to the fleeting sensation) and the filling required by emptiness. But this variation depends on whether the soul is an I or not; the mere soul cannot manage being without expelling it, whereas the I can accommodate being while keeping it at a distance. On the I's 'self-intuiting' in 'its Other', cf. §§413 ff.; 457, n. 1.

NOTES TO §413

1. 'Consciousness' (*Bewusstsein*) in Hegel (though not always in ordinary German) is intentional, consciousness *of* something, or that something is the case. *Reflexion* does have the sense of reflecting on or thinking about something, but Hegel also has in mind the reflection of light by a surface: cf. Enc. I, §112Z. 'Relationship' (*Verhältnis*: also 'ratio', 'proportion') denotes a close relationship between two things, here the mind and its object. (The mind's infinite 'relation' to itself is a *Beziehung*, not a *Verhältnis*.) 'Appearance' (*Erscheinung*) does not mean 'seeming' or 'semblance' (*Schein*); it is literally 'shining forth', and refers to the mind's coming out of its shell. (It is not unlike the appearance, or publication, of a book, as in: 'The appearance of the book is delayed', 'The book appeared last year', in contrast to: 'The book has an attractive appearance', 'The book appeared difficult'.) Three stages of the mind are in play: (1) the 'immediate identity of the natural soul' or its 'natural life', where it is aware only of its own sensations, not of external objects; (2) the mind's 'infinite' self-relation, its 'pure ideal self-identity', where the mind is aware or 'certain' only of itself, not yet of external objects; (3) the mind of stage (2) makes the 'content' of stage (1) its 'object' (*Gegenstand*) and turns it into an self-subsistent 'object' (*Objekt*), i.e. it transforms the subjective sensations of stage (1) into (consciousness of) external objects. On Hegel's two words for 'object', *Gegenstand* and *Objekt*, see §387, n. 15. Here the difference is that a *Gegenstand* is essentially an object *of* a mind, while an *Objekt* is independent. Nevertheless, the I is aware of this independent *Objekt*. The I is distinct from, other than, any and every *Objekt*, distinct even from itself, as the *Zusatz* explains, hence it is 'absolute negativity'. But it establishes a sort of 'identity' with

the *Objekt* in that it 'extends over' it, thereby sublating it as an *Objekt*, since it takes away its independence.

2. Hegel is here trying to explain how the I can be both universal and individual. As the I, it is a universal, featureless, relating only to itself, etc. But the I is also an 'individually [*individuell*: cf. §412, n. 4] determined universal': it is distinct from any of the objects of its awareness and from other I's (though these have not yet come on the scene explicitly: see §§430 ff.). The I is not a universal that *turns into* a determinate individual; it remains throughout *both* universal *and* individual. But universality and individuality are not unproblematically compatible; they are opposites. Hence the I somehow oscillates between them. It is an 'immediately negative relation' to itself as indeterminate universality, and is its 'unmediated opposite': 'abstract, simple individuality', i.e. an individuality marked out simply by difference, not by any specific property that it uniquely possesses. The negative relation and the opposition are immediate: the I does not swing from one extreme to the other by stages or continuously, like a pendulum. It veers between universality and individuality, with no intermediate steps.

3. The distinction between us or 'we' (Hegel and his attentive readers) and the phase of the mind under consideration is important in PS, where Hegel is careful to distinguish between what *we* can see and what the form or 'shape' of consciousness under consideration can see. This is a special case of a more general distinction between 'us' (or 'me') and the object under consideration. For example, in his Logic, Hegel stresses that the unfolding of a thought or category and its development into another thought or category is accomplished by the category itself, not by Hegel. It is not usually the case that an object itself distinguishes the 'moments' that we distinguish in it: it is we, not the pebble itself, who differentiate its smoothness, brownness, and hardness. But the I does so. To explain how it does so, Hegel finds it convenient to focus on the I's individuality. This individuality is 'exclusive': cf. §404, n. 1. An individual is not this, not that: it excludes other individuals. But as an I, this individuality relates to itself. It therefore turns its exclusivity against itself and excludes itself, thereby reverting to universality. The argument conflates different types of exclusion. An exclusive club excludes *most* people from membership, but as long as it does not exclude *everyone*, it does not exclude itself from being a club. Even if exclusive individuality does exclude itself from individuality, why must it become universality? Hegel's answer is that it is because universality is the 'opposite' immediately 'joined together' with it. The conjunction of individuality and universality is not a result of individuality's self-exclusion, but a constant background factor explaining why exit from the one is automatically entry into the other.

4. 'Being' (*Sein*) here contrasts primarily with 'thinking'. In the case of most things a distinction can be drawn between their being, on the one hand, and thought about them, on the other. We think of a pebble, for example, first as smooth, then as hard and finally as brown; but the pebble itself has all three qualities simultaneously and immediately, and it would have them even if we did not think about it: cf. §413, n. 3. Conversely, the thought of, or thinking about, pebbles, or this pebble, does not guarantee the existence or 'being' of pebbles, or of this

pebble; the thought of a hundred dollars, as Kant argued, does not guarantee their reality: cf. Enc. I, §51. I can distinguish in these ways even between myself as an embodied individual and my thought about it; I might exist as an embodied individual even if I lacked or had lost the capacity to think of myself as such, and I might conceivably think of myself as an embodied individual without being one. In a manner reminiscent of Descartes (cf. Enc. I, §64), Hegel argues that, in the case of the I, no such distinction between the I itself (or the 'being' of the I) and thought about it (or the I itself) can be drawn. (The uncertainty over whether the I is being or, alternatively, thinking stems from the disappearance of the usual distinction between thought and being, though Hegel here identifies the I with thinking.) Thus the 'determination of abstractly universal individuality' is a thought, a thought about (or applicable to) the I. Does this thought guarantee the existence of the I? Does it exhaust and thereby 'constitute' the being of the I? After all, one might think of a pebble as an 'abstractly universal individual', as simply 'this (individual)'; this thought does not constitute the being of a pebble, since there is far more to a pebble's being than simply individuality. But the I is just an abstractly universal individual and its being is therefore exhausted, and also guaranteed, by this thought. A distinction of sorts can, however, be drawn between being and thinking. Being is 'absolutely immediate, etc.'. Hegel here has in mind not so much the concrete being of, say, a pebble, which is somehow 'immediate', flat, just *there*, in contrast to thinking about it, as the abstract concept of being with which Logic begins, and which therefore has no mediating antecedents within Logic: Enc. I, §§84–6. (We might ask: Why not concrete being? But abstract or 'pure' being seems not inappropriate to the bare I.) Thinking, by contrast, is not just *there*: it differentiates and mediates itself, by, e.g., thinking about thinking, or by moving from premises to a conclusion. In a similar way, so does the I: I am aware of myself, of me, but the me of which I am aware is identical with the I that is aware. (Hence Hegel identifies the I with thinking rather than with being.) But thinking is not sheer movement without pause. It settles on the conclusion it has reached, it resolves a problem and focuses on the solution. The conclusion or the solution is somehow immediate; it has an intrinsic nature of its own that can be considered independently of the process by which it was reached. This stage of thinking is 'being'. So thinking, and consequently the I, involves being. This explains how the I can be self-aware. The I qua thinking 'posits' the I qua being as its 'other', but also as identical to itself. Hegel goes beyond Descartes to try to explain how one and the same I is aware of itself, and he uses the thought–being contrast to do so. 'Awareness' is *Wissen*, 'certainty' is *Gewissheit*, introduced both because of its affinity to *Wissen* and in reminiscence of Descartes and his epistemological concerns.

5. If we do not think philosophically about the I, but use pictorial 'representation', we tend to represent the I's certainty as a 'property' (*Eigenschaft*: cf. Enc. I, §§125-6) of the I or a 'determination in [*an*] its nature'. If certainty were a property of the I or in its nature, the I could exist without being certain of itself. But the I cannot exist without self-differentiation and self-identification, nor therefore without self-certainty. Moreover, self-certainty is not simply one among several essential

features of the I; it is its whole 'nature', there is nothing more to the I than such self-differentiation and self-identification. The I is essentially and exclusively self-certain, as the will is essentially and exclusively free. But there are at least two types of freedom, 'subjective' and 'objective'. Subjective freedom, the freedom to do what one likes, is more properly described as 'wilfulness' (*Willkür*) than 'will' (*Wille*): cf. §§443, 473 ff. 'Genuine' (*echten*) freedom is objective, involving acquiescence in an objectively rational order, especially the ethical and political order. The self-certainty of the I has more affinity to subjective freedom than to objective freedom. It does not immediately involve acknowledgement of an objective order, whether in logic or in the world. Descartes, after all, decides that *he* exists before he infers that God and an objective world exist.

6. When the I is aware of itself, it is free, since it is related only to itself; the I of which it is aware is only 'formally', not 'actually', distinct from itself. So the 'difference' is only 'in itself' or implicit. But an implicit difference must be 'posited', become actual: cf. Enc. I, §§116 ff. So the I must become aware of something that is actually distinct from itself. It cannot do this by reverting to the anthropological level, for there the mind is not conscious of an object distinct from itself, but merges into the 'natural'. The I has to remain a distinct, self-certain I, yet conscious of an 'object in the strict sense', a *Gegenstand*, something that stands over 'against' (*gegen*) the I. (*Objekt* also has this connotation in accordance with its Latin roots, *iectum*, 'thrown, and *ob*, 'against', but this is less obvious to a German speaker.) The object is a *Totalität*, since, like the I, it is a self-contained, independent whole.

7. The difference or distinction is between the I and the object, not between one object and another. But only the object has a 'determinate content', while the I lacks content. So the difference lies on the side of the objects. But because the I has a non-actual difference within itself, the I relates to the actual difference, i.e. the object, and is then 'reflected' back into itself and has the object 'posited ideally' within itself. So now there is an actual difference between the pure I and the I qua consciousness of an object. Awareness of oneself as an I is both sufficient and necessary ('Only when I apprehend, etc.') for consciousness of an object. The light-analogy suggests that I am only genuinely self-aware when I am conscious of objects: light is only visible when it encounters 'darkness' or a dark object (cf. Enc. II, §275Z.).

The view that consciousness of objects and self-consciousness require each other is more plausible than Hegel's argument for it. Like many of Hegel's references to the logical underpinning of his moves, this reference to the Logic (cf. §413, n. 6) is not very informative or compelling. Even if it is reasonable to suppose that a *potential* difference must become actual, it is not clear why the difference between the I and itself is *an sich* in the sense of 'potential'.

NOTES TO §414

1. On the soul's 'substantial universality' see §396Z. The soul is universal in a way in which the I is not: it is not developed into a distinct individual. 'Substantial(ity)'

contrasts with 'subjective': the soul as such is not a subject confronting an object, but a substance with accidents, i.e. sensations or feelings (cf. Enc. I, §§150-1). These sensations are transformed, at the stage of consciousness, into independent objects, correlative to the mind's 'reflection-into-itself'. (This is the 'self-division' of the mind discussed in §414, n. 2.) Hence the relation of the mind to its objects is similar to its relation to the soul's substantial universality. The latter is its 'negative', 'dark and beyond it'. So consciousness is related to its *objects* as its negative, dark and beyond it. Thus consciousness does not involve the 'identity' of itself and its objects: that would either be a return to the anthropological stage or an advance to a higher stage (cf. §414, n. 2). Consciousness and its objects are joined by a 'relationship'(*Verhältnis*), the two sides of which hover uneasily between independence and identity. Another such relationship is the relationship of the parts to the whole: to be parts of the *whole* they have to be identical to it, but to be *parts* they have to be separated from each other, and from the whole, and thus independent (Enc. I, §§135–6). 'Essence' (*Wesen*) contrasts with 'appearance' (*das Erscheinen*), which is quite different from 'semblance' (*Schein(en)*). 'The essence must appear' (Enc. I, §131), i.e. manifest itself in external phenomena; only then is it really an essence. The I is the essence of mind, consciousness its appearance. 'Reality' (*die Realität*) refers to the mind's objects, which are involved in the 'contradiction': they are 'posited' as both 'in immediate being' (*unmittelbar seiend*), i.e. mind-independent, and as 'ideal', i.e. objects of *consciousness*. Hence mind is here 'only' (*nur*) appearance, an uneasy combination of 'reflection-into-self and reflection-into-another, ... still divided against itself and without intrinsic stability' (Enc. I, §131Z.). In Enc. I the deficiency of appearance is repaired at the stage of 'actuality' (§§142 ff.), perhaps an analogue of 'psychology' in Enc. III (§§440 ff.).

2. The *Zusatz* expands on the 'contradiction' mentioned in the Paragraph. The contradiction depends on the expressions 'within me' (*in mir*) and 'outside me' (*ausser mir*). For something to be literally in me and outside me (not just half in and half out) would be contradictory. But the object is not literally *in me*, I am simply conscious of it; it might be said to be in my consciousness, but then it is not simultaneously outside my consciousness. That the contradiction is only apparent is suggested by Hegel's problematic use of the light-analogy. What is the 'darkness' (*das Dunkle*) 'outside the light'? Is it (1) a dark area or object not illuminated by the light, (2) an object illuminated by the light but not inside the light or inside the source of the light, or (3) those parts of an illuminated object that the light does not reach, its inside and its back? A readily recognizable contradiction requires that it be (1), giving an object that is both illuminated and not illuminated. But that does not apply to consciousness, whose object, as an object of consciousness, is illuminated. If the darkness is (2), there is no contradiction: an illuminated object need not be inside, i.e. a part of, the light that illuminates it. (3) is more promising, since it is true that illuminated opaque objects have unilluminated parts and aspects, that illumination is usually only partial. This also applies to consciousness: my knowledge of an object independent of myself is usually only partial. There is the difference that when I am conscious of e.g. a rock by

seeing it, I am usually also conscious of, or conscious that it has, parts and aspects that I cannot at the moment see. Light, by contrast, does nothing to illuminate those parts that it leaves in darkness, though it may, by illuminating *some* parts, indicate *to an observer* the presence of *other* parts left in the dark. That an object has parts of which I am not fully conscious indicates the independence of the object from myself, and my hazy consciousness of such unknown parts sustains my belief that the object is independent of myself. If the I were to exert 'absolute negativity' on its 'Other' there would be no such contradiction or incongruity. The Other would either be wholly outside the I and not known to it at all or, more likely, entirely dependent on the I and known through and through. In fact, Hegel implies, the object is 'posited' by the I, 'in itself' identical to the mind, and projected by the mind's 'self-division' (*Selbstteilung*). We, i.e. Hegel and his readers, can see this, because we have reached the 'Idea' (*Idee*) of mind, i.e. the stage at which the gulf between the mind and its objects is closed. On the Idea as the unity of concept (in this context, consciousness) and reality (objects) see §410, n. 11; on the distinction between 'we' or 'us' and the stage of mind under consideration, see §413, n. 3.

Hegel sounds here as if he is proposing an idealism of a Kantian sort, namely that the objects that I normally take to be independent of myself are really constructions of my own. If so, his argument for it is fallacious. Even if we grant that we become conscious of objects by means of a 'self-division' of the mind, it does not follow that the objects are not independent of the mind. We can grant too that our consciousness of objects requires a large contribution from the mind itself, especially of general concepts or thoughts, such as causality. But again it does not follow that objects do not intrinsically conform to such concepts, e.g. are not really causally related to each other. However, at bottom Hegel agrees with this. He does not believe that objects are constructed by ourselves. He does not, like Kant, suppose that things-in-themselves elude our thoughts and our sensory apparatus. (For one thing, Kant wants to leave space for a world-transcendent God accessible to faith, whereas Hegel's God is not transcendent.) It is important to remember that the 'mind', for Hegel, extends far beyond individual minds, so that what objects are and do can be attributed to the mind, without being attributed to the mind of the individual.

NOTES TO §415

1. To the I, the development of consciousness does not seem to be its own doing. 'For itself' the I is just 'formal identity', and thus too thin and frail to generate and guide the development. The I regards the development as depending on changes in its object. The syntax and meaning of 'the progressive determination . . . is in itself [*an sich*], etc.' are uncertain. It does not mean that the determination *really* or *in fact is* alteration of the object, but rather that *to the I* it seems to be really (*an sich*) alteration, etc., and/or that at this undeveloped stage (*an sich*) it is alteration, etc. The final sentence of the Paragraph gives Hegel's own view, rather than that of the I: the object develops, but its development is 'logical' (*logische*),

i.e. determined by the 'dialectical movement of the concept'. This development is driven by the subject, since this is 'thinking'. But the object shares the same logical development, shadowing the subject as it were. Because the object has the same underlying structure and development as the subject, it is 'the subject's own' (*das Seinige des Subjekts*), i.e. its object. Cf. §417, n. 2.

2. On Hegel's view of Kant, see Enc. I, §§40–60. 'Consciousness' (*Bewusstsein*) is not a word especially favoured by Kant, but he did, in the *Critique of Pure Reason*, explore the conditions of our 'objective experience' or 'experience of objects', and this is more or less what Hegel means by 'consciousness'. In *Critique* Kant did not consider other stages of mind that fall within the scope of Hegel's 'philosophy of mind', especially the soul, 'objective mind', and 'absolute mind'. Kant does in other works speak about morality and political institutions, but he does not view them, in the way that Hegel does, as a phase of the mind's objectification or as helping to close the gap, in consciousness, between subject and object and thus rising towards the 'Idea' of mind: cf. §§410, n. 11; 414, n. 2. The object of our experience is not, for Kant, straightforwardly the 'thing-in-itself'. The thing in itself is the thing or object as it is quite independently of the I or the knowing subject. It is known by us, in so far as we know it at all, only as it appears to us through our subjective forms of space and time, and through the 'categories' that we apply to our 'intuitions'. Thus what 'I' primarily stands in 'relation' to is not the thing in itself as such, but an 'appearance' or 'phenomenon'. An appearance is not conceived by Kant as wholly dependent on the particular individual who experiences it, like a dream image or an illusion; that would be a *Schein*, 'illusion, semblance' rather than an 'appearance', *Erscheinung*. An appearance can, for example, be experienced by others, and has an inner depth (e.g. an atomic structure) that may only be discovered after long investigation. (Kant's idealism differs in this respect from that of Berkeley, whose idealism requires the rejection of such entities as 'matter' and atoms.) There is, therefore, a sense in which the objects of our experience are 'in themselves', *an sich*, independent of any particular mind and its current experiences, even though they are not strictly things in themselves. Hegel may mean that the I, for Kant, stands in an essential relation to the thing in itself strictly conceived; the I could have no object at all, and could thus not be an I, unless it were affected in some way by the thing in itself. But it is more likely that he is, for brevity's sake, conflating the two types of object. The 'intelligence' (*Intelligenz*) is roughly the theoretical mind: see §§387, n. 18; 443 ff. Hence it more or less coincides with the subject matter of Kant's *Critique of Pure Reason*, except that Kant is accused of considering it only in relation to its object, and so 'according to [*nach*] this finitude', since it contrasts with, and is bounded by, an object different from itself, and does not have itself as its object: cf. §406, n. 9. The will is the subject matter of Kant's *Critique of Practical Reason*, where it is less obviously related to phenomenal objects than the intelligence is, since although it does will particular, phenomenal actions (such as repaying a debt), it is, if it is working properly, guided by the 'categorical imperative' to e.g. act only on a maxim that it can will to be a natural law. For Hegel, by contrast, the truly free

will wills itself or wills 'freedom', not anything other than itself: cf. PR, §§21 ff.; Enc. III, §481-2. Hegel's general idea is that intelligence and will should be considered in the way in which they overcome the cleavage between themselves and their objects, so that in dealing with their objects they are somehow dealing with themselves.

In his *Critique of Judgement* (1790), Kant introduced several ideas that, in Hegel's view, repaired some of the deficiencies in his first two Critiques. The 'faculty of reflective judgement [*Urteilskraft*]' is at work, according to Kant, in our judgements of nature as a purposive system, of beauty, and of organic natural wholes. While the 'faculty of subsuming judgement' (*subsumierende Urteilskraft*) is our ability to decide whether something stands under a certain universal rule, concept, etc., reflective judgement is the capacity to think of the particular as contained in a universal (a rule, law, concept, etc.) that is not immediately given: cf. Enc. I, §55, where Hegel plausibly, but against Kant's intention, claims that Kant ascribes to reflective judgement the 'principle of an intuitive intellect'. An 'intuitive intellect' or understanding, which Kant also refers to as 'intellectual intuition', is an intellect that supplies not only concepts, but also the 'intuitions' required for the application of them, and does not rely, as our intellect does, on intuitions supplied from outside. On Kant's view, the concept of an intuitive intellect is not contradictory, but we do not have such an intellect ourselves nor do we know whether there is a god who has such an intellect, though it may well be reasonable to view nature *as if* it were the creation of an intuitive intellect. For an intuitive intellect, a concept would immediately guarantee its realization in intuition. Hence it involves 'subjectivity-objectivity' (*Subjekt-Objektivität*), the automatic realization (objectivity) of a concept (subjectivity). This, in turn, amounts to an Idea (*Idee*), where the concept (subjectivity) involves its own reality (objectivity): cf. §377, n. 4. A 'reflective judgement' is, then, in Hegel's view, a judgement that presents a concept or universal as entailing its own realization. (It is distinct from what Enc. I, §174 calls a 'judgement of reflection', which is a judgement that relates something, such as a plant, to something else, such as a disease, as in 'This plant is medicinal', in contrast to a 'qualitative judgement' such as 'This rose is red'.) The concept of a plant, for example, involves its own realization—a claim that Hegel makes more plausible by identifying the concept with the plan or code embedded in the seed. By contrast, Kant regards a reflective judgement as a substitute for such claims. We would do well (Kant believes) to regard a living organism *as if* its realization were secured by its concept, *as if* it were the product of an intuitive intellect, but this is a 'subjective maxim' for our inquiry, not a genuinely objective claim. Moreover, we can think of God as having an intuitive intellect, but not ourselves. Hegel, by contrast, tends to attribute an intuitive intellect to *us*. *We* can derive nature from its concept, and mind from its concept, though we do so by a sequence of stages, not immediately as Kant supposes God would do.

Karl Leonhard Reinhold (1758–1823) published *Versuch einer neuen Theorie des menschlichen Vorstellungsvermögen* (Attempt at a New Theory of the Human Faculty of Representation) in 1789.

Inspired by Kant's claim that 'The *I think* must be able to accompany all my representations' (*Critique of Pure Reason*, B131), Johann Gottlieb Fichte (1762–1814) attempted, especially in his *Wissenschaftslehre* (Theory of Science) (1794), to derive the fundamental characteristics of the world from the I or ego. In doing this he tried to dispense with the unknowable thing-in-itself, which, like many of Kant's contemporaries and successors, he found objectionable. However, the first thing that the I has to do is 'posit' a 'Non-I' (*Nicht-Ich*) which gives the I an 'impetus', impulse, or shock (*Anstoss*), goading it into activity. The I then develops in interaction with the Non-I. The impetus is 'infinite', in that it is total and all-embracing, not one localized impetus among others, and that it impels the I to endless activity. Hegel's critique of Fichte is unfair. Whereas Reinhold gives a subjective psychological turn to Kant's doctrine and is dealing with the individual I, Fichte's I is not an individual I. Individual I's emerge only later, as a result primarily of the practical or moral requirements of the I: moral restraints and prescriptions presuppose another I. Hence the Non-I is not an 'object' (*Gegenstand*) of the I in the ordinary sense nor is it 'in consciousness'. Unlike Kant's thing in itself, the Non-I is not independent of the I; it is a product of the I itself and has no intrinsic nature beyond what the I posits in it. A rough analogy is this: an actual rival may spur me on in my academic, sporting, or amatory activities, but so may a rival whom I invent or imagine, perhaps for this very purpose; Fichte's Non-I is more like an imaginary rival than an actual rival. (Whereas for Kant, God, if he exists, is a thing-in-itself, for Fichte God, if he exists, is the I, not the Non-I.) Since Fichte's I is not the mind and the Non-I is not really 'an Other' standing 'in relation' to the I, Hegel has not substantiated his case against Fichte.

3. In his *Ethica ordine geometrico demonstrata* (Ethics demonstrated in geometrical order) (1677) Benedict or Baruch Spinoza (1632–77) argued that there is only one substance, with two attributes known to us, extension and thought. A human body is a 'mode' of substance in the attribute of extension, while the human mind is a mode of substance in the attribute of thought. Since the attributes and their respective modes run parallel to each other in every detail, Hegel inferred that the mind could not, on this account, be an I, a unitary self; it must be as dispersed as the body is, somewhat similar to the self as Hume views it, a bundle of impressions and ideas. According to Spinoza, the mind is, in its usual state, not free; it gets its ideas from the impacts of other bodies on its own body. We can however attain a certain freedom by acquiring philosophical knowledge of the whole of substance, thus breaking loose from our immediate surroundings. This is the third and highest of the grades of cognition described in *Ethics*, II. 40, Scholium 2, the *scientia intuitiva* that 'proceeds from an adequate idea of the formal essence of certain attributes of God [i.e. substance] to adequate cognition of the essence of things.' Now the mind views everything *sub specie aeternitatis*, and has what Spinoza calls *amor Dei intellectualis*, 'intellectual love of God' (*Ethics*, V. 32), which is, since the mind is still a mode of God or substance, 'part of the infinite love by which God loves himself' (*Ethics*, V. 36). Hegel refers to this intellectual love of God in Enc. I, §158Z., agreeing with Spinoza's view that freedom is the

understanding of necessity. Possibly he has it in mind here. If so, his argument is this: the mind does, in Spinoza's view, constitute itself as I, as 'free subjectivity', but this is incompatible with Spinoza's substance doctrine. But it is more likely Hegel is thinking more generally, arguing that proper I-awareness is incompatible with Spinozism. He regards Spinozism not as simply wrong, but as an essential phase of philosophy that needs to be overcome or 'sublated'. He regards the concept of substance as adequate for describing the early stage of the human individual before it reaches I-awareness (the 'soul'), the early stage of human society before individuals attained (modern) I-awareness (the Presocratic Greek city-state), and the early stage of the universe as a whole before self-conscious humans emerged. Hence Spinozism has a necessary place in our understanding of things, but it cannot accommodate the self-conscious 'subject'. The 'judgement' (*Urteil*) by which the I is constituted is not a proposition but an 'original' (*ur-*) 'division' (*teil*), by which the mind extricates itself from its substantial life and from its surroundings: cf. §407, n. 1.

4. After Fichte's I has posited itself and posited the Non-I, its third and final preliminary step is to posit in the I a 'divisible' Non-I in contrast to the 'divisible' I, i.e. it parcels out the available territory between the I and the Non-I. Hegel is not primarily referring, however, to the difficulties involved in this step. Fichte believed that after the I has, in interaction with the Non-I, produced the material world, individual I's, human societies, etc., it somehow reclaims them by its moral activity. This reunification can, however, only be achieved at infinity; the unity of the I and the Non-I 'ought to be', but is approached only asymptotically. It is not indisputably true, however, that Fichte here makes the I and the Non-I each something finite, bounded by the other, yet 'absolute'. The Non-I is produced by the I, which remains the dominant partner.

NOTES TO §416

1. Consciousness involves a bifurcation between the self-certain I and an object, which, though it is an object of the mind, has no special affinity to the mind or to the I, and has a content that is apparently quite different from and not determined by the mind. This bifurcation results from the 'appearance' (*Erscheinung*) of the mind's 'essence', its manifestation of the essence in consciousness of objects. The mind's *Existenz* (literally 'stepping forth': cf. §403, n. 2, and thus similar to its *Erscheinung*, literally 'shining forth': cf. §413, n. 1) is finite in that it is bounded or limited by alien objects. The 'goal' of the mind is to bridge this gulf, by a transformation both of the I and of its object. The elevation of self-certainty 'to truth' means, as Hegel explains below (cf. §416, n. 2) the sublation of this defect.

2. Ordinary German distinguishes between *gewiss* and *wahr*, as ordinary English distinguishes between 'certain' and 'true': 'I'm not quite certain, but I think it's true'. But Hegel's point is that when one is certain of something (or thinks that it is certain), one says that it, or 'a subjective state' (*ein Subjektives*) corresponding to it, is true. If I am certain that this rose is red, I say it is true that this rose is red; if

I am certain that I exist, I say it is true that I exist. Hegel, by contrast, denies that the statement or belief that this rose is red is true, for the reason that its 'content' is 'trivial' or 'bad' and, ultimately, in some way 'contradictory': cf. Enc. I, §172. So it is with self-certainty. The mind is certain of 'being together with itself' (*bei sich selber zu sein*) and also certain of being related to something other than itself. (The contradiction is not just between self-certainty and the object, but between two 'opposite' certainties; this makes it look more like a standard contradiction than it initially does.) The problem is not that these certainties are not true in the ordinary sense. They are in a way, since the mind is both together with itself and related to an other. But this is because the mind itself is, at this stage, in a self-contradictory condition, and this precludes the mind and its own certainties about itself from being true in Hegel's sense. The case is not unlike Catullus' claim to hate and love the same woman (at the same time: *odi et amo*). He is certain that he hates her and certain that he loves her. His certainties are no doubt true in the ordinary sense. But they are not true in Hegel's sense, because they contradict each other, correctly describing a mind, that is itself in a contradictory state.

Neither Catullus' condition nor that of consciousness looks much like a standard contradiction. (Hegel's colloquial expression for that is 'wooden iron', as ours is 'a square circle'.) It is more a tension or conflict. (There is perhaps a suggestion that just as for standard truth the 'subjective state' and the object must 'agree', so Hegelian truth requires the 'agreement' of subject and object. But Hegel does not stress this parallel here.) Why must such a contradiction be 'sublated'? The standard view is that a contradiction should be eliminated, because it cannot be true in the standard sense. Hegel's answer is that it is because it is not true in Hegel's sense. But he adds that the contradiction itself contains the 'urge to resolve itself'. Catullus's contradiction seems to involve an uncomfortable instability that invites, if it does not actually demand, resolution. So does consciousness's, if we see its problem as, for example, having an object that is quite alien and unintelligible to it.

3. The contradiction is to be resolved by a convergence of the subject and the object. The subject becomes objective, the object ceases to be alien and becomes wholly 'mine'. On 'reason that believes in itself', see §393Z. on the 'self-conscious reason' of the European mind; on reason's 'knowledge' (*Wissen*) and 'conceptual cognition' (*begreifenden Erkennen*), see §§437–9, and 465–8.

NOTES TO §417

1. In §416Z. reason is presented as the solution to the contradiction between self-certainty and certainty of the object. Here the procedure starts with consciousness of an 'object' (*Gegenstand*), then moves to self-consciousness, and concludes with the unity of the two. Reason is the 'concept of mind', in the sense that it is the fully developed mind, the full-grown oak-tree rather than the acorn or the sapling. Here 'concept' (*Begriff*) is roughly equivalent to 'Idea' (*Idee*), in contrast to the use of 'concept' discussed in §383, n. 8.

Why does the mind intuit the 'content of the object as itself', but intuit itself, not as the object, but as 'determined in and for itself'? The mind is now determinate, not simply I-awareness. But it is determined independently, not simply a mirror-image of the object. The mind is the dominant partner in the subject–object relationship.

2. Cf. §415: 'the progressive logical determination of the object is what is identical in subject and object'. The stages are 'judgements' (*Urteile*: 'original divisions') because the 'concept' is divided into two terms, the subject and the object.

3. The reference is to §415: cf. §§413, n. 3; 414, n. 2; 415, n. 1 on the distinction between what we know and what consciousness or the I knows. Initially the object is a sensory individual, and is thus plausibly regarded as independent of the I (§418). Gradually, but more especially in §§422–3, the sensory object is regarded as an expression of universals—force, laws, etc.—which constitute its 'internality' or inner nature, a 'recollection' (*Erinnerte*: 'recollected', but also 'internalized': cf. §§401, n. 2; 406, n. 26) that consciousness 'receives'. The I too undergoes a parallel 'internalization' (*Innerlichwerden*, lit. 'becoming internal'), since in general the subject and the object mirror each other. But the I regards its own internalization as an 'internalization' (*Innerlichmachung*, lit.'making internal') of the object. That is, the I does not appear to itself as undergoing an internalization; it attributes the internalization to the object alone. (The text might alternatively mean that the I regards its own internalization as brought about by the object.) Roughly speaking, the I regards the theoretical entities that emerge (laws, etc.) as empirical discoveries, rather than as its own contributions to the object by way of the concept active in both the subject and the object. Thus the I does not regard itself as having undergone any essential internalization apart from whatever it needs to register its discoveries about the object.

4. By a difficult transition discussed in §423, the object becomes the I and consciousness becomes self-consciousness. There follow four steps: (1) Self-consciousness has consciousness as its 'object' (*Gegenstande*); it both 'confronts' and involves consciousness. (2) By self-repulsion self-consciousness confronts another self-consciousness as its 'object' (*Objekt*), an 'immediate, individual I'. Steps (1) and (2) correspond to stage (**b**) in the Paragraph. (3) This 'object' loses its 'one-sided subjectivity' (namely its exclusive I-hood) and is conceived as Idea, i.e. as reality pervaded by the (non-one-sided) subjectivity of the concept. (4) Now that the object of consciousness is pervaded by the concept, self-consciousness no longer opposes consciousness. It unites with it, not immediately, but in a way mediated by step (3). Self-consciousness is no longer just the self-contained, exclusive I that cannot accommodate consciousness and its object. It is the 'concrete being-for-self' of the I, reason 'that recognizes' (*erkennenden*) itself in the world. Steps (3) and (4) correspond to stage (**c**) in the Paragraph.

Step (1) presents a difficulty: granted that self-consciousness has consciousness as its object, why must it 'confront' (*stellt sich ... gegenüber*) it, stand in 'opposition' (*Gegensatze*) to it? Hegel introduces this feature under the cover of the ambiguity of *Gegenstand* ('object', but literally 'stand(ing) against'). Is this simply a revival of the 'contradiction' between I-awareness and object-awareness discussed in §416 and nn. 1 and 2, or is there more to it? Possibly Hegel expects us to remember the youth of §396, nn. 2 and 8, whose growth to adulthood seems to require opposition to the world he finds before him. Step (2) involves a special difficulty: why is it necessitated (*daher*, 'therefore') by step (1)? Perhaps Hegel's train of thought is this: since self-consciousness is dissatisfied with consciousness, yet still involves it, it needs an object that is as little like an ordinary object of consciousness, i.e. as much like itself, as possible. This too reminds us of youth. Youths need companions, rivals, lovers, etc. Step (3) is also difficult: how does the awareness of another I necessitate (or facilitate) the conceptualization of 'reality'? The youth in §396 gradually comes to understand and accept the world in which he finds himself. This world is a world shared with others, including earlier others who have already structured the world in an intelligible way. Conceptualization is, Hegel realized, a collective enterprise. Step (4) coheres naturally with step (3). Self-consciousness, united with consciousness, is 'concrete', not abstract, and 'being-for-self' or actualized, not simply in itself, or potential.

5. Cf. §387, n. 17 on the centrality of 'reason' (*Vernunft*) to the mind. That the 'last term' (*das ... Letzte*) is also the 'first term' (*das Erste*), propelling the movement by which it is reached, is a fundamental schema for Hegel, corresponding to the idea that the third term is a restoration of the first on a higher level: cf. §381, nn. 4, 18. Hence e.g. the full-grown oak realizes its concept, having 'sublated' the 'one-sided' stages of acorn, sapling, etc. But the concept is also embedded in the acorn and propels the growth of the tree. So the concept is the first term as well as the last.

NOTES TO §418

1. The subject, object, and the 'relation' of subject to object are parallel to each other: cf. §417, n. 3. So all three are 'immediate', not reached by inference or by any other roundabout route. The object is determined as just 'being' (*seiender*) and as 'reflected into itself', i.e. cut off from other things, self-contained, and so 'immediate' in the sense that it is not 'mediated', produced or affected, by anything else. In Enc. I, §163, individuality is mediated, derived from universality and particularity. But in Enc. I, §20, universality is mediated, while discrete individuals are what is immediately given, a sensory given whose essential feature is individuality.

2. Consciousness is here a 'relationship' (*Verhältnis*), a sort of ratio or proportion in which subject and object stand to each other (as in a numerical ratio, $a:b$), with no complex interaction between them: cf. §413, n. 1. Hence consciousness has available only categories derived from its own side of the relationship, the 'abstract I', not categories presupposing interaction between entities, such as reflexion, causality, difference, etc. (In Enc. I, §§122–3, 'existence' is a complex category, involving mediation, and so, in Enc. I, §§124–5, is 'thing'. But 'existing thing', *existierenden Dinge*, is here used in a non-Hegelian sense.) Consciousness is aware of the object in other ways too—as red, fluffy, etc. But redness and fluffiness are not 'categories'. They are at best 'representations', empirical specifications

of general categories or thoughts. Such representations as enter consciousness's awareness here must conform to the thoughts available to consciousness; this might exclude its regarding one and the same thing as both red and fluffy, since this involves a complex thought: cf. §419, n. 1. This rich 'content', but not the meagre categories applied to it, comes from the feeling soul: cf. §§403 ff. But the feeling soul did not distinguish the 'determinations of feeling' from itself. Now the mind does so. It is reflected into itself as I and consequently separates off the 'material', giving it the 'determination of being [*des Seins*]', a lowly category, but sufficient to distinguish an entity from itself.

3. In PS, pp. 59 ff. (Hegel's pagination is that of the first edition) 'sensory consciousness' refers to its object as 'here' and as 'now'. Hegel now repudiates this. Such terms belong to 'intuition' (*Anschauen*), which is not dealt with until §449, where, in the Zusatz, Hegel explains the relation between intuition and sensory consciousness. The 'relationship' (cf. §418, n. 2) of the object to consciousness is just to be 'something external' to it, and this limits what can be said of the object. It is not external 'within itself' (*an ihm selbst*) or 'being outside itself' (*Aussersichsein*). If it were, we could refer to one part of the object as 'here', in contrast to other parts of it or to other objects to which it is spatially related. We could locate the object as 'now', in contrast to other preceding and subsequent objects. But the object is not regarded as spatially extended or as related to other things. So 'here' and 'now' cannot be applied to it. Hegel's unacknowledged reason for now excluding space and time from sensory consciousness is that he wants to distinguish consciousness in general from 'free mind' and, more specifically, 'sensory consciousness' from 'intuition' (§§ 448–9), which is responsible for the projection of sensations into space and time. On this, see §449, n. 5.

4. On the defect of sensory consciousness, see §419Z.

5. On perception, see §§420–1 The object, though individual, is 'related' (*bezogen*) to a universal in that it shares universal properties with other things.

6. On the 'intellect', see §§422–3 The universal is now incorporated into the individual object as 'an interior [*Inneren*] that is for itself'. The transition from the object as the 'appearance' of such an interior to the object as 'the living creature' is somewhat abrupt. It perhaps conflates two ideas: (1) The inner nature of the (possibly inanimate) object is seen as something projected into the object by consciousness. (2) The inner nature of the (living) object is seen as similar to consciousness, even as a second consciousness, but not presumably as projected into the object by the first consciousness.

7. Cf. §418, n. 2, where the 'content' is derived from 'feeling' (*Gefühl*) rather than 'sensation' (*Empfindung*). On these two words, see §402, nn. 1 and 2.

8. Cf. §400 and Z., and nn. 1–4; also Enc. I, §§61–78, where the doctrine of immediate 'knowledge' (*Wissen*) of God, etc. is associated with F. H. Jacobi. Here and elsewhere, Hegel's main objection to immediate consciousness or knowledge of such things is not that the consciousness and its claims are unsupported and unreliable, but that the 'content' is inevitably diluted by the 'form' in which it is accommodated. It is not obvious why this should be so. An ethical intuitionist might profess to be immediately aware, say, that it is always wrong to lie. This is

a 'universal' claim, in the traditional sense of 'universal', not conspicuously 'individualized' (*Vereinzelten*). Perhaps Hegel would say that intuitionism inevitably misses the interconnections or mediations between lying and other actions, institutions, etc., that it can only focus on things piecemeal; that it cannot, or can only with difficulty, allow exceptions to the general rule; and that it can at best give an account only of 'morality' (*Moralität*), not of the rich texture of 'ethical life' (*Sittlichkeit*). Immediate knowledge of God can only affirm that he is, etc., applying the categories to which sensory consciousness is restricted in virtue of its 'relationship' to the object: cf. §418, n. 2. The 'properties' of God are derived from feeling or 'sensation', and are equivalent to the 'content' discussed in §418, n. 2. A 'property' (*Eigenschaft*) of a 'thing' is a more complex category, that strictly oversteps the boundaries of immediate consciousness: the self-aware I is not a thing with properties (cf. §419 and Enc. I, §125).

NOTES TO §419

1. 'The sensory' (*Das Sinnliche*) is the object of sensory consciousness. It is a 'something' (*Etwas*) and so, by a process described in Enc. I, §92Z., it 'becomes an other'. When reflected back into itself, 'the something' is a 'thing' (*Ding*), which though still 'an individual' (*Einzelnes*) has many 'properties' and corresponding 'predicates': cf. Enc. I, §125. Properties and predicates are universal, not individual: they belong or apply, in principle at least, to indefinitely many things or individuals, not just to one. 'Thing' and 'properties' are 'determinations of reflexion', since the thing is reflected back into itself out of its external properties, in something like the way in which a 'ray of light in a straight line impinging upon the surface of a mirror is thrown back from it' (Enc. I, §112Z. Cf. Enc. I, §125 and Z.). It is this reflexion that makes it a single thing and not just a collection of properties. 'Relations' are presumably the relations of the something to the other. But it is not clear whether the other is the properties of the thing or other things. Perhaps it is both. A thing's properties involve other things in various ways: the properties are shared with some other things; a thing (sometimes) manifests and/or acquires its properties by interaction with other things; a thing's boundaries are established by adjacent things with different properties. It is also not clear why the immediate sensory object becomes a thing with properties. (The parallel passage in the PS, pp. 67 ff., is more explicit.) Perhaps it is because the properties are needed to establish the boundaries between the object and other entities.

2. The ambiguity in my translation reflects an ambiguity in Hegel's German: *für dasselbe als erscheinend hat der Gegenstand*, etc. If 'appearing' (*erscheinend*) qualifies the I (*dasselbe*), it perhaps means that the I is only making its first appearance or that it is shining forth (cf. Enc. I, §131 and Z.), not reflected back on itself, so that it cannot recognize its own activity. If it qualifies the object, it means that the object appears to the I as having undergone the change, as in §415Z.(1). Hegel is presumably not reporting an actual change. His idea is that the difference between a sensory object and a thing with properties is made by

the thinking I, and, hypothetically, *if* a consciousness were to progress in the way Hegel describes, it *would* change the object without recognizing its own handiwork.

3. On 'dialectical', see also §415, n. 1, where it contrasts with 'formal identity'. The force of the word is best seen in Hegel's applications of it. Here the dialectical movement involves two steps: (1) The content 'is supposed' (*soll*) to be 'the individual' (*das Einzelne*), i.e. the individual that sensory consciousness focuses on. But any and every individual can be referred to as 'the individual'. So the object is not 'an' (or 'one': *ein*) individual, but 'every individual'. (2) The 'individual content' excludes 'the other' and thus has the other in itself, i.e. specifying that I am conscious of *this*, not *that*, involves an essential reference to *that* as well as to *this*. As in §419, n. 1, it is unclear how this relation to an other (content or object) generates a thing with properties. The 'proximate truth' (*nächste Wahrheit*) of something, x, is something else, y, such that (i) x involves some intrinsic contradiction, (ii) y resolves this contradiction for the time being (though not ultimately, since y is likely to involve a contradiction of its own), and (iii) there is nothing else, z, such that z resolves the contradiction of x as directly and obviously as, or more directly and obviously than, y does. E.g. the 'contradictory' condition of the woman who swallowed a fly has its 'proximate truth' in her swallowing a spider. She then swallowed a bird, the proximate truth of her spider. The bird is the proximate truth of the spider, not the fly, since (let us suppose) a bird would not eat the fly, only a spider does that, and, in any case, it is more obvious and easy to swallow a spider than a bird. Hegel simplifies the problem of condition (iii) by supposing that the proximate truth of x, is not something we or consciousness need to look for among several candidates, but something that x 'becomes' or turns into—as if the spider were generated by the fly itself and then devoured its own progenitor. It is, in Hegel's view, not Hegel himself who produces dialectical arguments; the subject matter is intrinsically dialectical: cf. Enc. I, §81 and Z.

NOTES TO §420

1. 'To perceive' is *wahrnehmen*, and 'perception' is here the infinitive used as a verbal noun: *das Wahrnehmen*. *Nehmen* is 'to take', and *wahr* is 'true'; so Hegel takes *wahrnehmen* to mean something like 'to take truly, in its truth'. (In fact, the *wahr* in *Wahrnehmen* comes from an obsolete noun meaning 'attention, heed', and is not related to *wahr*, 'true'. So *wahrnehmen* originally meant 'take heed of', which explains why it also means, in current German, 'look after, protect'.) Because of this supposed connection between perception and truth, Hegel here suppresses the main feature of perception—that a single thing has many properties—and introduces more advanced scientific ideas that properly belong to the intellect and thus to §§422–3: cf. §420, n. 4.

2. 'Identity' (*Identität*) is used loosely for a sort of identity in difference. Consciousness and its attitude to its object vary in accordance with the nature of

the object: cf. §418, nn. 1, 2, and 8. *Gewissheit*, 'certainty', and *Wissen*, 'awareness' or knowledge, are close relatives, but *Wissen* is the nominalized infinitive of
wissen, which can be used for knowing about something, etc., and is thus more
appropriate for knowledge of a complex thing and its properties.

3. 'Apperception' was introduced by Leibniz (1646–1716) to distinguish self-
conscious perception from passive sensation. Kant distinguished between empirical and transcendental apperception. Empirical apperception is the unity of our
mental experience as we observe it, transcendental apperception is the intellectual activity that makes this unity possible. However, 'apperceptions' (*Apperzep-
tionen*), and 'observation' (*Beobachtungen*), are here closer to the objects of
sensory certainty, and to what Kant calls 'intuitions' (*Anschauungen*), than to
'perception' in Hegel's (or Kant's) sense. They are converted into 'experiences',
the objects of perception, by the application to them of categories, etc. 'Necessary and universal' refer not simply to an individual object of perception, but
also to the necessary laws, etc., which on Hegel's and Kant's view, need to
govern all our experience if we are to perceive an individual, objective thing:
cf. §420, n. 4. Hence 'ordinary consciousness' of things is not sharply distinct
from 'the sciences' that study the interconnections between things.

4. Hegel distinguishes between 'show' (*weisen*) and 'demonstrate' (*erweisen*). 'Perception' involves not just the ability to attribute qualities perceived by different
senses to a single object (a step taken by 'ordinary consciousness'), but scientific
explanation of the object's internal unity in terms of e.g. 'force' (*Kraft*) and of
the object's relations to other things by law-like generalizations. 'To demonstrate
things as true' (*die Dinge als wahr zu erweisen*) is thus both to reveal the truth
about things and to explain it by deriving it from laws about the interconnection
of things.

5. A demonstration in the sciences makes presuppositions, of laws, empirical
facts, etc. So demonstration can in principle go on ad infinitum. Philosophy
advances from 'demonstration' (*Erweisen*) to 'proof' (*Beweisen*) of the 'absolute
necessity' of things, i.e. a necessity that is not conditional upon or relative to
any presupposition. Philosophy cannot, however, dispense with 'experience'.
'Things' have to be experienced empirically and 'demonstrated' by the sciences,
before philosophy can 'prove' their absolute necessity. If Hegel undertakes this
proof, he does so not in Enc. III, but in Enc. I, the *Science of Logic*, and Enc. II:
cf. Enc. I, §147 on necessity.

6. Consciousness 'sublates the individuality of things' by revealing them to have
many universal properties (cf. §419), to be 'expressions' of a universal force, and
to be connected with other things by universal laws. It 'posits them ideally' by
imbuing them with universal thoughts or categories. It thus 'negates the externality' of the object's relation to the I by making the object as thought-laden as the
I and, in PS, pp.67 ff., by the interplay between the *many* properties of a *unitary* thing and the *many* sense-organs of the *unitary* self. The I 'withdraws into
itself', etc. in that it retrieves more of the categories implicit in itself. According to §418 (cf. n. 2) it can only deploy these categories when it is no longer
externally related to its object by a 'relationship'.

NOTES TO §421

1. Hegel reverts to the main theme of perception, a single thing with many properties: cf. §§419; 420, n. 1. Perception involves two 'contradictions', which are
   species of a third, more general type of contradiction:

   (1) 'Experience' sets out from empirical observations of individuals, and on
       this 'foundation' (*Grund*) bases its claims about universal properties,
       forces, laws, etc. But these universals are supposed to ground or constitute
       individual things. (The 'individual things' here are the 'sensory certainties
       of individual apperceptions, etc.' of §420 Remark, not necessarily fully
       fledged things with properties: cf. §420, n. 3.) This 'contradiction' is, on
       the face of it, only apparent. Sensory individual things and 'universality'
       are each supposed to be the 'foundation', but in different senses of the
       word. Individual things are the *epistemic* or epistemological foundation of
       the structure, whereas 'universality' is its *ontological* foundation.

   (2) The individual thing has 'independence' or self-subsistence (*Selbständig-
       keit*), it stands on its own two feet 'in its concrete content', not just as
       a bare individual. However, the thing has properties. It is not simply
       identical with its properties in the way that 'the something' (cf. §419,
       n. 1), the object of sensory certainty, is identical with its quality:
       cf. Enc. I, §125. It can change its properties without ceasing to exist. It
       is relatively independent of its properties and, conversely, the properties
       are relatively independent of the thing. This leads to the idea that the
       properties of a thing are really types of stuff or matter; scientists had
       postulated, for example, electrical matter, magnetic matter and 'caloric'
       or heat matter: cf. Enc. I, §126; Enc. II, §§304–5, 334. Now it is the
       properties that are independent; the thing is just a congeries of matters.

   (3) The pervasive 'contradiction of the finite' is explained in Enc. I, §92Z.
       A finite entity has a boundary or 'limit' (*Grenze*) that makes it what it
       is. A meadow of 3 acres, for example, has a quantitative limit making
       it 3 acres and a qualitative limit making it a meadow, not a wood or a
       pond. The limit makes the 'reality' (*Realität*) of the entity, but is also its
       'negation': beyond the limit lies what the entity is not, and this too is
       bounded by the limit. (This is why the thing is the 'negative' bond of its
       properties.) The reality of a finite entity is thus essentially dependent on
       its 'other', on what it is not. Hence, Hegel infers, a finite entity is sus-
       ceptible to alteration, to becoming other than it is. In Enc. I, §§194 ff.,
       'the object' (*das Objekt*) contrasts with the 'concept', and Hegel exam-
       ines three increasingly satisfactory versions of 'objectivity' in contrast to
       'subjectivity': mechanism, chemism and teleology. Each of these versions
       involves intrinsic defects—such as that a mechanical object has distinct
       parts that have no affinity to each other—and these are overcome only by
       the Idea, the unity of concept and objectivity (Enc. I, §§213 ff.).

NOTES TO §422

1. On 'the proximate truth', see §419, n. 3. The contradiction between the unity of the thing and the multiplicity of its properties is resolved by regarding the 'object' (*Gegenstand*) as the 'appearance' (*Erscheinung*) of an 'interior' (*Inneres*) that is 'for itself', i.e. independent: cf. §414, n. 1. The variety is in the appearance, the unity in the interior. On the universality of the interior, see §422, n. 2. On the 'intellect' (*Verstand*) and its contrast with 'reason' (*Vernunft*), see §§378, n. 1; 422, n. 5.

2. The appearance involves multiplicity, in that it is diverse at any given time and it changes over time. This multiplicity is is contained in the interior, but in a static uniformity. For example, a person's behaviour varies. He grovels to superiors, but is overbearing and merciless to inferiors. But his inner character need not change with every change in his behaviour. His character involves a relatively constant disposition to appease superiors and intimidate inferiors; changes in his behaviour depend on the activation of this disposition by changing circumstances. The disposition can be represented by law-like propositions: For any person x, if A encounters x, and A regards x as inferior to A, then A bullies x; for any person y, if A encounters y, and A regards y as superior to A, then A appeases y. Or we can put the two laws together thus: for any person y, if A encounters y, the courtesy of A's treatment of y increases in direct proportion to what A perceives to be y's rank in relation to A. The simultaneous diversity of a person's behaviour can also be explained by an interior character that is not diverse in the way that the behaviour is. If I blush, stutter, and spill my drink, this can all be explained by my nervousness, together with variable external circumstances such as a job interview and my having been given a drink. The laws are 'universal', in that they can be expressed in 'universal' propositions concerning a particular individual person, A, and help to explain the individual bits and pieces of A's behaviour. They are 'universal' too in that these, or similar, laws partly constitute the character not only of A, but of many other people. My nervousness on this particular occasion is no more 'universal' than my nervous behaviour on this occasion; my nervousness in general is more 'universal'; nervousness in general, not just mine but other people's too, is still more 'universal'.

3. Enc. I, §§135 ff. deal with 'essential relationship'. The first such relationship is that of whole and parts, which is similar to the relation of a thing to its properties, now reified into 'matters', and presents a similar problem: we vacillate between regarding the whole as self-subsistent and the parts as inessential, and regarding the parts as self-subsistent, the whole being inessential to them. This is the contradiction between 'reflection-into-self' (the thing, the whole) and 'reflection-into-other' (the matters, the parts). We have as yet no reason for assigning priority and thus self-subsistence to either factor. Hence the endless vacillation. But the vacillation is terminated when we convert one of the factors (the unified thing or whole) into the 'interior' and the other (properties, parts) into its 'appearance'. Then we can assign priority to the unity of the thing and prevent it from

dispersing into the 'other'. The most obvious way of doing this is by regarding the thing as a 'force' and its sensory properties as the 'expression' of the force: the relationship of 'force' (*Kraft*) and its 'expression' (*Äusserung*) is the immediate successor of whole and parts in Enc. I, §136. Now the sensory properties have become an essential aspect of the thing, indissolubly tied to the inner force and no longer liable to dispersal in different directions: the 'whole ceases to be a whole when it is divided, whereas a force only shows itself to be a force when it expresses itself, and in its expression only comes back to itself' (Enc. I, §136Z.(1)). The object is a unity in something like the way in which the I is a unity: a unitary centre (the force, the I) generating and controlling its own sensory states. This is a stage in the progressive assimilation of the object to the subject: cf. §422, n. 5.

4. A force, such as gravity, is initially conceived as internally undifferentiated. The same is true of a 'cause', though in his account of causality in Enc. I, §153, Hegel does not treat a cause as something inner that causes an outer effect: his main example of a cause is an outer process, rain, which causes the wetness of the streets, where, he argues, the cause is really the same as the effect, the same water disposed in different ways. Hegel does not say why a differentiated interior is better than an undifferentiated interior. No doubt it is because an undifferentiated interior cannot explain the variety of the exterior. Nor does he explain why a differentiated interior can only be a law. In Enc. I, §136, and PS, pp. 92 ff., he mentions polarized forces such as electricity and magnetism, but he does not deal with them here. No doubt he would say that if such forces are to explain phenomena, they must operate in accordance with a law, the law that like poles repel each other, while unlike poles attract each other. Hegel assimilates, but also differentiates, two types of law, (1) laws enjoining, prohibiting, or permitting certain types of action in a human community and (2) laws that constitute or express invariable sequences of events: cf. PR, Preface and Z. He wrongly implies that laws of type (2) determine only 'external nature'; there may be invariable sequences in, hence laws determining, our psychological, economic, social, etc. behaviour. Conversely, laws of type (1) concern only human conduct; non-human creatures, things, and events are not responsive to human legislation. Not all laws of type (1) are criminal or penal laws: laws of marriage, of contract, etc. primarily *enable* us to do something rather than *enjoin* or *prohibit* doing something, though they also prescribe penalties for offences such as bigamy, breach of contract, etc. At any rate, Hegel assumes that laws of type (1) necessarily prescribe a punishment for a crime. This is analogous to such type (2) laws as that the ratio of the square of a planet's sidereal period (i.e. the time it takes to complete one revolution of its orbit measured against the background of the stars) to the cube of its distance from the sun is a constant for all planets. (This is one of the three laws of planetary motion formulated by Johannes Kepler (1571–1630): cf. Enc. II, §270. The other laws are that each planet orbits the sun in an ellipse with the sun at one focus, and that each planet orbits the sun in such a way that an imaginary line joining the planet and the sun sweeps out equal areas in equal times.) Here the 'distinct determinations' are (the square of) the time and (the cube of) the

distance. How are these parallel to the crime and the punishment? Planets do not deviate from the laws governing them and, since they commit no 'crimes', they are not threatened with punishment. If humans infallibly and invariably obeyed whatever type (1) laws were promulgated they too would not need the threat of punishment. But the laws would still unite 'distinct determinations'. They would say, e.g., that no person is to assault another person. Here there are three determinations, one person, assault (prohibited), and another person. Why does Hegel ignore these determinations in favour of crime and punishment? Perhaps because they cannot easily and non-arbitrarily be reduced to two, let alone to two 'opposite', determinations, and because they do not stand in any obvious proportion to each other: the law forbids any assault on another, it does not e.g. prescribe an assault whose viciousness is to vary with the height of the victim. Punishments, by contrast, should bear a proportion to the gravity of the crime in something like the way that the time is proportional to the distance. On crime and punishment, see also §§496 ff. and PR, §§90 ff.

5. The 'intellect' (*Verstand*) or 'intellectual [*verständige*] consciousness' frames type (1) laws and realizes that crimes need punishments; it also discovers type (2) laws. The unity and its necessity cannot, however, be 'comprehended' (*begriffen*, the perfect participle of *begreifen*: cf. §§378, n. 3; 406, n. 9) by the intellect, only by 'reason' and its 'speculative thinking': cf. Enc. I, §§79 ff., esp. 82. Hegel attempts to comprehend this unity in e.g. PR, §§90 ff. and Enc. II, §270. Intellect is 'inherent' in the world; this is why the world is governed by type (2) laws. So in discerning type (2) laws, our intellect becomes its own 'object' (*gegenständlich*). By contrast, the object of sensory certainty is quite distinct from the I, though it is subject to the same categories as the I: cf. §418, n. 2. The object is progressively assimilated to the subject, though this requires a development of the subject as well as the object.

NOTES TO §423

1. In §422 'interior' and 'inner' refer primarily to what is inside things, in contrast to their outer 'appearance'. When laws are introduced as the interior of things, they involve a 'difference' or 'distinction' between two 'determinations' such as crime and punishment or the time of a planet's revolution and its distance from the sun. However, implicitly in §422Z. and explicitly in §423, Hegel claims that the determinations are not only inside things, but *inside each other*. What is the connection between these two types of interiority? There seems to be no connection if the inner determinations are not related by a law. If someone has blue eyes and fair hair, the hair and the eyes are external, both in the sense that they are apparent and in the sense that they are different from each other. No doubt there is some 'inner' thing or things producing the fair hair and blue eyes, I(fair hair) and I(blue eyes). If fair hair and blue eyes were lawfully related to each other, then I(fair hair) and I(blue eyes) might be internally related to each other, even the same thing. But since there are dark haired people with blue eyes, and fair haired

people with dark eyes, this is not obviously so. At most we can say the distinction between I(fair hair) and I(blue eyes) is 'inner' in the sense that it is not externally expressed. When the determinations are linked by a law, this objection to regarding them as internally related is removed. But that they are internally related does not follow from the fact that they constitute the 'interior' of things. Crime and punishment do seem to be internally related. Punishment is essentially *for* a crime or an offence. A crime is essentially punishable by law. These statements are supported by dictionary definitions of 'crime' and 'punishment'. But the relationship between the sidereal period and distance from the sun is not usually recorded by dictionaries. Hegel may be right in supposing it to have some deep necessity, but this does not follow from its constituting the interior of things.

2. For the 'distinction [*Unterschied*] which is no distinction', cf. the 'difference [*Unterschied*] that is no difference' of §413Z. and n. 4. There it refers to the I's difference from its own being, while here it refers to the difference between the 'determinations' of a law. The object, the law, is parallel to the subject, the I. Because the distinction is 'inner' (i.e. primarily in the interior of things), it is 'what it is in truth' (i.e. fulfils its true nature), when it is a distinction 'within itself' (*an ihm selbst*), i.e. a distinction not between two things, but within one thing, hence not a real distinction at all. For a similar idea, cf. Enc. II, §§312 ff. on the difference between the two poles of a magnet.

3. Now another distinction collapses, the distinction between subject and object. The I has itself as an 'object' (*Gegenstand*). So it is not really 'consciousness' any more. The reason for this collapse seems to be that with the collapse of the distinction between the determinations of the law, the law, as a distinction that is no distinction, is similar, if not identical to, the I, another distinction that is no distinction. (The distinction between the subjective distinction that is no distinction and the objective distinction that is no distinction is itself a distinction that is no distinction.) 'In its judgement' is *als urteilend*, literally 'as judging', but also 'as primally dividing': cf. §§388, n. 1; 389, n. 4; 467. Since the distinction is 'inner' and especially since the distinction is between the I and itself, it is produced by the I's dividing itself from itself.

4. 'Inner difference' or 'distinction' has by now accumulated three senses: (1) a distinction between determinations in the 'interior' of a thing; (2) a distinction between determinations which lie inside each other and are thus internally related; (3) a distinction within a single thing, i.e. between it and itself. Let us grant that when I am aware of myself, of I, there is no difference between the I that is aware and myself, the I of which it is aware, and that the distinction between I and myself is an inner distinction, produced by the I's dividing itself into I and myself. Let us also grant that if the determinations of the law, e.g. crime and punishment, lie inside each other, i.e. if the distinction between them is an inner distinction in sense (2), then they are differentiated by a distinction within the law, i.e. the distinction between them is inner in sense (3). Why does it follow that the determinations so distinguished are the same in the way that I and myself are the same? Punishment is not the same as crime. The sidereal period is not the same as distance from the sun. Countries, political parties, etc. often

divide against themselves, into Left and Right, etc. The division is internal to the country or party, not just a distinction from some other country or party; the distinction is inner in sense (3). Arguably, the segments into which it is divided are internally related: the distinction is inner in sense (2). There cannot be a Left without a Right or a Right without a Left. (If a country or party is wholly on the Left, with no Right, this can only be with reference to some other country or party.) But why must Left and Right be as similar as I and myself? Perhaps Hegel's tacit argument is this: If the Left is really different from the Right, then it has a nature of its own independently of its relation to the Right. For if its nature depended only on its relation to the Right, it would not differ from the Right, whose nature is determined by the same relation, only to the Left. But if the Left has an independent nature of its own, it can in principle exist without the Right, as, say, a woman might exist as a woman, though not as a wife, without a man. But since the distinction is inner in sense (2), the Left cannot exist without the Right. So it differs from the Right only in the way, say, that the North pole of a magnet differs from its South pole, a difference determined by their relation, not an intrinsic difference (cf. §423, n. 2). Or, as Hegel suggests, they differ in the way that I differ from myself.

Even if the determinations of law do differ from each other in the way that I differ from myself, why does it follow that the distinction between the I and the law collapses, i.e. that the law with its difference differs from the I with its difference only in the way that I differ from myself? Perhaps, after all, the poles of a magnet differ only in the way that I differ from myself. But it does not follow that I differ from a magnet only in the way that I differ from myself. Again, Hegel's argument seems to be this: If the natures of the north and south poles depend only on the relation between them, neither has any intrinsic nature apart from their relation. But the relation between them is the same as the relation between I and myself. Does it not follow that the north and south poles (and, in general, the determinations of the law) are flatly identical to I and myself? No. To infer this would be to forget that the subject and the object are themselves related in something like the way in which I and myself are related, and also north and south, etc. So the subject and object are never flatly identical with no difference whatsoever, but at least involve a 'difference which is no difference'. Nevertheless the arguments I have attributed to Hegel are flawed. If (i) each member of these pairs of determinations were determined only by the relation between them, (ii) the relation were the same for every pair, and (iii) the relation were wholly symmetrical, how could the north–south pair differ from, say, the crime–punishment pair, and how could, say, crime differ significanly from punishment? Premiss (iii) and premiss (i) and/or premiss (ii) must be rejected. It does not follow, however, that the arguments do not correctly represent Hegel's train of thought.

5. 'Comprehending' (*begreifen*) the ego-like unity of a law's determinations is a specialist business beyond the resources of 'intellectual consciousness'. But in a 'living creature' the unity of distinct determinations is on open display. On life, see also §§389, n. 3; 398, n. 9; 418, n. 6; PS, pp. 106 ff; Enc. I, §§216–22; Enc. II, §§337 ff. Here Hegel refers to the 'positing and sublating' of three sets

of 'distinct determinations': (1) life as the 'interior' and its outer 'expression' (*Äusserung*); (2) the living creature and the environing things it consumes 'by the negation of the immediate', and sublating its 'mediation into immediacy', i.e. assimilating the external objects on which it depends; (3) the distinct parts of the organism. With respect to (1) and (2), a living creature differs from an inanimate object, such as a magnet. A magnet may not attract or repel anything, since there may be nothing close enough to be repelled or attracted. By contrast a living creature must continually express its life if it is to remain alive, especially its 'sensibility', 'irritability', and 'reproduction': cf. §401, n. 23. A bar of iron must have a certain molecular structure, etc. if it is to retain its 'appearance'. But the connection between its 'interior' amd its appearance is not manifest to an observer. By contrast the transformation of inner life, e.g. hunger, into its outer expression, e.g. eating, and the converse transformation of the outer, e.g. food, into the inner life by digestion, etc. is manifest. With respect to (3), like any 'material entity', a living creature has parts separate from each other (their 'asunderness'). But none of the parts of a living creature can survive on its own. Each part is sustained and regenerated by the others. So the parts are not really distinct from each other: cf. §403, n. 3. The 'individual', i.e. each separate part, becomes 'ideal': cf. §§379, n. 3; 403, n. 2. Since each part is sustained by the activity of other parts, it is an 'end' (*Zweck*) to which they are means. But this part is, in turn, a means to other parts that it sustains. Since each part of the organism is both end and means to the others, the organism as a whole is an 'end in itself' (*Selbstzweck*). This does not mean that the organism, e.g. a cow, cannot serve any further purpose, e.g. human nutrition. It means that we do not need to appeal to any such further purpose, or to a purpose in the mind of an external planner, in order to explain a cow's structure and activities; every part and every activity is explained by other parts and activities within the cow. Kant called this 'inner purposiveness' (*innere Zweckmässigkeit*) in contrast to the 'outer purposiveness' that requires an external end and an external planner: cf. Enc. I, §§57–8, 204, and Kant, *Critique of Judgement*, §§61 ff.

6. Since a living creature, unlike a law, sublates the distinctions it involves, it is a closer approximation to the self-awareness of the I, the 'truth of the natural'. Hence it sparks off 'self-consciousness'. This is not just the self-aware I that is implicit in all consciousness, but an explicit consciousness of the self-aware I. It can, in Hegel's view, only be attained by one's becoming conscious of an object that mirrors the self-aware I: cf. §387, n. 14.

NOTES TO §424

1. On 'the truth of . . .' see §419, n. 3. Self-consciousness follows consciousness in Hegel's exposition, but it is really the 'ground' of consciousness, and 'in existence', i.e. in actual reality, all consciousness of an object other than myself is self-consciousness, because I am aware of the object as 'mine', i.e. as my 'representation' or as the object of which I have a representation. If it is true that all consciousness is self-consciousness, then self-consciousness cannot be explicit

reflection on oneself, since people often lose themselves in an object, wholly absorbed in it at the expense of everything else. In such a condition I am hardly aware even that the object is *mine*. Perhaps Hegel would dilute his claim to something like: 'If anyone is conscious of an object, then they are able to become self-conscious.' (Cf. Kant's 'The *I think* must be able to accompany all my representations'.) But even this weaker claim faces the difficulty that animals are presumably conscious and yet unable to become self-conscious. Hegel's response to this, however, is to deny that animals are conscious; what they have is 'sensation' (*Empfindung*). 'Consciousness', in Hegel's view, requires a fairly explicit distinction between oneself and the world (cf. §412, n. 1). So self-consciousness is implicit in it from the start.

2. The expression 'I = I' (*Ich = Ich*) or 'I am I' (*Ich bin Ich*) is especially associated with Fichte: cf. §379, n. 4. It is not immediately obvious why it should be taken to express self-consciousness. After all, it is equally true, if unilluminating, to say that 'this (e. g. pen) is/= this (pen)', but this does not imply that this pen is self-conscious. The force of the formula depends on its being thought or asserted. If I seriously think or assert 'I am I' I focus in a peculiarly intense way on my own self, regardless of my particular properties, etc. I do not think or assert 'I am a writer', 'I am hot', but simply 'I am I', and this, while not denying that I am a writer, hot, etc., excludes such features from consideration. Often Hegel associates the formula with emptiness; something that is only self-identical and nothing else does not amount to much more than pure being: cf. Enc. I, §86. Here he links it with 'abstract freedom', the sort of freedom that consists not in doing something positive, but in the ability to withdraw, to detach oneself, from everything. (In PR, §5, Hegel associates it with the mystic's withdrawal from everything and with the revolutionary's destruction of everything.) The use of 'pure ideality' is similar to the use of 'absolute ideality' mentioned in §401, n. 24.

   'In this way' (*So*), 'it' (*es*, presumably the I, but possibly self-consciousness) is 'without reality [*Realität*]'. This does not mean that self-consciousness does not occur. *Realität* contrasts with *Idealität*; it does not here mean 'existence' in the usual sense, but something like 'substance' or 'embodiment'. Such self-consciousness is empty, a gesture into the void. 'Object' is here *Gegenstand*, which, especially when italicized, stresses the sense of 'standing over against'. Thus, although the I stands over against itself, it is not an object in the sense of 'mine (... my representation)'. See also §424, n. 3.

3. In the Paragraph, the formula 'I = I' was taken to express 'abstract freedom', withdrawal from or rejection of everything other than oneself: cf. §424, n. 2. Here it expresses 'absolute ... freedom', which involves consciousness of the world as conformable to oneself, the objective world of §§402, nn. 4, 5; 408, n. 5; etc. Absolute freedom presupposes something like abstract freedom, the 'form of I = I', since only to the extent that I deepen my subjectivity can I gain access to genuine 'objectivity': cf. §402, n. 8. 'Absolute ... freedom' is freedom, since rational comprehension of the world makes it my own, no longer an alien restraint or intrusion, and because it lets the world develop in relative independence of myself, no longer right on top of me and crowding me in. It

is 'reason', since it involves unification and interconnexion rather than simply the separation characteristic of intellect: cf. §378, n. 1, etc. The formula 'I = I' is implicitly interpreted in two different ways: (1) 'I am immediately identical to myself, with no intermediate steps'; (2) 'I am identical to myself (not only immediately, but also) by a roundabout route via the world', which can be briefly if not quite accurately expressed as: 'I = world = I'. Sense (1) expresses abstract freedom; sense (2) expresses absolute freedom.

4. It is not clear what 'immediate self-consciousness' lacks. There are two possibilities: (i) Immediate self-consciousness is aware of the I and of the world in conformity to each other, but it has not reflected on this in a philosophical way. (ii) Immediate self-consciousness is aware of the I and also of the world, but it is not yet aware of the conformity of the I and the world; the world is still alien to it. Interpretation (ii) is supported by the fact that this is what Hegel goes on to describe in §425 and by the fact that immediate self-consciousness has 'only the I' 'for its object' (*zum Gegenstande*); its awareness of the world is only consciousness, not self-consciousness, since it does not recognize itself in the world. It may then have abstract freedom, the 'basis' (*Grundlage*) of freedom, but not absolute freedom. Hegel tends to regard abstract freedom as freedom 'in itself' or 'for us', while absolute freedom is 'for itself' or 'actual': cf. §383, n. 1; PR, §10 and Z. If immediate self-consciousness has the I as its object, why not the I = I? The 'I = I' here has sense (2) of §424, n. 3: 'I = world = I', I–world conformity. But in view of Hegel's tendency to equate actuality and self-awareness, both embraced in the concept of 'being-for-itself', his train of thought is probably this: When self-consciousness has just the I as its object, its I-awareness can be expressed as 'I = I' in sense (1). If it reflects on, takes as its object, its simple I-awareness, 'I = I' in sense (1), then it moves up into awareness of I-world conformity, 'I = I' in sense (2). The general principle is that someone is actually, not just potentially, in state S if, and only if, they are aware that they are in S. The principle is flawed. Someone losing their hair is potentially, not actually, bald. Becoming aware of one's potential baldness does not make one actually bald. Conversely, one may think one is actually bald, when one is not. Why should it be any different with mental states?

Throughout the Paragraph 'object' is *Gegenstand*. In the *Zusatz* 'object' is *Objekt*, except where self-consciousness has not the I = I, but only the I as its object. Perhaps a *Gegenstand* is more closely tied to the subject than a relatively independent *Objekt*.

NOTES TO §425

1. The 'first negation' contrasts with the negation of the negation, the second negation: cf. §381, n. 18. What it negates is consciousness and especially the external object *of* consciousness. It is hard to see, from the formal mechanics of negation, why the first negation should still be burdened with the term negated (or 'with the negation of itself', since if x is the negation of y, y is the negation of x). After all, the negation of the negation is a sort of return journey back to the

first term, only on a higher level (cf. §381, n. 18), so we might expect the first negation to be further from the term negated than the second negation is. The best that can be done formally is to suggest that in 'not-(not-p)', 'p' is in a way more thoroughly negated than it is in 'not-p'—and even more thoroughly negated in 'not-(not-(not-p))'! But Hegel's idea is not adequately captured by this symbolism. His idea is that first negation is a rejection of, or retreat or withdrawal from, the term negated, in this case a withdrawal from the world into one's own I, the 'abstract freedom' of §424. This still leaves the undigested world hovering in the background. This uncomfortable bifurcation or 'contradiction' between I and world is overcome by the second negation, which brings I and world into conformity with each other. See also §425, nn. 3 and 4.

2. If something is 'implicitly' (*an sich*) the case, then a movement is underway to 'posit' (*setzen*) it or to make it explicitly, or for itself, the case. If e.g. a very clever student is implicitly a professor, then s/he is on the way to becoming an actual professor. Confronted with this example Hegel's principle seems false. A clever student may be implicitly or potentially many other things besides a professor, and cannot be on the way to becoming them all. But what is implicitly the case is, in Hegel, characterized more generally than this, not so specifically as to be only one among several equally good alternatives. A clever student is e.g. implicitly wise. S/he may not become actually wise. But wisdom is not one among several equally desirable things to become. Nor is wisdom a straightforward object of rational choice; it is a precondition of a fully rational choice. Similarly, escape from 'abstract self-consciousness' is not one among several equally desirable alternatives; it is a precondition of rational aims and choices rather than something deliberately chosen.

   Why are consciousness and 'negation in general' (i.e. any duality, in which each of two things is the negation of the other) 'implicitly sublated in the I = I'? This is the 'I = I' in sense of immediate self-identity, sense (1) of §424, n. 3. When I am just aware of myself, I am not conscious of an object distinct from myself, and I and myself do not negate each other. This generates an impulse or 'urge' to extend this solution to the I–world bifurcation, by making them conform to each other in something like the way that I and myself do—not of course in exactly the same way, for then I would still have no proper object different from myself: cf. §425, n. 3. Thus 'I = I' in sense (1) is the implicit version of 'I = I' in sense (2).

3. The 'contradiction' discussed in §425, n. 1 now becomes clearer. There are two oppositions: between self-consciousness and consciousness, and between I and world. Self-consciousness is I-awareness, consciousness is world-awareness. But here Hegel assigns to consciousness awareness both of the I and of the world, and to self-consciousness only I-awareness. He does so, because he wants to argue that there are three connected problems in 'abstract self-consciousness': (i) The sheer disparity between self-consciousness and consciousness, between I and world. In the Paragraph the solution to this was their 'identification' (*Identifizierung*), but now this is weakened to 'reciprocal equilibrium' (*sich ... gegenseitig ausgeglichen haben*, for which Miller's 'made themselves equal to each other' may be right) and, for I and world, 'genuine mediation'. Like two wholly incompatible

occupants of the same house, they need to come to terms with each other, but need not become alike. (ii) When two disparate things need to be combined or mediated, Hegel usually finds a defect in each thing taken separately. Thus, consciousness on its own suffers from 'finitude' (cf. §379, n. 3 etc.) because in it I and world bound or limit each other in their unmediated 'opposition'. (iii) Self-consciousness too suffers from finitude because of the disparity between what 'ought to be' (*sein sollende*) and what actually is. On 'ought' cf. §472.

4. Cf. §425, n. 1. The first negation is 'conditioned' (*bedingte*) in the sense of 'conditional, qualified, limited, partial'.

5. Cf. §425, n. 2. Self-consciousness has itself 'for its object' (*zum Gegenstande*), not only 'as I', but 'as consciousness'. Perhaps this is intended to explain how consciousness is involved in self-consciousness, not just 'alongside' (*neben*) it, and how self-consciousness can posit the 'object' (*Objekt*) 'subjectively', as well as give itself 'objectivity' (*Objektivität*). The rough idea is that I need to view myself as one person among others in an objective world ordered according to categories that are derived from the mind itself and hence to that extent 'subjective': cf. §402, n. 8, etc. The self is then no longer empty and the world no longer alien to it. But this is reached only after a long detour.

6. Cf. §§426–9. This self-consciousness is 'individual' (*einzelne*) in the sense that it is solitary and self-centred. *Selbstbewusst* does not, like the English 'self-conscious', mean 'embarrassed, bashful', but 'self-confident, self-assured'. So it is easier in German than in English to associate self-consciousness with 'certainty' of one's own importance and of the 'nullity' of everything else.

7. Cf. §§430–5. The 'objective I' is the I that gets objectification by satisfying its desire: cf. §428. In §430 this new self-consciousness is described as 'particular' (*besonderes*), but in §425 the triad individuality–particularity–universality is only implicit: cf. §379, n. 5, etc.

8. Cf. §§436–7

NOTES TO §426

1. This Paragraph (and the *Zusatz*) explains why self-consciousness is 'desire' (*Begierde*), but not why it is individual. It is desire, because it involves two contradictions, though these are really two sides of the same coin: (1) Its 'abstraction', i.e. abstractness and/or abstractedness, i.e. I-awareness, 'is supposed' (*soll*) to be objective, i.e. have a real object, not just the I itself; (2) Its 'immediacy', i.e. object-awareness, is supposed to be subjective, not having an object external to it. Desire arises from and attempts to resolve these contradictions by eliminating two things: the persisting 'object' (*Objekt*) of consciousness, which 'certainty of itself', i.e. I-awareness, regards as a 'nullity', and 'abstract ideality', i.e. the bare I or I-awareness, which the 'relation of self-consciousness to the object', i.e. immediate object-awareness or consciousness, regards as a nullity. Each component of self-consciousness regards the object of the other component as a nullity worthy of elimination. So the contradiction within each component is also a contradiction between the components.

2. On 'urge' (*Trieb*), cf. §§425 and 473–8; Enc. II, §359. An urge gives rise to a transient desire for some individual thing for oneself, not a thoughtful desire for some impersonal object, such as world peace. It is close to what Reid calls 'appetite': 'If we attend to the appetite of hunger, we shall find in it two ingredients, an uneasy sensation and a desire to eat. The desire keeps pace with the sensation, and ceases when it ceases. When a man is sated with eating both the uneasy sensation and the desire to eat cease for a time, and return after a certain interval. So it is with other appetites.' (*Essays on the Active Powers of the Human Mind*, Essay III,. ii, ch. 1) What gives rise to the drive or desire for Hegel is not just an 'uneasy sensation', but the 'feeling' (*Gefühl*) of its 'inner contradiction'. To the question why this necessarily gives rise to a drive to sublate the contradiction, Hegel replies that self-consciousness also has a feeling of its implicit self-identity. But it is not clear that this helps. Presumably a feeling of self-identity contradicts a feeling of contradiction. But unless we are already convinced that any contradiction, even the first one, necessarily calls for sublation, why should we be convinced that this new contradiction does so?

3. Sometimes Hegel implies that non-living things are contradictory, that e.g. acid and base or alkali are each contradictory, since each exists only in relation to the other, and that 'contradiction is what moves the world' (Enc. I, §119Z(2)). But an acid cannot 'endure' contradiction of the sort that a living creature can, since if its 'Other . . . forces its way into it', i.e. if it is combined with an alkali, it ceases to be an acid and is neutralized to form a salt. Hegel does not specify the contradictions endured by non-human living creatures, but they presumably include hunger, pain, disease, etc.—states which if sufficiently intensified would kill the creature and can thus be seen as its 'other', but which at a lower intensity give rise to a drive to eliminate them. The claim that an 'ensouled', i.e. living, creature must have contradiction in it is most plausible for hunger, thirst, and sexual desire. In these cases the intrusive 'Other' is not the desired object (food, drink, mate) but the lack of such an object: cf. §426, n. 4.

4. 'In itself' or potentially self-consciousness is a 'totality', a fully rounded whole with a subjective and an objective aspect. But it can only become such a totality 'in and for itself', actually rather than just potentially, by satisfying its desire. At present it is actually and essentially, by its 'concept', just immediately related to itself, I = I in sense (1) of §424, n. 3. So the external object is an intrusive 'other', as long as it is not 'posited ideally', intellectually digested.

What 'self-consciousness' does to the intrusive 'other' is primarily, Hegel implies, to eat it. The urge to eat is thus motivated by a desire to remove an intrusive object as much as, or more than, to satisfy hunger. One can be hungry when there is no food around. But there are always objects of some sort around, and an infant might try to eat them, though an adult usually does not. If it is implausible to ascribe this motive for human eating, it is still less plausible to ascribe it to animal eating, since an animal is not an I = I and should not therefore feel the same discomfort as we do from the presence of an external object. The drive-generating contradiction in an animal seems to be mainly its lack of a desired object rather than the object itself: cf. §426, n. 3. Hegel might say that what animals do instinctively we do voluntarily. We do not have to eat when hungry, any more than we have to stand upright: cf. §§396; 410, n. 8; 411. We choose whether and when to eat. Some people choose not too, though it is hard to break the habit once it is formed. So a general self-assertion against the alien 'other' can be introduced to account for our choice. Some people, too—perhaps Hegel was one of them—do eat food because it is there, not just because they are hungry; the food is seen as a disturbing presence that needs to be removed, to avoid 'waste' perhaps. Cf. §427, n. 1.

NOTES TO §427

1. It is unclear what supports ('therefore') the claim that self-consciousness 'is aware of itself' (*weiss sich*) 'in the object' (*im Gegenstande*). It may be the last sentence of the preceding Paragraph, which said that *both* the object *and* the I were nullities. More generally self-consciousness has two seemingly distinct problems with the external object: (1)the sheer presence of the object contradicts its simple I-awareness; (2) simple I-awareness is intrinsically defective and objectless, so it needs somehow to assimilate the external object in order to complete itself. Problem (1) would be solved by simply eliminating the object, if that were possible. That would not solve problem (2), however; for that I need to assimilate the object. Assimilation, or 'sublation', of the object solves both problems; it eliminates the disturbing presence of the object and fills out the empty I-awareness. (It is as if in hunting rabbits one both eliminates a nuisance destroying one's crops and gets something to eat.) Here Hegel is thinking of problem (2). The object is seen as a necessary complement of self-consciousness, hence as appropriate or 'conformable' to its urge. The object is 'the selfless' (*das Selbstlose*) in two senses: it is not a 'self' in the way that self-consciousness is and it has an intrinsic tendency to sacrifice its own 'self', a 'dialectic of self-sublation', that makes it cooperate passively with the I's active sublation of it. (Rabbits are not selves; being killed and eaten by a hunter is just one of the ways in which rabbits die, death being the inevitable fate of every rabbit.)
2. On 'end in itself' (*Selbstzweck*), see §423, n. 5.
3. If one eats something then it must 'perish'. But why can self-consciousness not deal with the obtrusive object in some less destructive way, by e. g. domesticating it or making love to it? That subject and object are 'immediate' does not adequately answer this question. In any case, unity is said to require only the 'negation' of the object's immediacy, not the destruction of the object. Hegel seems to be relying on the fact that eating is a more fundamental and pervasive human activity than domesticating or sexually abusing non-human animals, and also on his perhaps exaggerated talk of the 'identity', 'unity', etc. of subject and object.
4. An individual rabbit is at odds with the 'universality of its concept', rabbithood. Unlike its concept, therefore, it must die in order to rectify this imbalance and to allow for the emergence of the genus: cf. §381, nn. 24, 25; 412, n. 3. This is the 'dialectic of self-sublation' of the Paragraph: cf. §427, n. 1. The rabbit dies by 'its own concept'. But there is always some more specific cause of its death. One

such specific cause of death is an external predator, including a human predator. The human predator, like any other cause of death, is the concept's agent. It is the 'appearing' (*erscheinende*) concept, whereas the concept itself is latent or 'internal'.

NOTES TO §428

1. When I am hungry, I am at odds with myself, not how I want to be. Satisfaction joins me together again. But I remain an individual 'on the external side' (contrasting with 'on the inner side' in §429). If my relation to the object were not purely 'negative', but one of e.g. friendship or love, I would not remain just as individual and 'self-centred' as before. But as it is, I do. Consequently desire re-emerges after each temporary satisfaction.

   Hegel does not explain why my relation to the object must be 'only negative': cf. §427, n. 3. Nor is it clear why desire has to re-emerge. The reason given is that satisfaction has only occurred 'in the individual case' (*im Einzelnen*) and 'this' (*dieses*) is transitory. 'Individual' here may refer to self-consciousness, or to the object consumed, or to the act of satisfying desire. (*Im Einzelnen* can mean 'in detail, in particular'.) Self-consciousness itself is not especially transitory; if it were it could not have new desires. The object is transitory and so is the act. But it does not follow that it cannot give lasting satisfaction. Might the consumption of one object not be enough for me? Further premises would be needed to show otherwise. But cf. §428, n. 3.

2. 'Fashioning' (*Bilden*) preserves the 'matter' of an object, while imposing on it the 'form of the subjective', i.e. the form that expresses the subject. Fashioning cannot wholly destroy the object, since the new form gains a 'subsistence' (*Bestehen*) in the object. Fashioning leaves the object its independence. Self-consciousness cannot endure an independent entity, so it does not fashion the object, it destroys it. Hence the 'form of the subjective' gets no 'subsistence'; the subject leaves no mark expressive of itself.

3. The subject, self-consciousness, is fundamentally universal. Owing to its (external) individuality it devours an individual object. But this 'objectification' (*Objektivierung*) does not adequately express its 'universality', its sheer I-awareness, capable of having a great variety of objects, not fixated on any single one: cf. §430Z. So it consumes one object after another in an attempt to objectify itself, but finds lasting satisfaction in none of them. This helps to explain why the consumption of one object is not enough: cf. §428, n. 1.

NOTE TO §429

1. Hegel is trying to explain self-consciousness's advance from repeated consumption of individual objects to its encounter with another self-consciousness on a par with itself. He locates repeated consumption on the 'external side' and encounter with another I on the 'inner side'. It is not clear what these two sides are. He does not, presumably, mean that repeated consumption is what I actually and overtly do, while encounter with another is what I imagine doing. In

reality, adults have always eaten food and encountered others contemporaneously, though perhaps infants eat food before they consciously encounter others. But for Hegel the two form logically, though not temporally, successive stages. The logical underpinning of the advance is that the 'bad infinity' of infinite progression ($1 = \frac{1}{2} + \frac{1}{4} + \frac{1}{8} + \frac{1}{16} + \cdots$) gives way to the 'good infinity' of a circular return to itself ($1 = 1$?): cf. Enc. I, §§94 ff. The encounter with another I is a sort of circular return, and it breaks off the endless consumption of individual non-I's, since it provides the I with a universal counterpart to its own universality.

The two sides are described in contrary ways. The inner side is associated with what is 'in itself', with the 'concept', and with universality; the outer side with 'being-for-self', immediacy, and individuality. 'Being-for-self' here indicates individuality, perhaps 'self-centredness', while 'in itself' and the 'concept' indicate what self-consciousness intrinsically is and should become explicitly. On 'judgement' as 'original division', here of the self-consciousness into two self-consciousnesses, see also §389, n. 4. *Diremtion* and 'diremption' come from the Latin *dirimo, diremptus*, 'to separate, divide'. On 'self-feeling' (*Selbstgefühl*), cf. §§407–1.

NOTES TO §430

1. The self-consciousnesses are there 'immediately' as physical entities, their encounter is not mediated by themselves or by anything else: they did not, e.g., arrange to meet, they are not yet in conflict, nor otherwise related to each other. Self-consciousness's 'individuality' has been sublated, but only by a 'first' sublation. The second sublation would transform it into universality, the fundamental characteristic of the self-consciousness: cf. §425, n. 1 on the first and second 'negation'. But the first sublation leaves it as 'particular' (*besonderes*): cf. §378, n. 10. 'Individuality' (*Einzelheit*) here suggests uniqueness, while particularity implies being just one thing alongside others of the same sort. Self-consciousness is not content with awareness of its own bare I. It wants to behold itself in external reality, to transform external reality into a mirror image of itself. But when it gets its wish, its mirror image is a distinct I confronting itself, and this makes each I just 'particular', not universal as they are supposed to be. Hegel knew Greek mythology, but he nowhere mentions Narcissus, the youth who fell in love with his own reflection. Probably self-consciousness would not be satisfied by its own reflection. That is too dependent on oneself, not a 'free object', nor really a proper I; what attracted Narcissus to his own reflection was its physical beauty, not its self-consciousness.

2. It is not clear why being recognized by the other will resolve the 'contradiction' or why there is no other resolution of it. The general idea is that self-consciousness feels bad about having lost its status as the only self-consciousness around, for which everything else is a 'nullity'. So it needs reassurance of its selfhood from the other I. This recognition needs to be more than just beholding the other as an I and beholding oneself in the other. One self-consciousness already views the other in this way and presumably the other does the same. But this minimal recognition

constitutes the contradiction, it does not resolve it. The recognition required will also remove the 'immediacy' of each self-consciousness, by establishing a relation between them. It looks as if the recognition required is unilateral, not reciprocal. I want my unique status confirmed. I do not want to be assured only of my particularity.

3. On the I's universality and the comparison with light, cf. §§381, n. 15; 396, n. 12; 409, n. 1; 412, n. 3. Here the 'contradiction' is intensified, but at the cost of an ambiguity in the account of the I's universality:

   (1) The I is 'interrupted by no limit'. For suppose there were a limit to my awareness. Am I aware of the limit? If I am, then it is no limit, since (according to Enc. I, §60) to be aware of a limit one must be aware of what lies beyond the limit and is not, therefore, limited by it. If I am not aware of the limit, then it does not interrupt my awareness, it does not appear to me as a limit. Moreover, in thinking about the possibility of a limit of which I am unaware, I have already gone beyond the possible limit by thinking about possible things beyond the limit of my thought. Why should this feature of the I imply that there cannot be more than one I? Because, Hegel suggests, each distinct I is 'impenetrable' to the other. I know that the other is an I and that he is thinking, but I do not know what he is thinking. So in encountering another I, the I comes up against a limit and knows that it does so. But why does another I limit me more than does, say, the molecular structure of a pebble? Because although the inner structure of the pebble may be unknown to me, perhaps for ever, there is something there to be known, and something within well-defined limits. The other I, by contrast, is unlimited in the way that I am. Whereas the pebble is a possible occupant of my world, the world as I view it, the other I is not. It is the focus of another world, the world as it views it. Perhaps the comparison with light helps: I am a light that illuminates my world and its inhabitants. How can I illuminate another light, illuminating its world? Can I even tolerate this rival light, illuminating the things that I illuminate from a different angle? Here a conflict may be stirring.

   (2) The I is 'the essence common to all men'. Everyone is an I. Prima facie this implies that there *is* more than one I or self. Perhaps there is a universal I-hood, selfhood or egoity which (like, say, rationality) is common to everyone, but not itself plural in the way that men are. But this is different from saying that there is a single I in which all men share. Perhaps there is such a single omnipresent I, but this does not follow from the fact that every man is an I. At any rate these claims are quite different from point (1). If (1) has any tendency to show that there is only one I, it is to show that *I* am the only person there is, not that there are many people, all sharing a single I.

The *Zusatz*, unlike the Paragraph, does not mention 'recognition' as the solution to the contradiction. This may be because, while in the Paragraph the problem seems to be that self-consciousness is 'particular' and needs to be assured that it is an I, in the *Zusatz* the I is decidedly universal and the problem is how there can be two of them. Hegel seems to hold that there are two selves only because of the persisting 'immediacy' of self-consciousness: cf. §431, n. 1.

NOTES TO §431

1. There are two aspects to the self-conscious I: (1) its 'immediacy', its natural, bodily 'reality' (*Dasein*); (2) its inner I-hood, its 'freedom'. Aspect (1) is an obstacle to 'recognition'. I 'cannot be aware of myself as myself in the other' when I regard him only under aspect (1). Conversely, he cannot recognize me under aspect (1). Why not? Why might I not become aware of my biological affinity to the creature confronting me, even of 'myself' in it? I might, but that is not enough. Aspect (2) is essential to me, and aspect (2) is not apparent in the other's aspect (1). For aspect (2) to become apparent, aspect (1) needs to be sublated. I somehow know that aspect (2) is there, for otherwise I would not be 'bent on the sublation of this immediacy'. But it is not manifest and I need it to be so, both to give and to receive recognition. But aspect (1) cannot be entirely eliminated. For it is not just an obstacle to recognition. I could have no relations to others if they or I had no body. Somehow aspect (1) must be sublated (cf. §381, n. 13), but not eliminated. It must be exploited to give expressive embodiment or 'reality' (*Dasein*) to our freedom.

    Nothing said so far supports Hegel's opening claim that the process of recognition is a 'combat' (*Kampf*). Might not smiles and greetings sublate aspect (1) to the required extent? The *Zusatz* attempts to explain why combat is needed.

2. These are aspects (1) and (2) of §431, n. 1. Under aspect (1) one is subject to 'alien power' or the power of another like any other 'thing'; under aspect (2) one is 'free' and ought not to be treated like a thing. This account has some affinity to Kant's view of the person. Kant might be less ready than Hegel to see a 'contradiction' between the two aspects, but he would not disagree that our bodily conduct should be brought into conformity as far as possible with our intrinsic freedom.

3. Hegel's argument is contentious. (i) Freedom 'consists in the identity of myself with the other'. So (ii) I am free only if the other is free, and (iii) I am free only if I recognize the other as free. If we assume that only two people are involved, myself and another, and if identity is a symmetric relation, so that I am identical with the other if, and only if, the other is identical with me, then (i) entails (ii): I am free, i.e. identical with the other, only if the other is free, i.e. identical with me. But (i) and (ii) do not entail (iii): 'I am free, i.e. identical with the other, only if I recognize the other as free, i.e. identical with me'—unless (i) is replaced with: 'Freedom consists in the identity, and the recognized identity, of myself with the other'. Hegel is perhaps conflating two distinct arguments:

    (1) If I am intrinsically free, i.e. if (roughly speaking) I have free will, then I am free simply as an I or ego, and not because of of some natural quality that I have, such as free birth (cf. §433, n. 4). But as Is or egos, human beings do not differ from one another (e.g. §430Z.). So if I am intrinsically free, then

as Is or egos all human beings are intrinsically free. Therefore, if I regard myself as intrinsically free, I must in consistency regard all human beings as intrinsically free. If I believe that some humans are not intrinsically free, owing to their possession or lack of some natural quality, then I do not regard myself as intrinsically free solely in virtue of my egohood. And then my own freedom is defective, for to be properly free I must regard myself as properly free. But if someone is intrinsically free, he should not be treated solely as a means, in particular he should not be enslaved. So if I regard myself as intrinsically free, I must in consistency believe that no other human beings should be enslaved. If I do not, then I do not, in the full sense, regard myself as intrinsically free.

This argument deserves at least two comments. First, one objection to it might be that, even if the argument is in general sound, someone may regard himself as intrinsically free, while nevertheless believing that some other people are not. This person's beliefs may be inconsistent, but this need not impair his belief that *he* is free and thus need not diminish his *own* freedom. But Hegel disagrees. If someone believes that he is free, but others are not, this must dilute his belief in his own freedom, so that he believes himself to be free not simply as an I, but in virtue, say, of his free birth (cf. §433, n. 4). Such a person's beliefs are, then, not really inconsistent. Consistency is preserved, but at the cost of diluting his belief in his own freedom, weakening the concept of freedom, and freedom itself. Secondly, the argument does not imply, and does not purport to imply, that no humans are enslaved. Someone might live in a slave-owning society and yet be himself fully and intrinsically free, as long as he does not believe that others *should be* enslaved. To exclude this possibility, we need to invoke a second argument:

(2) A human being is intrinsically free. But his freedom is not fulfilled in 'reality' except in a society where citizens recognize each other's freedom. A solitary individual cannot be genuinely free, nor can an individual who associates only with his own slaves. But might not such a society contain slaves too, as long as it contains a fair number of free men? Hegel doubts the possibility of this as well as its desirability. If a proposition of the form 'x is intrinsically free' is interpreted in such a way that it does not entail 'x ought not to be enslaved', then some *natural* feature (such as free birth) must be invoked to differentiate those whom it is permissible to enslave from those whom it is not. Then this natural feature is incorporated into the concept of intrinsic freedom or is, at least, assigned a disproportionate weight in comparison with intrinsic freedom, rationality, and egohood. This debases the freedom of free citizens as well as that of slaves. However, two replies are available to a supporter of slavery:

(a) Those whom it is permissible to enslave are not fully human. Despite their human exterior, they lack intrinsic freedom, rationality, and egohood.

(b) The slave and the free are distinguished by no natural feature. There are no natural slaves. Whether one is slave or free depends on a lottery. But since we (or 'civilization') need slaves, the lottery should nevertheless be held.

Neither of these responses involve the adulteration of freedom with 'nature'. So Hegel needs to find other reasons for rejecting them.

On freedom generally, cf. §§480 ff., 539. On slavery, cf. §§433, n. 4; 435, n. 5.

4. Owing to 'need' (*Bedürfnis*) and 'necessity' (*Not*) people cooperate. But they need not regard each other as free in order to do so. Equally, I can cooperate with a dog or a horse, without regarding them as free. I need not feel any deep affinity to those with whom I cooperate. Conversely, there are many people whom I regard as free, but with whom I do not cooperate, mainly because I have no occasion too. On needs, cf. §§524 ff.

5. Men are already free in some sense before they recognize each other's freedom. This is what makes another man, but not a chimpanzee, an appropriate candidate for recognition. But this is not yet true or genuine freedom. For that, recognition is required. But recognition is obstructed by 'immediacy', now also referred to as 'naturalness'. Our naturalness cuts us off from each other. So each party has to risk death to show his indifference to 'reality' (*Dasein*) and his capacity for freedom.

Hegel is open to two criticisms:

(1) Even if each party must risk death, this need not involve combat. In the circumstances combat is the most obvious way of risking death. But there are other ways of doing it. Each might, in full view of the other, hurl himself off a palm tree or swim in crocodile-infested waters. However, this too might be regarded as a combat of sorts.

(2) It is not clear why risk of death is required. Certainly, death is not required. Hegel is not suggesting that if each party dies, they will be united in the afterlife. The death of either party ends the game and it has to start again. So why risk of death? Readiness to risk death is not sufficient to establish 'capacity for freedom': a crocodile or a chimpanzee may risk death by attacking a man, but that does not show it to be free. Perhaps it is unaware that it is risking death. Well, so may the other humanoid fighting me be unaware of the risk it is taking. To know that it really is consciously risking death I already need to know that it is properly human and fairly familiar with the risks of combat. Perhaps I already need to know that it has the capacity for freedom. Nor does readiness to risk death seem necessary. It shows, Hegel implies, my indifference to what I risk, my life. But why does my freedom require indifference to my life? There are three possibilities:

(i) My life is my existence. To be truly free I must be indifferent to my own existence. Then nothing and no one can compel me to do anything, since I can always choose martyrdom or suicide instead. For signs of this somewhat specialized, Stoic conception of freedom in Hegel, see my 'Hegel on Death', *International Journal of Moral and Social Studies*, 1 (1986), 109–22.

(ii) My life is my external side, in contrast to my inner self-consciousness. The point of risking it is not to show that I could exist without it or that I do not mind whether I exist or not, but to show that I have inner self-consciousness and that it is not entirely absorbed in my outer side. (But, as we saw above, my opponent already needs to know this to be sure that I am consciously risking my life.)

(iii) My life is my 'naturalness'. What distresses me about it is that it is raw animal life, with none of the refinements that both result from and sustain the interconnection of people in a social order. I cannot at this stage express my distress in these terms nor can I see any solution to the problem except a somewhat raw animal rejection of my raw animal life.

Probably each of these ideas plays a part in Hegel's thought here.

NOTES TO §432

1. As the *Zusatz* shows, the 'new' and 'higher' contradiction is that the combatants have 'proved' their 'inner' freedom but do not get any recognized 'reality' (*Dasein*) of their freedom. This is debatable. The dead combatant can obtain posthumous recognition for the freedom he has demonstrated, though not now any 'reality' of it—unless a posthumous medal or monument counts as such a 'reality'. The survivor does not obtain recognition, at any rate from his dead opponent.

2. In the 'state of nature' (*Naturzustand(e)*) men have to fight for recognition, since they would otherwise not receive it. In 'civil society' (*bürgerliche(n) Gesellschaft*) and the 'political state' (*Staat*) they do not need to, since recognition is given to them without a fight: cf. §396, n. 17. Children need discipline (§396, n. 14) and adolescents rebel (§396, n. 8), but they do not usually fight 'in the extreme form'. If it were true the state rests on 'force' (*Gewalt*), then opportunities for combat would be frequent, since the state would not treat people as 'rational' and 'free'. But it does not rest on force. Whatever the origin of the state may have been, this is not relevant to what the state in reality is: cf. §433; PR, §258. We tend to think that the state rests on force because we forget how much we owe to it: 'habit blinds us to that on which our whole existence depends. When we walk the streets at night in safety, it does not strike us that this might be otherwise.... [It is not] force [that] holds the state together, but... the fundamental sense of order that everyone possesses' (PR, §268 Addition). It is not clear whether the recognition conferred in the state is equal and reciprocal recognition for all law-abiding citizens or whether, in addition, the 'citizen' or *Bürger* (which also means 'bourgeois, member of the middle class') receives special recognition, 'honour', from his position. The latter alternative is suggested by the contrast with the state of nature, where individuals claim recognition 'whatever they may be and whatever they may do'. But the implication of this may simply be that in the state those without

employment or who break the law are excluded from honour, not that people receive differing honour depending on their status. So far Hegel has given no hint that the combatants want non-reciprocal recognition, to receive a type of recognition that they do not give in return. On law as the 'will that is in and for itself', cf. §§485, 529 ff. On civil society, cf. §§523 ff. On the state, cf. §§433, 535 ff.

3. On feudalism, see also PH, pp. 366–89. Feudalism was, Hegel argues, barely a 'lawful condition' (*rechtlicher Zustand*); it was an egoistic, individualistic system, in which people wanted honour for themselves in their 'immediate individuality'. Because of the lawlessness, wrongdoers could get honour by success in a duel, while slandered innocents could often retrieve their honour in no other way. Apart from hand-to-hand fighting in battle and in military training, ancient peoples (Hegel is thinking mainly of the Athenians) did not have duelling, because the individual did not want respect or honour as a bare individual, but as a member of the state; the citizen was, on Hegel's view, too enmeshed in his community to want anything for himself outside of his social context. The point of the final sentence is that by fighting a duel for his honour a soldier establishes that he is not just fighting for money. Duelling was forbidden in the army by Hegel's time, but permitted earlier, and still prevalent in German student associations.

NOTES TO §433

1. The 'negation' is the negation of immediacy, as in §432. The 'relation to himself' which the victor holds on to is presumably his bare I-awareness in contrast to the life preferred by the vanquished. It is not clear why the vanquished does not get recognition from the victor. Neither party wants to die. So the victor would probably have given in if the vanquished had not. The victor did *risk* death, however. And it is risk of death that negates 'immediacy' or 'naturalness' and thus demonstrates one's 'capacity for freedom': cf. §431Z., and n. 5. But the vanquished risked death too: he could not be sure that he would not be killed before he surrendered or that his surrender would be accepted. So why does the victor not recognize him? Why does he take him into servitude? It is no doubt plausible that a victor would behave in this way in the state of nature, but it is equally plausible that the two would become mutually respecting friends: bonding rather than bondage. But bondage harks back to the freedom stressed e.g. in §431Z.

2. Cf. §432, n. 2. 'Appearance' (*Erscheinung*) often contrasts with 'essence' (*Wesen*): cf. Enc. I, §131. So it does here: force belongs to the appearance of the state, not to its essence or 'substantial principle'. Hegel's idea is that what is required for the state to begin or appear on the scene need not be a persistent or essential feature of the state. On 'universal self-consciousness', where everyone recognizes everyone else, see §436.

3. The bondsman abandons any will of his own and does what the master wants him to do. So the 'immediacy' of his 'particular self-consciousness' is 'sublated'. The master, by contrast, takes no account of what the bondsman wants; he tries to keep him alive and healthy, but for his own purposes, not because the bondsman

wants it. So the immediacy of the master's particular self-consciousness is not sublated. Hence the implicit 'mutual identity' of the two self-consciousnesses has become explicit or 'posited', but only in a 'relative' or 'one-sided' way. The bondsman is subservient to the master but the master is as self-willed as ever.

This is what happens while the 'naturalness of life . . . persists', i.e. while they remain in the state of nature. §431Z suggested that 'naturalness' would be sublated by the risk of death. But this has not happened to either party, even though the master was the last to blink: cf. §§431, n. 5; 434, n. 1. It looks as if Hegel has moved the goal posts. However, the 'contradiction' here, is the same as that discussed in §430 and nn. 1, 2, and 3.

4. Cf. §431, n. 3. Greeks and Romans, like other ancient and some not so ancient peoples, had slaves. But they did not hold that man is free 'only if he was born as a free man'. Slaves could be, and sometimes were, liberated. Conversely, people born free could be, and often were, enslaved. (Hume in his essay 'On the Populousness of Ancient Nations' argued plausibly that most slaves were captured in war rather than bred.) So slavery and its opposite, freedom, were not normally regarded as natural conditions in this sense. Aristotle, in his *Politics*, argued that slavery was natural in the sense that some people, mostly non-Greeks and most non-Greeks, were natural slaves, i.e. intellectually and morally ill-equipped to look after themselves and suitable for domination by others. But Aristotle's view was not the only view available. Other Greeks, including Euripides, questioned the naturalness of slavery. They did not, however, necessarily conclude that it should be abolished, since they could not think of an alternative way of meeting their needs. Arguably, however, Greek philosophers laid the basis for the abolition of slavery by framing and reflecting on such universal concepts as 'man as such', though Hegel reserves the credit for abolishing slavery for Christianity: see §482, n. 3; Enc. I, §163Z.(1).

Hegel opposed slavery, because of the deprivation of freedom, not because of the hardship involved: 'The Athenian slave perhaps had an easier occupation and more intellectual work than is usually the case with our servants, but he was still a slave, because he had alienated to his master the whole range of his activity' (PR, §67Z.). His main argument against it is that in so far as man is intrinsically free, i.e. has free will, he should have the outer 'reality' of freedom, which is similar to the Kantian argument that a rational being should be treated not just as a means but as an end: cf. §§385, n. 7; 431, n. 2. Aristotle would object that some biological humans do not have fully fledged free will or rationality. Hegel would perhaps agree with this, conceding that complete free will is not an invariable possession of all men at all times, but developed over time (PR, §57). Slavery is, in his view, always wrong, but justified in earlier times: 'Slavery occurs in man's transition from the state of nature to genuinely ethical conditions; it occurs in a world where a wrong is still right. At that stage wrong has validity and so is necessarily in place' (PR, §57Z.). Aristotle might again object that it is not only in prehistoric times that some men are deficient in free will and rationality; there are such people at all times and in all places. But Hegel's fundamental egalitarianism would resist this objection. What matters for Hegel is mind, not nature. He could well agree that slavery is natural, even that there are natural slaves, but he would respond that mind, especially in the form of Christianity, trumps nature and overcomes it.

In this paragraph Hegel uses the words *Sklave(rei)*, 'slave(ry)', while elsewhere he speaks of *Knecht(schaft)*, 'bondsman, bondage'. A *Knecht* may be a labourer, a servant, a serf, not necessarily a slave. But Hegel seems not to draw a significant distinction between the words here.

NOTE TO §434

1. It is unclear whether the immediate 'object' (*Objekt(s)*) that is no longer destroyed is the bondsman or a non-human object. It should be a non-human object, since it unites 'independence' (*Selbständigkeit*) and 'non-independence' (*Unselbständigkeit*), i.e. master and bondsman. But it should be the bondsman, since his life is maintained. Perhaps it is both: the preservation of the bondsman requires the master not just to eat things himself but give them to the bondsman, and this gives rise to the idea of preserving other things for the future. The satisfaction of need is 'universal' in two ways: the needs of all, in this case both, parties are satisfied reciprocally, and their needs are satisfied over a long period by provident thrift. Hegel seems to draw a connection between these two features.

NOTES TO §435

1. The master has an 'intuition' (*Anschauung*), almost a visible demonstration, of the 'validity' (*Gelten*) of his individual being-for-self, but he has not shed his 'immediate being-for-self', i.e. his self-centredness and self-importance, except by proxy. The bondsman, by contrast, works off his immediate being-for-self, i.e. his 'individual will and self-will'; this 'alienation' (*Entäusserung*) and 'fear of the master' is the 'beginning of wisdom', an allusion to Psalms 111: 10; Proverbs 9: 10: 'The fear of the Lord is the beginning of wisdom'.
2. In the bondsman, the master 'beholds' his own 'immediate will', not the bondsman's. His recognition by the bondsman is only 'formal', because it is extracted by force.
3. On the need for discipline in childhood, cf. §396, n. 14.
4. On the sixth-century lawgiver Solon and the subsequent tyranny of the Pisistratids, i.e. Pisistratus and later his sons, Hippias and Hipparchus, see also PH, pp. 258–92. On Rome and its kings, see PH, pp. 296 ff. That a people needs a period of tyrannical discipline may be plausible, but it does not follow ('therefore') from the fact that an individual needs discipline. Individual Athenians and Romans were no doubt disciplined by their parents, etc. in childhood. A tyrant is not needed for that purpose. So he is needed to subject the people to some further discipline, analogous but not identical to the discipline of a child. Hegel's argument is based on a tenuous analogy between an individual and a people.

To his first argument for the relative justification of bondage—the benefits of discipline—he adds another: anyone, or any people, who really wants to be free, can be free, and anyone, or any people, who does not really want to be free, does not deserve to be free. This is connected to the first argument: wanting to be free and the courage to win freedom are among the supposed benefits of the discipline of bondage. Cf. PR, §57Z: 'if a man is a slave, his own will is responsible for his slavery, just as it is its will which is responsible if a people is subjugated. Hence the wrong of slavery lies at the door not simply of enslavers or conquerors but of the slaves and the conquered themselves'.

5. In the preceding paragraph (cf. §435, n. 4), freedom was contrasted with slavery or bondage. Here bondage is said to be the beginning, not of wisdom, but of freedom, and its negation of 'egotistic individuality' is one 'moment' of freedom. The pursuit of one's egoistic individuality is, in Hegel's view, a type of freedom, but an unsatisfactory type: if I simply do as I like, I am really in bondage to by likes and dislikes, which are not chosen by me but just happen to be what they are ('contingent'). So although bondage deprives me of one sort of freedom, it gives me one essential ingredient of true freedom: freedom from my self-centred likes and dislikes. Hegel sees little value in freedom from slavery if it means simply the freedom to do as one likes, and he assumes in §433Z. that rebellious slaves are seeking 'recognition of their eternal human rights', not just the ability to do whatever they like. If they sought only the latter type of freedom, they would not deserve to be free.

The other, 'positive', ingredient of true freedom is submission not to the will of another individual, but to the 'universal, rational will that is in and for itself', 'what is in and for itself rational in its universality', or the 'law of the will that is in and for itself'. This is the laws and constitution of one's state. It is called 'will', because Hegel believes, under the influence of Rousseau and Kant, that it is what everyone at bottom wills. It embodies a rationality that expresses the rational core of the human mind, so that submission to it is genuine freedom. The bondsman and the master arrive at the same destination by different routes: the bondsman by escaping from the master's individual will as well as his own, the master escaping his individual will by looking after the bondsman and seeing the sublation of the bondsman's individual will.

Hegel tends to assume that true freedom must be for all: cf. §431, n. 3. Might not the master sublate his own selfish will and submit to the universal will, while continuing to own bondsmen? The master would then be genuinely free, but with a freedom not extended to the bondsmen. No doubt slavery tends to corrupt and brutalize free persons as well as the slaves, since slaves are exposed to violence and to sexual assault. But relatively few free persons would come into contact with slaves in public works, such as the Athenian silver mines, and at least some free persons, such as Plato and Aristotle, were not seriously corrupted by their house-slaves. Hegel oversimplifies matters by assimilating the slavery of highly civilized societies to the master–bondsman relation in the state of nature, where the master has not yet submitted his individual will to a rational, objective order and where, in Hegel's version of the story, there are no other free people around for the master to fraternize with. Perhaps a free person needs other free persons to associate with, but it does not follow that he needs everyone to be free: cf. §436, n. 4. Hegel might deny that one free person can immediately associate with another free person, without going through conflict and subjugation. But it is conceivable that some people could be liberated without everyone being liberated, especially if the slaves are subjugated at a later time.

NOTES TO §436

1. 'Affirmative' contrasts with 'negative'. Negative 'awareness' (*Wissen*) of oneself in the other self would be awareness of oneself as what is not (like) the other self. Affirmative awareness of oneself in the other self is then awareness of oneself as what is (like) the other self. Hegel may also have in mind affirmation as the negation of the negation: cf. §425, nn. 1 and 4. First, I am just aware of myself, then of myself as distinct from the other, finally of myself as the same as the other.
2. I know that you, as a free person, recognize me (freely, not under compulsion). I know this (namely that you recognize me), 'in so far as' (*insofern*) I recognize you and know that you are free. The clause beginning with 'in so far as' does not say how I know that you recognize me. Conceivably, I might recognize you even though you do not recognize me, whether or not I know that you do not recognize me. The clause just says that recognition is reciprocal. The final clause, 'and is aware that it is free' (*und es frei weiss*) could mean: 'and is freely aware of it'. This would perhaps make better sense, because Hegel has already said that it knows the other to be free ('in the free other self') and because he has not yet said that it recognizes the other freely. But it would be odd to speak of free awareness or knowledge, rather than of free recognition.
3. 'Mirroring' translates *Widerscheinen*. But this does not appear in the editions published by Hegel himself. The first (1817) and second (1827) editions had *Wiederscheinen*, the third (1830) had *Wiedererscheinen*. *Wiederscheinen* could mean 'shining back, reflection', but this would more usually be *Widerscheinen*. *Wiedererscheinen* means 'reappearance', as Wallace translates it from the third edition. 'Reappearance' would fit the context well enough, but 'mirroring' (in the sense of 'reflection') is more appropriate: cf. §§430, n. 1; 435, n. 5.
   A concept is primarily subjective; when it acquires objectivity or reality, it is an Idea: cf. §436, n. 5. Here the 'objectivity' of the 'concept' is a group of mutually recognizing individuals, e.g. a family, while 'subjectivity' is the individual's inner self. This inner self is now merged into the group, but it is nevertheless 'identical with itself', not lost or alienated, since the individual is entirely at home in the group. Because the subjectivity is merged into the group, the concept, and the subjectivity, are 'universal', shared by all, not the self-centred, individual subjectivity that has now been shed: cf. §435, n. 1. The objectivity of the concept is virtually the same as the 'substance' of a spiritual institution such as the family or love. (Often Hegel contrasts 'substance' with 'subject': cf. Enc. I, Preface to second edition, where Spinozism is the philosophy, in which 'God is determined only as *substance* and not as subject and spirit'.) The individual identifies himself with the institution and, regardless of his private interests, devotes himself to the purposes of the group. He displays courage on behalf of the group and receives

honour and fame for having done so. Honour and fame are the 'appearance of the substantial', its outward manifestation, but they can become detached from it, so that one receives undeserved honours and fame, or one's pursuit of them has a selfish motive.

4. This argument depends on the assumption that there is only one master: cf. §435, n. 5.

5. The use of 'reflected' (*reflektiert*) supports the reading *Widerscheinen* in the Remark: cf. §436, n. 3. On the 'speculative', cf. §§378, n. 4; 403, n. 3. It involves the unification of apparently contradictory features in a single, coherent whole. The 'concept', here equated with the 'subjective' (cf. §436, n. 3), is each independent self, the 'objective' is the same selves 'merged together'. But in fact there are three stages: (1) A single mind or mind as such, which (2) undergoes 'diremption' (cf. §429, n. 1) into several independent selves, which (3) are also merged together. Stage (1) is the subjective or the concept, (2) is the objective, and (3) is the unity of the subjective and the objective. Hegel speaks of the 'diremption of mind into different selves', rather than of different selves that happen to encounter each other, because he regards the mind as essentially requiring several selves. One self on its own cannot be a fully fledged self or mind.

NOTES TO §437

1. Consciousness and self-consciousness are united, since I am no longer conscious of an object that is quite different from myself. I am conscious e.g. of my family and conscious of myself, self-conscious, as a member of the family. 'Shining into each other' (*ineinander scheinende*) is equivalent to 'mirroring' or being reflected into each other: cf. §436, nn. 3 and 5. It seems wrong to say that the 'distinction' (*Unterschied*) between the individuals is now an indeterminate 'diversity' (*Verschiedenheit*). §436Z stressed the continuing independence of the selves, and e.g. family members occupy distinct roles: father, mother, brother, sister, and so on (cf. §§518–22; PR, §§158 ff.). Nevertheless, in one of his less perspicuous transitions, Hegel here exploits the 'identity' of the selves to move on to their 'truth' (cf. §419, n. 3): 'reason', the ideal rational structure that all the selves share in.

2. The Idea is the unity of concept and reality in general: cf. Enc. I, §§213 ff. The Idea need not involve consciousness. In Hegel's Logic, the Idea has three stages: 'life', 'cognition', and the 'absolute Idea'. Life is the lowest stage of the Idea, where the intimate connection between the whole organism (the 'concept') and its parts (its 'reality') does not depend on the organism's being conscious: cf. §423, n. 5. Nevertheless, reason is associated with the Idea from the start, since this type of concept-reality unity involves the structure of reason, not intellect. But reason at the first stage does not require consciousness on the part of the organism: the concept is too closely intertwined with its reality for consciousness to emerge. At the second stage of the Idea, cognition, a rift has opened up between the concept and its reality, that is, between cognition and its objects. Cognition aims to close this rift by disclosing the rational structure of its objects. (See Enc. I, §§223 ff.) In that context, Hegel does not speak of 'consciousness'. But cognition is similar

to consciousness as it is considered here. Here the concept is 'existing for itself', i.e. not intertwined in its reality as it is in a living organism: on one side is consciousness, on the other the 'object' (*Objekt(es)*). The concept and the reality or object are to be unified by discerning the rational structure involved in both. But so far they are still distinct from each other. Cf. §437, n. 4.

3. The two 'particularities' (*Besonderheiten*) are self-consciousness, initially individual self-consciousness (the 'subjective'), and its 'Other', another self-consciousness (the 'objective'). They are 'particularities' rather than 'individualities', because they are not really distinct individuals, at any rate not just two individuals, but two different aspects of a group of individuals: each individual acquires a unity-in-difference with the others. By overcoming these particularities each individual becomes merged in a single universal self-consciousness. But then it ceases to be self-consciousness 'in the narrower sense' and 'becomes reason'.

4. Hegel often distinguishes between 'truth' (*Wahrheit*) and 'correctness' (*Richtigkeit*): e.g. §379, n. 7; Enc. I, §§172 and Z., 213. Here he similarly distinguishes the 'truthful' (*Wahrhaft(en)*): more or less the 'true') from the 'correct' (*Richtige*). If I say 'That is a (poor) painting', my remark is 'correct', if it agrees with its object, i.e. if it is in fact a (poor) painting. But my remark, and more importantly my thought, is not true or truthful, since the painting does not measure up to its concept. To do that it would at least have to be a good painting. Hegel does not clearly explain the relevance of this point at this stage, but it seems to be this. As the Remark said, consciousness and its object are distinct, confronting each other. Hence the 'unity of self-consciousness with its object' is still 'abstract or formal'. Reason has not really got to grips with the object and displayed its rational structure. (§467 says more about how this is to be done.) But why does it follow that the object has 'hardly any truth'? Surely I can have a correct, but superficial representation of a good painting and, conversely, I can rationally get to grips with a bad painting. The abstractness or concreteness of my reason seems independent of the 'truth' of its object. Possibly Hegel is confusing two distinct ways in which an object 'only remotely corresponds to its concept': (1) my concept(ion) of it is thin and abstract, so that it and the object do not correspond well; (2) the object does not correspond well to the concept of it, e.g. a painting does not correspond well to the concept of a painting and is thus a poor painting. But these two correspondence-failures are not always as independent as this suggests. If the *artist* has only a thin conception of the painting to be produced, the painting is likely to be both (1) relatively independent of the artist's conception of it, and (2) a poor painting, thin or at least ill-organized. Analogously, a society whose members have only a thin conception of it is likely to be both (1) relatively independent of its members' conception of it, and (2) a thin, unstructured society.

NOTE TO §438

1. Permeating, encompassing, and overarching are, on the face of it, asymmetric relations, such that if x encompasses, etc. y, then y does not encompass, etc. x.

Hegel is perhaps thinking of a case where the object and the I both encompass, etc. each other. Yet here the 'universality of reason' 'signifies' (*hat . . . die Bedeutung*, lit. 'has the meaning of'): (1) the 'object' (*Objekt*) that permeates, etc. the I, and (2) the I that overarches, etc. the object. The solution is that Hegel has in view two different types of identity between subjectivity and objectivity. In (1) the 'object' is the social group to which the I belongs. This is no longer just 'given' to the I (as it was to consciousness), but permeates, etc. the I. The individual is imbued with the mentality or culture of his society. In (2) the I is a *pure* I, a thinker, not specifically the I permeated by its social group. Its object is any object of investigation, not necessarily the society to which the I belongs or the members of it. This I overarches, etc. the object by thinking about it and discerning rationality in it. Both processes are involved in the progress of the mind. (But see also §457, nn. 1 and 4.) Hegel's abrupt juxtaposition of these two exemplifications of the Idea is explained by the fact that he is trying to effect a transition from the socio-political concerns that are the natural conclusion of the section on Phenomenology to the investigation of the mind of an individual that occupies the section on Psychology. See also §457, n. 4.

NOTE TO §439

1. Hegel believes that the thoughts or thought-determinations that form the core of the human mind are also 'objective' (*gegenständlich*), constituting the 'essence of things'. Self-consciousness's 'certainty' of this has more to do with the second type of subjectivity-objectivity identity distinguished in §438, n. 1 (the I's takeover of the object) than the first (the object's takeover of the I). The essence of things is more or less the 'absolute substance', while the truth as 'awareness' is the mind: cf. §440, n. 6. The core of the mind is the I, 'the pure concept existing for itself', which is certain of its 'infinite universality' in that it constitutes the essence of things and is thus not bounded by anything external. But it cannot substantiate this certainty at once. The mind has to ascend and unravel 'its own thoughts' before it can discern them in things. Hegel traces this ascent in the following Paragraphs.

NOTES TO §440

1. Cf. §419, n. 3 on 'the truth of'. There, however, the truth was the 'proximate' truth of only one item, while here mind (in a narrower sense) is the 'truth' of two opposing, large-scale stages of 'mind' (in a wider sense). Soul and consciousness were opposite to each other. Soul is a 'simple immediate totality', a self-enclosed whole. Consciousness is 'knowledge' (*Wissen*) of an object distinct from itself, an object whose 'content' was derived from the soul: cf. §413, n. 1. Mind too is knowledge, but it is aware of itself, not of an external object. Hence it is 'infinite form', the infinity that goes round in a circle, not on for ever: it is not 'restricted' by anything else, only concerned with the mind itself. So it reverts in a way to a soul-like 'totality', only now it is a 'substantial', not a 'simple immediate',

totality. Since it is, unlike the soul, aware of itself, it is 'neither subjective nor objective', though perhaps Hegel could equally have said that it is both subjective and objective. Mind is a sort of return journey to the soul on a higher level, the negation of its negation, consciousness: cf. §§381, n. 18; 425, n. 1.

What Hegel here says of consciousness applies only to 'consciousness as such' (§§418–23), not to consciousness in the wider sense in which it includes self-consciousness. This indicates the uneasy relationship between 'phenomenology' and 'psychology': cf. §§440, n. 2; 446, n. 1.

2. *Psychologie* is, by its etymology, the study of the 'soul' (the Greek *psuchê*), but Hegel appropriates it for the study of the mind: cf. nn. to §378. 'In appearance', i.e. in real life, people do not just intuit, represent, desire, etc., they intuit, represent, desire particular things, such as a house, a drink, and so on. Psychology disregards such 'content' and focuses only on the 'faculties' (*Vermögen*) or 'universal modes of activity'. Psychology's disregard of the 'forms' is less straightforward. Consciousness perceives a house. Psychology disregards the actual house, the object. It is interested only in the faculty of perception or the activity of perceiving. It also disregards the occurrence of a content as a 'natural determination' in the soul, as a sheer sensation not yet projected as an independent object. But the soul does not have the faculties that Hegel mentions. It does not intuit, represent, think, or will. In this case Hegel is not just disregarding the 'form' of 'natural determination'. He is assuming that the content does not take this form. Is he treating the soul and consciousness differently? Is he, in effect, assuming that the mind is a *conscious* mind, not just a soul, and only disregarding the specific independent objects that a conscious mind has? Hegel does not think that he is discriminating in this way. He thinks that the mind has ceased, or is on the way to ceasing, to be simply consciousness, just as it has ceased to be simply a soul. It ceases to be consciousness because it believes, as 'reason', that its objects are not independent of itself, but are at bottom 'identical' to itself, that they are imbued with its own thoughts, and because as the mind ascends to higher faculties, such as thought, it becomes increasingly independent of external objects: cf. §439, n. 1. But Hegel does discriminate between the content and the forms. The content is simply disregarded (but cf. §440, n. 3), the forms are sublated. See also §440, n. 6.

3. The concept of mind involves its 'freedom', its 'elevation' above nature and external objects. But initially the mind does not fully accord with its concept, any more than an acorn is an oak-tree or an infant an adult. Thus the faculties of the mind form a hierarchy that ascends away from dependence on nature and external objects ('the form of immediacy') towards 'freedom' from them. Near the bottom are 'its sensations'. Sensations are natural determinations of the soul. They are decidedly '*its*' sensations, the sensations of the individual mind; they are simply subjective, with no objective or interpersonal status. These are elevated to 'intuitions' (cf. §§446 ff.). These are still 'its' intuitions, but less decidedly so, since 'its' (*seine*) is not italicized: my intuition depends on the presence of an external object, but others would have an intuition of it too if they were present. Intuitions are converted into 'representations' (cf. §§451 ff.), general ideas which,

though they depend on the prior intuition of objects, do not depend on the current presence of an object, and which are shared with others, hence no longer 'its'. Finally, representations are turned into 'thoughts' (cf. §§465 ff.), which not only do not depend on the immediate presence of an object, but are relatively independent of our past encounters with objects: if our intuitions of objects, even our representations, had been quite different, our thoughts would still be the same. Hence mind itself gradually extricates *itself* from what Hegel disregards: sensory content, 'nature', and objects.

Here, as elsewhere, Hegel tends to speak as if mind develops over time, when in this context it does not.

4. Here Hegel can reasonably be interpreted in either of two ways: (1) The mind has 'knowledge' (*Wissen*) of itself; the knowledge is 'boundless' in that it does not come up against any barrier in its exploration of itself; it 'embraces . . . all objectivity' in the sense that all the objectivity that concerns it, namely the objectivity of the mind itself, is immanent in it. (2) The mind has, at least potentially, knowledge of everything, since everything is somehow immanent in the mind.

5. Here Hegel endorses a diluted version of interpretation (2) in §440, n. 4., that the mind is confident that that it will find itself in the world, etc. So far, however, Hegel has said nothing to justify this confidence or his claim that the mind has it. That the mind has to seek reason in the world, that it will find it, or that it is confident that it will find it—these claims do not follow in any obvious way from the fact that the mind knows itself or from the fact (cf. §440, n. 3) that the higher phases of the mind are relatively independent of sensory material. 'Reason', the 'unity of the subjective and the objective', might be realized *within* the self-knowing mind, without being realized between the mind and the world. Hegel's idea, however, is that as the mind ascends to thought, i.e. to the 'concept', it becomes free of objects not only in the sense that it withdraws from them, but also in the sense that it finds its own thoughts to be 'determinations of the essence of things' cf. §439, n. 1. The mind must free, extricate itself from objects before it can take them over.

The biblical reference is to Genesis 2: 23: 'And Adam said, This is now bone of my bones and flesh of my flesh: she shall be called Woman, because she was taken out of Man'.

6. Cf. §440, n. 1 on mind as a unification of soul and consciousness. Here Hegel is speaking of the mind's knowledge not just of itself, but of any object of which we can be conscious. The mind aims to turn 'the beings' (*das Seiende*, 'what is', with the suggestion that it is just there) of consciousness into 'something soulful' (*ein Seelenhaftes*), i.e. into something mental or spiritual—he uses 'soulful' here instead of 'mental' in view of the mind's relation to the soul. (For the sake of symmetry Hegel adds that it turns the soulful into an object, though consciousness has already done that.) The mind does this by discerning in objects the 'determinations of free mind' which are both subjective ('its own thoughts', §439, the thoughts that it gradually extricates from 'the material' (*das Materielle*, §440)), and objective ('determinations of the essence of things', §439). When the object is seen in this way, it is 'true', in the sense of corresponding to its concept (cf. §437,

n. 4) and the mind's knowledge is true, since its own thoughts correspond exactly to the transformed object. In fact the mind and the object are really the same, since both involve the same determinations. Hence the mind is the 'self-knowing' (*sich wissende*) truth.

7. The doctrine Hegel criticizes is not global scepticism, but theological (or metaphysical) scepticism. This is not simply a 'modern' phenomenon. Aquinas believed that we can only know what God is not, not what he is—a view which, though not a thoroughgoing scepticism, Hegel wishes to reject. It is not obvious that Hegel has refuted theological, or even more extensive, scepticism. Even if we grant that the mind does discern its own thoughts in such objects as it encounters, it would not follow that there is no range of objects that elude its conceptual grasp. Suppose, for example, Hegel were dreaming, but retained his power of discerning thoughts in the dream-objects; the 'true' objects would then be unknown to him. Hegel has at least two replies: (1) The 'unknown' objects would not be 'true' or 'the truth', since, if they remain unconceptualized by us or by me, they do not correspond to the(ir) concept and are thus untrue. And to this the sceptic might reply: 'By "true" I do not mean "corresponding to (y)our concepts" in this sense'. (2) As soon as I become aware of the possibility of objects beyond my conceptual reach, they *ipso facto* become objects of my thinking, and then I can go on to conceptualize them; if I cannot get very far in conceptualizing them, this means that there is not very much to these objects; objects, *my* objects, cannot exceed my conceptual reach; so the objects are thin, and therefore not true. To which the sceptic can reply: 'I do not see why objects, even objects about which I can think sufficiently for them to be my objects, should not exceed my conceptual reach.'

The scepticism Hegel opposes is different from brain-in-a-vat or even Cartesian scepticism. The brain-in-a-vat sceptic can perfectly well describe the 'true' state of affairs unknown to the hypothetical subject: the subject is a brain in a vat manipulated by scientists to have our everyday beliefs about its surroundings, beliefs of the same type, though different in detail, from the beliefs that the scientists have about their surroundings. But for the theological sceptic the truth is of a quite different order from our everyday beliefs, so different that the sceptic can hardly describe it, at least in non-metaphorical terms. If the sceptic can describe, i.e. conceptualize, it, then Hegel is halfway to victory. Only halfway, because he still needs to negotiate the gap between conceptualization and knowledge, knowledge that things are that way.

8. Cf. §439, n. 1. 'Verification' (*Bewahrheitung*) here does not mean 'ascertaining or proving the truth (of)' in the ordinary sense. The deficiency of mind's 'certainty' of the 'identity of the subjective and objective' is not that it might be wrong, but that it has not yet carried out the identification in detail. As one might be quite certain that, say, a chess problem has a solution of a certain type, without yet having worked out the solution in detail. The verification involves the following steps: (1) The identity between the subjective and objective is developed into an actual 'difference' (*Unterschied*). That is, in its ascent from sensation and intuition to thought, the mind progressively disengages itself from the object, opening up

an apparent gap between the subjective and objective. (2) When this gap reaches its greatest extent, then it closes up again, not to give the original 'formal' identity, but the sort of identity that unites both formal identity and difference, an identity-in-difference. (3) The mind 'thus' becomes a differentiated totality, not the simple certainty with which we began. These steps exemplify the general principle that to grasp something properly we have first to distance ourselves from it: cf. §389, n. 6.

NOTES TO §441

1. Hegel has two apparently different accounts of finitude: (1) Something is finite if and only if it is bounded or limited by something else: cf. Enc. I, 92Z. (2) Something is finite if and only if its reality fails to correspond to its concept. The two accounts are connected in that if something fails to correspond to its concept, then it is not fully determined by its concept, but by something else. Conversely, if it is determined by something else, it does not fully correspond to its concept, since it is not determined wholly by its concept. Even an oak-tree is not fully determined by the concept of an oak but also by other things that interact with it. Account (1) explains the finitude of soul and consciousness: they are determined or limited, respectively, by nature and by an object. Account (2) is more prominent in the finitude of mind. Mind has a 'determinacy' (*Bestimmtheit*) in its 'knowledge' (*Wissen*), i.e. the content of its intuitions, etc. is determined from without. This is finitude of type (1), but it is 'the same thing' as finitude of type (2): a mismatch between the concept of mind and its 'reality' (*Realität*). The mismatch is between 'objective reason', i.e. the mind's own thoughts' constituting the essence of things (cf. §439), and the mind's own 'knowledge' or 'intelligence' (*Intelligenz*). The mind does not, at its current level of awareness or knowledge, discern its own thoughts in the nature of things. Hegel insists on viewing this as a mismatch between concept and reality, but it 'makes no difference' which is taken as which. Hegel's favourite analogy helps here: There is a mismatch between an acorn and the oak-tree that is to emerge from it. If this is a mismatch between concept and reality, which is the concept and which the reality? There are reasons for giving either answer. The acorn is the current reality or state of the plant, while the oak is the concept or plan that the reality is striving to realize. The acorn is the concept of the plant, since it embodies the concept or plan of the full-grown oak; the oak is the reality that will, but does not yet, fulfil the concept. The reason why either factor can assume the role of the concept is that the concept is both the fully developed entity and the plan of the fully developed entity that is implicit in its initial stage and, in a way, in every later stage of it. The initial stage or 'immediacy' of the mind involves both its current knowledge (corresponding to the acorn) and the abstract or indeterminate 'certainty' that its reason is in the world (corresponding to the concept in the acorn): cf. §440Z. Whichever of these, knowledge or certainty of reason, is taken as the concept, the mind is subjective or 'as the concept' (*als der Begriff*). Why does Hegel insist on that, rather than saying that 'it makes no difference' whether the mind is taken as subjective or objective,

concept or reality? After all, knowledge and reason (though not the mere *certainty* of reason) can equally be taken as reality. If so, why cannot the mind be taken as reality? Because the concept does not refer only to the initial stage of the mind in contrast to its developed state, but also to the subjectivity of the mind in contrast to the objectivity of the world and things in it. Initially the mind is distinct from the world as well as undeveloped. When it is fully developed, it ceases to be merely subjective and becomes both subjective and objective, closing the gap between itself and the world. The oak-analogy falters at this point: the full-grown oak hardly sublates the distinction between itself and its surroundings.

2. Reason is 'infinite', not bounded or conditioned by anything else. If it simply emerged at a certain stage of mind from preceding stages, it would not be infinite, since it would be dependent on these preceding stages. So it has to generate itself, or rather be entirely ungenerated, and thus 'absolute freedom', not conditioned or dependent freedom. It thus 'presupposes itself in advance of its knowledge' (*sich ihrem Wissen voraussetzt*). *Voraussetzen* is 'to presuppose, assume', but literally 'to place ahead, in advance'. So reason both takes itself as a presupposition and places itself 'in advance' of 'its knowledge', i.e. the mind's current state of knowledge, now regarded as belonging to, because generated by, reason; though it is conceivable, but not likely, that 'its knowledge' means 'knowledge of it, viz. of reason'. In either case, reason 'makes itself finite' (*sich verendlicht*), i.e. becomes a particular state of knowledge and then strives to overcome this finite state, 'comprehending' (*begreifen*) and becoming aware of itself.

   Hegel's account has theological overtones, recalling God's making himself finite as Christ: cf. §§441, n. 3; 568. More prosaically, the full-grown oak 'presupposes itself in advance' of every particular stage in its growth, since it, or its plan, is embedded in the acorn; a completed book 'presupposes itself in advance' of every stage in its completion, since the conception of the book is, at least in rough outline, implicit in the author's mind, driving the author on from one finite paragraph to the next until the conception is realized. It is not clear why the 'movement' is 'eternal'. The point may be that while the mind, the plant, or the author's manuscript undergo a change or development that is propelled by the plan in the mind, the acorn, or the author, the plan itself does (or need) not change along with its progressive realization. This would not entail that reason or the plan is everlasting; it may well have arisen at some time, only not in the course of its own realization. But Hegel may also mean that reason is everlasting or, more probably, timelessly eternal, a logical structure that somehow generates its own physical and/or psychological embodiment.

3. Hegel is here describing the final form of mind as it appears in the last Paragraph of Enc. III: §577, where the mind thinks (about) pure thoughts, and is Aristotle's God or at least the Hegelian logician. The thoughts involved in the mind's thinking are the same as the thoughts it thinks about, so the 'subjective' ('form') coincides with the 'objective' ('content'): cf. Enc. I, §133 on form and content. Another reason for the unity of form and content is that the thoughts are now devoid of empirical content, so that they have no content except the content determined by their form; this is why the mind is 'free'. The mind is now an

'absolute totality', 'infinite' in the sense that it circles back on itself in seclusion from the external world. Hegel also believes, perhaps too readily (cf. §440, n. 7), that the same thoughts constitute the essence of things, but that type of objectivity is not immediately in play here: the mind is here the 'infinite being-for-self of subjectivity', i.e. it descends into the depths of its subjectivity, disregarding the external world rather than discerning reason in it. (But cf. §441, n. 5.) The mind is 'eternal' in the sense of 'timeless' rather than 'everlasting': the thoughts mind thinks are timeless, so therefore (Hegel contentiously infers) is the mind that thinks them. All along, even at its lower stages, mind involves this subjective-objective unity implicitly or 'in itself', but it only becomes 'for itself' when the mind fulfils its 'concept'.

4. Hegel combats two apparently distinct theological doctrines, that nature is the highest manifestation of divinity (cf. ILA, pp. 3 ff.) and that the appropriate vehicle for religious content is feeling or 'sensation' (cf. §380, n. 2), with the same objections, that they involve contingency, 'formal, abstract' infinity of the sort that goes on for ever, and so on. It is mind rather than nature that is the 'image of God', and what makes it so is not its nature-burdened sensations, but its capacity for thinking about its own thoughts. This is the mind's 'concept', its 'truth' or fulfillment, the oak-tree for which sensation and other stages of mind are mere preliminaries. That mind is the 'image of God' does not imply that it is second-rate in comparison to a deity transcending it. Aristotle's God, in the account quoted after §577, is the spitting image of the Hegelian logician.

5. Unlike an oak, the mind develops by coming to 'know' (*weiss*) what it already 'is'. This is why the expression 'for itself' means, when applied to the mind, both 'actually', in contrast to 'potentially', and 'conscious(ly)', in contrast to 'unwitting(ly)': cf. §383, n. 1. So mind is 'in absolute agreement with its concept' if and only if it has 'grasped its concept'. So far mind has a hazy 'certainty' of reason, and therefore of its own concept, but no definite 'cognition' (*Erkenntnis*: cf. §445, n. 6) of the rationality of the 'object' (*Gegenstandes*). Here the object is in the external world. The mind proceeds as follows: First, it strips away the 'contingency', etc. of external objects, and uncovers their rational structure. This liberates the mind from the 'Other', so that it can now contemplate the rational structure of its own thoughts independently of external objects: cf. §441, n. 3.

6. Cf. §441, n. 2, where it is reason that makes itself finite and then sublates its finitude. The 'finite mind' is 'a contradiction, an untruth', but this does not imply its non-existence. The mind is like a prince who disguises himself as a beggar, adopting an 'appearance' that does not accord with its 'essence'. The disguise, we might suppose, will make him a better king, with insight into his subjects' condition and empathy for them, but he needs to shed the disguise before he can mount the throne. The 'limits' (*Schranken*) of reason involve a different sort of contradiction, a flat contradiction, 'wooden iron' or a square circle. Such a contradictory entity cannot exist: reason has no limits. (Hegel never refers to 'wooden iron'-contradictions as 'contradictions'.) A prince, unlike reason, is limited in power, but his power is not limited in the way that a beggar's is.

7. The I of consciousness develops and as it does so its objects alter too. The object alters because of the alteration of the I. But the I does not see its own alteration or its effect on the object. It thinks that the object alters independently of itself, rather like someone who thinks that policemen are getting younger. So only 'we' (Hegel and his readers) can discern the logical structure of this alteration: cf. §§413, n. 3; 414, n. 2. The objects of the 'free' mind alter too, but now the mind knows that it is responsible for their alteration, that it 'makes objectivity subjective' by discerning thoughts in things, and 'makes subjectivity objective' by realizing its will in the world. For the mind there is nothing 'immediate', no sheer facts that just have to be accepted as they are; everything can be explained as the work of mind itself.

It is not quite clear, even in the extended account of PS, why the I or consciousness under consideration is unaware of its own role in the change of its object from, say, the object of sensory certainty to the object of perception. Perhaps Hegel's idea is that we tend to attribute the change from one 'form of consciousness' or outlook to another to the emergence of new empirical information and this requires nothing more of us than a tendency to look for empirical information. To this Hegel's response might be: No empirical information can count as evidence for a new outlook unless we are ready to see it *as* evidence of something for which we are already somehow geared up, for e.g. forces, other people, or the historical past. The outlook is always severely underdetermined by the empirical data. Another factor may be that the I of consciousness is insufficiently reflective to ask why it moves from one outlook to another or to suppose that it contributes anything to the change.

'Facts' (*Tatsachen*) of consciousness are also mentioned disapprovingly in §444 and Enc. I, §§16 and 64. The expression was used not by Kant himself, but by followers of Kant, such as Karl Leonhard Reinhold, who spoke, in his *Über das Fundament des philosophischen Wissens* (On the Foundation of Philosophical Knowledge, 1791), both of 'the fact of consciousness' and of 'facts of consciousness': 'We know, not by any rational inference, but by mere reflection on the fact of consciousness, i.e. by comparison of what occurs in consciousness, that: *the representation in consciousness is distinguished by the subject from the object and subject and related to both*' (p. 78). Even if Hegel were to endorse this claim, he would say that it is not, as Reinhold believes, a rock-bottom given, but something brought about and explicable by the mind. Wilhelm Traugott Krug also appealed to 'facts of consciousness'. In his *Allgemeines Handwörterbuch der philosophischen Wissenschaften* (2nd ed., Leipzig: Brockhaus 1832), i. 350–1, he says that the origin of consciousness is entirely inexplicable, but that we can analyse consciousness: 'the philosopher discerns and exhibits the facts of his consciousness, compares them with one another, analyses them into their constituents, which are nothing but the I's activities or modes of expression, and finally seeks and exhibits the laws on which these activities depend, as well as the faculties from which they stem'. Thus for Krug the facts of consciousness do not 'remain an unmediated given', though Hegel can claim that he does what Krug regards as impossible, namely to reveal the origin of consciousness itself. Hegel

uses 'consciousness' in a narrower sense than Krug. For Krug, the facts of consciousness are explained not by 'natural consciousness', but by 'philosophical consciousness'. For Hegel, consciousness itself cannot explain the 'given material';
only the 'free mind' can do so. Hegel restricts 'consciousness' to consciousness
of an object conceived as independent of oneself. A philosopher as such is not
'conscious' in this sense.

The last sentence involves an untranslatable pun. The word for 'fact', *Tatsache*,
is formed from *Tat*, 'deed, action', and *Sache*, 'thing'. Hegel says that these facts,
Tatsachen, must be regarded as 'deeds', *Taten*, of the mind, not left as *Sachen*,
'things'.

NOTES TO §442

1. 'Progression' is *Fortschreiten*, 'advance'; 'development' is *Entwicklung*, literally
'unfolding, unrolling'. So a progression that is a development is an unfolding of
what is already latent in the developing entity, as an acorn unfolds into an oak.
'Knowledge' (*Wissen*) is the mind's *Existenz*, i.e. its stepping forth or emergence:
cf. §§403, n. 2; 416, n. 1. The progression of knowledge is development, since
knowledge involves 'determinedness [or 'being-determined'] in and for itself' (*das
an und für sich Bestimmtsein*), i.e. it is determined autonomously, not by (wholly)
external things. This is because it involves rationality or 'the rational', which itself
develops autonomously. (To take a partial analogy, pure mathematics develops
without (much) external input, and so therefore does the mind of the pure
mathematician when he is doing pure mathematics.) 'Translation' is *Übersetzen*,
usually translation from one language into another, but also carrying or ferrying
across, usually across water. (These are two different words, pronounced with a
different stress, but orthographically identical.) The advance from one stage of
mind to the next is a manifestation of what is already implicit in the mind or
in knowledge, something like a translation or deciphering of the code inscribed
in the mind. Hence it is a 'return into itself', a return to what is implicit in
the mind. The 'initial determinacy' of knowledge is quite different from its
'determinedness in and for itself'. It is the alien object with which the mind is
'encumbered' at its lowest level, the object of sensation or intuition: cf. §440,
n. 3. Knowledge is at that stage only 'abstract' or 'formal', since it operates on
content given to it from outside without producing content of its own. 'To
produce' (*hervorzubringen*, literally 'bring forth') objective 'fulfilment' (*Erfüllung*,
also 'filling', approximating to 'content') also gives 'freedom of knowledge', since
knowledge is no longer dependent on what is externally given to it.
2. In anthropology (§§388–412) human faculties develop successively in the 'individual'. In psychology, the study of the faculties of the adult, they are not regarded
as developing successively over time. Étienne Bonnot de Condillac (1715–80),
especially in his *Traité des sensations* (Paris and London, 1754), considered the
faculties in the order in which they supposedly emerged in the individual and
attempted, in the manner of Locke, to reduce every mental activity to sensations, the earliest mental phenomenon. Hegel endorses his aim of showing the

intelligible unity of the mind and the necessary interdependence of its activities, and also his belief in the primacy of sensation, but makes two criticisms: (i) The order in which faculties or activities emerge in us is not the key to explaining them. (ii) Sensations are the 'initial foundation' (*anfangende Grundlage*) of our other powers, the 'empirically primary' (*das empirische Erste*), but not (as Condillac holds) their 'substantial foundation'. Sensations are subjected to 'negative', not just 'affirmative' treatment; they are 'spiritualized and sublated': cf. §440, n. 3. To handle this requires richer categories than those deployed by Condillac.

3. Hegel rejects the view that mental 'activities' are 'expressions' (*Äusserungen*) of 'forces' or powers, i.e. faculty psychology (cf. Enc. I, §136). The view takes insufficient account of the mind's unity. Even if each power or activity is useful for some other power or activity, the powers are left taking in each other's washing and no account is given of the 'ultimate purpose' (*Endzweck*). (The 'heart' is *Gemüt*, the seat of emotions, hence contrasting with the *Intelligenz*.) This involves two objections: (1) An *ad hominem* objection: faculty psychology purports to give functional or teleological explanations of each faculty in terms of its service to other faculties, e.g. that perception, memory, and intelligence require each other. But that does not explain the faculties as a whole nor, ultimately, each individual faculty. Why do we have perception, memory, and intelligence? Why do we have memory, instead of lacking perception, memory and intelligence altogether? Faculty psychology does not answer these questions. Perhaps it can disclaim any intention of answering them. But (2) Hegel himself believes that we can answer these questions in teleological terms. The 'concept', the logical structure underlying the mind (as well as the world as a whole), is striving towards knowledge of itself, gradually shedding the 'immediacy' or 'subjectivity' (sensations, etc.) with which it is initially encumbered. That is, the mind is impelled by the concept to think about the concept, to study logic—somewhat like Aristotle's God: cf. §441, n. 4. The faculties are stages on the way to this 'ultimate purpose'and are ordered for this purpose, not just distinct from each other: cf. §440, n. 3.

Hegel's theory has the merit of taking account of the capacities of the psychologist or the philosopher, not just our everyday capacities: philosophy of mind concludes with an account of the capacities of the philosopher of mind, in particular the logical expertise that informs the philosophy of mind. But even if this account is the 'ultimate purpose' of the philosopher of mind, why should we regard it as the ultimate purpose of the mind or of the concept? Why should the mind have one ultimate purpose rather than several or none at all? Nevertheless, such teleology is deeply embedded in Hegel's thought and we need to recognize it to understand him.

4. (1) When the mind thinks pure, i.e. non-empirical, thoughts, as it does in §§465–8, it supplies its own content, namely the thoughts (about) which it thinks. Its 'productions' remain thoughts, however, 'more or less ideal', since it is not yet objective mind (cf. §§483 ff.) and it has not yet realized its thoughts in the world. In advancing to the level of pure thinking, the mind gradually distances

itself from external objects and content, is the 'infinite negativity' of them: cf. §440, n. 3. (2) The mind creates not only its own pure thoughts, but also 'all content', 'all reality', namely the objects of lower faculties such as perceptible things, whose externality and independence of the mind is a 'semblance' (*Schein*) to be sublated. This claim is not obviously entailed by claim (1). That the mind can ignore external objects does not immediately entail that their externality is an illusion, that they are really created by the mind. As §443 explains, the mind progressively imposes its thoughts on, or discerns them in, external objects and thereby eliminates their externality. One difficulty is that even when Hegel has ascended to the heights of science, lower levels of the mind persist. When he goes home to find someone greeting him on the doorstep, he knows that it is Mrs Hegel, not Mrs Schelling and, however thought-laden his perception of her may be, his ability to discriminate between his wife and other people arguably involves an ineliminable externally given content.

NOTES TO §443

1. The natural soul is a simple unity, drawing no distinction between subject and object, but simply aware of its sensations. The natural soul bifurcates into a conscious subject and its object, and the object is constructed from the sensations of the natural soul. 'In itself' the conscious I is identical with its object, but consciousness is unaware of this identity. Hegel believes that the mind develops by successive reflections on itself, by taking its preceding stage as its current object. So mind does not (as we might suppose) have the same object as consciousness, but takes as its object consciousness as a whole, the conscious I together with its object. This is because the mind is reflective in a way that consciousness is not. Consciousness focuses only on its object. Mind reflects on its own state or 'determinacy' as well, and on the relationship of its determinacy to the determinacy of the object. Unlike consciousness, the mind is now convinced that the I is identical with its object. So it tries to show this identity by bringing together these two determinacies. In this way mind restores, on a higher level, the unity of natural soul disrupted by consciousness.

Hegel exploits the similarity between *des Seienden*, 'of what is', and *des Seinigen*, 'of what is its own'.

2. The first way in which the mind brings the two determinacies together is 'theoretical' rather than 'practical'. Its procedure here is that described in §440, n. 3. Confronted initially by an external object of sensation or intuition, it transforms this into a representation, and eventually into a thought. The representation, and still more the thought, is 'its own' (*das Seinige*) in a way that the intuition is not. 'Knowledge' (*Wissen*) is thus liberated from 'presupposition', no longer reliant (to the same degree) on external input, and thus 'determined in and for itself within itself', developing autonomously: cf. §442, n. 1 on 'determinedness in and for itself', and §441, n. 2 on presupposition. The presupposition in §441 is reason itself, whereas here it is an 'immediate determinacy'. But the two presuppositions

are connected in that it is 'the rational' that assumes the form of the immediate determinacy.

A difficulty for this interpretation is that 'its (own)' plays different roles in §§440 and 443. In §440, sensations and intuitions are 'its', i.e. the mind's, while representations and thoughts are not. In §443, representations and thoughts are 'its own', while sensations and intuitions, or their objects, are not. But there is no real conflict here. The sensation or intuition is 'its', the mind's, but it belongs to this particular mind, not to any and every mind. In another sense, the intuition and the intuited object are not the mind's, not even this particular mind's: they are not produced by the mind but come from outside. In this sense representations and thoughts do belong to the mind: they are produced by the mind. In another sense they are not the mind's: they do not belong to any particular mind, but to any and every mind of the appropriate sort. They are thus objective in a way that sensations and intuitions are not.

3. 'Will' or 'practical mind' proceeds in the reverse direction. It starts not from an external 'content' or determinacy, but from 'its own' content. I want e.g. to build a house. The house does not yet exist and the building has not yet begun. The content is 'only' my 'own'. Then I build the house, and become 'objective' (*gegenständlich*) to myself as 'free mind', basking in my own product.

Schematically, theoretical and practical mind are related in the following way: Theoretical mind begins with an external object or state—a 'one-sidedness'—and then sublates it, so that it becomes only a state of the mind itself—another 'one-sidedness'. Practical mind begins with this one-sided state of the mind. It actualizes this state in the external world, e.g. builds a house, and sublates the 'double one-sideness': there is now an actual house conforming to the mind's will. In this account practical mind resolves a problem left by theoretical mind, its 'one-sideness'. Hegel does not always favour practical mind in this way. The highest phase of mind, philosophy, is theoretical rather than practical. Theoretical mind is often seen not (as seems to be the case here) as a retreat into oneself that leaves the external world unredeemed, but as a way of structuring the world so that it conforms to the mind, being governed by laws, etc: cf. §398, n. 6. Practical mind also structures the world in conformity with mind, only in a different way, by building houses, setting up states, etc. How do these two ways of spiritualizing the world relate to each other? And why do we need both? If theoretical mind has already spiritualized the world, what need is there for practical mind to do the same job? These questions tempt Hegel to describe theoretical mind as one-sided and to subordinate it to practical mind. In reality (as Hegel would agree) the relation between them is far more intricate than this Paragraph suggests. It is, e.g., hardly plausible that the 'content' that the mind wills is the abstract thoughts with which Hegel's account of theoretical mind concludes. It is not really necessary for the account of theoretical mind to precede that of practical mind; in life the two go hand in hand. But in an Encyclopaedia, one of them has to come first, and then (according to Hegel's general procedure) the mind that comes second has to be dominant, resolving problems left by its predecessor.

4. On 'urge' or drive (*Trieb*), cf. §§425, n. 2; 426, n. 2. Consciousness lacks urge: it just accepts whatever objects present themselves. The objects change, but consciousness is unaware of its own part in this. By contrast, mind knowingly makes immediate objects 'subjective'—because they now involve a larger contribution from the mind itself—while retaining, even enhancing, their 'objectivity'—because they no longer reflect only the mind's chance encounters with external things and because the mind now discerns the essence of things rather than their superficial exterior. 'Recollected' translates *Erinnerten*, the perfect participle of *erinnern*, which Hegel interprets as 'internalized': cf. §401, n. 2. 'Information' translates the plural of *Kenntnis* ('cognizance'), *Kenntnisse*, which 'suggests detailed knowledge (i.e. pieces, items of knowledge) of (a) any specified matter, whether of ordinary matters or in a branch of learning; (b) unspecified general knowledge' (DGS, p. 179). Hegel is making two claims about the mind: it actively seeks detailed knowledge about e.g. the motions of planets, and it transforms these objects by discovering the laws and forces that govern their behaviour. In both respects the object is no longer 'negative' towards the I: it is actively sought rather than simply encountered and it becomes thought-laden rather than 'alien'.
5. Theoretical mind remedies object-oriented consciousness, while practical mind remedies subject-oriented self-consciousness—a point that did not emerge clearly in the Paragraph. In the account of theoretical mind, 'subjective' meant (roughly) 'thought-laden'. Subjectivity in this sense does not exclude objectivity; the two go together. If one opposite, e.g. subjectivity, is pushed to its extreme, it veers over into the other opposite, e.g. objectivity. In this account of practical mind, 'subjective' means (roughly) 'only in the mind', also with the suggestion of 'belonging to a particular individual'. What is subjective in this sense cannot be at the same time objective, though it can be made objective.
6. Practical mind starts out from 'its own determinations', e.g. the wish for an ice cream. Theoretical mind does not start out from its own determinations, but it does deal with them eventually and imposes them on (or discerns them in) external objects in something like the way that practical mind realizes its plans in the world. Thoughts, however, are implicit in all humans, as well as the objective world, not 'something pertaining to the particular subject', while my wish for an ice cream is idiosyncratic. But the 'aims of the rational will' are not idiosyncratic, but are, like thoughts, something 'in and for itself', something justified independently of the wishes of any particular individual, such as payment of taxes, a law against murder, or a political state. When such an aim is realized, the product is a 'unity of the subjective and objective', an objective entity conforming to the 'rational will': cf. §435, n. 5. So too is the product of theoretical mind, e.g. planets conforming to the laws imposed on them by the mind. So theoretical and practical mind approach the same goal from different directions and thus 'complement each other' (*integrieren sich*).
7. Mind is not a substance, 'a being' (*ein Seiendes*), but essentially the activity of sublating a 'presupposition' (cf. §§381, n. 23; 441, n. 2), the subjective–objective opposition. This presupposition is made, most immediately, by the bifurcation of the soul into subject and object: cf. §416, n. 1.

NOTES TO §444

1. On the activity of both theoretical and practical mind, see §§442Z. and 443Z. Here the 'subjective mind', which includes the soul and consciousness, is said to be 'productive' (*hervorbringend*, lit. 'bringing forth'), but in §444Z. it is the 'free mind', in contrast to the 'soul', that is 'productive' (*produzierend*, the Latin-derived equivalent of *hervorbringend*). This discrepancy stems from the fact that Hegel is drawing two distinct contrasts: (1) the free mind (productive) and soul/consciousness (relatively unproductive); (2) subjective mind (with only 'formal' productions) and objective mind (with 'fulfilled' productions: cf. §444, n. 6). Subjective mind includes soul and consciousness as well as free mind. That the mind's 'productions' (*Produktionen*) are 'formal' (*formell*) means that they are not filled or 'fulfilled' (*erfüllt*) with appropriate 'content'. But this can be taken in two different ways: (1) The mind's internal production or determination lacks a content appropriate to it within the mind itself. (2) The mind's internal production lacks an appropriate external content or embodiment. When the mind intuits an object, it is formal in sense (1): cf. §442, n. 1. When its 'production' is 'only its ideal world, etc.', it sounds as if Hegel's complaint is that it is formal only in sense (2), that the mind is concerned only with its own thoughts, though before it reaches this stage it is formal in sense (1) as well. By contrast, practical mind determines itself from the very start, but its content (e.g. the ice-cream I desire) is 'restricted' (*beschränkten*), it lacks the 'universality' appropriate to the mind; so its productions are formal in sense (1). Theoretical and practical mind differ more than Hegel suggests. Theoretical mind achieves an internal content appropriate to itself without any obvious external embodiment, since it can think about its own thoughts, live in its own 'ideal world'. But practical mind cannot do this. As long as it remains internal, it has only a restricted content. It gains 'universality' for its content only by realizing its productions in the external world. Hence 'inwards' practical mind remains formal in sense (1), but theoretical mind does not.

2. 'Enjoyment' is, in contrast to 'deed and action', a relatively inappropriate content for the practical mind: cf. §469, n. 8. The 'word' too, Hegel implies, is an inappropriate content for theoretical mind: an uttered word is fleeting. But the parallel breaks down. It is difficult to think of a more appropriate expression for theoretical mind than words, whereas practical mind can go on to express itself in deeds. (Hegel is thinking here of John. 1: 1, 'In the beginning was the Word', and Goethe's response, in *Faust* I: 'In the beginning was the deed'.) In the *Zusatz* theoretical mind's production of the word is regarded as an advantage over practical mind; enjoyment is not mentioned. Words and enjoyment have something in common: neither is fully external to the mind, in the way that deeds and actions are, but neither is fully internal. This may be why their production is explained by the fact that 'subjective mind' is a 'unity of soul and consciousness': they are both internal, like the soul's determinations, and external, like the object of consciousness.

3. On the 'facts of consciousness', see §441, n. 7, and for a similar attack on psychology, §442, n. 3.
4. My desire for an ice-cream is just 'given': I did not choose or decide to want it and there is no rational justification for my wanting it. If my desire is to be 'posited' by the 'rational will', thoughtful or 'thinking' knowledge has to intervene, e.g. by showing that my health or life depends on some constituent of ice-cream or that it is no bad thing to satisfy one's harmless whims.
5. The theory criticized is most famously found in Descartes, *Principles of Philosophy*, 35: 'the perception of the intellect extends only to the few objects presented to it, and is always extremely limited. The will, on the other hand, can in a certain sense be called infinite, since we observe without exception that its scope extends to anything that can possibly be an object of any other will—even the immeasurable will of God. So it is easy for us to extend our will beyond what we clearly perceive; and when we do this it is no wonder that we may happen to go wrong' (*Descartes: Selected Philosophical Writings*, trans. J. Cottingham, R. Stoothoff, and D. Murdoch (Cambridge: Cambridge University Press, 1988), 171-2). Descartes's point about the will is, roughly, that I can will anything: that the sun should revolve around the earth, that I should believe that the sun revolves around the earth, and so on. Hegel's point about the will is that I cannot do whatever I will, owing to the resistance of matter and of other people. Descartes's point about the intellect is that it cannot perceive things about remote objects not presented to it, and it cannot perceive obvious falsehoods such as that the sun revolves around the earth, since it does not have a clear and distinct idea of this. Hegel might have objected that Descartes is unfairly discriminating between intellect and will, that he places rational constraints on the intellect from which the will is exempted. I may after all *believe* or *imagine* unlikely things about remote objects and obvious falsehoods about objects presented to me, and I cannot *rationally* will that the sun should revolve around the earth. But Hegel sidesteps this question, saying instead that, while matter and other people can stop me doing what I will, they cannot stop me thinking what I do and expressing my thoughts in spoken words. (Intelligence does go further 'in its expression' than spoken words, since it is involved in the rational will, but this is not intelligence 'as such'.) One reason why Hegel sidesteps Descartes's point about intellect is that he operates with a different notion of infinity from Descartes's. For Descartes the intellect is 'limited' or finite, because it cannot perceive anything and everything without end or limit. For Hegel it is infinite because it circles back on itself, especially in 'conceptual cognition', where it entirely permeates its objects, whether these be its own thoughts or external objects. (On conceptual cognition, see also §§445, n. 1; 465 ff.) However, Hegel himself unfairly discriminates between intellect and will, since he here applies to it Descartes's notion of infinity and does not (as elsewhere: cf. §§415, n. 2; 480, n. 2; 482, n. 1) consider whether it too circles back on itself. Hegel does not share Descartes's concern to avoid error, believing that error is an essential step on the path to truth.
6. Theoretical and practical mind both begin with a content that does not 'correspond to' or 'fulfil' the form, which is 'infinite' not in the sense that it circles back

on itself, but in the sense that it transcends any particular and definite content. e.g. the object I intuit has qualities that are just given and cannot be rationally accounted for; my desire for an ice-cream pertains to the 'singularity of the individual' (*Einzelheit des Individuums*: cf. §377, n. 7). Within subjective mind, this defect is overcome, by theoretical mind in §§465–8, and by practical mind in §§481–2. The 'Idea', the unity of concept (the subjective) and reality (the objective), is reached within subjective mind. At this point subjective mind 'passes over' to objective mind, i.e. roughly social and political institutions: cf. §482. That is, the subjective union of subjectivity and objectivity passes over into the objective union of subjectivity and objectivity, or rather (because Hegel wants to regard objective mind as somewhat one-sided and thus requiring absolute mind to supplement it) into objective objectivity. The rough idea is that only when the mind has perfected itself internally can it proceed to secure its occupation of the external world, transforming it, both theoretically and practically, into an abode in which it is at home and free, i.e. relatively unconstrained by non-mental things and events.

NOTES TO §445

1. On the process described here, cf. §440, n. 3. In e.g. intuiting an external object, intelligence (roughly, theoretical mind) just 'finds' itself determined in a certain way over which it has no choice or control: cf. §§401, n. 1; 402, n. 2 on 'finding'. This is 'its semblance' (*ihr Schein*), its outward appearance in contrast to its reality. Given the contrast between 'knowledge' (*Wissen*) and 'cognition' (*Erkennen*) (cf. §445, n. 6), it is not clear why the fact that intelligence is *knowledge* should explain why it engages in an activity which turns out to be *cognition*. But the expression 'positing what is found as its own' is ambiguous. It could mean either (1) simply 'becoming aware of what is found', or (2) 'realizing that what is found is its own product' or, a variant of this, 'converting what is found into its own product'. (1) is knowledge, (2) is cognition. Perhaps the ambiguity helps the transition from knowledge to cognition. What the intelligence finds is also 'reason' or 'the rational'; this is assumed from §§438–9. But presumably intelligence does not, initially, realize that reason is what it finds, since it is only when intelligence becomes 'reason for itself' that 'the content also becomes rational for the intelligence'. What intelligence is aiming at is that 'its concept should be for the intelligence'. This means both that it should fulfil its concept, become what it is meant to be (as a child becomes an adult) and that it should recognize what its concept is, what it is meant to be (as an adult recognizes that this is what s/he is meant to be). (This ambiguity might be conveyed by speaking of 'realizing its concept'.) Then intelligence becomes reason, both actually and wittingly, instead of the 'empty form' of 'finding' it, and imposes its rationality on the 'content'. 'Cognition' is not inappropriately described as an 'activity' (*Tätigkeit*), since *Erkennen* 'indicates a process of realization, a coming to know' (DGS, p. 291). Hence *Erkennen* can apply to the gradual unearthing of reason in oneself and one's object. By contrast, 'knowledge' (*Wissen*) is not an activity:

it is the awareness that one has at any given stage in *Erkennen*'s ascent. Initially, knowledge is simply 'formal', but at higher stages it becomes, under the guidance of *Erkennen*, 'conceptual' (*begriffgemässen*, lit. 'concept-appropriate'). Hegel generally regards 'certainty' (*Gewissheit*) as immediate and non-conceptual and also as thin, with a relatively indeterminate object: cf. §§413, n. 4; 420, n. 2. Immediacy and indeterminacy are connected: it is conceptual elaboration that fleshes out the object.

2. The powers of the mind do not have 'a fixed and separate existence' such that any one could occur without the others: cf. §445, n. 3. The relevance of this to the Paragraph is that the intelligence involves striving to fulfil an aim, i.e. will, and that its elevation from one 'faculty' to the next establishes a rational connection between the faculties. Hegel moves from willing or 'volition' (*Wollen*) and 'intelligence' to 'heart' (*Herz*) and 'intellect', presumably because of a common belief that the intellect and the heart (usually the seat of the emotions rather than of the will) can be cultivated separately. If there were 'intellectless hearts' or 'heartless intellects' this would not, he suggests, affect the nature of the 'matter' (*Sache*)—rather as the existence of freak or damaged dogs with three or five legs would not impair the truth that a dog is a quadruped or a four-legged animal. This is doubtful. If someone had a decent intellect but no heart whatsoever, or a decent heart but no intellect at all, this would show that heart and intellect are independent of each other. A better response is that while there are people (such as Isaac Newton) whose intellect is more developed than their heart, and others whose heart is more developed than their intellect, there is no one who has one of these powers but entirely lacks the other. Why should someone with no will or no heart ever manifest their intellect by applying it to a problem?

3. A *Reflexionsform* is not just a form by which we reflect on something, but a form in which outer appearances (e.g. our memories and recollections) are reflected back into themselves, i.e. regarded as manifestations of an underlying ground or force (e.g. the faculty of memory): cf. Enc. I, §112Z. This 'reflexion-into-itself' as a 'power' (*Kraft*) or 'faculty' (*Vermögen*) is made possible by the 'fixed determinacy of a content', i.e. by treating e.g. memory, whether as a faculty or as an activity, as distinct from other faculties or activities and as operating independently of them. (Phrenology reinforces this distinctness by assigning each faculty to a separate area of the brain: cf. §411, n. 2.) A force, faculty or 'power' has 'infinity of form', because it circles back on itself: at first it is latent or 'inner', then it expresses itself as 'outer' appearance, then it retreats again into inner latency. But it also has 'finitude': a force does not e.g. express itself spontaneously; it needs stimulation or 'solicitation' (*Sollizitation*, Enc. I,§136 Remark) from outside. This explains the 'indifference of content to form'. This means not only that a variety of different contents—memory, magnetism, gravity—can all take the same form, the form of power and its expression, but that the postulation of a power makes no significant difference to the content: it is like explaining why opium sends us to sleep by invoking its 'dormitive power'. But what Hegel primarily objects to here is 'isolating' the mind's activities; this tends to accompany the postulation of powers, but does not strictly require it.

4. If cognition were only one among several activities of intelligence, then cognition might be an 'option' (*Willkür*), something which, if we decided it was impossible, we might discard in favour of other mental activities. But cognition is not optional. Other mental activities, such as intuition, are of no use, or limited use, in the search for truth if they do not involve or subserve cognition. As the *Zusatz* suggests (cf. §445, n. 6), Hegel is responding to what is, among other things, a theological position: that we cannot know or cognize the real nature of God, or for that matter the real nature of the world; we can only gesture towards it in more or less intuitive, imaginative ways. Adherents of this position might allow that we can go through the motions of cognition, of demonstrative argumentation, but insist that this will only ever scratch the surface of things, never getting to the bottom of them: cf. §§380, n. 2; 400, n. 1; 418, n. 8 on F. H. Jacobi. (The 'place' where the issue gets 'cleared up' may be Enc. I, §§61 ff. on Jacobi or, less probably, Enc. I, §§223 ff. on cognition.) But, Hegel says, this criticism of cognition is 'external', criticism conducted from the outside. This is somewhat like assessing a car before one has driven it; one discovers all sorts of faults which will not necessarily impair the performance of the car. His own approach is internal: to drive the car and see whether, and why, it breaks down: cf. Enc. I, §81 on dialectic, and PS, Introduction, on knowledge or cognition. Hegel seems to have more success in arguing against the proposed alternatives to cognition than in defending the claims of cognition itself. We might agree, for example, that other mental activities derive such value as they have from cognition and that 'genuine' cognition, or the 'concept of cognition', is the goal to which intelligence tends, but nevertheless doubt that 'genuine cognizing' (*wahrhaftes Erkennen*) amounts to 'cognition of truth' (*die Erkenntnis der Wahrheit*). Might the truth not elude all our faculties? To this Hegel's implicit reply is that the truth is not distinct from our cognitive procedures and products, from our thinking and thoughts, in the way that traditional theologians suppose. Because of this Hegel does not distinguish sharply between 'true' or 'genuine' cognition and cognition of the 'truth': see also §445, n. 5.

The reference to '§445, Remark', which appears in all the editions I have consulted, is baffling. Presumably Hegel intended to refer to the Remark of another relevant Paragraph, such as §440 or §455.

5. Hegel seems to describe two stages in the mind's progress. First, by its 'sublation' of the soul and consciousness it has 'shown itself' as 'that which mediates itself with itself', etc. It has 'come to itself' and 'implicitly' contains the object as sublated. At this stage, however, the intelligence's activity is 'formal, unfulfilled' and the mind is 'unknowing' (*unwissend*). So secondly, intelligence 'fills itself with the object immediately given to it', and progressively strips away its externality and contingency by the process described in the Paragraph. This involves both the 'internalizing' of the object and the 'recollection', i.e. internalizing (cf. §401, n. 2), of the mind. The mind first withdraws into itself and becomes, within itself, 'unity of the subjective and the objective'; then it tries to give body to this by turning towards the external world and producing a more substantial subjective-objective unity. The mind first withdraws into itself to

rehearse its plan and muster its forces for an assault on the external world. The dual structure of this process is similar to that of self-consciousness, where I first become aware of myself as I, and then try to substantiate this I-awareness by consuming objects, etc: see §§424 ff., esp. 426, n. 1 and 427, n. 1; cf. also §444, n. 6. This is a more elaborate explanation of the mind's turn to cognition than the Paragraph supplied (cf. §445, n. 1). The mind engages in 'cognition' not just because it is already 'knowledge', but because the mind (which unlike soul and consciousness is thoroughly self-reflective) has already *implicitly* performed the task that cognition will perform *in reality*. It must go on to perform this task in reality, both because its knowledge will otherwise remain 'abstract, formal' and because it needs to sublate the obtrusive external objects.

6. *Wissen*, 'to be aware (of), to have information (of), as a fact', is distinct from *kennen*, 'to be acquainted, familiar, with a person or thing' (DGS, p. 178). *Kennen* has little significance for Hegel: but cf. §448, n. 2. He prefers the compound *erkennen*, 'to come to a mental understanding, realization', 'to come to know', and also 'to recognize' (DGS, p. 273). Hegel implies that *wissen* is the wider term, *Erkennen* being a special type of *Wissen*. *Wissen*, but not *erkennen*, applies to (1) knowing that something, e.g. God, is or exists; (2) knowing what something is in a hazy, representational way, e.g. knowing that God is our Father, the creator, etc; (3) knowing the superficial features of something, e.g. that God is powerful, etc. *Erkennen*, but not *wissen*, applies to (4) knowing the 'determinate, substantial nature' of e.g. God. Hegel is here criticizing contemporary theologians, but the doctrine that we cannot know the essence of God (in this life) goes back at least as far as Aquinas—who can hardly be accused of superficiality. Hegel himself believes that the essence of God, and the essence of things as a whole, is fully knowable to us.

7. Somewhat schematically, the mind is presented as advancing from naive objectivity to withdrawal into subjectivity, and then to the combination of subjectivity and objectivity. The second stage, representation, involves universality, but abstract universality: cf. §§448Z., 455. The third stage, 'thinking', involves 'the concrete universal' (*das konkret Allgemeine*, lit. 'the concretely universal'): cf. §§456Z., 469Z. An abstract universal results from the selection or 'abstraction' of one superficial feature of objects and is therefore felt to be a product of our mind, not intrinsic to the object (§448Z.), such as the redness of a rose (§456Z.). A concrete universal, such as 'plant' (§448Z.), constitutes the very nature of the object and is therefore objective in a way that an abstract universal is not. The concrete universal thus has some affinity to the natural kind. The distinction between abstract and concrete universals might be drawn in terms of the relative ease or difficulty of counterfactual suppositions. Pointing to a red rose, I say: 'Suppose this were not red'; this is a fairly easy supposition to make. Then: 'Suppose this were not a plant'; this supposition is hard to make without also supposing the rose not to exist. Unfortunately, Hegel neglects the intermediate case: 'Suppose this were not a rose'; this supposition is relatively hard to make, though 'rose' is an empirical 'representation', not a pure thought. Hegel

over-optimistically assumes that the distinction between abstract and concrete universals coincides with the distinction between representations and thoughts. See further §387, n. 18.

NOTE TO §446

1. Hegel has little difficulty in distinguishing the role of feeling here from its role in consciousness, where feelings are projected outwards to form an external object: cf. §418 Remark. But he has some difficulty in distinguishing feeling here from feeling in the soul. §400 describes 'sensation' (*Empfindung*) in similar terms to those now applied to its close relative, 'feeling' (*Gefühl*): 'Sensation is the form in which the mind weaves its sombre web, etc.' Moreover, the soul too 'finds' sensations or determinations in itself: cf. §§401, 402 Remark, and 446Z. The Remark to §446 locates the difference in the fact that feeling in the soul is a natural or bodily determination, whereas feeling in the mind is not. The *Zusatz* gives a different answer: the feeling in the mind is 'in itself both subjective [as in the soul] and objective [as in consciousness]'. The addition of 'in itself' avoids a clash with the Paragraph's claim that the mind is now 'ordinary subjective mind' (*gemein-subjektiver*). The real solution to the difficulty is this: there is no significant distinction between the soul's feeling and the mind's feeling. Hegel's account of the mind follows on naturally from his account of the soul and, if the section 'Phenomenology of Mind' (§§413–39) had been omitted altogether, we would hardly notice any discontinuity in Enc. III. In fact the transition from soul to mind would, in this case, be considerably smoother than the existing transition from soul to consciousness. So has the section on phenomenology any other function than to enable Hegel to pay homage to his earlier work on the theme and to accommodate concepts otherwise inexplicably omitted from his account of 'free' mind—such as consciousness, perception, and self-consciousness? Perhaps it is this: The 'Phenomenology of Mind' also follows on naturally from the account of the soul. It shows how we emerge from the soul's self-enclosedness to consciousness of an external world of increasing order and complexity. But it does not show, in any great detail, the mental activities that enable us to do this. This is where Psychology, the account of mind, comes in. It covers roughly the same ground as the Phenomenology, but explains in more detail the mental activities that make consciousness of objects possible. So why does Hegel not say this more clearly? It is because he wants to present Phenomenology and Psychology not just as accounts of the same terrain from different points of view, objective and subjective respectively, but as successive stages on the unilinear progression of mind. Whereas Phenomenology presents consciousness as a naive realist, unaware of its own part in the formation of its objects, Psychology presents the mind as burgeoning philosopher, aware of its own role in the constitution of the world. This does not entail, however, that feeling in the mind significantly differs from sensation in the soul. Cf. §449 n.5.

NOTES TO §447

1. A feeling is a determinate 'affection' (*Affektion*) since e.g. the feeling that lying is wrong differs from other feelings, such as the feeling that lying is not wrong and the feeling that theft is wrong. What constitutes this determinacy is ultimately the conceptual arguments that underly the feeling. But the feeling disregards all rational justification for the wrongness of lying, and thus compresses the 'determinacy' into simplicity: 'I just feel that it is wrong'. Hence the wrongness of lying is presented as a 'contingent particularity', not rationally promoted above the permissibility of lying, which can equally serve as the 'content' of a feeling: 'Well, I feel that it is not wrong'.

2. Both Hegel and his opponents (cf. §§380, n. 2; §400, n. 1 on Jacobi and Schleiermacher) endorse the claim that 'the mind has in its feeling the material [*Stoff*] of its representations', but they interpret it in different ('opposite') ways. The opponents take it to mean that feeling discloses an independent 'object' (*Gegenstand(e)*), e.g. God or moral values, and that the feeling derives its content or determinacy from its contact with this object, not from the mind itself. The feeling then contains the 'material' of representations, in that one forms a representation of God on the basis of the feeling of his existence, presence, etc. Hegel takes the claim to mean that 'the material of feeling' is 'immanent in the mind', not derived from an independent object. Feelings are then developed into representations, etc., and these (we learn from the *Zusatz*) are first subjected to 'explication' (*Auslegung*), and then 'concentrated in the simple form of sentiment [*Empfindung*, i.e. feeling]'. So there are, for Hegel, two types of feeling or sentiment: elementary feelings and sophisticated feelings. Elementary feelings contain the 'material' of representations in the sense that the 'material of feeling' is derived from the mind and develops into representations, etc. Sophisticated feelings contain the material of representations, in that they presuppose the explicit development of representations, etc., and compress it into simple sentiments. Hegel's opponents make two mistakes. First, while the feelings to which they appeal are in fact sophisticated feelings, presupposing representations, rational argumentation, etc., they take them to be elementary feelings, bypassing rational argumentation. Secondly, they assume that these elementary feelings get their content from an independent object, not from the mind itself. The feelings they postulate are thus not exactly elementary feelings as Hegel conceives them (which pertain to the 'soul'), but feelings at work in the realm of 'consciousness', where the 'judgement' or original division (cf. §389, n. 4) has produced an object and a subject that is directly or naively aware of the object, in this case by feeling. Hegel's own view is roughly this: (1) we are aware of objects in a quasi-direct manner; (2) we are not aware of God, values, etc.—the matters of interest to his opponents—in this quasi-direct way; (3) our knowledge of God, etc. presupposes rational thought; (4) even our quasi-direct awareness of perceptible objects presupposes a large intellectual input from the mind. In no case do we simply read off information from the object.

Earlier I translated *Empfindung* as 'sensation': see §402, nn. 1 and 2. But here and in the *Zusatz*, where *Empfindung* is more or less interchangeable with *Gefühl*, I translate it as 'sentiment', which is closer in meaning to 'feeling', but preserves a connection with 'sensation'.

3. Hegel believes that there is, in a sense, not more, but as much in feeling as in thinking. Feeling, whether elementary or sophisticated, contains 'the determinedness of reason in and for itself' (*das an und für sich Bestimmtsein der Vernunft*). But feeling is the wrong form for this content. It is the form of 'selfish individuality', of 'particular self-feeling'. A feeling pertains to a particular individual; to justify something by appeal to a feeling is to justify it by appeal to a state of oneself: 'It is so, because I feel it to be so (in my bones)'. Thinking or rationality, by contrast, is communal: I justify Pythagoras' theorem or God's existence by arguments that involve no essential reference to myself. Nevertheless Hegel allows a place for 'cultivated sentiment' ([*g*]*ebildete . . . Empfindung*), a sentiment that acknowledges rather than by-passes conceptual refinements.

4. The 'ancient' referred to is probably Xenophanes (*c*.570–478 BC), who said that 'if horses or oxen or lions had hands or could draw with their hands and accomplish such works as men, horses would draw the figures of the gods as similar to horses, and the oxen as similar to oxen' (fragment 15, trans J. H. Lesher, in *Xenophanes of Colophon: Fragments* (Toronto: University of Toronto Press, 1992), 25) and that 'Ethiopians say that their gods are snub-nosed and black; Thracians that theirs are blue-eyed and red-haired' (fragment 16, ibid.). Xenophanes no doubt intended to express scepticism specifically about the existence of the gods. But Hegel does not present it in this way; our 'concepts of external nature' also stem from our sentiments. The fact that 'the rational'—ethics, etc.—is immanent in the mind does not mean, for Hegel, that it is not real or objective. The mind does not simply project its rationality into an intrinsically non-rational or chaotic world; it goes out to meet the inherent rationality of the world.

NOTES TO §448

1. On 'diremption', i.e. division, separation, see §429, n. 1. 'Finding' (*Finden(s)*) refers to *Empfindung*, 'sensation, sentiment', by which we simply find a content, without inferring or creating it: cf. §§402, n. 2; 445 n. 1; 446 Remark. The 'immediate finding' of sensation splits into two 'moments' or factors: (i) 'Attention', the 'identical' (approximately 'unwavering') direction of the mind on something. This is active 'recollection' or internalization: cf. §402, n. 6 on *Erinnerung*. By attending to something I internalize it and make it my 'own'. Hence attention is the moment 'of its own possession' (*des Seinigen*). But the 'self-determination' of the intelligence is only 'formal' or abstract, since what it attends to and possesses is only in the mind and has as yet no external embodiment: cf. §444, n. 1. (ii) The 'content' is projected as 'a being' (*ein Seiendes*) into time and space. It thereby becomes not simply other than, 'outside', the intelligence, but other than, and outside, itself. In space and time the entity is dispersed: different parts of it are located in different places, and different stages of it at different

times: cf. Enc. II, §247 on the self-externality of nature and §254 on space. So whereas for consciousness the object is only a 'relative other', i.e. other than the conscious subject, for mind the object is other than the object itself. Hegel agrees with Kant (in *Critique of Pure Reason*, 'Transcendental Aesthetic') that space and time are forms of sensory 'intuition', but he rejects Kant's view that they are 'subjective': cf. Enc. II, §254 Remark. It is unclear why Hegel denies space and time to consciousness, when consciousness, especially perception, obviously involves space and time. Their introduction here is probably inspired by the topic of 'intuition' (*Anschauung*), which has Kantian overtones, even if it has a sense somewhat different from Kant's: cf. §449, nn. 2 and 3.

Roughly speaking, the two moments involve *both* appropriating the object for oneself *and* alienating it from oneself (as well as from *itself*), two processes which, on Hegel's view, invariably go together. If something is too close to me, I cannot get a grip on it. The idea is comparable to Heidegger's notion of *Entfernung*, getting closer to something by putting it at a distance.

2. 'Cognizance' is *Kenntnis*, 'cognition' *Erkenntnis*. On the difference, see §§377, n. 3; 443, n. 4; 445, n. 6.

3. It is not clear why what is attended to should be 'objective' as well as 'subjective'. I can after all attend to a pain or an itch that I have without supposing that others have or feel this pain or itch. Hegel would reply that in attending to a pain I distinguish it from myself and myself from it, implicitly regarding it as independent, if not of myself, at least of my act of attending to it. The pain becomes an object of my mind in a way that the other multifarious stimuli to which I am subjected are not. Perhaps he would add that our natural tendency is to regard an object of our attention as wholly objective, a tendency that is, however, sometimes checked by our general knowledge, e.g. that pains are not shared. Even if Hegel admits that attention is sufficient for objectivity only in this attenuated sense, he might still claim that our capacity for attention is a necessary condition of objectivity.

4. The claim that 'I am only attentive when I will to be so' looks false. Sometimes attention is voluntary: I 'pay' attention. Sometimes it is involuntary: something 'catches' or 'attracts' my attention; someone 'calls' or 'draws' my attention to something. (Animals seem to attend to some stimuli, but not to others; their attention is presumably not voluntary.) Nevertheless, attention often depends on our will or 'wilfulness' (*Willkür*). It is not clear what Hegel thinks 'implies' (*Darin liegt*) this. Perhaps he is thinking of undivided and sustained or unwavering ('identical') attention. Usually I do not attend to something for very long unless I 'will' to do so; I get used to attention-grabbing things and they soon lose my attention, even if I could not help attending to them in the first place.

5. In recommending attentive absorption in the 'subject matter' (*Sache*), Hegel is describing his own philosophical procedure. The reference to the 'botanist' is suggested by the example of Goethe, whose *Versuch die Metamorphose der Pflanzen zu erklären* (Attempt to Explain the Metamorphosis of Plants) appeared in. 1790. Cf. Enc. I, §24Z.(2) on Goethe's way of experiencing things, and Enc. II, §345 on his *Metamorphosis of Plants*.

6. This is Hegel's answer to the problem raised in §448, n. 3. When I attend to my pain, it becomes 'objective' only in the sense that it is an object of my inspection. If I am to 'intuit' the pain, it must become objective in a stronger sense, e.g. expressed in a poem: cf. §448, n. 7.

7. The distinction between 'inner' and 'outer' sensations is traditional. An inner sensation, e.g. pain or anger, is a sensation whose content we do not normally ascribe to an external object, even to an object that gives rise to it. A pin caused my pain, a colleague made me angry; the pin is painful, but not in pain; the colleague is irritating, but not necessarily angry. An outer sensation is a sensation whose content we normally ascribe to an external object, usually the object that causes the sensation. Thus in the first of Berkeley's *Three Dialogues between Hylas and Philonous*, Hylas says that the heat we feel from a fire is not only in us, but also in the fire, whereas the pain we feel when the heat is intense is only in us, not in the fire. That is, pain is an inner sensation, while heat is an outer sensation. Both types of sensation are, in Hegel's view, in us or 'subjective', but both are made objective in intuition. They become objective, however, in quite different ways: heat is attributed to an external object such as a fire, while a pain is expressed in poems or groans.

8. Goethe's *Die Leiden des jungen Werthers* (The Sorrows of Young Werther, 1774) was inspired by his unrequited love for Lotte Buff. Goethe recovered, but his work is said to have driven some of his readers to suicide. On Hegel's belief that the objectification of feelings releases us from them, see also ILA, pp.52 ff.

9. On the five senses, cf. §401, and nn. 3 and 9. In both passages Hegel classifies the senses in terms of their 'ideality' and 'reality' or 'materiality', but the classifications differ. In §401Z. sight and hearing go together as distance senses; smell and taste are grouped together for the same reason as they are here; touch or feeling is in a class of its own. Here, by contrast, sight and touch go together, as do taste and smell, with hearing in the middle. This is because in §401Z. Hegel is not concerned, as he is here, with the 'separability' of sensations, i.e. with their assignment to external objects and their consequent detachment from ourselves, but with the intrinsic nature of the various sensations. But given that his interest is now in the objectification and separability of sensations, he does not revise his earlier classification enough. Sight and touch are rightly grouped together, since although they differ with respect to distance and materiality, they are of central importance in the formation of our conception of objects. Smell and taste are of little importance in this respect, but not for the reason Hegel gives. Smelly objects and their smells may be quite persistent. Most objects do not, for us, have a distinctive smell. It is often difficult to tell what, or who, is making a smell. Smells may persist even when the object responsible for it is removed. Tasty objects may also persist. Most objects do not have a distinctive taste, at least not one that we are ready to savour. It is usually not difficult to tell what object is responsible for a particular taste, though it may be hard to say what ingredient in it produces the taste. Tastes may persist in the mouth, though not in the room, even after the object responsible for it is removed. (Sights and feels do not outlast the removal of the object in the same way as smells and tastes do. This is

an important factor in their 'separability'.) Apart from language, sounds are relatively unimportant. Many objects do not make distinctive sounds, not at least
unless we strike them. It is sometimes difficult to locate the source of a sound.
Sounds, unlike colours and textures, are usually intermittent.

10. It is not quite true that the externalization of what is sensed leaves the 'content'
    of the sensation unaltered. I may suppose e.g. that the faint hum that I hear is
    much louder in the proximity of its source or that something I see as shimmering
    in the sunlight is in fact uniformly brown. But Hegel is perhaps assuming that
    the hum or the shimmering is regarded as an objective phenomenon, perceivable
    by any normal perceiver occupying my vantage point, and not e.g. the result
    of some peculiarity of my ears or eyes. Since the content remains the same, it
    cannot be responsible for the 'transformation' of the sensation into an external
    object. So intelligence is the 'determining' factor. Its determining is 'formal',
    since it leaves the content unaffected.

11. In becoming external to the mind, sensory content becomes 'external-to-itself',
    since self-externalization, a mental or rational operation, is intrinsic to the nature
    of objects: cf. §448, n. 1. Since this self-externality is generated by the mind,
    it must be abstract, involving a 'formal, contentless universality', i.e. the sort
    of universality that belongs to space and time. Usually we think of 'discrete'
    quantity (e.g. 'There are six people in this room') as distinct from 'continuous
    quantity' (e.g. 'This room is 10 metres long'): cf. Enc. I, §100. But space and
    time are both discrete and continuous, since they can be divided into discrete
    units (metres, hours, etc.), but any such unit is adjacent to the next (unlike
    the people in a room) and can in turn be divided into smaller units ad infin-
    itum. Space and time are 'universal' in the sense that they can be occupied by
    an indefinite number of objects, yet are homogeneous: no region of space differs
    intrinsically from any other region, and no period of time differs intrinsically
    from any other. This universality has 'not yet developed to any actual indi-
    vidualization', since space and time are intrinsically empty, just uniform media
    ready to receive actual objects and events. See my 'Kant and Hegel on Space and
    Time', in S. Priest (ed.), *Hegel's Critique of Kant* (Oxford: Oxford University
    Press, 1987).

    Hegel is trying to answer the following questions: (1) Why are sensations relo-
    cated onto external objects? (2) Why are external objects spread out in such
    'universal' media as space and time? (3) Why are there two such media, space
    and time, rather than only one? His questions are better than his answers.

12. On Hegel's disagreement with Kant, cf. §448, n. 1, and on Kant as a 'subjective
    idealist', see Enc. I, §§42Z.(3) and 45Z. In §45Z. Hegel distinguishes subjective
    idealism from his own 'absolute idealism', and he does so here implicitly: things
    are ideal not because they or their characteristics are produced by us, but because
    they are produced by 'the infinite mind . . . , by the creative eternal Idea'. What
    this means in literal terms is that things are as they are owing to the logical struc-
    ture that pervades and sustains them, the structure that is described in Enc. I.
    and which is regarded as a 'mind' because it lies at the core of our minds as well
    as of things. This may be why in spatializing and temporalizing our sensations

'our intuitive mind' is 'assimilating them to itself': it gives them the same categorial structure as it itself has. But Hegel's point may be simpler: that our *intuitive* mind, not our mind in general, makes them into *intuitable* objects for itself. In general, Hegel's view of space and time is not unreasonable: they are *both* subjective *and* objective; we have to intuit objects as spatio-temporal but they also really are spatio-temporal. Hegel here places space and time on an equal footing: there is no hint of Kant's doctrine that while time is the form of 'inner sense', space is the form of 'outer sense'.

13. On the subjective–objective contrast, cf. Enc. I, §41Z (2), and on the relative unimportance of the question whether something is objective or subjective, cf. Enc. I, §42Z(3). Space and time are 'sublated' in two ways: (i) in nature, by the 'dialectic' of their 'immanent' concept, they are sublated into 'matter', a process described in Enc. II, §261; (ii) 'free intelligence' sublates them by rising above the level of spatio-temporal intuition to the level of 'cognitive thinking', i.e. Hegelian logic, where things are considered in their 'concept' or essential nature independently of their location in time and space. 'Dialectic' is here the negative principle at work both in our thought and in reality described in Enc. I, §81; it sublates space and time both from within (i) and from without (ii). Since space and time are sublated in any case, it matters little whether they are subjective or objective in the first place. Relegation of the question whether something is subjective or objective is a constant theme of Hegel's thought: what matters e.g. is not so much whether God exists or not as what conception we have of God: cf. §564, n. 3.

NOTES TO §449

1. The two moments are the 'recollection' or internalization of the content of sensations and their externalization as a being: cf. §448, n. 1. The two moments are intertwined into a 'concrete [i.e. 'grown together': cf. §396, n. 3] unity', not merely juxtaposed. In the 'external being of this material' (*in diesem äusserlich-seienden Stoffe*) the intelligence is recollected, and in its recollection it is sunk in 'self-externality' (*das Aussersichsein*).

2. Cf. §440, n. 3 on the relationship between intuition and representation. In §440 representations or general ideas are not characterized as 'its', namely the mind's, representations and are felt to be more impersonal, less 'my own', than intuitions are. Here, however, it is the 'object' (*Objekt*), not the intuition or representation, that is said to be 'my own' (*das Meinige*). It is 'detached' from me, an independent object, but my own, since I intuit or represent it. This does not mean that others cannot intuit or represent the same object, but 'intuition' and 'representation' have a subjective flavour lacking in, say, 'concept': '*Vorstellung* is a mental picture of a thing. It draws attention less to the thing in its objective aspects than to the state of mind of the subject' (DGS, p.156)—as we speak of 'the concept of . . .', but 'my conception of . . .'. In intuition, however, I focus primarily on the object; I look at a rose and do not reflect on my looking. Hence here 'object-hood' (*Gegenständlichkeit*) predominates and the mineness of the object is only 'in

itself', not for itself or 'posited'. When I reflect on the fact that it is my looking, I enter the domain of representation.

3. To judge from what Hegel has said so far about intuition, there is little or nothing to distinguish it from the sensory certainty described in §418. Hegel succeeds in differentiating them only by attributing new features to intuition and by appealing to types of intuition that are too sophisticated to appear at this stage: cf. §449, nn. 4, 5. The main new feature attributed to intuition is that its object is a 'cohesive fullness' (*zusammengehaltene Fülle*) of determinations, while the object of sensory consciousness is 'disintegrating' (*auseinanderfallende*) or 'torn asunder' (*auseinandergerissenes*) into various 'aspects' (*Seiten*, lit. 'sides'). The object of sensory certainty turns into the object of 'perception', the thing with many properties, a 'mixture' of individuality and universality: cf. §§418Z.; 419, n. 1. The object of intuition does not disintegrate in this way, but only because Hegel does not let it happen. There is no obvious reason why an object of intuition located in space and time should not be regarded as an object of perception and then undergo the same disintegrating analysis that Hegel applied earlier. But Hegel avoids this objection by implicitly restricting intuition to a special sort of object (such as a living organism, which cannot be split up into various 'aspects') or to a special way of viewing things. 'Reason' and rationality are invoked to justify this restriction, primarily as a ruse for assigning *Anschauung* a more elevated sense than is appropriate at this stage. He exploits the fluidity of *Anschauung*, which

> means 'view' in the sense of a 'conception' and can include a theory. This meaning is connected with other uses of the term: (i) contemplation in the sense of seeing into the inside of things; (ii) 'intuition' as a philosophical term (e.g. Fichte's 'intellektuelle Anschauung'); (iii) experience of the concrete, the visible, ... In the sense of 'view' it suggests origin in the inner life, the workings of intuition on experience, ... In strict use it is applied to the great spheres of knowledge and experience (e.g. life, art, love, ...)' (DGS, pp. 236-7).

> Anschauung means 'view', 'opinion', but beyond that ... 'concreteness', 'in the concrete', a direct vision as opposed to 'in the abstract' (DGS, p. 387).

4. On 'intellectual' (*intellektueller*) intuition, cf. §§394, n. 11; 415, n. 2. ('Intellectual' does not here carry the unfavourable connotation of *Verstand* and *verständig*, which I have also translated as 'intellect' and 'intellectual'.) Kant, who coined the term, contrasted it with 'sensory' intuition. He argued that while intellectual, i.e. wholly non-sensory, intuition is not impossible and might be possessed by God, human beings do not have it. If they did have it they would, like God, have knowledge of things in themselves. Kant's successors, however, were reluctant to allow that we do not have intellectual intuition (or something that can appropriately be called 'intellectual intuition'), though they do not usually suppose that we have the full-scale version that Kant attributes to God, an ability to create objects by thinking about them. Fichte argued that self-awareness, awareness of oneself as I (which is, in a way, created by its awareness of itself), is intellectual intuition. Schelling used 'intellectual intuition' to refer to the philosopher's awareness of the absolute, of the identity of the subject and the object. On Schelling's intellectual

intuition, see HP iii. 427 ff. Schelling's intellectual intuition is quite remote from the intuition that Hegel primarily has in mind. Although it dispenses with 'concepts' it presupposes conceptual knowledge, whereas Hegel's intuition is here preconceptual.

5. 'Mindful' (*Geistvolle*) intuition is close to 'intellectual' intuition. It is not reserved exclusively for philosophical intuition, but is required by a respectable historian or biologist as well: cf. §448, n. 5 on Goethe. It enables us to get to the heart of the matter and to see the wood as well as the trees. It contrasts with 'mindless' (*geistlose*) intuition, purely 'sensory consciousness', and also with the 'separating' intellect. On 'external' purposiveness, or 'end and means', and its inappropriateness for living organisms, see §423, n. 5.

Again, 'mindful intuition' is not what Hegel introduces in §448Z. The intuition involved in the projection of sensations into space and time is the 'sensory consciousness' from which Hegel tries to differentiate it. The account of intuition given in the Paragraph of §449 is sufficiently general to apply to both types of intuition, the 'mindful' as well as the 'mindless'. 'Mindful' intuition presupposes intellect and conceptual thought in a way that the 'mindless' variety does not. Hegel is here putting a high-grade content into what might be considered a low-grade form: cf. §380, n. 2. He does so in part because he has a higher regard for mindful intuition than he does for Schleiermacher's religious feeling and thus does not really think of intuition as a low-grade form, in part because of his need to distinguish 'consciousness' and its stages from 'free mind' and its stages. The answer to this second difficulty is that Hegel is mistaken in representing consciousness as a more primitive phase of mind than 'free mind', in the way that soul is more primitive than both consciousness and mind. Roughly speaking, psychology gives an account of the mental faculties that underly our consciousness of objects, ourselves and each other. There is no good reason for the assignment of 'perception' to phenomenology and its exclusion from psychology. 'Intellect' and 'reason' are officially included in phenomenology rather than psychology, but implicitly they are dealt with by psychology, under the heading of 'thinking' (§465 ff.). 'Consciousness' does not of course include, in Hegel's usage, everything that we would call a state of consciousness, only such states as have an object conceived as distinct from the subject. Thus when I do logic or think about thoughts, I am not, in Hegel's sense, conscious, since the object of my thinking is not distinct from myself. Thus the faculties considered by psychology do not underlie consciousness exclusively; they also underlie higher states and activities. Again, when Hegel is studying the mind itself, his state is not one of consciousness, since the mind is not an object distinct from himself. This may be one reason why he regards psychology, the explicit study of mind, as higher than phenomenology. But this is a mistake. Hegel's *study* of consciousness is no more consciousness than psychology is. His main reason for including phenomenology in his philosophy of mind is to find a place in his Encyclopaedia for the main findings of PS, and once this is done the structure of the Encyclopaedia imposes an order of priority on phenomenology and psychology. Then, since psychology considers some activities that are higher than consciousness, phenomenology is subordinated to psychology. Cf. §§440, n. 2; §446, n. 1.

6. Hegel refers to four states or activities:

(1) 'Immediate intuition'. This is the preliminary vision of e.g. a historical epoch. It is 'immediate' not in the way that 'sensory consciousness' is, but in that it is not preceded by 'cognition' or even by 'reflective thinking'. It gets at the 'substance' or essence of the object, but does not enable one to see how the 'inessentials' derive from the substance. It is equivalent to the 'wonder' (*to thaumazein*) from which, according to Aristotle, *Metaphysics*, I. 2, 982ᵇ12-13, philosophy begins. Earlier, in *Theaetetus*, 155d, Plato has Socrates say that 'wonder [*to thaumazein*] is the only beginning of philosophy'. Hegel also ascribes this saying to Aristotle at PH, p. 234.

(2) 'Contemplative thinking' (*Nachdenken*). *Nachdenken* is literally 'after-' or 'meta-thinking'. It is similar to, and sometimes equated with, 'reflective thinking' (*das reflektierende Denken*): cf. Enc. I, §2. But it does not carry the unfavourable connotation often found in 'reflective thinking'. In Enc. I, §2 *Nachdenken* is associated especially with philosophy, but here it is required of an educated person and of an artist for their intuitive vision to have any clarity.

(3) 'Cognition', especially the 'pure thinking of conceptual reason' required of the philosopher.

(4) 'Perfectly determinate, genuine intuition', which presents the subject matter as an 'internally articulated, systematic totality' in which the relationships of the contingencies to the essence are entirely clear. This intuition is cognition in a concentrated form; hence it is not 'immediate'. The educated man's and the artist's intuition is a lesser version of this, made possible by 'contemplative thinking' rather than by 'completely developed cognition'.

NOTES TO §450

1. This direction of attention is distinct from that referred to in §§448 and 449. There attention was needed in order to externalize the content. Here the attention is directed towards or 'against' (*gegen*) the externality itself, and involves a sort of retraction of the externality. Intelligence internalizes the content and makes it its own, especially in a representation, which is initially an image. Then intelligence can dispense with the bodily presence of the object. But cf. §450, n. 2.

2. On 'the dialectic that is for itself', see also §448, n. 13. This dialectic is negative, it sublates spatio-temporal externality. It is 'for itself' in the sense that it is actually at work, not merely potential, and perhaps also in the sense that it knows what it is doing.

We can become 'unfree' in intuition if we are entirely absorbed in the object, transfixed by it, as a moth is transfixed by a flame. But Hegel seems primarily to have in mind the different idea that we are unfree if we are unfamiliar with the object, if we encounter something of which we have as yet no representation.

Conversely, we become 'free' if we internalize the intuition and form a corresponding representation, so that the object is no longer alien and unfamiliar. It is unclear whether the words 'mind posits the intuition as its own, etc.' refer to the representation itself or to the external intuition now recognized as corresponding to the representation. See also §450, n. 3, which suggests the former interpretation.

3. The German verb *haben* corresponds closely to the English 'have'. Thus it is used not only as a transitive verb meaning roughly 'possess', but also as an auxiliary verb used to form the perfect tense of other verbs. Thus *ich habe [etwas] gesehen*, 'I have seen [something]', indicates a completed action or event viewed in its bearing on the present. Hence *haben* and 'have' are here in the present tense. Hegel takes this as an indication of 'sublation' (cf. §381, n. 13), the simultaneous abolition and preservation of something. For this idea of the living past, the past that casts a shadow on the present, Heidegger coined the terms *gewesen* and *Gewesenheit*, 'having- been' and 'having-been-ness'. But Hegel has only one word for 'past' and 'the past', *vergangen* and *Vergangenheit*, which come from the verb *vergehen*, 'to pass away', and hence suggest the past that is dead and gone, 'passed away' (*Vergangenes*). To avoid this suggestion, Hegel speaks of a 'relative past' (*relative [Vergangenheit]*), which also involves 'presence' (*Gegenwärtigkeit*). The intuition is past not absolutely, but only relative to our current representation. This, together with the example of 'I have seen', suggests that Hegel has in mind a representation in the absence of any actual intuition corresponding to it; the intuition is present in the sense that it has been converted into a representation, not in the sense that it persists alongside the representation. Hence the intuition is not fully past, but it is past in comparison with the representation, it is not present in the way that the representation is.

The perfect tense sometimes suggests that the past is still preserved in the mind, but it is hardly a 'universal sign' of this. If I say 'I have (already) seen this film', I suggest that I remember it, or at least enough of it not to want to see it again. But I may add: 'But I have entirely forgotten it' and this, despite its use of the present tense 'have', implies that the film is not preserved in my mind, except to the minimal degree required for me to know that I have seen and forgotten it.

NOTES TO §451

1. 'Recollected' (*erinnerte*) means roughly 'internalized': cf. §401, n. 2. When intelligence finds itself determined, it has not recollected its intuition. When it thinks, it has broken loose from intuitions altogether. So representation is in the middle. Intelligence still has intuitions, but it has internalized and mastered them. The representation still involves a subjectivity that is 'one-sided', i.e. not counterbalanced by objectivity, since it is 'conditioned by immediacy'. That is, as an image the representation is dependent on what I happen to have intuited. Others are unlikely to have intuited it as well, so it is peculiar to me. Moreover, the representation is still in my mind, not yet given any objective embodiment. When it ceases to be conditioned by immediacy, it will be 'self-contained being' (*an ihm selbst*

das Sein). 'Being' here contrasts with 'conditioned'; being has cut loose from its conditions and become independent. But representation has not yet reached that stage.

2. As the *Zusatz* explains, representation passes through three ascending stages. The tasks proposed in this sentence correspond to those three stages. At stage (1) intelligence forms an image of the intuition, so as to 'make the immediacy inward, etc.' At stage (2) we 'sublate the subjectivity of the inwardness' by forming a universal representation on the basis of the image, and also by devising a sign for this representation. At stage (3) intelligence has a language created by itself, in particular a name, which it commits to memory, and is thus 'within itself in its own externality': the name denotes what is external to the mind without any intuition or image: cf. §462, n. 6. The reference of the pronouns in the latter part of the sentence is unclear. I have supplied 'within inwardness itself' for Hegel's *in ihr selbst*, which could equally refer to intelligence or to subjectivity. What intelligence is to divest itself of, *ihrer* ('it'), is presumably subjectivity rather than inwardness.

3. The *Differenz* is the 'difference' between intelligence and the material of intuition. Words and the corresponding representations still involve intuitive material as well as the creativity of intelligence, and are thus 'syntheses': cf. §457, n. 2. Concepts, by contrast, are not. They are immanent in the mind, their content supplied by thinking alone: cf. §467Z.

4. On Hegel's criticism of faculty psychology, cf. §§378, nn. 8, 9; 442, n. 3; etc.

5. *Erinnerung* usually means 'recollection' of something (a name, a face, an event, etc.) one really knew or remembered all along. This is a 'peculiar' (*eigentümlichen*) sense of the word, since the basic meaning of *Erinnerung* is, in Hegel's view, 'internalization', 'making inner' (cf. §402, n. 6), whereas in the 'peculiar' (though standard) sense it is an 'arousal' (*Hervorrufen*, lit. 'calling forth'), an externalization more than an internalization. How do these apparently opposite senses of *Erinnerung* square with each other? *Erinnerung* as arousal, Hegel replies, presupposes a prior internalization of an intuition, the formation of an image whose content is the same as that of the intuition. The image then recedes from my consciousness, but is aroused if e.g. I see the same person again: cf. §454Z. When I see the person, my image receives its 'verification' (*Bewährung*) from my present intuition. The content of the intuition 'proves its worth' (*sich . . . bewährt*) in the representation in the quite different sense that it needs to be interesting to be remembered and recalled: cf. §452Z. Recollection as arousal is initially 'involuntary' (*unwillkürlichen*); it is provoked by an intuition and not in our control: cf. §453, n. 5.

6. In recollection, the content of the intuition and of the representation were the same. 'Imagination' (*Einbildungskraft*) forms a universal representation (the 'subjective') whose content differs from that of the intuition that inspired it (the 'objective'). At stage (1) the subjective image and the intuited object are in immediate unity: I recognize the person I see as corresponding to my image. It might be thought that something similar happens at stage (2), that I recognize an intuited object, e.g. a giraffe, as an instance of my universal representation. But Hegel

takes a different route, since he is trying to move representation away from an external content that is simply *given* or *found*. The 'intuited external content' is made a 'sign' (*Zeichen*) of the 'represented content'. This intuited content need not be an actual instance of the representation, e.g. a giraffe, or even a picture of a giraffe. It may just be a hieroglyph or the word-sound 'giraffe'. Then the representation is externalized and 'rendered imageable' (*verbildlicht*), i.e. we have an image of the universal representation, not just of individual instances of it.

7. 'Memory' is *Gedächtnis*, especially, in Hegel's view, memory of signs and words: cf. §§410, n. 3; 461–4. The distinction between *Gedächtnis* and *Erinnerung* in its usual sense corresponds roughly to the distinction between 'remembering' as (1) 'having learned and not forgotten', and (2) in the sense in which 'a person is said to have remembered, or been recollecting, something at a particular moment, or is said to be now recalling, reviewing or dwelling on some episode of his own past' (Gilbert Ryle, *The Concept of Mind* (London: Hutchinson, 1949), 272–3.) But here, a sign is 'recollected' not in the sense that it is 'recalled', but in the sense that it is committed to memory or memorized, i.e. 'internalized'. Hegel attaches great importance to mechanical memory, our ability to memorize a list of intrinsically senseless signs without regard to their meaning or their customary context. The signs are 'external', namely unrelated, to each other. They are also external to the intelligence in that they have no meaning for it and it means nothing by them. The signs are thus 'objective' with respect to the intelligence, even though they are created by the intelligence and need not be expressed externally, e.g. as sounds. This mechanical memory 'forms the transition to thinking' in that it exercises us in dealing with items wholly within the mind, without reference to external objects or intuitions. Consequently Hegel regards learning by rote or by heart as a crucial ingredient of a proper education. cf. §395, n. 2 on education. The nursery rhymes that some children learn by heart are often nonsensical; any coherent meaning they have can be appreciated only by an educated adult.

NOTES TO §452

1. I see someone, dressed in a particular way, with a certain expression on his face, standing in a group outside a church at a certain time. In 'recollecting', namely internalizing, this intuition, I form an image of the man which omits much of this detail: the dress, the expression, the church, the rest of the group, the time. I shall recognize him if I meet him again at another time and place, even if he is dressed differently, has a different expression and is in different company. My image is discretionary or 'wilful' (*willkürlich*): I decide what goes into the image and what does not. The image is 'contingent' (*zufällig*), not fully determined by the intuition that inspires it. Hegel seems to be qualifying his claim, in §451Z., that the 'represented content is still the same as in intuition'. Why does he speak of the intuited content as the content of 'feeling' (*des Gefühls*)? Perhaps it is to stress its warm and colourful immediacy in contrast to the relatively sparse image. By intelligence's 'own' space and time, Hegel seems to mean primarily the space

483

and time in which intelligence can revive the 'content of feeling' or recall the corresponding image, i.e. anywhere and at any time (during the remainder of one's life), not just the place and time of the original intuition and its object: see §452, n. 2.

2. If I see someone standing outside St Paul's church at 6 p.m. on 4.7.02, then I see him at 6 p.m. on 4.7.02 , my intuition occurs at 6 p.m. on 4.7.02. Moreover, my intuition occurs fairly near to St Paul's church. Intuition requires the spatial and temporal proximity of its object. There are therefore at least two ways in which intelligence can 'lift the content out of the particularity of space and time': (1) My image of the person omits the facts that he was standing outside St Paul's church and was doing so at 6 p.m. on 4.7.02: cf. §452, n. 1. (2) I can call up my image of him at other places than St Paul's church and at other times than 6 p.m. on 4.7.02, in fact more or less anywhere and at any time. These ways are quite different: I may be able to recall him anywhere and at any time, even if my image of him is an image of him standing outside St Paul's church at 6 p.m. on 4.7.02. Conversely, if my image of him does omit his spatio-temporal location, I am still likely to be able to recall him anywhere and at any time, though this has little to do with the abstractness of my image. (By contrast my ability to *recognize* him in other contexts does have something to do with the abstractness of my image. But I may be able to recognize him, lying on a beach in Dorset, as the man I saw outside St Paul's church two years ago. Here my image hovers between an abstractness that enables me to recognize him in a different context and a concreteness that enables me to recall him in a definite context.) Hegel does not distinguish (1) and (2) sufficiently. My ability to call up the image anywhere and at any time does not depend on how determinate the image is, but on the fact that it is an image rather than an intuition. The 'universal' space and time of intelligence are primarily the space and time in which intelligence can recall the intuited event, i.e. anywhere and at any time, in contrast to the particular time and place of the original intuition: cf. §452, n. 1.

3. 'Duration' is *Dauer*, how long something lasts for. Corresponding to the distinction drawn in §452, n. 2, the duration acquired by something, e.g. a person's standing outside St Paul's church, could in this context be either of two things: (1) how long he seems, as I imagine or recall him, to have stood outside the church; (2) how long I retain the image of him standing outside the church and am able to recall it. These are quite distinct. I may remember for a long time an event that seems to have lasted only a short time, e.g. an earthquake. I may soon forget an event that, as long as I remember it, seems to have lasted a long time, e.g. waiting for a late train. Here Hegel seems to have (2) in mind, whereas in the next paragraph he is thinking of (1): cf. §452, n. 4. As an image, an image lacks the 'clarity', 'freshness', and 'determinacy' of intuition. But the length of time for which I retain an image does not depend on the relative obscurity, etc. of the image. I am more likely to remember events that I picture with relative clarity, etc. than those that I do not.

4. Cf. W. James, *The Principles of Psychology*, 619–27. Hegel's explanation of this phenomenon is problematic. In 'recollection' (*Erinnerung* in its usual sense) we

look at our 'subjectivity' as well as the events, measuring the time by our 'interest' in it. Then a crowded period will seem long, since our interest was intense, and a barren period short, since our interest was slight. In intuition we focus only on the events. So we cannot now measure the time by the intensity of our interest. But why does a crowded period seem short and a uniform period long? All that Hegel says is that 'deficiency of material drives us to the contemplation of our empty subjectivity'. By his previous argument this should make a barren period seem short at the time, given that our interest is slight.

NOTES TO §453

1. The image 'for itself' is the image consciously attended to by intelligence. This conscious image is 'transient', short-lived. It occurs when and where intelligence attends to it. 'Reality' (*Dasein*) is here the explicit, overt reality of which we are conscious. It contrasts with 'the in-itself' (*das Ansich*), the latent underlying essence or bearer of 'determinations'. (The 'in-itself' may also contrast with the image 'for itself', though this may simply mean 'of/by itself'.) Similarly 'consciousness' contrasts with 'the subject' (*das Subjekt*), the underlying bearer of consciousness. The image is 'recollected', *erinnert* in the sense of 'internalized'. It is not 'existing' (*existierend*), stepping forth, since it is merely latent: cf. §403, n. 2.
2. The 'requirement' to conceive the intelligence in this way is 'universal' or general, in that it applies to every case where the 'concept' is involved, not just the intelligence but also the seed, etc. On the comparison of the mind to a seed, cf. §§378, n. 11; 379, n. 5. A seed grows into a tree with a trunk, branches, leaves, etc. It is therefore 'concrete'. But it is also 'simple'. If an acorn is cut open it is entirely homogeneous. It does not contain miniature versions of the trunk, etc., nor does it contain specific areas in which the potential trunk, the potential leaves, etc. are separately located: cf. Enc. I, §161Z. for Hegel's rejection of the theory that a seed or egg contains the organism in miniature. What the seed contains is a sort of plan or 'concept' of the tree that will emerge from it. The mind or intelligence too stems from a 'concept' and this is also concrete, yet simple. It is wrong to suppose that different ideas, memories, etc. are situated in different parts of the brain, to locate different faculties in different parts of the brain: cf. §411, n. 2 on phrenology, whose founder, Gall, also distinguished in the brain between nerve fibres, cortex, and ganglia.
3. On this difference between a seed and a mind, see §379, n. 6. An acorn grows into an oak-tree, but the oak-tree does not withdraw again into the same simple acorn that it emerged from. What it does is to produce new acorns, the 'existence of being-in-itself' (*Existenz des Ansichseins*)—a paradoxical expression, approximating to the 'explicit emergence of implicitness'. Intelligence too is the 'existence of being-in-itself'. But it does not become so by generating another intelligence as an appendage of itself. It is so 'as such', just as intelligence, not in virtue of something else. So the existence of being-in-itself is now 'free', not dependent on a prior intelligence in the way that the new acorn depends on the old acorn. Moreover, whereas one acorn is much like another, the intelligence develops, continually

absorbing new material and consigning it to, and occasionally retrieving it from, the 'nocturnal pit'.

4. 'On the other hand' contrasts with 'on the one hand' at the beginning of the Remark. But how does what Hegel say here differ from what he said earlier? Clearly he wants to differentiate the intelligence from other cases involving a concept, such as a seed. A seed is 'unconscious', but it is not a 'pit' (*Schacht*), a mine, from which ore is extracted and into which (if we pursue the analogy) things can be deposited or 'recollected'. We must not, however, think of what is in the pit as 'discrete', scattered around as separate lumps. The interior of the pit is entirely homogeneous, as is (in Hegel's view) the inside of an acorn. Hence the pit, along with its contents, is 'universal', blank and undifferentiated. This is different from the more familiar 'form' of universality, the universality of e.g. the conception of redness, which applies to indefinitely many red things. But this form of universality has not yet presented itself, and is not, moreover, 'existing', since it depends on red *things*. So pit-universality is the first form to appear.

5. According to the Remark intelligence is the 'free' existence of being-in-itself, in that it does not, like an acorn, depend on another intelligence or on something analogous to an oak-tree. But it is not free in the sense of being able to summon up its images 'at will' (*willkürlich*): cf. §451, n. 5.

NOTES TO §454

1. As the *Zusatz* explains, when I see Mr Smith; this is a real or 'occurrent' (*daseienden*) intuition. This calls up an image of Mr Smith acquired in a previous intuition, thus giving the image 'reality' (*Dasein*). The new intuition is subsumed under the image, which is universal 'in form' not in the sense that it is a general image of man as such, enabling me to classify any man I meet *as a man*, but in the sense that, although it is an image specifically of Smith, it enables me to recognize Smith in any of my indefinitely many encounters with him. In enabling me to do this, my image of him is 'proved' or verified (*bewährt*): cf. §451, n. 5. This is 'recollection' in the standard sense.

2. My 'property' (*Eigentum*) may not be in my 'possession' (*Besitz*) (and what is in my possession may not be my property). Since the image is my property (but mostly not in my possession), it is distinct from the intuition, which is always, whenever it occurs, explicit, 'real', and thus not my property, even though I recognize it as my 'own' in virtue of its correspondence to my image. Since the image can come into my possession, it is distinct from the 'simple night', the 'pit', in which it usually resides. Hegel infers that intelligence can summon up an image at will: the 'existence' of the 'property', for which an 'external intuition' is no longer needed, is the explicit occurrence of the image in consciousness.

3. *Vorstellung* ('representation') comes from *vorstellen*, which is formed from *vor*, 'before, in front of', and *stellen*, 'to put, place', and thus means literally 'to put before'. The verb is often used reflexively: *sich vorstellen*, 'to put before, present to, oneself'. But here *Vorstellung* means that 'what is internal' can be put or 'presented' before the intelligence. The recollected 'reality' (*Dasein*) is perhaps e.g.Mr

Smith rather than my present intuition of Mr Smith, and Hegel is saying that an image can be presented before intelligence in the absence of a corresponding intuition.

4. It is not clear what reason Hegel has given for saying that retention of something requires 'repeated' intuition. I may have seen Mr Smith only once, yet recognize him when I see him again. Nor is it obvious that repeated arousal of an image by an intuition is needed before I can summon it at will. Perhaps this is needed initially to develop my capacity for image-summoning, but I do not need to repeat this process with every image I acquire. Hegel's attack on curiosity is reminiscent of Heidegger's in *Being and Time*.

NOTES TO §455

1. On 'reproductive imagination' (*reproduzierende Einbildungskraft*), cf. §455, n. 12. It differs from recollection in that the emergence of an image, e.g. of Mr Smith, does not depend on a current corresponding intuition. The second sentence is ambiguous. It could mean: (1) 'The nearest [*nächste*, i.e. immediate] relation of each image is its relation to the place and time of its original acquisition', e.g. the relation of my image of Smith to St Paul's church and 6 p.m. on 4.7.02. Or it could mean: (2) 'The nearest relation between images is the relation between the places and times of their original acquisition', e.g. the relation between my image of Mr Smith and my image of Mrs Smith is that I first saw them both outside St Paul's church at 6 p.m., etc. Hegel seems to be thinking of (2), since he goes on to speak about a different type of relation between images. But he also has (1) in mind, since reproductive imagination does not essentially involve a relation between images, only the emergence of a single image. But Hegel is perhaps trying to assimilate reproductive and associative imagination by suggesting that both involve a relation between images. In fact, since the space and time are also 'stored up with them' (*mit aufbewahrten*), (1) also involves a relation between images, between e.g. my image of Smith and my image of St Paul's church, etc. Hegel said earlier (cf. §452, n. 2), and says again in the next sentence, that an image omits the space and time of the original intuition. But he needs it to be 'stored up' somehow, since otherwise I could only recall or imagine Smith, not Smith outside St Paul's church. This spatio-temporal relation between images facilitates the transition from reproductive to associative imagination: one type of relation between images gives way to another type.

2. Hegel seems to feel some difficulty over the way in which, or the extent to which, an image omits space and time, perhaps for the reason suggested in §452, n. 2 and §455, n. 1, that an intuition of Smith in one context enables me both to recall him in that context and to recognize (or even imagine) him in different contexts. This perhaps explains why he here speaks of the 'subject' (rather than the I or the intelligence), a term that he has not used since §453 (cf. §453, n. 1). As 'a unit' (*Eines*) in intuition, i.e. as one thing among others, Smith is related to St Paul's church, Mrs Smith, etc. But as an image 'in the subject', Smith

retains only the 'individuality' (*Individualität*) that links his determinations, his portly figure, his pale colouring, etc. What his determinations are to include is a tricky matter. He cannot be imaged simply as bare individual, since this will not enable me to recognize him again. The image should include his portliness, since I will be able to recall him as portly. But it cannot include it too decisively and irrevocably, since I shall recognize him again even if he loses weight in the meantime. It is no doubt not easy to say what it is about a person that enables us to recognize them in different contexts.

3. Now that the image has been stripped of space and time, something else is needed to relate images. This is a 'universal representation', 'universal' in a different sense from that in which the 'pit' is universal (cf. §453, n. 4). Hegel's main idea here is that an image of e.g. Smith and an image of e.g. Jones are associated in virtue of their common exemplification of the universal representation of e.g. 'man'. The 'former' (or 'other': *sonstigen*] circumstances on which the relative abstractness and concreteness of the images depends are presumably the circumstances of the intuition that gave rise to the image.

4. The association of ideas was expounded by Hobbes, in *Leviathan*, ch. III, and also by Hume, *Treatise of Human Nature*, I, §iv, who says: 'The qualities from which this association arises, and by which the mind is after this manner conveyed from one idea to another, are three, viz., Resemblance, Contiguity in time or place, and Cause and Effect'. The doctrine was developed by Hartley (*Observations on Man*, 1749) and by James Mill (*Analysis of the Phenomena of the Human Mind*, 1829). 'In Germany, the same mythological supposition [of 'atomistic "ideas" which recur'] has been more radically grasped, and carried out to a still more logical, if more repulsive, extreme, by [Johann Friedrich] Herbart [1776–1841, especially in *Psychologie als Wissenschaft*, 1824] .... 'For Herbart each idea is a permanently existing entity, the entrance whereof into consciousness is but an accidental determination of its being. So far as it succeeds in occupying the theatre of consciousness, it crowds out another idea previously there. This act of inhibition gives it, however, a sort of hold on the other representation which on all later occasions facilitates its following the other into the mind. The ingenuity with which most special cases of association are formulated in this mechanical language of struggle and inhibition, is great, and surpasses in analytic thoroughness anything that has been done by the British school' (W. James, *Principles of Psychology*, 603).

5. Hegel objects to calling '*Ideen*' what are, in his terminology, *Vorstellungen*, 'representations', or *Bildern*, 'images'.

6. When I see or think of St Paul's church, does it call to mind Smith, whom I once saw there (here the link is 'something pictorial), or St Paul's Cathedral (here the link is the 'intellectual category', *Verstandeskategorie*, of likeness), or its architect (the intellectual category of ground and consequent)? This is contingent. So the 'laws of association' are not really laws, but at most tendencies jostling for supremacy.

7. 'Formal' (*formelle*) universality contrasts implicitly with the particularity of the content, e.g. St Paul's church, perhaps even a church in general. Intelligence is

universal in that it is not fixated on any particular content, but passes from one to another.

8. Hegel here uses 'representation' in two senses, a narrower sense in which it contrasts with 'image' and a wider sense in which an image is a representation, though not every representation is (or involves) an image. It is not very clear where Hegel has given a 'more precise determination' of image and representation 'in terms of their form': cf. §§453, n. 4; 454, n. 3. A *Vorstellung* in the narrow sense may be a general idea, such as the idea of a church (in the sense of a building); then its 'content' is 'pictorial', though it need not be so 'sensorily concrete' as an image (either of a church in general or, e.g., of St Paul's church). Its content may be a 'concept' such as causality, or an 'Idea' such as God. Even then it is 'given and immediate': unlike a 'thought', it presents its content in a pictorial way (as God the Father, e.g., rather than as the absolute) and it presents it immediately, without tracing, or even suggesting, its derivation from other concepts. This immediacy of the representation is also implied by Hegel's reference to 'the being' (*Das Sein*) of intelligence. 'Being', in Hegel's logic, contrasts with 'essence' and with 'concept'. To say that something *is*, is just to say that it is (or to say that it just is), without explanation or conceptual derivation. Thus the representation of a church is universal, it applies to, even represents, indefinitely many churches. But its universality is just 'abstract', not concrete. That is, the content of the representation is not intrinsically universal, not derived from the intelligence itself, but from encounters with one or more particular churches.

9. On the 'syllogism' or *Schluss*, see §§389, n. 4; 399, n. 5. 'Being' and 'universality' are the extremes which representation links up. 'Being' is the starting-point of intelligence, and it indicates that intelligence (as sensation and intuition) or its object (what is sensed or intuited) just is, without explanation: cf. §455, n. 8. Being is thus one meaning of 'relation-to-self' (*Beziehung-auf-sich*). The relation-to-self is in this case direct and immediate: intelligence and its object are not related to anything else as their cause or essence, they just are that way. 'Universality' is the finishing-point of intelligence. Here the relation-to-self is indirect and mediated, albeit self-mediated. The universal is not just there. It has emerged victorious from a conflict with its other, the sensory material that underlies intuition and representation. It no longer depends on this material for its determinacy; it determines itself from its own resources. Being is comparable to the contented, self-contained infant, universality to the contented, self-contained old man, whose contentment stems from his emergence from the struggles of life: cf. §396, n. 2. This universality is concrete, not 'abstract'. A version of 'being' and of 'universality' appeared in 'consciousness', where being is the object, simple and self-contained, while universality is the subject, equally simple, but with a simplicity extricated from its entanglement with its sensory states. At the stage of consciousness, however, there is, Hegel implies, no mediating link between object and subject. Here representation supplies that link, and itself involves both being and universality. 'What is found' is being, the sensory stuff that just is. Intelligence supplements this with universality, turning it into e.g. the representation of a church. Then, conversely, we might expect Hegel

to say: intelligence supplements 'what is its own, the inner', namely universality (the universal form), with being, which equally gives rise to a representation, e.g. of a church. But this cannot be what he means, since the being is 'posited by itself', by intelligence. And the sensory stuff that goes into the representation of a church is not 'posited' by intelligence, it is just 'given'; intelligence may select it for attention, but it does not posit it. So what Hegel most likely means here is that intelligence supplements 'the inner', namely the universal representation, with an external sign, such as '+' or the word 'church'. So 'being' comes in twice: first as the sensory given, secondly as a piece of sensory stuff adopted or created by intelligence as a sign.

As noted in §§446, n. 1 and 449, n. 5, Hegel's attempt to integrate phenomenology into the philosophy of mind and to differentiate it from psychology are not very successful. Universal representations are involved in consciousness, e.g. the 'properties' or 'predicates' of a thing in §419.

10. This theory of concept-formation first appears in Aristotle, *Posterior Analytics*, B19, 100^a4-$^b5$, though Aristotle's stages—perception, memory, experience, understanding—differ from Hegel's. Since anything is 'similar' to anything else in some respect or other, the superimposition of images might be a matter of 'chance'. I see e.g. Mr Smith, St Paul's church and a butterfly, and then frame the idea of an entity seen by M. J. Inwood at 6 p.m. on 4.7.02 or of a composite entity, man-church-butterfly. To avoid such random combinations we postulate something like a force of attraction between similar images, e.g. the images of Smith, Brown, Jones, etc. The differences between the images are 'rubbed off' to leave the general idea of a man. It is not clear why Hegel thinks that he has already shown that intelligence 'by its recollection [viz. internalization] immediately gives the images universality' in the relevant sense. He has shown that the image is consigned to a universal 'pit': cf. §453, n. 4. He has shown that my image of Smith is sufficiently abstract or universal to enable me to recognize him on different occasions: cf. 454, n. 1. But where has he shown how my Smith-image acquires the type of universality that enables me to apply it to any man I meet, not just Smith? Hegel wants to transfer the universalizing force from the images themselves to the intelligence or I. But he does not explain how it universalizes the image in the relevant way. Presumably the answer to the question how we avoid eccentric ideas such as that of an entity seen by Inwood at a particular time or of a man-church-butterfly is that the latter combination is insufficiently frequent to be noticeable or for the idea of it to be useful, and the former idea is too egocentric to be socially shareable. Despite his interest in education and society, Hegel tends to neglect the communal character of our mental acquisitions.

11. On the distinction between 'symbol' and 'sign', see §§457Z. and 458. *Phantasie* ('fantasy') is not a derogatory word. Hegel reserves it for the higher, more creative imagination. '*Einbildungskraft, Vorstellungskraft*: the faculty of imagination. These terms are used chiefly in analyses of the nature of this faculty. Otherwise *Phantasie* is the usual equivalent of "imagination" [e.g. "He has a vivid imagination"]' (DGS, p. 157, n. 1).

490 *Commentary*

12. Cf. §§451, n. 5; 453, n. 5 on voluntary and involuntary emergence of images.
13. If something is 'finite', it is bounded by, and therefore related to, something else. The content of an image is finite and so related to something else, though it is not obvious that this is due to its 'immediacy or sensoriness', since a thought may, in Hegel's view, be finite and so bounded by and related to other thoughts. The content of one image is objectively related to the content of other images. For example, the content of my image of Hegel, namely Hegel himself, is objectively related to the content of my image of Stuttgart, his birthplace. But I need not relate my image of Hegel to my image of Stuttgart. I can replace this 'objective bond' by a 'subjective bond'. I may associate my image of Hegel with my image of my computer, though there is no objective bond between the two contents. The image of my computer is 'connected quite externally' or superficially to my image of Hegel. But not every subjective bond is so external. If I relate my image of Hegel to my images of Plato, Aristotle, etc., these images are not 'connected quite externally', though the bond is here subjective rather than objective: Hegel had no physical contact with Plato, etc.
14. On 'emotional moods' (*Gemütsstimmungen*), cf. §401Z. If I am in a cheerful mood, my image of Hegel reminds me of an enjoyable day in Heidelberg, etc. 'Passions' (*Leidenschaften*) include especially love: 'Every little breeze seems to whisper Louise', which involves a pun as well as association of images. An example of a significant witticism is Feuerbach's *Der Mensch ist, was er isst*, 'Man is [*ist*] what he eats [*isst*]'.

NOTES TO §456

1. It is not very clear what supports ('hence', *daher*) this claim. Hume (cf. §455, n. 4) mentioned three sources of the association of ideas: resemblance, contiguity in time or place, cause and effect. Association of two individual representations by their contiguity in time or place does not in any obvious way require a universal representation under which they are both subsumed. It might be argued that they are subsumed under some such universal representation as 'encountered at the same time' or 'encountered at St Paul's church'. But this does not seem to be Hegel's line of thought, since he argues that intelligence strips the images of their spatio-temporal specificity: cf. §455, nn. 1, 2. Then there is nothing left to associate the images except their suitability for subsumption under a universal representation. In Hegel's view, intelligence universalizes the image, preparing it for such subsumption, before universal representations come on the scene. Aristotle makes a similar move, but with regard to perception rather than images. He argues that while what one perceives is e.g. the individual Callias, what one strictly perceives is only a man of a certain sort, hence a type of universal: *Posterior Analytics*, A31, 87^{b}29–33 and B19, 100^{a}17–^{b}1. Hegel does not mention association by cause and effect. He perhaps assumes that this relation presupposes subsumption under universal representations.
2. Hegel now moves from 'reproductive imagination', the theme of the Paragraph §455, to what he calls in the *Zusatz* 'productive imagination': cf. §456, n. 5.

(But the witticisms and puns referred to in §455Z. fall under the heading of productive imagination.) The distinction between reproductive and productive imagination corresponds roughly to Hobbes's distinction between 'simple imagination, as when one imagineth a man, or a horse, which he hath seen before', and 'compounded imagination, as when from the sight of a man at one time, and of a horse at another, we conceive in our mind a Centaure' (*Leviathan*, p. I, ch. 2). To explain reproductive imagination we do not, on the face of it, need to postulate anything in the intelligence apart from a tendency to retain images and to universalize them. But to explain productive imagination we need to assume that the intelligence has a 'content' (*Gehalt, Inhalt*) of its own, which it then expresses by delving into its 'stock' of images and representations. This content is distinct from its current stock of ideas. What this content might be in the case of imagining a centaur is not very obvious, though presumably there is some content that explains the formation and persistence of this image. The content is more obvious when intelligence adopts the cross as a symbol for its Christianity or allegorizes it in the *Pilgrim's Progress*. It 'imaginatively impresses' (*einbildend*) its idea of the cross or the various ideas that make up the pilgrim's journey onto its Christianity. In these 'individualized structures' (*individualisierten Gebilde*) Christianity, the 'subjective content', gets an intuition-derived 'reality' (*Dasein*).

3. Images are more universal than intuitions because they omit the spatio-temporal context, etc: cf. §452, nn. 1, 2. They are not yet, however, universal representations such as the idea of redness or of a plant. The formation of a universal representation has, as a necessary condition, something 'common' to a group of images. But this common element is not sufficient, as e.g. Herbart implies: cf. §455, n. 4. Intelligence needs to analyse the 'concrete individuality' of the images and strip away the 'empirical connection, etc.', i.e. those features of the images that they do not have in common. On the distinction between 'the concrete universal' (*das konkret Allgemeine*, lit: 'the concretely universal') and an abstract universal, such as redness, see §445, n. 7.

4. On the distinction between 'abstract representations' and 'concepts', see §§451, n. 3; 467Z. Concepts are not derived by abstraction from empirical objects or images, but are formed by the mind alone. Here 'abstract representations' are those universal representations, such as redness, that are not 'concrete'. Hegel disliked and despised Jakob Friedrich Fries (1773–1843), whose main work, *Neue Kritik der Vernunft* (1807: New Critique of Reason), fused Kantian doctrines with the psychology of the day.

5. Both the representation and the image are in the mind, the 'subjective sphere', but the image is 'external', in relation to the representation, both because it is closer to the sensory surface of the mind and because it is capable of and destined for direct externalization in e.g. art. In a chemical combination an alkali and an acid neutralize each other, producing a salt that is neither acid nor alkaline. When, by contrast, a universal representation expresses itself in an image, it does not cease to be universal, nor does the image cease to be an image. In the image, the representation becomes 'for itself', i.e. both actualized and aware of itself, and 'recollects itself', i.e. draws itself together and becomes self-aware. When the

image is externalized in e.g. a painting, it is once more an intuition rather than a mental image. It regains the specificity that the image lost, so the 'totality present in intuition' is restored. Now, however, it is a 'proven' (*bewährte*) totality. It is not just an object that we happen to come across, as Smith was. It is selected for its fitness to express our idea and is charged with meaning. This is what an artist does: selects a sensory image to express not, in this case, a commonplace representation, but a 'genuine universal', such as God. This is just 'the formal aspect' (*das Formelle*) of art. The content of art, in particular the image selected, is up to the artist. But the type of art that Hegel has in mind is more likely to express a representation derived from 'the sphere of reason, of law, ethics, and religion' than a representation of e.g. a tree or a house. Hence Hegel introduces representations derived from reason, etc., even though they are less directly related to intuition than representations derived from the 'external world'. The image that expresses the representation may be an instance of the representation, a man for example. But it need not: a cross is not itself an instance of the Christianity that it expresses.

NOTES TO §457

1. As a prefix, *selbst*, 'self', usually (though not invariably) has reflexive force. Hence *Selbstanschauung*, 'self-intuition', implies that intelligence intuits itself. This does not mean that it intuits some external object (such as a painting) that expresses its universal representation: the reference to art in §456Z. was an anticipatory digression. It means that it contemplates a mental image expressing its representation. This is regarded as *intuition*, since the object contemplated is 'pictorial' (*bildlich*), but as *self*-intuition, since the image is derived from intelligence itself. The 'structure' (*Gebilde*) is not simply the image, but the combination of representation and image: cf. §456, n. 2 on the 'individualized structures'. Intelligence as 'reason' moves in two apparently contrary directions. First, it withdraws inwards, transforming what it 'immediately' finds (sensations, intuitions) into universals—images and then representations. This process sublates 'immediacy'. So intelligence is not at this stage in 'identical self-relation', or relation to itself, as immediacy. It is in a way alienated from its own immediacy. However, the formation of a representation-image 'structure' or complex 'implicitly' restores intelligence's relation to itself in its immediacy. This implicit return is made explicit by the second movement. Here intelligence ventures outwards, giving external embodiment to its inner achievement, making it into 'a being' (*Seiendes*), making itself 'into being, into the thing' (*zum Sein, zur Sache*), into an external, intuitable entity that is just immediately there. That is, intelligence devises intuitable signs for its representations. On 'being' and its contrast with 'universality', see §455, n. 9.

2. The universal is 'one's own' (*das Eigene*), and the inner. 'Being' (*das Sein*) is 'being-found' (*das Gefundensein*) and the outer. Previously, in 'intuition, recollection, etc.' these two 'moments' have been synthesized. A synthesis is a combination or compound of two or more ingredients, in which, Hegel implies, each

element retains its own nature: cf. §§451, 454, 456. In particular, the element of being, the sensory material I find (e.g. Mr Smith), remains just 'found', only now I apply my image or my representation to it. But with fantasy it is different. The two moments are not just synthesized, they are 'completely welded into one' (*vollkommen in eins geschaffen*). Previously, intelligence was the universal element, the 'indeterminate pit'; whatever being it had it got from outside. But now it is 'individuality', in being as well as universal. That is, signs enable intelligence to step forth into the world as a concrete, discernible individual, entering into relation to others, not just itself; it makes its mark in and on the world. Signs are not simply found, they are created by fantasy. They are intuitable entities, but they are not just there, they are charged with universal significance.

3. 'Everywhere' the 'structures' or products of fantasy are unifications of 'the mind's own', its universal representation, with 'the intuitive' (*des Anschaulichen*), and are recognized as such. Not everyone recognizes specific signs, since these vary from department to department. e.g. the sign 'x' may be a letter, a St Andrew's cross, a multiplication sign, a mark on a ballot paper, an indication of error, or a mark of affection. Hegel is dealing only with the 'abstract moments', such as 'own', 'inner', 'intuitive', 'universality', 'being', which do not vary from department to department.

4. In §438 reason is said to be the identity of the concept's subjectivity and objectivity, of the I and the object. Fantasy's sign-making satisfies this condition. Hence fantasy is reason. But only 'formal' reason, since it does not matter what the 'content' is. In its first occurrence in this sentence 'content' is *Gehalt*, in its second *Inhalt*, and Hegel's italics suggest that he is distinguishing between the two words. The 'indifference' of the 'content' (*Gehalt*), as far as fantasy is concerned, might refer to either of two things: (1) it does not matter whether Christians symbolize their beliefs with a cross or Nazis symbolize their beliefs with a swastika; (2) it does not matter whether Christianity is symbolized with a cross or with a fish. The 'content' (*Inhalt*) that reason determines to truth is more likely to be the content involved in (1), the content of the universal representation. It matters to reason whether one is a Nazi or a Christian. But the content involved in (2), the intuitive sign, may also matter to reason. Some ways of expressing an idea are better, more adequate expressions, than others. However, this still leaves unclear what the difference between *Gehalt* and *Inhalt* is, since the contrast between fantasy and reason 'as such' requires that one and the same content matters to reason, but not to fantasy.

5. When Hegel says that fantasy determines the 'content' (*Gehalt*) 'as being' (*als seiend*), this expression is not especially surprising. What might seem 'surprising' (*auffallend*) is the claim that intelligence 'makes itself be, makes itself the thing' (*sich seiend, sich zur Sache mache*). But, Hegel argues, the second expression is no more surprising than the first. For the 'content' (*Gehalt*) of intelligence is intelligence itself, and the 'determination' it gives to the content, namely being, is also intelligence itself, or at least a determination given to intelligence itself. Hence when intelligence (in the form of fantasy) determines its content as *being*, it *ipso facto* makes itself *be*.

Hegel's 'point' remains unclear. Why is intelligence the same as its content? I may, after all, have a variety of ideas, some of which I embody in images, some I do not. I might have had different ideas from those I actually have. I have, according to Hegel, many images that remain dormant. So there is more to me or to intelligence than I express in images. On the other hand, when I express my ideas, I am said to express myself, my mind, etc. Hegel is stressing that intelligence is not a distinct faculty that underlies its activities and persists unchanged throughout changes in its activities. Intelligence is what it does, or at least: what it does reacts back on it and alters intelligence itself.

6. Here Hegel implicitly distinguishes (as in the *Zusatz*) between symbols, which involve an image of something that shares some characteristics with the object of the representation, such as the strong eagle symbolizing the strength of Jupiter, and signs, which do not: cf. §457, n. 8. The image is only subjectively 'intuitive' (*anschaulich*), not because it is not expressed externally, but because it is an image and therefore has a content that depends on what we happen to have encountered and is not chosen by us. I cannot, for example, symbolize Jupiter's strength by a dove, or indeed by an eagle, if the only eagles I have ever come across have been dilapidated and lethargic. Perhaps Hegel also has in mind that for this reason symbols may not be intersubjective, not at least intercultural, since different cultures may have different conceptions of eagles, even if they have encountered any.

The sign, by contrast, need share no characteristic with the object signified. So there need be no intervening (and controlling) image; it is sheer 'intuitability' (*Anschaulichkeit*): cf. §457, n. 8. But because the sign provides no intrinsic clue as to its meaning, signs, especially linguistic signs, just have to be learned by heart. In this process, the meaning of the signs is repressed. So they come closer to sheer, i.e. meaningless, being. On memory, see §§410, n. 3; 451, nn. 2, 7.

7. 'Proves itself' (*sich . . . bewährt*) means something like 'proves its worth', 'stand the test', 'enters the realm of public discourse'. 'Proof' (*Bewährung*) has a corresponding sense throughout this *Zusatz*: cf. §456, n. 5. On the subjectivity of the 'proof', see §457, n. 6. The 'plastic' (*bildenden*) arts include primarily painting and sculpture.

8. A 'symbol' (*Symbol*) is an 'image' or picture (another meaning of the word *Bild*) of something that shares some features of what the representation is of. It is a sort of picture of the representation. It is intuitable, though it may only be expressed in words, in for example a poem that represents Jupiter as an eagle. Hegel's argument for the transition to non-pictorial signs is this. Since the content of the representation and of the image are so similar, the representation 'joins together only with itself' (*sich nur mit sich selber zusammenschliesst*) in the image. So the image is really dispensable. The representation can 'prove itself' without the intervening image, immediately and 'in and for itself'. This does not mean that it can prove itself without any external embodiment. It means that it can adopt almost any intuitable entity, such as a piece of red cloth, as its 'sign' (*Zeichen*), giving it an entirely different meaning from any that it intrinsically has. By contrast, something adopted as a symbol, such as the eagle, retains at least some of the properties

or meaning that it initially has. (The eagle need not really be strong to symbolize Jupiter. But it must be supposed to be strong.) Hegel's description of this transition as a 'dialectical movement' is somewhat overblown. No clash or unification of opposites is involved. It is simply that the image is so closely attached to the representation that it is no longer needed—as I might, e.g., become so familiar with my lectures that I no longer need notes to give them.

NOTES TO §458

1. A cockade is a badge worn on the hat, especially by servants of court officials. If it is, say, black, we need to have seen black things in order to adopt this colour. But the black colour has no significance in itself. It signifies a certain status, which has nothing to do with blackness. This is quite distinct from the use of black as a symbol of grief or mourning, owing to its tendency to arouse a sombre mood: see §401, nn. 4,16, 17.
2. Two features of the pyramid make it an appropriate metaphor for a sign, that in ancient Egypt it served as the tomb of a king, and that it has a geometrical shape with no intrinsic connection or similarity to the dead person inside it. It is not, e.g., shaped like a person.
3. On space and time, see §448, nn. 1, 11, 12. Intelligence 'generates' (*erzeugt*) the 'form of time and of space' in the sense that it spontaneously projects the content of its sensations out into space and time. It does not read *off* the form of space and time from intrinsically spatio-temporal intuitions; it reads space and time *into* them. (Hegel does not infer that objects are not really spatio-temporal; he believes that they really are spatio-temporal.) With the 'sensory content' that fills space and time, it is otherwise. Intelligence does not generate it or read it into things. It reads it off them. The distance of a tree from myself is in some sense my own doing in a way that its green colour is not. Hence intelligence 'appears' (*erscheint*), i.e. makes its appearance, as receiving (rather than generating) sensory content and forming ideas from it. (It does not just *seem* to do so. *Erscheinen*, 'to appear', is quite different from *scheinen*, 'to seem'.) Once its ideas are formed, they become self-subsistent or 'independent' of sensory intuition, and intelligence can thus use intuition as it likes, to give them determinate embodiment or 'reality' (*Dasein*).
4. 'Productive memory' (*das produktive Gedächtnis*) is not mentioned elsewhere in Enc. III, and in particular it does not appear among the types of memory listed in §461Z. It does appear, however, in Hegel's *Philosophical Propaedeutic*, the notes of his lectures to schoolboys between 1809 and 1811, which were published by Karl Rosenkranz in. 1840:

> [III, sect. 2,] §156. Thus the productive memory produces the connection [*Verknüpfung*] of intuition and representation, but a free connection, where the preceding relationship, in which the intuition forms the basis of the representation, is reversed. In the connection of productive memory the sensory reality [*Dasein*] has no value in and for itself, only the value that the mind gives it.

> §157. The sensory reality is related to another reality through its determinations in general. But in so far as a representation is made into its determination through productive

memory, the reality essentially becomes the relation of representations to other representing beings [Wesen] and it begins therein the theoretical communication of these beings with one another.

§158. Language. The highest work of the productive memory is language, which is partly spoken language, partly written language. Since the productive memory or mnemosyne is the origin of language, we can speak of a further origin only with regard to the invention of determinate signs.

'Productive memory' contrasts with 'reproductive memory', the ability to remember and recall the signs produced by productive memory (*Philosophical Propaedeutic*, III, sect. 2, §162)—as in Enc. III, except that reproductive memory includes all the types of memory mentioned in Enc. III, §461Z., not just what is there called 'reproductive memory'. 'Mnemosyne' comes from *mnêmosunê*, the Greek word for 'memory, remembrance'. It was personified as Mnêmosunê, the mother of the Muses, the nine sister goddesses responsible for inspiration in the arts: history, comedy, tragedy, etc. (Hesiod, *Theogony*, 52–4; Plato, *Theaetetus*, 191d). She owed this status to the fact that, before the invention of writing, poets needed a good memory. Mnemosyne is 'initially abstract', since it is empty until signs are invented.

This raises two questions: Why does Hegel restrict memory to signs? Why does he make memory responsible for the invention of signs rather than simply for their retention and recall? The answers are as follows. *Gedächtnis* and the verb *gedenken*, 'to remember', are etymogically close relatives of *denken*, 'to think' with its perfect participle, *gedacht* ('thought'). Correspondingly, Hegel associates *Gedächtnis* closely with thinking, which follows it immediately in Enc. III (§§465 ff.). Thinking is, for Hegel, pretty much detached from sensory material. Hence *Gedächtnis* too needs to be detached from sensory material, in so far as this is compatible with its retaining at least some of the functions of memory, enough, that is, to deserve the name *Gedächtnis*. Signs are, in Hegel's eyes, far enough removed from sensory material to serve as the objects of *Gedächtnis*. What about other objects of memory, such as people's faces and trips to the seaside? At least some of these are assigned to *Erinnerung*, 'recollection' in the usual sense—remembering a familiar face in a crowd or dwelling on one's memories: §454Z. Hegel retains *Erinnerung* in its usual sense as well as giving it the new sense of 'internalization'. So since we already have a decent word for the memory of things other than signs, why not use *Gedächtnis* for another purpose? Once *Gedächtnis* is reserved for signs, it is then natural to attribute to it the invention of signs as well as their retention and retrieval. 'Productive' imagination or fantasy is responsible for symbols. So why not attribute to it the production of signs? After all, it is far easier to regard imagination as 'productive' than 'memory'. Memory is usually conceived as simply reproductive; if it is productive in the way imagination is, it amounts to misremembering, to 'imagining things'. But in inventing signs, memory is not imagining things. There is nothing to imagine in a sign. A sign is just any old intuition harnessed to a representation, whereas imagination, *Einbildungskraft*, is irretrievably 'pictorial' (*bildlich*). Sign-creation calls for inventiveness, but not for imagination, at least not for the type of imagination required for the creation of symbols, allegories and metaphors. So memory, or rather *Gedächtnis*, takes on the task of sign-creation.

NOTES TO §459

1. The intuitions used for non-linguistic signs are mostly 'spatial' and 'given'. A red flag, e.g., is spatial and, although it is made by us (though not usually by the individual wielding it), its red colour and its shape are found in artefacts not used for this purpose (such as a tablecloth) and even in natural entities (such as blood). Intelligence sublates this intuition, reducing its specific shape and colour to intrinsic insignificance. So it is more appropriate if the intuition serving as a sign sublates itself, surrenders of its own accord to the purposes of intelligence. This happens if the intuition is (1) temporal rather than spatial, since then it disappears as soon as it has served its purpose, and (2) 'posited' or produced by the sign-users from their own resources rather than 'given'. Sounds satisfy these two conditions. We make our own sounds; we do not just imitate naturally occurring sounds such as bird-song. They emerge from our 'own (anthropological) naturalness'. That is, the sounds we make depend on our physiological and emotional make-up; they are not intrinsically intelligent. On sounds and 'voice' as expressions of inwardness, see §401, nn. 27, 28.

2. 'Speech' is *Rede* ('speech, talk, etc.'); 'language' is *Sprache*, which comes from *sprechen*, 'to speak', but here (and mostly) means 'language', the 'system' governing, and actualized by, particular utterances, including written statements. The distinction is similar to Ferdinand de Saussure's distinction between *parole* and *langue*. Why does Hegel say that they give a higher 'reality' (*Dasein*) to 'representations' as well as 'sensations' and 'intuitions'? If he is using 'representations' in the narrow sense (as 'universal ideas'), these are given a higher reality in a quite different way from sensations and intuitions: representations are expressed, while sensations and intuitions are sublated. He is more probably using 'representations' in a wider and looser sense, whereas the realm 'of representation' (*des Vorstellens*) is the realm of representation in the narrow and strict sense.

3. Hegel considers three possible explanations of the 'material' (*Material*) of language, i.e. why we use the range of sounds we do and why we use a certain sound for a certain 'representation':

   (1) The 'idea' (*Vorstellung*) of 'mere contingency'. This 'has disappeared' (*hat sich . . . verloren*). This presumably means that no one, not even Hegel himself, believes that there is no rhyme or reason to the sounds we use.

   (2) Our sounds depend on a 'symbolism relating to external objects', in particular on 'imitation' of their sounds or noises. This applies only to a few, not very important words, such as *Rauschen* ('rustling, hissing', etc.), *Sausen* ('blowing, buzzing', etc.), and *Knarren* ('creaking').

   (3) Our sounds depend on 'inner symbolism'. A vowel, for example, is a sound pronounced without stoppage or friction of the breath, and one

vowel differs from another, depending on the height of the tongue in the mouth, on whether the tongue is at the back or the front of the mouth, and on whether the lips are rounded or unrounded. In this theory, the utterance of a certain sound is conceived as a 'gesture' (*Gebärde*), as a bodily movement with a specific significance: cf. §§401, n. 20; 411, n. 4. Similarly, each of the elementary movements or positions into which the sound can be analysed (such as rounded lips) is a gesture with a specific significance. Hegel agrees that this may be so. But he adds that whatever symbolic meanings these gestures may have originally had, in virtue of being intuitions of a certain sort, has been suppressed by the reduction of the gestures to signs, since this sublated the intuitive content that carried the symbolic meaning.

4. Wilhelm von Humboldt (1767–1835) delivered *Über den Dualis* as a lecture to the Academy of Sciences in Berlin on. 16 April 1827. It was published in 1828 in Berlin in the *Abhandlungen der historisch-philologischen Klasse der königlichen Akademie der Wissenschaften zu Berlin aus dem Jahre 1827*. In Greek, Latin, and German, words—nouns, adjectives, pronouns, and verbs—are inflected, that is, modified to express a grammatical relation. For example, the endings of nouns, etc. vary according to number, the number, that is, of entities to which they are currently applied. Latin and German have only two numbers, singular and plural. A noun, etc. will have different forms depending on whether it is singular, denoting only one object, or plural, denoting more than one object. But no other numerical difference is indicated by inflection. However, ancient Greek had a third number, the dual. A noun, etc. may have a special form if it denotes just two objects, though this usage is not compulsory and the plural form is commonly used to denote two objects. Some languages have a 'trial' as well as a dual and a plural, that is, a special form for denoting three objects. Humboldt considered the dual in other languages, as well as Greek, and classified its uses. Friedrich von Schlegel (1772–1829) also associated the grammatical complexity of a language with its antiquity: 'If we examine the grammar of the old dialects, considering the Gothic and Anglo-Saxon as examples of the German; and the Icelandic of the Sclavonian branch of our language—we shall not only find a perfect with an augmentative, as in the Greek and Indian, but a dual, and also an exact definition of gender, and relation of participle, and declension, which are now lost; as well as many inflections, which are already somewhat modified, and less easy of recognition. . . . In short, the study of these old monuments of the German language will undeniably establish the fact, that their grammatical structure was originally the same as that of the Latin and Greek' (*On the Indian Language*, in *The Aesthetic and Miscellaneous Works of Friedrich von Schlegel*, trans. E. J. Millington (London,: Bohn 1849), 442). Hegel is right, at least to the extent that every known language has a complex grammar, however culturally primitive its speakers may be in other respects. It is, however, hard to say that the grammar of one language is 'less complete' than that of another. The dual seems superfluous; its lack can easily be compensated for by using a word for 'two'.

5. The second part of the sentence involves three ambiguities: (1) Is the 'particular province' language itself or a province within language? The italicized 'particular' suggests that it is a province within language, rather than language as such, which we would expect to be described as 'universal'. (2) Does 'which' (*welche*) refer to 'a further development' (*eine weitere Fortbildung*) or to 'language'? (3) Is 'which' the subject of the subordinate clause or is it the object, giving e.g. 'which an externally practical activity summons to its aid'? (A script both requires practical activity, namely writing, and assists such practical activities as trade and government.) At all events, it seems to give Hegel's reason for considering script only 'in passing', meaning something like: 'There is a province of language which, unlike plain speech, makes use of practical activity, e.g. gestures and gesticulation. Writing is a development within this particular province. Hence it deserves to be mentioned only in passing'. This is mildly at variance with his later suggestion that an alphabetic script clarifies the pronunciation of a language: see §459, n. 11.
6. Writing consists of marks, usually visible marks, on a surface, so all writing 'proceeds to the field of immediate spatial intuition'. But there are two main types of writing: (1) Non-phonological, where there is no clear relationship between the written marks and the sounds of the language. Usually the written marks directly indicate things or ideas, sometimes pictorially, sometimes more conventionally. Hegel calls this 'hieroglyphic script', since Egyptian hieroglyphics was the example most familiar to him. ('Hieroglyphic' comes from the Greek for 'sacred carving'; the script was found most commonly on tombs, temples, etc.) Hegel classifies Chinese as a hieroglyphic script, but this is inaccurate, since the characters refer to words or other linguistic units, not directly to things or ideas. But he is right in thinking that the characters do not usually relate to the sound of spoken words. (2) Phonological, where there is a clear relationship between the written marks and the sounds of the language. Hegel calls this 'alphabetic script' (*Buchstabenschrift*). He passes over another type of phonological script: syllabic writing, such as Mycenaean Greek and Japanese katakana, where each character stands for a spoken syllable, usually a consonant followed by a vowel. In an alphabetic script, spoken words are analysed into distinct phonemes and the characters directly correspond to the phonemes. For more on writing systems, see *The Cambridge Encyclopaedia of Language*, by David Crystal (Cambridge: Cambridge University Press, 1987), 194–203.
7. Gottfried Wilhelm Leibniz ((1646–1716) proposed a '*characteristica universalis*' ('universal characterization') that would display the structure of concepts and their relationship to other concepts by analysing them into basic elementary concepts, which were to be represented by symbols, a sort of alphabet of thoughts. See *Die philosophischen Schriften von Gottfried Wilhelm Leibniz*, ed. C. J. Gerhardt (Berlin: weidmann, 1890), vii. 3–247: 'Scientia Generalis. Characteristica'. As a more recent example, Gottlob Frege's idea of a *Begriffsschrift* ('conceptual writing') is similar; formal logic represents ideas and their relationships without regard to the sound of the spoken words symbolized. Leibniz had two aims: logical transparency and ease of communication. Hegel tries to show

that neither aim would be fulfilled. In addition, these two aims are likely to conflict with each other.

As Hegel says, our signs for numbers and operations on them are non-phonological, if not hieroglyphic: '2 + 2 = 4' does not refer directly to the sounds in the way that 'Two plus two equals four' does. Again, the expression 'H$_2$O' bears no relation to the spoken word 'water', but unlike the latter it displays the chemical composition of the substance—in a manner not wholly unlike the way in which Chinese represents a 'crowd' by three occurrences of the symbol for 'man'. On chemical symbolism, see also Maurice P. Crosland, *Historical Studies in the Language of Chemistry* (New York: Dover, 1962).

8. According to Crystal, *Cambridge Encyclopaedia of Language*, 202: 'The earliest-known alphabet was the North Semitic, which developed around 1700 BC in Palestine and Syria. It consisted of 22 consonant letters. The Hebrew, Arabic, and Phoenician alphabets were based on this model. Then, around 1000 BC, the Phoenician alphabet was itself used as a model by the Greeks, who added letters for vowels. Greek in turn became the model for Etruscan (*c*.800 BC), whence came the letters of the ancient Roman alphabet, and ultimately all Western alphabets.'

The embassy of George Macartney, Earl (1737–1806) to China is recorded in *An authentic account of an Embassy from the King of Great Britain to the Emperor of China . . . Taken chiefly from the papers of his Excellency the Earl of Macartney*, ed. Sir George Staunton (London, 1797). This was translated into German as *Des Grafen Macartney Gesandtschaftsreise nach China, welche er auf Befehl des Königs von Grossbritannien, George des Dritten, in den Jahren. 1792 bis 1794 unternommen hat; nebst Nachrichten über China und einen kleinen Teil der chinesischen Tartarei, etc.* (Berlin, 1797–9).

9. By 'name' (*Name*) here, and elsewhere in §459, Hegel means not a proper name, but a common noun or substantive, such as 'lion', though the points he makes are applicable to words of other types, such as verbs. A 'sensory object' such as water can be designated by a permanent 'hieroglyphic' sign, 'H$_2$O', now that we have settled the chemical composition of water and are unlikely to change our view on it. But 'spiritual matters', such as the state, art, religion, God, etc. cannot be definitively analysed in this way. At any given time reasonable people hold different views about them and our views of them change over time. Hence we need a name that is non-committal as to their nature, as a sort of peg on which to hang our diverse and changing views of them. Otherwise we would have only different and changing 'hieroglyphic' signs for them. On changes in chemical terminology, see M. P. Crosland, *Historical Studies in the Language of Chemistry*, esp. 102–4, 294–6.

Hegel perhaps also has in mind different approaches to philosophical terminology. Christian Wolff, under the inspiration of Leibniz, attempted to give each philosophical term a clear, unequivocal definition, to use any given term only in the sense defined for it, and to use no other term in that sense. By contrast, Hegel's terminology is fluid and developing. The meaning of a term such as 'being' develops as his system unfolds.

10. Hegel has an oversimple view of Chinese script. According to Arthur Cooper's 'Chinese Evidence on the Evolution of Language', in Richard L. Gregory (ed.), *The Oxford Companion to the Mind* (Oxford: Oxford University Press, 1987), 143: Chinese 'symbols or characters each represent a *logos* or unit of meaning.... In Chinese this is always a grammatically invariable monosyllable, which may be a word used independently, like "house" or "boat", or "man" or "kind"; or may be combined with other such monosyllables to form polysyllables, like "houseboat", "boatman", or "mankind". All words of more than one syllable in Chinese were at least originally of this type; word-forming syllables such as "-er" in "farmer" and so on, which never existed as independent words, do not feature in Chinese word-making. Furthermore, grammatical inflexions which also had no independence as words, like our plural "-s" and past tense "-ed", had no place either. Chinese lacks the kind of grammar that makes them necessary: expression of plurality, tense, and the like in Chinese is voluntary, and when necessary is performed by means of independent syllables such as "two-three", "some", "just now", "long since", and so forth.' Chinese is an 'analytical' language, in which grammatical relationships are shown by word order, not by word endings. Chinese script is more appropriate to such a language than it would be to 'synthetic' or inflecting languages, such as Latin or Greek.

It is thus not true that Chinese lacks words; it has basic words. Nor is it true that compound words are in effect definitions. The Chinese character for 'bright' is composed of the character for 'sun' and the character for 'moon'; this is not a definition of 'bright'. Compound words need not prevent us changing our view of what they designate. 'Philosophy', for example, originally meant 'love of wisdom', but Hegel argued that philosophy is in fact wisdom, not the love of it, while nevertheless advocating the retention of the word 'philosophy': PS, p. 3. Similarly, the expression 'Holy Roman Empire' did not prevent Voltaire from saying that it was neither holy, nor Roman, nor an empire. It is not obvious therefore that the Chinese script hampers cultural development.

Hegel is on firmer ground when he turns to its suitability as a means of communication. An alphabet has around 20–30 characters, whereas Chinese once had nearly 50,000, and today 'basic literacy requires knowledge of some 2,000 characters' (Crystal, *Cambridge Encyclopaedia of Language*, 200).

11. Hegel's view about the effect of script on spoken language conflicts with his view that written language is a side issue: cf. §459, n. 5. The German language is also vulnerable to his complaints about Chinese. Hegel himself was renowned for his strong Swabian accent rather than the 'purity' of his articulation. Ideally, an alphabet provides just one 'grapheme' for each 'phoneme'. But this ideal is not usually met, often because spelling has not kept up with changes in pronunciation. English is particularly irregular in its grapheme-phoneme pairings, with e.g. umpteen different pronunciations of '-ough'. Elsewhere Hegel makes a virtue of the opposite meanings that some German words, such as *aufheben* (cf. §381, n. 13) have: Enc. I, §96Z. 'Parler sans accent', 'speaking without accent', is a stock French expression for speaking without a peculiar, e.g. regional

or foreign, mode of pronunciation, but Hegel also takes it to mean speaking without emphasizing particular syllables and words by stress, pitch, or intensity.

12. Alphabetic script analyses a word such as 'cat' into its 'elements', which are here the complete phonemes represented by 'c', 'a', and 't', not the rounded lips, etc. referred to in §459, n. 3. They are 'brought to the form of universality', since they are not individual tokens, but universal types, that appear not only in different occurrences of the word 'cat', but also in other words, such as 'mat'. A written word encourages 'reflexion' on the word as such, because it is a sign of the word, a sign of a sign. However, according to Crystal (*Cambridge Encyclopaedia of Language*, 200) and Cooper (see §459, n. 10) Chinese script is 'logographic': each grapheme represents a word. Can we not say, then, that a Chinese grapheme too is a sign of a sign and that therefore Chinese script too makes the word an 'object' (*Gegenstand*) of reflexion? Hegel might reply that the word or logos of which the Chinese grapheme is a sign is not the spoken word, but a neutral word that may be either spoken or written but is intrinsically neither. Hence the grapheme is not the sign of a *sign*, since the neutral word is not a sign until it is spoken, written, or expressed in some other way. In practice, Chinese script is dependent on and posterior to Chinese speech. But it is not logically and essentially dependent on and posterior to speech in the way that alphabetic script is. Logically, the written and the spoken language run parallel. Moreover, even if we agree that Chinese script does encourage reflexion on words, it is, Hegel might say, the wrong sort of reflexion. Simple characters tell us next to nothing about the word, while compound characters give a sort of definition and hence break up the unity of the word in a way that phonological analysis does not. The matter is too complex for a definitive verdict here. Many Chinese characters, for example, involve, in addition to a semantic element, a phonetic element to remind readers how the word is pronounced.

13. Hegel does not comment on the great facility of the German language for forming compounds of the 'houseboat' type. It is often no easier than in the case of Chinese compounds to infer the meaning of the compound word from its constituents. *Schein*, for example, is 'shine; semblance, seeming', and *heilig* is 'holy, pious'. These words are compounded in two ways: *scheinheilig*, 'hypocritical, sanctimonious', and *Heiligenschein*, 'a halo'.

A Kua is not a Chinese character, but a type of symbol found in the I Ching ('Book of Changes'), one of the 'five classics' of Confucianism, though it was originally a system of divination traditionally dated to the twelfth century BC. The symbols are formed from two types of line: a solid line, _____, representing yang (the male cosmic principle) and a broken line, __ __, representing yin (the female cosmic principle). The ceaseless interaction of yang and yin explain all being and change; this is represented by the diagrams formed from their lines. The basic diagrams are trigrams, formed from three horizontal parallel lines, in all the possible combinations of the two types of line. Hence there are eight of those, the pa kua or 'eight diagrams', said to have been discovered by the emperor Fu Hsi on the back of a tortoise in the twenty-fourth century BC:

Each trigram has a name, a root meaning, and a symbolic meaning; Thus the first is Ch'ien, Heaven; it is active and represents the father. The eighth is Tui, Lake, is joyful, and represents the youngest daughter. And so on. Pairs of trigrams are then placed one above the other to form hexagrams, of which there are thus sixty-four. For example, two occurrences of Ch'ien gives:

This is also called Ch'ien. As a combination of heaven, active and heaven, active, it stands for creativity, success, perseverance, etc. And so on. These hexagrams, attributed to Wen Wang in the twelfth century, supposedly contain profound meanings applicable to life, if they are rightly interpreted. After devising the binary system of arithmetical notation, published in his *De progressione dyadica* (1679), Leibniz was introduced to the I Ching and was intrigued by the parallel it presented to his own binary system. See Alfred Douglas, *The Oracle of Change: How to Consult the I Ching* (London: Gollancz, 1971), app. 1.

14. Hegel does not object to analysis of a representation or a thought as such. To take a simple case, we can analyse the idea of man into the 'abstract moments' *rational* and *animal*. What he objects to is the proposal that we then dispense with the word 'man' and use instead the combination 'rational animal' or whatever more complex expression might result from the analysis of rationality and animality. Similarly we can analyse water as H_2O, as long as we retain some such word as 'water'. The reason Hegel gave for this above (see §459, n. 9) was that our analysis of the thing or representation may change over time, so that we need a neutral name as a peg to hang our varying analyses on. The reason he gives here, by contrast, is that a simple, non-committal name is required for a simple, unified representation or thought. He does not give an argument for supposing that we need simple thoughts, but arguments such as the following are available: (1) The claims 'Water is H_2O' or 'Man is a rational animal' presuppose the simple thought of water and of man. (2) Teaching the language to children or foreigners as yet unacquainted with our analyses involves focusing their attention on a unitary thing, prior to its analysis. (3) Even if we dispense with the words 'water' and 'man', and make do with 'H_2O' and 'rational animal', we still need to focus on hydrogen, oxygen, rationality, and animality as unitary notions. If hydrogen in turn is analysed in terms of its atomic structure, and if e.g. the proton is again analysed, and so on indefinitely, our thought can never get a grip on anything. We have, at some point or other, to focus on a unitary thing, even if things are in principle analysable ad infinitum.

Such arguments as these may tell against Leibniz's project, but they are not especially effective against Chinese. Chinese does have simple words, it does not analyse thoughts or things ad infinitum, and spoken Chinese, at least, is as teachable as English. The Chinese need have no more difficulty in using their compound words than we have in using 'houseboat', etc. However, to the extent that a compound word comes to express a unitary idea, it is likely to cease to involve a perspicuous definition or analysis. 'Houseboat' gives an analysis of sorts. But the word 'ringleader', though originally compound, hardly does. It is difficult to say what type of ring, or what sense of 'ring', it involves; it expresses a unitary idea that resists analysis in terms of its component words.

The 'representing' (*vorstellende*) intelligence is the intelligence involved in ordinary language use. 'Thinking' and 'thought' refer primarily to Hegel's logic and its analytical and synthetic procedures: see Enc. I, §§227–9.

15. Here Hegel reverts to his earlier point, that 'concrete', i.e. complex, spiritual representations admit of various and changing analyses. Perhaps he would have done better to say that their 'relations', e.g. the relation between the ideas of state and of society, are in any case 'complicated and confused', whether or not we have a 'hieroglyphic' script. But an alphabetic script can ignore these complications by using simple words for them and forgoing the semantic analysis that a hieroglyphic script might require. He adds (as in argument (3) in §459, n. 14) that analysis can proceed indefinitely.

According to Crosland, *Historical Studies in the Language of Chemistry*, 99, 222, 'hydrochloric acid' (*Salzsäure*, lit. 'salt acid') was called 'philosophical spirit of vitriol' (in seventeenth- and eighteenth-century chemical works), and 'muriatic acid' (until the early nineteenth century); the name 'hydrochloric acid' was proposed by Gay Lussac in 1810. Since 'muria' is Latin for 'brine', 'muriatic acid' is equivalent to *Salzsäure*.

16. On the educational value of the alphabet, cf. §396, n. 15.

17. On the question whether reading requires 'phonic mediation' or is solely 'by eye', see Crystal, *Cambridge Encyclopaedia of Language*, 210-11. Crystal supports a compromise similar to Hegel's: 'The "ear" approach (sometimes referred to as a "bottom-up" or "Phoenician" theory, because of its reliance on basic letter units) is evidently very important during the initial stages. Perhaps after several exposures to a word, a direct print-meaning pathway comes to be built up. But the "eye" approach (sometimes referred to as a "top-down" or "Chinese" theory, because of its reliance on whole-word units) is certainly needed in order to explain most of what goes on in fluent adult reading' (ibid. 211).

Hegel's train of thought is hard to follow, in part because he is trying to have his cake and eat it. Reading of an alphabetic script becomes 'hieroglyphic' or 'Chinese', and so 'for itself' a dumb reading, etc. ('For itself' seems to mean here 'of/in itself', i.e. leaving aside the non-hieroglyphic reading that precedes it and the consequences of this non-hieroglyphic stage, rather than 'as far as consciousness goes'.) So might not writing/reading and speech/listening be equal and parallel in status? After all, sounds and sights are intrinsically of equal status, neither dependent on the other. (We might add that the congenitally deaf can learn to read, albeit with difficulty, and that the Chinese can read, though again with some difficulty.) But, says Hegel, sounds and sights are not equal when it comes to 'intelligence': speech, not 'visible language', is its immediate and unconditional mode of expression. Hegel's main argument for this claim is that temporal sounds, unlike spatial sights, are self-sublating (see §459, n. 1) and are 'less sensory' than sights (see §459, n. 18).

18. On the etymological affinity of *Denken* ('thinking') and *Gedächtnis* ('memory') see §458, n. 4. Memory is the transition from representation to thinking, and the 'mediation of representations by the less sensory element' is essential to it.

NOTE TO §460

1. Hegel speaks here as if there were three items in play, the 'name', the 'intuition produced by intelligence', and the 'meaning' of this intuition, e.g. the name 'cat', an utterance of the sound 'cat', and the representation of a cat. But at this stage the name is just an 'individual transient production'. So the name amounts to the same thing as the intuition. The name is nevertheless the 'connection' (*Verknüpfung*) of the intuition and the representation, since it expresses or connotes the representation. The connection is external. The individual, perhaps an infant, said 'cat', when it saw a cat, but it could equally have said 'tac' or 'dog', and there is as yet no guarantee that it will say 'cat' next time it sees a cat or wants to express its cat-representation. This externality is in need of internalization or 'recollection' (*Erinnerung*) by 'memory'.

NOTES TO §461

1. As 'representation in general', intelligence internalized and universalized 'the first immediate intuition', i.e. intuitions that do not serve as symbols or signs of anything else, in three stages: forming an image of it (§452), storing the image in its 'nocturnal pit' (§453), and reviving the image to recognize something it has encountered before (§454). Memory does something similar to intuitions serving as signs in three (very roughly) parallel stages: name-retaining memory, reproductive memory, and mechanical memory.
2. Having uttered the sound 'cat' to express its cat-representation on one occasion, intelligence makes this 'cat'-cat connection its own or 'takes' it 'into its possession' (*zu dem Ihrigen machend*), resolving, as it were, to use the sound 'cat' on future occasions when it needs to express its cat-representation. This makes the 'cat'-cat connection 'universal' and it also turns the individual 'cat'-sound into a universal 'representation', a name that can be used on indefinitely many occasions. The 'cat'-representation and the cat-representation, the 'meaning', are now 'objectively combined'. They will in future go together, as long as we do not change the name.

So far we have two representations combined, a cat-representation and a 'cat'-representation. This means that 'the content, or meaning' (*der Inhalt, die Bedeutung,*), i.e. the cat-representation, and 'the sign', i.e. the 'cat'-representation, are 'identified' (*identifiziert*), are 'one representation'. This single representation, or 'the representing' (*das Vorstellen*) it involves, is internally complex or 'concrete', since it fuses together the representations of cat and of 'cat'. It is not clear what Hegel means by saying 'with the content as its reality' (*der Inhalt als dessen Dasein*). He seems to be taking the concrete word-meaning complex as a case of the concept-reality complex discussed in §437, n. 2. But if (as I have assumed) the 'content' is equivalent to the 'meaning', we would expect the word to be the 'reality' rather than its meaning. One answer to this might be that the 'content' is now not so much the meaning, i.e. the cat-representation, as the things denoted by the word, i.e. actual cats. But it is more likely that the 'content' is still the 'meaning' and that Hegel treats the meaning as the 'reality', because the highest stage of memory, 'mechanical' memory, disregards the meanings of words, concentrating only on words as such, and this, in Hegel's view, is the transition to *conceptual* thinking.

Hegel supplies no good argument for his claim that the two representations fuse into one. He might have done so by referring back to what he said about habit: see §410, esp. nn. 3 and 9. He explains what he means by the claim in §461Z: hearing a word and understanding its meaning are not two distinct, successive events. Moreover, understanding a word does not require any intuition or image of what it denotes: §462 Remark.

3. Hegel's belief that comprehension precedes production seems to be supported by one's experience of learning a foreign language, and also by the fact that in one's native language one's passive vocabulary (the words one can understand) is usually much larger than one's active vocabulary (the words one readily uses). But 'there is increasing evidence that this simple relationship does not always obtain. Production may precede comprehension, or the two processes may be so intimately connected that they develop in parallel. There is certainly a great deal of evidence to show that children produce a word or construction without having a full understanding of it' (Crystal, *Cambridge Encyclopaedia of Language*, 232).

The distinction between comprehension and production possibly corresponds to the distinction between name-retaining memory and reproductive memory, a distinction which is otherwise not very clear. A difficulty in supposing such a correspondence is that Hegel speaks throughout of 'intelligence' (*Intelligenz*) in the singular, and in §460, etc. intelligence is regarded as producing signs. But if comprehension precedes production, we must suppose that one intelligent being understands the signs produced by another intelligent being, but cannot yet produce them itself. If this is what Hegel meant, one reason why he did not make it clear may be his predilection for abstract terms such as 'intelligence'. But another reason is that he is trying to explain how language emerges from more basic capacities. If what emerges first is language comprehension, he cannot explain the emergence of language as such, since no one can comprehend words unless someone has first produced them. At most he can explain the emergence of language in a single individual, in particular a child born into an existing linguistic community.

A more likely possibility is that both the understanding of a word encountered and the production of a word fall under the heading of reproductive memory, while retentive memory simply keeps the signs in readiness for use. At any rate, §462 shows no sign of reviving the disparity between comprehension and production.

NOTES TO §462

1. Throughout §462, 'thing' is not *Ding*, but *Sache*, which has the flavour of 'the thing that matters', as in 'The thing is that . . .' or 'That's the thing!' The *Sache* is the thing denoted by the name, e.g. the lion(s) denoted by the word 'lion'. No distinction is drawn here between understanding a name ('recognizes [*erkennt*] the thing in the name') and producing it ('with the thing it has the name'). Name and thing are inextricably linked. This is why the name-representation and the thing-representation are one representation: cf. §461, n. 2. The name is the *Existenz* (the 'existence' but also the 'emergence': cf. §403, n. 2) of the 'content', i.e. the name 'cat' points outwards directly at cats. Hence the name is the 'externality' (*Äusserlichkeit*) of intelligence within itself. So the 'recollection'-cum-internalization (*Erinnerung*: cf. §402, n. 6) of the name is also the 'self-externalization' (*Entäusserung*) or alienation of the intelligence.

2. The *Assoziation* in question is not the 'association' of each 'particular' name with its meaning or the thing it denotes, but the association of names with each other. Ferdinand de Saussure distinguished two types of relationship between words. In the sentences 'She may swim' and 'He will ride', the words 'she', 'may', and 'swim' are related *syntagmatically*, and so are the words 'he', 'will', and 'ride'. The words 'he' and 'she', on the other hand, are related *associatively* or *paradigmatically*, and so are the words 'may' and 'will', and also the pair 'swim' and 'ride'; the words in each pair contrast with each other, and each might replace its partner to produce a grammatical sentence. Thus, we can replace 'she' with 'he', giving 'He may swim', but we cannot replace 'she' with 'will'.

   If Hegel has either of these relationships in mind, it is likely to be the syntagmatic relationship, since this is (more or less) what he discusses under the heading of 'mnemonics'—only in that case the association of the names depends on the association of a series of images, not on the 'meaning of the determinations, etc.' It is true that in learning grammar, e.g. the cases of a noun, one is learning words that are related *associatively*. But the 'series' that intelligence most obviously runs through 'as it senses, etc.' are series of syntagmatically related words. Perhaps the 'association' of names is introduced as a counterpart to the association of ideas: cf. §455, n. 4, and on the parallel between 'representation in general' and memory, see §461, n. 1. See also §463, n. 1.

3. The mnemonic system to which Hegel refers was known to the Greeks (who attributed its invention to the sixth-century poet Simonides of Ceos) and was described by Cicero in his *De Oratore* (55 BC). The first step is to memorize a series of 'places', such as landmarks on a journey or the rooms of a large building. Secondly, the series of words or ideas to be remembered is broken down into units, and each of these is associated with an image. If for example the first word to be remembered is 'Hegel', I form an image of Hegel and imagine him at the first landmark (e.g. waiting at Oxford railway station) or in the first room of the building. And so on. The same sequence of places can be used and reused for

indefinitely many series of words or ideas. The method and its history is described by F. A. Yates, *The Art of Memory* (London: Routledge, 1966).

4. The German for 'by heart, by rote, inside out' is *auswendig*, which primarily means 'outward(ly), external(ly), outside'. Thus what is mnemonically impressed is not really produced *outwards* or 'by heart' (auswendig), i.e. 'from the inside' (*von innen heraus*). The opposite of *auswendig*, *inwendig*, means 'inward(ly), etc.'. It has no common figurative meaning corresponding to that of *auswendig*, but Hegel plays on the contrast. The name is a 'reality' (*Dasein*) produced by intelligence. This reality is 'known inside out' (*einem . . . Auswendigen*, lit. 'an outward') but enclosed 'in the inside' (*in das Inwendige*) of intelligence. It is intelligence's 'outside, its existing side' (*auswendige, existierende Seite*), but 'within intelligence itself' (*innerhalb ihrer selbst*).

The wordplay depends on two points: (1) *Auswendig* and *inwendig* look like opposites, and are opposites in their literal sense. But in its figurative sense *auswendig* is not opposite to *inwendig*. What is known by heart lies within. (2) Even when they are taken literally, *auswendig* and *inwendig* do not necessarily exclude each other. 'Inside' and 'outside' are relative terms: what is outside the bedroom may be inside the house and what is inside the intelligence may be outside its 'nocturnal pit'. But Hegel seems not to mean this, but rather that if something is really outside, then it is also fully inside. That is, if something is properly remembered, i.e. outside, then it comes from deep within us, i.e. inside. The point is similar to the earlier claim that intelligence's 'recollection' of the name is also its 'self-externalization': cf. §462, n. 1. There, however, the externalization depends on the fact that the name points towards external things, whereas here it refers to our overt utterance of names. But Hegel gives a different account of this internal-external dialectic in the *Zusatz*: see §462, n. 5.

5. A word is both 'external', something uttered perceptibly and publicly, and 'internal', having (unlike e.g. a sneeze) a meaning impressed on it by intelligence. There are three areas of difficulty: (1) It is unclear why thought requires words. Hegel gives three reasons: (i) If I think without words, I am not 'aware of' (*wissen von*) my thoughts; (ii) if I think without words, my thoughts are not 'determinate, actual'; (iii) 'the ineffable' (*das Unaussprechliche*) is 'murky, fermenting'. His implicit argument for (i) is that our thoughts need to get the form of 'objectivity' (*Gegenständlichkeit*), of 'being distinct' (*Unterschiedenseins*) from our inwardness, for us to be aware of them. This argument perhaps depends on the ambiguity of 'objectivity', which means both 'being a real object' and 'being an intentional object', i.e. an object of our awareness. It has, nevertheless, some plausibility. The idea is that if I am too close to my own thoughts I am not aware of them—like the spectacles on my nose. His argument for (ii) is that the verbal expression of a thought gives it definiteness, actuality and clarity; it completes it into a fully fledged thought. A child, e.g., does not have determinate thoughts until it is able to express them outwardly: cf. §411, n. 1, and Enc. I, §140 on the inner and the outer. Points (i) and (ii) show how the expression *für sich*, 'for itself', came to refer, for Hegel, both to actuality and to self-awareness: cf. §383, n. 1. Point (iii) differs from (ii) in that what a person thinks without words need not be

intrinsically 'ineffable' or inexpressible. (2) It is not clear whether what thought requires is publicly uttered words or only thought words. When Hegel speaks of the 'articulated sound', this suggests that the words need to be uttered. But what Mesmer (see §379, n. 3) attempted was thinking without any words at all, not even thought words. Moreover, the idea that we have to think in words, even if we do not utter them, would give a good sense to his claim that the word is the 'outside' of intelligence, only 'within intelligence itself'. Hegel probably believes that for there to be words at all words have on occasion to be publicly uttered; that one cannot have proper thoughts without thinking in words; that one can have thoughts without uttering the corresponding words; but that the public utterance or inscription of the relevant words often clarifies one's thoughts. (3) Hegel arguably underrates non-verbal modes of expression: painting, musical notes, and so on. For more discussion of this, see ILA.

On the question whether thought is possible without words, see W. James, *Principles of Psychology*, 260–8.

6. The claims that 'the genuine thought is the thing' and that 'the word' is the thing are ambiguous. *Sache*, 'thing', is used widely (as in 'The thing is, that . . .') and need not contrast with 'thought' or 'word'. So the claims could mean that the thing in question is just the thought or the word, and that we are not here concerned with any further thing, such as a lion, that the thought or the word denotes. But this would mean that Hegel is here considering thoughts that are about thoughts themselves or words that are just words, regardless of their connotation or denotation, and he does not seem to be doing this at this stage, though he is moving in that direction. More probably, then, he simply means that one does not need an intuition of the 'thing' (such as a lion), or even an image of it, in order to think or speak about it. I can e.g. think about two billion unicorns or two trillion electrons without having, or ever having had, any intuition or image that corresponds more than remotely to the object of my thought.

7. Sache was originally a 'lawsuit', but came to mean 'thing, subject matter, etc.' It gave rise to two adjectives, *sächlich* ('pertaining to the thing', and also '(grammatically) neuter') and *sachlich*, 'pertaining to the thing, relevant, impartial, etc.' Intelligence here makes itself 'into something thingly' (*zu einem Sächlichen*). At first it sounds as if this means not that the intelligence is itself a thing, but that it is wholly absorbed in things, making no contribution of its own. Now, however, the words have become united with 'my inwardness' and have, moreover, shed their 'objectivity' (*Gegenständlichkeit*), i.e. their reference to external things such as lions. The words have become 'thingly' or thing-like, rather than meaningful, and correspondingly my memory has become thing-like, rather than mind-like. This is why it can become 'mechanical'. Strictly speaking, only things can be mechanical, not minds. But in memory the mind becomes a thing and so becomes mechanical.

As in the Paragraph (see §462, n. 1), *Erinnerung*, 'recollection'-cum-internalization, contrasts with *Entäusserung*, 'alienation' or (self-)externalization. This is Hegel's usual view of the transformation of opposites into each other: when one opposite is taken to 'excess' it veers round into the other opposite. Here the opposites apply to different things: what is recollected is the word, while what is alienated is the intelligence. But Hegel's general idea is clear enough: as the word and its meaning become very familiar to me, its meaning 'can disappear'. Does this mean that I use it meaningfully without thinking about its meaning, or that I really do forget about its meaning? For more on this see §463.

NOTES TO §463

1. This refers back to the last sentence of the preceding Paragraph, discussed in §462, n. 2. If (as §462 suggests) the 'interconnection' (*Zusammenhang*) of names with each other depends on the meaning of the names, then the 'connection' (*Verknüpfung*) of a name with its meaning is only a 'synthesis' (*Synthese*, 'putting together'): cf. §451, n. 3; 457, n. 2. Thus we have two things conjoined or synthesized: the meaning and 'being as names' (*mit dem Sein als Namen*). So when the intelligence externalizes itself by uttering or thinking a sequence of meaningfully interconnected names, such as 'She may swim', it has not 'simply returned into itself', because the names it has uttered are not intrinsically meaningful; their meaning lurks behind them in the depths of intelligence. This is made even clearer in §462, where the meaning responsible for the interconnection of the names is the meaning of the 'determinations of the sensing, . . . intelligence', i.e. the meaning conferred by non-verbal features of intelligence.

   Why does Hegel claim that the meaning-dependent interconnection of words implies that a word and its meaning are only synthesized? One argument might be this: If I utter a meaningful sequence of words, such as 'She may swim', I could just as well have uttered the different sequence 'He will ride'. That I uttered the one and not the other, depends on my meaning, what I meant or what I meant to say. But that sort of meaning is only contingently connected to the words taken separately, even to the meaning of the whole sequence. The words 'she', 'may', and 'swim' can be used in quite different sequences, and used by people who mean to say quite different things. To this argument the reply might be made that we need to distinguish between two types of meaning, between what a given speaker means to say on a given occasion, and the meanings of the words that enable the speaker to use them to say what he means. The latter type of meaning, word-meaning, does not vary from occasion to occasion and from speaker to speaker in the way that the former type, speaker's meaning, does. To this objection Hegel can reply: I agree that there are these two types of meaning. My problem is to find out how intrinsic word-meaning comes about. It cannot arise simply from the utterance or consideration of meaningful sequences of words. What these give us is, at most, the speaker's meaning.

2. This is the response to the supposition ('In so far as . . .') made in the preceding sentence. Intelligence is 'the universal', 'the being [*das Sein*], . . . the universal space of names as such', 'this abstract being' (*dies abstrakte Sein*), 'the empty bond', etc. It would not be like this, if a name was distinct from its meaning and only synthesized with it. So in its 'particular self-externalizations', i.e. its utterance or thought of particular names, and in the 'appropriation that it carries

out' (*ihr durchgeführtes Aneignen*), i.e. its appropriation of its self-externalizations or namings, the name-meaning distinction is sublated. The names are 'senseless words', in 'complete externality' with respect to each other, i.e. not related syntagmatically to form intelligible sentences (cf. §462, n. 2). Hence the memory is mechanical: 'The mechanical feature in memory lies merely in the fact that certain signs, tones, etc. are apprehended in their purely external association, and then reproduced in this association, without attention being expressly directed to their meaning and inward association' (Enc. I, §195Z.).

This raises three questions: (1) Why should the intelligence be 'the universal', etc? Even if it sometimes is, our ability to utter intelligible sentences relevant to their context implies that it usually is not, that we retain interests, etc. over and above the words at our disposal, enabling us to combine them in non-arbitrary ways. (2) What is the connection between the universality of intelligence and the sublation of the name-meaning distinction? (3) What are the 'senseless words' that memory accommodates?

The answers are as follows: (1) Hegel does not believe that the intelligence remains permanently devoid of interests, contextual knowledge, etc. but that the repression of interests, etc. is a crucial feature of childhood education and that it enables us, as adults, to retain the ability to disregard our interests. (2) If the intelligence is reduced to 'the universal space of names as such', etc. it does not have the resources from which to confer meaning on the names. The names 'just are' (*nur seiend*), with nothing added; whatever meaning they have is intrinsic to them. (3) Hegel does not describe the words as 'meaningless' (*bedeutungsloser*), but as 'senseless' (*sinnloser*). '*Sinn* differs from *Bedeutung* . . . in that *Bedeutung* is more objective and more exact, whereas *Sinn* is more subjective . . . *Sinn* differs from "sense" in one point. While it is possible to refer to the "sense" of a word or its various senses as listed in a dictionary, *Sinn* only denotes the sense of a word either in a context or in reference to an idea as conceived by a person or a group of persons' (DGS, p. 294). Hence in a nursery rhyme, such as 'Sing a song of sixpence, pocketful of rye', each word has a *Bedeutung*, but lacks a *Sinn*, since the sequence does not make much sense. (Some writers use *Sinn* for the meaning of a whole, such as a sentence, and *Bedeutung* for the meaning of a part, such as a word.) In this case the sequence, or at least its first clause, has a grammatical structure. But some sequences do not: e.g. 'Eucalyptus concession tarnish Hegel'. Here the whole sequence lacks *Sinn* entirely, and so consequently does each word in the sequence. If I remember the sequence, my memory is 'mechanical', not jogged by the *Sinn* as when I remember 'Hegel was born in Stuttgart'. Each word in the senseless sequence has a *Bedeutung*, but it does not get it from the memorizer or from the accompanying words. In memorizing the sequence we tend to forget the meanings of the individual words, since they contribute nothing to the overall sense of the sequence.

3. In a meaningful or senseful sequence various words can take a 'stress' (*Akzent*), depending on the context: '*Hegel* was born in Stuttgart', 'Hegel was *born* in Stuttgart', and so on. In a senseless sequence, such as 'Eucalyptus concession tarnish Hegel', there is no room for a significant stress. If I stress words in a poem I have

learned by heart, this means I am attending to the sense, and that means I have not really learned it by heart, since my memory is jogged by the sense. In Hegel's view, too, I will not recite it so flawlessly, not word for word. If I think of the meaning I may say 'We are such stuff as dreams are made of' instead of 'We are such stuff as dreams are made on'.

4. In 'intuition' the mind is not really 'in its right mind' (*bei sich*: 'at home with, together with itself, not beside itself'); it just 'finds' things: cf. §§449 f. So it has objectivity at the expense of subjectivity. In 'representation' the mind recollects 'this find' (*dieses Gefundene*) and so is 'in its right mind', with an appropriate 'unity of subjectivity and objectivity'. In memory the mind goes out of its mind again, it regards 'what is its own', names, as if they were found, in the way that what is not its own is found in intuition. So subjectivity is repressed and objectivity takes over, but this time 'within intelligence', since the objectivity is self-imposed, not imposed by external objects.

5. Memorizing poetry, Latin verbs, multiplication tables, etc. is not just useful because it enables one to recall these things when needed and also to memorize other useful items. It plays a crucial part in clearing the mind for abstract thinking and for the objectivity that thinking requires. Perhaps we should compare Hegel's blank intelligence with the intellect as conceived by Aristotle—the intellect that can think about anything and for that reason cannot have the nature of any of the things it can think about (De anima, III. 4, 429$_a$22–430$_a$9)—or with the nothingness that Sartre ascribes to the *pour soi*. If the mind is to grasp things it cannot be cluttered up with them.

NOTES TO §464

1. That the name is 'the being' (*Das Seiende*) implies here that the name just is, bereft of meaning and pointing to nothing beyond itself. It needs the meaning 'of', i.e. conferred by, representational intelligence to be the 'thing' (*Sache*), etc. 'Thing' is here ambiguous: cf. §462, n. 6. It might refer to the name itself, conceived as the 'main thing', the 'subject matter'. But it more naturally refers to the thing denoted by the name, such as lions or a lion. So the natural reading of the sentence is that a name, such as 'lion', needs to be given a meaning by intelligence if it is to refer to such things as lions. Or schematically: name + meaning = thing. But, as often with Hegel, we need to read further before we finally make up our minds.

2. The second sentence is naturally read as saying that, as mechanical memory, intelligence is (i.e. is aware of) the thing, e.g. the lions to which the word 'lion' refers, and is (i.e. confers) the meaning of the word 'lion' that enables it to refer to lions. Intelligence is, as it were, poised between the word-meaning and the object referred to. But this natural reading cannot be right, since mechanical memory disregards the meanings of the words it remembers and also the things that the words are about: cf. §463. So the sentence means something like this: as mechanical memory, intelligence takes the place of, or does duty for, the 'external objectivity' and the 'meaning'. As 'reason', intelligence is 'implicitly'

(*an sich*) the 'unity of the subjective and objective' (§440Z.). But initially it is
not such a unity 'explicitly' (*für sich*), it has to go through a series of stages to
get there: cf. §440, n. 3. Now, as mechanical memory, it is explicitly this unity
or 'identity', since it is both the 'external objectivity' and the 'meaning', i.e. the
subjective. We might expect such a unity or identity to be a unity or identity
of real, external things (such as lions) and our words or thoughts referring to
them, but this is not what we get. The unity is achieved not by bridging the gulf
between things and meanings, but by effectively eliminating things and meanings, and replacing them with the bare intelligence.

3. Here Hegel reveals his hand. 'Memory' (*Gedächtnis*) is a step on the way to the
   'thought' (*Gedanke(ns)*), and the thought has no 'meaning', that is, it does not
   mean, denote, or refer to anything other than itself. If I think about or represent lions, the lions are distinct from my thinking about them. But if I engage in
   the kind of activity that (in Hegel's eyes) qualifies as thinking in the strict sense,
   if I think, say, about opposition, the opposition that I think about is not distinct from my thought about it. So 'the subjective', the thinking, is not distinct
   from 'its objectivity', opposition. This 'inwardness', i.e. the subjective 'space' in
   which thinking occurs, is 'in being' (*seiend*), i.e. is itself a sort of objectivity,
   with no subjective interests, etc. to impede or influence the course of thinking:
   cf. §464, n. 4.

   Hegel's argument is that our utterance or private recital of words without
   regard to their meaning, interconnections, and reference prepares the ground
   for our thinking of pure thoughts, thoughts which have no 'meaning'. (Hegel
   discomfortingly switches from speaking of the meaning of words to speaking
   of the meaning, or meaninglessness, of thoughts. But that probably does not
   unduly disturb his argument.) *Bedeutung* here perhaps approximates to *Bedeutung* in Frege's sense, i.e. 'reference'. The word 'lion' has a meaning, it refers to
   or denotes lions. So too the word 'opposition' has a meaning, it admits of para-
   phrase, such as 'antithesis, contrariety'. But what does it denote or refer to? If we
   leave aside concrete uses of the word (such as Her Majesty's Opposition, which
   is not the object of a pure thought), it just denotes opposition, and that (Hegel
   assures us) is simply the thought we started with. On thought, see §§465–8.

4. Pure thinking is, in Hegel's view, somewhat like reciting words one has committed to memory. Just as one recites the words without imposing any interpretation on them, so one lets 'the thing' (*die Sache*), in this case the thought itself,
   unfold the content that is implicit or 'in itself' without any subjective interference. Hegel seems to have shifted from one type of objectivity to another, from
   the sense of 'objectivity' in which real lions are objective, in contrast to our representation of them (as in §464, n. 1), to the sense of 'objectivity' in which it
   means something like 'impartiality, disinterestedness'. The word *Sache* is related
   to both types of objectivity, since the adjective *sachlich*, 'pertaining to the Sache',
   also means 'impartial, objective': cf. §462, n. 7. One might take an objective or
   impartial attitude towards things, such as lions, which are also real or objective.
   But one can also take an impartial attitude towards 'thoughts', which are not real
   or objective, not at least in the way that lions are.

5. Thinking involves two 'moments'. One of these is 'the merely external mode' (*die nur äusserliche Weise*), 'thinking's existence', or 'the mode of existence'. 'Existence' is here used in its sense of 'stepping forth, emergence' (cf. §403, n. 2). This is what memory is. But on its own this moment is 'one-sided', since it omits the other moment, namely, reason. In Hegel's explicit discussion of existence at Enc. I, §§122–3, 'existence' is contrasted with the 'ground' (*Grund*), roughly the essence, from which existence emerges. Perhaps here, then, reason is conceived as the ground from which thinking's existence emerges, though Hegel does not use the word 'ground' or 'essence' in the vicinity. 'For us' or 'in itself' (but unbeknown to the thinker), the transition from memory to thinking involves the identification or fusion of these two moments. (What is only 'in itself' and thus not *for* intelligence at its current stage, is nevertheless *for us*, philosophers who are at a higher stage and can thus see things that lower stages of intelligence cannot: cf. §§381, n. 1; 424, n. 4; 413, n. 3; 441, n. 7 on 'we'.) Then reason 'exists in the subject' (*im Subjekte existiert*).

Hegel is not content to show that mechanical memory is a necessary condition of thinking in that it clears the space for thinking. He also wants to display the 'transition' from memory to thinking, which at least involves showing what transformation memory has to undergo to give the sufficient condition of thinking. Mechanically we memorize more or less any old words in any old order. They need not be words for thoughts, such as 'opposition', and even if they were, memorizing a list of words for thoughts does not amount to thinking. Even if I memorize the whole of Hegel's logic from beginning to end, this does not amount to thinking. I need in addition to follow the argument or the train of thought. Perhaps this is what Hegel means by saying that reason 'exists in the subject', that the subject pursues a train of thought, or follows the thought's self-unfolding, while curbing its 'subjective inwardness', i.e. its non-rational feelings, etc. It might then be objected that someone who memorizes a random list of words or numbers meets this condition, but is still not thinking. But to this Hegel can reply that unless there is some rationality, some rhyme or reason, in the object of thinking, there cannot really be reason in the subject of thinking. The mindless memorizer of random names is rational in the crucial, but incomplete, sense of being totally absorbed in what is memorized: cf. §464, n. 2. But such rationality can hardly be said to 'exist' in the subject, to be the subject's 'activity'. The subject secures this type of rationality at the cost of self-immolation to the object.

NOTES TO §465

1. 'Recognitive' is *wiedererkennend*, the present participle of *wiedererkennen*, 'to recognize', formed from *erkennen* and *wieder*, 'again'. *Erkennen*, 'to cognize, know' also often means 'to recognize'. Hegel slides from *erkennen* in the sense of 'recognize' to *erkennen* in the sense of 'know, cognize'. Thus when intelligence 'cognizes' (*erkennt*) an intuition, it recognizes an intuition, e.g. a person, it has encountered before: cf. §454, n. 1. When it 'cognizes' the 'thing' (*Sache*) in the

name, it (re)cognizes e.g. lions or the lion when it hears the name 'lion'. This
differs from the first case in that one need never have encountered a lion in order
to recognize the lion in the name. In thinking, what is 'for intelligence' (*für sie*)
is not an intuition or a thing, but 'its universal' (*ihr Allgemeines*). The force of
'its' is perhaps that the universal is not external to intelligence in the way that an
intuition or a thing (such as a lion) is, or even that the universal is the 'product' of
intelligence. At any rate, 'its' answers to 'its own' (*die ihrige*) above: as intelligence
recognizes an intuition when it is 'its own', i.e. corresponds to an image of it, so
intelligence (re)cognizes 'its' own universal. This universal is universal in a double
sense. First, it is universal 'as such', i.e. it contrasts with what is 'immediate' and
with beings, with specific individual things such as lions (or, possibly, thoughts).
The universal in this sense is comparable to the acorn that has not yet opened up
into an oak-tree: cf. §441, n. 1, etc. Second, it is the universal 'as immediate or
as being' (*als Unmittelbaren oder als Seienden*). This is the universal embedded
in real entities such as lions (or, possibly, thoughts). It is comparable to the
oak-tree, which embodies the 'universal' (in the first sense of 'universal') in the
acorn. If the intelligence's universal were universal in only one of these senses, it
would be either one-sidedly 'subjective' or one-sidedly 'objective'. But since it is
both at once, it is the 'genuine' (*wahrhafte*) universal, embracing or 'overarching'
(*übergreifende*) both itself (as universal 'as such' or in the first sense) and its 'other',
'being' (*das Sein*): cf. §455, n. 9.

2. Intelligence is 'for itself intrinsically cognitive' (*für sich an ihr erkennend*), because
the universal that it is, by its very nature overarches its other, being, and cognizes
or recognizes itself in it. It is the 'identity of the subjective and objective'. But
what is the 'objective'? Is it such external entities as lions? Or is it thoughts? The
latter answer is suggested when Hegel implicitly distinguishes between the universal, which intelligence 'intrinsically' (*an ihr selbst*) is, and the 'thought' (*Gedanke*),
which is intelligence's product. It is also suggested by the claim that the thought
is the 'thing' (*Sache*). However, this claim is ambiguous: cf. §462, n. 6. It could
mean that the thought as such (not lions, etc.) is the (main, important) thing.
Or it could mean that the thought is the thing, such things as lions. If we take
it in the first sense, then the identity of the subjective and objective is the identity of the intrinsically universal intelligence with the thoughts it produces. If we
take it in the second sense, it is the identity of the universal thought(s) with other
things, lions, etc. Hegel's reference to Enc. I, §§5 and 21 favour the second interpretation, since in those paragraphs he argues that the true nature of something
(such as thunder and lightning, or plants) is revealed by thinking about it and by
transforming it into pure thoughts (such as the thought of the force that underlies
thunder and lightning). If this is right, then the claim that 'what is thought, is'
(*was gedacht ist, ist*) means not that the thought as such *is*, but that what thinking
reveals about an entity is that entity's true nature. (It could possibly mean that
pure thoughts must be embodied in some external reality or other. But that claim
does not figure in Enc. I,§5 or §21). Conversely, the claim that 'what is, only is
in so far as it is a thought' means that an external object only is, in so far as it
embodies a thought (such as force). (It does not of course mean that something

only exists if and when it is thought about.) Intelligence 'knows' (*weiss*) all this, it is what it is 'for itself'. The final two clauses ('the thinking.... object of intelligence') seem to revert to the first interpretation, that the 'thing', the 'other' of the 'genuine universal', is thoughts as such, not thoughts as embedded in external reality. But the second interpretation is not strictly excluded: the thoughts that we 'have' are, in Hegel's view, also embedded in things. The point of the seeming tautology, 'the *thinking* of intelligence is *having thoughts*', is to distinguish this 'pure', explicit thinking from the subdued thinking involved in all everyday activity: cf. §465, n. 4.

Hegel's words in this Paragraph are, then, ambiguous. They waver between an account of pure thinking, the type of thinking attempted by Hegel's logic, and an account of the way in which our thought about things transforms our world into an objective world: cf. §402, nn. 4, 8.

3. The other main stages of intelligence are 'intuition' (§§446–50) and 'representation' (§§451–64). On the recurrent pattern of simple unity–opposition–restored unity, see §§387, n. 14; 443, n. 1, etc. Initially, intuition takes the form of feeling or sensation, where the distinction between intelligence and its object is barely made. This unity is only 'in itself', not *for* intelligence. If the unity were for intelligence, intelligence would have had to disentangle itself from its object. But it has not yet done this. A gap opens up between 'the subjective and objective' in §448, when intelligence pays attention to its objects and projects them out into space and time, and the gap persists throughout the account of representation, despite representation's successive attempts to close it. (This gap is presumably *for* intelligence, though Hegel does not say so explicitly.) These attempts produce a unity of the subjective and objective that is still subjective: on an objectivity that is still 'subjective', cf. §408, n. 5. The words I commit to memory are objective in relation to my memory of them, but they are still *my* words, perhaps even signs capriciously invented by myself. Such reference as they may have to external reality is repressed by mechanical memory. Imagination too can, and often does, operate within one's 'individual world' and need have little bearing on the fully objective world: cf. §402, n. 7. Symmetrical, unqualified unity of the subjective and objective is finally restored by thinking. But now the unity is for itself as well as in itself, since thinking knows that it is the nature of the 'thing' (*Sache*) as well as actually being the nature of the thing.

4. Cf. §§389, nn. 5,6; 413, n. 4 on the unity of thinking and being. We think 'in all circumstances', because e.g. wanting to sit on a comfortable chair involves such pure thoughts as those of a thing and its properties. Abstract thoughts are, in Hegel's view, implicated in all our rational activities. Thought is thus not just one of our faculties among others, but the underlying structure of our mental and practical life. (Hegel thus disagrees with the view perhaps suggested by Plato's *Republic*, IV—though not by *Republic*, X—that we are brute animals with reason added on top. For Hegel, we are rational all the way down.) However, as long as we remain at the lower levels of everyday thinking, we may not be aware that we are thinkers. We become aware of this only when we ascend to 'pure thinking', thinking e.g. about the notion of a force. Then we realize that

the 'truth' of 'things' (*Dinge*) is given by thinking, that e.g. the essential nature of thunder and lightning is the force responsible for them, not the sound and the flash.

Hegel's account of Epicurus (341–270 BC) is misleading. Epicurus held that knowledge derives from sensations, and that our theories about invisible things must be tested against what we can perceive. But he also believed that perceptible things (including our sensations) depend on the shape, size, and arrangement of invisible atoms. Hegel, though not himself very fond of atomism, would regard atoms as 'thoughts', and he need not disagree that the postulation of such thoughts in reality presupposes sensations. After all, we could not know that lightning was the manifestation of a force, if we did not also see the flash, etc. Hegel might reply that while sensation may be a necessary condition of thought, Epicurus wrongly regards sensation as a sufficient condition of his belief in atoms, since according to Epicurus repeated sensations alone give rise to concepts, and these, together with more sensations of the appropriate sort, give rise to judgements. But though Epicurus believes that sensations ultimately give the truth about things, he does not believe that they are, in Hegel's sense, the 'truth of things'.

5. 'Abstract' originally meant 'drawn away, removed', and 'concrete' meant 'grown together': cf. §396, n. 3. Here Hegel means that if thinking is to grasp the truth of things, then its thoughts must not be severed from each other and presented piecemeal (as they are by the intellect) but interconnected with each other in the way described in §467. *Begreifenden*, 'conceptual', also has the flavour of 'comprehensive, inclusive': cf. §378, n. 4. Roughly speaking, Hegel believes that if thoughts are cut off from each other, then they are cut off from perceptible reality, whereas if they are appropriately interconnected with each other, they coincide with reality.

NOTES TO §466

1. That cognition is 'formal' implies that it ('likewise', i.e. like lower faculties) lacks a content of its own. Hegel is qualifying the statement at the end of the Paragraph of §465, that 'thoughts' are the 'content and object' of thinking intelligence. Initially these thoughts are not determined 'in and for themselves', i.e. independently and in their own right. Thinking gets its content from representations, 'recollected' or internalized, but simply given, not generated by thinking itself.

2. See §467.

NOTES TO §467

1. Hegel presupposes the traditional triad (found in Kant and in logic textbooks of the day, and also—with radical revision—in Hegel's logic): concept, judgement, syllogism. In the traditional view, a concept, such as the concept of a man, is formed by the 'intellect'. Concepts are then put togther to form a 'judgement', such as 'All men are mortal'. This too is the work of the intellect. Finally, judgements are related to each other in a syllogism or 'inference' (*Schluss*), such as 'All

men are mortal; all Greeks are men; so all Greeks are mortal'. A syllogism is the work of 'reason' rather than the intellect.

Hegel retains this basic framework, but alters its details considerably. First, he breaks the link between intellect and the 'concept'. The concept acquires a different sense and status in Hegel and is reserved for reason. Hence the intellect brings representations not into concepts, but into 'categories' or 'thought-forms' (*Denkformen*): see the similar account of the intellect in §422 and Z. The intellect is 'formally identical' in that it deals with things piecemeal and sets up hard and fast barriers between things, between, for example, distinct genera and between distinct species.

2. Another revision introduced by Hegel is to regard judgement not as a combination of concepts, but as a 'diremption', a division or separation: cf. §429, n. 1. If the judgement were a diremption in the sense that it 'breaks up the concept into the previous opposition, etc.', it would simply undo the work done by the intellect at stage (1). Nevertheless, it does 'differentiate', but does this by following the 'interconnections' (*Zusammenhängen*) of the 'concept'. The *Zusatz* expands this somewhat uninformative account: cf. §467, n. 10.

3. Hegel interprets the syllogism or inference as a closure, closing, that is, the gap opened up by judgement: cf. §389, n. 4. The 'form-determination' (*Formbestimmung*) sublated by thinking is the same as the 'form-distinction' (*Formunterschied*) below. What thinking now does is to obliterate the distinction between form and content involved in stages (1) and (2). The 'differences' (*Unterschiede*) whose 'identity' it posits are the differences or distinctions drawn by judgement. Then it is 'formal reason', a low level of reason, or 'concluding' (*schliessender*: also 'closing, inferring, syllogizing') intellect, a high level of intellect.

4. The three stages are now repeated, to show how thinking involves cognition as well, cognition initially of individual entities. At stage (1) the intellect 'explains' (*erklärt*) the individual 'by' (*aus*) its *own* categories. This suggests that the intellect is initially somewhat overbearing, imposing its own categories and ignoring what it regards as inessential, disregarding the thunderclap, for example, and the lightning flash in favour of the underlying force. The final clause (*so heisst er sich begreifend*) is ambiguous: *heisst* (from *heissen*) could be intransitive ('is said, called') and then *sich* would go with *begreifend*, giving 'is then said to comprehend or understand itself', as Wallace translated it. The point might then be that the intellect comprehends itself, rather than the individual, since the categories are those imposed by the intellect. But if Hegel meant this, the stress should be on *sich* rather than *begreifend*. So I prefer the alternative reading: *heisst* ('calls') is transitive and, in this case, reflexive. Hegel does not call this intellect 'comprehending' or conceptual: it calls itself that, in view of the traditional schema presented in §467, n. 1.

5. *Erklären* means 'to explain' and also 'to declare [something to be something]'. So the intellect here explains the individual 'as' (*für*), or declares it to be, a universal. A fuller account of this is given in the *Zusatz*: see §467, n. 10.

6. At stages (1) and (2) the intellect works on something, a 'representation' or 'the individual', given to it from outside, but now 'the intellect' (*er*) determines

content for itself. This shows the content to be necessary rather than contingent. The connection between this and the 'inference' (*Schluss*) is not obvious, but is explained more fully in the *Zusatz*: cf. §467, n. 11.

7. According to Hegel, thinking appears in at least three places in 'science': in Logic (Enc. I), at the end of the 'Phenomenology of Mind' section (§437), and at the end of the 'Psychology' section. In logic thinking forms an 'unopposing' (*gegensatzlosen*) medium for the unfolding of reason. That is, thinking is, in logic, 'pure' thinking: it deals only with thoughts, not with recalcitrant external objects. It does not follow that logical thinking has nothing to do with 'opposition'. First, because Hegel's science forms a circle, logic, though it appears at the beginning of the system, itself develops out of, and as a response to, oppositions that emerge at the end of the system, i.e. at the end of the Philosophy of Mind. Secondly, oppositions emerge within logical thinking, and reason develops in an attempt to overcome them. But in logical thinking, all the hurdles that reason has to surmount are set up by reason itself.

In consciousness, thinking plays a fairly subdued role, though 'reason' is prominent and §437Z. refers to §467. Reason resolves the opposition between the subjective (i.e. the self-conscious individual) and the objective (i.e. other self-conscious individuals). 'Here' (i.e. in §§465 ff.) thinking or reason also resolves the subjective-objective opposition, only now this opposition is not between different individuals, but between the mind and its sensory input, hence an opposition that develops 'within the mind itself'. Reason is 'the truth' of an opposition in the sense that it resolves or reconciles it: §419, n. 3. Reason or thinking is an arbitrator of disputes, a sort of marriage guidance counsellor.

8. The distinction between reason and intellect, or understanding, antedates Kant. Aquinas, for example, distinguishes between *intellectus*, 'understanding', and *ratio*, 'reasoning'; we have both these faculties, but God lacks *ratio*, since he grasps everything at once and does not need to reason from premises. But Kant drew a distinction more to Hegel's liking. For Kant, the intellect or understanding is the faculty that actively conceptualizes our sensory intuitions. It produces categories and applies them to intuitions, thereby transforming intuitions into perceptions of a world of law-governed objects. The intellect conceptualizes, judges, and generalizes, but it gives us knowledge only of the 'conditioned'. It does not give us knowledge of the 'unconditioned', final and complete knowledge and rock-bottom explanations. Reason proposes an ideal of such ultimate knowledge, an ideal which we can pursue either (rightly) by expanding our empirical scientific researches and theories or (wrongly) by trying to deduce the ultimate nature of things by pure, non-empirical reasoning. Kant also believed that reason provides moral certainties, not only binding moral laws, but also a belief in free will and in God's moral governance of the world.

Hegel's version of the distinction has some affinity to Kant's. Kant would agree on the following points: For the intellect, (i) the 'form' of the object is distinct from its 'content': the form is provided by intellect itself, while the content comes from 'sensibility': that there are causal regularities is ordained by intellect, but that water expands when it is frozen is an empirical matter, dependent on sensibility; (ii) the individual, Jumbo, and the particular species, elephant, are distinct from the universal, animal, under which they fall; (iii) the determinate qualities of a thing depend on its interactions with other things ('outside'), though by the 'thing in itself' Kant usually means not the thing independent of its interactions with other things, but the thing independent of its interaction with us: intellect and sensibility give us not the thing in itself, but the thing as it appears to us. Each of these dichotomies leaves unanswered questions: Why does water always expand when frozen? Granted that animals exist, why are there elephants, and why Jumbo? Granted that Jumbo is as he is because of his interaction with other things, why are these other things such as they are and such as to make him what he is? What are things like apart from us? Reason, ideally, answers all such questions. So for reason none of these dichotomies obtain. In its objects, e.g. God or the world as a whole, no gap remains between form and content, etc. Kant might wonder why Hegel expresses this by saying that the 'content *produces* its form *from its own self* ', rather than saying that the form produces the content or that there is no form-content distinction at all. He would also question the equation of 'rational' cognition with 'conceptual' (*begreifenden*) cognition, since Kant links conceptualization with the intellect, not reason. Above all, he would object to Hegel's assumption that rational cognition of this sort is possible at all, after all Kant's efforts to show its impossibility. But he might also notice that, beneath Hegel's surface agreement with him, Hegel gives a rather different sense to 'reason' and 'rational cognition': cf. §467, n. 11.

9. Here Hegel gives a traditional rather than a Kantian account of the intellect. Rather than imposing objective order on our chaotic sensations, intellect produces Linnaean-type classifications of things, abstracting from their contingent features (such as the duck's bill, duck's feet, and egg-laying of the platypus) to focus on the essential (the fact that it suckles its offspring and is thus a mammal). On the one-sidedness of intellect, see §394, n. 10. It can, especially in practical affairs, focus exclusively on one feature of a thing, without a balanced, all-round view, and the 'sense for the essential' that common sense has.

10. The intellect, in classifying the platypus as a mammal, ignores its duck's bill, feet, and eggs. But judgement brings them all back in again and considers their interrelationships. Judgement has now lost its function of 'diremption', to which Hegel briefly paid homage in the Paragraph. It is more like judgement as it appears in Kant's *Critique of Judgement*, especially in its account of our appreciation of living organisms: cf. §415, n. 2, §423, n. 5. But the disparity between the one-sided intellect and the more comprehensive judgement is found in other areas too. Arguably, Max Weber gives a one-sided definition of the state, when he says: 'A compulsory political association with a continuous organization will be called a "state" if, and insofar as, its administrative staff successfully claims the monopolization of the legitimate use of physical force in the enforcement of its authority' (M. Weber, *Basic Concepts in Sociology*, trans. and introd. by H. P. Secher (New York: Citade, 1964), 119). Hegel disagrees that force is central to the state: cf. §432, n. 2. He gives a more rounded account of the state, considering it in its relationship to the family and civil society. (This does not deter

Secher from claiming that Weber's 'definition seems to echo the influence of Hegel, Treitschke and the high-pitched nationalism of the Wilhelmine empire', Weber *Concepts in Sociology*, 19.)

Nevertheless, the sort of judging that Hegel has in mind is not 'comprehension' (*Begreifen*), i.e. it is not based only on the 'concept', the *Begriff,* of the object, but considers it as dependent on external circumstances. Suppose for example I consider the platypus in relation to its environment, and ask: Why in this (or a former) environment, should a creature have fur, a duck's bill, a duck's feet, lay eggs, and suckle its young? Then I am treating its environment—predators, food, climate, etc.—as 'independent existences'. The 'identity' or relationship of the platypus to these other 'phenomena' (*Erscheinungen*) is a 'merely external' relationship, not a conceptual relationship. If the relationship were conceptual, the phenomena would cease to be 'independent existences' with respect to each other; they would be moments of a single concept. At bottom, Hegel implies, the relationship is conceptual. But the concept does not 'show itself'. So the relationship is 'merely inner', i.e. hidden from us, and that is what makes it 'merely external'.

11. For a general account of universality, particularity, and individuality, see Enc. I, §§163–5. The triad appears frequently in Hegel's thought, especially in the development of the mind: cf. §§379, n. 5; 385, n. 2; 387, n. 8. In §§541 ff. the schema is applied to the state. (Hegel himself would jib at the expression 'applied to', insisting that universality, etc. are intrinsic to the nature of the state.) This is possible, because the state, in Hegel's view, develops from its own intrinsic nature, relatively independently of its environment. The government is the universal moment (§541). The unity and unifying activity of the government makes the state 'one' and thus introduces the moment of individuality (§541 Remark). This individuality is confirmed by establishment of a (constitutional) monarch (§542). Finally, the government entrusts its particular types of business to particular powers or branches of government (§543). The universal is not here something that we outsiders impose on the state, as we imposed the concept of a mammal on the platypus. The state is intrinsically universal, but a universal that particularizes and individualizes itself, thus producing its own 'content': cf. the universality of the seed or acorn in §453, n. 2, etc.

To think about something in this way is real 'comprehension' (*Begreifen*), since it follows the self-developing 'concept' (*Begriff*) of the 'thing' (*Sache*). But the way in which the thing develops mirrors the way in which we think. Our thinking too proceeds in terms of the concept and its moments of universality, particularity, and individuality; and, in Hegel's view, we too develop the content of our thought from a universal concept. Hence, in viewing the 'object' (*Gegenstand*) in this way, thinking 'finds only itself'. The object does indeed differ from our thinking about it, but it differs 'only by having the form of *being*, etc.', not in its essential structure. Hence thinking is now in an entirely 'free' relationship to the 'object' (*Objekt*). That is, the object is not in the least alien to thinking, getting to grips with it requires thinking to perform no unnatural contortions, nor, conversely, do our thought-patterns distort the object at all. Hegel has an identity theory of knowledge, but the identity obtains only at the highest level of knowledge, not at lower levels.

12. 'Objective reason' is the reason immanent in, the rational structure of, such things as the state, and even oak-trees. This is now 'posited' as 'knowledge' (*Wissen*), not just implicitly knowledge as it was at the beginning. Conversely, knowledge is the 'subjectivity of reason'. So reason as subjective cognizes itself as objective. (One difference between *erkennen*, 'to cognize', and *wissen*, 'to know, be aware', seems to be that *erkennen* is here more or less restricted to this conceptual knowledge, whereas *wissen* is used more widely.) This is what the mind was 'supposed' to be 'in its immediacy', i.e. on its first appearance at §440 and Z. That is why the mind was there said to be 'free': cf. §440, n. 3. In his Foreword to *Hegel's Philosophy of Mind*, trans. W. Wallace and A. V. Miller (Oxford: Oxford University Press, 1971), Findlay says:

> What is important in this stage of the Philosophy of Mind is that the inner life of the subject, its life of reflection, judgement, memory, deliberation, etc. . . . presupposes the prior capacity to see oneself as a free man among other free men. A man who envisages himself as a slave, an inferior, cannot judge, decide, imagine, agree, nor even have the dreams of reason, or rather, the fact that he succeeds in having them, shows that he is no longer envisaging himself as a mere slave. The possession of an ordered inner life is the prerogative of a free individual, recognized as such by an ordered society (p. xvi)

It is difficult to see why this should be true. If someone can 'envisage himself as a slave', why should he be unable to perform any other mental function? Aesop (sixth century BC) and the Stoic philosopher Epictetus (*c*.55–135 AD) were originally slaves, though later freed. Did their 'ordered inner life' begin only after their liberation, or did they cease to envisage themselves as mere slaves earlier? At all events, there is no sign of this doctrine in Hegel. Freedom, in this context, is having oneself as one's object, i.e. not being determined or restricted by an alien object. Presumably not all free persons are capable of this, not at least without the help of scientists, philosophers, etc. Conversely, there is no a priori reason for thinking that a slave would necessarily be incapable of it.

NOTES TO §468

1. All along, intelligence 'appropriates' (*sich . . . aneignet*) the 'immediate determinacy', i.e. the intuitions, etc. that it just finds: cf. §445, n. 1; 457; 463, n. 2. Now it has taken complete possession. This occurs through the 'last', i.e. final, negation of immediacy. (This refers back to 'the last immediacy' that has 'vanished' in stage (3) at the end of the preceding Paragraph: cf. §467, n. 6.) By this negation it is posited that the content is determined 'through the intelligence' (*durch sie*)—because the rational structure that determines the content is the same rational structure that informs intelligence—and that this fact is 'for the intelligence' (*für sie*). But this is posited only 'implicitly', not explicitly or for itself, since intelligence need not yet be actually aware that it determines the

content, or indeed that it is now 'in its own property'. At earlier stages of thinking, stages (1) and (2) in the Paragraph of §467, thinking was 'the free concept', or free in form. But it got its content from outside. Now it is 'free in the *content*' as well, since it determines the content. Now intelligence becomes 'aware' (*wissend*) that the content is determined by itself. Moreover, the content is not only determined 'as being' (*als seiend*), it is the content of intelligence itself. But this amounts to the will. When I will something, I form a plan—the 'content' of my will—and then I fulfil my plan, determine it 'as being'. The plan is, often at least, all my own, I decide what the plan is. I am aware of this. When I realize the plan, I know that it is I who am bringing about this new state of affairs, a state of affairs that I recognize as my 'own property'.

This transition raises obvious questions. Why, for example, is thinking of stage (3) unaware that it determines the content? And how does it become aware of this? If it were aware of it all along, it would be will all along, and there would be no distinction, and therefore no transition, between top-grade thinking and willing. The *Zusatz* tackles these difficulties with little success: cf. §468, n. 2.

2. Since pure thinking is initially 'self-effacing' (*unbefangenes*), it does not consider the question whether or not it determines the content of its thinking. It is just not 'objective' (*gegenständlich*) to itself. It is lost in thought. But this thinking must become objective to itself, and then it must 'recognize' (*erkennen*) the identity of its own determinations with those of the 'thing' (*Sache*). Here Hegel gives no good answer to the question: 'Granted that the determinations of cognition and the thing are the same, why must cognition recognize this?'

3. Thinking is a necessary condition of willing. This claim can be supported by least two considerations. First, I must have some conception of what it is that I will to do, such as marking examination scripts or dealing with my tax return. Second, I must be able to resist my inclination to do something more enjoyable, in view of prudential or moral considerations, and this too requires thought. (But see §469, n. 5 for Hegel's own reason for the claim.) However, the fact that thinking is a necessary condition of willing does not entail that a 'transition' can be made from thinking to the will. For that to be possible, thinking would have to be a sufficient condition of willing. No doubt thinking is a sufficient condition of willing, and so there could not be a pure thinker incapable of willing. But Hegel does not actually say this, let alone argue for it.

If thinking is a sufficient condition of willing, then there would no doubt be a plausible transition from thinking to the will. But it need not be the transition that Hegel proposes, namely, that thinking 'determines itself into will'. It might take the form of arguing, e.g., that a pure thinker must will to do something (something other, that is, than thinking itself) or it would starve to death. Or we might take the more roundabout route of arguing that a pure thinker must have desires (as animals do) to ensure its survival, but that if it is to think at all it must be capable of occasionally resisting its desires, and of deciding, i.e. willing, to think rather than to eat or copulate. The transition Hegel offers is not the only, or the best, available transition.

NOTES TO §469

1. 'Reaching a conclusion' is *beschliessend*. *Beschliessen* means both 'close, finish, etc.' and 'resolve, decide, etc.' Hence the mind both encloses itself within itself and comes to a decision. Then it 'fulfils' (*erfüllend*) itself by realizing its decision.

2. 'Being-for-self' (*Fürsichsein*) conveys both that the mind is self-aware and that it is now actualized, not just in itself: cf. §383, n. 1, etc. 'Individuality' (*Einzelheit*) contrasts with the 'universality of the concept'. What the will produces, even if it is what any decent will would do (such as paying its debts), is nevertheless an individual state of affairs, *this* payment of *these* debts. On the 'Idea' (*Idee*) as the combination of concept and 'existence'(*Existenz*) or 'reality' (*Realität*), see §377, n. 4, etc.

3. The will makes up its own mind about the 'content' and is therefore self-contained or 'together with itself' (*bei sich*). This makes it free 'in general', i.e. in a wide sense, and freedom in this minimal sense is required by its concept. But it is formal and therefore finite. It is formal, because its content is defective. While the thinker contemplates the universal vista of 'developed reason', the willer realizes only some definite, restricted goal, initially something that will give it pleasure. In realizing such a goal it does not express its nature, its concept, namely freedom, but only something it happens to want at the time.

4. The will therefore, even as it achieves these finite goals, is still '*in itself*', it has not realized its full potential, its concept. Its 'determination', its destiny, is to actualize the will's formal freedom, not just by achieving particular goals, but by making freedom its goal and actualizing it as freedom.

5. It is not obvious that it requires thought simply to do what one wants. But to make freedom itself one's purpose surely does involve thought. This is the only way in which the will can become 'objective' (*objektiven*) mind, i.e. to fulfil itself in objective, interpersonal institutions. That requires universal goals (such as payment of debts) whose formation requires thought, as well as the self-restraint that thought makes possible: cf. §468, n. 3. Granted that such a will must think, why must it be 'a will that thinks itself' (*sich denkender*)? Perhaps because the will ascends by thinking about its lower stages: to make freedom one's explicit goal one has to think about the freedom of the formal will.

6. '*True* freedom' contrasts with the freedom of the formal will. 'Ethical life' (*Sittlichkeit*) corresponds roughly, though not exactly, to 'objective mind', the morality embodied in social institutions. It contrasts with 'morality' (*Moralität*), individual or personal morality. Participation in ethical life involves respect for universal norms, not just doing what one likes.

7. 'Mind . . . recognizes its inwardness as what is objective' (*seine Innerlichkeit für das Objektive erkennende Geist*) has at least two, and perhaps three, meanings: (1) Mind 'recognizes its inner determinations as the same as the determinations of its object'. This applies to thinking, not the will. The will need not come into play if the mind's inwardness is already objective in this sense. (2) Mind 'recognizes its inner determinations as what is to become objective'. This applies to the

will, not to pure thinking. (3) The distinction between these two meanings is mediated, or perhaps obscured, by the notion of 'objective mind'. When I will to pay my debts, I do so in the context of an objective system of credit (an aspect of objective mind), which corresponds to my will. In this sense, even before actually paying my debts I recognize my inwardness as what is objective, as embodied in social morality or 'ethical life'.

8. The 'objectification' (*Objektivierung*) of the will's inwardness is also ambiguous. (1) If I do something for 'enjoyment', such as pick and eat a banana, I objectify my inwardness in the sense that I actually do what I want to do. But my action need neither presuppose nor produce 'objective mind', e.g. a rule-governed system of banana-production. Apart from my own enjoyment, the state of affairs I produce, a banana-skin on the ground instead of a banana on the tree, shows barely a trace of the work of mind. This type of objectification is called, in the next sentence, 'externalization' (*Äusserlichmachung*). (2) As the will progresses, it 'becomes', i.e. both presupposes and contributes to the production and maintenance of, objective mind, a world of norms, institutions, etc. infused with mind. Objective mind expresses or objectifies the will's inwardness in a stronger sense than mere 'externalization' does. It also enables me to have elevated, 'universal', purposes that express the nature of my will more adequately than does the desire for a banana.

It is perhaps odd to contrast 'enjoyment' with 'deed' (*Tat*: 'the completed act or action, the result ... [I]t is vivid, dramatic, refers to something of imposing proportions, and is personal in that one thinks of the doer as an individual', DGS, p. 4) and 'action' (*Handlung*: 'a conscious expression of the will. It is only possible in statements which describe, judge or by implication draw attention to the motives of 'acts' or 'actions'', DGS, p. 3). To enjoy something one usually has to do something and, conversely, enjoyment is often part of the motive for actions of which it is not the primary purpose. In objective mind, however, the deed or action itself is of public significance, whereas in mere 'externalization' it is not. In the context of a system of banana-cultivation, my picking and eating a banana may be an act of theft (*Tat* 'may be used of a crime', DGS, p. 4) or a sample tasting by an agent of a supermarket. cf. §444, n. 2.

9. As 'practical feeling' the will has an 'individual content' (such as a desire for that banana) and is just 'individual, subjective': it acknowledges no general principles or purposes governing its acts, it just wants a banana for itself. It 'finds' or 'feels' itself as 'objectively determining', as able e.g. to get the banana it wants. But because it lacks a content 'genuinely objective, universal in and for itself', does not e.g. regard itself as contributing to the production and marketing of bananas and acknowledges no moral restraint on its banana-picking, it has not '*posited* itself as intelligence freely and objectively determining'. The connection here between the restrictedness of the content of the will and the implicitness (rather than positedness) of its determining is this: if I have a 'universal', say a moral, purpose, I can do something in the absence of a desire or urge to do it, even in the face of a desire or urge not to do it. I may e.g. eat regularly, even if I do not

feel like it. Self-restraint, the overcoming of recalcitrant urges, etc. 'posit' my free
and objective determining in a way that just doing what I want does not. But
cf. §469, n. 10.

10. Initially then the will is free only 'by its concept' or in germ. But it has to
advance to the 'Idea' of freedom, giving reality to the concept. Hegel gives three
apparently distinct accounts of how this happens: (1) the will makes 'its concept,
freedom itself, its content or aim'; (2) it 'constructs... a world of its freedom'
by becoming objective mind; (3) it gets a universal content. The connection
between these accounts is as follows. I can only escape from self-centred individuality and acquire universal aims, namely (3), by participating in an interpersonal social order, namely (2). Conversely, if I respect moral constraints, by
e.g. exchanging my goods with a stranger instead of clubbing him to death and
stealing his goods, I implicitly contribute to the emergence or maintenance of a
system of exchange that is an aspect of objective mind. In both (2) and (3) freedom is, in a way, my aim: my adoption of a universal content liberates me from
my hitherto irresistible urges and the social order gives me a mind-infused environment corresponding to my own mind and will instead of the raw natural
order that, as an alien 'Other', impaired my freedom. Freedom, for Hegel, is
being determined by oneself, not by an other. It is best achieved, in Hegel's view,
not by withdrawing from the world, but by making it like myself. Hegel also
introduces account (1) because he likes the idea that just as the mind in general
advances by successively reflecting on its previous stage, so the will advances by
making its previous stage its present aim.

11. On the difference between 'practical feeling' and 'urge' (*Trieb*: 'an innate disposition towards a thing and ... therefore thought of as permanent', DGS, p. 363),
see §473, n. 1.

12. On happiness, see §§479–80 and PR, §20. 'Universality of reflection' is the sort
of universality that does not constitute the items to which it applies, but presupposes their independent existence: cf. §410, nn. 2 and 10; PR, §24 Remark.
Thus 'All the people in this room are under 40 years old' involves a universality of reflection, assuming that the people have not been preselected by age.
Happiness is a sort of universal, in that it depends (roughly) on satisfying one's
various urges in accordance with their strength. But what my happiness amounts
to depends on what urges I already happen to have. Happiness, at this stage
at least, does not determine what urges I have. So happiness is 'external to the
particularity of the urges'. 'Wilfulness' (*Willkür*) is (roughly) the freedom to do
what I like, and doing what I like most is what this type of happiness consists in:
cf. §§477–8.

13. The triad of universal happiness, particular urges, and individual wilfulness,
whose 'mutual externality' is marked by the adjectives 'indeterminate',
'immediate', and 'abstract', contrasts with 'the concrete universal' (*das konkret
Allgemeine*), which fuses together universality, particularity and individuality:
cf. §§387, n. 18; 393, n. 8; 410, n. 10; 445, n. 7; 456, n. 3. On freedom,
or the concept of freedom, as the goal of the will, cf. §469, n. 10. Since the
concept of freedom is concrete, it involves particularity and individuality; hence

it does not differ significantly from freedom itself, i.e. the 'world of its freedom' or objective mind.

NOTES TO §470

1. I want a banana. This is the determinacy posited 'from out of' (*aus*) myself. But I have no banana. This is the immediate 'determinedness' (*Bestimmtsein*), my 'reality' (*Dasein*) and 'condition' (*Zustand*). This comes in again owing to its discrepancy with the determinacy I posit. My want involves an 'ought' (*Sollen*) addressed to my banana-less reality: I ought to have a banana. The relative pronoun, 'what . . .' (*was . . .*), probably refers to the whole situation: just as practical mind sets up an antagonistic relationship between itself and external reality, so consciousness sets up a relationship, in desire an antagonistic relationship (cf. §426), 'towards' (*gegen*) external objects. It is unlikely to refer to the 'determinedness' or the 'reality'—the only neuter nouns in the vicinity; how could either of those alone develop into a relationship to objects? Possibly it refers to the 'ought': a discrepancy of sorts is involved in our relationship to objects.

2. The 'self-determination' (*Selbstbestimmung*) is the positing of the determinacy 'from out of' oneself. This is immediate: I just want a banana. I do not justify my want in universal terms. I do not, for example, claim that everyone has a right to a weekly banana. So from the point of view of the 'universality of thinking' my want is defective in form: I ought to justify my claim in universal terms. My want may also be defective in content: perhaps I should not have a banana. But even if I should have a banana, the form-deficiency still remains. This 'ought' or 'opposition' is only 'in itself', only 'for us' onlookers. Practical mind itself is not yet in a position to acknowledge this 'ought', since it does not yet participate in the universality of thinking. Only the first 'ought' is *for* the practical mind itself: it knows there is something wrong with not having a banana when it wants one.

NOTES TO §471

1. Practical 'feeling' is primarily the state in which 'I (just) feel like (eating) a banana', etc. It is the counterpart in practical mind of feeling in theoretical mind: cf. §§446–7 and also 399 ff. 'Formally' (*formell*) implies that the self-determination is not actual or substantial: what I feel like is not really in my control. On the relationship of practical feeling to reason, see §470, n. 2.

2. Here 'objective' is *objektive*, while 'objectivity' is *Gegenständlichkeit*. The variation may be only stylistic, but perhaps 'to which consciousness . . . ascribes *Gegenständlichkeit*' means 'which consciousness makes its object'. This is clearly a different matter from whether the content is 'objective' rather than 'subjective'. Consciousness can make into its object something (such as a feeling) that is subjective, rather than objective. But no content can be put into the form of feeling unless it is an object of consciousness.

3. On the overall theme of this Remark, see also §§400 (with regard not to *Gefühl*, 'feeling', but its near-synonym, *Empfindung*, 'sensation') and 447.

NOTES TO §472

1. This is the 'ought' (*Sollen*) of §470, n. 1. Practical feeling involves two factors: (1) its self-determination 'as being in itself' (*als an sich seiend*), i.e. as only implicit and unrealized: e.g. my wish for a banana. (2) 'an individuality that is in being' (*eine seiende Einzelheit*), i.e. the current individual state of affairs, such as my not having a banana, though there is one on the tree, etc. (2) is assessed only in terms of its adequacy to (1). Hence (1) addresses an 'ought' to (2), implying that (2) ought to be in conformity to (1). However, since neither (1) nor (2) has 'objective determination', i.e. neither is objectively right or wrong, the 'ought' takes the form not of a judgement of rightness or wrongness, but just a feeling of the pleasant (if I get my banana) or of the unpleasant (if I do not get my banana).

2. On 'remorse' (*Reue*) and other emotions, cf. §401, n. 19. Delight, joy, contentment arise when the current state of affairs conforms to the ought involved in my feeling; grief, shame, remorse arise when it does not conform to my feeling. But grief and shame, for example, differ in their 'content'. Shame is displeasure at my own defects, in view of the actual or possible disproval of others, while grief is displeasure arising from a sense of loss. These differences give a different 'determinacy' to the implied 'ought'. The 'ought' whose violation results in shame is something like: 'My person and my conduct ought to be such as to command the respect of others'. The 'ought' whose violation results in grief is something like: 'The goods and the people I cherish ought to remain in my possession'. (*Schmerz* can mean physical 'pain', as well as 'grief', but this does not affect Hegel's general point.)

3. 'Evil' here is *Übel*, which 'expresses an emotional dislike, particularly with reference to what is offensive to the senses, but mostly points to no objective characteristic of the person or thing that is rejected' (DGS, p. 36). It is not 'evil' or 'wicked' in a moral sense, as *böse* is: cf. §382, esp. n. 5. 'Evil' here is just the 'inadequacy of *being* to the *ought*', that things *are* not how they *ought* to be. If I want a banana, the 'meaning' of the implied 'ought' differs from that of the ought involved in my wanting an orange. Presumably Hegel believes that a prudential or felicific 'ought' ('I ought to eat healthy food, though I rather dislike it') and a moral 'ought' ('I ought to hand over the money I've found, even though it would make a big difference to my life if I could keep it') differ in 'meaning' both from each other and from the 'ought' implied in 'contingent purposes' more radically than different purposive oughts differ from each other. But at this stage he focuses on purposive oughts. He wants to maintain that there is no unjustifiable or inexplicable evil in the world, and so argues that purposes that are frustrated get no more than their just deserts. To someone who complains that an illness, an accident or the death of a loved one is an incomprehensible evil, Hegel replies that the desire for exemption from such mishaps is itself an evil, given that they are an intrinsic feature of life in general.

4. 'Judgement' (*Urteil*) here combines the ideas of division or bifurcation (cf. §389, n. 4, etc.), and of a judgement or assessment of oneself. Life and mind are finite

because they have an 'Other' separated from them, as do other finite things. But they also have this other 'within them'. It is not quite clear whether the 'Other' is other, surrounding entities or, alternatively, injury, whether, that is, the Other of life is its environment or illness and death, and whether the Other of mind is its surroundings or the frustration of its purposes, etc. But this may not matter, since both are obviously involved. The environment that sustains life also brings illness and death. The environment that enables mind to fulfil its aims may also frustrate them. So life and mind are a sort of 'contradiction', the co-presence of themselves and their 'negative'. Unlike dead, i.e. non-living, things, living things involve a confrontation between the concept and its 'reality' (*Dasein*), while the concept remains 'its' subject, the subject of the 'distinction'. That is, a living thing, especially a mind, is aware both of itself (the concept) and of its potentially discordant other (the reality). ('Its', *dessen*, might, alternatively, refer to the 'reality'.But this is less likely.)

A natural non-living thing, such as a rock, may crumble, but here there is no clear-cut concept–reality distinction, no way in which the rock ought to be, unless we consult the interests of living things involved in its fate. The rock has an 'Other', namely crumbling and/or the things that cause it, but it does not contain this Other within itself; it just undergoes a change. An artificial non-living thing, such as a wall, may crumble. Here there is a definite concept–reality distinction, some way the wall ought to be. But this depends entirely on the purposes and needs of human beings. An animal may become ill. Here too there is a definite concept–reality distinction, but in this case the distinction and the disparity depend on the animal itself. The animal feels the disparity between its concept and its reality as pain. It does this because the concept remains the 'subject' of the distinction between itself and its substandard reality (or perhaps of simply of the reality). By contrast, the concept of the original rock does not remain the 'subject' of the disparity between its pristine and its crumbled state (or perhaps just of its crumbled state); if the rock has a concept all, its concept just changes in line with the rock, leaving no disparity. In the case of the mind, the concept is 'subjectivity, I' and perhaps 'freedom', while 'this negativity' is the discrepancy between the concept and its reality. Hence the 'ought', evil, and pain. On pain, see also §§381, n. 9; §382, nn. 1 and 4.

A difficulty in this account is that the concept plays a double role. It is (1) the ideal nature of the creature, and (2) it is what is aware of the discrepancy between the ideal nature and the reality, and addresses an 'ought' to the reality. Perhaps this is what Hegel has in mind when he implies that the concept remains the 'subject' of the distinction, not just one term of the distinction. He would no doubt say that the concept 'overarches' its Other: cf. §465, n. 1. But often the two roles are separated. Suppose, for example, that I am stupid, sufficiently stupid for there to be a significant discrepancy between my concept and its reality. I may be aware of my stupidity, and perhaps distressed by it. In that case, I span both my concept and its reality. Perhaps then we can can say that I am my concept, that my concept is aware of the concept–reality discrepancy. But

I may, on the other hand, be unaware of my stupidity. Then my concept qua ideal nature is in play, since otherwise I could not be assessed as stupid by a third party; there would be nothing wrong with me; I would just be different. But the concept qua I is, with respect to this issue, in abeyance. How can that be, if I *am* my ideal nature? At the very least, if I can remain unaware of and unperturbed by a discrepancy between my concept and my reality, the existence of such a discrepancy cannot by itself account for pain and distress.

5. Cf. §411, n. 2. Jakob Böhme (1575–1624) was a Lutheran mystic much exercised by the problem of evil. He was also addicted to wordplay. He connects *Qual* ('torment') with *Quelle* ('source'), especially in *Aurora oder Morgenröte im Aufgang* (*Aurora or the Dawn in its Rising*, written 1612, published 1634). Hegel deals with him at length in HP. As well as admiring the wordplay, Hegel agrees with his overall message, that evil is an essential ingredient of 'I-hood' (*Ichheit*).

6. The will is 'simple identity with itself' because it just feels like something, with no detour through reasoning or justification. The 'difference' (*Differenz*) is between what it self-determinedly wants and what it is currently getting 'from outside', namely 'affections' (*Affektionen*) such as hunger. On the pleasant and unpleasant, cf. §§401, nn. 4 and 16; 471, n. 1.

7. The pleasure I get from eating a banana does not depend on my believing that it is a banana I am eating, nor need the feeling it satisfies be anything so definite as wanting a banana; it may just be wanting that over there or wanting something to eat. By contrast, my 'joy' (*Freude*) at getting good examination results depends more on my belief that I have done so, and less on definite, localizable sensations. Hence it gets its 'content' from 'intuition or from representation'. This is even more evident in the case of 'fear' (*Furcht*), where my immediate sensations may be intrinsically quite pleasant, marred only by my belief that there are tigers in the vicinity. 'Terror' (*Schrecken*) assails me when I identify the attractive striped creature beside me as a tiger, knowing its likely behaviour from my tiger-representation.

   Hegel does not explore all the complexities of these emotions. His account of fear, for example, does not cater for fearing for the safety of another. Perhaps he would say that fear is primarily fear for oneself and that fear for another either involves fear for oneself (one's loss of a loved one, say) or belongs to a higher stage of practical mind. Again, his description of joy does not distinguish between the case where I previously wanted a certain outcome, such as the good examination results that I have been anxiously waiting for, and the case where I did not, such as my unexpectedly winning a lottery with a ticket I had forgotten about. In the former case my 'determinedness-in-and-for-itself' is a definite desire for good results and it addresses an 'ought' to the external world. In the latter case I have no such desire and do not address an 'ought' to the world in advance, only register my approval afterwards: I might have been quite happy if I had not won the lottery, even unaware of it.

8. This seems to refer both to the second class of feelings, joy, etc. and to the first class, feelings of pleasure and displeasure. Whether I am afraid or not and what I am afraid of depends on my environment (the jungle, the dentist's surgery) or on

my beliefs about it ('intuition' and 'representation'). Whether I feel pleasure or not depends on whether I eat the banana. Both these classes are contrasted with the third class of feelings: see §472, n. 9.

9. Hegel's distinction between this class of feeling and the previous two classes involves two points: (1) What is 'determined-in-and-for-itself', such as my duty to pay my debts or my belief that I have such a duty, is intrinsically and objectively right or, perhaps, wrong. If I do not much care about my examination results or do not fear tigers or dentists, I am not in the wrong, only unusual. (I may have a duty to develop my talents or to take care of my safety, but this need not involve concern for examination results or avoidance of jungles and dentists and, in any case, such a duty raises these feelings to the ethical plane.) I *am* in the wrong if I do not care about debt-repayment. (2) What conflicts, or perhaps agrees, with what is thus 'determined-in-and-for-itself' is not something 'from outside' but, in Hegel's examples, my own activity. The contrast with fear, etc. is somewhat weakened by the fact that in the cases of shame or remorse, the activity may well be my past activity, not activity over which I now have control. I may be ashamed or remorseful because before my conversion I helped to stone Christians, even though that is not something I can alter now.

When Hegel says that 'these feelings . . . are distinguished from one another by their own *peculiar content*', whereas the first two classes 'have no *content immanent* in them', he may mean that whether an emotion is one of joy or of fear is determined solely by its external object (good results/success or tigers/danger), but whether an emotion is one of 'remorse' (*Reue*) or 'regret' (also *Reue*) is determined not only by one's activity (non-payment of debts) but by whether it is viewed as conflicting with one's 'duty' or with one's 'advantage'. It is true that the presence of danger may arouse exhilaration rather than fear, but this does not depend on any content that it is 'determined-in-and-for-itself'.

10. Feelings are neither sufficient nor necessary for morally appropriate attitudes and responses. Remorse over what is in fact a 'good deed' might result from defective moral attitudes: e.g. I feel remorse for having declared some income that I could have concealed from the tax-inspector. But Hegel more probably has in mind cases where, in a difficult situation, I choose the lesser of two evils (e.g. I shoot one of the hostages myself in order to save the rest from being shot by their captors) but nevertheless feel remorse over my deed. My remorse is here in conflict with what Hegel would probably regard as my duty, though it is likely that if I had performed the alternative action (e.g. refrained from shooting anyone myself, and thus allowing all the hostages to be shot) I would also have felt remorse. Still, since it is likely that in such a situation I would feel remorse whichever alternative I chose, a feeling of remorse is not a reliable indicator of what I should have done.

11. Hegel endorses the Stoic ideal of *ataraxia* or imperturbability, at least in the face of one's own good or bad fortune. Excessive concern about one's own fate belongs to one's 'individual world' rather than the objective world favoured by 'science': cf. §402, n. 8. From an 'objective' point of view, it does not matter whether it is I who win the lottery or someone else relevantly similar to myself.

In principle perhaps I should not care in the least who in particular wins the lottery, but only about impersonal matters, such as the overall effect of the lottery
on the national spirit and the causes supported by the lottery. In practice this is
asking too much of us. We all need to make some concessions to our individual world and to the particular ego at its centre. That is why most people enter
lotteries in the first place. But we should not get too carried away by our own
successes and failures.

NOTES TO §473

1. In §472 Hegel dealt with the case where something I happen to come across,
   a 'current [*seienden*] determinacy', just happens to answer to my need. But the
   will is essentially self-determining, and so it ought not simply to rely on chance
   encounters to actualize the harmony between its own 'universality' (or 'inner
   determination') and the 'determinacy' (or 'reality', *Dasein*). It should bring
   about this harmony itself. This is where the 'urge' or drive (*Trieb*) comes in. I
   do not simply come across a banana and find it pleasant. I want a banana and
   set about getting one. This is what Hegel means by saying that the practical
   'ought' (*Sollen*) is a 'real' (*reelles*) judgement. It does not just passively reflect on
   my want, the objective state of affairs, and the relationship between them. It sets
   about actively modifying the state of affairs so that it harmonizes with my want.
   Thus 'judgement' (*Urteil*) here has the force of bringing two things together,
   rather than (as often in Hegel: cf. §389, n. 4) of prising them apart.
2. The 'content' of my will is an urge for, say, a banana. This content could take a
   variety of forms. I might want a banana for a dietary reason, even perhaps for a
   moral, or a religious reason. I might have submitted my want to a dietary, moral,
   or religious test before giving way to it. But here none of these factors are in play.
   I just want a banana and so my will is 'natural', 'immediately identical with its
   determinacy', with no moral or other supervision. But I may not have placed the
   'totality of the practical mind' in this determinacy. That is, I may want other
   things that would divert me from my pursuit of a banana. If I find something
   better, a pineapple say, or if a ferocious stranger bars my way, I shall give up my
   pursuit. If however I do place the totality of my practical mind in some such
   object, so that I cannot be diverted or deterred from its pursuit by anything else,
   then what I have is not just an urge, but a 'passion' (*Leidenschaft*). The object
   of a passion might be a banana, though it is more likely to be, say, a beloved or
   a political cause. But in any case, the object of a passion is only one of 'many
   restricted determinations'. My beloved is only one of many possible objects of
   desire, my cause only one of many worthy causes. Any such determination is
   'posited . . . with the opposite', that is, I opt for Catholicism in preference to its
   opposite, Protestantism, for socialism rather than capitalism, and so on. I throw
   my whole weight into one of the scales rather than its opposite.
3. *Trieb* ('urge') is 'an innate disposition towards a thing and is therefore
   thought of as permanent. It is therefore a close synonym of *Instinkt*', but it

is 'a wider term than *Instinkt*. As a psychological term it is translated and introduced into English by American psychologists as "drive" ' (DGS, p. 363). Wallace's 'impulse' is not a very appropriate translation of *Trieb* in this sense, since 'impulse' suggests 'suddenness and capriciousness' (DGS, p. 363). An 'inclination' (*Neigung*) is similar to a *Trieb* in its 'universality'; Kant regarded it as a 'habitual sensory desire'. *Begierde* ('desire') 'refers only to strongly emotional desires and is thus more restricted in application than "desire". *Begierde* concentrates attention on the subject'. The corresponding adjective, *begierig*, means 'desirous of getting possession of something which satisfies an appetite or insistent desire, for oneself, not for others' (DGS, p. 18). Hence *Begierde* fits well into the account of self-consciousness.

Hegel's distinction between *Trieb* and *Begierde* is thus confirmed by ordinary usage. Here he applies the distinction in the following way. In §426 consciousness does not yet conceive the external world as a stable, regular objective order. The world is a baffling chaos of sensory entities. Thus consciousness does not regard the world as a reliable source of satisfaction for its long-term urges, as providing, for example, a regular supply of bananas. It just encounters individual entities and desires them on the spot. Correspondingly, consciousness, though it regards itself as 'I', does not view itself as the bearer of long-term urges needing regular satisfaction. It has only momentary impulses in the face of individual objects it encounters. Desire and the satisfaction of desire is consciousness's first attempt to establish an intelligible relationship between itself and the external world. By now, however, such an intelligible relationship has been established. The I has long term urges and it can satisfy them in the world. No doubt the I still has desires, but the desires are now expressions of an urge, not (for the most part) fleeting whims.

As compared to desire and to 'practical feeling', an urge is universal. The urge to eat, for example, is satisfied not just by eating on one occasion but by eating on indefinitely many occasions throughout one's life. The urge to eat is, however, only one urge among others: the urge to drink, the sexual urge, and so on. Such urges may conflict with each other; I may, for example, be unable to satisfy on a given occasion my sexual urge and my urge to eat. For this and for other reasons (such as the fact that the satisfaction of an urge on this occasion may impede the satisfaction of the same urge on subsequent occasions) we need some way of assessing the claims of various urges and deciding which to satisfy on which occasions. The notion of happiness (see §479) is one way of deciding these matters, and happiness will be 'universal' in a way that an urge is not. In comparison to happiness, each urge will be 'particular' (see §378, n. 10), one particular urge alongside other particular urges. This stems from the fact that urge is only the first 'negation' of individuality, not its second negation, the negation of the negation: cf. §425, n. 1. Someone absorbed in urges is 'unfree' in that he is, as it were, jostled this way and that by a crowd of urges, unable to rise above them and decide where his best direction lies.

NOTES TO §474

1. A practical feeling is e.g. the pleasure one feels at getting something to eat on a particular occasion. An inclination (here equivalent to an urge) is one's long-term disposition to eat when one wants to. A passion is an obsessive tendency to eat, regardless of all other considerations. Hence they have the same content, e.g. eating, but differ in form. On the contingency and particularity of inclinations, cf. §§471, n. 2; 473, n. 3. They 'stand . . . in an external relationship' to each other, because they are not intelligibly connected or ordered with respect to each other. There is as yet no way of answering the question 'Which of my inclinations should I satisfy now?' They are externally related to the individual because the individual plays no part in the creation or formation of his own inclinations. They are simply there, with no rhyme or reason to them. Hence in satisfying an inclination the individual is determined by, or at least submitting to, an alien power, something other than himself. To be determined by something other than oneself is, in Hegel's view, to be unfree.

2. Passion is a sort of monomania: cf. §473, n. 2. The impassioned person throws his whole weight into one cause (the Guelphs, say) against the opposing cause (the Ghibellines), neglecting or subordinating the many other worthwhile pursuits that have nothing to do with this particular dispute. One might object to passion for three reasons. (i) The cause chosen might be bad or wholly unworthy of single-minded devotion, such as food or drink. Hegel agrees with this. That is why some passions are 'evil' (*böse*). (ii) A passion is inevitably one-sided. Should a philosopher or a historian not be impartial, at least less obsessively partial than the people he studies? To this, Hegel would reply that even if the philosopher or historian is not a single-minded Guelph or a single-minded Ghibelline, he must be devoted to philosophy or to history at the expense of other pursuits. If people were not one-sided in the appropriate way, conflicts would not occur and conflicts would not be studied. (iii) It is possible to support a cause, even to support it with unswerving loyalty, without *passion*, just as it is possible to want to win a lottery without feeling joy when one does so: cf. §472, n. 11. So we might endorse partisanship, while condemning passion. We might argue, as the Stoics did, that passion upsets the balance of the mind. Hegel agreed with the Stoics in condemning joy and grief at one's own good and bad fortune, but he did so for the reason that this makes too much of *oneself*. He disagrees with their condemnation of passion *in general*. Great achievements depend on single-minded partisanship, and this can only be motivated by passion. Reason alone can rarely supply a watertight case for supporting one cause rather than another, and in any case it is not obvious that a rationally watertight case alone can motivate whole-hearted partisanship unless it is accompanied by, or somehow generates, passion.

    Hegel's thesis that nothing great is ever achieved without passion (cf. PH, p. 23) looks false. Newton made great achievements in science, though his main interest was theology. If science and theology are two distinct 'contents' and if

Newton was interested in both contemporaneously, then he had no passion, since he did not place the whole vitality of his mind, etc. in one content.

3. It is not clear why the 'situation' (*Bewandtnis*) of the 'numerous urges, etc.' is the same as the situation with the 'powers of the soul'. The powers of the soul are not said to be good or evil, nor do they conflict with each other in any obvious way—unless Hegel has in mind such things as perceptual illusions, where e.g. a stick in water looks bent, but our previous experience and our calculations tell us that it is straight. Moreover, Hegel's solution differs in the two cases. He orders the collection of soul-powers by discerning a rational organization of them within the 'subjective' mind itself. He does not in this case appeal to anything like 'objective' mind. It is true that the subjective mind becomes aware of an objective *world*, but this is a consequence of the rational order within the mind rather than a cause of it. By contrast the disorderly array of urges is reduced to order by objective mind. This difference is related to the fact that whereas the soul-powers form, in Hegel's view (cf. §440, n. 3), a hierarchy, progressing towards greater independence of sensory input, the urges and inclinations do not. They all stem from the same soul-power, or at any rate the differences between them are not of such generality that philosophy can put them in order. The potential conflict between e.g. the sexual urge and the urge to eat can only be averted by non-philosophical means, by, say, one's own conception of happiness or by the provisions of objective mind. Philosophy can tell us that this is where the solution lies, but it cannot itself provide it.

4. The 'formal' rationality of urges, their common or 'universal' urge to be realized, is not 'genuine' rationality, since in cases of conflict, between one urge and another or between the present satisfaction of an urge and its future satisfaction, it does not tell us what to do. 'External reflexion' (*äusseren Reflexion*) does not help, since that just leaves the urges as they were before. What is needed is the kind of reflexion that will induce a development of the mind itself, and this can only be a reflexion within the mind in question. This type of reflexion alters what is reflected, as a light ray is altered by being reflected back from a mirror: cf. Enc. I, §112Z., discussed in §402, n. 1. It is not just that the mind itself transcends the particularity and immediacy of the urges; that still would not tell us whether or how to satisfy them. Rather, the urges themselves are transformed into 'rights and duties'.

This account leaves two questions:

    (i) The reflexion of a ray alters the direction of the ray. But how does that apply to my urges? The most obvious application would be that in attempting to realize my urges, I find that I cannot do so satisfactorily, and that a frustrated urge is reflected back from an impervious world into the mind. But there is little sign of that idea here, though it does occur elsewhere: cf. §§396, n. 14; 410, n. 7. Hegel's idea is rather that in reflecting *on* my urges, I disclose the 'essence' that lies behind their immediate surface. But a sheer urge does not have an appropriate essence all along. Finding the essence of an urge is not like finding that water is H_2O. It is more like finding that I am a violinist by learning to play the violin, a transformation as much as a discovery.

(ii) Why does reflexion on urges convert them into rights and duties? Hegel's aim is not simply to order the urges so that disputes between them can be settled. It is to transcend their immediacy and contingency. The sexual urge is something one contingently happens to have. As an urge it involves a general drive to satisfy itself. But one does not have a right, let alone as duty, to satisfy it and others have no duty to provide such satisfaction. But when it is 'objectified' in objective mind, specifically in the family (cf. §§518 ff.), one acquires a right to sexual satisfaction from one's spouse and a corresponding duty to satisfy one's spouse's sexual urge. One's urge has left the realm of private subjectivity and entered the objective public economy. At the same time, urges acquire an ordering that settles disputes between them; the sexual urge, for example, is not to be satisfied at mealtimes. Analogously, the bits of metal in one's private collection may be exchanged for goods, but others have no duty to accept them and they have no fixed value, until they are publicly recognized as valid currency.

5. In Books II–IV of his *Republic* Plato, through the mouth of Socrates, describes first the ideally just state or city and then the ideally just person. The reason given for describing the just state first is that since the state is larger than a person, it is easier to discern justice in a state than in a person (*Republic*, II, 368b–369a10). Justice has the same form or structure in a just state and a just person: the just state is a state in which rational, educated guardians, assisted by disciplined and courageous warriors, rule over the class of workers; a just person is one in whom reason, assisted by disciplined emotion, rules over desires. A just state requires just persons: the guardians are just persons in the full sense, while the warriors and the workers are just in a derivative sense: they are ruled not by their own reason, but by the surrogate reason of the guardians. Plato does not say that a just person requires a just state, however. It is possible, though no doubt more difficult, to be a just person in an unjust state, though not, perhaps, in no state at all. Correspondingly, it would have been possible, though perhaps more difficult, for Plato to describe a just person without describing a just state. (Plato's real reason for starting with justice in the state is that it enables him to present the justice of a person as an internal condition of the soul, rather than a matter of external conduct, since the justice of a state is primarily an internal condition of the state.) Hegel's account differs from Plato's. He does not describe the state before describing a just person; he begins with the person and reveals problems which, he argues, can only be resolved by viewing the person in the context of a society. It is more plausible for him to suppose that an individual cannot be just unless he is in the society described, since the society that Hegel introduces is not an ideally just society. (In Hegel's view, the state that Plato described was not an ideal society but simply the existing Greek city-state in its fundamental structure. For criticism of Hegel's interpretation, see my 'Plato, Hegel, and Greek

Sittlichkeit', in Z. A.Pelczynski, (ed.), *The State and Civil Society* (Cambridge, Cambridge University Press, 1984))

The last part of the sentence, 'and also . . . right of the mind' (*auch insofern er unter dem Rechte des Geistes seine ganze Natur befasste*—the words appear earlier in the German sentence, not at the end) presents two problems: (i) Do the words *seine ganze Natur*, literally 'its whole nature', refer to the whole nature of the mind or the whole nature of 'right'? The latter interpretation is possible, but the former makes more sense. (ii) But what sense? Is the whole nature of the mind that is included in the 'right', i.e. approximately 'justice', the whole nature of the *subjective* mind, i.e. reason, emotion, and desire, or does it also cover *objective* mind, i.e. society, as well as subjective mind? On the latter interpretation, Hegel is making the same point as before, namely that in Plato's view the justice of the mind involves the social order as well as the individual mind. On the former interpretation, he is making a distinct point, that the right or justice of the mind involves the whole of the individual subjective mind. This could be an implicit criticism of Kant, who, as Hegel interpreted him, argued that emotions and desires play only a negative role in morality, and that someone who obeys the commands of reason may be morally impeccable, even if his emotions and desires are thoroughly unruly.

NOTES TO §475

1. The subject 'joins together with itself' in the 'objectivity' of its satisfied urge, because it gets what it wants. The 'important thing' is the *Sache*, 'thing' as used in such expressions as 'The thing is that . . .' and 'The (main, great) thing is to get started'. It may be distinct from the activity of producing it, though presumably the activity itself (e.g. eating) may be one's purpose rather than the upshot of the activity (e.g. repletion), in which case the activity itself is the 'thing'. 'Interest' is *Interesse*, here in the sense in which it is compatible with disinterest or impartiality. Interest is the subject's favourable attitude towards the *Sache*, which is required to motivate the subject's activity.
2. 'Most unselfish' is *uneigennützigsten*. An action's unselfishness is entirely compatible with the subject's having an interest in it.
3. Each of the positions criticized suggests that action is possible without an urge or inclination. In utopian 'natural happiness' (*Naturglück*) 'needs' are immediately satisfied without any delay and without any activity on the subject's part, so that urges are superfluous. In the second position, 'morality' or 'the ethical' (which are not differentiated here), the subject's recognition of his duty, motivates the subject to activity without any urge or inclination. Hegel's objection to this (Kant's) view is ambiguous. It might mean:
   (i) A subject's recognition of his duty is never alone sufficient to motivate action. He must in addition *want* to perform the action, though this want may simply result from his desire to do his duty. If the subject wants to do his duty, this is in effect an urge or an inclination, albeit an urge or inclination to do one's duty.

(ii) A desire to do one's duty is never alone sufficient to motivate action. The subject must always have some other urge or inclination if he is to do his duty.

(iii) A desire that duty be done is never alone sufficient to motivate action. What is needed to motivate a given subject to do *his* duty is that subject's urge to do it, whether this stems from a general urge to do his duty or from some other urge.

Criticism (i) still allows that some people do, in a sense, do their duty for duty's sake, namely those who do their duty only from an urge to do their duty, with the assistance of no other urge. It does nevertheless vitiate Kant's claim that such people attain a special sort of freedom, freedom from the motivating influence of their contingent urges and inclinations. The urge to do one's duty now looks like only one among other contingent and motivating urges. Criticism (ii) implies that no one does their duty *exclusively* for duty's sake. Criticism (iii) suggests that no one does their duty for the sake of duty *as such*, but at most for the sake of their *own* duty. A general desire to maximize the performance of duty may lead me to neglect *my* duty. If, for example, I go to a shop with two companions, they may say to me that if I pay for my goods, they will shoplift, whereas if I shoplift, they will pay for their goods. If I believe them, then my desire to maximize duty-performance (or to minimize neglect of duty) may induce me to shoplift. It is only if I have a desire to do *my* duty that I will disregard their offer and stick to my own devices.

4. The will is essentially free. Hence freedom is the concept of the will. Normally, however, a will has other 'content' apart from freedom, e.g. a desire for food. A selfish person will satisfy his desire for food by shoplifting, if he thinks he can get away with it, since he prefers the 'particular content' (his desire for food and money) to the 'objective content' (the wrongness of shoplifting). A good person, let alone the 'purest . . . will', will not shoplift if he does not face starvation. But what will he do if shoplifting is the only way to avoid starvation? Hegel's words allow three different answers:

(1) He will, and ought to, shoplift in order to avoid literal 'perishing' (*zugrunde gehen*), i.e dying.

(2) He will not, and ought not to, shoplift, even though he does 'not wish' (*will . . . nicht*) and ought not to suffer the inevitable consequence. (That x ought not to happen and that my φ-ing is the only way of preventing the occurrence of x do not entail that I ought to φ. That I ought not to be tortured and that my revealing next year's examination questions is the only way to avoid this do not entail that I ought to reveal the examination questions.)

(3) His prospective starvation is irrelevant to the question whether he will or ought to shoplift, since *zugrunde gehen* does not mean literally 'perish'. He may shoplift or, more likely, he may not. What he will not do is something that he does not *want* to do, in a wide sense of 'want'.

NOTES TO §476

1. Someone who does not transcend his urges in this way is 'unfree': cf. §§473, n. 3; 474, n. 1. The will that does transcend the urges and reflect on them is only 'implicitly' (*an sich*) free, since it is as yet empty, lacking any resolve of its own. It only becomes free 'for itself', when it adopts an urge as its own: cf. §§477–8.

NOTES TO §477

1. If I have an urge to eat and an urge to drink but cannot do both and then decide to drink rather than eat, the 'particularity' of the urge to drink has been endorsed or adopted by the will and thus gives the otherwise indeterminate will a determinacy of its own. 'Wilfulness' is *Willkür*, a word formed from *Wille* ('will') and which has not yet acquired its modern sense of 'arbitrariness'. In Kant and Hegel it is not generally a term of disapproval. It indicates a phase of the will, though not the highest phase: free choice.

NOTES TO §478

1. The 'immediate self-determination' of the will is its adoption of some particular urge, say the urge to drink, as its own. But the will is not wholly absorbed or engrossed in the urge to drink, as is someone who without reflecting at all simply gives way to his urge to drink. The will could have chosen to eat rather than drink. It could perhaps have chosen to indulge neither urge but to fast instead. Hence the will is 'reflected into itself as the negativity, etc.'.
2. The 'contradiction' is between the fact that the will is 'reflected into itself, etc.', not identical with or absorbed in any particular urge, and the fact that if it is to actualize itself, i.e. will to do anything definite, it can only adopt some particular and contingent urge. As often in Hegel, the initial resolution of the contradiction is an infinite progression, moving from the satisfaction of one urge to the satisfaction of another urge: cf. §426 n. 1, etc. on 'desire'. 'Distraction' is *Zerstreuung*, literally 'dispersion, scattering, strewing (an English relative of the root verb *streuen*)', hence 'diversion, amusement'. Happiness resolves both the contradiction and the infinite progression.

NOTES TO §479

1. Happiness requires the sacrifice of one urge to another; e.g. I do not eat as much as I would like, since I need to drink too. It also requires the sacrifice of the present satisfaction of an urge to the future satisfaction of the same urge; e.g. if I forgo one chocolate now, I will be given two chocolates later on. It is not clear what Hegel means by the sacrifice of an urge 'directly' (*direkt*) to happiness. Perhaps he is thinking of such urges as an urge to drink a litre of whisky a day,

though one might equally regard the sacrifice of this urge as a sacrifice to a negative urge, such as an urge not to have hangovers, rather than as a direct sacrifice to happiness.

2. If offered a choice between a banana and a chocolate, I may choose a banana, since I prefer them to chocolate. This is presumably a 'qualitative . . . determination'. But if offered a choice between one banana (or one chocolate) and a whole box of chocolates, I may prefer the chocolates—a 'quantitative determination'. Urges are limited by each other, but they have the final say, since what my happiness consists in depends on what urges I happen to have.

NOTES TO §480

1. In contrast to the particular urges happiness is universal, but its universality is only 'represented' (*vorgestellte*) by us, superimposed on a collection of urges whose intrinsic nature is not constituted or affected by it. It is also intrinsically empty, with no content of its own except what it derives from the urges. It is thus 'abstract', not concrete universality: cf. §§387, n. 18; 445, n. 7; 456, n. 3; 469, n. 13. When Hegel says that this universality 'only ought to be' (*nur sein soll*), it is not clear whether he means (i) that it *ought* to be, but is not actual *now*, or (ii) that it is only *supposed* to be real, but is not actually real. Claim (ii) would follow naturally from the fact that happiness is only represented and abstract: happiness is not real, since it has no content of its own and is not inherent in the urges. Claim (i) would present a new point: happiness is always something that ought to be realized, but never actually is so. Perhaps Hegel combines the two claims. They are after all not unrelated. Claim (i) seems to entail (ii), though (ii) does not entail (i).

2. Happiness is described in paradoxical ways. The 'particular determinacy', viz. the urge, is sublated as much as it is, i.e. it counts towards happiness but is sacrificed to other urges. Wilfulness gives itself a purpose, i.e. it reaches a decision about what to do, but it does not give itself a purpose, i.e. it derives this decision from the urges. There is, however, something for the will to aim at which is not simply a function of the urges. This is the will's own freedom, its 'self-determination'. This is universal in a way that a particular urge is not ('pure'). But it is also determinate, not simply a blank cheque waiting to be filled in by the urges ('concrete'). If the will makes its own freedom its purpose, it will be more fully self-determining, free, than hitherto, since the 'concept', the will, and the 'object', the purpose of the will, are the same, namely freedom or the will itself. The will now gets its content or purpose from itself alone, and does not depend on contingent urges. Truth, as well as freedom, consists in the identity of concept and object: cf. §§379, n. 5; 381, n. 7; 382, n. 3. The formula makes better sense in the case of theoretical mind than in the case of the will. We can see, at least roughly, what is meant by saying that thought thinks about thought, or that the mind thinks about the mind. But what does it mean to say that the will wills itself or wills freedom? For further explanation of this, see §482, n. 1.

NOTES TO §481

1. On the 'unity of theoretical and practical mind', see §443, n. 3. That free will is *'for itself as free will'* means: (i) it is actual free will, not just potential free will; (ii) it is aware of being free will; and (iii) it has itself, free will, as its object and purpose. Previously, the content of the will was 'mediated' by contingent, limited urges. This involved 'formalism', since the will's content was simply a function of the contents, and relative strengths, of the urges. The emergence of the pure will was also mediated by the formalism of wilfulness and its sublation. Now all that has been 'sublated', and the will pulls itself up by its own bootstraps as an *'immediate individuality'*, as an individual that has left behind the mediation that previously supplied its content and also the mediation that led to its emergence.

2. Hegel earlier associated 'intelligence' (*Intelligenz*) with theoretical mind and distinguished it from the will: see §445. In §443 (see n. 2) and §448 (see n. 13) 'free intelligence' refers to the highest phase of theoretical mind. Hence Hegel here stresses the convergence of theoretical and practical mind in the will. The will 'thinks [of, about] itself' (*sich denkt*), rather in the way that thought thinks about thought. It is difficult, however, to see what the practical implications of this are.

NOTES TO §482

1. The difficulty of this Paragraph stems from the fact that Hegel is trying to construct, or discern, the logical transition from the free will as expounded in §§480 and 481, the will that wills its own freedom, to 'objective mind'. 'Idea' (*Idee*) in Hegel's technical sense is the concept together with its 'reality' (*Realität, Dasein,* etc.). Hence the will that wills itself as its own object and purpose is an Idea, not just a concept, but a concept together with itself as its object. There are, however, Ideas and Ideas, and Hegel notes two deficiencies in this Idea:

   (1) It is the rational will *'in general'* (*überhaupt*), i.e. not embodied in specific, concrete institutions and procedures. It is *'in itself'* the Idea, but not for itself, let alone in and for itself. Hence it is only a concept—the concept of 'absolute mind'. Absolute mind combines subjective and objective minds: cf. §§381, n. 18; 553, n. 1. If subjective mind is the concept of absolute mind and objective mind its reality, then to say that the will is here only the concept of absolute mind implies that it requires completion by objective mind.

   (2) As abstract rather than concrete, the Idea exists only in the 'immediate' will, i.e. in the will of an individual, but not in concrete institutions and procedures, not in what might be called the 'social' will or the 'general' will, a will that is mediated by individual wills. The individual will is a 'finite' will, whereas the social will is, by contrast, implied to be infinite. This abstract Idea is thus not merely a concept, it is the 'reality' of reason, since it is embedded in individuals who work to realize the Idea as 'reality' (*Dasein*) and as 'actuality' rather than mere potentiality.

The two deficiencies seem at odds with each other. In (1) the Idea is the rational will in general; in (2) it exists in the 'immediate' will. In (1) the Idea is a concept, albeit the concept of absolute mind; in (2) it is reason's reality. The reason for the discrepancies is this. In (1) the Idea of freedom is regarded as a general account of free human beings, disregarding the social context to which they belong. The account could well apply to any human being at any stage of history. But this Idea is an abstraction. There cannot be a human being who is aware of and aims at freedom alone, but does not aim at anything more specific and does not belong in any social context. Hence we need to bring in the social context, 'objective mind', to complete our account of the free human being. In (2), by contrast, the Idea of freedom is an Idea in people's minds, an 'idea' in the more usual sense. Here Hegel moves from his technical sense of *Idee* to the usual sense, in which it 'has all meanings of "idea", from its philosophic use to that of "notion", whether vague or clear, "belief", "fancy", "plan"' (DGS, p. 155)—though Hegel's use of '*Idee*' still marks the fact that it is the idea of something especially elevated and significant. The Idea of freedom in this sense applies to all human beings, but it does not exist in the minds of all human beings. As Hegel explains in the Remark, it arose with Christianity and was then gradually realized in European institutions. Its existence in the minds of individuals is a sort of 'reality', but it acquires 'reality' in objective mind only gradually, through the activity of individual wills. The expression 'objective mind' involves a corresponding ambiguity. It refers both to (i) the social institutions of any and every time and place, in contrast to the individual human mind, and to (ii) specifically modern social institutions that realize and express the essential freedom of every human being. What Hegel goes on to describe is more or less (ii) rather than (i).

The ambiguity of *Idee* facilitates the transition from subjective to objective mind. To the question: 'Why does the Idea of will willing its freedom require completion in objective mind?' there is no obvious answer except that this Idea is hard to make sense of without some more concrete interpretation and that, in any case, there cannot be human subjective minds without objective mind. In this case the transition will be made by Hegel himself, dissatisfied with the incompleteness and near senselessness of the picture he has produced. To the question: 'Why do people with the Idea of freedom endeavour to realize it in objective mind?' the answer is that people with a potent and practicable idea try to realize it. Here the transition is not just from the Idea of freedom, but from the Idea of freedom in an objective mind discordant with it to an objective mind that embodies it. This is not a transition made by Hegel alone; it is made by individual wills transforming their social order.

2. In speaking of 'misconceptions' and the 'uncontrollable strength' of the 'abstract concept of freedom' Hegel is thinking especially of the French Revolution. It is not clear how the identification of the 'free mind' with the 'actual' (*wirkliche*) mind explains the 'practical consequences' of mistakes about it. After all, fundamental mistakes about the mind, about thought for example, need not have momentous practical results. Perhaps it is because freedom is the point of connection between the subjective mind and objective mind, which is more or less

identified with 'actuality' (*Wirklichkeit*) at the end of the Paragraph. The affinity of *wirklich* to *wirken*, 'to work, have an effect', may also influence Hegel's claim.

3. On ancient views of freedom, see §433, n. 4. Hegel here attributes two views of freedom to the Greeks and Romans: (i) Freedom acquired by birth, i.e. citizenship, and (ii) freedom acquired by one's own efforts, an inner freedom or self-mastery that is indifferent towards one's bodily enslavement. (Hegel over-simplifies: e.g. in Athens a resident alien—such as Aristotle—was free, i.e. not a slave, though he did not enjoy civic rights.) The view of freedom introduced by Christianity, the Idea of freedom, is that (iii) freedom belongs to all human beings regardless of their birth, social status, and intellectual attainments. The introduction of this Idea involves two stages:

   (1) 'In religion' God assigns 'infinite value' to each individual, and 'man *in himself*' (*der Mensch an sich*), i.e. man as such regardless of birth, intellect, etc., is 'destined' (*bestimmt*) to supreme freedom, presumably in heaven.
   (2) In 'worldly existence', i.e. outside the sphere of religion proper, God is also somehow present, and social and political institutions are arranged so as to realize the freedom promised in religion, making man 'actually free'.

In principle it would be possible for stage (1) to occur without its being followed by stage (2). This is, roughly speaking, what Karl Marx believed had happened: the heavenly freedom and equality promised by religion are a consolation for the absence of worldly freedom and equality. Hegel disagrees. In his view, heavenly freedom and equality are realized in worldly existence, not through equality of income or of social status, but through the equal recognition as a person that is withheld from the slave (cf. Enc. I, §163 Z.(1)). The religious symbol for the transition from stage (1) to stage (2) is, in Hegel's view, the incarnation, the descent of God into 'worldly existence'. The fundamental Christian aversion to slavery (which was not of course shared by everyone called a 'Christian') extended to the enslavement of non-Christians as well as Christians.

4. This sentence might be taken in either of two ways: (i) The 'if'-clause is concessive: 'knowledge' (*Wissen*) of the Idea, which is only 'speculative', is contrasted with the Idea itself, which is the 'actuality' of men. 'Speculative' then means something like 'theoretical, non-practical'. (ii) The 'if'-clause is conditional: that knowledge of the Idea is speculative implies that the Idea itself is men's actuality. 'Speculative' then means something like 'pertaining to the nature or essence of things'. In either case, Hegel is referring to the transition from stage (1), the religious conception of freedom, to stage (2), the worldly realization of freedom: cf. §482, n. 3. Another difficulty in the sentence is that it equates 'knowledge of the Idea' with knowledge 'of men's knowledge, etc.', and the Idea itself with men's knowledge, etc. Perhaps Hegel is stressing the second-order character of speculative knowledge, that it is knowledge about knowledge and hence remote from actuality. But the second 'of' (*von*) may be an oversight, induced perhaps by the ambiguity of *Idee*, which means men's idea of freedom, hence their knowledge, etc. as well as freedom itself: cf. §482, n. 1. The Idea that men 'have' is their idea of freedom; the Idea that they are is freedom itself.

5. That the Idea is men's 'actuality' and that they 'are' the Idea means not just that they happen not to be slaves, but that they take freedom, both in the sense of not being a slave and in other senses, for granted as their fundamental characteristic. This claim is restricted to 'adherents' of Christianity. Non-Christians may well regard enslavement as a tolerable misfortune. Christians do not. If they were to be enslaved, this would shatter their whole world, the substance of their 'life' (*Dasein*). Their 'will to freedom' (*Wollen der Freiheit*) is not one urge among other urges, not an urge that they might not have, but something that constitutes their very 'being' (*Sein*). It does not, of course, follow that a Christian will not be enslaved. The guarantee of that requires the historical developments referred to in the next sentence.

6. The will to freedom of the preceding sentence is 'initially only a concept', i.e. not yet realized in objective reality, where Christians might be enslaved, despite their profound aversion to it. This profound, 'urgeless' aversion may account for the abolition of the enslavement of Christians, but it does not account so well for the abolition of the enslavement of non-Christians. 'Scientific' (*wissenschaftlichen*) actuality is presumably the systematic, philosophical attack on slavery and other violations of freedom mounted by Hegel and others.

NOTES TO §483

1. On the 'absolute Idea', see Enc. I, §§236–44. If objective mind were the absolute Idea *for itself* rather than merely 'in itself' (*an sich*), it would be (Hegel implies) 'infinite', in the sense of 'self-contained', and would have no need of 'external appearance'. For example, when one engages in logic, thinks about thinking, one can dispense with appeals to 'external' empirical phenomena; rationality supplies all its own needs. Free will, by contrast, cannot get by on rationality alone. It requires 'external appearance', namely an 'external objectivity', and this involves (i) 'particular' (*partikulären*) needs that belong to the level of 'anthropology', e.g.the need to eat, (ii) external 'things of nature' (*Naturdinge*), such as cows and corn, and (iii) the relationship of individual wills, whose awareness of each other amounts to 'self-consciousness' in contrast to the 'consciousness' that we have of natural things. Objective mind thus presupposes and involves lower phases of mind: anthropology, consciousness, and self-consciousness.

NOTES TO §484

1. The aim of the will is to overcome the sheer externality described in §483, by transforming anthropological needs into rights and duties, etc. (cf. §474, n. 4), natural things into artefacts, and individual wills into citizens, etc. Then the concept of will, freedom, becomes an Idea, by acquiring a realization appropriate to itself. Necessity is often contrasted with freedom, but for Hegel freedom involves certain types of necessity: cf. Enc. I, §35Z. For example, someone who freely does his duty feels that he *must* do it (Enc. I, §158Z.). So it is too on a larger scale. It is necessary that society should be organized in a certain way, and

necessary that individuals and groups should behave in certain ways in this society. What makes this necessity, namely the 'interconnexion' (*Zusammenhang*), operates at two levels, the 'substantial' or fundamental level and the 'apparent' (*erscheinende*) or surface level. Why, for example, is it necessary for children to be educated? At the substantial level, it is owing to the 'determinations of freedom', it is because the continuance of objective mind requires the enlistment of new citizens into its norms and institutions. At the apparent level, it is owing to 'power' (*Macht*), it is because the authorities make parents educate their children. The power is not, however, brute force. The power is recognized or acknowledged as legitimate power and its requirements as legitimate requirements. Hence it is has 'validity' (*Gelten*) or efficacy in the consciousness of the individual. Grammar and sense would be satisfied if 'its' (*ihr*) were taken to refer to 'necessity', but 'valid power' in §485 tells against this.

NOTES TO §485

1. The 'rational will' needs individual wills for its 'operation'. But it does not achieve its appropriate realization if individual wills are still at the level of practical feeling and urges. So it gets individual wills to actualize the intrinsically universal 'content' in a universal form. It does this in two ways: by 'law' (*Gesetz*, from *setzen*, 'to put, set, posit'), in which the content is 'posited' (*gesetzt*, also from *setzen*) for the 'consciousness of intelligence', i.e. in an explicit and intelligible manner, and by 'custom' (*Sitte*), in which the content is 'impressed' (*eingebildet*) on the will as its habit, etc., i.e. not in the explicit and intelligible form of a law, but nevertheless universal.

NOTES TO §486

1. The German *Recht*, usually translated as 'right', has no exact counterpart in English. In the 'restricted juridical' sense it is close to 'law', as in 'law and order' or 'the law is an ass', but not as referring to a particular law or laws. In Hegel's usage it is wider than 'law', since it also includes custom. In Enc. III, it initially contrasts with 'morality' and with 'ethical life', though in a wider sense it covers these areas too, as it does in PR, especially since morality and ethical life are also 'determinations of freedom'. It also means *a* 'right', in contrast to a duty.
2. The difficulty of this passage stems from the ambiguity of 'right' and also from the different types of 'will' in play. In its wider, abstract sense 'right' does not contrast with 'duty' or 'duties', but rather embraces them. In a narrower, concrete sense, 'right' contrasts with 'duty', even if Hegel goes on to argue that rights and duties are at bottom the same. 'Right' in the wider sense is not something that an individual will has, it is a system to which the individual will belongs and which it, together with other individual wills, sustains and activates. Hence when Hegel introduces the 'subjective', i.e. individual will, arguing that it is needed to embody the 'determinations of freedom', he ascribes to the subjective will not right or rights, but 'duties' and 'custom'. 'Right' has not yet acquired the more

concrete sense in which it can be ascribed to an individual will. (Hegel may also feel that a duty motivates a will to action more obviously than a right does, and the individual wills need to go into action if they are to actualize right in the abstract sense.) Next, however, rights and duties are identified with each other: 'That which is a right is also a duty, and what is a duty is also a right'. Here 'right' is used in the sense in which it is coordinate with, and is usually held to contrast with, 'duty'. Then Hegel gives a reason for his identification of rights and duties: 'For an embodiment [*Dasein*] is a right only on the basis of the free substantial will . . . in individual wills'. 'A right' (*ein Recht*) sounds like a right that is coordinate with a duty. But Hegel does not ascribe it to individual wills; to them he again ascribes only duties. *A* right is ascribed to, or at least based on, the 'free substantial will', which is not the subjective, individual will, but something more like the general will embodied in the institutions and practices of a society. Hence here 'a right' is not primarily a right in the narrower, concrete sense, but is something like an aspect or feature of right in the wider, abstract sense. So Hegel's argument seems to be this: Right (in the abstract sense) generates, in individual wills, duties with the 'same content' as itself; so these duties are also rights (in the concrete sense) and rights (in the concrete sense) are duties. The argument suffers from the fallacy of equivocation. 'Right' in the abstract sense has no more to do with 'right' in the concrete sense than it has to do with duty. Concrete rights, as well as concrete duties, embody right in the abstract sense. But this no more implies that rights are the same as, or have the same content as, duties than that one duty is the same as another duty.

The 'objective will' that is distinct from individual wills is more or less the same as the 'free substantial will', and even as 'objective mind'. In each of the cases dealt with in the Remark, there is a 'semblance of a distinction' between rights and duties, despite their fundamental identity. Hegel's central point is that, despite appearances, in a satisfactory social order rights and duties intermesh with each other in such a way that everyone gets what they have a right to if and only if everyone fulfils their duties.

3. The Remark deals successively with duty and right in the three main stages of objective mind: right (or what PR calls 'abstract right'), morality, and ethical life. Property and the person belong to the sphere of right: cf. §§488–502. Right is seen as a 'concept' developing into its 'appearance' or manifestation: cf. §484, n. 1 on the distinction between the 'substantial interconnexion' (namely the concept) and the 'apparent interconnexion'. At the level of the concept one and the same individual has both a right and a duty to what is, more or less, the same thing. He has a right to a particular 'thing' (*Sache*) that he has acquired, and also presumably a right to acquire property in general. He also has a duty to acquire property, and, since one is a property-owner if and only if one is a person, he has a duty to be a person. Here the right and the duty are not 'correlates' (*Correlata*); they are more or less the same thing. 'Property' (*Eigentum*) is not just 'possession' (*Besitz*), but 'lawful' (*rechtlicher*) possession, or, Hegel insists, possession by a 'person' (*Person*). But it is not clear how this entails that one has a duty to own things or a duty to be a person, rather than simply a duty to abstain from *unlawful* possession.

One may have a duty to acquire property for a specific purpose, such as to feed one's family, but this introduces a consideration from ethical life and is not relevant here. Hegel's idea is this. Humankind has a deep general duty to actualize freedom in the world: cf. §484. A fundamental part of this actualization is the existence of persons owning property. Hence we have a duty to acquire property and become persons.

At the level of appearance, where the concept radiates into a diversity of individuals, rights and duties become 'correlates': the right of one corresponds to the duty of another, as parenthood in one individual corresponds to childhood in another. It is not clear, however, why it is the duty to possess property and be a person that 'develops into' the duty to respect another's right. This implies that at the level of appearance one no longer has a duty to possess property, since this duty has developed into a different duty. Perhaps this is so. One is punished for infringing another's property rights, but not for failing to acquire property oneself.

4. In morality duty and right coincide: I have a duty to perform moral acts (and abstain from immoral acts) and I also have a right to perform acts that I regard as moral and abstain from acts that I regard as immoral. This is a right of the 'subjective' will, since it depends not on the objective rightness or wrongness of the acts, but on how the subject views the acts. On the whole or prima facie, people should not be forced to perform acts that they regard as immoral or to abstain from acts that they regard as moral. But now a new gap opens up, between the subject's intention, his 'subjective duty' (i.e. a duty that is not yet objectively performed or actualized), and external reality, which presents all sorts of obstacles to the actualization of duty. I may, e.g., kill someone in my dutiful attempt to rescue or cure him. The 'moral standpoint' requires an agent to be held responsible only for what he intends, not for e.g. the unintended consequences of his action, but adverse consequences cannot simply be a matter of indifference to it: cf. PR, §118. Not only is reality intrinsically resistant to the moral agent. It is essential to morality that it should be so. Morality involves the attempt to bring about what ought to be the case. If ever reality were to become fully and exactly as it ought to be, morality as such would cease to exist, since it would no longer be able to bring about what ought to be, only to relish what is and then it is no longer morality: cf. PR, §108 and Z. This makes the moral standpoint 'one-sided', not, that is, to be rejected altogether, but to be supplemented by and integrated into another standpoint.

5. 'Ethical life' is the higher standpoint that resolves the difficulties involved in abstract right and in morality. 'These two sides' (*beides*) should refer to the 'inner determination of the will' and the 'actuality of that determination', between which a gulf opened up in morality. But what Hegel goes on to discuss is not the 'absolute unity' of these two sides, but the mediated convergence of rights and duties. This takes place in the following way: One party, x, has a right with regard to the other party, y, and also a duty towards y. Conversely, y has a right with regard to x and also a duty towards x. Hegel omits to say that this formula applies to property owners in abstract right. One property owner, x, has a right

to have his property respected by another property owner, y, and also a duty to respect y's property; conversely, y has the same right and the same duty with regard to x. Hegel's omission is not simply motivated by his desire to reserve the fully satisfactory relationship of duties and rights for ethical life. Unlike a father and his children or a government and its citizens, two property owners are, in the relevant respects, equal in status and have exactly the same right and duty with respect to each other. Moreover, their right and duty are merely negative, simply a duty to leave each other alone and a right to be left alone. By contrast, a father does not have the same right and the same duty as his children, and the rights and duties are positive: they are duties to do something to someone else and rights to have something done to oneself. The father's right to be obeyed is not the same as the children's right to be educated; the father's duty to educate them is not the same as their duty to obey. But the right of each party involves a correlative duty of the other party, and the duty of each party involves a correlative right of the other party. Thus x has a right to be φ-ed (e.g. obeyed) by y, and y has a duty to φ (e.g. obey) x, while y has a right to be ψ-ed (e.g. educated) by x and x has a duty to ψ (e.g. educate) y. Here rights and duties lock the parties into a structure of reciprocal exchange. So do the rights and duties of a government and its citizens, but, as Hegel presents the case, the rights and duties do not have the same transparent logical structure as those of a father and his children. The rights and duties of a government are more or less the same. The government, x, has a right to φ (e.g. to punish, to administer) with respect to y (citizens) and also a duty to φ. The citizens, y, do not have rights and duties *exactly* correlative to those of x, a right to be punished and administered and a duty to be punished and administered, but rights and duties that are only roughly correlative to those of x, namely, a duty to provide taxes and military service that enable the government to do what it has a right and a duty to do (punish, administer, etc.) and also a right to have done what the government has a duty to do, administration, the punishment of wrongdoers, etc., i.e. the activities necessary for the protection of property and their 'substantial life'. Again, however, two unequal parties are locked into a system of reciprocal exchange. Because private citizens have to perform arduous duties, such as paying taxes and military service, and are recompensed for these only in a roundabout way and in a different form, the protection of their property and of their way of life, it looks as if the government and the citizens have different purposes, as if the purposes of the state—to punish, administer, collect taxes, etc.—are different from the purposes of private individuals. But this is only an 'appearance'. (Here *Erscheinung*, 'appearance', is close to *Schein*, 'semblance'.) At bottom these are also the purposes of private individuals, since they are necessary conditions of what private individuals want.

This resolves the problem involved in morality. The moral subject has duties and also a right to perform these duties. But his performance of his duties does not depend on others' performance of their duties, nor does it guarantee that they will do so. The moral subject believes he has a duty, say, not to lie to others and that they have a right not to be lied to. If he fulfils his duty this will not ensure that others will not lie to him and to each other. If they do so, this does not relieve *him* of his duty not to lie. So he need not receive any compensation for his dutifulness. He may not even get any credit for it, or even have much of an effect at all. Others may believe that he is lying, even believe the contrary of what he tells them. But none of this exempts him from his persistent and fruitless truthfulness. In ethical life it is different. If citizens do not pay taxes, the government does not administer; if the government does not administer, the 'substantial life' withers. So Hegel feels entitled to claim that 'whoever has no rights has no duties, and vice versa', even if we might raise objections about infants and horses.

Despite the reference to 'appearance', ethical life does not seem to involve a distinction between the concept and appearance in the way that abstract right does. The concept of right envisages only a single property owner. If the rights and duties of property owners with respect to each other are only negative, it is possible to conceive of a single property owner, a Robinson Crusoe who regards it as his duty to cultivate a plot and to harvest its produce. We cannot, by contrast, conceive of a dutiful father without children or of a dutiful government without citizens. Here the rights and duties of one party essentially involve the rights and duties of the other party.

NOTES TO §487

1. Property makes one a 'person' (*Person*). Hegel's general idea is that a fully fledged human being requires various levels of cultivation. The most basic of these levels is our ability to mould and stake out as one's own a portion of the material world—including one's own body: cf. §410, n. 13. Property ownership is an appropriate starting-point for objective mind, since a single isolated property owner (who is more easily conceivable than an isolated moral or ethical subject: cf. §486, n. 5) is closer to the unique concept of freedom with which Hegel begins than are the plural subjects of morality and ethical life, but property nevertheless makes us into a plurality of discrete individuals and thus prepares us for morality and for ethical life.

2. That the will is 'particular' (*partikulärer*) has two implications:

    (1) It withdraws from the objective world and becomes simply 'subjective' will, not objective will. (In §486, by contrast, 'subjective will' applied to the individual will in general and was not restricted to the moral will.)

    (2) Unlike the 'person', the moral will has inner determinacy and is not just a bare individual: since it no longer depends on an external embodiment, it has to develop a nature of its own.

3. The 'substantial will' is the will embodied in social institutions. It conforms to the 'concept of the will' in that it fully actualizes this concept, whereas abstract right and morality are only stages on the way to its actualization. It is both 'in the subject', i.e. in the individual, and a 'totality of necessity' embracing many individual subjects.

NOTE TO §488

1. The 'person' is simply a bare human individual, dependent for its identity on an external 'thing' (*Sache*). It reduces this thing to an 'accident' (*Akzidens*) of itself, in the sense of an 'accessory' or an accident of a substance. In one sense of the word 'absolutely' (*absolut*) the person is not yet 'absolutely free will'; that comes at a later stage. But the person is aware of an incipient version of absolute freedom: it has boundless freedom within the domain of its possessions, unrestrained as yet by the demands of others and of the social order.

NOTE TO §489

1. To take possession of a thing is to make a 'judgement' about the thing, applying to it the predicate 'mine' (*des Meinigen*). ('Judgement' here does not have the meaning of 'division': cf. §389, n. 4.) But this predicate has two meanings: (i) 'For itself', i.e. by itself or intrinsically, it is just 'practical'. I simply physically seize or appropriate the thing and use it for my present purpose. Then the thing is a possession and a means to whatever purpose I may have. (ii) I make the thing mine by putting 'my personal will' into it. Here I need not physically grasp the thing or do anything in particular with it. In fact, I cannot usually grasp physically the whole of what I lay claim to: cf. PR, §§54Z., §55 and Z. I make it mine by forming it (cf. PR, §§56–7) or by simply putting my mark on it (cf. PR, §58). My bookplate, for example, marks the whole book, not just the page on which the mark appears, as mine, even when I am not reading it. The book is an 'embodiment' (*Dasein*) of my 'personality' or personhood. (My *Persönlichkeit* is simply my being a person. It does not refer to my distinctive character; as a *Person* in Hegel's sense, I have no distinctive character.) As the embodiment of my personality, the book is an 'end' (*Zweck*), not a means to some further purpose of mine. I may well have lost interest in the book *as a book*, but it is still *mine*.

NOTE TO §490

1. There are two ways in which a person is 'joined together with' or returns to himself in property. (i) The person is related only to his property, not to other persons. Both the thing and the I are here 'abstractly external', 'external' because the thing and the I are external to each other, 'abstract' because the thing is not related to other things and the I is not related to other I's. This joining together with oneself is like gazing at oneself in a mirror. (ii) The I is 'infinite relation of me to myself': cf. §412, n. 1; Enc. I, §96Z. The relation is infinite, because I am related to myself and the relation is thus entirely self-contained, with no other entity involved. However, the single I repels itself from itself and thus encounters other I's: cf. §417, n. 4. This self-repulsion exemplifies the dialectic of the 'one' and the 'many' at Enc. I, §§97–8, where the one (e.g. atom, I, etc.) repels the many, but is equally attracted to them, since each of the many is itself one. Hegel's idea is

that there cannot be one that is not one of many. This is open to the objection that the universe might have contained only *one* atom or *one* steel ball, though in such a case we would not be around to describe it as 'one'. But it is hardly credible that there could be only one I or one person: an I needs to bounce off other I's, to contrast itself and compare itself with them, to be recognized or acknowledged by them and to recognize them in turn. This return to myself out of other persons is 'concrete' rather than 'abstract'. It is concrete not only because of the roundabout route I take back to myself, but because the I has acquired a richer identity from its encounter with other I's: it is no longer just *me* as opposed to *it*, the thing, but me as opposed to the other I's recognizing me and recognized by me.

NOTE TO §491

1. In §490 the person joined together with himself. In §491 different 'mutually independent' persons join together with each other, though it is already implicit in §490 that they do so. The three ways of acquiring a thing—seizing it, forming it, and marking it (cf. PR, §§54–8)—are ways of acquiring something that is not currently owned by anyone else. Acquisition by purchase, etc. falls under the heading of 'contract': see §§493–5. I cannot legitimately acquire a book by seizing it, forming it (e.g. writing in it), or marking it as mine. Unless I make it myself, I have to buy it or be given it, and then it is mine, even if I do not seize, form, or mark it. But land and raw materials with no current owner are acquired in the ways Hegel mentions.

NOTE TO §492

1. On the distinction between 'will' (*Wille*) and 'wilfulness' (*Willkür*), cf. §§469, n. 12; 477, n. 1. Wilfulness is roughly the freedom to do as one likes, whereas will has to meet certain standards.

NOTES TO §493

1. Suppose that two parties, Tom and Joe, agree that Tom will give x (e.g. a piece of land) to Joe in exchange for Joe's giving y (e.g. 1,000 marks) to Tom. The contract has been agreed to, but not yet fulfilled. Tom still retains possession of x, and Joe still retains possession of y. Nevertheless, x is now the property of Joe and y is the property of Tom. PR, §79 ascribes to J. G. Fichte a different view, namely, that Tom's obligation to fulfil the contract begins only once Joe starts fulfilling his side of the bargain and, similarly, Joe's obligation begins only once Tom starts fulfilling his side. So the contract is not 'valid' (*gültig*) or binding until one of the parties begins to fulfil it. The reason for this is that Tom cannot be certain that Joe will fulfil his side of the bargain, after he, Tom, has fulfilled his. Against this view, Hegel presents four arguments:

    (1) Perhaps neither party is prepared to begin. Then the performance will not take place. But suppose that one party, say Tom, begins the fulfilment of

the contract. He will not give the whole of x to Joe, since, if he does, Joe may keep it and not hand over y. So Tom gives to Joe a tiny piece of x (e.g. a square centimetre of land). Then Joe gives Tom not the whole of y, since he does not trust Tom, but a tiny fraction of y (say, 20 pfennigs). It will take a long time to fulfil the contract in this way, but it does not yet 'imply an infinite regress'. However, Tom may decide that a square centimetre of land is too much to put at risk. Why not half a centimetre? Or a square millimetre? Tom can select any fragment of x, however small, to begin the exchange. This is where the infinite regress sets in. Presumably the 'labour' and the 'time' are the labour and the time required to make the exchange. The labour is divided up in the same way as the 'thing', and so is the 'time', unless we suppose that the whole time taken increases as the thing is divided into ever smaller fragments. Knox rightly says: 'Hegel's point here is that the infinite divisibility of time, etc., makes impossible any clear answer to the question: at what precise point, in Fichte's view, does the contract become legally . . . binding?' (PR, p. 329).

(2) If a 'deed' (*Tat*) is required to make x Joe's property, then in this realm of 'representation' (*Vorstellens*) the word is a deed and the 'thing'. §462, where Hegel says that the 'name' is the 'thing' and that we think in names, is hardly germane. Tom may well mention x to Joe by *name*, or give him the *name* of x, without thereby giving him x. A more relevant consideration is this. Suppose that Tom promises to give x to Joe unconditionally. Then Tom is obliged to give x to Joe simply in virtue of his word. We can hardly say that Tom is only obliged to give x to Joe once he has already started to give x to Joe. If that were so, no one would ever break a promise, at least not completely. So if the word of a promiser is binding on its own, why is the word of a contractor not binding on its own?

(3) If the 'stipulation' were not 'complete and exhaustive', if e.g. Tom agreed to give x to Joe at some unspecified time or other and Joe agreed to give y to Tom at that time, then Tom or Joe would have to make the first move towards fulfilling the contract before the other party acquired a definite obligation. But contracts are not so indeterminate. They specify the date on which the exchange is to take place, etc.

(4) Tom and/or Joe may not mean the contract seriously, and either may suspect the other of not intending to fulfil his side of the bargain. But this is not relevant to Tom's and Joe's contractual obligations. Tom is under an obligation to give x to Joe, whether or not he intends to do so, and whether or not he believes that Joe intends to give him y. In any case, Fichte's proposal does not provide absolute security against deceit. If Tom hands over a part of x, Joe may keep it and not hand over the corresponding part of y; or if Joe hands over y in return, Tom may withhold the rest of x. If Tom, after signing a contract with Joe, learns that Joe is an inveterate confidence trickster, Tom may be *morally* entitled not to fulfil his side of the bargain. But this does not affect Tom's *contractual* obligation; he has already given x to Joe and is contractually obliged to hand it over.

NOTES TO §494

1. The two distinctions are clear enough: (1) The 'stipulation', i.e. what the contract requires each party to do, contains the 'substance' of the contract, while the 'performance' or fulfilment is just a consequence of this. (2) What Tom surrenders is e.g. such and such a plot of land, its specific 'constitution' (*Beschaffenheit*), but it is also worth 1,000 marks, and this is its substance or 'value'. It is less clear what Hegel believes to be the relationship between these two distinctions, and why distinction (2) is posited in the 'performance' as well as in the 'thing'. Perhaps he thinks that the two distinctions are simply analogous. But 'thereby' (*damit*) suggests that distinction (2) depends on distinction (1). This seems wrong. Surely distinction (2) is implied in the stipulation itself, in the substance of the contract, and does not depend on the performance. Why should Tom and Joe contract to exchange x and y unless they believe x and y to be more or less equal in value? Perhaps Hegel means that *after* the fulfilment each party owns the same value as he had *before* the fulfilment. So the fulfilment itself is really an exchange of two equal values, not just of two things with a different constitution.

   In fact, x and y need not be of equal value. Tom and/or Joe may be mistaken about their value. PR, §77 refers to *laesio enormis*, 'excessive damage', a provision in Roman law that if one sells e.g. a farm for less than half its value, the contract is not binding. However, Tom and Joe need not even believe that x and y are of equal value. Joe may want x for sentimental reasons and be ready to give y for it, though it is worth less on the open market, because it is worth y *to him*.

NOTES TO §495

1. The 'accidental' (*akzidentellen*) will, the will of an individual, contrasts with the 'substantial' will, the will embodied in objective norms, in this case the common will of the two parties embodied in the contract: cf. §§486, n. 2; 487, n. 3. Accidental wills are needed to activate the substantial will in contracts, etc., i.e. contracts would not be made unless individuals just wanted certain things that they could not otherwise obtain. It is not clear why the possibility of 'wrong' (*Unrecht*) depends on the 'wilfulness' (cf. §492, n. 1) of the contractors or the contingency of the thing. Wilfulness and contingency are not explicitly involved in the law against murder, but the law can be infringed. Hegel would perhaps reply that because wilfulness and contingency are not explicitly involved here, it is possible to conceive a community whose members infallibly respect the prohibition on murder, are never even tempted to infringe it, since in this respect their wills entirely conform to the substantial will. But the wills of contractors do not entirely conform to the substantial will. They each want something that the substantial will does not require them to want. Each has a will of his own; this is presupposed ('posited') by the contract. Since this is so, it must be possible for each of them to deviate from the substantial will still further, to be tempted to cheat the other party and then to actually cheat him. But this does not 'sublate' right, which is 'in and for itself', i.e. stands on its own two feet.

NOTES TO §496

1. Right *in abstracto* is unambiguous and clear-cut. But when it is applied to the 'external sphere', conflict may arise between divergent 'legal claims' (*Rechtsgründe*). A man bequeaths his property to his neglectful son rather than to the daughter who cared for him, or to his mistress rather than his wife; and so on. In such cases two or more parties each have a claim to a single property. Only one of these claims is 'the right', and, Hegel implies, at least one of the claims is the right. But since we do not yet know which is right, each of the claims is only the 'semblance' of right, in contrast to the right 'in itself'.

   Why not divide the property between the claimants? Or why not give the claimants joint ownership of the property? There may in such cases be no definite answer to the question: Who really owns it? But, says Hegel, property is exclusively 'individual' (*individuell*). His reason for discounting joint ownership is that he regards property as the embodiment of one's individuality as a 'person'.

NOTE TO §497

1. PR, §86Z. gives, as an example of a simple negative judgement, 'This rose is not red'. This judgement does not deny that the rose has a colour, only that its colour is red. Analogously, a non-malicious or 'inadvertent' (*unbefangene*) wrongdoer, Tom, does not deny that this property, x, rightfully belongs to someone or that the property should go to its rightful owner. He simply denies (Joe's claim) that x belongs to (him,) Joe. Neither Tom nor Joe is a denier of property rights in general or a criminal, who believes that the property rights of others should be overridden in his own favour. So the dispute requires a civil lawsuit, with an impartial judge who can enforce his own judgement.

NOTES TO §498

1. The fraudster, e.g. a bogus claimant to an inheritance, pretends to respect the right in itself, but in reality prefers his own semblance of right. Hegel wants fraud, like inadvertent wrong and crime, to involve a specific type of judgement. This is the 'infinite judgement as identical' or, as PR, §88 puts it, an 'infinite judgement expressed positively or as a tautology'. The examples given of this type of judgement in Enc. I, §173 are: 'A lion is a lion' and 'Mind is mind'. In his note on PR, §88 Knox explains this as follows:

   > The predicate should be a universal and tell us something about the subject, but in this case the the subject is qualified by itself, and the judgement is bogus, a show, because it professes to be a judgement, to tell us something, and it does not. The same is true of fraud. Fraud as the sale of *this* article, e.g. this share certificate, which the purchaser voluntarily accepts, is prima facie a genuine transaction. But as a sale it should contain a universal element, i.e. value. The seller professes to sell this universality of which the printed paper is supposed to be only a symbol, and the transaction is fraudulent because the universality is absent. (PR, 330)

This may be what Hegel in fact means, but it is not what he ought to mean. What the fraudster tries to sell need not be valueless; it may have, say, half the value he attributes to it. In that case it is not true that 'universality is absent' altogether. The main problem is that, unlike inadvertent wrong and crime, fraud operates on two levels. Overtly, the fraudster resembles the inadvertent wrongdoer and makes the same overt judgement as he does: a simple negative judgement that denies not the right as such but only its applicability to, say, Joe's claim that x is his. Covertly, the fraudster resembles the criminal and makes an infinite negative judgement, denying the right as such: cf. §499, n. 1. It is hard to see how these two judgements could be fused into a single type of judgement peculiar to fraud.

NOTES TO §499

1. Enc. I, §173 gives examples of the negative infinite judgement: 'The mind is no elephant' and 'A lion is no table'. The mind is not just not an elephant, it is not an animal at all. A lion is not just not a table, it is not a household implement at all. Whereas the rose, though it is not red, is of some colour, the mind is not red, nor is it any other colour. A negatively infinite judgement denies of the subject not just the determinate or specific property (e.g. redness, elephanthood), but (implicitly at least) the determinable or generic property (colouredness, animality). This why it is an 'infinite' judgement: it is a negation of the *indeterminate*, i.e. the boundless, the generic, not just the determinate or specific. This is what the criminal does. He denies Joe's claim to x, a claim which, though only a claim and thus only a semblance of right, nevertheless has won 'recognition'. He also denies right-in-itself, since he claims x for himself whatever the rights and wrongs of the matter. He denies generic right as well as Joe's specific right.

   Hegel tries to find types of judgement in the three types of wrong, because he wants to display the logical structure of social, as well as natural, phenomena. The attempt fails in the case of fraud, which is perhaps why Enc. I, §173Z. in discussing the involvement of judgements in wrong, does not mention fraud.

NOTES TO §500

1. This Paragraph applies only to the violent criminal discussed in §499, not to the fraudster. The criminal implicitly sets up a law such as: 'One can take whatever property one likes without regard to legal ownership'. This is the law that governs his action. Others do not, for the most part, recognize this law. However, since the criminal has acted on the law, he has made himself subject to it. So others are entitled, if not obliged, to treat him in accordance with the law he has set up. Others, his victim in particular, take whatever they like from the criminal, without regard to legal ownership. In this way they implement *both* the criminal's own law *and* right-in-itself, since the victim gets his property back and the criminal gets his deserts. The criminal act is thus shown to be 'null and void', because, although it has really occurred, it is self-defeating, generated by a principle that provokes

its own nullification. (Hegel neglects the fraudster, perhaps because his theory implies that one can only avenge or punish a fraud by fraudulent means.)

The victim's revenge does not make him a criminal, since he applies the law 'One can take whatever property one likes without regard to legal ownership' only to the criminal, not to those who do not recognize this law. But the revenge is a 'violation', since it is taken by a private individual in his own interests. So someone else, the original criminal himself or one of his friends or relatives, takes revenge on the first avenger, and so it goes on unless and until a disinterested judge intervenes and punishes the original trangressor, as well perhaps as the subsequent vigilantes.

When it comes to morality, Hegel criticizes Kant's categorical imperative, formulated as e.g. 'So act that the maxim of your will can at the same time always be considered as the principle of a universal legislation': cf. §§415, n. 2; 508, n. 1; 511, n. 1. But he accepts something like it in his own account of revenge and punishment. Revenge or punishment involves treating the criminal as if the maxim of his act were a universal law, i.e. doing to him what he did to others. Given that the criminal legislates for his own retribution, is not clear why revenge is a 'new violation', as long as it is proportionate to the offence and inflicted on the actual offender. The criminal and his adherents may well object to the revenge. But why should they not equally object to punishment, even seek revenge on the judge? After all, it is, according to Hegel, a defining feature of the criminal that he rejects 'right in itself', and it is only right in itself that entitles us to prefer punishment to revenge. Participants in a vendetta (cf. Aeschylus' *Oresteia*) might welcome the intervention of a disinterested arbitrator to end their blood-feud. But that is because they have not rejected right in itself, but are caught up in a messy and costly attempt to execute it. What prevents the genuine criminal, the wholehearted right-rejecter, from taking revenge on the judge is the power at the judge's disposal rather than the judge's disinterestedness.

NOTES TO §501

1. The victim of a criminal may have no interest in 'turning against' the crime. He may be a criminal himself and do a deal with his assailant. He may not be 'in conformity with right'; he may, e.g., exact a grossly excessive retribution for a slight offence. The judge is free of these faults.
2. The criminal's victim may be unable to take revenge. But the judge has the power and resources to exact retribution. He wants to 'negate' the criminal's 'negation of right'. This negation of right resides in the criminal's will. So it is no use appealing to the criminal's better nature; he has to be coerced. But the judge cannot coerce the criminal's will directly. The will is embodied in a 'thing', either an ordinary thing (the criminal's property) or 'bodiliness' (his 'person'). So the criminal's will can be 'seized' or affected only by attacking his property or person, i.e. by confiscation, imprisonment, etc.
3. The will cannot be coerced directly, only by way of what it cares about. If I do not care about confiscation of my property, imprisonment, etc., then I cannot be

coerced by such means. I may even cease to care about my life, killing myself or letting the authorities kill me. Then I cannot be coerced at all. 'Only the will which allows itself to be coerced can in any way be coerced' (PR, §91). On Hegel's debt to the Stoics, see §431, n. 5.

4. PR, §93 defends this doctrine by arguing that breaking a contract or neglecting one's duties to one's family or the state amount to 'coercion' (*Zwang*), as does the 'natural will' of children who need to be coerced by their teacher.

NOTES TO §502

1. The 'subjective' will is the will of the individual: cf. §487, n. 2. Right, i.e. 'right-in-itself', cannot be realized without the help of subjective will. In the case of the 'personal will', i.e . the will of the person, the distinction between right and the subjective will hardly arises. Individuals get the 'reality' (*Realität*) of right 'in an immediate manner', by doing what they want to do in any case, by taking possession of things. But with the emergence of contracts, crime and punishment, right and the subjective will become distinct factors or 'moments'. The subjective will may actualize right or it may oppose it. Here the realization of right is no longer immediate; it is mediated by subjective will as a distinct and often unreliable moment. The reality of right is now in a precarious position.

2. The subjective will is also in a precarious condition. So far it is just the 'power over right'. It alone can decide whether right is realized or not, but it is not equipped with any way of deciding what right consists in. Hegel does not explain why this makes it 'a nullity' (*ein Nichtiges*). He means that the subjective will, isolated from the value system it is supposed to operate, is just empty, deciding everything by the toss of a coin. Nor does Hegel explain why 'morality' is the only way of getting it out of its dilemma. He believed that there have been societies, especially ancient (archaic and classical) Athens, that did not have 'morality' in the modern sense, but in which individuals were wholly absorbed in their 'ethical life', their conduct guided by the shared values of their society rather than by their individual conscience: see my 'Plato, Hegel, and Greek Sittlichkeit'. But, he would argue, we have no hope of restoring such a society. If the subjective will is to be kept on the straight and narrow in our individualistic times, it can only be by morality. On the 'rational will', in contrast to the subjective will, see e.g. §485, n. 1.

3. 'Nature' denotes (among other things) (i) what is natural and unspoilt in contrast to the artificial accretions of culture, society, and civilization, and (ii) the nature of something, in a sense roughly equivalent to its 'essence'. This generates an ambiguity in the term *Naturrecht*, 'natural right': (1) The right that would obtain if human beings were entirely uncultivated. This gives rise to the idea of a 'state of nature'(*Naturzustand*), a condition in which humans would be (and, as some supposed, once actually *were*) untouched by culture, etc. Natural right is then the right that obtains in the state of nature. (2) The right determined by the nature of the 'thing' (*Sache*), by the 'concept'. The 'thing' here is not the thing owned as property, but is more like the 'case' or 'subject-matter'. The 'concept' is the

logical development of right, not the simple, primitive stage of right obtaining in the state of nature.

Roughly speaking, each type of natural right depends on the 'nature' of man: (1) regards the nature of man as man's primitive, uncultivated condition (the acorn), while (2) regards it as it the eventual condition of man as a social, political, etc. creature (the oak-tree). But they are not simply two different types of natural right. Advocates of each type of right downgrade the other type. Advocates of (1) argue that society and the 'political state' (*Staat*) curtail natural right. Hegel replies that, first, right is based on 'self-determination', not 'determination by nature', where 'nature' is used in approximately sense (i), not sense (ii), and, secondly, natural right in sense (1) depends on strength, violence, etc. and is thus wrong, not right. Hegel's first argument lacks adequate support and is difficult to assess. He perhaps means that if men do only what they are naturally determined to do, rather than what they freely choose to do, there is little point in speaking of 'right' at all, since there can be no divergence between what right requires and what men actually do. It is unclear why Hegel thinks that his first argument supports the second, as 'therefore' (*darum*) implies. Even if some men are naturally stronger than others, why might they not also be by nature generous and non-violent, unwilling to use their strength to secure advantage? For Hegel's belief that the state of nature was or would be violent and oppressive, see his account of the struggle for recognition in §§430–5.

More generally, the connection between this Remark and the preceding Paragraph is unclear. Perhaps the Remark is simply an appendix on the notion of right in general. Or perhaps Hegel is anticipating the objection that if he is concerned with *natural* right, he need not go on to morality, but can stop at this point.

NOTES TO §503

1. 'Person', from the Latin *persona*, a 'mask' worn by actors, suggests a public persona or role. By contrast, 'subject', from the Latin *subicio*, 'throw, put, under', suggests inner depth. This is appropriate to morality, where what matters is the will's 'determinacy', one's purpose and intention, rather than one's external goods.
2. Persons are numerically distinct individuals, but are not 'particular', i.e. not differentiated from each other by their inner 'determinacy', but all alike persons as long as they own property. Morality differentiates people. The further 'particularizations' (*Besonderungen*) are 'purpose', 'intention', etc. See §§504–12.
3. The determinacy of the will, its reason-derived view of 'what is lawful' (*das...Rechtliche*), is initially 'in itself' or potential, but then it is actively expressed and eventually 'comes into relationship' with, i.e. corresponds to or realizes, the will's inner purpose. It does not do so immediately or as soon as it 'sets out', since intervening *means* are needed to fulfil the will's *end*. 'These determinations' include the will's inner determinacy as well as its outer expression: to be morally free the will must be in full control both of what it wills and of what it does. What one freely does is one's 'action', *Handlung*, a term which implies a 'conscious expression of the will. It is only possible in statements

which describe, judge or by implication draw attention to the motives of "acts" or "actions"' (DGS, p. 3). *Morally*, one is responsible only for what one did knowingly and willingly. Oedipus killed an old man, but since he did not know it was his father, and presumably would have refrained from killing him if he had known who he was, he was not morally responsible for killing his father. Not only is Oedipus innocent of parricide. His 'action' is not parricide. By contrast, his 'deed' (*Tat*) is one of parricide: cf. PR, §§117Z.; 118.

4. This suggests that a latter-day Oedipus might defend himself against the charge of parricide not only by saying, as in the Paragraph, (1) 'I did not know the man I killed was my father', but also by saying (2) 'Like an animal or an infant, I did not know the difference between good and evil in general, and so I did not realize that there was anything wrong with parricide', or (3) 'I knew that parricide was forbidden by the customary ethical code, but I did not approve of this prohibition myself'. (1) and (2) are credible defences, but (3) is, on the face of it, absurd; one could evade responsibility for any sin or crime by simply disapproving of its prohibition. However, Hegel's justification of punishment removes the sting from this absurdity: cf. §500, n. 1. A thief who deploys defence (3), saying 'I did not approve of the prohibition on theft, so I acted on the principle of taking whatever I like from others', is exposed to the reply: 'You may not be morally culpable for your theft, but we are entitled, indeed we owe it to you, to apply your own principle to yourself and to take whatever we like from you.' (More ingenuity would be needed to deal with a wilful parricide in this way.) This reply would not work against defences (1) or (2), i.e. it would not justify punishing the unwitting wrongdoer or someone who does not know the difference between right and wrong, since neither of these bases his wrongdoing on a general principle.

5. The French usage (cf. 'the moral sciences') is quite different from Hegel's. He means that 'morality' (*das Moralische*, lit. 'the moral') includes the immoral, moral evil, as well as the morally good, and thus the subject's 'purpose' and 'intention', even if the subject himself is not concerned with morality in the narrower sense.

NOTE TO §504

1. 'What is mine' (*das Meinige*) is 'formal' (*formell*) in that it does not include extraneous *material* or content from external 'reality' (*Dasein*). Suppose I light a fire to form a clearing, and unintentionally set light to the forest. All these alterations, the forest-fire as well as my original fire, are included in my 'deed' (*Tat*). However, only some of them are included in what I recognize as my 'action' (*Handlung*), namely those that were my 'purpose' (*Vorsatz*): my original limited fire, but not the forest-fire.

NOTES TO §505

1. Hegel distinguishes three things: (i) all the alterations I bring about, my 'deed'; (ii) that segment of these alterations that figured in, and is structured by, my 'intention'(*Absicht*), e.g. forming a clearing; (iii) what I immediately proposed to

do in order to realize my intention, e.g. to light a tuft of grass, my *Vorsatz. Vorsatz* is used more restrictedly than in ordinary German, more narrowly in fact than we would expect from §504. It is even less plausible to suppose, in the case considered, that the forest-burner can disclaim responsibility for everything except his immediate 'purpose', to light a tuft of grass, than that he can admit responsibility only for what he intended, to form a clearing. Here the 'intention' is equivalent to the 'aim' (*Zweck*). On this whole topic, cf. PR, §§119 ff.

2. 'Happiness' (*Glückseligkeit*) was considered in §§479–80, but it was not there considered in relation to action nor as something to which we have a moral 'right'. When considered in this light, it is 'well-being' (*Wohl*). The subject has a right to derive satisfaction from his action. 'Particularity' (*Besonderheit*) refers primarily to the subject's 'needs, etc.', which are peculiar to the subject and of little concern to anyone else, but it also contrasts with 'essential determination'. I should e.g. perform my professional duty, the 'essential determination'. But I am also entitled to do so in a way that gives me pleasure and that will advance my career.

NOTES TO §506

1. 'When St. Crispin stole leather to make shoes for the poor, his action was moral but wrong and so inadmissible' (PR, §126 Addition). St Crispin's deed involves at least two aspects, stealing leather and helping the poor. In reflecting on it, we (or indeed St Crispin himself) might say that his intention is to steal leather, elevating this 'particular aspect' to the 'abstract form of universality'. Or we might say that his intention is to help the poor. In the latter case, we bring the 'supposed essentiality of the intention' into 'contradiction' with the 'genuine essentiality of the action', as a theft. Hegel does not say how we are to decide that theft is the 'genuine essentiality' of this action and not to be excused by a good intention. Several arguments are available. If St Crispin's venial offence is justified by its intention, it is hard to see why other, far worse acts would not be justified by a good intention. If theft for the poor were to be *legalized*, hardly anyone could be convicted of non-charitable theft, except a thief who blatantly used his loot to enrich himself or other prosperous people; other ways of helping the poor, less detrimental to security of property, are available, such as welfare benefits. See further PR, §140 and Remark.

2. An intention, e.g. to steal, to help the poor, is abstract and universal, because it selects only one aspect of an 'empirically concrete action' and might in principle be the intention of any number of concrete actions: only St Crispin performs this concrete action, but many others can act with the same intention. Hegel sees a parallel with well-being. Different people may all get well-being, but from different things; *my* well-being and what I get it from is peculiar to *me*.

NOTE TO §507

1. This is a brief summary of Kant's moral philosophy, which is meant to resolve the problems involved in these 'particularities', namely intention and well-being,

and to make their 'formalism' concrete. Morality so far is only formal. It tells me that I have a right to be held responsible only for what I intend, but it does not tell me what my intention should be. It tells me that I have a right to well-being, but it does not say what my well-being consists in. It does not tell St Crispin whether or not he should steal to give to the poor, only that he should have a good intention. The 'universal will' (cf. §§408, n. 26; 435, n. 5; 443, n. 6), 'the good', and 'duty' (cf. §475) supposedly answer these questions. The 'final aim' (*Endzweck*) of the world is, for Kant, the moral perfection of rational beings, with happiness in proportion to their goodness. Hegel disapproves of Kant's tendency to situate it in the unattainable future.

NOTE TO §508

1. Since the good is 'determinate', it not only tells me to do my duty, it also tells me to do my *particular* or specific duty. But this 'particularity' is still abstract: telling me to do my particular duty is no more helpful than simply telling me to do my duty. How can I discover what my duty is? Not, in Hegel's view, by an inspection of the universal good: cf. PR, §135 Remark. I have to turn *outside* the universal good, to current social practices, say, to utility, or to God, to find any specific duties. That is a problem in itself, because the free will is supposed to determine itself, to be 'for itself', not determined by extraneous factors. This problem leads to a contradiction. For what I discover is not some single particular good or duty that I have to pursue, but a variety of goods and duties. Such duties (the duty to my country, say, and the duty to my family) may well conflict. They 'ought' (*sollen*) to harmonize, but they do not in fact: each duty makes an unconditional claim on me that is incompatible with the other. So I 'ought' to 'decisively conclude' (*beschliesse(n)*, both 'decide on' and 'end, close') a harmonious combination of them. But I can only do this by sublating the unconditional claim of one of the duties. I cannot simply toss a coin to decide which duty to pursue. If I take duty seriously I 'ought' to assess their claims 'dialectically', i.e. rationally. *Sollen* ('ought', but also 'to be supposed to') is often a derogatory term in Hegel, especially in the context of morality. It suggests that Kantian morality rests content with saying that such and such *ought* to be the case, but provides no realistic account of how it might be brought about or of what we are to do if it is not.

NOTES TO §509

1. This is loosely based on Kant's doctrine: while one's own happiness or well-being cannot be one's motive for doing one's duty—'honesty' motivated solely by my self-interest is of no moral worth—people ought to be happy in proportion to their moral merit. Hegel's version runs as follows. The good as such, which the moral agent aims to realize, is 'universal'. By contrast, interest and well-being are essentially particular; they are always *someone's* interest and well-being. Hence they 'ought' to play no part in the good as such or in the motives for pursuing

it. *My* interest and well-being are of no more relevance to the realization of the good than they are, say, to the truths of mathematics. However, I am not just a universal, not just a disinterested actualizer of the good. I am a 'particular' human being, with my own interest and well-being. As such, I have a duty to seek my own interest and well-being. But because pursuit of the good and self-interest are quite independent, they may well not coincide: good people are often unhappy, while bad ones prosper. They *ought* to coincide, because a subject is not just a loose composite of a universal good-actualizer and a self-interested particular; it is 'in itself', *at bottom*, a unitary individual.

This is open to criticism. The reason for the irrelevance of my well-being to the pursuit of the good cannot be the universality of the good. I am, after all, a particular moral agent, but what matters is not just that the good should be realized, but that *I* should play my part in its realization by doing *my* duty: cf. §475, n. 3. So why should *my* well-being not be relevant to the good? If I, as a particular, really have a duty to further my well-being, my performance of this duty would surely be as relevant to my pursuit of the good as is my performance of my duty to pay my debts. But it is not obvious that I do have a duty to further my own well-being, not at least a duty on a par with the duty to pay my debts, since (in Kant's view) the duty to pay one's debts should always override considerations of self-interest. It might be unrealistic and unreasonable to expect someone to pursue the good to the extreme detriment of their long-term interest, but this is what morality might on occasion demand.

However, well-being is not as irrelevant to the good as the analogy with mathematics suggests. The well-being of a particular mathematician, or of anyone else, is clearly irrelevant to the truths of mathematics. Mathematics, as such, does not even require any particular individual, or anyone at all, to be a good mathematician. But the good as such does require individuals to do their duty and to improve themselves, and it also requires (in Kant's view) that they be happy in proportion to their merit. Does this imply that I have a duty to further well-being, either my own or that of others? Not my own: morality allots to me the well-being I morally deserve, not the well-being I manage to get, and I must establish my desert independently. Not the well-being of others, except when it is required by a specific duty such as the duty of charity: I cannot reasonably hope to make people happy in proportion to their merit; this is something that ought to come about, but not something that any individual ought to bring about.

In general, Kant and Hegel have different concerns. Kant insists that morality requires that good people be rewarded and bad ones punished. Hegel wonders how a single unified individual can be both self-interested and morally good.

2. The subject has to be at least a 'particular in general' if it is to realize the good, even if it were to do nothing but realize the good. However, as we have seen in β), as a particular, the subject has interests of its own, though it may subordinate them to its pursuit of the good. But now the subject is more than a particular in general. It is not identical with the 'reason of the will', nor irresistibly governed by it. It withdraws from it, and stands above it, so that what reason prescribes is only

one among several alternatives between which it is free to choose. It is not clear from Hegel's language whether he means:

(1) I can choose evil knowing it to be evil, e.g. be fully aware that it is wrong to murder for money, yet decide to murder someone for their money
or:

(2) I can choose evil after deciding that it is not really evil, e.g. decide that it is not wrong to murder for money after all and so murder someone for their money.

Perhaps he would say that either is possible.

NOTES TO §510

1. The external world can frustrate morality in several ways. It can prevent the performance of a virtuous act: a traffic jam keeps me from an appointment, the coin I toss to a beggar falls down a drain. It can pervert the consequences of a virtuous act: the beggar catches a disease from the coin or uses it to finance his vices; a fire engulfs the scene of our appointment. It can make virtuous people unhappy. Evil is conceived as the negation or deficiency of good, hence as intrinsically 'null' (*nichtig*). By rights then evil should be nullified by the world: the murderer should fail in his attempt or at least fail to inherit the victim's wealth after all. But evil often prospers in the world and vicious people get the happiness denied to the virtuous. It 'ought' not to be so.

NOTES TO §511

1. The 'ought' (*Sollen*) expresses (as well as attempting to resolve) a 'contradiction'. If two unconditional duties contradict each other, the subject 'ought' to reconcile them; if the distribution of happiness 'contradicts' the distribution of merit, this ought to be put right. This 'multiple' ought is the absolute 'being' (*Sein*): it is unconditional, with no restrictions on it. Yet it 'is not': it only *ought* to be. This unsatisfactory state of affairs leads the subject to withdraw into itself, away from any objective constraints, so that it becomes infinite, i.e. unbounded, unconstrained, subjectivity. It stands above such objective factors, now in disarray, and conceives itself as entitled to choose between them.

Hegel gives a more detailed account of this degeneration of Kantian morality in PS, pp. 364–409 and PR, §§136–40. However, it is not clear which, if any, of the 'contradictions' that he unearths necessitates the degeneration. Contradiction α)—that whatever procedure I use to discover my particular duty, reveals to me different duties conflicting with each other (cf. §508)—naturally suggests that it is up to me to choose which of the conflicting duties to fulfil. But this still leaves me subject to objective constraints. I may be free to choose, on occasion, between my duty to my country and my duty to my family. But I am not free to choose to betray *both* my family *and* my country. Moreover, such conflicts are perhaps less frequent than Hegel implies. Hegel might respond: if I am free to choose in some cases, why am I not free to choose in every case? But this is like asking: 'If I am free to choose between tea and coffee, why am I not free to choose between helping people and murdering them?' Contradiction β)—that (my duty to pursue my) interest and well-being conflict with (pursuit of) the good (cf. §509, n. 1)—would suggest that conflict of duties is more widespread, if it were the case that I have a *duty* to pursue my interest and well-being. But Kant need not recognize such a duty. Kant's belief that happiness and virtue *ought* to coincide does not entail that I have a duty to pursue my own happiness, still less that I am entitled to choose between my duty and my happiness. Contradiction γ)—that the subject is able to choose between good and evil (cf. §509, n. 2)—is only a more moderate statement of §511. Contradiction δ)—that the world can frustrate morality in various ways (cf. §510)—might suggest the following argument: 'I cannot be sure what the upshot of my actions will be. Acts done with the best intentions may end in disaster; vicious acts may turn out for the best. So it really does not matter what I do. I should just choose what takes my fancy and hope for the best.' This no doubt exaggerates the unpredictability of things. Moreover, Kant would reply that it is the good intention, or at least the good will, that matters: ensure that your will is good and leave the consequences to themselves. Here the objector replies: 'That is just my point! It is the good intention that matters. You, along with the tradition, believe that a good intention is a necessary condition of virtuous action, but not a sufficient condition. You still have regard for objective rules of conduct which, you believe, are sustained by rationality. For me there are no binding rules. Any rule that is in force is only one factor that I take into account in making my decision. So for me a good intention is sufficient for virtuous action. Nothing else matters.'

2. The shift from 'certainty' (*Gewissheit*) to 'conscience' (*Gewissen*) is facilitated by the similarity of the words: cf. PR, §136. Conscience is here the subjective certainty that a particular action is right. It does not acknowledge any binding objective standard. It does not make universal claims, of the form 'It is always right for any subject S to perform act A in circumstances C'. What it prescribes is 'the indescribable' (*das Unsagbare*) in that the subject cannot give explicit reasons for its decision. However, it is not clear why conscience in this sense should 'immediately pass over' into evil. According to the doctrine in question, an evil decision could only be a decision against the subject's conscientious conviction, not an act against objective standards, since it acknowledges no objective standards. In his longer discussion in PR, Hegel makes the following claims: (1) Possession of a conscience, in the sense of an awareness of the difference between good and bad, is a necessary condition of evil; a creature lacking a conscience may do bad things, but it is not evil: cf. PR, §139 and Addition. (2) The stress on conscience leads to moral laxity, typified by the 'probabilism' attacked by Pascal in his *Lettres provinciales*, the doctrine that an act is permissible and can be done with a good conscience, as long as *some* reason or authority can be found in its favour: cf. PR, §140 and Addition. Still more extreme is the doctrine that conscientious conviction of the rightness of one's act is a sufficient condition for the rightness of the act, regardless of any reason or authority in its favour: PR, §140 and Addition.

Such doctrines may well permit acts that are evil, as judged by objective standards that the doctrines themselves do not acknowledge. But they can be seen to be defective even by someone who acknowledges no objective standards, since they allow more or less any act, hence obliterate the distinction between good and evil and defeat the very purpose of morality.

The final sentence ('But *evil*... to the good') seems to involve claim (1). It refers to a subject who opts for a 'subjective interest contrary to [*gegen*] the good', not to someone who conscientiously decides that his subjective interest *is* good. But this does not square well with the fact that in the preceding sentence ('Conscience... decision') conscientious conviction is implicitly regarded as sufficient for the rightness of an action. Claim (1) does not presuppose that conscientious conviction is sufficient for the rightness of an act: even if a right act needs to meet certain objective standards, it is still the case that someone whose act contravenes those standards is evil only if he has a conscience, i.e. awareness of the difference between good (right) and bad (wrong). Hegel seems to conflate a general reflection on the human condition, namely claim (1), with criticism of the fairly modern, especially (though not exclusively) post-Kantian, doctrine that conscience alone is an infallible guide to right conduct. He also implies that, whatever the conscientious subject may decide, it is evil, or at least arrogant, to set up oneself, an individual unconstrained by any universal, as the arbiter of good and bad.

NOTES TO §512

1. *Phänomen* is 'appearance, manifestation', perhaps also a 'wonder' or 'spectacle'. *Eitelkeit*, 'vanity', suggests both 'conceit' and 'emptiness'. The 'absolute vanity' of the will is distinct from its collapse, but is immediately followed by its collapse. Hegel often says that things turn into their opposites when they reach their extreme point, as when we go as far north as we can, we start walking south. The will is here at its highest peak, because it has broken free of any objective or rational constraint and set out on its own.
2. Someone who decides what to do regardless of any objective or universal standards, and who is therefore 'evil' is in the same position as someone who aims to do good in the abstract, but always has to make up his own mind what the good requires of him. Both of them are 'evil' in that they make up their own mind what to do; each of them is likely, though not bound, to perform acts that are, by the objective standards that they do not acknowledge, 'evil'. 'Semblance' has changed sides: at first objectivity, etc. is a 'semblance' (*Schein*) for subjectivity, but then subjectivity becomes the 'semblance' (*Scheinen*), just an outward show with no inner substance.
3. The 'absolute vanity' of the will consists in its complete detachment from the good, from objective standards or criteria. Willing is then vacuous, with no foothold from which to make a decision; I just do whatever I feel like at the time. The good is correspondingly vacuous, supplying no guidance, at least no incontestable guidance, for my decisions. That is the negative side. The positive

side is that 'in concept', i.e. at bottom, the will and the good are the same 'simple universality'. The deficiencies of the wholly independent will and the wholly abstract good are repaired by the emergence of their fundamental identity.

Hegel's argument operates at the level both of the individual and of society. As regards the *individual*, the argument is suggestive, but not compelling. An individual may well find satisfaction in simply following his convictions. In PR, §141 Addition, Hegel notes that many 'Protestants [notably Friedrich von Schlegel] have recently gone over to the Roman Catholic Church, and they have done so because they found their inner life worthless and grasped at something fixed, at a support, an authority . . .'. But many Protestants did not convert, and those that did usually did so only after they had enjoyed a dissolute (though not usually a violent or criminal) youth. However, individuals such as Schlegel operated in a society where most people followed an established code of conduct. Hegel does not suggest that there could be a whole *society* whose members act solely on their own convictions, with no respect for authority or tradition, though revolutionary France, according to his accounts (PS, pp. 355–63; PR, §5 and Addition), came close. By contrast, there have been societies, such as ancient Athens, that (in Hegel's view) lacked an individual moral conscience. With respect to a society, then, the problem is not: 'Why does a society whose members act only according to their private convictions come to respect objective, universal norms?' Few, if any, societies have made this transition, while many have travelled in the reverse direction, from 'ethical life' alone to ethical life tempered by 'morality'. The problem is rather: 'Why is a society unable to get by with morality alone, why does it need ethical life?' The transition from morality to ethical life is not, then, a historical transition. It is a transition in Hegel's thought.

4. In the morality of conscience, subjectivity and the good are merely in 'relationship', *Verhältnis*, a sort of ratio or proportion in which they stand to each other (as in a numerical ratio, a : b), with no complex interaction between them: cf. §§413, n. 1 and 418, n. 2 on the *Verhältnis* between consciousness and its object. This is now replaced by an 'identity' between them: subjectivity is now thoroughly imbued with the norms that govern its society. In the morality of conscience, subjectivity was 'infinite': it was not bounded or constrained by any norms, etc., because it was entirely detached from them: cf. §511, n. 1. Now it is the 'infinite form': it is not bounded or constrained by norms, etc., because it has absorbed them completely and become entirely at home in them. It is 'form', because it gets all its content from these objective norms. All that it does is activate and develop the norms. The 'ought' is no longer relevant. I only feel that I *ought* to φ if φing does not come naturally to me and I have some reason not to φ. I feel that I ought to pay my debts, but I do not feel that I ought to breathe. Since subjectivity is now thoroughly imbued with the objective norms and has no will independent of them, it can hardly feel that it *ought* to activate them. It just does so.

This account is exaggerated, perhaps beyond Hegel's intentions, though not beyond the implications of his language. It makes 'ethical' people sound like fanatical devotees of painting by numbers, or soldiers on a parade-ground, willingly and mechanically obeying every command of their officer, so enthusiastic in fact that they hardly need commands at all. But ethical life, as Hegel describes it, is not like this. At least its second stage, 'civil society' (see §§523 ff.), enables an individual to go his own way, to decide how to fulfil his duties and even to wonder whether he should fulfil them. Hegel's idea is that it is only on the basis of a thorough absorption of the norms of one's society that one can become an independent agent, relatively detached from those norms.

NOTES TO §513

1. 'Ethical life' translates *Sittlichkeit*, a word which, before Hegel, was generally used as a synonym of *Moralität*. Hegel stresses its affinity to *Sitte*, 'custom', and uses it for social or customary morality, whereas *Moralität* is reserved for individual morality. *Sittlichkeit* is the third and final stage of objective mind or spirit, the others being '(abstract) right' and 'morality'. Since subjective mind is coordinate with objective mind, and ethical life is a stage of objective mind, we might not expect ethical life to be 'the truth of' subjective and objective mind. The truth of x, or the truth of x and y, is not usually a part of x: cf. §§381, n. 2, and 388, n. 1, on mind as the truth of nature; §419, n. 3 on the 'proximate truth'; and §440, n. 1 on the truth of two items, x and y. However, it is clear what Hegel means. Ethical life resolves defects both in subjective mind and in the earlier stages of objective mind. Abstract right locates freedom in an external 'thing' (*Sache*), property. Morality offends in a different way. It also locates freedom outside the individual subject, only not in 'reality' (*Realität*), but in a universal that is cut off from reality and therefore 'abstract'. Subjective mind does the opposite. It makes the individual mind self-determining, without regard to the 'universal', i.e. primarily the universal norms, etc. of a shared culture, and therefore also 'abstract'. There are two quite distinct ways in which it does this: (1) In Hegel's *account* of subjective mind, the mind is considered without regard to the 'universal'. (2) In so far as the subjective mind, in Hegel's account of it, seeks freedom, it seeks it without regard to the universal; it seeks only the satisfaction of its urges and it seeks freedom only for itself: see e.g. §469. It may be because he has (1) in mind, rather than (2), that Hegel does not say that subjective mind locates '*freedom*' in the individual mind. Although freedom, for him, usually amounts to 'self-determination' (in one or another sense of this expression), the type of self-determination attributed to the subjective mind is not intended to confer freedom upon it. It is simply a defect or limitation in the account given of the mind that it ignores the universal. One might say (corresponding to (2)): 'People are free if, and only if, they can satisfy their own urges', but one could not reasonably say (corresponding to (1)): 'The subjective mind is free, because we can consider it without regard to external factors'. By contrast, one might intelligibly say: 'People are free if, and only if, they own property' or 'People are free if, and only if, they aim at the good.' The defects of subjective mind and those of objective mind are of radically different types.

2. The rational will is both subjective and objective. On the subjective side is the rational will's 'awareness' (*Wissen*) of itself and also the 'disposition' (*Gesinnung*), the attitude or principles that guide the individual's conduct. On the objective

side is 'custom', the actualization of the rational will in social life. The objective and the subjective have come together. Freedom hs become 'nature' in that it is now established in the individual's environment.

NOTES TO §514

1. 'Substance' is (roughly) a shared culture in contrast to the individuals who belong to it and activate it. The absolute 'ought' (*Sollen*) is 'being' (*Sein*) because what ought to be the case actually is the case. When people do their duty (voting in an election, say) they do not bring about what ought to be the case but is not yet the case; they sustain a system of practices that is already in being. As the *Geist* of a 'people' (*Volk(es)*), *Geist* is more appropriately translated as 'spirit' than as 'mind'.

2. *Diremtion*, from the Latin *dirimo*, 'to separate, break up', with the perfect participle *diremptum*, is often used by Hegel (though by few other authors) for significant cases of division, usually self-determined division. The 'diremption' into 'persons' (cf. §487, n. 1) is 'abstract', because every person is, as a person, identical to every other person. It contrasts with the division into the different realms: family, civil society, and state (cf. §§517 ff.). Persons are relatively independent of each other and of the spirit of their people. But they are sustained and controlled by this spirit. We can compare the relation of persons to their language. A language requires speakers. Their use of the language does not create it; it keeps it in being. Speakers have absorbed the language, and because of this are relatively independent of it. It is the speaker, rather than the language, that decides what words to use on a given occasion. A speaker can also, within limits, use words in innovative ways while remaining a speaker of the language.

3. Traditionally, 'substance' and 'accident' are correlative terms: cf. Enc. I, §§150–1. A substance has accidents (which may, however, change over time), and an accident belongs to a substance. A substance has independent existence, while accidents depend on their substance. For Aristotle, an individual man is a substance, his colour, shape, etc. being accidents of it. For Spinoza, by contrast, only 'God or nature' is a substance, and such individual entities as men are accidents of it, though Spinoza uses the word 'mode' rather than 'accident'. When Hegel speaks of 'substance' he usually has Spinoza in mind, even when (as here) he does not apply the term to the same entity as Spinoza does. However, Hegel argues that since a person is aware that the substance is his essence he thereby ceases, in that 'disposition' or mindedness (*Gesinnung*), to be a mere accident or mode of substance. Nevertheless, a person does not reflectively choose to do his duty, any more than we generally, in ordinary conversation, reflectively choose our words. The duty is 'something that is' (*Seiendes*), i.e. automatically assigned to me by the social order. On freedom, cf. §484, n. 1.

NOTES TO §515

1. The relation between individuals and the whole is reciprocal. Each individual is 'for himself', relatively independent, and takes care of himself; but his doing so

is conditioned by the whole. Conversely, the activities of individuals continually produce or regenerate the 'universal product', namely the whole that conditions their activity. However, the 'universal product' may be the 'trust' or confidence mentioned in the next sentence.

2. Each individual is aware that his own interests coincide with the interests of the 'whole'. Each individual is aware that every other individual is also aware that his interests coincide with the interests of the whole. No one could serve his interests better by violating the general interest than by serving it, and everyone knows this. So everyone trusts everyone else. Everyone, as it were, trusts everyone else to remain at his post.

NOTES TO §516

1. An individual's ethical duties are established by his 'relations' (*Beziehungen*), such as being a sergeant in command of a platoon, in particular social circumstances or 'relationships' (*Verhältnissen*), such as the army. His virtue is the disposition or character that enables him to fulfil these duties.

2. Virtue takes different forms, depending on the type of situation facing the individual. 'In relation to external immediacy', it is something like courage, endurance, or imperturbability. 'In relation to substantial objectivity', it is something like trustworthiness or reliability, though Hegel qualifies it as 'trust' (*Vertrauen*). In relation to the others we happen to deal with it is justice and benevolence. In the individual's attitude to his own 'reality' (*Dasein*) and 'bodiliness' (*Leiblichkeit*), it is presumably temperance, a tendency to restrain one's bodily (sexual, etc.) appetites. 'In this sphere', i.e. the sphere of our contingent encounters with others, and in our attitude to our own bodies, 'virtues' express one's 'particular character, etc. Hegel may mean that in the first two spheres, concerning hardship and working for the common good, virtue is not an optional matter, but is prescribed by the social order. By contrast, benevolence and temperance are matters on which individuals may vary, depending on their 'temperament' and 'character'. But it is hard to see why he should take this view of *justice*.

NOTES TO §517

1. The triad family–civil society–state exemplifies the pattern of simple unity–opposition–restored unity discussed in §§387, n. 14; 443, n. 1; and 465, n. 3. Individuals in civil society are not necessarily opposed to each other, but they are 'independent' of each other, not closely united as in the family, or 'organically' united, as in the state. The qualification of the 'totality' and the 'relations' (*Beziehungen*) as 'relative' (*relative(n)*) indicates their independence. 'Formal [*formellen*] universality' makes the same point: this universality makes them all persons and members of civil society, but it does not knit them together in the way that a concrete universal would. For 'formal universality', cf. §455, n. 7. It is similar to 'abstract' universality.

2. A 'political constitution' (*Staatsverfassung*, lit. 'state-constitution') is a society's consciousness of itself, because it subjects the social order to explicit reflection, codification, and control. Hence at this level substance is 'self-conscious'.

NOTE TO §518

1. 'Intimate trust' is *Zutrauen*, which is 'more intimate and personal than *Vertrauen*' (DGS, p. 358).

NOTES TO §519

1. This refers to the intellectual and 'ethical' differences between the sexes alleged in PR, §§165–6. Such differences are required, in Hegel's view, to explain the 'ethical', and not just the 'natural' or biological, appropriateness of a union between a man and a woman. If there is no *ethical* difference between men and women, then a union between a man and a man or between a woman and a woman is as appropriate *ethically* as a heterosexual union, whatever its *biological* disadvantages may be.
2. In their union a man and a woman each abandon their 'exclusive individuality' and become one person rather than two. They have *subjective* 'intimacy' (*Innigkeit*), i.e. they love and/or desire each other, and this leads them to 'substantial' or 'ethical' unity, not just a subjective unity based on their private passions, but a socially and morally significant objective bond.
3. If a person, x, is married to two persons of the opposite sex, y and z, neither the bond between x and y nor the bond between x and z is 'undivided': x's attention and affection are divided between y and z. Assuming that y and z do not unite to become 'one person', neither x and y together nor x and z together, nor all three together, can form one person. x will reserve some part of him- or herself for the other spouse.

NOTE TO §520

1. A family's property is not just a means for satisfying the needs of its members. It represents the unity and permanence of the family: cf. PR, §170. A marriage might be ended by divorce, but it is permanent in the sense that it outlasts the ebb and flow of sexual passion.

NOTE TO §521

1. Children were mentioned only obliquely in §519, perhaps in the reference to 'physical union'. But §519 does stress the fulfilment (or sublation) of the natural by the ethical. Education is perhaps a secularized version of the rebirth mentioned by Christ: 'Except a man be born again, he cannot see the kingdom of God.... Except a man be born of water and of the Spirit, he cannot enter into the kingdom of God' (John 3: 3–5).

NOTE TO §522

1. Hegel speaks as if civil society emerges from the dissolution of the family. This dissolution happens in three ways: (1) children leave home; (2) parents die; (3) the family members as one person break up into several persons and invoke 'legal regulations' (*rechtliche Bestimmungen*) to resolve their disputes—presumably a reference to divorce, etc. However, this is only a device for presenting the transition to civil society. Hegel knew that the family persists in civil society: 'Marriage, and especially monogamy, is one of the absolute principles on which the ethical life of a community depends' (PR, §167 Remark). Equally he knew that animals persist, even after the emergence of spirit, but that does not prevent his suggesting that spirit somehow arises from the death of an animal, i.e. of the natural: see Enc. II, §§375–6. But these two cases differ. However many animals die, their deaths need not presuppose, or give rise to, the emergence of spirit or human beings. But the dissolution of a family in ways (1) and (3) naturally presupposes a society into which the independent children or the estranged spouses disperse. Alternatively, if there is as yet no society, but only a few isolated families, the dispersal of family members to found new families will, if their numbers increase sufficiently, give rise to a society. Thus in PR, §181, Hegel presents the transition to civil society in both these ways: as the dispersal of family-members into a pre-existing civil society and as the pre-historic emergence of civil society from the expansion of a single family or from the interaction of scattered families. On Hegel's conflation of historical transitions and logical transitions or transitions in his thought, see also §512, n. 3.

NOTES TO §523

1. On atomism, see Enc. I, §98, especially: 'In recent times the atomistic conception has become even more important in the *political* sphere than in the physical. According to this conception the will of *individuals* as such is the principle of the state; the attractive force is the particularity of needs, inclinations; and the universal, the state itself, is the external relationship of the contract.' In this conception the whole of society, including the state and perhaps even the family, is atomistic. In Hegel's view, by contrast, civil society is atomistic, at least in its lower stages, but civil society is only one aspect of society, not the whole of it. Before Hegel's time, the expression 'civil society' had long been used to denote a civilized society in contrast to barbarism and despotism. Adam Ferguson used it in this way in *An Essay on the History of Civil Society* (1767). In German, 'civil society' became *bürgerliche Gesellschaft*, which means 'bourgeois society' as well as 'civil society'. This suggested that civil society was only one type or realm of modern society, not civilized society in general.

Hegel usually distinguishes civil society from the state, but here he calls it the 'external state' (*äusserer Staat*). He also does so in PR, §157, and in PR, §183 he explains: 'This system may be prima facie regarded as the external state, the state based on need, the state as the Understanding [or intellect] envisages it'. This state is external, in that its members are 'external' to each other. This use of 'external state' is distinct from its use in §534, where the 'external' (*äusserliche*) state is the governmental regulation of (and therefore 'external' to) civil society, and also from 'external public law' (*das äussere Staatsrecht*, §547), which deals with foreign affairs.

NOTE TO §524

1. §523 spoke of the 'mediating interconnection' of 'extremes', namely persons, and their 'interests'. In §524 the mediation occurs between a person's needs and the goods that satisfy the needs. In civil society a person can only rarely satisfy his needs by taking possession of unowned natural objects. (Hegel was not much influenced by the American experience.) So a given person, x, has to persuade the owners of goods to give him what he needs. The owners of goods are also trying to satisfy needs that they cannot satisfy with only the goods they own. So they are willing to give him the goods he needs in exchange for goods that they need, but which are owned by him. The goods that the owners need from him are either his labour or goods that he has acquired by his labour. So he has to work. It is also quite likely that the owners of the goods he needs have also had to work in some way to acquire them. So the 'general resources' (*allgemeine Vermögen*) are in a way constituted by the 'labour of all'. But not, of course, labour alone. The labour has to produce 'exchangeable' goods such that needs can be satisfied by its 'mediation'. Hegel seems to neglect raw materials, which, though they have owners and are extracted by labour, are not initially created by labour. But raw materials are mentioned in PR, §196.

NOTES TO §525

1. Needs are initially 'particular'. They are needs for particular things and the needs of particular persons. Four persons, w, x, y, and z, all need, say, bread and wine. There may be a division of labour here, with, say, w and x producing only bread, and y and z producing only wine. But there need not be a division of labour. Even if each of the four produces both goods, they may still need to exchange their surplus in one of them to repair their deficiency in the other. Suppose that their tastes become more refined: w comes to need white bread and red wine, x prefers brown bread and red wine, y brown bread and white wine, and z white bread and white wine. Then a division of labour is more likely, both because of the greater number of goods to be produced and because, in this case, each good is needed only by two persons, so that the others are unlikely to produce it (unless they can exchange it for goods they do need). The needs have become more 'abstract': a need for red wine 'abstracts' from the need for wine in general, excluding white wine. Their 'content' has been narrowed down by specialization or 'individualization' (*Vereinzelung*): cf. §378, n. 10 on the distinction between 'particular' and 'individual'. But individualization gives rise to a sort of universality: division of labour. Particular persons are locked together in a universal system

of interdependence. (Increasing division of labour does not result only from more refined needs. Adam Smith's pin factory intensified the division of labour not primarily to meet a demand for more specialized varieties of pin, but because it is a more efficient way of producing ordinary pins in the large numbers now needed: cf. §526, n. 1.)

2. People are less likely to enjoy the same things, know the same things, and behave in the same ways. Their pleasures, etc. become more specialized. This is 'culture' (*Bildung*), but only 'formal' culture, because it makes no claim about the content of what they enjoy, etc; this may not be especially elevated.

NOTE TO §526

1. An artefact, say a pin, can be produced by a single worker, and this is usually the most efficient way of producing a small number of pins for a small market. But the production of a pin can be broken down into a sequence of detailed tasks, and these can be assigned to different workers. A worker can acquire great facility in the performance of his allotted task, and does not waste time in moving from one task to another. Hence this is a more efficient way of producing a large number of pins. The labour of, say, fixing the head onto a pin is more 'abstract' than the labour of producing a whole pin in something like the way in which a need for red wine is more abstract than a need for wine. The worker is now more dependent on the 'social system'; given his specialized skill, he cannot become a solitary pin-maker. His simple physical operation can be performed by a machine as well as a human being, because it is 'mechanical', i.e. it does not require even implicit thought or judgement.

NOTES TO §527

1. The universal or 'general' (*allgemeine(n)*) resources are also a 'universal' (*allgemeines*) business. This can be taken in two ways: (1) The stress is on 'universal': the general resources are, like ('also', *ebenso*) the division of labour discussed in §525, a universal matter, i.e. to be distributed universally, to all. (2) The stress is on 'business': the resources are not just 'resources' (*Vermögen*, literally 'ability, capacity'), but also a *Geschäft*, a settlement, arrangement or transaction, i.e. a distribution or something to be distributed.

2. As Hegel points out in PR, §303 Remark, *Stand*, 'estate', signifies both a social 'class' in civil society and a politically significant 'estate'. Here only the social sense of *Stand* is relevant. The political sense comes into play in §544. §528, like PR, §202, distinguishes three 'estates' (*Stände*): the agricultural class, the business class, and civil servants. Estates differ from social classes in that they include both employers and workers in the relevant sector. 'Masses' (*Massen*) is not used derogatively, but as a neutral term for a relatively homogenous and distinct collection of people, whereas '*Stand*' suggests one's social standing or status. That there are these three 'masses' is, in Hegel's view, determined by the 'concept': cf. §528.

3. 'Actual existence' contrasts implicitly with 'concept'. One can, in the ordinary sense of 'exist', exist simply as a person. One can only properly *exist*, step forth into the world and make something of oneself, if one becomes a person of some particular type, belonging to a particular estate: 'When we say that a man must be a "somebody", we mean that he should belong to some specific social class, ... A man with no class is a mere private person and his universality is not actualized' (PR, §207 Addition). See also PR, §207 Remark: 'At first (i.e. especially in youth) a man chafes at the idea of resolving on a particular social position, and looks upon this as a restriction on his universal character and as a necessity imposed on him purely *ab extra*. This is because his thinking is still of that abstract kind which refuses to move beyond the universal and so never reaches the actual'. On *Existenz* as 'stepping forth', cf. §403, n. 2.
4. Why could there not be a society consisting of only peasant farmers and their families? Hegel has already stipulated that there is civil society and a state. If there is a state, there must at least be politicians, and if there is a civil society there must be a theatre of significant activity outside the family, most obviously trade, run by a class of traders. Might not political affairs and trade be managed by the peasants themselves, without a dedicated class of politicians and of traders? Presumably so, as long as the society is small and the interactions of is members simple. Size and complexity require specialization. Hegel compares a society to a living creature, which, if it is large and complex, requires different particular organs. The 'centre' (*Mittelpunkt(e)*) of the estates is the state itself.

NOTES TO §528

1. The agricultural class. 'Substantial' implies unreflective, down-to-earth stolidity.
2. The business and manufacturing class. 'Reflected' (*reflektierte*) means reflected or turned back into itself, i.e. no longer guided by nature as the farmer is. It also suggests reflectiveness, in contrast to 'faith and trust'.
3. Civil servants. In §543 and PR, §§202 and 205 they are called the 'universal' class or estate.

NOTES TO §529

1. Civil society arises from the 'principle of contingent particularity'. People just happen to need certain things and they make unregulated choices about what to produce, what to buy, what to sell, and so on. But this mass of contingencies develops into a system involving 'universal relationships' between, for example, the three estates. It also involves 'external necessity', such as (perhaps) the need to reduce the price, or improve the quality, of one's produce if one wants to sell more. The transition from this to 'formal right' is not very clear. Hegel's general idea is that the necessity implicit in this system should be made explicit in *laws*. This would include laws specifically concerned with the economy, such as laws enforcing contracts (§§493–5), against price-fixing or laws controlling the

quality of goods (see PR, §236). But it would also extend to laws against theft, murder, and so on, practices which, if they become too widespread, undermine economic life.

2. 'Intellectual' (*verständigen*) suggests that what is needed here is stability and clarity, not the fluidity of 'reason'. The informal practices that the system requires are to be brought to explicit 'consciousness' by laws, in something like the way in which the formal grammar of a language brings to consciousness, and also sharpens and stabilizes, informal linguistic usage. *Gesetz*, 'law', is *gesetzt*, 'posited' or laid down, from the verb *setzen*, 'to posit, put, etc.'

3. 'The positive aspect' translates '*Das Positive*'. This contrasts not with 'negative', but with 'rational'. A law is essentially 'posited', laid down. It is then 'in force' (*gültige*) and known to everyone. A law is still a law if its content is 'irrational'. But it is not a law if it is not promulgated.

4. It is rational, 'determined by reason', etc. that there should be a law against, say, murder, imposing a harsh penalty for this offence. Suppose the penalty imposed is 10 years imprisonment. But why 10 years? Why not 11 years, or $10\frac{1}{2}$ or $10\frac{1}{4}$, and so on? Here we can go on ad infinitum, devising a more and more refined penalty. Clearly no rational reason can be given for making the penalty 10 years rather than 11 or 9 or any other number within this range. So the legislators just have to dig in their heels at some point and impose a penalty which, if not irrational, cannot be rationally justified over an infinity of alternatives. In PR §214 Hegel points out that the law is likely to impose not a fixed penalty, but a penalty within the range bounded by a maximum and a minimum. Thus the law will prescribe that a murderer is to be imprisoned for, say, no more than 20 years and no less than 7. But this, as Hegel there says, raises the same difficulty at two points. First, the maximum and minimum are themselves round numbers arbitrarily selected from within a certain range. Why not a maximum of $19\frac{1}{2}$ years and a minimum of $6\frac{3}{4}$? Second, the judge has to select a definite penalty within the range bounded by the maximum and minimum, and this again cannot be rationally justified over an infinity of possible alternatives. Legislators and judges (and perhaps everyone else) are constantly and inevitably faced by problems of the type that confronted 'Buridan's ass', who, situated exactly midway between two equally delectable piles of hay, starved to death because he had no reason to prefer one of the piles to the other. Judges and legislators have to choose between alternatives, none of which is discernibly preferable to the others.

5. The view Hegel criticizes in this paragraph was proposed by K. L. von Haller's *Restauration der Staats-Wissenschaft oder Theorie des natürlich-geselligen Zustands* (Winterthur, 1816–20; 2nd ed. 1829–22) (*Restoration of Political Science: Theory of the Natural Social Condition*). Hegel also attacks von Haller in PR, §§219 and 258. On Hegel's assimilation of human laws enjoining, prohibiting, or permitting certain types of action in a human community and natural laws that constitute or express invariable sequences of events, cf. §422, n. 4. His argument against von Haller seems frail, both because the two types of law are arguably quite different, and because it might be objected that humans display their superiority to stars and

cattle by breaking free of laws. However, Hegel's criticism is quite appropriate to von Haller, who himself appeals to the laws supposedly governing non-human entities in such claims as the following: 'Just as, in the inorganic world, the greater dislodges the less and the mighty the weak... so in the animal kingdom, and then amongst human beings, the same law appears in nobler forms' (Restauration, i. 342 ff. (2nd ed., 361 ff.); 'this, therefore, is the eternal, unalterable, ordinance of God, that the mightier rules, must rule, and will always rule' (2nd edn, p. 375). (The translation and the pages of the 2nd edn. are taken from Knox, PR, p. 158).

6. The 'same empty requirement of perfection' refers back not to von Haller in the preceding paragraph, but to the first paragraph of the Remark, which dealt with people who argued that the law and its application can be rationally and/or intellectually determined down to the finest detail. The people criticized in the present paragraph argue that a law-code is impossible, because it would have to distinguish between, say, different types of crime. The law would have to distinguish not just, say, burglary from street robbery, but the burglar who enters by the front door from the burglar who enters by a window, the theft of a video from the theft of a wallet, and so on. Since individual actions always differ from each other in some respect, this distinguishing can proceed indefinitely. Because the required distinguishing can never be completed, it is argued that a law-code is impossible.

This distinguishing is comparable to the division of a line or a spatial area. This too can proceed indefinitely. But there is the difference that while each successive segment of the line is *qualitatively* the same as its larger predecessor, the division of a wider offence (e.g. burglary) into two or more narrower offences (e.g. burglary after entry by the front door, the back door, or a window) results in more specific varieties of the wider offence. Thus in the case of spatial division, there is no obvious reason (apart from practical convenience) for differentiating between one stage of the division and the next, for saying that the division should not proceed beyond a certain point or that after a certain point the division has a different significance from that which it had earlier. By contrast, there is good reason for differentiating between earlier and later stages in the distinguishing of different offences. For example, we need a law against robbery and another law against murder. These are two distinct types of offence, neither being a species of the other. Hence they require two distinct laws. There is also a significant distinction between burglary and street robbery, and between robbery with and robbery without violence. But neither of these distinctions require a distinct law for each type of offence, since the distinct offences are species of the wider, more general offence of robbery or theft. Only one law is needed, with the relevant distinctions and their consequences specified within the single law. If the original law did not mention the distinction between robbery with and without violence, it needs to be improved in this respect. But the improvement is an improvement of the single law, not its bifurcation into two new laws. To produce a new law every time we feel the need for a new distinction would be like building a new house every time a door needs replacing. Other distinctions, by contrast, need not be made at all. It makes no difference whether the burglar entered by the back door or the front, whether his violence was inflicted with a baseball bat or a cricket bat. Or, at any rate, if such distinctions are found to be relevant to a particular case, they can be left to the judge and his 'decisions'.

There are societies in which there is a confused mass of distinct laws, with no apparent attempt to simplify matters by classifying specific types of offence under more general headings. In PR, §211 Remark, Hegel cites English law as an example of this and also the later Roman Empire. These situations arose, however, not because a single overzealous legislator produced a new law for every distinction that occurred to him, but because a number of different legislators (judges in England, jurists in the Roman Empire) each produced laws without, at least for a time, adequate supervision and sytematization. Hegel says that 'an Emperor' (according to Knox, p. 357, Valentinian III in 446 AD) remedied this situation in the Roman Empire. Sir Robert Peel (1788–1850) was Home Secretary in a Tory administration from 1821 to 1827 and from 1828 to 1830. In the first of these ministries Peel reformed the penal code. Hegel was writing in 1827. (I owe this information to F. Nicolin and O. Pöggeler, in their edition of G. W. F. Hegel, *Enzyklopädie der philosophischen Wissenschaften im Grundrisse* (Hamburg: Felix Meiner, 1969), 494.)

NOTES TO §530

1. Of laws that forbid actions, some forbid actions that are wrong in themselves, independently of the existence of a positive law forbidding them, e.g. laws against rape or murder. Others forbid actions which are not wrong in themselves, but become wrong in virtue of the existence of a law forbidding them, e.g. laws forbidding parking on a double yellow line. If a law against murder is not suitably promulgated, we nevertheless have an obligation not to commit murder, since this concerns the 'moral or ethical will'. But this obligation does not depend on the positive law against murder; since this law is not known to us, we have no 'external' obligation to obey it. This is seen in the case of the second type of law. If the law forbidding parking on double yellow lines has not been promulgated, then we have no obligation whatsoever not to park on them, unless some specific feature of the situation (such as a narrow road or a sharp bend) prohibits the action. In the absence of a promulgated law, the moral or ethical will has no reason to follow this rule. A law as such appeals only to the 'abstract will', requiring only external conformity to itself, and so it must be promulgated. It cannot rely on the 'moral or ethical will', except in so far as obedience to promulgated laws is itself a requirement of the moral or ethical will. That is, although it is not immoral to park on a double yellow line unless there is a law against doing so, it is immoral to disobey the law once it is promulgated.

In PR, §215 Remark, Hegel says that 'Dionysius the Tyrant' of Syracuse hung laws too high up for anyone to read and then punished them for disobeying them. (In his note on p. 358, Knox says that he 'has been unable to trace this anecdote in any writer on Dionysius. The story is more commonly told of the emperor Caligula.')

2. This 'subjectivity' is contrasted with the subjectivity involved in 'morality': cf. §§511, n. 1; 512, nn. 2 and 4. In pure morality, subjectivity and its rights were unrestricted. A pure moralist might say, for example, that someone is not obliged to obey a law unless he assents to it or agrees with it, that a law as such imposes no obligation whatsoever, but is just one factor in the situation that the agent needs to take account of in coming to a decision. Hegel disagrees. The only right that subjectivity has here is the right to know what the law is, or at least to be able to discover what the law is without excessive difficulty. This knowledge is the subjective 'reality' (*Dasein*). But it is also an objective 'reality', since it is knowledge of objective laws that are the same for everyone and independent of the agent's personal feelings, etc.

3. This refers back to the account of property in §§488–92, where law was not mentioned. In civil society one's title to one's property is recognized and guaranteed by law, as long as it is acquired in accordance with the legal 'formalities'. Cf. PR, §217.

NOTES TO §531

1. Hegel says: 'Die *Notwendigkeit*, zu welcher das objektive Dasein sich bestimmt, erhält das Rechtliche in der *Rechtspflege*.' As I translate the sentence, Hegel's point is this: If there were laws but no courts and, in particular, no judicial punishments for breaches of the law, compliance with the law would be patchy and contingent. In the last resort, compliance would be secured by the threat of revenge, and non-compliance met with actual revenge. But whether revenge is taken and, if so, in what form, are contingent matters: see §§500, n. 1; 501, nn. 1 and 2. The law-court confers 'necessity' on these contingencies by transforming revenge into punishment.

   Hegel's sentence could also be translated as: 'The *necessity*, to which the objective reality determines itself, acquires legality in the *administration of justice*.' Then Hegel's point would be this: if there were laws but no courts or punishment, the laws would still be enforced by revenge and the threat of it; law courts confer legality on this necessity. However, this translation does not square well with the reference to contingency in the final sentence of the Paragraph.

2. In §§496–502 'right-in-itself' (*das Recht-an-sich*) or 'right in itself' (*das Recht an sich*) was contrasted with the 'semblance of right' proposed by the fraudster and to the non-fraudulent criminal's denial of right: see §§496, n. 1; 498, n. 1; 499, n. 1; 500, n. 1; 502, n. 1. Here it is distinguished from 'provable' right. Hegel may be suggesting that right-in-itself and provable right are sometimes in conflict with each other. But he cannot mean that right-in-itself *often* loses because it cannot prove its claim, whereas a mere semblance of right *often* wins because it can prove its claim. If that were so, he could hardly say that the law court 'deprives the existence of right of its contingency'. His main point is that, by proving itself, right-in-itself completes or fulfils itself, transforming itself into proven (and recognized) right.

3. Two distinctions are in play here. (1) In the first sentence, the distinction is between learning the facts of the case from witnesses and other evidence, and learning them from the defendant's confession or guilty-plea. (2) In the second sentence the distinction is between discovering the facts and applying the law to them, i.e. declaring the law and deciding the sentence. The connexion between the two distinctions is that if the defendant confesses, the facts of the case are agreed in advance and all the court needs to do is to apply the law to them. In that case, no jury is needed and the case is tried by a judge or magistrate. If the defendant does not confess, then the court has to perform the two tasks distinguished in (2), and it is believed that they should be performed by different people. Usually, the facts are determined by a jury of laypersons, while the law is applied by a judge. It is assumed that no special legal expertise is required to judge the facts of the case. But Hegel seems to doubt whether the two tasks need to be performed by different people. A legal expert may not, after all, be a worse judge of the facts than a lay person.

4. There are two types of confession: a confession of guilt preceding the trial itself, which avoids the need for a jury, and a confession of guilt during the trial, which may be required before a penal sentence is imposed. When Hegel says that the jury-court 'abstracts' (*abstrahiert*) from this 'condition', he means that if the defendant confesses, a jury is not needed, and so, conversely, if a jury is needed, a confession is not needed. However, Hegel is arguing that a confession should be required, in order to help the jury reach their decision. His argument runs as follows. (My own comments on the argument appear in brackets.) The jury is trying to find the 'truth' of the matter, what actually happened. But their inquiry is not like an investigation in mathematics, where the truth can be definitively demonstrated. All that the jury can hope to obtain is (a feeling of) certainty, and this is subjective; it may not correspond to the (objective) truth. A confession produces certainty as great as can be hoped for. (Why so? As Hegel says in PR, §227 Addition, the defendant may lie. It may be hard to disbelieve someone who, with apparent sincerity, confesses his guilt, but someone can easily confess a guilt that they have not incurred. Conversely, the guilt of a person who refuses to confess may be obvious from other evidence.) If the defendant's right is to be respected, the evidence of his guilt and the 'persuasion' (*Überzeugung*) of the judges must be 'conclusive'. That is, the evidence against him must be so strong that it leaves no room for reasonable doubt, that it could not be strengthened by further evidence, and that it cannot be weakened by further evidence. The judges must be so strongly convinced of his guilt that they have no residual doubt, etc. Hence a confession is required. However, a confession alone is not enough to secure a conviction. (Why not, if it produces the 'highest degree of assurance'?) 'Objective' proofs, from testimony and circumstances, are also needed. (Earlier, 'assurance' or certainty was said to be 'subjective', in contrast to 'truth' and presumably to knowledge. But here 'objective' proofs contrast not with subjective certainty, but with the defendant's confession, which supposedly *produces* subjective certainty.) But these alone are not enough. They

do not establish the defendant's guilt or innocence conclusively: 'the jurors are essentially judges', making a judgement according to the balance of probability, not definitively demonstrating a conclusion. The certainty produced by objective proofs is incomplete, because it is only 'in them', in the jurors. (Certainty is only complete, if it is also *in the defendant*.) To rely exclusively on *objective* proofs and *subjective* certainty (but not subjective *proofs*) is a confusion, reminiscent of the ancient Teutonic trial by ordeal, in which the guilt or innocence of the accused is established by requiring him to hold red-hot iron, etc., without harm.

Hegel's argument is a muddle. In so far as a confession is used by the jury to infer the guilt of the defendant, the confession is as 'objective' as testimony and other evidence. It may produce *subjective* certainty in the jury, but so too may objective proofs. Apart from this, what makes a confession subjective is that a confession, if it is sincere, shows that the defendant himself accepts his guilt, whereas 'objective' proofs do not. However, a confession is, in itself, no more reliable than other sorts of evidence. A defendant may for some reason (e.g. to protect someone else) confess to a murder that he knows he did not commit, or he may mistakenly believe that he committed a murder. Hegel's main reason for requiring a confession is not that it is either sufficient or necessary for establishing the defendant's guilt, but that 'the right of self-consciousness thereby attains a measure of satisfaction; consciousness must chime in with the judge's sentence, and it is only when the criminal has confessed that the judgement loses its alien character as far as he is concerned' (PR, §227 Addition). The defendant then accepts the legitimacy of the legal process and its outcome, and is thus reconciled to them. So-called 'objective proofs' are required to ensure that the confession is genuine. For Hegel's belief that a criminal, as a free man, is entitled and required to accept the punishment meted out to him, cf. §500, n. 1, though this concerns the law to be applied to him rather than the fact that he did something to deserve its application to him.

5. Hegel is perhaps correcting a remark he made in 1821: 'The objective truth which emerges from material of this kind [namely testimony and circumstantial evidence] and the method appropriate to it leads, when attempts are made to determine it rigidly and objectively, to half-proofs and then, by further deductions from these—deductions which at the same time involve formal illogicality—to extraordinary punishments' (PR, §227 Remark). In his note on this, Knox quotes from the second, 1827, edition of the Encyclopaedia, §531: 'materially, all punishments inflicted as a result of the verdict of a jury are what have been called extraordinary punishments—there may be a confession here too but that is something accidental in these circumstances and outside the essence of the matter'. Knox adds: 'Ordinary punishments then are those inflicted, by judges who sit without juries, on criminals who confess their guilt' (PR, p. 360). So here, in the third, 1830, edition of the Encyclopaedia, Hegel is saying that it does not matter whether the punishment is imposed with or without a jury; what matters is whether the defendant confesses or not. He still insists, erroneously, that a confession involves absolute 'assurance' (*Vergewisserung*).

NOTE TO §532

1. Administration of justice confers 'necessity' on freedom, and does not leave it to chance. It punishes and annuls violations of one's person and property, if they occur, and also deters other such violations, which would occur if it were not for legal penalties. However, two deficiencies remain. First, this 'activation' of freedom depends on the 'subjectivity' of the judge. This ought to coincide with 'right-in-itself', but it may not: the judge, and especially the jury, may give a mistaken verdict or ruling. Second, administration of justice deals with only the 'abstract' side of freedom, the side considered in §§488–502. The judicial system oversees, and attempts to guarantee, the security of one's person and property. But it is not concerned with the 'system of needs'. This system works by a 'blind' necessity. No one has an overall 'consciousness' of its workings and no one oversees it, guides it, or corrects its malfunctioning.

NOTES TO §533

1. This is a somewhat perfunctory account of what administration of justice excludes. For example, everyone sleeps at some time or other. So sleep is, in one sense at least, a universal rather than a particular matter. But it is of no concern to the judge, unless it is relevant to the case in hand. Conversely, particular details of a person's life may well be relevant to the case in hand. 'Belonging to particularity' amounts to 'whatever does not pertain to the inviolability of a person and his property'. Crime too is a universal phenomenon. But the law court as such is not concerned to reduce (or to increase) the incidence of crime, only to annul such crimes as occur.
2. It is not clear what Hegel's reason is for saying that the aim is not just the satisfaction of need, but the stable, universal satisfaction of it. His German (. . . *die Befriedigung des Bedürfnisses, und zwar zugleich als des Menschen* . . . literally: 'the satisfaction of the need, and in fact at the same as of the man') might be taken in either of two ways: (1) 'the satisfaction of need, and in fact the need of a man as well', i.e. the stability of satisfaction is required by the fact that the need is a *human* need; (2) 'the satisfaction of need, and in fact the satisfaction of the man as well', i.e. the stability is required by the fact that the satisfaction is the satisfaction of the *whole* man, not just of the need. Wallace opts for (1). But this does not give a very good reason for requiring stability: animals, as well as men, have recurrent needs requiring stable satisfaction. (2) gives a better reason: the enduring man requires satisfaction, not just his temporary need.
3. Two things are required of the system of needs, that it satisfy needs regularly, not sporadically ('stable'), and that it satisfy the needs of everyone ('universal'). These requirements are not always fulfilled, for two main reasons. First, the system malfunctions. It responds sluggishly to changing needs, supplies from abroad are disrupted, and so on. Secondly, the system itself does not essentially aim at the regular satisfaction of all individuals. Its efficient operation often involves

bankrupting inefficient enterprises and depriving superfluous workers of their livelihood. Individuals whose needs are not satisfied are not consoled or compensated by the overall efficiency of the system: they regard themselves, not the overall system, as the 'morally justified end'.

NOTES TO §534

1. On the 'external state', cf. §523, n. 1. Here it is governmental regulation of civil society. It is 'external', because it regulates civil society from outside civil society, and 'universality', because it is not associated with any particular segment of civil society but oversees it as a whole. It depends on the 'substantial state', the state that is above and distinct from civil society. The word *Polizei*, from the Greek *polis* ('city', city-state, state') now means 'police', but originally meant something like 'government' and retained this wide sense down into the eighteenth century. In Hegel's day it still covered the provision of 'public alms-houses, hospitals, street-lighting' (PR, §242 Remark), in general things required for public order, for the smooth functioning of civil society and for the relief of its victims. PR, §§231–49 deal with this at greater length.
2. A 'corporation' is a body to which people engaged in a particular sector of civil society belong. Unlike a trade union, it included employers as well as employees. Unlike the *Polizei* it is an institution within civil society, not external to it, and is concerned with the interests only of a particular segment of civil society, not with civil society as a whole. The corporation has, Hegel suggests, three functions: (1) it serves the private interests of its members by helping them in hard times; (2) it encourages them to work not just for their private interests but for the interests of their trade as a whole, a 'relatively universal end'; (3) it provides a professional ethic.

NOTE TO §535

1. The family is a close unity; its members do not pursue their own separate interests. This unity is based on love, however, not on a conscious, rational strategy. By contrast, a member of civil society adopts a conscious rational strategy, but he seeks his (or his family's) own interests, not the interests of civil society as a whole. The state combines these two principles, restoring the unity of the family at a higher, consciously rational level. It is concerned with the interests of the state as a whole, including the 'determinations of it which develop in knowledge', i.e. those determinations that Hegel develops in the following §§.

NOTES TO §536

1. See §§537–46. 'State-law' is *Staatsrecht*, i.e. 'constitutional law'.
2. See §547. The state is an *Individuum*, a more emphatic word than *der Einzelne*, which is the 'general term for "the individual". *Das Individuum* is used in more

strictly philosophical contexts, and not like English "individual" in the sense of "person"' (DGS, p. 297, n. 1). The other individuals are other states.

3. See §548–52. Each individual state is a mind or 'spirit', which Hegel later calls a *Volksgeist*, 'national spirit' or 'spirit of a people': §§548, 552, 559. National spirits all belong to a larger spirit, the *Weltgeist*, 'world-spirit': §549. Hence they are 'moments' in the 'development' or unfolding of the universal 'Idea' (*Idee*: cf. §377, n. 4) of spirit. It is universal because it embraces all the particular national spirits; it is Idea (rather than 'concept') because it gradually actualizes itself.

NOTES TO §537

1. The state is one 'individual' (*Individuum*), because it is ruled by a monarch: cf. §542.
2. Cf. PR, §265 Addition: 'It has often been said that the end of the state is the happiness of the citizens. That is perfectly true. If all is not well with them, if their subjective aims are not satisfied, if they do not find that the state as such is the means to their satisfaction, then the footing of the state itself is insecure'.
3. Individuals tend to become absorbed in their private interests and to lose touch with the general interest. The most striking way in which the state remedies this is warfare: cf. §546.

NOTE TO §538

1. On 'objective freedom', cf. §484, n. 1. On the role of the 'estates' (*Stände*) in legislation, see §544. On 'custom', see §§485, n. 1; 513, n. 2. Laws do not simply restrict us. They enable us to do things that we could not otherwise do, such as make binding contracts and walk the streets in safety. Obedience to them becomes, for most people, more or less habitual and they are thus not felt as restrictions.

NOTES TO §539

1. Hegel implicitly compares the mind, and hence the state, to a living creature, as earlier he compared society to a living creature: cf. §527, n. 4. On the mind or 'spirit' as a rationally articulated structure, deriving from a single 'concept', see §378, n. 11. A mind or an organism is not a composite of distinct parts, any of which might be removed without detriment to the others. It grows out of a single plan or 'concept', which unfolds into various organs, serving to maintain the whole organism. In the case of the state, the concept is the rational will.
2. The 'constitution' is not identical to the 'rational will' nor is it the 'concept' from which the state develops. It is the overall structure of the state as it has developed from the rational will. In this sense a living organism, such as a tree, has a constitution or something analogous to a constitution: its overall structure. However, a tree never becomes conscious of its own concept: the concept of a tree does not develop to consciousness of itself. By contrast, the concept of

the state, the rational will, becomes fully conscious of itself in the constitution. Private individuals fulfil the rational will with only implicit or tacit awareness of it, but the government makes it fully explicit and pursues it consciously.

3. Taken in their abstract form, i.e. without drawing essential distinctions and making essential qualifications, the categories of freedom and equality stifle or undermine constitutional government. They might be taken to imply that no one should have authority over anyone else, that everyone should have an equal say in public affairs, and that everyone should be free to do whatever they like. In this abstract form these categories are very 'familiar'. The distinctions between different types of freedom and equality are less familiar. But it is only when such distinctions and qualifications are made that equality and more especially freedom can be regarded as 'foundations' of the state.

4. Why are men 'only unequal' 'by nature'? Hegel might mean either of two things: (1) In their natural qualities, i.e. strength, intelligence, etc., men are unequal. (2) As a matter of empirical fact, men are not regarded and treated as equal in every society, let alone in the state of nature: cf. §433, n. 1, etc. If he means (1) it is unclear why he says they are 'only unequal' (*nur ungleich*). Men are 'equal' (or at least 'similar', another meaning of *gleich*) in some respects, in their humanity for example and in their mortality. Moreover, it would be more accurate to say that, by nature, men are neither equal nor unequal. They are *dissimilar* in various ways, and they are unequal *in certain respects*, in height for example. But neither dissimilarity nor inequality in certain respects entails inequality *simpliciter*: ten pound coins are dissimilar to a ten pound note and unequal to it in weight, yet both are of equal value. The coins and the note are of equal value, however, only because they are assigned an equal value by human society; and a single pound coin and a single ten pound note are of unequal value because of the value assigned to them by society. None of the three is either equal or unequal to the others 'by nature'. Similarly men, whatever their differences and specific inequalities, are neither equal nor unequal to each other by nature, unless, of course, God is supposed to assign value to them in some such way as we assign value to coins and notes. It is more likely that Hegel has (2) in mind. This is, in any case, suggested by his reference to slavery and by his shift from 'equality' to 'freedom'. By nature men dominate other men and deprive them of their freedom, as in the struggle for recognition and also in Greece, Rome, and almost every preChristian society: cf. §433, n. 4, etc. A slave need not be inferior to his owner in physical or mental qualities; he just happened to lose the fight, to be captured in war, to be born to a slave, or whatever. Hence position (2) does not entail or presuppose position (1).

Equality first comes about in society, when all men are recognized as persons 'capable of property'. This is equality in freedom, freedom to acquire property and to do what one likes with it, not equality in the amount of one's property: cf. §488, n. 1. This equality is conferred by the 'concept', not by nature. The concept is the concept of freedom, since man is essentially free. Hence the concept of freedom converges with the concept of man. But not all men are actually free, any more than all cows have four legs—despite the fact that the cow is, by its concept, a quadruped. The concept of man tells us what men ideally are, not what they actually are. But freedom, unlike four-leggedness, is a complex matter, involving stages and levels. Personality or personhood is only the lowest level of freedom, before the concept has been determined and developed, before it has expanded into the Idea of freedom. Nevertheless, to work our way out of nature even to this level of the concept required a great effort, to reach 'consciousness of the deepest principle of the mind, etc.' For Hegel it is freedom, both at this and at higher levels, that is essential to man. Equality is simply a consequence of freedom.

5. 'Men are equal before the law' is a tautology in the sense that if men are not equal before the law, then to that extent the laws are not applied. The laws presuppose inequalities, between for example rich and poor. If the law imposes higher taxes on the rich than on the poor, the rich and the poor are not unequal before the law; the law is being properly applied to them. It might be argued that equality before the law requires more than simply the application of the law as it stands. The law should, in addition, not discriminate between people in perverse or irrelevant ways and it should also be accessible to all. For example, if a law were to impose a higher tax on the poor than on the rich, or a higher tax on Jews than on Christians, it might be claimed to infringe equality before the law even if the law is strictly and impartially enforced. Again, if the poor are deterred by the high cost of legal representation from defending their legal claims, this too could be thought to infringe equality before the law. But Hegel might reply that an unfairly discriminatory law is not a proper law, and that if the law is not accessible to all then it is not properly enforced.

6. Hegel implicitly divides freedom in two ways, into (1) negative and affirmative freedom, and (2) objective and subjective freedom. Negative freedom is freedom *from* interference; affirmative freedom is freedom *to*, freedom *to* do various things. But this affirmative freedom is also subjective freedom. *Objective* freedom is the freedom embodied in rational laws: cf. §§484, n. 1; 539, n. 7. Subjective freedom consists in the freedom allowed to the individual subject by the laws. It falls into two broad types, private and public. First, the subject is left free to do many things as he pleases. He can, for example, marry whoever he wants and choose his own career. (Hegel believed that these freedoms were denied to the citizens of Plato's 'republic' and also to the citizens of Athens: see my 'Plato, Hegel and Greek Sittlichkeit'.) As long as he does not disturb others, he can get drunk, and indulge in other private follies. Secondly, the citizen has a right to 'insight', to understand the justification of laws he is expected to obey, a law requiring, for example, the education of children: cf. §484, n. 1. He also has a right to a say in legislative and other public procedures.

7. This section deals with objective freedom. The privileges of a city, etc. or its exemptions from taxes and other services were called its liberties or 'freedoms' (*Freiheiten*). But this is collective negative freedom (from), not the freedom that is embodied in 'every genuine law'. The common idea of freedom is that it is freedom to do as one likes ('contingent preference and wilfulness'), i.e. the first type of subjective freedom discussed in §539, n. 6. Since not everyone can do as

they like without infringing the freedom of others to do as *they* like, laws are then regarded as restrictions of one's freedom in the interests of the freedom of others. Hegel grants a place to freedom to do as one likes, but he does not regard it as the only or even the highest type of freedom: §413, n. 5. When one does as one likes, one follows urges that just come and go with no rational justification, and hence one is not fully self-determining and does not fulfil one's rational nature. This is achieved by obedience to 'genuine' laws, laws that correspond to our rational nature.

8. The 'assumed definition' of freedom corresponds roughly to the second type of subjective freedom discussed in §539, n. 6, participation in public affairs. The proponents of this definition had in mind ancient Athenian democracy, in which all male citizens were supposed to participate in public affairs. This does not happen in 'modern states', though since modern states, at least in Europe, have abolished slavery, they are 'more capable of equality'. But, Hegel insists, it is wrong to confront 'actuality' or reality with a definition of freedom such that we cannot hope to find freedom in actuality. He does not mean that we must find freedom in modern states at all costs, if necessary by scaling down our ideal of freedom so that modern states measure up to it. Rather, since actuality is 'rational' (cf. PR, Preface and Enc. I, §6: 'What is rational is actual and what is actual is rational'), we shall, if we are persistent enough, find in modern states a type of freedom that surpasses the freedom of antiquity. He does not, at least in this section, explain his discrimination between freedom and equality. If the rationality of modern actuality guarantees the existence of freedom in it, why does it not guarantee the existence of equality as well? After all, the freedom that Hegel values should be equal freedom for all. Hegel gives a more restrictive definition of equality than he does of freedom, and thus finds equality wanting where freedom luxuriates. Equality in freedom is a necessary, but not a sufficient condition of equality *simpliciter*.

9. In modern societies, objective freedom, i.e. rational law, is more developed than in earlier societies. This in itself increases inequality, since a strong state with a complex legal code requires hierarchy and expertise. But it also enables modern societies to allow and promote *subjective* freedom, both in the sense of doing as one likes and in the sense of forming one's own moral views, to a greater extent than earlier societies. This too increases inequality: the education that individuals need to acquire to exercise this freedom, as well as the exercise of freedom itself, enlarges the distance between them. The advance of freedom cannot be halted *before* it threatens equality. Once we establish freedom by securing property, etc., we take this as 'a matter of course' and think we are not really free unless we are allowed to 'venture in every direction', etc. Freedom has an intrinsic drive to expand, since each increase in it comes to be taken for granted and not regarded as freedom. Cf. PR, §268 Addition: 'habit blinds us to that on which our whole existence depends. When we walk the streets at night in safety, it does not strike us that this might be otherwise'. It might be objected that equality too has a similar intrinsic drive to expand. But equality does not usually have the same appeal to the individual as freedom does. For example, it

matters to me far more whether my income is sufficient to enable me to do what I want to do (i.e. freedom) than whether it is greater than, less than, or equal to someone else's income (i.e. equality). Egalitarians are generally less concerned about inequality *as such* than about deprivation, more troubled by the difference between the rich and the poor than by the difference between the very rich and the moderately rich. But the relief of poverty, Hegel would argue, has more to do with freedom than with equality.

10. Cf. PR, §302 Addition: 'The constitution is essentially a system of mediation. In despotisms where there are only rulers and people, the people is effective, if at all, only as a mass destructive of the organization of the state. When the multitude enters the state as one of its organs, it achieves its interests by legal and orderly means. But if these means are lacking, the voice of the masses is always for violence'. 'Constitution' is here contrasted with 'despotism', an essential feature of which is the exclusion of the people from formal participation in public affairs. Hence Hegel regards such participation as a necessary feature of a constitution, though only a part of the constitution, not the whole of it.

NOTES TO §540

1. Cf. PR, §§273–4. Following Montesquieu and also Aristotle, Hegel is implicitly arguing against the view that it is possible to devise a constitution a priori and to impose it successfully on a people, without regard to their existing character, customs, laws, etc. Account must be taken of the 'spirit' of a people. However desirable a constitution may be in the abstract, it will not generate rational laws and secure compliance with them, unless it is buttressed by the spirit of the people, of the 'whole' people, not simply a few enlightened individuals.

The mind or 'spirit' of an individual involves consciousness both of the surrounding world and of the individual itself. Analogously, the mind or spirit of a people implies a consciousness of the world and of the people itself. It is conscious of rationality or 'reason' (*Vernunft*), though of 'its' (*seiner*) reason, not of reason in the abstract. This consciousness is expressed in the ethical life of the people, but its ultimate basis, Hegel seems to say, is the religion of the people. He may have in mind the religion of a Greek city-state, such as Athens: cf. PR, §257: 'the mind of a nation [or 'spirit of a people'] (Athene for instance) is the divine, knowing and willing itself'. But Enc. III, §552 Remark indicates that religion is also the basis of the spirit of a modern people. However, the spirit of a people cannot dispense with a constitution. The 'principle' involved in it needs to be developed and organized, if the people is to be conscious of it. Roughly speaking, the spirit of a people and its constitution need each other, and fit each other, like a plug and a socket.

2. The answer to the question 'Who has to make the spirit of a people?' is 'No one' or perhaps 'Everyone'. Hence the answer to the question 'To whom . . . belongs the power to make a constitution?' is 'To no one' or 'To everyone'. Hegel is not opposing constitutional reform. His argument, clarified in PR, §273, is this. If we devise a constitution and try to impose it on a collection of people who do

not already have a constitution, we will not succeed. For a collection of people without a constitution is not a people with a single spirit; it is just a collection of isolated individuals incapable of a constitution. So a constitution can be successfully imposed only on a people that already has a constitution. But the constitution we impose cannot be very different from the constitution they already have. If it is, then our new constitution will jar with the people's spirit, which conforms to the old constitution, not our new one. So a new constitution can be successfully imposed on a people only if it is fairly similar to their existing constitution. But then the new constitution is not really a new constitution. It is a development of the old constitution, and we are in fact altering the old constitution rather than imposing a new one. In PR, §274 Addition, Hegel cites Napoleon's attempt, in 1808, to impose a more 'rational' constitution on the Spaniards, who 'recoiled from it as from something alien, because they were not yet educated up to its level'. But Hegel's general claim is not easily testable, owing to the inevitable vagueness of such notions as 'success' and 'similarity'. Moreover, how long a time is allowed for the test? To Edmund Burke (whose appreciation of the interconnexions between culture and institutions was comparable to Hegel's) in 1790 the revolutionary attempt to rebuild French society from scratch looked like a disaster; by the 1830s a restoration of the *ancien régime* seemed neither desirable nor possible. Hegel might reply that the constitution prevailing in the 1830s was not itself devised by anyone, but 'grew' out of previous post-revolutionary constitutions.

NOTES TO §541

1. The 'government' (*Regierung*) preserves the 'state in general', i.e. the whole state, not just the specific state institutions. This involves two functions. First, it preserves the family and civil society with its 'estates' (cf. §527, n. 2), which, unlike the government itself, are the 'naturally necessary' organization. Second, it fulfils 'universal aims' transcending the family and civil society, especially warfare. For both these reasons the government is, in contrast to the family and civil society, 'universal' rather than particular. Just as ethical life or the 'state in general' is divided into family, civil society, and state (or 'government'), so the government is 'likewise' divided into 'powers'. These powers are determined by the 'concept': they are related to each other as universal, particular, and individual (cf. §541, n. 2). The powers are not simply distinct from each other, but closely united. The concept is something like a plan, which, in so far as it is not yet realized or actualized, is 'subjective' rather than objective, but subjective in the way that the plan in a seed is subjective, not in the sense of being in the human mind: cf. §379. The elements in the plan are not simply distinct from each other, but interpenetrating. Hence when the plan is realized the elements form a unity prescribed by the plan.

2. If I say 'This rose is red', an individual (this rose) is subsumed under a universal (red). This is applied to the powers in the state as follows. The legislative power is universal. The executive power, by contrast, is divided into two, the governmental

and judicial powers, and each of these is subsumed under, and therefore subordinate to, the legislative power. The governmental power differs from the judicial in that it applies laws to universal, not private, affairs. Nevertheless, it is, together with the judicial power, a power 'of the individual', not, like the legislature, a power 'of the universal'.

Hegel objects to the excessive 'independence' of the powers in this organization. In PR, §272 Remark, he suggests that the executive and the legislature did become so independent after the French Revolution. But such independence and the attendant strife lead either to the destruction of the state or to the dominance of one power over the others.

3. The different functions of the state should be organized 'separately'. This is a requirement of freedom. Hegel does not say why the 'depth' of freedom requires the development of 'differences'. One obvious answer would be that different powers check and restrict each other. But Hegel rejects this idea in PR §272 Remark: 'This view [namely that of the intellect or understanding] implies that the attitude adopted by each power to the others is hostile and apprehensive, as if the others were evils, and that their function is to oppose one another and as a result of this counterpoise to effect an equilibrium on the whole, but never a living unity'. The functions of government must be organized separately, but not independently. This requires a reversal of the hierarchy proposed by the 'intellect'. The legislature is still 'universal', as it was for the intellect. But if we make this universal power supreme, as the intellect did, then the state cannot be 'one'. The individual power, the government, must be supreme, embracing and supervising all the other powers.

Hegel again appeals to the 'concept'. The intellect thinks of the concept in terms of the subsumption of individuals under universals. Reason (or Hegel) thinks of it in terms of the fundamental structure or plan of a living organism. If the functions of the state are not organized separately, the state is like an immature or a simple organism, whose diverse functions are not allocated to distinct organs. If the functions are assigned to independent powers, the state is like a diseased organism, whose organs, with their functions, do not properly communicate with each other and may even be in conflict: cf. §406, n. 27 on disease. A complex, healthy state, with different functions assigned to different bodies, 'joins together with itself': it diverges into different organs, but constantly retrieves its unity.

Why does the 'depth' of freedom require the separate organization of functions? What is wrong with a simple state, with a single body performing a variety of functions? Several answers are available. A simple state will either perform fewer functions than a complex state or it will, as a jack-of-all-trades, perform its functions badly. A simple state with a diversity of functions will not be fully intelligible to its citizens, it will not display the functions 'as existent' to their consciousness: cf. §540, n. 1. A complex, unified state can give a freer rein to its citizens than a simple state; a simple state preserves its unity by imposing uniformity on its citizens, a shared religion for example or a shared creed, since it lacks the unity-in- difference of the complex state: cf. §539, n. 9.

With respect to the government, the legislature is as much particular as universal, simply one function among others needing unification by the government. It is regarded as universal by the intellect for three reasons: (1) It is the supreme power, subsuming all the others; (2) 'everyone' participates in it; (3) it passes 'universal' laws. Hegel can accept only the third of these reasons. (1) and (2) are accepted by the intellect (and the French revolutionaries), but not by Hegel himself.

NOTES TO §542

1. 'Subjectivity' expresses the unity of the state, in contrast to its differentiation: cf. §541, n. 1. A 'subject' is literally something 'underlying', hence the unitary subject of predicates, the unitary self underlying its states and activities, and so on. The state, like the concept, has an 'infinite' unity, in that it returns to itself out of its differentiation and thus forms a sort of circle: cf. §429, n. 1, etc. In principle, the 'princely power' embodying this unity need not be an individual person. It might be a 'moral person', a unified body of people, such as a family, a state, a church, or a committee. Or it may be a popular assembly, reaching decisions by majority voting. But in a 'perfect' state the princely power is a single individual. A moral person has no single 'resolving will', just a collection of individual wills to be counted up. If this 'moral person' is to unify the state, what unifies the moral person? Why should the dissenting minority accept the majority verdict? Such problems are, Hegel believes, resolved by a monarch. Any viable constitution involves a princely power. Only the most advanced constitution has a monarch.

2. The monarchy is a limited, constitutional monarchy, distinguished from the 'patriarchal system' in which all power is concentrated in a single person. It is clear why Hegel disapproves of democracy in the sense of 'participation of all in all affairs': it excludes a division of powers. It is less clear why he objects to an elected monarch (or president) in favour of a hereditary monarch. In PR, §281 Remark, he criticizes elective monarchy for the reason that it surrenders the 'power of the state at the discretion of the particular will'. He has in mind the Holy Roman Empire rather than the USA: Knox writes, 'In the sixteenth century, by compelling the man of their choice to accept such a compact [of election], the Electors acquired a distinct preliminary control of both the internal government of the Holy Roman Empire and its foreign policy, and so circumscribed the Emperor's authority' (PR, p. 370, n. 54).

NOTES TO §543

1. Legislation was considered in §§529–30, judicial power in §§531–2, and the 'police' in §534. The fact that the relevant authorities have these powers assigned to them by law means both that they can act independently and that there are legal constraints on what they do.

2. The 'universal estate' is the 'thinking estate' of §528, the class of civil servants.

NOTES TO §544

1. The 'council of the estates' (*ständische Behörde*) is a bicameral parliament with representatives of the agricultural class, i.e. the landed nobility, in the upper house, and representatives of industry in the lower house: see PR, §§306 ff. 'Universal opinion' is roughly public opinion: cf. PR, §§316–18.

2. In his *Politics*, III. iv, Aristotle distinguishes three 'correct' types of constitution, together with three degenerate constitutions corresponding to them. 'Kingship' is rule by one individual; so is its corresponding degeneration, 'tyranny'. 'Aristocracy' is rule by a few people, as is its degeneration, 'oligarchy'. 'Republic' (or 'constitutional rule': *politeia*) is rule by many people, as is its degeneration, 'democracy'. In the correct constitutions, the rulers govern in the interests of all, while in the deviant constitutions they govern in their own interests. Later in the work, Aristotle qualifies this classification, tending to focus on monarchical, aristocratic, and democratic features, which often appear together in existing constitutions. 'Ochlocracy' is 'mob-rule'. It is a stock word for the corruption of democracy, when the word 'democracy' is used in a relatively favourable sense.

   'Oriental despotism' is hardly a monarchy at all in Hegel's sense of the word: 'an oriental despotism is not a state, or at any rate not the self-conscious form of state which is alone worthy of mind, the form which is organically developed and where there are rights and a free ethical life' (PR, §271 Remark). In a 'feudal monarchy' the 'relationships recognized in its constitutional law are crystallized into the rights of private property and the privileges of individuals and Corporations. In this type of constitution, political life rests on privileged persons and a great part of what must be done for the maintenance of the state is settled at their pleasure' (PR, §273 Remark). Hence feudal monarchy is a *konstitutionelle(r) Monarchie*, but not sufficiently regulated by laws, etc., to count as more than a transitional form on the way to monarchy in Hegel's sense. The nature of a constitution depends not only on the number of people holding supreme power, but also on the principles governing the state as a whole.

3. Hegel has two different conceptions of a 'private person' (*Privatperson*): (1) 'Individuals in their capacity as burghers in this state [namely civil society or the "external state": cf. §523, n. 1] are private persons whose end is their own interest' (PR, §187); (2) 'A man with no class [or "estate", *Stand*: cf. §527, n. 2] is a mere private person and his universality is not actualized' (PR, §207 Addition). The members of estate assemblies are private persons in sense (1). They are members of civil society with no political office. But they also belong to estates and corporations that educate them to look beyond their own interest to the general interest: cf. §534, n. 2. Private persons in sense (2) lack any such education. The 'people' (*Volk*) consists of private persons. So there are two relevant senses of 'people': (1) *populus* (the Latin for '(the) people'), the politically organized and disciplined people; (2) *vulgus* (the Latin for 'crowd' or 'mob'), the people as an undisciplined mass, an *Aggregat* (rather than a structured whole) of

592 *Commentary*

individuals who have abandoned their allegiance to their estate and corporation
and forgotten the lessons they learnt from them.

4. The 'private persons' who participate in English state affairs are the *populus*, not
(as in revolutionary France) the *vulgus*. On popular participation in England,
cf. PR, §302 Addition: 'in despotic states, the despot always indulges the mob
[which] in such states pays only a few taxes. Taxes rise in a constitutionally governed state simply owing to the people's own consciousness. In no country are
so many taxes paid as in England'. On the chaotic state of English law, cf. §529,
n. 6. On 'formal right' or legal formalities, cf. PR, §217 Remark. Hegel does not
establish that the deficiencies of English law were the result of popular participation. His earlier remark that Peel 'gained the gratitude, even the admiration, of his
countrymen' for his legal reforms (§529 Remark) suggests the contrary.

5. Hegel refers to the two conceptions of a people discussed in §544, n. 3: (1) the
people in its 'substantial universality', an organic whole organized into estates;
(2) the people in 'external universality' or 'universality of reflexion'. On 'universality of reflexion', see §410, n. 2 and PR, §24R. On 'substantial universality',
cf. §414, n. 1 and PR, §24 Remark. 'Universality of reflexion' applies to *all* the
instances of certain type; so Hegel sometimes calls it the universality of 'allness'
(*Allheit*): see PR, §24 Remark. For example, all the members of an army are soldiers. But an army is not just a collection or 'aggregate' of soldiers. It is divided
into regiments, brigades, platoons, etc., and the soldiers differ in rank: privates,
sergeants, captains, colonels, etc. An army so organized is a substantial universal. If, by contrast, we consider the army simply as a collection of soldiers, then
we treat it (or 'soldierhood') as a universality of reflexion. But there are now two
possible forms that the army may assume. First, while we consider it only as a
collection of soldiers, it may retain its discipline, ranks, and organization, and
not actually be just a collection of soldiers. Second, its discipline and organization may break down, so that it dissolves into a mere collection of soldiers. The
same is true of the 'people'. It may preserve its orderly division into estates, and
then it can be considered either as an organized people or as simply a collection of
individuals. Alternatively, its organization may break down, so that it becomes a
disorderly mob. At all costs, the breakdown of order must be avoided. The people
on the rampage, like an army on the rampage, threatens the dissolution of the
state. But this does not automatically resolve the question whether, given that the
people should 'share in public affairs', this participation should be achieved by the
'democratic mode of election', on the 'principle of plurality and number', i.e. by
a simple one-person-one-vote system without regard to rank or status, or, alternatively, by a procedure that takes account of the estates, giving perhaps a greater
say to landowners than to their workers. Hegel seems to waver on this question.
He begins by implying that the people should have a say simply as a 'multitude
of free individuals'. But then he retracts this and suggests that the participation of
the people must take account of their organization into estates. He is motivated in
part by a fear of a breakdown of order.

6. On the legislature and the roles of the estates in it, see PR, §§298 ff. Rational
laws need to be made by rational people. So given the deficient 'insight' of private

persons, Hegel wants to minimize their role in legislation. He argues, that is, not that they *should* have less power of legislation than they currently do, but that they *in fact* have less power of legislation than they are sometimes thought to have. The budget involves a universality of reflexion in that it deals with *all* the revenues required in a given year, which, first, have no intrinsic connection with each other and, secondly, are different (though, according to Hegel, only marginally different) from the revenues required in other years.

7. Hegel is arguing not against the annual grant of budget, but against the doctrine that the point of it is to function as a check on the power of the government. He presents four arguments against this doctrine: (1) It is not, in normal circumstances, a live possibility that the budget as a whole will be rejected, any more than it is a live possibility that the government will withdraw the forces of law and order. The threats are empty because the consequences of carrying them out would be disastrous for everyone. (2) The doctrine presupposes that the state depends on a contract between government and people, and that it involves a balance of distinct powers. These presuppositions are false. They are false, primarily because a people and its government, and the different powers in the state, share a common 'spirit'; they are made what they are by their membership of the state and are not simply distinct from each other. (3) If the government and the people diverge in spirit sufficiently for such a threat to be necessary, the divergence is too great for there to be a coherent constitution and stable government. (4) If the threat were carried out, the result would be anarchy and then autocracy.

Hegel thinks of the state as a cooperative enterprise, with a shared spirit and goal, rather like a well-functioning army or orchestra. An orchestra may have originated in a contract, but that is not relevant to its present functioning if it is functioning well. The conductor and the different sections of the orchestra do not view themselves as distinct powers, each trying to protect itself against the encroachments of the others. They do not think of themselves as playing their part only on condition that the others play theirs. *If* the other sections *were* to stop playing their parts, then my section would not play *its* part. But it does not follow that each section plays its part only because of the threat that others will stop performing. If that is the case, the orchestra is malfunctioning in a way that cannot be repaired by threats. Similarly, if the government or the people were to misbehave radically, threats—to reject the budget, to fire on the crowd, etc.—would be made and perhaps carried out. But this does not entail that the government and the people are, and need to be, deterred from misbehaviour by such threats. See also §467, n. 10, on Max Weber's view that the state is based on force, and on Hegel's denial of this, §432, n. 2.

NOTES TO §545

1. A 'people' (*Volk*) is not, as in §544, the common people in contrast to the government, but one people or nation in contrast to other peoples or nations. A people in this sense is 'naturally determined', i.e. it is a group united by language, culture, race, and religion. (Cf. DGS, p. 245: ' "People" in the sense of a "community"

bound together by common customs, sentiments, language'.) However, Hegel supported civil rights for Jews and toleration of sects such as Quakers, who refuse military service: PR, §270 Remark. He believed that a strong state can accommodate 'anomalies': cf. §539, n. 9. Such a relatively homogeneous group is not made a people by the state; the German people did not in Hegel's day have a single state. But the state makes the people 'actual': cf. §§517, n. 2; 549 Remark.

2. The relationship of states to each other is comparable to that of individual 'persons'. But states 'are not private persons but completely autonomous totalities in themselves' (PR, §330 Addition). Between individual persons within a state, the 'universal of right' is 'actual': there are established rules for settling disputes between them and established authorities to propose and enforce a solution that is distinct from the particular wills of the parties to the dispute. But 'since the sovereignty of a state is the principle of its relations to others, states are to that extent in a state of nature in relation to each other' (PR, §333). There are rules of sorts, mainly that treaties should be kept (PR, §333). But there is no established neutral authority able to propose and enforce a solution to disputes between states. Such a 'universal of right' *ought to be*, but it is not an actual reality. So disputes between states are settled by war. This involves the 'universal estate', 'the thinking estate' (§528), which 'has for its task the universal interests of the community' (PR, §205). Hence the 'military class is that universal class which is charged with the defence of the state' (PR, §327 Addition).

NOTE TO §546

1. The state unifies itself into a single individual by getting its individual members to put at risk their lives and their property: cf. PR, §324 and Addition.

NOTES TO §547

1. §430 opened the account of the struggle for recognition by individual combatants. Here the recognition is won by 'national individualities' (*Völkerindividuen*), not by individual people. They gain this recognition not by winning the war, but simply by risking their independence in war. Whereas, however, the victor in an individual combat enslaves his opponent if he is still alive, a nation does not generally lose its independence after a war and become enslaved to the victor. The recognition it gained from its readiness to fight is enshrined in a peace-settlement, as are the particular 'entitlements' (*Befugnisse*) of the combatants: '*Befugnis* is a formal, official term, and means the "power to act" conferred legally, constitutionally on an individual or a body by virtue of his office, or special circumstances' (DGS, p. 255).

2. The treaties are 'positive', not in contrast to 'negative', but in the sense that they are actually made. The rights enshrined in the treaties lack 'genuine actuality', since, as §545 noted, there is no neutral authority to declare that such a right has been infringed and to enforce respect of it: 'There is no Praetor to judge between states' (PR, §333 Remark). PR, §338, speaks of the 'proviso of the *jus gentium*

that the possibility of peace be retained (and so, for example, that envoys must be respected), and, in general, that war be not waged against domestic institutions, against the peace of the family and private life, or against persons in their private capacity'. PR, §339, adds: 'relations between states (e.g. in war-time, reciprocal agreements about taking prisoners; in peace-time, concessions of rights to subjects of other states for the purpose of private trade and intercourse, etc.) depend principally upon the customs of nations,' and not on enforceable laws.

NOTES TO §548

1. The spirit of a people must be actualized in a particular geographical region with a particular type of climate. This alone does not entail that it has a history. Species of animals and plants are often confined to a particular geographical region, and they sometimes become extinct, but they do not, in Hegel's view, have a history. Human societies do not simply become extinct. They also, often at least, have a history. But this is not primarily because of their natural environment or their particularity; such factors could explain only their impermanence, not their historicity. It is because human beings are to a lesser extent than other animals restricted to a fixed pattern of behaviour: they make choices between significant alternatives. They are also aware of what previous generations have done and this awareness informs their choices. They may, for example, try to outdo their ancestors or they may become bored and want to do something different. Hegel was aware of such considerations: in history the mind's 'act is to gain consciousness of itself as mind, to apprehend itself in its interpretation of itself to itself . . . and the completion of apprehension at one stage is at the same time the rejection of that stage and its transition to a higher' (PR, §343).
2. There are two types of history: first, the history of a given national spirit 'within itself' and, second, the historical sequence of national spirits (in PR, §§354 ff., the 'oriental', the Greek, the Roman, and the 'Germanic'), 'universal world-history'. The history of a particular national spirit does not of itself entail its impermanence. Why should a national spirit not continue to change, even develop, for ever? In a sense, Hegel believes it can. The Chinese and Indian civilizations have not become extinct, though they are, in his view, relatively unchanging. He believes, however, that only one civilization can occupy the centre of the stage of world history at a time. This is in part because he believes world-history to be the work of a *single* 'world-spirit' or mind: cf. §536, n. 3. So one national spirit, e.g. the Greek, is supplanted at the centre of the stage by another, the Roman. This, Hegel believes, can only happen in virtue of the internal history of the Greek spirit. It could not be ousted by the Roman spirit if it remained at the height of its power; it has to go into decline internally if it is to make way for its successor. Hence the ambiguous expression 'dialectic of the particular national spirits' applies both to the internal dialectic of each national spirit and to the dialectic of all the national spirits collectively; the two aspects of dialectic mesh with each other. But here 'dialectic' has primarily a negative sense (cf. Enc. I, §81). Hegel is stressing the decline and fall, or at least withdrawal,

of each national spirit. 'Judgement of the world' is *Weltgericht*. A *Gericht* is a lawcourt, a trial or a judicial sentence. Hence *Weltgericht* is the 'last judgement', the process in which the world is judged. But Hegel also has in view the process in which a particular national spirit is judged *by* the world. According to Knox's note on PR, §340, Schiller anticipated Hegel in his poem 'Resignation', with the words: 'World history is the world's court of judgement'.

NOTES TO §549

1. A particular national spirit or mind goes through a process of rise, decline, and fall, followed by its replacement by another national spirit. The whole succession of national spirits is, by contrast, a progression towards a goal, the realization of the 'final aim' (*Endzweck*) of the world. The final aim and the advance towards it involve two aspects. First, 'spirit' becomes progressively more conscious, more self-aware. This is a 'liberation' (*Befreiung*): cf. §552, n. 1. Spirit is initially 'in itself', embedded in human societies and guiding them more or less subconsciously or instinctively. Gradually it becomes self-aware and thus liberates itself from its immersion in the mundane world. Secondly, spirit orders the mundane world more effectively and thus becomes the 'externally universal spirit'. On the dual process by which spirit detaches itself from the world and then returns to it and imbues it with thought, cf. §393, n. 10. In PR, §§359-60, the 'Germanic realm' is characterized by a bifurcation into an other-worldly religion and a barbaric mundane world, which are eventually reconciled to form a harmonious whole. Here, as elsewhere, Hegel speaks as if the 'final aim' of the world is fully and finally realized in his own time. But it is not clear whether he means that his own time is especially significant, in contrast to other times, or whether, alternatively, he means that any historian is entitled to believe that the final aim of the world is realized in his *own* time, whatever time that may be. The second alternative would imply that the world has no 'final aim' in the sense of a dramatic conclusion towards which it progresses: its final aim always lies in the historian's present.
2. Each national spirit plays a part in the realization of the 'final aim' of the world. But each national spirit plays only one part; it cannot come round for a second time. This is open to dispute. Did not Italy make two appearances, once as the Roman republic and empire, then again at the Renaissance? Hegel has at least two replies to this. First, the geographical area may be the same, but the national spirit is not: the spirit of Renaissance Italy is quite different from that of ancient Rome. Second, Renaissance Italy was not the predominant national spirit of its age. The centre of gravity of the 'Germanic realm' is northern Europe, whose barbaric tribes overran Italy and which had not previously taken the lead in world-history. Since national spirits cannot be individuated clearly and sharply, hardly anything short of a more or less exact replay of an earlier phase of history would refute Hegel's claim.
3. Hegel might have argued that his belief that world-history has an aim is not a priori, but a posteriori, based, that is, on records and observations that suggest

that history is heading in a certain direction, even if it is not strictly *aiming* at it. He has at least three reasons for not arguing in this way. First, he argues that one cannot write a satisfactory history without presupposing an aim, such as the fall of Rome. (To this the reply might be that before we write the history we already know, and know a posteriori, that Rome fell. The apriority consists only in adopting this fact as the focal point of our history.) Second, he argues that since the question of history's aim must be settled by philosophy, the aim itself must be 'necessary' and therefore not discoverable only a posteriori. (To this the reply might be that philosophy can surely declare some matters to be a posteriori.) Finally, he associates the final aim of the world with divine providence, and this presumably involves a necessity that goes beyond what could be established by empirical observation alone.

It is not very clear why Hegel says that the final aim is 'in and for itself'. It looks as if it is intended to imply that the aim is really intrinsic to history and is not simply assumed, or read into events, by the historian for the sake of producing a good story. But Hegel does little to justify this belief in this paragraph.

4. Cf. PH, pp. 57–8, where this view is attributed to Friedrich von Schlegel: cf. § 405, n. 9.

5. 'Sacerdotal peoples' is *Priestervölkern*, lit. 'priest-peoples'. Cf. PH, pp. 57-8: 'The biblical account [of Adam] by no means justifies us in imagining a *people*, and a historical condition of a people, existing in that primitive form; still less does it warrant us in attributing to them the possession of a perfectly developed knowledge of God and Nature'.

6. Hegel refers to Barthold Georg Niebuhr's *Römische Geschichte*, 3 vols. (Berlin, 1811–32). Niebuhr's predecessors tended to accept the account of early Roman history given by such historians as Livy. Niebuhr rigorously assessed and criticized the literary sources in order to discover the true history of Rome behind the legends. Niebuhr was enormously influential, particularly on Ranke, who applied his method more generally. But Hegel disliked him: 'This "higher criticism" has been the pretext for introducing all the anti-historical monstrosities that a vain imagination could suggest. Here we have the other method of making the past a living reality; putting subjective fancies in the place of historical data; fancies whose merit is measured by their boldness, that is, the scantiness of the particulars on which they are based, and the peremptoriness with which they contravene the best-established facts of history' (PH, p. 7). Niebuhr is also attacked at PH, pp. 280, 296, 297, and 302.

7. On 'pragmatizing' or pragmatic history, see §377, n. 7.

8. A judge is supposed to be impartial or disinterested with respect to the contending parties. But this does not mean that he favours each party equally. He has an overriding commitment to justice, which is likely to lead him to support one party against the other. Similarly, a historian of philosophy is impartial with respect to the ideas he considers, but this does not mean that he has no preferences among them. He has an overriding commitment to truth (but cf. §549, n. 11), which is likely to lead him to prefer one idea to another.

These cases differ from each other. Justice is the intrinsic aim of the practice in which the judge is involved. The contending parties seek, or purport to seek, justice, and it is the judge's job to give it to them. Philosophy and its history are a different case. Truth, at least in the sense in which Hegel uses the term, is no doubt the intrinsic aim of philosophy. But the historian of philosophy is not in the same position as the judge. His primary task is to give a correct account of the philosophies he considers. It may not be his job to adjudicate between competing philosophies, nor need he even be a participant in the practice of philosophy, as long as he knows enough about it to give an account of it. He needs to know enough about philosophy to exclude from his history what is not philosophy and to include what is philosophy; he needs to have an idea of what is philosophically important and what is not. But that may be all. He is not needed to settle philosophical disputes. Others do that, or perhaps no one does. Still, if the historian does resolve philosophical disputes, that is all well and good. He is not required to do it, but no one will complain if he does.

It is far from clear how either of these examples can be applied to ordinary history, let alone world-history. The most obvious application would be this: A historian should be impartial with respect to contending parties in history, between, say, Greece and Rome or between Caesar and Pompey. He should record the relevant facts about each of the parties without fear or favour. But he can, indeed should, prefer one contending party to another in view of an 'objective' aim. This must be an aim that is intrinsic to historical events and processes in the way that justice is intrinsic to legal cases and truth is intrinsic to philosophy. But is there such an aim? It does not look as if there is. One might prefer Greece to Rome, or Rome to Greece, for a variety of reasons. Greece produced better philosophers, Rome had better engineers. Rome threw Christians to lions, but had better roads than Greece. Even if we restrict the objective aim to, say, freedom, the concept of freedom looks too diverse and amorphous for us to decide unequivocally in favour of Greece or of Rome. Women (someone might say) had more freedom in Rome than in Greece, but Rome (the reply might be) had more slaves than Greece.

9. A historian cannot simply write history. He has to have a subject or an 'object' (*Gegenstand*), something to write the history *of*. Suppose this is Rome. But that alone is not enough. The historian cannot simply write down everything there is to be known about Rome in the order in which it occurs to him. He 'selects' (*aussondere*), deciding that some events are irrelevant to his theme; he 'arranges' (*stelle*), recording this event before that event, relating that event to other events, and so on; he 'assesses' (*beurteile*), judging that this event is more important than that event, and so on. To do all this, the historian needs a theme, say, the decline of Rome, or Roman architecture, or Roman coinage, or Roman slavery. Can such a theme be called an 'aim' (*Zweck*)? It is no doubt the historian's aim: it is what he is aiming to write about. But Hegel implies that it is an aim in a stronger sense than this, namely that, first, the historian views the events he narrates as tending towards a goal or a conclusion, and, secondly, this goal or aim 'lies at the basis' (*zum Grunde liegt*) of the events themselves. Each of these

claims is contestable. A historian may, but need not, view the events as tending towards a goal. A history of the city of Rome from its beginnings to the present, for example, has no definite goal, apart from the *present* state of the city or its state at whatever other point the historian chooses to end. Moreover, even if the historian does view events as tending to a goal or aim, the aim may not lie at the basis of the events, except in the sense that just these, and no other, events have been selected by the historian for their relevance to his aim. After all, Rome in the present can be regarded, with equal legitimacy, in a variety of ways: as the centre of the Catholic faith, as the capital of modern Italy, as a tourist resort, and so on. If these are aims, they are quite different aims, yet the past events relevant to them (e.g. its conquest in antiquity of the rest of Italy) overlap to a great extent. Which of these aims lies at the basis of past events? Arguably, any such aim is chosen by the historian from a set of plausible alternatives and does not underly the events themselves. Fairy tales usually have a beginning, a middle, and an end. Often they have a moral, that, for example, a pig should build its house with bricks, if it wants to avoid being eaten by a big bad wolf. In history, by contrast, there are no clear-cut beginnings or endings, and (as Hegel knew) no morals except those read into events by the ('pragmatic') historian and his readers.

10. Hegel here produces an argument against the objection (raised in §459, n. 9) that the historian of e.g. Rome can select from a variety of equally legitimate 'aims', none of which 'lies at the basis . . . of the events themselves'. The historian might study the architecture of Rome, its coinage or its slaves. But one aim has priority over all other supposed aims, namely the aim of a 'people' to form a state. Whatever other aim a historian may select presupposes the state: without a state there is no significant architecture, no coinage, no slavery capable or worthy of the attention of the historian. Unless a people has a state no history of it can be written, since no records or documents will be produced. Whatever other aim may 'lie at the basis' of historical events presupposes the aim of 'state-formation'. Unless a people has a state it does not *have* a history, not even a history of which no record remains. A people without a state, since it keeps no record of its activities, cannot (in Hegel's view) develop by building on its past achievements. So if it aims at anything, it must aim at a state. A people without 'state-formation' is a 'nation [*Nation*] as such', i.e. a nation in the literal sense of something like a 'breed', since the word derives from *nascor, natus sum*, 'to be born', and is thus associated with 'nature' in contrast to culture.

Hegel distinguishes between peoples with a state and 'savage nations', but he has surprisingly little to say about a single people dispersed throughout several distinct states, such as the Jews or, in a different way, the Germans. There is in such cases no lack of documents and records, and there is certainly development.

11. 'Truth' is used in two senses: (1) 'So-called truth' is what Hegel elsewhere calls 'correctness': cf. §§379, n. 7, 408, n. 13; 437, n. 4. If a historian reports that Napoleon said 'Not tonight, Josephine', this may well be 'correct', but it cannot, without more ado, be regarded as 'true' or as an 'objective truth', since both Napoleon's remark and the historian's report of it are trivial. (2) If a historian

reports Napoleon's remark that the fate of the ancients has now been replaced by politics (PH, p. 278) or his claim that 'the French Republic needs recognition as little as the sun requires it' (PR, §331 Addition.), this is 'true', since it relates to 'objective truth', namely, the formation of a state. In this sense of 'truth' it is things and events that are primarily true. Statements about such things and events are true secondarily and derivatively. 'Objective truth' thus more or less coincides with the 'objective aim'and suggests what is of fundamental necessity and importance. Hegel has moved from a sense of 'truth' in which a philosophy may be true (cf. §549, n. 8) to a sense of 'truth' in which the state may be true.

12. The exclusion of a presupposed objective aim is 'more explicit' (*ausdrücklichere*) in the case of the histories of philosophy and religion, because it is clear in these cases what is being excluded: a preference for one philosophy or religion over others in view of the 'objective aim' of truth. By contrast, it is not clear what impartiality excludes in the case of political history. Even the most impartial historian writes a history *of* something, and it is likely to be a history of a state, rather than, say, of umbrellas. Such impartiality is not, as Hegel interprets it so far, intended to exclude a preference for one state over another: cf.§549, n.8.

13. The analogy between the state and truth seems strained. It suggests the idea that different philosophies or religions are related to truth in the way that particular events and characters in Roman history are related to the Roman state. The political historian here under consideration writes a history of a single state. By contrast, the historian of philosophy or religion whom Hegel has in mind is writing about several philosophies or several religions, on the merits of which he may, or may not, pass judgement. To adjudicate between different philosophies or religions, the historian needs some standard or 'aim'. This is most likely to be truth, since presumably truth is what the philosophies and religions under consideration were themselves aiming at. A historian of Rome does not essentially require such a standard, since he is not comparing Rome with other states. He may, however, criticize Rome, just as a historian of a single philosophy may criticize that philosophy. Then he will need an aim or standard by which to assess Rome. But this cannot be the Roman state itself: that would enable him to assess particular events and characters, but not Rome itself. It will have to be some wider standard, perhaps freedom, as Hegel suggests later: cf .§549, n.15.

14. It is easy enough to imagine a historian of religion who denies that any religion is true and treats different religions as simply interesting stories. Perhaps we can also imagine a historian of philosophy who takes the same view of philosophies; at any rate a historian of philosophy may well refrain from passing any final verdict on the philosophies he considers, either because he does not regard it as relevant to his enterprise or because he does not regard himself as competent to deliver such a verdict. It is, by contrast, hard to imagine a historian of Rome, even a historian of Roman umbrellas, who denies the existence or the relevance of the Roman state. This is another respect in which the analogy between the state and truth falters. What Hegel has in mind, however, is this: A historian of Rome may accept the existence of the Roman state, yet fail to use it as a standard for the selection, arrangement, and assessment of particular events

and characters. He might, for example, consider Mark Anthony's dalliance with Cleopatra simply as a moving love story rather than in view of its implications for the Roman state. In that case he may make 'correct' judgements, but he cannot make genuinely 'true' judgements.

In traditional logic, the 'quality' of a judgement depends on whether it is positive, negative, or 'infinite', while the 'quantity' of a judgement depends on whether it is of the form 'All x's are F', 'Some x's are F', or 'This x is F'. Hence 'quality' and 'quantity' do not designate types of judgement, but rather aspects or features of a judgement. But Hegel regards the qualitative judgement as a specific type of judgement, exemplified by 'This rose is red' (cf. §415, n. 2 and Enc. I, §172). In Enc. I Hegel does not explicitly discuss the quantitative judgement, but he does discuss the singular judgement, the particular judgement, and the universal judgement in Enc. I, §175, under the heading of the judgement of 'reflexion', a term that fluctuates in Hegel's usage. It seems likely that what he has in mind here is a judgement involving the universality of 'allness': (cf. §544, n. 5) and also particular judgements of the form 'Some x's are F'. Hence the aimless historian can make judgements such as the following: 'Caesar was a consul', 'All of Caesar's troops were hardened veterans', 'Some of them had fought with him in Gaul', 'Kant was an idealist', and so on. But he cannot make judgements of 'necessity'. The primary judgement of necessity, according to Hegel's classification, is the 'categorical' judgement, which ascribes an essential property to a thing ('Caius is a man') or to a type of thing ('Gold is a metal', 'The rose is a plant'): see Enc. I, §177 and Z. Nor can the aimless historian make judgements of the 'concept', the primary type of which is the 'assertoric' judgement, in which something is said to be 'good, bad, true, beautiful, etc.', i.e. is assigned a value depending on how closely it conforms to its concept: see Enc. I, §178. Hegel is not denying that the aimless historian can make judgements of the sort: 'Caesar was a man', 'Caesar was a good general', and 'Mark Anthony was a good lover' or 'His affair with Cleopatra was a wonderful love affair'. His point is this. Apart from being a man, Caesar was many things: a general, a ruler, a husband, a lover, a writer. Which of these roles was essential to him? Was he necessarily a ruler, but only incidentally a lover? The aimless historian has no answer to this. Apart from his manhood or humanity, everything that Caesar was or did is equally essential and equally inessential. Only if we appeal to some fundamental 'aim', such as the development of the Roman state, do we have a standard enabling us to give an answer: he was essentially and necessarily a general, a ruler, while his marriage and love affairs are incidental contingencies. Similarly with judgements of the concept. Caesar was good in many respects and bad in others: a good general, a good lover, a bad husband. But what is his value all things considered? Was he good, bad, or indifferent? Again the aimless historian has no answer. Only if we refer to a fundamental aim or standard, can we give an answer. Similar considerations apply, in Hegel's view, to the history of philosophy. Was Berkeley a good philosopher? He writes well, his illustrations are vivid, his arguments are intriguing and at first glance compelling, his conclusions are implausible. But what, Hegel asks,

602 Commentary

was his contribution to the 'truth'? That is what enables us to give a definitive evaluation of a philosopher.

It might be objected that even if we presuppose the Roman state as the 'aim', this does not automatically enable us to evaluate Caesar's contribution to it. Suppose, for example, that Pompey had defeated Caesar or that Brutus had defeated Mark Anthony. The development of the Roman state, if it survived, would then have taken a different course. Would it have been very different? And if so, would it have been better, worse, or much the same? Caesar's value and importance needs to be assessed not simply in terms of the actual development of Rome, but in terms of possible alternative developments. However, Hegel's view of history is sufficiently necessitarian to exclude the possibility of significant alternatives to the actual course of events.

15. If a historian writes about Rome, he must take the Roman state as his aim, since it is a necessary condition of any other aim he might adopt. The state is an objective aim, since it is a necessary condition of anything of historic significance, even of history itself. Cf. §549, n. 10. Is there a parallel argument to suggest that if a historian writes a 'universal history', i.e. a history of the whole succession of states, he must adopt an overall aim which he views as progressively realized by these states? Or that this overall aim is an objective aim, underlying and driving on the successive state-formations? If there are such arguments, they are hard to find. Suppose that the succession of (dominant) states is this: China, India, Egypt, Persia, Greece, Rome, 'Germanic'. Suppose, in addition, that a historian regards each of these states as interestingly different from the others, but as neither better nor worse than the others as measured against any aim or standard that he is prepared to endorse. Why would this prevent him from writing a coherent history of all these states? Since they are states, they leave documents and records enabling him to write about them, and they provide him with events and characters worthy of the historian's attention. (The intervening periods remain somewhat dark, but so they do in any case.) His account of each individual state will have an aim and will constitute a story with a beginning, middle, and end (somewhat like an account of the growth of a plant), but his account of the whole sequence of states will have no aim or direction (somewhat like an account of different plant or animal species). There are, however, some objections that Hegel might raise:

(1) The course of the historian's work is determined only by the temporal succession of states: first China, then India, and so on to the present. This would be alright if there were, at any given time, only one state in existence. But that is not so. When a state loses its historic dominance, it does not usually disappear; it continues to exist alongside its successor. It also continues to change, so that it does not cease to deserve a historian's attention. So in any given period there are several states in existence. In principle, the universal historian might record the history of every state from its beginnings to the present. But this is an impossible task for one person. A single historian will need to decide when to turn his attention

from one state (say, Greece) to another (say, Rome). How is he to decide this if he has no aim or standard in view? One answer might be: power. If one state withers and weakens, while another grows and flourishes, it is natural to turn from the first to the second. This need not presuppose that power increases throughout history, in which case power would be the aim; it need only assume that states tend to lose the power they originally had.

(2) A state is not usually enclosed within itself. Its citizens, or some of them, know of other states, including previous states, and even write histories of them. If this were not so, it would be impossible to write a universal history, since no one would know about any state except their own. But this, in Hegel's view, is how mind advances. In becoming aware of an earlier stage of itself, it *ipso facto* moves to a higher stage: e.g. PR, §343. So we would expect each state to advance beyond its immediate predecessor simply in virtue of knowing about it. And if there is advance or progress there must be some aim or standard in terms of which the progress occurs. However, this is vulnerable to the response that not every human product or activity that is informed by knowledge of its past exhibits indisputable progress. Some of them, most notably science and technology, do. But others do not. Artists and writers know about their predecessors but, as Hegel well knew, art and literature do not get better and better: see Hegel's ILA. Might not states be one of those things that do not exhibit progress?

(3) Hegel might insist that people want to form a state because of certain values or 'aims' that the state serves, and that it is blinkered, perhaps inconsistent, to appeal to these values only with respect to each state individually and not with respect to the whole sequence of states. Any state worthy of the name provides a security of person and property that does not obtain in a stateless condition. A state perhaps solves more specific problems such as irrigation or redivision of land after the floods have receded. Some states may be better than others in solving such problems as these. Then again states may give rise to internal problems. Even if a state protects its citizens from external and internal predators, it may treat its citizens in an overbearing way, allowing them little 'subjective' freedom or little say in the running of affairs. Is it not reasonable to suppose that, just as a people is impelled to form a state for the benefits it provides, peoples in general are impelled to form states that improve on those of their predecessors? But there are at least two difficulties. First, even if a people is impelled to form a state, it is often not impelled to improve on what went before. Many peoples, in Hegel's view, continue to live in states that are relatively static and that have long since been superseded by the progress of the world-spirit. The drive to improvement is not simply an extension of the drive to form a state in the first place. It is the world-spirit that moves on, humanity as a whole, not any given people. Secondly, it is hard to believe that there is only one aim or value

for the assessment of states. There seem to be several, potentially conflicting values. Some states might provide greater security, while others
provide more freedom. Hegel has a tendency to lump all values (except
equality: cf. §539, n. 4) under the heading of freedom, but this makes it
hard to view freedom as a single 'aim'.

16. Cf. Genesis, 1: 2: 'And the Spirit of God moved upon the face of the waters'.
Spirit strives to actualize its concept in a manner roughly analogous to the way in
which a plant strives to actualize the concept implanted in its seed: cf. §379, n. 5.
Spirit's development is free, because it is determined by the concept of spirit, not
by external factors. (It is also necessary: the freedom in question is not liberty
of indifference.) When spirit fully actualizes its concept, spirit will attain 'truth'.
'Truth' here has two senses: (1) Simply in virtue of actualizing and conforming
to its concept, spirit will be 'true', since for Hegel something is true if, and only
if, it conforms to its concept: cf. §§379, n. 5; 437, n. 4. In this sense of 'truth'
an oak-tree too attains truth when it becomes fully grown: it is a true oak-tree.
(2) When spirit reaches its own 'concept', it does not simply conform to its
concept; it also becomes aware or conscious of its own concept, it discovers, that
is, the truth about itself. A 'true' spirit or mind (in sense (1)) is a spirit or mind
that knows the 'truth' about itself (in sense (2)).

Earlier (cf. §549, n. 15) it looked as if the aim of world-history was something
like the perfection of the political state. Now it looks as if the aim has to do with
our acquisition of knowledge, especially philosophical knowledge. At first glance
there seems little connexion between these aims. But Hegel's idea is roughly this.
Complete philosophical insight into spirit or mind and its workings in society
and in history can be attained only in a certain type of state, a state that is possible only after the world-spirit has run its course. Or more briefly: the aim of
world history is the writing of world history. There is a parallel here, albeit not
an exact parallel, between the aim of world history and the aim of, say, Roman
history. The primary aim of Roman history is the formation of the Roman state.
A people acquires consciousness of itself in its 'political constitution' (*Staatsverfassung*): cf. §§517, n. 2; 539, n. 2. The documents, etc. that the state provides
may even enable a Roman, such as Livy, to write a history of the Roman people.
Such documents and histories as survive in turn enable a modern historian (such
as the much maligned Niebuhr) to write a history of Rome. The modern historian is unlikely to regard any particular ancient history of Rome, let alone his
own modern history of it, as the aim of Roman history. But he might regard the
overall knowledge, that the Romans acquire of themselves in the course of forming and developing their state, as a substantial part of the point or significance of
Roman history. Similarly, the primary aim of world history is the formation of
states and their replacement by better states. In the course of this process humanity discovers more and more about itself, about its political skills and foibles,
about the variety of states it is capable of forming, and so on. Some of this knowledge appears in written histories, including works that purport to be histories
of the world, such as St Augustine's *City of God* (413–25) and Ibn Khaldun's

Muqaddimah (1377) and *Universal History* (1377–82). But for a really satisfactory history of the world the world has to wait until the nineteenth century, when spirit and its historical workings become plain to all. Whereas the modern historian's knowledge of Rome is not a part of the history of Rome, this knowledge of world history is itself a part of world history. Hence it can plausibly be regarded as at least a part of the aim of world history, in the way that a Roman historian's knowledge of Rome is a part of the aim of Roman history.

NOTES TO §550

1. 'Task' is *Geschäft*, also 'business', etc. It refers to the human activity required for the liberation of spirit, discussed in §551. There is, in Hegel's view, a historic justice that overrides the justice of any particular state. This implies, first, that we have no right to complain about the fall of empires, etc., and secondly, that a historian should not condemn a 'world-historical individual', such as Caesar or Napoleon, for breaches of ethical and moral norms, which serve the purpose of the world-spirit: cf. §377, n. 7. This is comparable to God's right to transgress ethical norms (as in commanding Abraham to sacrifice Isaac and in the suffering inflicted on Job) and also to more recent appeals to history and/or posterity for justification, as well as the assignment of defunct regimes to the 'rubbish dump of history'.

2. In any given period, a particular people, e.g. the Romans, is the chosen vehicle of the universal spirit. There are other national spirits contemporaneous with Rome: Greeks, Germans, Chinese, and so on. But none of these has any rights against Rome, the current possession or 'property' (*Eigentum*) of the universal spirit. However, the universal spirit moves beyond Rome, delivering it over to invasion by Germanic tribes.

NOTE TO §551

1. The universal spirit needs to be actualized by individuals. It looks like their work, but in reality it is somewhat like a musical score or a dramatic script, which is 'prepared and determined independently of them', but needs them to perform it. Like musicians or actors they have their own peculiar 'subjectivity', the passions, etc. that motivate them to play their part and the idiosyncracies of their performance of it. But the 'substantial content' of their performance, in contrast to their motivation, the 'empty form of the activity', is determined by the score or script. Actors and musicians may achieve fame, though this is usually no part of the score or script they perform. Historical actors also achieve fame, but their fame is presumably prescribed by the universal spirit itself. Fame is 'universality', because a famous person is stripped of individual features and preserved as a sort of abstraction, perhaps also because everyone knows about the famous person. This universality is 'formal', in contrast to the person's 'substantial' performance. The 'subjective representation' is people's image or knowledge of the famous person.

NOTES TO §552

1. 'Within itself' (*in sich*) ethical substance is 'infinite': it is self-contained and embraces the whole lives of the citizens, rather as a lake embraces the fish swimming in it. 'For itself' it is finite, however. It is one among many such ethical substances and one day it will give way to a successor. Unlike fish in a lake, the inhabitants of an ethical substance are conscious that their ethical world will come to an end. This finitude depends partly on the natural surroundings of the substance (one day the lake will dry up, one day the volcano will erupt, the barbarians will come), and partly on its contingent particularity, the fact that it is only one among many ways of organizing human life. Thinking spirit, however, rises above this finitude. This happens in two stages. First, its 'awareness' of its 'essentiality' still has the limitations of a national spirit. This refers to the religions of the Greeks, the Jews, and other peoples whose religions were the religions of a particular people, not of all mankind. Secondly, spirit gradually sheds these natural and local limitations to rise to awareness of 'absolute' spirit. This refers primarily to Christianity, especially Protestantism: cf. §408, n. 7 on Hegel's disdain for pilgrimages to holy places. The word '*absolut*', like its Latin prototype '*absolutus*', usually means 'perfect, complete, unconditional'. But '*absolutus*' is the perfect participle of the verb *absolvo*, which means 'to loosen, set free', as well as 'to complete'. Hence 'absolute' spirit is not only perfect or complete spirit. It is also liberated spirit, spirit set free from the limitations of space, time and particularity.

2. Traditionally, there were supposed to be several different proofs of the existence of God. Each proof begins with a premiss that states an obvious fact, usually a fact about the world, such as that motion occurs. Hegel regards what is stated in the premiss, or rather the phenomenon mentioned in the premiss, as a starting point for our rise or 'elevation' to God. The 'cosmological' proof, for example, starts from the premiss 'Something is (or exists)' and proceeds from there to argue that if there are corruptible and contingent beings, there is a necessary and incorruptible being on which they depend. The 'physico-theological' proof begins with the premiss 'The universe is an orderly system which looks as if it were designed' and argues that it was designed by a purposive agent. Kant, who established these (not especially appropriate) names for these proofs, rejected both proofs as invalid, arguing that it is impossible for us to acquire theoretical knowledge of what transcends our sensory experience. Hegel disparages these proofs, not because they are invalid, but because they give rise to an impoverished concept of God. An argument for the existence of an entity not only establishes its existence; it also tells us what that entity is. Thus the cosmological proof sets out from the 'being' of (finite) entities and thus tells us that God is a being, albeit a necessary being. The physico-theological proof sets out from the apparent design of the universe and thus tells us that God is a purposive designer. Neither of these characterizations of God is adequate, in Hegel's view. God is the spirit or 'mind', etc. To achieve this concept of God, the appropriate

starting point is the one Kant preferred, namely 'practical reason', which, for Kant, goes beyond what is required for 'purposive activity', since it essentially involves respect for moral laws that do not depend on the contingent desires that we happen to have. A robber who efficiently cracks open a safe to extract the money he desires displays purposive activity. But he is deficient in practical reason, since he pays insufficient respect to the moral prohibition of theft.

A first response might be that Hegel is unfair to the physico-theological proof. If God is a purposive designer, then surely he must be a 'mind', etc. But there are at least three respects in which the conception of God as a purposive designer looks inadequate: (1) A designing God may nevertheless be an immoral God. Entities that are apparently designed, such as the liver fluke, need not be especially benign; indeed, they may look as if they were designed by an evil demon to plague human beings. Moreover, in Kant's view, an immoral God would not be 'self-determining': he would, like an immoral man, be determined by desires that he has, but does not choose to have. (2) 'Purposive activity' is less than fully 'self-determining' in another respect. A human designer is dependent not only on his desires, but also on the materials available to him, materials that he does not create. If God is a purposive designer, then, he too may be dependent on raw materials that he did not create. (3) A human designer does not usually design or create human beings. God too, if he is a purposive designer, need not create or design human beings. If there are human beings, then no doubt a designer God designed them. But the universe might have contained no human beings, that is, no minds. It might have contained mountains, trees, and butterflies, but no minds. Then God would be a designer, but not a designer of minds. The physico-theological proof does not essentially start from the existence of the mind.

Hegel's main objection to the physico-theological proof seems to be (3): a proof of God's existence that gives an adequate concept of God must start from the human mind or spirit, not from nature. The physico-theological proof, taken in the traditional way, may well, if it is valid, show that God is a mind, even though its premises do not refer to a mind. But Hegel does not take the proof in the traditional way. God, for Hegel, is not an entity sharply distinct from the finite entities referred to in the premises of arguments for his existence. God is a continuation or development of these entities. (Thus the expression 'mind's elevation [*Erhebung*] to God' means not only mind's becoming aware of God, but mind's becoming God.) Hence if God is to be seen as a mind or spirit, the entities from whose existence his existence is derived must be minds. Hegel does not flatly reject the proofs he criticizes. To prove that God is (a) being or that he is purposive activity is at least something. Such proofs are seen as steps on the way towards an adequate concept of God. But the most adequate concept is provided, in his view, by a proof that starts from mind or spirit.

3. Kant did not regard the proof of God's existence from practical reason as the same sort of proof as the cosmological and physico-theological proofs. The latter two proofs are proofs of 'theoretical reason' and, if they were valid, they would give us theoretical knowledge of God's existence on a par with our knowledge of,

say, Newtonian physics. The former proof, by contrast, does not give us theoretical knowledge, only practical or moral conviction. Kant's argument runs thus: If we take morality seriously, we are obliged to pursue the *summum bonum*, the supreme good. The supreme good is a state in which happiness is distributed in proportion to our moral virtue. Such a state is a forlorn hope if the world is a godless mechanical system: bad men are happy and good men unhappy. Only if there is a God who organizes the world in such a way that happiness is proportioned to desert is the supreme good a reasonable goal to aim at. Kant concludes not that God in fact exists, but that morality is only fully reasonable if we believe in God. Hence he presents the 'existence of God as a postulate of pure practical reason' (*Critique of Practical Reason*, P I, bk II, sect. 2, subsect. v). A 'postulate' was originally a 'demand', hence something one is required or 'ought' to accept, not necessarily because it is true or self-evident, but sometimes, as in this case, because it is a prerequisite of doing something else. Hegel rejects this limitation of the proof. Such a limitation involves 'finitude's opposition', the opposition between what we believe (the subjective) and what is the case (the objective) and also the opposition between what actually is the case and what ought to be the case: the supreme good is, in Kant's view, a state whose realization is postponed into the indefinite future. But, Hegel argues, these oppositions conflict with the nature of what we are arguing for, God and the supreme good. In God himself there is no opposition between what he believes and what is the case, no opposition between what he ought to bring about and what he actually brings about. In the supreme good, again, everything that ought to be the case actually is the case, and whatever we believe is true: there is no room for error in the supreme good or in God. Clearly, however, there is no such contradiction in Kant's limitation of the proof as Kant interprets it. God, as traditionally conceived, has knowledge, not probable belief or conjecture. But that does not prevent me from having a merely probable belief or from conjecturing that God exists. In the supreme good there is no disparity between what is so and what ought to be so. But again, that does not prevent me from believing that the supreme good ought to be realized, though it is not yet realized. However, Hegel does not conceive God (or the supreme good) in the way they are traditionally conceived. God, for Hegel, is a development of the human mind: cf. §552, n. 2. It is no doubt an oversimplification to say that Hegel believes that we become God, but it is nearer the mark than to attribute to him Kant's belief in a wholly transcendent God. If we do suppose, for argument's sake, that he does believe that we become God, then his rejection of Kant's limitation of the moral proof becomes intelligible: in God himself, there is no place for a disparity between the objective and the subjective, or between the 'is' and the 'ought'. A similar effect is achieved if we suppose that, for Hegel, the 'elevation' to God consists not in knowledge of a transcendent entity, nor exactly in our becoming God, but in our having a certain type of Godlike thought. Such thought too, if it is appropriately Godlike, would exclude the oppositions of subjective–objective and is–ought. Hegel's own view of God is hard to pin down, but it is at any rate quite different from Kant's and so, correspondingly, is his interpretation of the 'proofs'.

4. We do not, in Hegel's view, have wholly immediate knowledge of God, nor indeed of anything else: cf. Enc. I, §§61–78. Our 'elevation' to God involves 'mediation', mediation by finite things, whether these are things that just are, things apparently designed, or our 'practical reason'. However, these finite things that form our starting-point must undergo a 'negation' if the elevation is to occur. But 'negation' here can be interpreted in three ways:

(1) In the proofs as traditionally conceived, God is a different type of entity from the entities forming the starting point. Even if the same term, such as 'being', is applied to both types the term is differently qualified: God is a necessary, infinite, pure, etc. being, while the others are contingent, finite, impure beings. So the entities from which we set out are 'negated' simply in virtue of the fact that the entity whose existence we infer is of a different type from the initial entities. Here neither the initial entities themselves nor our view of them undergoes any change.

(2) Our conception of the entities from which we started alters once we infer the existence of an infinite God. Initially we regarded them as solid, independent entities. When we have inferred from them the existence of God, we regard them as dependent on God, etc. Here the initial entities do not change, but our view of them changes.

(3) When we undergo our elevation to God the entities that form the starting point for this elevation themselves undergo a change that amounts to 'negation'.

Negation of types (1) and (2) could, and probably would, be agreed to occur by someone who interpreted the proofs or 'elevation' in the traditional way. Negation of type (3) could not. Someone who argues from the existence of contingent beings to the existence of a necessary being does not thereby change contingent beings, except in so far as he changes himself from, say, from someone who does not believe in God to someone who does. Someone who argues from the existence of apparent design to the existence of an actual designer does not change apparent design in any way, except in so far as he perhaps adds to it an extra theist. These changes are insignificant: they do not alter the broad fabric of contingent beings or of apparent design. But perhaps it is otherwise if the proof starts from the mind itself. Someone who argues from the existence or nature of his own mind to the existence of God does alter his own mind; it changes from a mind that does not believe in, and perhaps has no conception of, God into a mind that does. This is a significant change, not simply a marginal addition, but a thorough change in the starting point of the proof. Hegel seems to regard the elevation that starts from 'practical reason', which has now become 'ethical life' (cf. §513, n. 1), as involving a negation of type (3). The 'purification' of the finite does not take place only in the mind of someone who argues for God's existence from the existence or nature of ethical life, as in a negation of type (1). The purification is 'actually accomplished' in the 'ethical world'. However, the purification is not so much a consequence of the elevation to God. It is what the elevation to God consists in. The purification is the emergence of 'genuine religion' in ethical life. This somehow involves the 'Idea' (*Idee*: cf. §377, n. 4) of God as 'free spirit', i.e. as mind or spirit that is self-determining and, more particularly, detached from the contingencies of time and place: cf. §552, n. 1. But God is not an entity distinct from human mind and society, or from our beliefs about him. This 'elevation' is a transformation of society and of our beliefs and practices, not a recognizable proof of the existence of God.

5. Traditional proofs of God's existence start from some feature of finite entities. Thus God or God's existence is 'mediated' by finite entities. Once God's existence is accepted, however, we realize that finite entities are produced or caused, i.e. mediated, by God. In fact God, since he is uncaused (Aquinas) or his own cause (Spinoza) is in a way unmediated or immediate, not mediated at least by the finite things that formed the starting point of our knowledge of him. On the face of it, the two types of mediation are different. God's mediation by finite things is epistemic mediation, mediation, that is, of our knowledge of God. By contrast, God's mediation of finite things is causal or ontological. (But the mediation of our *knowledge* of God by finite things is also causal or ontological.) Hegel does not draw this distinction, partly because he does not distinguish sharply between God and our knowledge of God, i.e. religion. For Hegel goes on to argue, not that God mediates ethical life, but that *religion* mediates ethical life: cf. §552, n. 6.

6. On 'ethical life' (*Sittlichkeit*), cf. §513, n. 1. Here it is close to the 'ethical disposition' (*sittliche(n) Gesinnung*), since it is the 'state drawn back into its substantial interior'. It plays a mediating role between religion and the state. Hegel is primarily arguing against the view that a people might have a religion that is indifferent to or in conflict with their ethical and political norms. It is easier to see why religion cannot (apart from marginal sects such as Quakers: cf. §545, n. 1) *conflict* with ethics and the state. If that were so, there would be two consciences, an ethical one (prescribing e.g. military service) and a religious one (forbidding military service). The individual has to choose between these consciences; he cannot obey both. Since religion is 'consciousness of absolute truth', the religious conscience would have to prevail, and this would undermine the state. It is less easy to see why religion and the state might not be 'mutually indifferent'. There seems no harm in having two consciences if they are guaranteed never to come into conflict. That religion is 'consciousness of absolute truth' may well entail that in cases of conflict it should override any ethical or political consideration. But it does not obviously entail that whatever counts as 'right, etc.' 'follows from' that absolute truth. Some duties, such as the duty to pay one's TV licence or not to drive on the wrong side of the road, surely arise from practical rather than religious considerations. But, Hegel will reply, although practical considerations explain why there are laws imposing such duties, the duty to obey the laws 'follows from' the absolute truth of which religion is the consciousness. Religion may have little to say about the details of traffic regulations, but it cannot be indifferent to the duty to obey the laws that are in place. If we ask why a religion might not be indifferent to this and other such matters,

Hegel's reply is that such a religion would not have a 'genuine content', a genuine 'Idea of God'. Genuine religion, in Hegel's view, is a religion that endorses the state and its requirements. He is not arguing for a theocratic state, but for what might be called, with considerable oversimplification, a 'political religion'. The mediating link between religion and the state is 'ethical life', from which the genuine Idea of God somehow emerges. To prepare it for this role, ethical life is itself described in somewhat theological terms: it is the 'divine spirit as indwelling in self-consciousness, etc.' (The conjunction of self-consciousness 'as a people' and as 'the individual members of that people' becomes significant shortly: cf. §552, n. 7.) Hegel has not as yet explained why ethical life might not be wholly secular or why a people without a 'genuine' religion might not nevertheless have a state. This omission stems partly from the religiosity of his age and partly from his scaling down religion so that it is hard to distinguish from ethical life.

7. Hegel seems to argue both that religion and the state are inseparable and that their separation occurs. So 'inseparable' (*untrennbar*) presumably means not strictly 'cannot be separated', but something like 'ought not to be separated'. An alternative possibility is that Hegel believes that even if a religion separates itself from the state, there is always another, underlying religion that is intertwined with ethical life and that is thus not separated from the state. On the face of it, nothing that Hegel says about Catholicism in this paragraph suggests that it need conflict with the state or even remain indifferent to it. Hegel no doubt believed that there could not be a large, viable state consisting mainly of Quakers. But he could hardly deny the possibility of a large, viable state consisting mainly of Catholics. His main objection to Catholicism is that it conflicts with what he regards as a central feature of modern ethical life, namely individual 'self-consciousness' and individual freedom or autonomy. A Catholic is required by an external authority to say certain things whether or not he really believes them, and to do certain things, regardless of whether he believes they are the right things to do. A Lutheran, by contrast, is required above all to believe certain things, to make them his own. (This might suggest that Lutheranism is more intrusive than Catholicism, if Lutheranism requires belief, whereas Catholicism allows one to maintain a respectable distance between one's inner beliefs and one's external actions. But Hegel takes Lutheranism to require one only to say and do what one believes, not actually to hold certain definite beliefs.) This need not jeopardize the Catholic's loyalty to the state, unless what the priest tells him to do conflicts with what the secular authorities tell him to do. A tendency to obey orders regardless of one's private beliefs or conscience is valuable, and perhaps essential to the state. But it is at odds with the individualism of modern ethical life.

Now for the details of the passage:

(1) The words 'God who is known in the *spirit* and in the *truth*' echo John 4: 24: 'God is a Spirit: and they that worship him must worship him in spirit and in truth'. Hegel takes this to imply that God is not dependent on

anything external, in particular on natural objects, and that consequently worship of God should not rely on anything external to the worshipper. This detachment, both of God and the worshipper, from externals corresponds to the 'liberation' of mind or spirit from particular times and places: cf. §§549, n. 1; 552, n. 4.

(2) 'Host' (*Hostie*) probably comes from the Latin *hostia*, a 'victim' or 'sacrifice'. The host is unleavened, consecrated bread in the form of a round wafer given to Catholics and Lutherans at the eucharist or holy communion. It symbolizes the sacrifice of Christ for the expiation of our sins, and derives from the words attributed to Christ in Matthew 26: 26: 'And as they were eating, Jesus took bread, and blessed it, and brake it, and gave it to the disciples, and said, Take, eat; this is my body.' (Cf. Mark 14: 22; Luke 22: 19; 1 Corinthians 11: 24.) Catholics, in Hegel's view, take these words literally, believing that the host really is a part of Christ's body. (Aquinas argued that the 'substance' of the host is Christ's flesh, but it retains the external 'accidents' of ordinary bread: Summa Theologiae, III, Q.75, articles 4 and 5.) Lutherans dispute this. For them the host has no independent significance besides its 'externality'; it acquires its significance only in our 'annihilation' and 'enjoyment' of it. Cf. PH, p. 415: 'Luther's simple doctrine is that the specific embodiment of Deity—infinite subjectivity, that is true spirituality, Christ—is in no way present and actual in an outward form, but as essentially spiritual is obtained only in being reconciled to God—in *faith and spiritual enjoyment*.' Roughly speaking, Hegel takes Christ to have meant: 'Do not make any special sacrifices on my behalf. Just eat and drink as usual, only think of me when you do so.'

(3) Hegel connects the 'externality' of the host with the 'externality' of the priesthood, the 'class' (*Stand*) that imparts knowledge to the laity and directs their conscience. Moreover, a priest acquires his authority to perform these functions not by the knowledge and wisdom he actually has, but by being consecrated or ordained in a ritual ceremony.

(4) According to Hegel, what matters for the Catholic is not whether one believes or even means the words one utters in prayer, but that one actually says the prescribed words. Hegel is thoroughly sceptical of miracles, condemning Catholicism's 'credulity of the most absurd and childish character in regard to *Miracles*, for the Divine is supposed to manifest itself in a perfectly disconnected and limited way, for purely finite and particular purposes' (PH, p. 413).

(5) There is conflicting biblical testimony on whether 'justification' (*Gerechtigkeit*, 'justice', the word used by Luther in this context) is by 'works' or by 'faith': 'Therefore we conclude that a man is justified by faith without the deeds of the law' (Romans 3: 28), but 'Ye see then how that by works a man is justified, and not by faith only' (James 2: 24). The issue was hotly disputed, but seems rather futile. Clearly, doing the right things, but for the wrong reasons, though it may be socially convenient,

does not constitute moral or religious merit. Equally clearly, to have faith, but to make no attempt to do the right things, is also unsatisfactory. Hegel is criticizing the performance of actions solely for the purpose of accumulating religious credit, and transferable credit at that. His criticism of the practice is justified. How widespread the practice was is another matter. It is not an intrinsic feature of Catholicism, but a symptom of the degeneration of Catholicism that provoked the Reformation.

8. Hegel's attack on Catholic states and their defenders is perhaps directed in part against Friedrich Schlegel who, after his conversion to Catholicism in 1808, went to work for the Austrian government. 'Worldly wisdom' (*Weltweisheit*, lit. 'world-wisdom') was often used for 'philosophy', in contrast to theology, 'sacred wisdom'. Its use probably goes back to the eleventh century. Hegel interprets the word in his own way. In Catholic societies the mind or spirit is, as it were, chained up. Philosophy releases it into the world, and this improves both the mind itself and the institutions that it now pervades. The word translated as 'presents', *vergegenwärtigt*, is ambiguous. Literally it means 'make present', usually (in the reflexive form) to one's own mind. But Hegel does not use it reflexively, so it also means 'make present in the world'.

9. The vows of chastity, poverty, and obedience were required of monks by St Benedict (*c*.480–*c*.543): a monk could have no sexual intercourse, could have no private property of his own, and had to obey his abbot. These vows were adopted by later religious orders, and celibacy was generally demanded of Catholic clergy. Chastity, poverty, and obedience were not, in this form, required of the laity: they are encouraged to marry and to acquire property, though they are expected to obey their priest. (Hegel tends to obscure this in the interests of a dramatic contrast between Catholicism and Lutheranism.) However, chastity, poverty, and obedience are, in Hegel's view, regarded as the 'holy', and in some sense the ideal, condition. There is, therefore, in Catholic societies a rift between the holy life and the secular life, between the 'divine spirit' and the world. It is not clear, however, what Hegel takes the connection to be between chastity, poverty, and obedience, on the one hand, and, on the other hand, the 'unfreedom of the form', the lack of awareness and 'self-consciousness'. His idea seems to be that chastity, poverty, and obedience do not come naturally to people, so that if they are adopted, this can only be because they are demanded of them by an 'external' authority, not because their heart is really in it. Conversely, if a code of conduct is to be adopted on external authority, it needs to be a code of conduct that does not come naturally to us, since otherwise the authority is superfluous. Chastity, poverty, and obedience are, moreover, so unnatural to human beings that even those who do adopt them tend to lapse from their high ideals and to become corrupt. Secular institutions too tend to become corrupt; they are neglected in favour of the pursuit of otherworldly holiness. Lutheranism, in Hegel's view, solves all these problems by giving ethical priority to marriage, property, and obedience to the law, and in effect abolishing, or at least secularizing, 'holiness'.

Hegel is wrong to suppose that there is a 'contradiction' in fulfilling one's vow of poverty by giving one's goods to others. Someone who takes the vow of poverty need not suppose that everyone else has taken, or ought to take, this vow. Even if he regards poverty as the ideal condition, he is not preventing the recipient of his goods from attaining it: the recipient can always give the goods to someone else or throw them into the sea. Arguably, he is giving the recipient the opportunity of making the supreme sacrifice that he himself has made, that of giving all his goods to the poor. Hegel's mistake implies that Catholicism required chastity, poverty, and obedience of *everyone*. He knew this was not so. His suggestion to the contrary may simply be dramatic hyperbole. Or it may stem from Hegel's residual Kantianism, the assumption that if I believe chastity, poverty, and obedience are right for me, then I should believe they are right for everyone.

10. Hegel quotes Luther's translation of Christ's saying in Matthew 22: 21 and Mark 12: 17. The saying is taken to imply that the religious and secular spheres can peacefully coexist, each taking care of their own concerns. Hegel has two arguments against this:

   (1) Each sphere tends to claim as its own concern matters claimed by the other. So we need some single authority to decide what belongs to each sphere. Given the intrinsic superiority of religion, it must be religion that makes this decision. But religion cannot simply take whatever it wants and leave the secular realm to its own sinful ways. Religion, the 'divine spirit', must descend into the 'worldly sphere' and sanctify the institutions it requires: marriage, property, and compliance with the laws. In doing this, Catholicism effectively becomes Protestantism.

   (2) A rational, secular constitution has to be operated by individuals. If this constitution coexists with a religion different in 'spirit' from itself, it will be operated by individuals whose primary allegiance is to their religion: cf. §552, n. 6. Then they will pervert the spirit of the constitution, even if they do not undermine it. Checks and balances, 'chambers' of parliament, etc. are not a sufficient antidote. These too have to be operated by individuals, individuals whose consciences need to be in tune with the constitution.

Hegel is thinking primarily of the French Revolution and its aftermath:

Thus Liberalism as an abstraction, emanating from France, traversed the Roman World; but Religious slavery held that world in the fetters of political servitude. For it is a false principle that the fetters which bind Right and Freedom can be broken without the emancipation of conscience—that there can be a Revolution without a Reformation.—These countries, therefore, sank back into their old condition—in [Catholic] Italy with some modifications of the outward political condition. . . . Material superiority in power can achieve no enduring results: Napoleon could not coerce [Catholic] Spain into freedom any more than Philip II [of Spain] could force [Protestant] Holland into slavery (PH, p. 453).

But it is not obvious that subsequent events support Hegel's thesis or, indeed, that the thesis is sufficiently precise to admit of empirical testing. On Spain, cf. §540, n. 2.

11. According to Hegel's interpretation of Plato's *Republic*, Plato saw the emergence of 'freedom' as a threat to the traditional Greek state. The new freedom is 'subjective' freedom, both the freedom to do as one wants ('wilfulness') and the freedom to make up one's own mind about the right thing to do ('morality'): cf. §552, n. 13. The traditional Greek state excluded subjective freedom, in Hegel's view, and so Plato proposed to eliminate this burgeoning freedom from his state. To this end the state must be modelled as closely as possible on the 'Idea' of justice. The Idea of justice can only be discerned by philosophers, in Plato's view. And so Plato argues that philosophers must be the rulers of the state: *Republic*, V. 473 c–e. Hegel agrees with Plato that subjective freedom is at odds with the Greek state. He does not, however, believe that subjective freedom can or should be eliminated: it must rather be accommodated in a new type of state. He agrees with Plato that it is the philosopher's job to discern the principles of justice. However, he does not agree that philosophers should rule. As he explains in the final sentence, Plato held (correctly) that if the Idea of justice is to be imposed on the state, those who impose it must be conscious of this Idea. But Plato held (incorrectly) that one can be conscious of the Idea of justice only in the way that philosophers are conscious of it, namely as a 'free self-determining thought', etc. Hegel, by contrast, implies that there are other, lower ways in which we can be conscious of this Idea, in particular in a new type of religion, which can itself accommodate subjective freedom as well as ethical life.

12. Hegel is here implicitly criticizing Plato's theory of 'Ideas' or 'forms' at least in its application to 'natural things'. In the case of, say, horses, there are three things to be considered: (1) the substance or genus 'horse' or equinity; (2) individual horses, the subjects in which the genus *exists*; (3) the abstract thought of the genus 'horse' formed by the human mind. Plato (according to Hegel's implicit interpretation of him) believes that the genus 'horse' is in some way separate from its instances, individual horses, and has 'universality and essentiality' prior to and independently of the mind's thinking of it. Hegel disagrees: whatever existence an Idea has independently of its instances is conferred on it by a thinker or 'representer'. In this he is closer to Aristotle than to Plato. 'Form' is not here used by Hegel in the sense of a Platonic 'form': it contrasts with 'content' (*Gehalt*). Plato himself used two words more or less synonymously, '*idea*' and '*eidos*', usually translated into English as 'idea' and 'form' respectively. Almost invariably Hegel speaks of Plato's 'ideas' (*Ideen*) rather than of his 'forms' (*Formen*).

13. The 'human content' (*menschliche Gehalt*) contrasts with the 'content of natural things'. The content of natural things needs a thinker external to itself in order to acquire existence as a universal independent of its instances ('for itself'). The content of a human being needs nothing external to itself to exist as a universal. It acquires such existence when the mind becomes self-conscious, conscious of

itself as a mind or as a human being. More specifically, the mind has as its 'content' (*Inhalt*), i.e. thinks about, thinking itself, which is the 'form' because it is the universal characteristic of all individual minds. The mind is thus the absolute 'content' (*Gehalt*), both because it is independent in a way that the content of natural things is not and because it is complete and self-contained: cf. §552, n. 1 on '*absolut*'. It is also concrete 'intrinsically' or within itself, since it generates its own internal duality.

14. 'Entelechy' (*Entelechie*) translates Aristotle's ἐντελέχεια, which comes from ἐν ('in'), τέλος ('goal, end'), and ἔχεια ('having'). Its root meaning is thus 'having its end in itself'. Aristotle uses it for the 'actualization' of something that would otherwise be merely potential. In *de anima*, II. 1, 412^{b}5–6, for example, the soul is said to be 'the first entelechy of a natural, organic body', i.e. it makes an organic body actually alive. (It is only the 'first' entelechy, since an actually living body may nevertheless be asleep and not currently engaged in the activities characteristic of living things—the second entelechy.) νοησις της νοησεως is 'thinking of thinking', an expression used by Aristotle at *Metaphysics* XII. 8, 1074^{b}34–5, where he is speaking about God's thinking: 'and thinking is thinking of thinking'. Aristotle himself does not speak of the 'entelechy of thinking'. Hegel could mean simply the 'activity' of thinking, or he may mean the thinking that actualizes something else, namely the mind. But more probably Hegel means that thinking of thinking is fully actualized or perfected thinking, in contrast to thinking that is not about thinking. Thinking of or about thinking is, for Hegel, logical thinking, thinking about non-empirical thoughts such as being, causality, etc., which pervade all our spiritual and intellectual activity. Thinking about, say, horses, by contrast, is not thinking of thinking.

It is not clear why Hegel believes that Aristotle 'soared above' Plato. For Plato the forms or Ideas are objects of thought as much as they are for Aristotle, though they exist separately, independently of our thought about them as well as of their instances: cf. §552, n. 12. Plato does not speak about 'thinking of thinking' nor, in the *Republic* at least, does he postulate a thinking god. Hegel values the notion of thinking of thinking. Whereas Aristotle attributes it only, or at least primarily, to God, Hegel attributes it to man: cf. §§441, nn. 3, 4; 442, n. 3.

15. Thinking involves two constituents, the conscious thinking self and the universal thought that it thinks of or about. Hegel believes that the system of universal thoughts constitute the core of the mind, and this may be what he has in view in saying: 'the genuine Idea . . . the same substantial content in the one as in the other'. The system of thoughts bifurcates, as it were, into a thinking self and the thoughts it thinks. The self, however, is not just a thinking self. It also feels, intuits, and represents, activities which, though they involve thought, do not amount to pure thinking, or thinking of thinking. The highest activity of the mind is thinking of thinking, thinking, that is, about the pure thoughts that structure the world and the mind (the 'absolute Idea') without any sensory input or pictorial trappings. But we cannot do that right away, either in our individual life or over the course of history. First we need to become conscious of the 'absolute Idea' in the form of intuition and representation. Perhaps in the

individual life, and certainly in the course of history, this means that the absolute Idea is first conceived in the form of religion. Philosophy, the thinking of naked, non-pictorial thoughts, emerges only later.

Elsewhere Hegel distinguishes between religion, the 'form' of representation, and art, the form of intuition: see ILA. But though he regards art as a simpler form than religion, he does not seriously propose that art precedes religion in time. It is, however, quite plausible that religion, or at least some pictorial portrayal of the nature of things, precedes philosophy in time. This applies to man, however, not to Aristotle's God. Aristotle's God does nothing but think: he does not feel, intuit, or represent. For Aristotle God and man are quite distinct, though we should model ourselves on God and try to do intermittently what he does constantly, namely think. Hegel blurs the boundary between God and man, attributing to man a capacity that Aristotle reserves for God.

16. Greek philosophers, most notably Plato in the *Republic*, but also Xenophanes of Colophon (*c*.580–*c*.485 BC) and the sophistic movement of the fifth century, attacked traditional Greek religion, whereas Hegel and other German philosophers found Christianity relatively congenial. Hegel stresses two respects in which Greek religion offended philosophy: it was polytheistic, in contrast to the 'unity of thought, etc.', and it was the product of 'poetic fantasy' (*dichtende Phantasie*) rather than of serious religious inquiry. There was no other religion available in Greek society. So Greek religion could not be improved or 'purified' at the level of religion, in the way that, say, Lutheranism improved and purified Christianity. This had two consequences. First, philosophers found themselves at odds with Greek society, with 'substantiality', in which Greek religion was 'immanent'. Second, Greek religion could only be improved by philosophy: no other remedy, in particular no religious remedy, was available. Hence philosophy 'burst forth' as 'subjective free thinking', in conflict both with Greek society and with the religious realm in general. The 'subjective free thinking' in question is primarily the thinking of the sophists and of Socrates rather than that of Plato. Plato was trying to remedy the state of affairs that Hegel describes.

17. On the emergence of the state from religion. cf. PH, p. 252: 'Athene the goddess is Athens itself—i.e. the real and concrete spirit of the citizens'. At PH, p. 267, Hegel says that the 'principle' of the 'corruption' of the Greek world was 'subjectivity obtaining emancipation for itself' (*die für sich frei werdende Innerlichkeit*, lit. 'inwardness becoming free for itself'). So the 'one-sidedness' involved in the Idea of the state is the predominant 'substantiality' of its ethical life, unable to accommodate 'subjectivity'. Hence when subjectivity does emerge, it takes the form of 'corruption' (cf. PH, p. 252). Of the very many Greek city-states, only some were democracies. The most notable of these was fifth- and fourth-century Athens, and it is Athens that Hegel primarily has in view here. In Athens the corruption stemming from subjectivity took the form of 'levity in public conduct' (*offener Leichtsinn*) (PH, p. 265). Hegel believed the democratic constitution to be the 'only possible one' for the traditional Greek state, whose 'citizens are still unconscious of particular interests' (PH, p. 252), whereas Plato objected to democracy root and branch. But Hegel himself perhaps regarded

democracy's inability to accommodate subjective individualism as a defect in its 'principle'. Plato's response to 'subjective freedom' is, as Hegel interprets him, to eliminate it entirely from his ideal republic. He could not therefore allow the citizens to reform the state of their own volition. They have to be organized from above by people especially qualified for this task. The reply to the objection that the organizers might be, say, priests rather than philosophers, is that there are no suitable priests available. Society is, in Plato's view, so thoroughly corrupt that anyone apart from a philosopher is a part of the problem rather than the solution. On subjective freedom, see §539, n. 6. On the 'infinite form of subjectivity', see §552, n. 18.

18. Hegel believes that only Christianity, and more specifically Protestantism, permits a stable social order ('substantiality') that allows and accommodates subjective freedom. Plato and his philosopher rulers could not secure such an order. They could not even conceive of it until religion prepared the way for it. However, Hegel somewhat exaggerates the difference between Plato and himself. The subjective freedom that Plato proposed to eliminate from the state consisted in such freedoms as the freedom to marry whomsoever one likes, to choose a profession, to express dissenting opinions from a platform or even in a philosophy lecture, and so on. The modern state that Hegel favours no doubt allows more freedom of this sort. But the freedom it permits is not unrestricted. However, Hegel does not here refer explicitly to freedoms of this type. He mentions instead the 'freedom of the self-consciousness that is for itself' and of the 'mind that is aware of its essence'. It is not obvious that Plato was deficient in this respect or that he would have failed to comprehend Hegel's meaning. But he would not have seen this as a good reason for granting subjective freedom to the citizens of his state. He would say that most citizens do not have minds of this sort, and cannot be trusted to behave properly if they are allowed too much subjective freedom; that even philosophers need to be restrained if they are not to misbehave and thereby impair their philosophical competence. In fact the mind that Hegel describes sounds more like the mind of the philosopher or even God's mind than the mind of the average citizen. But this, Hegel might reply, is precisely my point. Plato had a good mind, 'aware of its essence', and so on. But no one else did, apart from the odd philosopher. The gods were shallow sensory creatures of the poetic imagination, incapable of sustaining a society as deep and complex as a modern state. The citizens were hardly any better, unfit to be trusted to run their own lives. So the philosopher is thoroughly alienated from his society and its religion, unable to respond to it except by withdrawing from it or else autocratically reforming it along philosophical lines. But a Christian society is different. The Christian God is a mind in which the philosopher sees his own reflexion. This God sustains and justifies a society whose citizens can be given considerable free rein. The citizens themselves are good Christians and thus have the inner depth and self-restraint to use their freedom wisely. So at long last the philosopher feels at home in his society and its religion. In fact, in Hegel's view, religion, the state, and philosophy all involve the same 'principle', the 'absolute truth', only in different 'forms'. Hegel's account follows the pattern

of immediate unity—opposition—restored unity: cf. §387, n. 14. Philosophy emerges from the immediate simple unity of Greek religion; it opposes this religion; Christianity restores the unity of religion and philosophy.

19. The pattern of immediate unity—opposition—restored unity (cf. §552, n. 18) is repeated within Christianity itself. Hegel does not give an adequate explanation for this, since it is 'religion', not specifically Christianity, that is said to develop the 'distinctions contained in the Idea' and Greek religion has already provided a phase of opposition. But Hegel needs to account for the degeneration of Christianity that he finds in Catholicism: cf. §552, n. 7. Why did this corruption of Christianity not require a new religion to remedy it, as the corruption of Greek religion did? It is because of the 'infinite elasticity of the absolute form' that Christianity, unlike Greek religion, is self-correcting. Hegel might have added: First, the 'corruption' of Greek religion was not really a degeneration from its original ideal condition; all along it was afflicted with 'sensory externality'. Its problem is that it has given rise to a 'subjectivity', in particular philosophy, that it cannot accommodate. By contrast, Catholicism is, in Hegel's view, a degeneration from an early Christianity, which has left records to which reformers can appeal. Secondly, Greek religion lacked the support of philosophers or even serious theologians. Philosophers tended to oppose it, except as a social convention. Christianity, by contrast, is a thinking religion. It commands the allegiance of a host of philosophers and theologians, who are ready to help it out of a tight spot.

NOTE TO §553

1. This is the third, culminating phase of mind: absolute mind. The 'concept' of mind already has its corresponding 'reality' (*Realität*) in objective mind. But the reality of mind does not yet amount to 'knowledge' (*Wissen*) of the absolute Idea, which is required for a genuine unity or 'identity' of concept and reality. If this is to come about, the intelligence must be liberated from its entanglement in social and political life: cf. §§549, n. 1; 552, n. 1. Only in this way can the intelligence be a worthy 'shape' (*Gestalt*) or vehicle of the concept. The Idea is the concept together with its reality: cf. §377, n. 4. '*Absolut*' is 'independent, unrestricted, unconditioned', from the Latin *absolutus*, 'complete, finished; unconditional', but also, as the past participle of the verb *absolvere*, 'to loosen, detach, free', 'loosened, detached': cf. §552, n. 1. It is thus connected with the implicitly 'free' (*freie*) intelligence and with its being 'liberated' (*befreit*) to its concept. 'Absolute mind' is, among other things, free mind. It has returned from its objectification in the external world to knowledge of itself.

NOTES TO §554

1. The 'identity' in question is the identity of the absolute mind and its self-knowledge. This identity is both an eternal logical structure and an achievement

accomplished in the course of time, both the self-knowing God and our knowledge of him, namely religion. Hegel speaks of '*das Urteil* [literally 'the judgement'] into itself and an awareness [*Wissen*]'. But he interprets *Urteil* as 'original (*ur-*) division (*teil*)', its supposedly original sense: cf. §389, n. 4. Wallace's 'discerning itself' (from the Latin *cernere*, 'to sift', and *dis-*, indicating separation, etc.) conveys this idea well. The discerning judgement is the converse of the identity. A single substance bifurcates into itself and knowledge of itself, and these are identical with each other.

2. Hegel calls this sphere 'religion', rather than 'art' or 'philosophy', because religion is the dominant theme on which art and philosophy are variations. *Geist*, 'mind' or 'spirit', as well as referring to the human mind and to God in general, is also used for the holy spirit, the third term of the Trinity, which descends into the Christian 'community' (*Gemeinde*): 'And they were all filled with the Holy Ghost, and began to speak with other tongues, as the Spirit gave them utterance' (Acts 2: 4). The community affected in this way consisted of the Apostles. But Hegel takes 'community' in a wider sense, covering the Christian community in general and also activities other than their specifically religious activities, such as art and philosophy (and sometimes also the institutions and activities of objective mind). In saying that religion comes both from 'the subject', i.e. human beings, and from the absolute spirit descending into the community, Hegel has more in view than the obvious point that knowledge and belief involve direction on an object as well as an attitude on the part of the subject or the orthodox theological belief that God is the fundamental cause or ground of whatever humans do, as well as of everything else. These considerations would apply to all our knowledge. If I know the Himalayas or that $7 + 5 = 12$, my knowledge is *of* the Himalayas or *of* the proposition that $7 + 5 = 12$. Moreover, if traditional theology is correct, God is ultimately responsible for my knowledge. Hegel means rather that God or the absolute mind has a drive or tendency to be known by man. It is not complete unless it is known by man. That is why it 'discerns itself' into itself and knowledge of itself. It essentially comes to meet us halfway. The Himalayas, by contrast, have no drive to be known by us; they are complete without our knowledge of them. The same is true (at least for a mathematical Platonist) of the proposition that $7 + 5 = 12$.

3. Hegel is not here concerned with the evidence for or justification of belief, though he does deal with that in Enc. I, §§61–78. That faith or 'belief' (*Glaube*) is a form of 'knowledge' (*ein Wissen*) implies that it is a mistake to focus exclusively on the subjective component of faith, neglecting the object of faith or knowledge, i.e. the truth. In Enc. I, §§61–78 he attributes this error to Friedrich Heinrich Jacobi, but he also has in mind, though he rarely mentions him, Friedrich Ernst Daniel Schleiermacher, who located religion not in any definite beliefs about God, but in a feeling of absolute dependency. ('In that case', Hegel is reported to have said, 'my dog is the best Christian'.) As Hegel implies, Schleiermacher did not neglect the third person of the Trinity, the Holy Spirit. But this served his emotional and anthropocentric pantheism. It did not give us access to a substantial God or to substantial knowledge about him. Hegel hated Schleiermacher. One source of his

hatred may be his fear of being assimilated to him. Hegel, like Schleiermacher, blurs the boundaries between God and man, between God and the world. But there are distinct differences. Hegel stresses reason rather than emotion. He does not share Schleiermacher's tendency to religious relativism, the view that it does not matter what one believes as long as one believes it with devotion and a feeling of dependency. Hegel distinctly prefers Christianity to other religions, and Lutheranism to Catholicism. On Schleiermacher, see also §§380, n. 2; 400, n. 1; §449, n. 5.

NOTE TO §555

1. The process of our 'subjective consciousness' of absolute mind or spirit involves three stages: (1) Faith or belief as 'immediate' certainty of the objective truth. (2) A 'contrast' (*Gegensatz*) emerges between the 'different determinations' involved in faith, i.e. between 'subjective consciousness' and 'objective truth'. (3) This gulf is bridged by the 'mediation' of worship or 'cult'; the 'contrast' between subjective consciousness and objective truth is sublated by the authentication of the original immediate certainty; and mind or spirit thus gains 'liberation', 'reconciliation' and 'actuality'. 'Implicit [*impliziten*] cult' refers to such things as art that is not specifically religious. Faith 'through the witness of the spirit' echoes Romans 8: 16: 'The Spirit itself beareth witness with our spirit, that we are the children of God'. 'Through' translates Hegel's *in*, to avoid the misunderstanding that the faith is a faith or belief in the existence or efficacy of the witness, which would be expressed by *an* rather than *in*.

NOTES TO §556

1. The 'finitude of art' is the finitude of symbolic (pre-Greek) and classical (Greek) art, the only types of art that Hegel considers in Enc. III. It contrasts with the 'infinite form' of Christianity: cf. §§561, n. 2; §563, n. 1. However, no art, not even Christian art, can adequately capture the infinite form.
2. This refers to one aspect of art, rather than to a distinct type of art. Art involves (1) a work, considered simply as a thing existing among other things, (2) an artist, and (3) an audience. Hegel returns to this in §560. This 'disintegration' (*Zerfallen*) stems from art's finitude.
3. This refers to another aspect of art, its meaning. On 'intuition' (*Anschauung*), cf. §§446–50. Sensory intuition is, in Hegel's view, the specific form in which art presents the absolute mind, in contrast to 'representation', the characteristic medium of religion, and thought, the medium of philosophy. Nevertheless, art also involves 'representation' (*Vorstellung*), since it conveys a meaning that goes beyond sensory intuition. The 'ideal' (*Ideal*) is an Idea in a sensory or imaginative form. On a 'sign' (*Zeichen*) see §§457Z. and 458. It is a sensory entity that represents something that resembles it in no significant respect. The flag of a country is a sign of it, since, while it represents or stands for the country, it is qualitatively quite different. And so the 'natural immediacy' that is only a sign of

the 'Idea' is qualitatively different from the Idea. It is e.g. a pyramid: cf. §458, n. 2. Hegel then refers to a further stage in which the 'natural immediacy' is so 'transfigured' that it 'shows' only the Idea, and not (like a pyramid) a physical shape that has no intrinsic connection to the Idea. This is Greek art, especially a statue of a god. Beauty arises from the perfect match between the Idea and the form that expresses it. In §561 Hegel calls pre-Greek art 'symbolic art', implying that the work resembles in some respect what it represents: cf. §§561, n. 2 and also 457, n. 8 on the distinction between a sign and a symbol. This is perhaps a third stage between the pyramid and Greek ('classical') art.

NOTES TO §557

1. Hegel has in mind a Greek statue of a god. Its form is sensory: it is a visible and tangible shape. But this form also affects the 'content' of the god. To be represented in this way he must be a 'unity of nature and spirit', not a purely 'spiritual unity' in which the natural element is overcome and transfigured. Unlike the Christian god the Greek god cannot dispense with its sensory form or be transmuted into a conceptual, philosophical form. Hence it is not 'absolute mind' or spirit, spirit detached from the sensory world and self-contained.
2. The Greek community is, like its gods, attached to externals. It is an 'ethical' (*sittliche*) community and it provides 'substantial' freedom, in that the citizen is at home in the community and in harmony with its norms and institutions. But this freedom is only a 'custom' (*Sitte*), not the subjective freedom discussed in §539, n. 6. The subject cannot withdraw into himself to ask what he really wants to do, or what he really ought to do, regardless of what the norms of the community prescribe. In particular the Greeks lacked the individual 'conscience' characteristic of the Christian era: 'The Greeks had no conscience'(PH, p. 253). In other words, the Greeks lacked inner depth and detachment from externals. This is why their gods lacked inner depth and detachment from externals. For the same reason, however, the Greek gods could, unlike the Christian God, be portrayed to perfection in sensory art. The 'reflection into itself' that the Greek subject lacked is 'infinite' because of the circular relation of the subject to itself: cf. §395, n. 2. On Greek religion see also §552, n. 16.

NOTES TO §558

1. The production of 'intuitions' requires stone, pigments, etc., but also 'subjective images and representations': cf. §556, n. 3. The expression of spiritual 'content' (*Gehalt*) requires in addition 'forms of nature' with a 'meaning' (*Bedeutung*), especially the human body, whose significance is considered in §411.
2. Art does not imitate nature 'in its externality', but nature in so far as it signifies spirit or mind. The 'characteristic . . . natural form' is the archetypal or ideal natural form, e.g. the ideal human body, stripped of idiosyncrasies and blemishes. Hegel sees no artistic merit in accurate pictures of sheer nature or, say, the production of noises indistinguishable from birdsong.

NOTES TO §559

1. The attempt to represent absolute mind in sculpture fails. What is represented is not absolute spirit, detached from any particular society, but a *Volksgeist*, a national spirit, the spirit of the Greek (or perhaps, more restrictedly, the Athenian) people. Even such a national spirit is 'implicitly universal', but the attempt to explicate this results in an 'indeterminate polytheism', the portrayal of an indefinite number of distinct gods, each representing as aspect of the *Volksgeist*, perhaps even an aspect of absolute mind, but with no clear principle of order among them.
2. This refers to the art of a later stage than that of 'indeterminate polytheism', perhaps to the art of the Hellenistic period (i.e. after the death of Alexander the Great), when non-religious art, such as individual portraiture, flourished.

NOTES TO §560

1. To view something as 'immediate' is to disregard the process by which it came about and view it just as it is in itself. Thus to view a work as immediate is opposed to viewing it as mediated or 'made by the artist'. On the 'ideal', cf. §556, where Hegel also distinguished between the work, the artist, and the audience.
2. The artist's relation to the work is both constrained and free. To express the god, the work must show 'no sign of subjective particularity', no idiosyncratic contribution by the artist. Hence the artistry is mere 'formality'; the artist is, as it were, just a midwife at the birth of the god. Artistry requires 'inspiration' (*Begeisterung*). If this involved thought, then the artist might be free in this respect, and that would introduce 'particularity' into his work. But the artist (like everyone else) is free only to the extent that he thinks. Inspiration does not involve thought, and so it is not free. Inspiration comes to a particular individual, but since it is like an alien force to which the artist does not succumb freely, the artist's particularity is not transferred to the work of art. The artistic activity thus has the 'form of natural immediacy': the deity expresses itself in it in much the way that it might be thought to express itself in an earthquake or a volcanic eruption. This is not the whole story, however. Inspiration and the consequent impulse to artistic production may not be free. But artistry requires technique as well as inspiration. The artist must make choices about the materials to use and about his way of fashioning them. At this point free 'wilfulness' (*Willkür*) enters in, and presumably an element of particularity, since the choices the artist makes do not depend only on the inspiring deity nor are they the choices that every other artist would make. Hence with respect to its inspiration, the work is constrained and the artist is a servant of the god. But with respect to technique the work is free and the artist is the master of the god. 'Master' translates *Meister*, which usually refers to the 'master' of a craft or a sport rather than the master of a slave or servant. Hence it suggests the artist's mastery of the subject matter more than his domination of the god, his artstic skill rather than his theological incompetence.

   In this and the following Paragraphs Hegel speaks as if the artistic portrayal of God or gods is as much the work of God himself as of the human artist. In theological terms he believes that God strives for an adequate manifestation of himself in the world, but that since he is dependent for this on human vehicles—artists, worshippers, theologians, philosophers, etc.—his manifestation is more or less imperfect. That God should be so manifest is essential to him: it constitutes his self-consciousness. Thus artists' portrayals of God are an essential aspect of God himself. God is not so clearly distinct from humanity as he is in traditional theology. Accordingly, our production and appreciation of portrayals of God correspond to our understanding of ourselves. Our own self-consciousness and God's self-consciousness (i.e. our portrayals of him) go hand in hand.

NOTES TO §561

1. Classical, i.e. primarily Greek, art achieves a 'reconciliation' (*Versöhnung*) between the deity and the means of expressing it. No prior search for a suitable expression, for a way of spanning the gulf between god and man, is required. No explanation of the symbols employed is need. When Greeks look at a statue of the god they immediately feel that their god has been suitably represented. They do not feel that there is any residual mystery, any underlying 'essence', that defies adequate expression. In this respect Greek art differs both from pre-Greek art and from Christian art. It is characterized by its supreme 'beauty' (*Schönheit*). On reconciliation in Hegel's philosophy, see M. O. Hardimon, *Hegel's Social Philosophy: The Project of Reconciliation* (Cambridge: Cambridge University Press, 1994).

2. *Erhabenheit*, 'sublimity', was regarded by Burke and Kant as a dimension of aesthetic value coordinate with beauty. It characterizes objects that are magnificent and awe-inspiring rather than pretty, such as the Niagara Falls or Dostoevsky's novels. Hegel assigns it to an inferior type of art, 'symbolic' art, primarily pre-Greek art, in which the reconciliation of form and content required for beauty is not yet attained. God is the object of 'pure thought', but a suitable expression has not been found. This shows that the 'meaning' or 'content', i.e. the god, is not yet 'free spirit' either for us or for itself: if it were it, or we, would supply a suitable form, an 'infinite' form in which God is free, i.e. complete and self-contained, not dependent on anything outside himself. On thought, cf. §562, n. 6. On symbolic art, cf. §556, n. 3.

NOTES TO §562

1. 'Romantic' art is roughly the art of the Christian era. Classical art, 'that first extreme', does manage to express its god adequately, but that is because the god is 'only superficial personality', lacking the depth of the Christian God and thus 'satisfying himself in an external shape'. Romantic art, like symbolic art, is unable to express the 'Idea' adequately. In symbolic art, this is because the Idea is too thin and indeterminate to allow adequate sensory expression; hence it is only 'seeking its shape'. In romantic art, it is because God is too profound to be susceptible of sensory expression. He does not need sensory expression, because he is

a pure, self-contained mind. God does, however, 'condescend to appearance', in the person of Christ, and artists can depict Christ. They can also depict worldly phenomena and events ('externality') in the belief that God constitutes their inner nature, their 'meaning'. But since the deity 'disengages itself' from such phenomena, they appear only contingently related to their meaning.

For Hegel, Christian art embraces apparently secular art (such as Shakespeare's plays), as well as explicitly religious art, because the secular world is imbued, though not very obviously and manifestly imbued, with the Holy Spirit.

2. Throughout history the being or 'essence' (*Wesen*) regarded as 'the absolute' is conceived in different ways, ascribed different 'determinations', by different peoples in succession. The determinations so ascribed and the order in which they appear are not haphazard, but governed by 'logical necessity'. Any given stage in the determination of the absolute belongs especially to a single 'people', and to any such stage there corresponds a certain type of worship, of secular or 'worldly' self-consciousness, of ethical life, of art, etc. A given people or nation makes a significant contribution to the development of the absolute only occasionally (or, Hegel sometimes suggests, only once: cf. §549, n. 2), but it invariably has all these elements or 'moments'—religion, art, etc.—and they form a single 'systematic totality' governed by a single 'spirit'. 'World-history' is the history not of a single people, but of all the peoples who have made a substantial contribution to the development of humanity. It coincides with the history of religions, owing to the correspondence between religion and other aspects of human life. This does not entail that religion is the basis, the fundamental substructure, of the totality or even that it is more important than other elements in the totality. Here Hegel claims only that religion closely coheres with the other elements in the totality. He might equally have said that the history of law or the history of ethics coincides with world-history. He believes, however, that religion is more fundamental than art or philosophy: art is motivated by religion, while philosophy presupposes religion. In his lectures on philosophy of religion, he implies that religion is more fundamental than morality and politics: 'According as the religion of nations is constituted, so also is their morality and government' (LPR i. 70); 'reverence for God, or for the gods, establishes and preserves individuals, families, states; while contempt of God, or of the gods, loosens the basis of laws and duties, breaks up the ties of the family and of the State, and leads to their destruction' (LPR i. 103). See also §552 on the potency of the religious conscience. Passages such as these suggest that for Hegel religion occupies, in human society and history, the same dominant position that Marx assigned to the forces of production.

3. Beauty is here restricted to classical art. This is confined to religions (especially Greek religion) in which 'spirituality' is 'concrete' and 'free'. It is concrete, because it has internal form and articulation, and this enables it to express itself in sensory material. It is free, because it is self-contained and self-developing, not at the mercy of sensory and natural entities. The Christian God is also concrete and free, but it eludes beautiful artistic expression, because it is 'absolute', so self-sufficient that it needs and admits no adequate sensory embodiment. Hegel tacitly

invokes the principle that to master sensory or natural material, mind or spirit must become free of it: cf. §393, n. 8. But mind can become too free of the sensory to master it in an artistically satisfactory way.

4. Pre-Greek religions need art since it is the only way in which they can become conscious of the 'essence'. But since the essence is inadequately conceived, it can only be laboriously squeezed into an unsuitable senory form. It is abstract rather than concrete, lacking the immanent form that blossoms into sensory form. It is too close to nature to master it. Beautiful art, by contrast, has taken its distance from nature and can therefore manipulate it freely.

As in §§560 and 561, Hegel blurs the distinctions between God and man, and between what God is and how God is conceived. God and man are closely connected. How we conceive God depends on how we conceive ourselves. God is not sharply distinct from our successive conceptions of him; he develops along with man. 'The idea which a man has of God corresponds with that which he has of himself, of his freedom' (LPR i. 79).

5. Pre-Greek religions are 'bound to sensory externality'. The Greeks perfect the artistic expression of sensory religion. But in doing so, they drive this religion beyond its 'limitation'. They purify spirit of its 'unfreedom' in the way philosophy does. Hegel appeals to the principle that to master the sensory, and to survey one's mastery of it, liberates one from it: cf. §562, n. 3.

6. The role of images in Greek religion reminds Hegel that Catholics also venerate images. He does not mean to compare Greek religion directly with Catholicism, since the Greeks did not, in his view, acknowledge a 'thoughtless and sensory beyond'. If they had done so, why would the artist and the spectator have been so satisfied with their statues? Nor does he believe that Greek 'idols' were 'unbeautiful' or regarded as 'wonder-working talismans'. Bones too play no significant part in Greek religion. So he is comparing Catholicism with religion *before* its redemption by Greek art, and also perhaps suggesting that Greek religion harbours the defects of Catholicism 'in its principle'. To the objection that his admiration of Greek images is inconsistent with his dislike of Catholic images, Hegel might reply that Greek images were the best available expression of their religious beliefs, whereas Catholic images are not the best available expression of Christianity, rather a distortion of it. On Hegel's aversion to Catholicism, see also §552, n. 7.

7. Both Christianity and philosophy locate 'objectivity' in 'thought' rather than in the sensory. Hegel's preference for thought unmixed with sensory nature might seem at odds with his reference to the pre-Greek 'abstract God of pure thinking' in §561. The difficulty stems from the fact that if pre-Greek artists unsuccessfully strive to express God in art, they must have some non-artistic conception of God against which to measure their failure, and this can only be a thought, not an adequate sensory image. But the pre-Greek God, and the thought directed on him, is 'abstract', not, like the Christian God, 'concrete'. The thought is thin and indeterminate as compared with Greek religion, let alone Christianity. The reference to the 'unbeautiful sensoriness' of pre-Greek religion stresses its difference from Christianity, though he does see some affinity to Catholicism.

NOTES TO §563

1. Greek art cannot, in Hegel's view, be surpassed *as art*. What is wrong with it is its restricted 'content' (*Gehalt*), its finite gods, who while they lend themselves to consummate artistic portrayal, lack the depth and 'universality' of the Christian God. Art and the religion that motivates it develop as follows: Pre-Greek religion has a thought of the essence that is too thin and indeterminate to dispense with sensory expression, but for the same reason is incapable of mastering the sensory and of finding adequate expression in it. It remains entangled in the sensory. Greek religion is sufficiently remote from the sensory to control it and find adequate expression in it, but not sufficiently remote from it to dispense with it altogether. Its adequate sensory expression entails the finitude of its content. One cannot produce an adequate painting or statue of the infinite. Christianity expands its content to such a degree that it bursts the bonds of the sensory, neither finding nor needing adequate expression in it. It can be adequately expressed in thought, and only in thought. Hence it is 'for the spirit' or mind, not for the eyes. The self, both the self of God and the self of the worshiper, has withdrawn into itself, away from the sensory, to become a thinker.

   It is not clear, however, why the Christian God has a monopoly on 'revelation' (*Offenbaren*). Pre-Greek religion may well be defective in this respect, since, in Hegel's view, it finds adequate expression neither in the sensory nor in thought. But if the Greek gods are adequately expressed in stone and paint, why are they not revealed? Hegel has two points in mind. First, neither we nor the Greeks themselves think that these sensorily portrayable gods are the whole story. There is something else, behind them, some residual mystery, that eludes plastic art. Second, a Greek god does not essentially need revelation. (St Paul saw in Athens an altar inscribed 'To the Unknown God' (Acts 17: 23), erected in case some god worthy of worship had been left out.) A Greek god is a relatively superficial mind, fully and adequately portrayed in sensory material. This means that he lacks inner depth, does not withdraw from his surroundings to reflect on himself, since reflective thought cannot be sensorily depicted in any detail. He is thus not an 'absolute', a *complete*, mind or 'spirit'. The Christian God is, by contrast, an absolute mind. He is self-aware and reflective. But God can only think and reflect with human help, just as Greek gods can only appear in stone and paint with human help. So God essentially requires revelation. He only becomes fully God in virtue of our knowledge of him. The requirement of revelation is symbolized, in Hegel's view, by the incarnation. See also §564, n. 1.

NOTES TO §564

1. 'To reveal' is *offenbaren*, from *offen*, 'open', and *offenbar*, 'obvious, etc.' 'Revealed religion' often means religion known by inspiration or by supernatural means, in contrast to 'natural religion', religion that is inferred by our natural faculties from the facts of nature naturally known to us. For Hegel, however, 'revealed religion' does not imply any special divine inspiration or dispensation, or anything more

than natural human faculties. But religion, i.e. Christianity, is revealed by God, both because no sensory or natural intermediary is now required and because it is essential to God that he should reveal himself in this way. As mind or spirit, rather than merely 'substance', God essentially reveals or manifests himself, keeping nothing back. This is implied by the fact that God is mind or spirit. Mind is not something in itself that may or may not be revealed, but essentially self-revelation: cf. §§383, 384. Hence God himself develops the 'knowledge' (*Wissen*) of himself, i.e. our knowledge of him. In previous religions God is revealed partially and laboriously (in symbolic art) or else only sensorily. But these gods are not wholly and exclusively spirit, i.e. not 'absolute spirit'.

2. Cf. Plato, *Phaedrus*, 247a and *Timaeus*, 29e; Aristotle, *Metaphysics*, I. 2, 982^{b}32–983^{a}5. The Greek word 'nemesis' means 'righteous indignation, jealousy, envy, etc.'. It was personified as the goddess of retribution, who overturns excessive good fortune.

3. Cf. 1 Thessalonians 4: 5: 'the Gentiles which know not God'. Hegel's quotes Luther's German. St Paul's Greek (*ta ethnê ta mê eidota ton theon*) refers to those who know nothing of the Judaeo-Christian God, but worship some other god or no god at all. Hegel's opponents are, by contrast, those who accept the existence of the Judaeo-Christian God, but deny that we know his nature or essence. Hegel offers two substantial arguments against their view. First, if God is unknown, then he cannot play the pivotal role in religion, since the content of religion cannot be derived from him or from statements about his nature. Secondly, if God is (as Hegel's opponents presumably agree) a mind, then he reveals himself, at least to himself, and this entails (in Hegel's view) that he reveals himself, eventually at least, to us. To the first of these arguments, Hegel's opponents (such as Aquinas) might reply that Hegel fails to consider an intermediate position between knowing nothing about God and knowing everything about God. To claim 'I know (or believe) that God exists, but I know (or believe) nothing else about him whatsoever' is incoherent. But one might claim to know something about God, on the basis of, say, his effects in the world, while disclaiming knowledge of his fundamental nature. To the second argument one reply might be that if God is a mind or spirit, God knows all about himself, but that this does not entail that *we* know everything, or even anything, about him. Hegel's argument relies on his own contestable views about God's self-knowledge and/or about the nature of mind.

4. 'Systematic knowledge' (*Erkenntnis*) of 'God as spirit' involves three stages: (1) 'simple representations of faith', such as God as our father, shepherd, king, etc., which it needs to transcend; (2) the thinking of the 'reflective intellect' (*reflektierenden Verstande*): cf. 378, n. 1; (3) 'conceptual thinking' (*begreifenden Denken*) or 'speculation': cf. §378, n. 4. Someone who believes that we know nothing of God might stop at stage (1), claiming that pictorial representations of God are the best we can hope for. But Hegel more probably has in view someone who invokes our ignorance as a reason for stopping at stage (2), claiming, for example, that while we can know that God is the ultimate cause of certain natural effects, we cannot know his real nature or essence: cf. §564, n. 3.

5. Hegel here advances at least four propositions, since his second proposition is complex:

   (i) God essentially 'knows himself' (*sich selber weiss*). This is argued in §563.
   (ii) Man knows (of) God. This is argued in §564.
   (iii) 'Man's knowledge *of* God' (*das Wissen des Menschen von Gott*) advances 'to man's self-knowledge *in* God' (*zum Sichwissen des Menschen in Gott*). This is not explicitly argued, but is implicit throughout: Man knows himself by knowing God, e.g. the Greeks in learning to portray their gods were learning about themselves, and the inadequacy of their portrayal goes hand in hand with a deficiency in their self-consciousness and hence in themselves. Religion is not, in Hegel's view, one activity among others that human beings engage in. It is an essential factor in their becoming human.
   (iv) God's self-knowledge is man's knowledge of God, God's 'self-consciousness in man' (*sein Selbstbewusstsein im Menschen*). This is not explicitly argued, but presupposed: cf. §§562, n. 4; 563, n. 1.

6. Carl Friedrich Göschel, *Aphorismen über Nichtwissen und absolutes Wissen im Verhältnisse zur christlichen Glaubenserkenntnis. Ein Beitrag zum Verständnisse der Philosophie unserer Zeit* [Aphorisms on Ignorance and Absolute Knowledge in relation to the Christian Faith: A Contribution to the Understanding of the Philosophy of Our Time] (Berlin, 1929), esp. 61 ff. Hegel reviewed this book in the *Jahrbücher für wissenschaftliche Kritik* for 1929. As a result of this review, Göschel, then a senior official in the appeal court at Nuremburg, initiated a correspondence with Hegel: see *Hegel: The Letters*, trans. C. Butler and C. Seiler (Bloomington, Ind.: Indiana University Press, 1984), 537–46.

NOTES TO §565

1. In pre-Christian religions the 'absolute' mind or spirit was known only in so far as it could be presented in a sensory 'shape'. In Christianity this sensory shape is 'sublated'. So now spirit is 'absolute' in a stricter sense: it is detached from the sensory and self-contained. It is 'in and for itself', the culmination of nature and mind or spirit. Spirit in nature is not 'in and for itself', but only in itself or implicit; spirit in the earlier phases of mind is for itself, but not in and for itself. But in this final stage of spirit, spirit is elevated to become in and for itself; it is independent of nature and the sensory, and fully self-conscious. That is its 'content'. The 'form' of something may be discordant with its content, as, for example, the poetic form of a didactic poem may be at odds with its prosaic content. This is the case with Christianity. 'Initially', before, that is, theologians and philosophers set to work on it, its content appears in an inappropriate form, that of representation.

2. When something is represented pictorially, its aspects or 'moments' are presented as separate from each other, either in space or, as in this case, in time. God (§567) is followed, and presupposed, by his incarnate son (§568), who is followed, and presupposed, by the descent of the Holy Spirit (§569). Each moment is distinct from the others, hence bounded by them and 'finite'. 'Determinations of

reflexion' are relational categories such as cause and effect: cf. §567, n. 1. The two terms of the relation are conceived as 'reflected' into each other: cf. §384, n. 2.
3. Faith and worship reunify what representation has separated. Hegel sometimes suggests that popular faith and worship are free of the defects introduced into Christianity by reflective theologians, and that his own version of Christianity is a restoration of simple faith on a higher level. (This is perhaps comparable to Berkeley's claim to be a defender of common sense.) However, while the 'determinations of reflexion' are no doubt introduced by theologians and philosophers, pictorial representation is rooted in popular faith.

NOTE TO §566

1. The 'content' of absolute spirit remains unitary. But the 'form' diverges into three 'spheres'. The 'content' appears in each of these spheres in a different form. In α) the content is universal and 'eternal'; it is self-centred or keeps to itself. In β) the content divides into the eternal 'essence' and its manifestation, which is not eternal: the phenomenal world into which the content (i.e. as Christ) enters. (As often, Hegel connects the creation and the incarnation: cf. §381, n. 20.) In γ) the 'alienated' world, the world of appearance produced in stage β, is reconciled with the eternal essence. This alludes to the descent of the Holy Spirit, while the 'withdrawal of the essence, etc.' is Christ's ascension. Since Hegel links the creation (of the world) with the incarnation (of Christ), he naturally links Christ's return to heaven with the redemption of the world by the dsecent of the Holy Spirit. (The words for 'reconciliation' and 'to reconcile', *Versöhnung* and *versöhnen*, are not etymologically related to *Sohn*, 'son', but Hegel probably connects them with it and sees, or half-sees, them as meaning 'making (someone) one's son': the world is a sort of prodigal son reconciled with its father.) The three forms correspond respectively to the concept, the 'judgement', and the 'syllogism'. The concept in α is unitary. In β it is divided in a 'judgement', an *Urteil* or, as Hegel sees it, an 'original division': cf. §389, n. 4. In γ unity is restored again by a syllogism, *Schluss*, which Hegel sees as a sort of conclusion or closure that brings together what the judgement divided: cf. §§389, n. 4; 399, n. 5. The three forms also correspond to the 'moments of the concept', viz. universality, particularity and individuality: cf. §§378, n. 10; 379, n. 5. The undifferentiated universal of α particularizes itself in β into two components, which are reunited in γ into a single individual.

NOTE TO §567

1. In the 'moment of universality', all three moments—universality, particularity, and individuality—occur in a non-temporal key. (1) The absolute spirit is the 'presupposition' (*das Vorausgesetzte*), the ungenerated starting-point of the process. (2) It generates something differentiated from itself, and becomes the 'universal essence' in contrast to its product. This is conceived in two ways. In the

'reflexion-determination of causality' (cf. §565, n. 2) it is the creation of heaven and earth. But causality has no place 'in this eternal sphere', so, properly speaking, it is the generation of the essence itself as its 'son'. (3) The essence and its son are identical in their difference; hence the difference between them 'eternally sublates itself'. So the 'mediation' between essence and son is 'self-sublating', and this, by a further 'mediation', transforms the absolute spirit from a 'substance' into 'concrete individuality and subjectivity', i.e. spirit.

Why is the absolute spirit the 'presupposition', when the whole process transforms it into 'spirit'? How is the 'first substance' related to 'absolute spirit'? Hegel's idea is this. The whole process must begin with spirit rather than simply with substance, because only spirit is sufficiently dynamic to initiate and oversee the process, whereas substance is too inert for the task. In the course of the process, however, absolute spirit demotes itself to a substance; this happens at stage (2), where it distinguishes itself as 'universal essence' from its 'son'. Then, at stage (3), by uniting with its son, it transforms itself back into spirit. The absolute spirit is comparable to a film-director, who acts the part of a character in his own film; at first the character he plays appears quite different from the director himself, but eventually it emerges that he is the director of the film we are watching.

The difference is that Hegel conceives this process to be a non-temporal logical movement or sequence, not a sequence of events in time. At the level of religion, he is influenced by texts such as John 1: 1: 'In the beginning was the Word, and the Word was with God, and the Word was God' and John 1: 14: 'And the Word was made flesh, and dwelt among us, . . .'. These texts imply that before the incarnation God was not simply the first member of the Trinity, entirely shorn of the second and third members. If that were so, it would be hard to explain how this simple deity manages to manifest himself in the world. Rather, God is, from the very beginning, internally complex, containing within himself in a non-temporal way the the other forms he will take in the course of time. Thus the 'Word' (in Greek the 'Logos') is both there at the beginning, and then becomes flesh at a definite time. Moreover, just as the 'son' in Hegel's Paragraph is both different from the universal essence and identical with it, the Word was both God (implying identity) and 'with God' (implying difference). The analogy of the film-director can shed light on this. Before making the film, the director has a plan in mind for the film he is to make. He himself as the maker of the film figures in the plan, and so does he himself as a character in the film. The plan prescribes a temporal sequence of events: he is to make his appearance only late on in the film. But the temporal sequence prescribed by the plan is not a temporal sequence of the parts of the plan: the director has it all in mind at the same time, both himself as director and himself as character. Something similar, Hegel believes, is involved in Christianity: a non-temporal Trinitarian order that is later realized as a temporal sequence of events. In Hegel's philosophical interpretation of Christianity, this non-temporal order corresponds to the 'logical Idea', which realizes itself in nature and mind: cf. §377, n. 4.

NOTES TO §568

1. *Urteil*, 'judgement', is taken as 'original [*ur-*] division [*teil*]': cf. §§554, n. 1; 566, n. 1.
2. The 'concrete eternal essence' is the result of the 'mediation' described in §567. It is 'presupposed', because process β begins with it.
3. In §567 the absolute spirit generated its own 'son' as an 'eternal', non-temporal 'moment' that mediated between absolute spirit as substance and absolute spirit as spirit. The 'son' suggests Christ, but here as elsewhere Hegel (perhaps with some help from St John's Gospel) fuses together the incarnation and the creation. The son, no longer eternal, bifurcates into two contrasting realms, nature and mind or spirit. Together these constitute 'appearance', the phenomenal world. The process corresponds to the way in which the 'logical Idea' portrayed in Hegel's logic passes over into the realms of nature and of spirit. This spirit is 'finite', since it is related to, hence distinct from, and bounded by, nature: cf. §379, n. 3.
4. To be evil spirit must be more than simply natural; it must be capable of reflective choices. An animal that acts by instinct and without knowledge cannot be evil (or good). To be evil spirit must, however, be involved in nature too. An angel lacking any natural desires to fulfil cannot be evil. Spirit's capacity for rational choice stems from its 'negativity'. It is negative because it asserts its independence, i.e. breaks loose from a merely natural condition so that it has knowledge of, and is thus capable of, both good and evil. This is described in the myth of the fall: cf. §405Z. and Enc.I, §24 Z.(2). On evil, cf. §382, nn. 4 and 5; §472. That spirit, though evil, is 'directed towards the eternal', implies that in β, as in α and γ, there is a reconciliation of sorts between the terms separated (God and 'appearance'), even if it is somewhat unsatisfactory.

NOTES TO §569

1. The third term of the triad, 'individuality' (*Einzelnheit*), removes the 'opposition' between the first two terms, 'universality' (roughly, God the creator) and 'particularity' (the created world). Its association with 'subjectivity and the concept' implies its unity, in contrast to the 'judgement' of §568 (cf. §554, n. 1), but it also suggests Christ. This unity results from three 'syllogisms' or conclusions: cf. §571. Each syllogism or *Schluss* (from *schliessen*, 'to close', as well as 'conclude, infer') unites two extremes by means of a middle term. Hegel's account owes something to a traditional syllogism such as: 'All men are mortal; All Greeks are men; All Greeks are mortal'. Here the middle term is 'men', which unites the two terms occurring in the conclusion, 'Greeks' (the 'minor' term) and 'mortal' (the 'major' term): cf. §399, n. 5. But a Hegelian syllogism does not consist of propositions or judgements, only of three terms. One of these terms is conceived as universal, one as particular and one as individual; one of these terms mediates between the other two. In the syllogisms that follow it not always easy to pick out the three terms, since Hegel is forcing his thoughts into a triadic pattern that does not readily accommodate them.

2. The middle term is the son, not the eternal son of §567, but this son 'transposed' into time. He can mediate between God and the world, since he has a foot in both camps. He is immediately 'identical with the essence', i.e. God, yet has 'sensory existence'. His 'putting' himself 'in judgement' immediately suggests Christ's judgement by Pontius Pilate, and his subsequent crucifixion, dying in the 'pain of negativity': cf. §382, n. 1. Christ survived this ordeal and returned out of negativity to spiritualize and redeem the world. But incarnation, passion and resurrection are here intertwined with other themes, which they symbolize. In §568 the son's 'judgement' was an 'original division', a bifurcation into nature and mind. Mind or man became evil owing to his detachment from nature, while nevertheless retaining natural desires to motivate his misconduct. In §§527, 537, and 546, the 'universal substance' referred not explicitly to God, but to the human social order, to ethical life. Here too it carries this suggestion. The 'individual self-consciousness' is then not simply Christ, but the individual citizen imbued with the norms of his society. In such a citizen 'evil' is 'implicitly sublated': raw natural urges are tamed and civilized by social norms. Another idea symbolized by Christ is this. The individual citizen suffers and dies, owing to his sensory, natural aspect. But the social order incorporates him into its tradition, and preserves his memory; it maintains and enhances itself through the death of the individual. In this sense too the syllogism is a unification of spirit with nature. For Hegel, Christ and his fate represents man and the human condition in general. Cf. §552 on the relationship between religion and ethical life.

NOTES TO §570

1. 'This objective totality' is the 'Idea of the eternal, but living spirit, present in the world', the conclusion of the syllogism presented in §569. This is not Christ as an individual, but the spirit that informs and redeems the world as a whole. However, since the individual 'subject' is as yet only 'finite', i.e. distinct from the spirit and not imbued with it, at first he regards the totality as other than himself, as something that he perceives or 'intuits'. This refers to eyewitnesses of the biblical events, perhaps especially to doubting Thomas ('Except I shall see in his hands the print of the nails, . . . , I will not believe', John 20: 25), and to the requirement that Judas's replacement as an apostle should have witnessed the resurrection (Acts 1: 22). What the subject intuits is the 'truth', but only the truth 'in itself' or implicitly, since what is intuited is only a perceptible model of a truth that is not perceptible.

2. Since what the subject intuits is the truth, he has not only the evidence ('witness') of his eyes but also the witness of the spirit 'in him'. (Cf. e.g. Romans 8: 16: 'The Spirit itself beareth witness with our spirit, that we are the children of God'.) At first he regards himself as bad and worthless in comparison to Christ. This is because of his 'immediate nature', i.e. his unredeemed natural urges, etc: cf. §569, n. 2, and also the 'unhappy consciousness' of PS, pp. 16–38. In Christ, by contrast, an individual man is united with the divine essence. The subject is inspired by this 'example' to shed his 'natural' aspect, thereby 'joining together'

(*zusammenzuschliessen*) with Christ and thus with the 'essence'. This involves the 'pain of negativity': the pain of the crucifixion symbolizes the pain of relinquishing one's 'natural' self. The middle term here is Christ as the Idea of the spirit. By his 'example', he unites the subject with God. If Hegel has in mind a particular passage of the Bible, it is perhaps Acts 2: 37–47, where converts to Christianity 'sold their possessions and goods, and parted them to all men, as every man had need' (Acts 2: 45).

3. In the second syllogism, the subject was the active party. In this third syllogism the 'essence', i.e. God, is the active party. It has, by the 'mediation' of Christ and/or the subject, brought about its own realization as the Holy Spirit. This third syllogism looks more like a summary of the other two (cf. 'the one syllogism' in §571, n. 1) than a distinct syllogism coordinate with the other two.

NOTES TO §571

1. It is not clear whether the 'three syllogisms' are presented respectively in §§567, 568, and 569–70, or whether they all occur within §§569–70, introduced by the numbers '(1)', '(2)', and '(3)'. The first alternative presents difficulties. §567 contains a syllogism, the joining together of God with the eternal son he generates, but §568 does not contain a syllogism: it presents the alienation of the world from God,—unless spirit's being 'directed towards the eternal' (cf. §568 n. 4) is meant to count as a syllogistic closure. The second alternative is also difficult, since (3) does not look much like a distinct syllogism.

   Probably Hegel has both alternatives in mind. He is working with at least two triads, not just one. The first consists of (α) God, the universal moment, (β) the created and fallen world, the moment of particularity, and (γ) the redemption of the world by spirit, the moment of individuality. The third moment of this first triad, (γ), involves a second triad consisting of (a) God the Father, (b) Christ, and (c) the Holy Spirit. The triads are easily confused, since God is the first term of each, (α) and (a), and the Holy Spirit, (c), also appears as the third term of each triad: it is what redeems the world in (γ). Where the triads differ is in their second term: the fallen world, (β), is hardly the same as Christ, (b). Hegel makes them look the same by referring to both (β) and (b) as the 'son'. One justification for this is that in Hegel's view Christ represents man in general; this is why in him 'evil' is sublated only 'implicitly' (*an sich*), not explicitly: cf. §569, n. 2.

   The first of these triads, (α)–(β)–(γ), obviously involves a syllogistic closure, and this takes place in §§567–70. There are, however, syllogisms within syllogisms. In §567, (α) itself involves a syllogism that provides a non-temporal model of the syllogism as a whole. There is no obvious syllogism in (β), but (γ), the ultimate reconciliation of (α) and (β), involves three syllogisms, deploying the terms of the second triad, (a), (b), and (c). The obvious middle term here is (b), Christ, who mediates between God the Father, (a), and the Holy Spirit, (c), which is more or less the same as (γ), the realization of spirit in the world. Why then does Hegel introduce three syllogisms into (γ)? His motive is his belief that if three terms are to be closely and definitively joined together syllogistically, then they must be joined by three syllogisms, with each term in turn serving as the middle term. Thus not only should (a) be connected to (c) by means of (b), but (b) should be joined to (c) by means of (a), and (a) to (b) by means of (c). This is how logic, nature, and mind are joined together by three syllogisms in §§575–7. In Enc. I, §198 and SL, pp. 723–4, civil society, the state, and the individual are said to be related by three syllogisms in this way. In this case each term in turn can be seen, with some plausibility, as the link between the other two. But this is not so in the case of God, Christ, and the Holy Spirit; only Christ looks like a plausible link.

2. As traditionally conceived the development of spirit forms a temporal sequence: first God, then Christ, then the Holy Spirit. But the closure of spirit with itself effected by the syllogisms results in two types of 'simplicity' incompatible with temporal succession: (1) 'faith and devotional feeling'; (2) 'thinking' or philosophy. The two types of simplicity differ. Faith and worship do not split up their object at all, though they still conceive it in representational rather than conceptual terms: cf. §565, n. 3. They result from the syllogisms because they are essentially involved in the Holy Spirit, they are in fact more or less equivalent to it. Philosophy, by contrast, splits its object into three, though the parts or moments are not successive in time and they are regarded as inseparable. Hegel's account of Christianity so far has been thoughtful philosophy, not simply presenting the conceptions of ordinary Christians or even of theologians, who do not usually conceive God as a triad of syllogisms. But it is a philosophical account of spirit, of the 'truth', as it appears in the form of pictorial representation, not in the form of thought. To assume the form of thought it has to undergo yet further revision, eliminating especially the temporal succession.

The transition from religion to philosophy is somewhat abrupt. Faith and worship are a necessary requirement of religion: if there had been no appropriate faith or worship, the Holy Spirit would not have descended. Philosophy is not in this way an intrinsic requirement of religion. It is a requirement of Hegel's own philosophical beliefs. First, spirit must, if it is to complete its development, join together with itself. Second, if spirit is to join together with itself it must become wholly transparent to itself in prosaic, conceptual terms. For Hegel's justification of these beliefs, see §563, n. 1.

3. Hegel wants to distinguish his own type of thinking from the 'irony' of such Romantics as Friedrich Schlegel (1772–1829). On Romantic irony and on its affinity to Hegel's thought, see ILA, pp. xxviii–xxx, 70–5, and 155–64. The ironist regards himself (and occasionally herself, since women held a respected position in the Romantic circle) as something like God. The ironist recognizes no objective moral norms, no ideals worthy of unequivocal commitment. He deals with the laws of logic as he pleases and, as an artist at least, can endorse any view he likes. He toys with ideas only to drop them when they no longer suit him. He surveys competing doctrines and causes from a superior, Olympian position. This sounds not wholly unlike Hegel. Hegel too does not stick to a 'one-sided' doctrine or cause, but surveys the development of the mind in all its facets and oppositions. Might irony be the ultimate phase of mind? Does the sublation of

Christian *Vorstellung* (which some Romantics welcomed, though they later converted to Catholicism in droves) leave man in a godlike position, able to dispose of things, in thought at least, as he will? What prevents this is that spirit is, and is known as, not simply 'for itself' but also as 'in itself' and 'objectively unfolding itself', that thinking is not just subjective, but has a 'content that is in and for itself' as its object. If spirit were only for itself, not in itself, this would mean that the third term of the Trinity had entirely supplanted its 'mediation', the first two terms. The third term would then simply amount to human thinking or, for that matter, human feeling, and would be free of any objective constraint. The ironist's thinking is thus 'infinite', unbounded and unrestrained, but merely 'formal': it considers any object, takes on any content it likes. Hegel's thinking is also infinite, without bounds or limits, but it has an 'absolute' content. It is free not in the ironist's sense that it can think what and as it likes, but in the sense that its object and the constraints it imposes are wholly appropriate to it and not felt as constraints. Hegelian freedom is analogous to the freedom of the skilled mathematician at home in the world of number; the ironist's freedom is the freedom to think that $2 + 2 = 5$. The ironist conceives of the thinking subject as quite distinct from and unaffected by the objects of thought. The Hegelian subject is deeply involved in the object of thought and indelibly marked by it; even when it passes on to a new object it carries its former object along with it. The ironist conceives of the field of thought, the world, as consisting of discrete islands such that thought can hop from one to another just as it pleases. Hegel conceives of the world as a system, knitted together by interconnections along which thought, itself systematic, must travel.

NOTES TO §572

1. Philosophy is 'science', *Wissenschaft*, a word used more widely than 'science' is in English. It implies that philosophy is a systematic, methodical discipline, but it leaves open the extent to which philosophy depends on empirical data. Hegel believes that philosophy has the same 'content' as art and religion, but presents it in a different 'form'. Art presents the content in the form of 'intuition', roughly sensations or perception: cf. §446 ff. Religion presents it in the form of 'representation', roughly pictorial images. Philosophy presents it in the form of thought. Thus art, religion, and philosophy form an ascending series. Art splits up the 'content' into 'independent shapes': the five arts (architecture, sculpture, painting, music, and poetry) present different aspects of the content, and different aspects again are captured by the three art-forms (symbolism, classicism, and romanticism). The form of art is 'external'—both in itself, because art presents the content to the senses, and also external to its content, because the content is essentially unitary and not adequately presented in sensory intuition. Artistic production is 'subjective', since it depends on individual artists, not on the content itself. Religion brings the content together into a single 'totality'. It unfolds the content in representation, but 'mediates' it: religion establishes syllogistic interconnections between Father, Son, and Holy Spirit. (Art as such establishes no

intelligible connections between the different arts or between the different art-forms.) Philosophy (like religion) keeps the content in a whole, while (like art) it surveys it in 'intuition', but now a 'spiritual' rather than sensory intuition. Philosophy is the 'concept' of art and religion, in that it explicitly thinks about the conceptual structure implicit in art and religion. Thus what looks contingent in art and religion is shown to be conceptually necessary, but also 'free', in that it is self-determining, not determined by external factors.

Hegel's claim that philosophy is the 'unity' of art and religion has more than one meaning. Philosophy incorporates the essential features of both art and religion: it unifies the content even more than religion does, while it preserves a spiritual intuition analogous to art's sensory intuition. (The introduction of philosophy's 'spiritual intuition' is designed to suggest that philosophy owes as much to art as it does to religion and that it effects a restoration of art on a higher level. Perhaps Hegel means that philosophy, like a painting, presents the content without the temporal succession associated with religion.) Again, philosophy sees that art and religion have their content in common; art and religion themselves cannot see this, since neither of them reflects significantly on the other. Philosophy can also see that it too shares this content, since it reflects on art, religion, and philosophy itself, while neither art nor religion reflects on philosophy.

NOTES TO §573

1. 'Absolute representation' is an unusual combination: representation is usually regarded as too lowly, and too dependent on sensory experience, to be described as 'absolute'. The absolute representation is primarily the Christian religion, which in §564 (and often in LPR) is referred to as the 'absolute religion'. But it is also meant to include art, which is an essential aspect of the 'revelation'. The two forms assumed by the content of the absolute representation are art and religion. The first form, art, is the 'objective and external revelation'. The second form, religion, presents the 'subjective' side; it is perhaps the 'subjective and internal revelation', though Hegel does not actually use this expression. This explains the necessity of the two forms. Art presents the content objectively, while religion presents it subjectively. Philosophy, we might surmise, presents it in both ways.

   The second form, religion, involves three stages: a withdrawal inwards, i.e. the beginnings of 'faith'; a movement outwards, towards 'the presupposition', i.e. towards God; and the 'identification' of faith with the presupposition, i.e. the unification of one's inner withdrawal, faith, with God. The first form, art, also has three phases or components. Art ascends from 'immediate intuition', by way of the 'poetry' (*Poesie*) of immediate intuition, to 'the presupposing representation'. Immediate intuition is the form common to all the fine arts, except poetry. Poetry, in Hegel's view, does not rely on intuition in the same way as other arts do; the sheer sound of poetry is relatively unimportant. Poetry depends on *Vorstellung*, 'imagination' or 'representation', rather than intuition: see ILA, pp. 95–7, 194–6. Hence poetry forms a bridge to the *Vorstellung* characteristic of religion. But what is the 'presupposing representation' and what does it presuppose? What it presupposes must be the 'presupposition' involved in the second form. That is God. So the representation that presupposes it is Christ. This coheres with Hegel's view of Christian art. Art, especially painting and sculpture, cannot portray God the Father adequately, but it can portray Christ: see ILA, pp.76–7, 165–60. It also coheres with the role of the incarnation within religion: Christ is the 'objective and external revelation' of God. Hence the intuitional form of art is required by religion itself. In portraying Christ, art provides the objective revelation that religion requires. It might be objected that, in the view of believers, Christ really appeared in the flesh, so that artistic portrayals of him are not necessary; if his appearance needed to be recorded and transmitted to later generations, this is achieved by prosaic accounts such as the Gospels rather than by art. Hegel disagrees. He believes that it hardly matters whether the events recorded in the Gospels really occurred or not. What matters is what the mind makes of those events. The real incarnation occurs not in Palestine two thousand years ago, but in artistic (and also prosaic) portrayals of it through the ages.

2. This 'cognition' (*Erkennen*) is 'recognition' (*Anerkennen*) of the content and its form in the sense of 'acknowledgement' or 'endorsement '. Philosophy accepts the content but liberates it from the one-sided forms, i.e. from the 'intuition' of art and the 'representation' of religion. The 'absolute form' is not one-sided, not one form in contrast to others. It is not a form at all in the way in which intuition and representation are, but simply the immanent structure of the content. To take a simple analogy, the mathematical content '2+2 = 4' can be presented to young children in the form of a picture (of, say, the addition of two apples to two pears) and to older children in the form of a representation (of, say, the increase of one's pocket-money from £2 a week to £4 a week). When '2+2 = 4' is presented without pictures or representations, it has no form at all comparable to these: it is just the naked, prosaic truth. It still has a form of sorts, 'x+y=z' or '2x+2x=4x'. But the 'content' is not detachable from this form in the way that it is detachable from pictures and representations. It is a limitation of this analogy that, in Hegel's view, the 'absolute form' is 'identical' with the content, whereas the arithmetical content ('2+2 = 4') is not identical with or deducible from its form ('x+y=z').

3. The 'movement' is the process of liberating the 'content' from the forms of intuition and representation. What philosophy (or the 'movement') then arrives at is its own 'concept'. Unlike art and religion, philosophy grasps its own concept or nature. But its concept (as Hegel explains in §574) is the logical Idea, the self-thinking logical structure with which philosophy begins. The logical Idea is, as it were, the seed or germ from which philosophy develops: cf. §379, n. 5. So at its highest stage, when it considers the content of art and religion, philosophy not only grasps its own nature, it also returns to its beginning. Philosophy needs to give a special account of art and religion. But it does not need to give a special account of itself. All it needs to do is look back on its earlier stages, in particular the Logic (Enc. I).

4. Hegel distinguishes three 'forms': (1) his own 'speculative thinking' (cf. §564, n. 4), (2) 'representation', and (3) the 'reflective intellect'. That he speaks of the 'forms' (*Formen*) of speculative thought' suggests that he has in mind not just one form that the content can assume, but also the 'categories' or 'thought-forms' to which he refers below: cf. §573, n. 6. He thus uses '*Form*' in two ways: for the form of speculative thought, in contrast to the forms of representation and intellect, and for the particular thought-forms, such as being and substance, that appear within speculative thought. The distinction between speculative thought, representation, and intellect emerges and is 'assessed' (*beurteilt*) in the Logic especially (cf. Enc. I, §§20, 80–2), but also in the Philosophy of Mind (§§422-3., 451 ff., 465–8). The distinction between the speculative and the non-speculative thus develops of its own accord within speculative thought, and there 'directs' (*richten*) itself. (*Richten*, lit. 'to straighten out', has a variety of senses, including to 'judge, pass a judicial sentence on'; the proximity of *beurteilt*, from *beurteilen*, 'to judge, assess', suggests that it here carries the suggestion of 'judge'.) The superiority of the speculative emerges of its own accord, and is not something imposed or presupposed by Hegel.

5. Apart from the details of nature (Enc. II) and the earlier part of Enc. III, the content of religion and philosophy is the same. But whereas only a few people study philosophy, religion is the 'truth for all men'. In the Preface to the second, 1827, edition of Enc. Hegel invokes Homer's Iliad (i. 401, ii. 813, xiv. 290, xx. 74): 'Religion is the mode and manner of consciousness, in which the truth is for all men, for men of every culture; but the scientific cognition of the truth is a particular mode of their consciousness, the labour of which only a few men, not all men, undergo. *The content is the same*, but just as Homer says of some things, that they have two names, one in the language of the gods, the other in the language of everyday men, so there are two languages for this content, one the language of feeling, of representation, and of intellectual thinking nestling in finite categories and onesided abstractions, the other the language of the concrete concept'. But here his language echoes the Bible rather than Homer: 'The same [namely John the Baptist] came for a witness, to bear witness of the Light, that all men through him might believe' (John 1: 7).The spirit on whose testimony or 'witness' faith rests is the Holy Spirit of Romans, 8: 16: 'The Spirit itself beareth witness with our spirit, that we are the children of God'. (Cf. §§555, n. 1; 570, n. 2) Prima facie this spirit is not identical with the human mind or spirit. But in so far as it witnesses, it is 'the spirit in man', hence present in all men, not just apostles or philosophers. This witness is 'in itself substantial', i.e. it is in us independently of any particular formulation. But it first expresses itself in terms of the 'culture' (*Bildung*) of the secular or 'worldly' consciousness of the time, i.e. in terms more appropriate to finite things than to religion. Hence there is a misfit between religious content, which is 'speculative' and 'infinite', and the 'finite' terms in which it is expressed. 'Finite' categories are categories applicable to finite entities, but also categories bounded by other categories, in that they exclude their application to the same entity. If, for example, God is different from the world, he cannot also be identical with the

world, if 'difference' and 'identity' are finite categories. But such categories do not readily accommodate religious content. If the content is retained, certain incoherencies occur in religious discourse, breaches of the principles of formal logic, which Hegel groups under the 'principle of formal identity'. In one of his early unpublished writings, 'The Spirit of Christianity and its Fate' (*Hegel's Early Theological Writings*, trans. T. M. Knox (Chicago: University of Chicago Press, 1948), 256; cf. PH, p. 331 and §567, n. 1), Hegel noted such an illogicality in John, 1:1: 'In the beginning was the Word, and the Word was with God, and the Word was God'. Here the 'word' (*logos*) is said to be both identical to God and 'with God' (*pros ton theon*). According to finite thought, if x is with y, then x is not identical to y. But Hegel regards such 'inconsistency' as an essential corrective to the finite categories in which religious content is inevitably expressed.

6. Speculative philosophy transposes religious content from sensory representations and finite categories into 'thought-forms' (*Denkformen*) that are entirely appropriate to the content. It is then attacked from three directions: (1) It has 'too little of God' for religious orthodoxy, i.e. it lacks the pictorial form of religion, and its religious content goes unnoticed. (2) It has 'too much' of God for a 'self-styled philosophy', presumably the same philosophy that attacks the incoherence of orthodox religion. However, the accusation now is not that speculative philosophy supports orthodox religion, but that it identifies God with the universe and thus makes everything God: pantheism. (3) A 'contentless piety' also attacks it for pantheism, for having 'too much' of God. These accusers have some connection with those referred to in §564 (see especially n. 3), who claim that the quest for knowledge of God is futile and impious. If God is fully knowable (they might argue), then God is identical, or at least intrinsically connected, with the world, since our cognitive powers cannot span the gulf between our world and a god entirely distinct from it. Conversely, if God is identical with the world, then God is as knowable as the world is.

   'Atheism' is the denial of God's existence, 'pantheism' the identification of God with everything. The words stem from the Greek *theos*, 'god', *a-* (the 'privative alpha'), and *pan*, 'all, everything'. Pantheism is usually associated with the belief that the universe has a special unity; hence it is also the 'All-one doctrine', *All-Eins-Lehre*.

7. The claim that God is identical with the world can plausibly be interpreted either as atheistic or as pantheistic. The claim is atheistic, if it has the force of 'God is no more than (or 'nothing but') the world', and thus implicitly denies the existence of God as traditionally understood or in any other acceptable sense. It is pantheistic, if it does not have this force, that is, if it implicitly ascribes to the world 'divine' features, features that an atheist would characteristically deny to it. The limiting case of non-atheistic pantheism is what Hegel calls 'acosmism', the belief that only God exists, whereas the world does not exist except as an appearance. Spinoza identified God with nature: *deus sive natura*. Hegel tends to interpret this as acosmism: Enc. I, §§50, 151Z. By contrast, Pierre Bayle in his article on Spinoza in his *Dictionnaire historique et critique* (1696–7) asserted that

Spinoza was an atheist. Hegel implies that to say that someone is a pantheist, one need not have any very 'determinate representation' of God. Since pantheism ranges from what is effectively atheism to theistic acosmism, and covers a variety of intermediate possibilities, the attribution of pantheism presupposes no definite conception of God. But does the attribution of atheism presuppose a determinate representation of God? There are many different conceptions of God: he may be conceived anthropomorphically or as, say, the ground of all being. One might say that someone is an atheist if he denies the existence of anything corresponding to *any* of these conceptions. All that is required for a significant attribution of atheism is that the conception of God in play should not be so vacuous as to exclude nothing, so that no one, or at least no sane person, could possibly count as an atheist. (In Enc. I, §71 Hegel argues that our conception of God has become so empty that it is hardly possible for anyone to be an atheist.) But such a minimally determinate conception of God is hardly more determinate than the conception of God presupposed by an attribution of pantheism. It is, of course, likely that someone who condemns atheism, regarding an attribution of atheism as an 'accusation', will have in view a more than minimally determinate conception God, regarding God as, say, a mind or person, rather than as simply the ground of all being; such believers usually have a conception sufficiently determinate for God to be worth believing in, and worth disbelieving in. But this is not logically required for the accusation to hit its target.

8. Any determinate representation of God has a counterpart in philosophy, but its philosophical counterpart is conceptual rather than representational. For example, the representation of God as the Lord of the world might have, as its philosophical counterpart, the thought of a unique substance, of which every finite entity is just a 'mode'. A religious believer in the Lord of the world regards Spinoza as an atheist, since Spinoza believes only in the unique substance. Conversely, however, Spinoza, or Hegel, do not regard the religious believer as an atheist on account of his denial of the unique substance. This is because they, as philosophers, think both about philosophy and about religion, and can therefore recognize the correspondence between the representation of the Lord of the world and the thought of the unique substance. The religious believer, by contrast, cannot *think* about religion, let alone philosophy. Hence he cannot discern the correspondence between his own representation and the philosophical version of it, and so regards the philosopher as an atheist.

9. Hegel is here trying to explain not so much why philosophy is accused of pantheism, but rather why philosophy is no longer accused of atheism. This is because the conception of God has been so diluted that hardly anyone can count as an atheist. Religion is regarded as just a 'subjective feeling' directed towards an indeterminate object of veneration. Hence veneration of a cow, etc. (also mentioned in Enc. I, §72) counts as worship of God, not only because it is worship of *something*, namely a cow, but perhaps also because the cow-worshipper himself has an indeterminate conception of 'God in general', which, in his view, the cow points towards. The theologians Hegel is criticizing (Schleiermacher in

particular) are not only ready to count cow-worship as a religion and as worship of God. They also have no interest in regarding such a religion as inadequate or in assessing one way of conceiving God as better than another. All that matters is that one has a religion and thus worships God in one's own way. Their indeterminate conception of God supplies no criterion or incentive for evaluation of religions. They grant that other people have had, and perhaps still have, a variety of determinate conceptions of God. But this is only of 'historical' interest. (Hegel here uses the word *historisch* rather than his usual word for 'historical', *geschichtlich*. For Hegel, *historisch* has a mildly derogatory flavour of unsystematic empiricism, whereas what is *geschichtlich* is of systematic philosophical importance. We might compare 'That is just history/only of historical interest' in contrast to 'That was a truly historic occasion'.) Hegel's objection to this indeterminate conception of God is not so much that it obliges us to count cow-worship as God-worship, but more that it does not allow us to prefer Christian God-worship to cow-worship. After all, it hardly matters where we locate the boundary between atheism and God-worship. What matters is that we should be able to distinguish worse forms of God-worship from better forms of God-worship. (Similarly, it does not matter if our concept of art is sufficiently inclusive for us to count an unmade bed as a work of art, as long as it enables us to regard it as bad art.)

If these theologians do not regard cow-worshippers as atheists, then a fortiori they are unwilling to regard a philosopher (such as Spinoza or Hegel) as an atheist. But why do they regard the philosopher as a pantheist rather than as a plain theist? For several reasons. First, these philosophers are obviously not plain theists in the sense that they believe God to be a distinct entity, an entity different from nature and humanity. Secondly, pantheism, though a lesser offence than atheism, is still an offence as compared with theism; philosophers are convicted of a lesser crime, not completely acquitted. Thirdly, however, the accusation of pantheism stems from the intrinsic nature of the 'new theology' itself. Although the words 'God . . . is supposed to be in fact everything and everything to be God' express the view attributed to philosophy by the new theology, the new theology itself has a tendency towards pantheism. If God is a distinct entity, different from nature and humanity, then someone who worships a cow does not worship God. If the cow-worshipper is to count as worshipping God, then God must be conceived as simply any object of appropriate worship, whatever it may be. If a cow is worshipped, then God is a cow. If a monkey is worshipped, then God is a monkey. And so on. God is in a way everything, though most worshippers are discriminating: they identify God with a cow, but not, say, with a cat, while others identify him with a cat, not a cow. But most worshippers identify God with some finite entity or other. There are two exceptions to this. First, the new theologians themselves do not identify God with any particular finite entity. They regard 'God' as a variable, an 'x', holding the place of any specification of a finite entity with which other worshippers may choose to replace it. Secondly, the philosophers do not venerate any particular finite entity at the expense of the rest. So if they, like everyone else, worship God, they must be identifying him with everything, with the world as a whole. And that is pantheism, 'too much God'. See also §573, n. 10.

10. Hegel here gives his own explanation of the charge of pantheism. The new theology involves a sort of dualism. On the one hand there is God, an indeterminate 'abstract universality'. On the other hand there are the determinate entities of the world, entities which exist just as much as God does. Since God is intrinsically so abstract, he, or our conception of him, cannot acquire any determinate content, unless he derives it in some way from worldly entities, in particular by being identified with some worldly entity or entities. This position looks similar to 'philosophy', especially to Spinozism. For philosophy too ascribes universality to God (as, say, the unique substance) and also acknowledges worldly entities. So the new theology assumes that for philosophy too the universality of God derives its determinate content from worldly things. But the new theologians have missed two differences between philosophy and the new theology. First, the universality postulated by philosophy is not 'abstract', but 'in and for itself'. That implies that this universality generates its own determinacy, and does not need to borrow it from worldly things. Secondly, for philosophy worldly things do not retain the being or substantiality that is usually attributed to them. According to Spinoza, for example, they are simply 'modes' of the divine substance. Hence they are not in a position to lend determinacy to God even if God needed to borrow it from them.

This account implies that philosophy amounts to 'acosmism' (cf. §573, n. 7), the denial of the reality of worldly things. This is a version of pantheism: if God alone exists, then God is 'all' or 'everything'. But it does not follow that God is a cow, since cows and other finite entities do not fall within the domain of 'everything': they lack 'substantiality'. Hegel often implies that he himself is an acosmist, and he certainly prefers acosmism to atheistic pantheism (the doctrine that only worldly entities exist) and to dualistic theism (the doctrine that both God and the world exist as distinct entities). But Hegel's own view postulates a complex identity-in-difference between God and the world rather than the sheer identity and sheer difference involved in acosmism, atheism, and theism.

11. 'Exoteric' (*exoterisch(e)*) means 'intelligible to outsiders', from the Greek *exō*, 'outside'. It was applied by Aristotle to his popular writings (now lost) in contrast to his 'esoteric' writings, writings meant for the initiated (from the Greek *esō*, 'inside'). Hegel's Remarks are often exoteric, in contrast to his esoteric Paragraphs. Here he connects the idea of an exoteric discussion with the discussion of 'fact(s)' (*Faktum, Fakta*). A fact is here a *mere* fact, something that just is the case, regardless of the explanation or justification of it. A 'fact' contrasts with a 'concept', at least when a concept is treated as it should be, that is, analysed, explained or justified. But as Hegel explains later (cf. §573, n. 30), a concept may be viewed in an 'external' way and then it is treated as a fact. For example, 'Hegel says he is not a pantheist', is a statement of fact, and so perhaps is: 'Hegel was not a pantheist', if it is based solely on the fact of his denial. If we say: 'Pantheism is true for such and such reasons', that is not a statement of fact, since it involves conceptual analysis and argument. Somewhere in between is a claim of

the sort discussed in §573, nn. 9, 10: 'Although Hegel does not say he is a pantheist and even says that he is not, he must really be a pantheist, since pantheism is entailed by other doctrines he endorses'. In this case the 'external view' of concepts falters, since the claim invites an analysis of the concept of pantheism. The question whether or not Hegel was ever a pantheist cannot be as factual as the question whether he ever grew a moustache.

The factual question which Hegel proceeds to discuss is whether anyone has ever accepted the following version of pantheism: each and every thing in the world around us (trees, pens, paper, etc.) is fully real, and all these things together constitute God. At most Hegel shows that some oriental pantheists have not held this view, not that no one has ever held it. His reason for doubting that anyone holds the view is conceptual rather than factual. The view in question does not differ from atheism, apart from conferring an honorific title, 'God', on the natural world. As soon as 'God' is taken in anything like the traditional sense, this diminishes the 'substantiality' of worldly things, reducing them to, say, thoughts in God's mind. Cf. §573, n. 16 on the distinction between 'Everything' and 'All'.

12. The *Bhagavad Gita*, the 'Song of the Lord', composed around the third century BC, is India's most popular religious text. It forms a part of a much larger Sanskrit epic, the *Mahabharata*. The *Bhagavad Gita* was edited by August Wilhelm von Schlegel (1767–1845), the elder brother of Friedrich von Schlegel, with this title: '*Bhagavad-Gita id est* ΘΕΣΠΕΣΙΟΝ ΜΕΛΟΣ *sive almi Krishnae et Arjunae colloquium de rebus divinis*. Textum recensuit, adnotationes criticas et interpretationem Latinam adiecit Aug. Guil. a. Schlegel. Bonn 1823'. (*Bhagavad Gita, that is, a sacred song or a conversation of the gracious Krishna and Arjuna about religion*. Aug. Wm. von Schlegel revised the text and added critical notes and an interpretation in Latin. Bonn, 1823.) Wallace replaced the 'citation given by Hegel from Schlegel's translation' with the 'version (in one or two points different) in the *Sacred Books of the East*, vol.viii' (Wallace, p.306, n. 1). I have reinstated Hegel's translation of Schlegel.

13. Krishna, the hero of the *Bhagavad Gita*, was regarded as an incarnation of Vishnu, one of the two deities immediately subordinate to Brahma, the divine essence or absolute which manifests itself in the world. Siva was the other deity subordinate to Brahma. Siva was the destructive principle, and Vishnu the conservative principle. The Rudras were a group of deities dealing with destruction. Meru was a mountain at the centre of the world. Indra, the god of storms and battle, was one of the nature-deities worshipped by the people who produced the Veda or sacred lore.

14. Maya, or Maja, is a godess who personifies deception and magic. In the Shankara (788–820 AD) it is the principle of distortion or illusion. 'Magia' is Schlegel's Latin translation of the name.

15. Vasudeva was a Hindu god, Krishna's father rather than Krishna himself.

16. Hegel distinguishes between 'this/the All' (*dieses/das All*) and 'the Everything' (*das Alles*). '*Das All*' was a regular expression for 'the universe', but for Hegel *das All* is not simply the universe, since 'the universe' can mean 'all existing

things', i.e. what Hegel means by 'the Everything'. 'The All' is the universe conceived as a single, unified entity, while 'the Everything' is the universe conceived as the collection of all existing entities, on the assumption that there are many such entities, not just one. If 'the All' in Hegel's sense is fully real, then the Everything, finite entities, are less than fully real, since they are somehow dependent on the All. (The singular All and the plural Everything cannot simply coexist, being equally independent and real, since then the universe would consist of two components, the All and the Everything, and thus lack the unity required for it to be the All.) The Eleatic school were followers of Parmenides (c.540–c.480 BC) of Elea in southern Italy. In the surviving fragments of his poetry, Parmenides denied the reality of motion, plurality, and change. On Spinoza, see §389, n. 6. Spinoza called the unique substance 'God'. A believer in the All, however, need not regard it as God. Someone who believes that the All is matter or energy or (like Schopenhauer) the will could well deny that it is God. But Hegel would perhaps disagree with them on this, arguing that they do believe in God, but the wrong sort of God.

17. According to Nicolin and Pöggeler, Henry Thomas Colebroke (1765–1837) expressed this view in *On the Vedas or Sacred Writings of the Hindus, Asiatic Researches*, 8 (1805), 369–476. Hegel's 'brief quotations' suggested that Indian religion is monotheistic, but they did not indicate the central role of Brahma, the divine essence of which the world is the manifestation. Immediately below ('proximate') Brahma are the gods, especially Vishnu and Siva, and below them the Everything. The gods are, in Hegel's view, not full 'substantialities', since they depend on Brahma and eventually disappear in Brahma. Nor are they even fully gods, only 'called' gods.

18. Brahma is a 'spiritual' (*geistigen*) god in that it is represented not as an embodied person, but as a creative principle, even as a mind. However, it is not conceived as internally 'concrete', so that no explanation is provided of its creative and destructive power. Hence the entities that are supposed to be dependent on and structured by Brahma retain a de facto independence. (Brahma is comparable to a nominally absolute ruler who lacks the means to prevent his provincial governors from operating independently.) So a disorderly polytheism persists alongside monotheism. This why the Indian worships the ape, etc. But even this does not amount to the pantheism referred to in §573, n. 11. No Indian worships everything; worship is reserved for some things and denied to others.

Hegel's criticism of Brahma is similar to his criticism of Spinoza's substance: cf. §389, n. 6. The abstractness of Brahma and of Spinoza's substance contrasts with the internal concreteness of the God of Christianity discussed in §567, n. 1.

19. To predicate 'empty numerical unity' of the world is to say that there is one and only one world. This tells us nothing about the intrinsic unity of the world. The world may nevertheless resemble a collection of bric-a-brac, which is counted as *one* collection, even though there is no cohesion or affinity between the items in it. If the world, as an all-embracing collection of bric-a-brac, is identical with God, then there is just one God, though he too is just a disorganized

collection of odds and ends. By contrast, a steel ball within the collection has a degree of intrinsic unity: it is uniform throughout and its parts cohere with considerable force. This is quite different from numerical unity. There may well be more than one such steel ball, but each of them has intrinsic unity. Brahmanism and Spinoza attributed to God an intrinsic unity comparable to, only far greater than, the unity of a steel ball. This will not do, however, because then there can be no intelligible relationship between the unitary God and the bric-a-brac of the world. In the case of Hinduism this leads to a confused world–God dualism. In Spinoza's case it leads acosmism. To establish an intelligible relationship between God and the world, we need to bring God and the world closer together, first by making God's intrinsic unity 'concrete', and secondly by regarding the world not as just a collection of odds and ends, but as a structured unity that can qualify as the All rather than just the Everything. The concrete unity of God is then comparable to, say, the unity of a plan, while the unity of the world is somewhat like the unity of a film.

The pantheism that identifies God with everything is, Hegel concludes, absurd. It can only have arisen owing to a confusion between the Everything and the All, between numerical unity and intrinsic unity. One possibility ignored by Hegel is that God may be an eccentric collector of bric-a-brac. This might have appealed to Hegel's Romantic contemporaries, but for Hegel it would be too anthropomorphic, and dualist.

20. Jalaluddin Rumi was the pen-name of Jalaluddin Muhammad Ibn Bahauddin Walad al-Khatibi al-Bakri al-Balkhi (1207–73), a Persian Sufi, poet, and thinker. His thought too has something in common with Spinozism. Like Spinoza, he held that in our ordinary condition we are cut off or 'veiled' from higher perceptions by lower stimuli, especially by our emotions. We can overcome 'veiling' and reach the ultimate truth only by a special love, of which worldly love is only a crude likeness. This is comparable to Spinoza's recommendation of 'intellectual love of God': cf. §415, n. 3.

21. Friedrich Rückert translated some of Rumi's poetry in *Mewlana* [i.e. Master] *Dschelaleddin Rumi* in *Taschenbuch für Damen auf das Jahr 1821* [Pocketbook for Ladies for 1821] (Tübingen, 1821), 211–48. According to Nicolin and Pöggeler, Hegel does not quote Rückert's translation with complete accuracy.

22. Friedrich August Gotttreu Tholuck published his *Blüttensammlung aus der Morgenländischen Mystik, nebst einer Einleitung über Mystik überhaupt und Morgenländische insbesondere* [Anthology of Eastern Mysticism, together with an Introduction to Mysticism in general and Eastern Mysticism in particular] in Berlin in 1825. In the Preface to the second edition of the Encyclopaedia (1827), Hegel criticizes Tholuck's philosophical position at greater length. See G. W. F. Hegel, *The Encyclopaedia Logic*, trans. T. F. Geraets, W. A. Suchting, and H. S. Harris (Indianapolis: Hackelt, 1991), 8-9, 12-13.

23. On the Eleatics and Spinoza, see §573, nn. 7, 10, and 16. Here Hegel dissociates his own view from acosmism, denial of the reality of the world. The acosmism of Eleaticism and Spinozism results from their conceiving the 'absolute', the fundamental nature of reality, as a substance, and 'only' as a substance. The acosmism

of oriental religions results from their conceiving the absolute as the 'utterly universal genus, etc.' Like Allness, a genus is universal, but it differs from Allness in the way that e.g. animality differs from the collection of all animals. The 'utterly universal' genus is the genus to which everything belongs, presumably the genus of being. This does not seem to differ much from conceiving the absolute as substance, since all these views (Hegel continues) fail to determine 'substance' as subject and mind. If, and only if, substance is determined as subject and mind, he implies, acosmism is avoided or at least diluted.

In Enc. I, §112Z. Hegel criticized Mohammedanism for its 'scant recognition of the finite, . . . be it as natural things or as finite phases of the mind', a defect that stems from conceiving God as 'the essence', and thus 'only as the universal and irresistible power; in other words, as the Lord'. In LPR, iii. 142-3, Hegel contrasts Mohammedanism with Christianity in two respects. First, 'in Christ the spiritual element is developed in a concrete way, and is known as Trinity, i.e. as spirit'. Secondly, in Christianity, the 'history of man, the relation in which he stands to the One, is a concrete history'; this history starts from the 'natural will, which is not as it ought to be, and the yielding up of this will is the act whereby it reaches this its essence by means of this negation of itself'. For Islam, by contrast, first, 'God is the absolute One', from which all concreteness is excluded, and secondly, as against God, 'man retains for himself no end, no particularity, no interests of his own': man's only 'specific aim' is 'self-absorption in the unity of God'. PH, p. 356 gives a similar account: 'This One has indeed, the quality of spirit; yet because subjectivity suffers itself to be absorbed in the object, this One is deprived of every concrete predicate; so that neither does subjectivity become on its part spiritually free, nor on the other hand is the object of its veneration concrete'. In Hegel's view, the Trinitarian concreteness of the Christian God implies the independence and freedom of man. God generates Christ as an aspect of himself. But Christ represents nature and, above all, man. Hence nature and man are phases of God himself, and thus have a relatively independent status. Because of his independence man has a concrete history: he is not absorbed in God from the start, but works his way up to God gradually. Conversely, the independence and freedom of man implies the concreteness of God. If man is free and independent, as well as being a phase of God, then man's developing knowledge amounts to God's self-consciousness and thus makes God into a fully fledged mind or subject. Islam lacks both of these features. Since God is not concrete, he cannot generate anything genuinely independent of himself. Conversely, since man is not independent of God, man cannot confer concreteness on God. On Hegel's account God is here comparable to a ruler, a 'Lord', whose subjects have no other wish than to obey his every command. Such a ruler has no incentive to develop 'concrete', articulated institutions by which to govern his subjects. Conversely, if the ruler has no other aim for his subjects than that they should obey his every command, then they will not develop into free and independent subjects.

24. In this passage Hegel uses three different words for the connection between God and the world:

(1) *Verhältnis*, 'relationship', which 'means primarily "ratio" and "propor-tion". Applied to a "relation" between things, it can only mean that they stand in a certain ratio to each other, i.e. that the relation is fixed in this way" ' (DGS, p. 278). *Verhältnis* is thus the appropriate word, when Hegel is emphasizing that God's 'relationship' to the world is determ-ined by God's nature. In a ratio, n : m, we know the ratio between n and m as soon as their values are specified. If, say, n = 9 and m = 6, then n and m are in the ratio of three to two. In this case both values must be specified for their ratio to be determined. This would suggest that God's relationship to the world is determined not by God's nature alone but by God's nature together with the nature of the world. However, Hegel's view is that the nature of God determines both the nature of the world and God's relationship to the world. In the ratio-schema n : m, n and m are independent variables: 'n' and 'm' can be replaced by any numbers we like. But in the ratio God : world, the value or 'determination' we give to 'God' will automatically determine the value we assign to 'world', as well as the ratio between God and the world. For example, if we regard God simply as the lord or master, then the world is simply his slave or vassal, and their relationship is one of domination. Hegel does not make clear whether the 'reflective intellect' denies that there is a *Verhältnis* between God and the world. It would presumably deny that there is an *intimate* relationship between them, but a *Verhältnis*, in the sense of a 'ratio', need not be an intimate relationship. Hegel himself believes that in postulating a God of a certain sort, the reflective intellect *ipso facto* determines the nature of the world and God's *Verhältnis* to it. But he may well think that the reflective intellect would deny this, or would even reject the question itself.

(2) *Zusammenhang*, 'interconnection', which 'indicates in a general way a close relationship between between things or ideas' (DGS, p. 279). The reflective intellect rejects any attempt to 'express' the *Zusammenhang* between God and the world, presumably because it believes there is no such *Zusammenhang*. God is to be kept quite separate from the world, though this does not exclude characterizing God and the world in correlative terms: God is, for example, the essence and/or infinite, while the world is appearance and/or finite. These correlative terms exemplify a part of Hegel's point about a *Verhältnis*. Assuming that there is nothing besides God and the world, if God is the essence, then the world is appearance, since there can be no essence that does not appear in some way. Conversely, if the world is appearance, God is the essence, since there can be no appearance that is not the appearance of an essence. Similarly, there is (in Hegel's view) no infinite without something finite, and nothing finite without an infinite.

(3) This alone, however, does not tell us much about the 'relation' between God and the world, about their *Beziehung*, 'relation', in which 'one thing influences the other, or where there is an interaction, . . . In the sense of

relations between people *Verhältnis* is much deeper and more intimate than *Beziehung* (DGS, pp. 378–9). One of the aims of the reflective intellect in characterizing God as infinite and as the essence is to emphasize the distance between God and the world. For the reflective intellect does not share Hegel's view about the close interrelationship between infinity and finitude or between essence and appearance. It may well hold, contrary to Hegel's view, that God existed before the world existed and that God could have existed even if the world had never existed, that the essence can exist without appearance and the infinite without the finite. Nevertheless there must be some 'relation' between God and the world, essence and appearance, infinite and finite. An unreflective believer can avoid asking what this relation is, but the reflective intellect cannot evade this question, if only to answer that the relation is 'incomprehensible'.

25. Hegel moves from 'relation' to 'unity' for three reasons. First, unity is a type (and, according to Hegel, several types) of relation. And he perhaps believes (though this is less clear) that, conversely, every relation is a type of unity. Secondly, he himself believes that the relation between God and world is 'unity' or oneness. Thirdly, his opponents accuse him of believing that God and world are related by unity, only they attribute to him the wrong conception of unity.

This passage alludes to two wrong conceptions of unity.

(1) The wrong conception of unity attributed to Hegel so far is this: each and every thing in the world around us (trees, pens, paper, etc.) is fully real, and all these things together are identical to God (cf. §573, n. 11). This type of unity is much like the identity of Cicero and Tully, except that this identification of God and the world amounts to atheism, whereas our antecedent conceptions of Tully and Cicero are sufficiently similar for our identification of Cicero and Tully not to imply a denial of the existence of either. Cicero exists and Tully exists, only they are the same man. But we cannot identify God and the world without somehow downgrading either God or the world or both.

(2) However, another wrong conception of unity is involved in the claim that philosophy is the 'system of identity' and postulates an 'empty absolute'. The philosophy of identity stems from Schelling, with some help from Spinoza. It claims that those aspects of the world that we usually regard as opposites and which are variously called 'nature' and 'mind', 'being' and 'thinking', or 'object' and 'subject', are at bottom one and the same thing, namely the neutral absolute, which nevertheless appears in two different ways. In the Preface to PS, p. 9, Hegel (without mentioning Schelling) describes this absolute as 'the night in which . . . all cows are black'. This type of identity differs from the identity of Cicero and Tully. When we say that Cicero is Tully, we do not suppose that there is, underlying Cicero and Tully, a neutral person who is neither Cicero nor Tully. It is more like the sort of identity involved in the claim that, say, good

and evil, or again beauty and ugliness, are at bottom the same, because they are both ways in which reality, which *in itself* contains neither good nor evil, neither beauty nor ugliness, appears to us or is conceived by us. This claim does not imply that good and evil, or beauty and ugliness, are the same in the way that Tully is the same as Cicero or in the way that, say, courage is much the same as bravery. Good and evil, beauty and ugliness, though they stem from the same neutral source, are also different from each other, as well as the same. In the Preface to the second, 1827, edition of Enc., Hegel considers the charge that 'speculative philosophy' is a 'system of identity', equating good and evil, as well as subject and object, and he denies that Spinozism, let alone his own philosophy, entails these equations. (See *The Encyclopaedia Logic*, trans. T. F. Geraets *et al.*, pp. 7–10.) Nevertheless, Hegel seems to deny that this type of unity, even when it is acquitted of these charges, is the unity he has in mind.

   Philosophy is concerned with unity for what initially look like four distinct reasons. First, there is the problem of the unity of entities within the world. What makes a tree one thing? What makes a squirrel one thing, distinct from the tree it is running up? Second, there is the problem of the unity of the world as a whole. What unifies the tree and the squirrel with each other and with other things, so that they belong to a single, orderly world? Thirdly, what is the relation between this world and God, the 'absolute' that sustains it? This relation will also be a type of unity, whether it be a close or a loose unity. Finally, what is the unity or other relation between the thoughts or categories that we apply to things, between, for example, infinity and finitude, or appearance and essence, or cause and effect? These look like four different reasons for our interest in unity, four different types of question. But the questions have, in Hegel's view, the same type of answer. Everything depends on the thoughts or categories and on the type of unity that we can establish between them. Take the third question, about the relation between God and the world. The answer to this depends first on the categories that we apply to God and the world respectively, and secondly on the type of unity that obtains between the categories applied to God and the categories applied to the world, between, for example, infinity and finitude, or between essence and appearance. The answer to the second question also depends on categories. The unity of the world depends ultimately on the relations between the categories we apply to it, cause and effect, for example, or force and its expression, and indeed on the coherent unity of the whole network of categories. So too the first question. The unity of things within the world depends on such categories as 'thing' and 'life', on their ability to unify diversity.

   This is why Hegel associates unity, 'concrete' unity, with the 'concept'. Something is made a unity by the concept it embodies. But concept-generated unity always involves an element of diversity, a diversity that is unified by the concept, but which nevertheless survives within the unity. Take, for example, our question 'What makes a tree one thing?' A tree is not a simple unity. It involves diversity, both over time—the stages of its growth—and at any given time—root, trunk, branches, leaves. Something is needed to explain why all this diversity constitutes one thing. What makes it a single organism is, in Hegel's view, the concept it embodies, not simply a concept that we impose on it, but a concept that is embedded in its seed and determines the nature and stages of its growth, while keeping them within the bounds of a single organism. (The word *Begriff*, 'concept', is especially suitable for this unifying function, since it comes from the verb *begreifen*, which, like the English 'comprehend', means 'include, comprise', as well as 'understand, grasp'.) Now contrast this with the identity of Cicero and Tully. There is no relevant diversity here, except in the person's name, 'Marcus Tullius Cicero', which explains why he is sometimes referred to as 'Cicero' and sometimes as 'Tully'. There is diversity within this person, since he is a developing, articulated organism. This diversity is relevant to the questions 'What makes this collection of limbs, etc. a single organism?' and 'What makes that infant the same individual as this elderly orator?' But it is not relevant to the question 'What makes Cicero the same individual as Tully?' We cannot, for example, ask: 'Which part or stage of him is Cicero and which part or stage is Tully?' Because the Cicero-Tully identity does not unify any relevant diversity, it is abstract identity or unity, not concrete unity. Since there is no diversity to be overcome, nothing makes, and nothing is needed to make, Cicero identical to Tully, except the application of those names to the same individual. Hence this unity is 'conceptless'. The same is true of the straightforward identification of God with the world that amounts to atheism. Here 'God' and 'world' are implied to be two different names for one and the same thing. It is less obviously true, however, of the 'system of identity', which claims that subject and object, etc. are rooted in the same neutral absolute. Something, no doubt the 'concept', would be needed to explain the emergence of subject and object from the same source. Hegel does not hold this doctrine. (He is more inclined to say that each of two opposites emerges from the extreme intensification of the other than that both emerge from a neutral source.) But in the 1827 Preface he is less concerned to attack the doctrine itself than to defend it against confusion with abstract Cicero-Tully identity, claiming that subject and object, good and evil, or for that matter God and the world are flatly identical.

Even when we exclude 'abstract unity', there are many conceptions of concrete unity, and these form a progression, culminating in 'absolute mind'. What is it that makes one type of concrete unity superior to another? It is the type of unity's ability to answer the questions that motivate our interest in unity. Take, first, things within the world. These form, in Hegel's view at least, a hierarchy, of which a simplified version is this. At the bottom are, say, minerals. Above these are plants. Then animals. Then the human mind. Each grade in the hierarchy presupposes the grade beneath it, but a lower grade can exist without the higher grades: there can be, for example, minerals without plants, but not plants without minerals. Each grade exhibits a higher type of unity, a unity that is *both* more intensely unifying than its predecessor *and* embraces greater diversity. A stone is fairly homogeneous. It can be broken into pieces that are much the same, and the pieces survive the fragmentation. A plant is not so homogeneous. The difference between roots, stem, leaves, flowers are essential to the plant. Nevertheless, some plants can be broken in two so as to produce two plants. A squirrel too contains diverse organs, and it cannot readily be divided into two squirrels or even into two living, enduring half-squirrels. In this respect a human body is much like a squirrel. But in Hegel's view a human mind has an even more intense, more concrete, unity. It cannot be severed at all, not even into two dead minds. It embraces within itself all the diversity of the world, not just the trees and nuts in its vicinity. Each of these grades of unity embodies, in Hegel's view, a certain set of categories. Minerals embody only lower categories, minds require higher, more complex categories.

Suppose next that we are trying to answer the second question, 'What unifies the world?' Not every type of concrete unity will be an appropriate answer to this question, and this for at least two reasons. First, a type of unity that is sufficient to explain lower grades of entity cannot be adequate for the world as a whole, since the world also contains higher grades of entity. The world cannot, for example, have only the unity possessed by a stone, since that would leave the minds the world contains unaccounted for. Secondly, some types of unity can only explain a finite entity within the world, not the world as a whole. A finite entity might be explained, for example, as the expression of a force. But why does a force express itself? Only because it is induced to do so or, as Hegel says, 'solicited', by some other force which is already expressing itself. We cannot, however, say that the world as a whole is the expression of a single force, since there can be no other force to explain why this cosmic force expresses itself. A force can explain, along with other forces, the unity of something within the world, but not the unity of the world as a whole. Many of the types of unity Hegel considers suffer from this defect, that they can account for only a part of the whole, not the whole itself. This is true, for example, of 'objective' mind or spirit. Objective mind is an especially concrete type of unity, embracing all the members of a given society, and the complex network of their institutions. It is not, however, the all-embracing unity needed to encompass the world as a whole. It leaves out raw nature, for example, and also other societies, societies contemporary with one's own and also societies of the past. Each society has its own objective mind. And according to Hegel, if a society attains the highest stage of objective mind, the state, there must be more than one society, since a state essentially belongs to a system of potentially warring states. So objective mind cannot unify the world. That leaves absolute mind, which is not tied to any particular society. Absolute mind has another advantage over objective mind and, indeed, over all the other types of unity that Hegel considers. Absolute mind, at least in its philosophical phase, is entirely self-aware. It plumbs its own depths and knows all the ins and outs of its own development. This is not true of objective mind. Membership of a society requires some knowledge of its workings, and officials need to know more. But no member needs complete knowledge of the society; even if everyone's knowledge is pooled together, it need not and probably will not amount to complete knowledge of that society. So objective mind is not fully self-conscious. But absolute mind, in Hegel's view, is fully self-conscious. Mind has, as it were, returned to itself, and thus acquired the most intense of all the concrete unities under consideration. But absolute mind does not simply bask in its own unity and leave the rest of the world to its own devices. It elicits the unity implicit in the system of categories embedded in the world and thereby brings out the unity of the world.

26. The parallel between Hegel's philosophical opponents and the physicists and chemists of the day consists in their focus on a single type of unity to the exclusion of other types. They do not focus on the same type of unity. Hegel's opponents focus on 'abstract identity', whereas physicists focus on 'composition'. (But cf. §573, n. 27.) Physicists tended to treat properties as 'stuffs'. For example, Antoine Lavoisier (1743–94) listed heat (and also light) among the elements. Heat was, he believed, an 'imponderable fluid' called 'caloric': cf. Enc. II, §§304-5 on caloric, and Enc. I, §126 on stuffs or 'matters' in general. Stuffs, the real as well as the illusory ones, are regarded as elements, which enter into the relation of 'composition' with each other. *Zusammensetzung* is both a general term for 'composition' of any kind and a specific term for chemical composition. (In a similar discussion at LPR i. p. 100, Hegel distinguishes between a mixture, such as mud produced from earth and water, and a compound, such as the salt produced, together with water, by the interaction of an acid and a base.) Thus we can say water is a 'compound' (*Zusammensetzung*) of hydrogen and oxygen, and also that an animal is composed of bones, muscles, nerves, etc. or a house is composed of a roof, walls, doors, etc. In Enc. I, §126Z. Hegel similarly complains about the use of the expression 'consist of' (*bestehen aus*) to say both that water consists of hydrogen and oxygen and that an animal consists of bones, muscles, nerves, etc. He rightly points out that an animal does not consist of bones, etc. in the same way as water consists of hydrogen and oxygen. Nor are the bones, etc. of an animal compounded in the same way as hydrogen and oxygen are compounded in water. An animal does contain chemical compounds, but it also contains organs that are related to each other in a different way. It is harder to accept Hegel's claim that the difference between, say, water and a pig depends 'solely on the different determinacy of this unity'. If the relations between the constituents of a pig are specified closely enough this does determine the nature of the pig, but, conversely, a sufficiently precise specification of the nature of a pig will determine the relations between its constituents. However, Hegel is not here thinking simply of the relations between the parts of an animal. He has reverted to 'unity', and has in mind the 'concept' that determines the nature of an animal, of its parts, and of the relations between the parts. See also Enc. II, §334.

Hegel's complaint about the physicists is ambiguous. It might mean that they believe that an animal is composed or consists of bones, etc. in the very same way as water consists of hydrogen and oxygen. It is hard to accept, however, that any respectable scientist did believe this in Hegel's day. The difference that hydrogen and oxygen survive the decomposition of water, whereas most of an animal's organs do not survive the dismemberment of the animal, is surely too obvious to miss. Alternatively, it may mean that physicists use the terms 'composition' and 'consist of' in an undiscriminatingly general sense for these different types of unity. This is a more plausible, but less serious complaint.

27. Two distinct views are in play here:

   (1) God is identical to the world

The opponents of philosophy attribute this view to philosophy, because they forget that identity is only one moment of the category of relation. The other moment is difference, which, when combined with identity, gives rise to 'concrete unity' of various kinds. But philosophy's opponents can make no use of concrete unity. Nevertheless, they find position (1) unsatisfactory, since it amounts either to atheism or to acosmism, whereas they believe that God and the world each have 'solid substantiality'. So they modify position (1) to:

   (2) God is composed of God and the world.

Position (2) looks incoherent. On the face of it, God can no more be composed of God and the world than water can be composed of water and hydrogen. But what the view amounts to is that God and the world are compounded together in something like the way in which hydrogen and oxygen are compounded together to make water. That the whole compound, as well as one of its ingredients, is called 'God', if it is not just a slip, expresses the fact that God is the dominant partner, giving form and unity to the other ingredient. This view is not wholly remote from Hegel's own view. But his philosophically incompetent opponents express it in terms of 'composition' and thus align themselves with the physicists: cf. §573, n. 26.

28. Hegel's opponents attribute to philosophy a determinate conception of the relation between God and the world, relying on such inadequate categories as identity and composition. They themselves offer only an 'indeterminate' conception of the relation, owing to the apparent 'contradiction' in it. The contradiction stems from the 'solid substantiality' they ascribe to both God and the world. This implies that God and the world are not just identical: cf. §573, n. 25. But they cannot just be different either, because, for example, God is omnipresent, i.e. is present everywhere in the world: cf. §573, n. 29.

29. Epicurus (342/1–271/70 BC) was a Greek atomist, who is said to have believed that the gods do exist, eternal and blissfully happy, but that they live in the empty space between worlds and do not concern themselves with human affairs. On 'pores', see Enc. I, §130. According to Hegel, pores are a requirement of the theory of composition: cf. §573, n. 26. Suppose that something is, say, red and warm throughout. Then it is a compound of red-stuff and heat-stuff, as well as other stuffs. But two stuffs cannot occupy exactly the same portion of space. So there must be pores in the red-stuff for the heat-stuff to fit into, and likewise pores in the heat-stuff for the red-stuff to occupy. (The pores are, of course, so narrow and so close together that to us the object seems to be red and hot throughout.) However, the pores-theory does not depend on the postulation of

illusory stuffs. Any compound, such as water, of two or more substances requires gaps within each substance which can be occupied by the other substance.

Hegel's ironical suggestion is that in a similar way God might be supposed to occupy the pores between and within material things. God can then have 'solid substantiality' and so can material things. Nevertheless, this is pantheism of a sort. Everything will have a bit of God in it, and God will be, in a way, everywhere. God has to be everywhere if he is to exert his influence on 'filled space', i.e. space occupied by matter, as well as on the gaps in between. But this theory, Hegel objects, splits God up in the way that matter is split up. God is like a very fine gas that seeps into every nook and cranny, but he is not everywhere, or anywhere, as a *whole*. Epicurus did not split up the gods in this way, since he does not require them to exert any influence on the world.

30. On the difficulties of an 'exoteric' discussion of concepts as 'facts', see §573, n. 11.

NOTES TO §574

1. According to Hegel, reality has main three parts or 'moments': the logical Idea, nature, and mind. These are respectively examined by the three parts of philosophy: logic, philosophy of nature, and philosophy of mind. The highest stage of mind, and the object of the final Paragraphs of the philosophy of mind, is philosophy itself. But philosophy begins with logic, the study of the logical Idea, and so the consideration of philosophy at the end of philosophy of mind takes us back to logic and the logical Idea: cf. §573, n. 3. Philosophy thus forms a circle, and so does reality itself. Each of the three moments can be seen as a middle term linking the other two, giving three linkings or 'syllogisms' considered in the following Paragraphs. In §575 nature is the middle linking the logical Idea and mind. In §576, mind links together nature and the logical Idea. In §577, the logical Idea links nature and mind. See also Enc. I, §187Z.

The details of the Paragraph are as follows. 'This concept of philosophy' refers back to the last sentence of the preceding Paragraph, which said of philosophy that 'at the conclusion it grasps its own concept, i.e. only *looks back* on its knowledge': cf. §573, n. 3. We might infer that Hegel expects us to start reading the *Encyclopaedia* over again, starting at §1 of the Introduction to Enc. I, or perhaps at §84 where the Logic proper begins with a consideration of 'being'. Instead he refers us to Enc. I, §236, which introduces the 'absolute Idea': 'The Idea as unity of the subjective Idea and the objective Idea is the concept of the Idea, the concept for which the Idea as such is the object [*Gegenstand*], the concept for which the object [*Objekt*] is the Idea; an object [*Objekt*] into which all determinations have converged. This unity is thus the *absolute and complete [alle] truth*, the Idea that thinks its own self, and here in fact *as* thinking Idea, as *logical* Idea'. All the 'determinations' or categories considered in the Logic have now come together to form a single system. This system is entirely adequate for thinking about itself. Some categories cannot be thought about in terms of themselves; we have to introduce a new category in order to think about them. For example, we use the category of 'cause' and 'effect' to think about events. But we cannot use only this category to think about the *thought* of a cause and the *thought* of an effect, since the thought of a cause and the thought of an effect are not related to each other as cause and effect. We have to think about these thoughts in terms of, say, the category of correlativity. This is one of the ways in which Hegel's Logic develops: our thinking about one thought or category involves some other thought or category. When we reach the absolute Idea, however, this is no longer the case. Thinking about the Idea as a whole does not require and does not generate any further thought or category besides those we already have; the absolute Idea is wholly self-contained. (Hegel overreaches himself in describing the absolute Idea as 'complete' truth: the Idea's self-containment does not entail that it includes *all* possible thoughts, that there *are* no other thoughts, only that no other thoughts can be discovered by reflection on our thinking about the Idea.) So Hegel's logic does not just think about logical structures; it also accommodates our thinking about logical structures within those logical structures. Now this feature of logic prefigures what happens in philosophy as a whole. Philosophy essentially reflects on itself, on its own thoughts and thinking. It reflects on 'the logical' (*das Logische*), i.e. the subject matter of Logic, but it is now concerned, in a way that Logic itself was not primarily concerned, with the embodiment of logical categories in nature and mind. Now that 'the logical' is a 'result', it is explicitly 'the spiritual' [*das Geistige*] in a way that it initially was not: it has emerged from and is sustained by the mind or spirit. The logical Idea divides into nature and mind. This is the 'presupposing judgement', the original division: cf. §§554, n. 1; 568. What this judgement presupposes is the logical Idea, which at that stage was only an 'immediate' beginning, i.e. not derived from, or mediated by, any prior stage. In nature and mind the 'concept', i.e. the logical Idea, was only 'in itself' or implicit, not present in its pure form. It was encumbered by 'appearance', i.e. it was manifested only in its natural and mental embodiments. Now, however, it has emerged from the highest stage of mind in its pure form, free of natural and psychological embodiments.

NOTES TO §575

1. The 'further development', namely of the logical Idea beyond itself, is grounded by the Idea's 'appearing'. But only 'initially', i.e. in the first two syllogisms (§§575-6), but not the third: cf. §577, n. 2. The first of these appearances follows the order traced by Hegel's *Encyclopaedia*, with the logical Idea becoming nature, and nature becoming mind: nature is the middle term of what Hegel regards as a syllogism or conclusion: cf. §569, n. 1. Enc. I, §187Z gives a similar account: 'Nature is the middle term which links the others together. Nature, the totality immediately before us, unfolds itself into the two extremes of the logical Idea and mind. But mind is mind only when it is mediated through nature.'

2. The three terms—nature, mind, and 'its essence', i.e. the logical Idea—are not distinct entities, like three links in a chain or three railway carriages. Links in a chain or railway carriages can in principle be separated from each other. But

nature essentially and necessarily joins together mind and the logical Idea, because the 'syllogism', i.e. the closure or joining, is 'determined in the Idea', i.e. prescribed in the logical structure or plan with which the syllogism begins and which is to be fully realized at the end. According to this plan nature is not an independent, self-contained realm, but a 'transit point' (*Durchgangspunkt*) on the way to mind and to the full realization of the Idea. Nature is the Idea 'in itself' or implicitly: it embodies the logical Idea in a natural, physical form. (Hegel's analogy of a tree perhaps clarifies this: the logical Idea corresponds to the plan in the seed; the sapling, say, corresponds to nature; the full-grown tree is mind, while the seeds on the full-grown tree correspond to the reemergence of the logical Idea in philosophy. The sapling is not distinct from the seed and the tree in the way that railway carriages are distinct from each other; its emergence from the seed and subsequent development into a tree is prescribed by the plan in the seed; and the sapling is implicitly this plan, embodying it in an undeveloped form.)

However, although nature is *in itself* the logical Idea, this does not become clear in this syllogism. This syllogism presents the transition from the logical Idea to nature simply as a *transition* and nature simply as a 'transit point' on the route from the logical Idea to mind. It does not display the logical structure of nature itself. It is only mind that can do this. But in this syllogism mind does not play an active part. Hence the syllogism does not display the attainment of 'freedom' effected by the mind: the extraction of the logical Idea from nature and the emergence of the logical Idea from mind. This deficiency is to be repaired by the next syllogism.

NOTES TO §576

1. Enc. I, §187Z. gives a similar account: 'Mind, which we know as the principle of individuality and as the actualizing principle, is the mean; and nature and the logical Idea are the extremes. It is mind which cognizes the logical Idea in nature and thus raises nature to its essence.' The mind discerns the logical Idea in nature, discovering laws, forces, causal connections, and so on. In this way the mind mediates between nature and the logical Idea, and joins them together. This syllogism does not follow the order of Hegel's *Encyclopaedia*. If we were to trace this syllogism through the *Encyclopaedia*, we would perhaps read first Enc. II (nature), then Enc. III (mind), and finally Enc. I (logic). The problem with this, however, is that Enc. II does not present *raw* nature, the nature that mind 'presupposes'. It presents nature as already ordered and conceptualized by mind. This difficulty suggests a conflict between this syllogism and the first syllogism. In the first syllogism the logical Idea becomes nature before mind appears on the scene, whereas in the second syllogism mind is required to join together the logical Idea with nature. This may be why 'this appearance', i.e. the first syllogism, is 'sublated' in the second syllogism. The solution is that what the logical Idea becomes (in the first syllogism) is raw nature, nature in which the logical Idea is only implicit, whereas mind (in the second syllogism) transforms this raw nature into the nature that is explicitly structured by the logical Idea. The *Encyclopaedia* does not

present this solution very clearly, since it inevitably provides only one account of nature, that is, of logically structured nature. Hegel does not, and cannot, give an extended account of nature as it is independently of mind's operations on it: in describing nature he automatically brings out its conceptual structure.

2. In Enc. I, §190 and in SL, pp. 686–95, the 'syllogism of reflexion' is one of the three main types of syllogism. Hegel divides it into three subtypes: (1) The syllogism of Allness (*Allheit*): e.g. 'All metals conduct electricity. Copper is a metal. Therefore copper conducts electricity.' But the major premiss of this needs to be established by: (2) the syllogism of induction: e.g. 'Gold is a metal; silver is a metal; copper, etc. Gold, silver, copper, etc. all conduct electricity. Therefore all metals conduct electricity'. The problem with this is that we may not know whether we have specified all metals in the premisses, and, in cases where the induction deals with individuals (e.g. 'Caius is a man, Titus is a man, etc. Caius is mortal, Titus is mortal, etc. Therefore all men are mortal') we usually cannot enumerate all the relevant individuals. Hence the syllogism of induction is replaced by: (3) the syllogism of analogy, some of which are acceptable (e.g. 'All planets so far discovered have been found to obey the laws of motion. Pluto is a newly discovered planet. Therefore it obeys the laws of motion'), while others are not (e.g. 'The earth is a planet and it is inhabited. Mars is a planet. Therefore Mars is inhabited.') Inferences of this type no doubt play a part in mind's recognition of the logical Idea in nature. This need not mean, however, that the syllogism in which nature and the logical Idea are linked by mind is itself of this type. There is only a single instance each of nature, mind, and the logical Idea; so they can hardly be related by Allness, induction, or analogy. It is more likely, then, that Hegel uses the expression 'syllogism of spiritual reflexion' in a looser way, meaning that the mind reflects on nature. The addition of '*geistigen*', 'spiritual' or 'mental', perhaps has the effect of distancing the whole expression from the more technical expression, 'syllogism of reflexion'.

On *Reflexion*, see §§384, n. 2; 389, nn. 9, 12. It is often a mildly derogatory term in Hegel. Also mildly derogatory is the reference to 'subjective' cognition: the scientific conceptualization of nature does not yet correspond to any parallel process in nature itself. Cognition aims at freedom, the conceptual domestication of nature, but does not yet seem to have achieved it. Whatever defects there are in this second syllogism will be remedied in the third.

NOTES TO §577

1. In Enc. I, §187Z., Hegel gives a much simpler version of this third syllogism: 'the logical Idea itself becomes the middle: it is the absolute substance both of mind and of nature, the universal and all-pervading principle'. The logical Idea is the core both of mind and of nature. Philosophy tells us that this is so, but otherwise philosophy is assigned no special role in this syllogism that it does not have in the other syllogisms, logic–nature–mind and nature–mind–logic. In §577, by contrast, the 'logical Idea' is replaced by 'self-knowing reason', perhaps harking back to the 'self-thinking Idea' of §574. Moreover, philosophy is implied to play a part

in this syllogism that it does not play in the preceding two. These differences stem from the fact that Hegel is now thinking about the structure of his system more explicitly then he was in Enc. I, §187Z. This third syllogism follows the order: mind (Enc. III), logic (Enc. I), nature (Enc. II). In this order the logical Idea emerges from mind, that is, from the climax of mind, philosophy. That is why the mind is the 'presupposition', and also why the logical Idea is called 'self-knowing reason' rather than the 'logical Idea', as in Enc. I, §187Z., or simply 'the logical', as in §§575 and 576. Nevertheless, it is the logical Idea that does the work here. It 'divides' itself into mind and nature, and 'makes' the mind its presupposition. This makes two additions to the comparatively straightforward account given in Enc. I, §187Z. First, the logical Idea acquires an active role. It does not simply form the core of mind and nature, it generates the very distinction between mind and nature. Secondly, the logical Idea can do this only because it has emerged explicitly in the highest phase of the mind, the mind that the logical Idea has itself produced. Hegel's circle is here a genuine circle of explanation, not just a way of reading the *Encyclopaedia* in a certain order. The logical Idea divides into mind and nature, but it can do this only because it emerges within mind. One might take this to be a heady idealism, according to which the logical Idea, nature, and the lower phases of mind are created not just by mind, but by philosophy. But this would be a mistake. Philosophy too has presuppositions. It presupposes and emerges from lower phases of mind, from nature, and from the logical Idea. Some of the oddity of this circle is removed if we cease to think of it as a temporal process, in which at one time, t_1, there is the logical Idea as yet undivided into nature and mind, then at a later time, t_2, it divides into nature and mind, but can only do this, indeed can only exist at all, because at some time before t_1, t_0, the logical Idea has been produced by philosophy: cf. §575, n. 2. The logical Idea is, like its theological counterpart (cf. §567, n. 1), non-temporal and therefore does not exist at any time apart from its manifestations. It is the deep logical structure of nature, mind, and their interrelationship. It is not, therefore, comparable to a seed that grows on the tree that grew from that selfsame seed or an egg laid by the chicken that emerged from that selfsame egg. The claim that it divides into nature and mind is comparable to the claim that 12 'divides into' 5 and 7 or that 3 'goes into' 12 four times, where the questions 'When does it divide?' and 'When does it go into it?' are inappropriate.

Hegel speaks as if mind and nature are two parallel processes, one 'subjective', the other 'objective'. This is not quite accurate. Nature does not, in Hegel's view, develop over time. Different levels of nature embody different stages of the logical Idea: space, for example, embodies pure quantity (Enc. II, §254 Remark), while organic nature embodies the Idea in the form of life (Enc. I, §§216 ff.; Enc. II, §337). Nature thus follows a certain logical order. But space does not precede organic life in time, nor does, say, plant life precede animal life in time. Mind, by contrast, develops over time. For example, the Greek city-state is a significantly different stage of mind from the modern state and it preceded it in time, just as Greek religion preceded Christianity. But not all stages of mind form a temporal sequence. For example, humans did not have intuition (§446) before they acquired memory (§461); these stages of the mind are contemporaneous. The climax of mind, philosophy, in which the logical Idea, nature, and mind itself, are explicitly examined, is temporal in several respects. It emerged relatively late in the development of humanity. It develops over the course of its history. And it forms a temporal sequence in the mind of the philosopher, who thinks about pure being, say, before he thinks about causality or space. There are, then, two difficulties in Hegel's account here. First, his use of the word *Prozess* suggests a temporal 'process', when only mind, and not even the whole of mind, involves this. Secondly, within the realm of mind, the logical Idea is manifested in two ways, not just one. The whole realm of mind, i.e. the subject matter of Enc. III, is structured by the logical Idea in roughly the same way as nature is structured by the logical Idea. Then at the climax of mind philosophy explicitly considers the logical Idea and also its embodiments in nature and mind. There are therefore three parallel 'processes', not just two: nature, mind and philosophy. They are parallel in the sense that even when one of the processes (philosophy, say) is temporal and the other (nature) is not, they follow the same logical order. Thus when Hegel speaks of the 'process of the Idea's subjective activity', he perhaps has in view two different parallel pairs: nature//mind as a whole and nature//philosophy. What the logical Idea divides into is the pair: nature//mind as a whole. (This is the theme of the third syllogism in Enc. I, §187Z.) What is most obviously a 'subjective activity' is not mind as a whole, but philosophy, and this runs parallel not only to nature, but also to mind as a whole: philosophy//nature and mind. Hegel has this parallel in view when he assigns a large role to philosophy in this syllogism. It also contrasts this syllogism with the second syllogism, in which 'cognition' was 'subjective', lacking the objective counterpart that mind has here (cf. §576, n. 2): philosophy follows the objective logical order of the realms it examines.

2. The 'self-judging', i.e. the original division, of the Idea is the same as 'self-knowing reason's' division in the preceding sentence. A 'manifestation' (*Manifestation*) is more revelatory than an 'appearance' (*Erscheinung*). Nature as such is an *appearance* of the logical Idea, since the logical Idea is embodied in it, but it does not *manifest* the logical Idea in the way that philosophy does. In the first two syllogisms nature and mind were appearances of the logical Idea, but not manifestations of it. The reason for this is that in the first syllogism the appearance emerged by 'transition' and in the second syllogism it emerged by 'reflexion', whereas here in the third syllogism both appearances emerge by a 'self-judging'. These three modes of emergence correspond to the three parts of the Logic. 'Transition' or passing over (*Übergehen*) is characteristic of the first part, the 'Doctrine of Being': see Enc. I, §111Z. Reflexion is characteristic of the second part, the 'Doctrine of Essence': cf. Enc. I, §112. Judgement belongs to the third part, the 'Doctrine of the Concept': cf. Enc. I, §§166 ff. Hegel seems to be saying that the division into the two appearances is now undertaken by philosophy itself, and this guarantees that they are 'its' manifestations.

A 'unification' takes place in 'it', namely in the Idea or in self-knowing reason. What is unified? It should be nature and mind, the two appearances into which the Idea divided or 'judged' itself. However, Hegel goes on to speak of the parallel between the development of the concept and the activity of cognition. This suggests that the unification is between the 'subject matter' (*Sache*), in which the concept is embodied objectively but implicitly, and cognition. As we have seen, the 'subject matter' cognized by philosophy is not simply nature, but also the lower stages of mind: cf. §577, n. 1. The picture that Hegel has in view seems to be this. Philosophy begins by considering the logical Idea. This then bifurcates into nature and mind, which are again considered by philosophy. Initially mind, as the soul, is embedded in nature, but gradually it disentangles itself from nature and rises above it. At its final stage—philosophy—mind is at its greatest distance from nature. However, at that stage too reunification takes place. Philosophy realizes that nature and mind are both structured by the same logical Idea. It realizes too that its own 'subjective' activity follows the same logical order as do the stages of nature and the lower stages of mind. There are, therefore, two unifications: between nature and mind and between philosophy and its subject matter.

What is the general significance of the triple syllogism? There are three items involved: the logical Idea, and its two 'appearances', nature and mind. Let us call these, respectively, 'L', 'N' and 'M'. We might expect this to result in six syllogisms, with each item appearing twice as the middle term, twice as the first extreme, and twice as the last extreme: L–N–M, N–M–L, M–L–N, M–N–L, L–M–N, and N–L–M. But Hegel provides only the first three of these syllogisms. Each item is to appear *once*, and only once, in each of the three positions: as the middle term, as the first ('presupposed') extreme, and as the last extreme. In the first two syllogisms, the relation between the terms determines the order in which they occur. In syllogism (1), the logical Idea 'becomes' nature, and nature becomes mind. Becoming is, on the face of it, an asymmetric relation. So the converse of syllogism (1)—mind becomes nature, and nature becomes the logical Idea—is excluded by this, apart from the intrinsic implausibility (in Hegel's eyes) of a degeneration from complexity to simplicity. Syllogism (2) starts with nature and the middle term, mind, connects it to the logical Idea by reflecting on it. The converse of this syllogism looks as if it may be possible. Why might the mind not begin with the logical Idea and then, by reflecting on it, construct or reconstruct nature? This suggestion is ambiguous, however. It could mean that the mind *constructs* nature from scratch on the basis of the logical Idea alone, with no reflection on a pre-existing nature. Hegel would deny that this possible. Or it could mean that the mind reconstructs or reinterprets nature, reflecting both on the logical Idea and on nature. This, Hegel would say, is possible, but the process described does not differ significantly from its supposed converse, syllogism (2).

Syllogisms (1) and (2) presuppose the distinctness of their three terms, and then the middle term effects a unification between the two extremes. By contrast, syllogism (3) does not presuppose that its three terms are distinct. It begins with a division or 'self-judging' of the logical Idea into 'mind and nature'. Hegel puts them in the order 'mind and nature'. But in so far as the logical Idea simply 'divides' into mind and nature, it does not matter in which order the two extremes occur. Dividing into mind and nature is the same as dividing into nature and mind. Apart from this, syllogism (3) looks, at this stage, similar to syllogism (1). In syllogism (1), the middle term, nature, does not *divide* into the logical Idea and mind. Nature simply forms a 'transit point' on the logical Idea's journey to mind. And this, apart from its implication that nature is prior to mind, hardly differs from the division, in syllogism (3), of the logical Idea into nature and mind. This is inconvenient, both because syllogism (3) should differ from syllogism (1) and also because the first extreme should be the mind, which has not so far occupied this position. But syllogism (3) also involves a unification that did not occur in syllogism (1). In this unification the mind takes the driving seat. The mind qua philosophy traces the development of the logical Idea, nature and mind. Thus it sees that nature and mind as a whole embody the same logical Idea. In its consideration of the development of the logical Idea, nature and mind as a whole, mind qua philosophy follows the same path as this development does, and it also sees that this what it does. In this respect syllogism (3) differs from syllogism (2). In syllogism (2) philosophy reflects on nature and discerns the logical Idea in it. But this is a 'subjective cognition', that is, it does not mirror the way in which the logical Idea and nature themselves develop.

This suggests that the three syllogisms are related in the following way. Syllogism (1) presents the *objective* order in which the three items occur: logical Idea, nature, mind. This is the order followed by Hegel's *Encyclopaedia*. What syllogism (1) does not tell us, however, is how we know that the three items occur in this order. It neglects the *subjective* aspect, because the mind plays no active role in the syllogism. The mind is simply the end-product of the process. Syllogism (2) remedies this by assigning the mind an active role. The mind now does what it could not do in syllogism (1): it discerns the logical Idea in nature and thereby joins nature to the logical Idea. However, this *subjective* process does not have any counterpart in the *objective* development recorded in syllogism (1). In syllogism (1) nature emerges from the logical Idea; the logical Idea does not emerge from nature. In this respect, mind or 'cognition' acquires a sort of 'freedom'. It does not simply follow the 'progression of necessity' presented in syllogism (1), where 'freedom of the concept' is situated only 'in the one extreme'—presumably in the logical Idea, which, since it initiates the progression of necessity, is in a way liberated from it. According to syllogism (2) the mind transgresses this necessity by reflecting on and conceptualizing the nature that gave rise to it. It does this, however, at the cost of remaining subjective, out of step with the objective process.

So syllogism (1) and syllogism (2) are each one-sided, respectively one-sidedly objective and one-sidedly subjective. Syllogism (3) remedies this. It is both objective and subjective, since in it the subjective development of mind qua philosophy follows the same path as the objective development of the logical Idea, nature and mind. Syllogism (3) achieves this effect not by presenting two parallel sequences, but by moving round in a circle. It begins with the division of the logical Idea into nature and mind. This follows the same course as syllogism (1), the objective sequence: L–N–M. But the last term of this sequence, mind, culminates in philosophy. Philosophy begins with the logical Idea. Then it proceeds to nature and it discerns the logical Idea in nature. Here mind qua philosophy does what it was presented as doing in syllogism (2), but it does not deviate (as it did in syllogism (2)) from the objective order L–N–M. It does not start with nature and then unite it to the logical Idea. It starts with the logical Idea and discerns it in nature. It then proceeds from nature to mind, and eventually concludes with philosophy itself. Hence in syllogism (3) the sequence L–N–M is repeated. Its first occurrence presents the objective order (the 'subject-matter'), while its second occurrence presents the subjective order. But there is no reason why the sequence should occur only twice. It can occur indefinitely many times. This is why Hegel says: 'The eternal Idea . . . eternally remains active, engenders and enjoys itself as absolute mind'. It follows from this account that the three syllogisms presented by §§575–7 are not on a par with each other. Syllogism (3) incorporates, or 'sublates', both of its one-sided predecessors, syllogisms (1) and (2). See also §553, n. 1. Cf. §§379, n. 7; 381, n. 23.

3. Hegel quotes the original Greek from *Metaphysics*, XII. 7, 1072^{b}18–30. 'In itself' here translates Aristotle's *kath' hautên* and *kath' hauto*. These expressions do not mean 'potential(ly)' or 'implicit(ly)' as Hegel's 'in itself' often does. 'Thinking that is *kath' hautên*' probably means thinking that, unlike human thinking, does not depend on sense and imagination, i.e. God's thinking. The object of such thinking must be 'what is best *kath' hauto*' and so, we are to infer, its object is God's thinking or intellect. This conclusion leads on to the question how the intellect can think itself. (My interpretation of the passage owes a great deal to W. D. Ross, *Aristotle's Metaphysics: A Revised Text with Introduction and Commentary* (Oxford: Clarendon Press, 1924), ii. 379–81.)

4. In Aristotle's view, an intellect, whether human or divine, has no nature of its own. Therefore when it thinks an object, it can take on the nature of the object, and this is how it thinks, by becoming identical with its object. (Aristotle's account is in this respect similar to Sartre's account of consciousness or the *en soi*, which also has no quality of its own, but is as it were entirely transparent.) Since when it actually thinks, the intellect becomes identical with its object and the object is thinkable, the intellect too 'becomes thinkable', i.e. becomes the object of its own thought. 'Touching' is reaching or coming into contact with the object of thought.

5. A human intellect can think about e.g. beauty, but does not always actually think about it. Hence Aristotle draws a distinction between being *receptive* of the thinkable, i.e. being able to think it or *potential* thinking, and *having* the thinkable, i.e. *actually* thinking it. Since Aristotle believes that actuality is higher than potentiality, his argument should run as follows: actual thinking is better than potential thinking, since 'contemplation', i.e. actual thinking, is pleasantest and best; so if there is anything 'divine' about thinking, it must be actual thinking ('the latter') rather than potential thinking ('the former'); so, we are to infer, God actually thinks all the time. Or alternatively: the divine element in thinking belongs to God (the former) rather than the human mind (the latter), assuming that God actually thinks always, while we do so only sometimes. However, Hegel's text

follows the surviving manuscripts in reading *ekeino mallon toutou*, i.e. the former rather than the latter. Ross amends this to *ekeinou mallon touto*, i.e. the latter rather than the former, a reading implied by Aristotle's ancient commentator, Alexander of Aphrodisias. If the manuscripts (and Hegel's) reading is retained, then it perhaps bears the second of the alternative meanings suggested above: the divine element in thinking belongs to God (the latter) rather than the human mind (the former), assuming that God actually thinks always, while we do so only sometimes.

6. God does better than we do in two respects. First, he always thinks actually, while we think only sometimes. Second, his actual thinking is better than ours: it is not dependent on the senses and he always thinks about God.

7. I have translated Aristotle's Greek in the spirit of Ross. Hegel would translate it differently. Nicolin and Pöggeler have attempted to reconstruct, on the basis of his account in HP, the translation that Hegel would have given (p. 496), and this in turn is translated by J. M. Stewart and P. C. Hodgson in Peter C. Hodgson, (ed.), *G. W. F. Hegel: Theologian of the Spirit* (Minneapolis: Fortress. 1997), 153-4. However, I do not translate this reconstruction here, since it does not differ markedly from more standard translations of Aristotle. For the most part Hegel translates Aristotle with reasonable accuracy.

The details of Aristotle's meaning are obscure. It is clear, however, from both this passage and the surrounding text, that Aristotle is not saying the same thing as Hegel. The primary function of Aristotle's God is to keep the heavens moving, without which movement everything would collapse into motionless potentiality. God moves things as a final cause, by attracting other things towards himself, and he therefore moves things without himself undergoing movement or change. What God himself does is to think continuously about himself, again without changing, since whatever he thinks about he thinks about all the time. Aristotle implies that God thinks about himself in virtue of thinking about other things. What God thinks about, apart from himself, is left in obscurity. It is likely that Aristotle had no definite answer to this question. (A plausible answer might be: something like Hegel's logic.) But at all events Aristotle draws a sharp distinction between God's thinking and human thinking, a distinction that Hegel rejects. In Aristotle's view, human thinking, as well as divine thinking, involves the identity of the intellect and its object. But none of us humans, not even Aristotle himself, engage in the thinking that God performs or, rather, *is*: we think only intermittently, and we do not think everything at once, we think one thing after another. Aristotle believes that human thinking, and especially his own philosophical thinking, gives us glimpses of what God's thinking is like. But he is, unlike Hegel, ready to leave the precise nature of God's thinking in obscurity. He does not believe that human thinking converges on divine thinking, let alone that divine thinking somehow emerges from human thinking: God was thinking long before there were any philosophers. Aristotle's God is the pinnacle of the cosmos, but he does not, like Hegel's God, complete the cosmos or return to its beginning; he simply keeps it on the move.

Index to Translation and Commentary

Note: 'fn' indicates a footnote in the text, 'n' indicates a note in the Commentary.

678 *Index*

worldly wisdom 252
world-soul 31, 35, 85, 86
world-spirit 246, 604 n. 16
worship 264, 641 n. 9
written language 195–7; *see also* spoken
   language
wrong 221, 222–3

Xenophanes of Colophon 334 n. 6, 472 n. 4,
   617 n. 16
Xenophon 39

youth 53, 55, 59